MOTIVATIONS
IN
PLAY, GAMES AND SPORTS

MOTIVATIONS
IN
PLAY, GAMES AND SPORTS

Edited by

RALPH SLOVENKO, B.E., LL.B., M.A., Ph.D.

Professor of Law
The Menninger Foundation and
The University of Kansas
School of Law

JAMES A. KNIGHT, A.B., B.D., M.D., M.P.H.

Professor of Psychiatry and
Dean of Admissions
Tulane University
School of Medicine

With a Preface by

KARL A. MENNINGER, M.D.

The Menninger Foundation
Topeka, Kansas

CHARLES C THOMAS · PUBLISHER

Springfield · Illinois · U.S.A.

Published and Distributed Throughout the World by

CHARLES C THOMAS • PUBLISHER
BANNERSTONE HOUSE
301-327 East Lawrence Avenue, Springfield, Illinois, U.S.A.
NATCHEZ PLANTATION HOUSE
735 North Atlantic Boulevard, Fort Lauderdale, Florida, U.S.A.

Library of Congress Catalog Card Number: 67-21778

With THOMAS BOOKS *careful attention is given to all details of manufacturing and design. It is the Publisher's desire to present books that are satisfactory as to their physical qualities and artistic possibilities and appropriate for their particular use.* THOMAS BOOKS *will be true to those laws of quality that assure a good name and good will.*

Printed in the United States of America
N-1

PARTICIPANTS

Ralph Slovenko and James A. Knight
Editors

Carl Adatto
Michael Balint
Warren J. Barker
Knute Berger
Arnold R. Beisser
William R. Burch, Jr.
Martin D. Capell
Robert A. Dentler
Helene Deutsch
Joseph P. Dolan
Dennis Farrell
Reuben Fine
Roy G. Francis
Marcel Heiman
Lawrence R. Herkimer
William R. Hogan
Charles S. Houston
Viggo W. Jensen
Thomas P. Johnson
Samuel Z. Klausner
James A. Knight
Gertrud Lederer-Eckardt
Jacob Levine
Joseph F. Lupo
Willard Manus
Karl A. Menninger
Russell R. Monroe
Robert A. Moore
Robert E. Neale
John S. Oelkers
Bruce C. Ogilvie
Ramon A. Oldenburg
Barry P. Pariser
Thomas A. Petty
Richard H. Phillips
Robert T. Porter
Norman Reider
Douglas A. Sargent
Vernon Scannell
John L. Schimel
Margaret N. Sidney
Ralph Slovenko
William R. Sorum
Arthur Sternberg
Stonewall Stickney
Adrian Stokes
Alan A. Stone
Gregory P. Stone
Sue S. Stone
Ted N. Thompson
Thomas A. Tutko
Clyde H. Ward
Stephen D. Ward
Simon I. Wenkart
Machiel Zeegers

Tell me what you play, and
I'll tell you who you are.

Roger Caillois

BIOGRAPHICAL NOTES

Ralph Slovenko, co-editor of the volume, holds B.E., LL.B., M.A. (philosophy), and Ph.D. (psychodynamics) degrees from Tulane University. He was a Fulbright scholar to France, and a former editor-in-chief of the *Tulane Law Review.* He was a sportswriter for the *New Orleans Item* and sports editor of the *Tulane Hullabaloo.* He was a varsity sports letterman in track and field at Tulane University and a cross-country runner for the New Orleans Athletic Club. He served as Professor of Law at the Tulane Law School from 1954 to 1964. He has served as United States Commissioner, Law Clerk to the Louisiana Supreme Court, member of the Board of Governors of the Louisiana State Bar Association, Director of the Program of Continuing Legal Education for Members of the Bench and Bar in Louisiana, and Chairman of the Standing Committee of the New Orleans Bar Association on Admission to the Bar and Continuing Legal Education. During 1964-65 he served as Senior Assistant District Attorney in New Orleans, and on the part-time faculty of the Tulane University School of Medicine, Department of Psychiatry and Neurology. He is currently Professor of Law at the University of Kansas School of Law and the Menninger Foundation, the first joint appointment by the two institutions. He is a member of the American, Kansas, Louisiana and New Orleans Bar Associations; the American Orthopsychiatric Association; the American Society of Criminology; the Association Internationale de Droit Penal; the Southern Society of Philosophy and Psychology, and the Academy of Religion and Mental Health. He has published fourteen books and over sixty major articles on law, psychiatry and philosophy. He is Editor of the American Lecture Series in Behavioral Science and Law.

James A. Knight, co-editor, is Professor of Psychiatry and Dean of Admissions at the Tulane University School of Medicine, New Orleans. He was educated at Wofford College (A.B.), Duke University (B.D.), Vanderbilt University (M.D.), and Tulane University School of Medicine (M.P.H.). Before assuming his present position, he was Assistant Dean and Assistant Professor of Psychiatry at Baylor University College of Medicine (1958-61), Associate Professor of Psychiatry at Tulane University School of Medicine (1961-63), Harkness Professor of Psychiatry and Religion, and Director of the Program in Psychiatry and Religion at Union Theological Seminary (1963-64). He is a Fellow of the American Psychiatric Association and a Diplomate of the American Board of Psychiatry and Neurology. He holds membership in the Academy of Psychoanalysis, American Public Health Association, Academy of Religion and Mental Health, and the Society for the Scientific Study of Religion. He is the author of numerous articles and books.

Carl Adatto, a psychiatrist in New Orleans, received his B.S. degree from the University of Washington and his M.D. degree from the University of Chicago. He is a graduate of the New Orleans Psychoanalytic Training Center. In addition to his private practice, he is Clinical Associate Professor of Psychiatry at the Louisiana State University Medical School, and Training and Supervising Analyst of the New Orleans Psychoanalytic Institute. He is a member of various professional organizations, and he has written several articles. At golf he is a 17-handicapper.

Michael Balint was born in Budapest, Hungary. He holds the M.D. degree, University of Budapest, 1920; Ph.D. in chemistry, physics and biology, University of Berlin, 1924; Hungarian State Diploma in clinical medicine, 1936; Hungarian State Diploma in psychoneurology, 1936; L.R.C.P., L.R.C.S., Edinburgh, 1944; M.Sc. (psychology), University of Manchester, 1945. In psychiatry, he was an assistant at the Berlin Psycho-Analytical Institute, 1922-24; Training Analyst and Lecturer, Hungarian Psycho-Analytical Institute, 1926-39; Deputy Director, Budapest Institute of Psycho-Analysis, 1935-39; consultant practice in Manchester, 1939-45, and since then in London. He is Editor of Mind and Medicine Monographs. His books include *Primary Love and Psycho-Analytic Technique, The Doctor, His Patient and the Illness, Problems of Human Pleasure and Behaviour, Thrills and Regressions,* and *Psychotherapeutic Techniques in Medicine,* and he has also published approximately ninety scientific papers in Hungarian, German, French and English.

Warren Jackson Barker was born in Oklahoma in 1910 among cowboys (working) and Indians (peaceful). He graduated from the Tulane University School of Medicine in 1935. After a rotating internship at Touro Infirmary in New Orleans, he engaged in general practice of medicine in Oklahoma for three years. In 1940 he took a commission in the United States Army Medical Corps and later served in the European theater of operation during World War II. After the War, he engaged in formal training in psychiatry and psychoanalysis at the University of Chicago. He joined the faculty of the University of Pittsburgh School of Medicine in 1954. He is currently an associate professor in the Department of Psychiatry and a training and supervising analyst in the Pittsburgh Psychoanalytic Institute. He is a Fellow, American Psychiatric Association; Diplomate, American Board of Psychiatry and Neurology; and Member, American Psychoanalytic Association.

Knute Berger, our cartoonist, was born in Seattle in 1915 and is still a Seattle-ite because of preference for the Pacific Northwest. He had much art training during high school, and he worked his way through college doing commercial artwork during the academic year and working in machine shops and logging camps during the summer. He graduated in 1937 from the University of Washington (premedicine) with a B.S. in chemistry. His interest in cartooning really developed during a stint as art editor and contributing cartoonist to the college humor magazine for two years. All the good college student cartoonists had graduated the previous year, and he began to try cartooning in many different styles (signing different names), so that it would appear to the student and faculty reading public that the magazine had a plethora of cartoonists. Through medical school (Yale, '41), and during internship and four years of service in the Army Air Force, he kept the avocation of art going when spare time permitted. His primary interests in medicine were surgery and pathology, and in 1949 he accepted a full-time position as Chief Surgeon of the Cerro de Pasco Copper Corporation in the Peruvian Andes. The demands of a surgical career were such that he could not see any happiness for himself except in becoming dichotomous and training in the field of art as applied to medicine – the discipline of presenting medicine on the printed page, screen or exhibit allowed for a satisfying creativity. Accordingly, he trained with Ted Bloodhart at the Good Samaritan Hospital in Los Angeles and with William Mortensen of Laguna Beach (in photography). He returned to Seattle and set himself up on a free-lance basis in the field of "medical depiction," a somewhat broader field than is implied by the term "medical illustration." He has engaged in this activity since 1951. He is also presently Vice President and Medical Director, John Slade Ely Center for Health Education Research, New Haven, Connecticut; Associate and Art Editor, *Pacific Medicine;* and Research Associate and Research Pathologist, Reconstructive Cardiovascular Research Laboratory, Providence Hospital, Seattle. In this volume he reacts to – not undoes – the various ideas expressed.

Arnold R. Beisser is Director, Center for Training in Community Psychiatry, State of California, and Professor of Psychiatry, California College of Medicine, Los Angeles. He holds the M.D. degree from Stanford University School of Medicine. He is a Fellow of the American Psychiatric Association and a Diplomate of the American Board of Psychiatry and Neurology. He is a former member of the medical faculty at the University of California at Los Angeles. He serves as consultant to a number of hospitals and agencies. He has published a number of professional articles in the psychiatric and psychoanalytic literature. He was a nationally ranked tennis player, and in 1950 he won a national championship. He has in publication a book entitled *Madness and Sports,* which deals considerably with clinical case histories.

William R. Burch, Jr., earned his B.S. and M.S. degrees from the University of Oregon, and in 1964, his Ph.D. degree in sociology from the University of Minnesota. He has taught at the University of Missouri, University of Minnesota, and Victoria University of Wellington. He is presently Research Associate at the State University College of Forestry at Syracuse University. He has spent five seasons doing varied recreational and fire suppression work for the U.S. Forest Service in the Mt. Hood National Forest, Oregon. He spent one summer as an interviewer for a Forest Service study of recreation in the Boundary Waters Canoe Area, Minnesota. From June, 1962, until July, 1964, he was a research sociologist for the Pacific Northwest Forest and Range Experiment Station in Portland, Oregon. In this job he did studies of forest recreation, of which some of the findings form a basis for his paper in this volume.

Martin D. Capell received his B.A. degree from New York University in 1951, his M.S. from City College of New York in 1952, and his Ph.D. from the University of Utah in 1957. He is presently Staff Psychotherapist at the Metropolitan Center for Problems in Living, a treatment center located with Metropolitan Hospital, Detroit, Michigan. In addition, he is in part-time private practice of intensive psychotherapy in Garden City, Michigan. He was formerly Staff Psychologist, Veterans Administration Hospital, Dearborn, Michigan, and Staff

Psychologist, Rehabilitation Institute, Detroit. He is a member of various professional groups.

Robert A. Dentler is Associate Professor of Sociology and Education, Department of Social and Philosophical Foundations, Teachers College, Columbia University. He is also Executive Officer, Institute of Urban Studies, Teachers College. He has served as Visiting Professor, Sociology Colloquium, Wesleyan University, 1964-65; Consultant, U.S. Urban Renewal Administration, 1963-64; Assistant Professor, Department of Sociology, Dartmouth College, 1961-62; Assistant Director, Bureau of Child Research, University of Kansas, 1959-61. He received his B.S. from Northwestern University, his M.A. from The American University, his Ph.D. from the University of Chicago. His writings include *The Politics of Urban Renewal* (with Peter Rossi), *Politics and Social Life* (with N. W. Polsby and P. Smith), *Hostage America* (with Phillips Cutright), *Big City Dropouts and Illiterates* (with M. E. Warshauer), and Staff Research and Writing on "Desegregation in the Public Schools of New York City" (*The Allen Report*). As far back as he can remember, he has always been interested in swimming. He took part in competitive swimming in high school, and he has also done lifeguard work.

Helene Deutsch, born in 1884 in Przemysl, Austria (now Poland), attended the Medical School of Vienna University, and soon after graduation in 1912, entered its Psychiatric Department and served there until 1919. The atmosphere in the official psychiatric world at the time was opposed to Freud, but she was very impressed with the lectures Freud gave as Professor of the University for a small group of participants. She was accepted for her personal analysis by Freud in 1918. With the end of her analysis she started intensive analytic practice and scientific work in psychoanalysis. Clinical observations were from the beginning the starting point of her work. She served as Director of the Vienna Psychoanalytic Institute, which was founded in 1925, for ten years, until her departure to America in 1935. She and her family followed the invitation her husband received from America, not knowing that the political situation in Europe would soon make it advisable to stay permanently in the United States. From the beginning she found her work in the U.S. exciting and productive. Presently, she is partly retired from teaching obligations but continues with her private practice and, above all, she uses as much of her time as possible for scientific work. She is the author of *The Psychoanalysis of Neuroses, Psychology of Women* (translated in eight languages), *Neuroses and Character Types,* and numerous papers in psychoanalytical and other journals.

Joseph P. Dolan is Chairman of the Divisions of Health, Physical and Nursing Education at Missouri State Teachers College. He received his B.S. and M.S. degrees from Purdue University and his Ed.D. degree in social psychology from North Dakota University. He has done postdoctorate work in epidemiology at Michigan University, in anthropology at Colorado University, and in child psychology at Tulane University. His master's and doctorate work for research was on athletic injuries, and he has authored a text on the subject.

Dennis Farrell is presently a staff psychiatrist at the Menninger Clinic and also an instructor in the Menninger School of Psychiatry. He graduated from the

University of Washington (B.S. in chemistry), studied at the Sorbonne, and then returned to the University of Washington for his medical training. His paper on parachuting stems out of personal experience. He has been a parachutist himself, and he was Division Psychiatrist, 1957-59, with the 82d Airborne Division.

Reuben Fine originally planned to specialize in mathematics and philosophy, but during the war his interests switched to psychology, and in 1948 he took a Ph.D. in that field at the University of Southern California. Since then, he has taught and practiced psychoanalysis in New York. He has been active in the training of nonmedical analysts. He served for five years on the Board of Directors of the National Psychological Association for Psychoanalysis, and in 1960 he helped organize the Institute for Psychoanalytic Training and Research and served as its first president. He has been regarded as one of the world's outstanding chess players, and his books on chess include *The World's Great Chess Games* and *The Psychology of Chess.* He is also the author of *Freud: A Critical Reevaluation of His Theories* and *The Logic of Psychology.*

Roy G. Francis is Dean of Letters and Science at the University of Wisconsin, Milwaukee. He has written extensively on statistical methods, sociological theory and large-scale organization. He took his doctorate at Wisconsin (1950) and had a postdoctoral fellowship (granted by the Social Science Research Council) in mathematics, which he spent at Harvard (1952-53). He was Acting Instructor at the University of Wisconsin, and Assistant Professor (and Research Associate) at Tulane University before joining the faculty at the University of Minnesota in 1953, where he served until 1966 as Professor of Sociology and Statistics. His contact with sports includes being a member of a University of Minnesota committee which studied the student athlete in comparison with the nonathlete, captain of a high school football team, pitching coach for a service team in World War II, and coach of Little League baseball. He was staff member and editor of student newspapers in high school, college and graduate school.

Marcel Heiman, born in Vienna, Austria, graduated in 1934 from the Vienna University Medical School, and had his neuropsychiatry residency there. He had psychoanalytic training at the New York Psychoanalytic Institute, 1944-48, and he is presently engaged in the private practice of psychoanalysis in New York City. He is a member of many professional societies and the author of numerous articles.

Lawrence R. Herkimer is presently the Executive Secretary of the National Cheerleaders Association. He and his staff of 186 instructors currently conduct training "clinics" for cheerleaders in forty-three states. To date, over 600,000 cheerleaders have attended his clinics over the past seventeen years. He has conducted clinics in South America, Central America, Canada, and the Hawaiian Islands. He is the author of *Pep Rally Skits and Stunts, Champion Cheers, Photographically Illustrated Cheer Routines,* and *Musical Cheers.* His organization also publishes a quarterly magazine, *The Megaphone.* He was a cheerleader himself for four years in high school, three years at Southern Methodist University, and one year at the University of Illinois. He holds B.S. and M.S. degrees. He was an AAU Tumbling Champion, and through his many training clinics he has become known as "Mr. Cheerleader," and has been featured in several national magazines and has appeared on several national television shows.

William R. Hogan, Chairman of the History Department of Tulane University, is the author of *The Texas Republic* (1946) and a number of essays in historical and literary journals, and co-author of three other books in the cultural and free Negro fields of United States history. He has been an archivist, National Park Service historian, and Army Intelligence officer in World War II. During the period 1958-1965, he was founder and faculty Administrative Chairman of the Archive of New Orleans Jazz, Tulane University (established with Ford Foundation grants of $156,000) . During the same period he has been engaged in studies of American leisure-time activities, including sports and recreation, in the nineteenth and twentieth centuries. A Guggenheim Fellowship supported his present publication goal — a book-length study of the historic attitudes of American churches toward recreation. He has also been awarded fellowships by the Rosenwald Foundation, the American Philosophical Society, and the Ford Foundation; and in 1962 he was elected an honorary member of Phi Beta Kappa.

Charles S. Houston, a Board-certified internist, is a member of the faculty of the Department of Community Medicine, College of Medicine, University of Vermont. He served as Special Assistant to the Director of the Peace Corps, in charge of volunteer doctor programs. He was Director of the Peace Corps program in India from September, 1962, until December, 1964, in charge of volunteers working in many different programs throughout that country. Prior to entering the Peace Corps in 1962, he practiced medicine in Aspen, Colorado, and before that was one of the founders of the Exeter Clinic in Exeter, N.H. He served as a flight surgeon from 1941-46 in the Navy and was active in high altitude studies. He has published many papers on various aspects of high altitude; he was the first to describe a "physiologic disease" called high altitude pulmonary edema, which has been a serious threat to those who reach altitudes above 8000 feet without allowing adequate time for acclimatization. Since 1959 he has been active in the development of a permanent intrathoracic replacement of the living heart and has developed designs which have been successful in maintaining life in experimental animals for long periods. He has also been a distinguished mountaineer. He took part in the successful ascent of Nanda Devi, which was the highest mountain climbed for many years. He was leader of the first and third American expeditions to K-2 in the Western Himalayas, second highest summit in the world. In 1950 he was a member of a small team that crossed central Nepal for the first time to have the first glimpse of the great south face of Everest, and photographed the route since used by all expeditions. He has an A.B. degree from Harvard and an M.D. degree from Columbia, and interned in medicine at Presbyterian Hospital, N. Y.

Viggo W. Jensen was born and educated in Michigan and graduated from the University of Michigan Medical School in 1946. He received his psychiatric education and psychoanalytic training in the Detroit area. He was on the staff of the Detroit Receiving Hospital, as Assistant Clinical Director, Department of Psychiatry, 1953-55, and as Clinical Director, 1955-58. His research on suicide, which began at the Detroit Receiving Hospital in 1953, continues to the present. He has been active in teaching psychiatry at Wayne State University Medical School since 1953, and there he is presently Clinical Assistant Professor of Psychiatry. He has been an active angler for thirty-five years, and his paper about fishing in this volume is a result of this experience.

Thomas P. Johnson graduated from the University of Minnesota Medical School in 1960. After interning at the Cottage Hospital in Santa Barbara, California, he returned to the midwest for four years of psychiatric training at the Menninger Clinic in Topeka, Kansas. The last two of these four years were spent in a child psychiatry fellowship. He has served as Lieutenant, USNR, Balboa Naval Hospital, San Diego, and is presently engaged in the private practice of psychiatry in San Diego. Sports of all types have been a lifelong hobby for him, primarily as a participant. His paper on coaching represents his first attempt at participation from a writing standpoint.

Samuel Z. Klausner is a psychologist (Ed.D. 1951, Columbia University) and sociologist (Ph.D. 1963, Columbia University) whose major fields of interest include research methods, social psychology, sociology of religion, education, and Middle Eastern society. He has taught at the City College of New York; Hebrew University, Jerusalem; Columbia University; and Union Theological Seminary. In 1953-54 he was a Ford Foundation Area Research Fellow, studying problems of immigrant absorption in the Middle East. This was followed by a year as Clinical Psychologist at the Government Mental Hospital in Jerusalem. During 1956-61 he was Program Director for Columbia University's Bureau of Applied Social Research program in psychiatry, religion, and alcohol. Since 1961 he has been Research Associate and Senior Research Associate of the Bureau of Social Science Research, Inc., in Washington, D.C. His research has included studies for the Air Force on the problem of self-control; the present paper, "Fear and Enthusiasm in Sport Parachuting," results from this work. He is also Executive Secretary of the Society for the Scientific Study of Religion. He is the author of *Psychiatry and Religion* (1964) and the editor of *The Quest for Self-Control* (1965). His articles on psychology, the religio-psychiatric movement, the acculturation of immigrants, and other subjects of social-psychological interest, have appeared in many professional journals.

Gertrud Lederer-Eckardt teaches gymnastics and body development, currently specializing in work with the handicapped and persons in psychotherapy. Trained both as a nurse and a physical education specialist, she was formerly at the Falke Schule in Hamburg, Germany (1925-30), Truempy Schule, Berlin (1930-35), and at the New School for Social Research, New York (1935-55), as well as at the Dramatic Workshop under Erwin Piscatur (1940-42) training actors in body movement. From 1945 to 1952 she was also the private secretary to Karen Horney and worked with many of her patients.

Jacob Levine received his B.A. in 1936 from Clark University, and his M.A. (1939) and Ph.D. (1941) from Harvard University. He was Parker Fellow at Harvard, 1940-41. He was Chief Psychologist, 1944-47, U.S. Army Rehabilitation for the Blind; Instructor of Psychology, University of Connecticut, 1946-47; Assistant Professor, Hartford College, 1947-48; Chief Psychologist, 1947-48, Connecticut Commission on Alcoholism. From 1948 to the present, he has been Chief, Psychological Services, Veterans Administration Hospital, West Haven, Connecticut; Associate Clinical Professor, Yale University, School of Medicine, and Department of Psychology. He is a graduate of the New York Psychoanalytic Institute; Fellow, American Orthopsychiatric Association; and member of the American Psychological Association and other associations.

Joseph F. Lupo received his M.D. degree from Tulane University School of Medicine in 1958. He interned at Charity Hospital, New Orleans, and also had his residency training in psychiatry at Charity Hospital and the Tulane School of Medicine. Prior to his psychiatric residency he served for two years in the Air Force. He is presently practicing child psychiatry in Tampa, Florida.

Willard Manus, a former college and semi-pro athlete, is the author of *The Fixers,* a novel based on the basketball scandals of the 1950's. He is former fiction editor of the literary quarterly *Venture,* and he has published short stories, satire and articles in many magazines, including *Greek Heritage, The Skindiver, Monocle, Dude, The Skier, Go!, Escapade, Help!* and *The Nation.* He has also written three books for young readers and has recently completed a new novel, *Mott the Hoople.* He is presently living in Rhodes, Greece, working on a new novel.

Karl A. Menninger, author of the preface, is chairman of the Board of Trustees of The Menninger Foundation, Topeka, Kansas, and Dean of The Menninger School of Psychiatry. He is also University Professor-at-Large at the University of Kansas, Visiting Professor at the University of Cincinnati, and Senior Consultant to the Stone-Brandel Center in Chicago. Dr. Karl, as he is affectionately known, was born in Topeka of pioneer parents, both of whom were teachers. He attended the Topeka Public Schools, Washburn University of Topeka, University of Wisconsin and Harvard Medical School, graduating from the latter *cum laude* in 1917. Following an internship in Kansas City, he returned to Boston to work with Professor Ernest Southard in the Boston Psychopathic Hospital of the Harvard and Tufts Medical Schools. In 1919 Dr. Karl returned to Topeka to practice with his father, Dr. C. F. Menninger, and after a few years of partnership, the two founded and began the development of the Menninger Clinic. In 1925 they were joined by Dr. Karl's brother, William, then by other physicians. They began in a remodeled farm house; in 1945 The Menninger Foundation was officially born. A man of great faith, vision and dedication, Dr. Karl was a prime force in changing the then prevailing attitude of hopelessness and prison-like treatment of troubled persons. On the other side of the globe from the birthplace of Freud, Dr. Karl in Topeka, Kansas has been the spirit behind the development of The Menninger Foundation — known by people around the world as the "World's Psychiatric Center," the "Vienna of the Plains." In addition to his teaching and professional work, Dr. Karl interests himself in conservation programs, orchestral and piano-forte music, comparative religion, philosophy, English literature, cultural history, American Indian problems, and chess and bridge. He holds honorary degrees from eight universities, and is the author of numerous books, including *The Human Mind, Man Against Himself, Love Against Hate, Manual for Psychiatric Case Study, Theory of Psychoanalytic Technique,* and *The Vital Balance,* and in addition, he has written several hundred articles for scientific and lay journals. More than any other individual, he has brought the knowledge of psychiatry to the public in understandable language. His colleagues generally regard him as the "Dean of American Psychiatry," and in 1965 the American Psychiatric Association awarded him its first Distinguished Service Award. "For forty-five years," the citation told, "he has made most singular and exceptional contributions to the advancement of psychiatry – As a great HEALER dedicated above all to helping those sick in mind and heart who turn to our profession for comfort and relief; As a great TEACHER with special genius for inspiring the young as he transmits to them new knowledge in perspective of the wisdom of the past; As a great SCHOLAR who has reached out to other disciplines that their knowledge may be joined to our own and ours to theirs in the service of mankind; As a great MAN OF LETTERS whose beauty and clarity of diction have made the very name of psychiatry a household word; As a great CRITIC who has shown how the shibboleths of the past blind us to promising pathways to the future; As a great ORGANIZER who first conceived the structure now underlying our dynamic Association; and As a great CITIZEN protagonist of fair play and foe of prejudice, discrimination and deprivation in all their forms. Reasons enough these – and there are still others unspoken here but deeply felt – that cause us thus to honor him."

Russell R. Monroe is Professor of Psychiatry at the Psychiatric Institute of the University of Maryland School of Medicine. He received a B.S. degree in 1942 and his medical degree in 1944 at Yale University, and was Assistant in Medicine there from 1944 to 1945. He had his psychoanalytic training at the Psychoanalytic Clinic for Training and Research, College of Physicians and Surgeons, Columbia University. He was Research Associate, 1949-50, and Associate Psychoanalyst, 1950-53, at Columbia University. He was Assistant Professor and Associate Professor at the Tulane University Department of Psychiatry and Neurology, 1950-60, and he has been at the University of Maryland since 1960. He is a member of numerous professional societies, including the American Psychiatric Association, Academy of Psychoanalysis, Group for the Advancement of Psychiatry, American Association for the Advancement of Science, and the N.Y. Association for Psychoanalytic Medicine. He is the author of numerous articles.

Robert A. Moore is Director, Department of Psychiatry, Swedish-American Hospital, Rockford, Illinois, and he is also Clinical Assistant Professor of Psychiatry at the University of Illinois College of Medicine. He received his medical degree at the University of Illinois. He interned at the University of Michigan Medical Center, and he had his psychiatric residency at the Neuropsychiatric Institute, University of Michigan Medical Center. Prior to his present position, he was Assistant Professor of Psychiatry, University of Michigan Medical School, and Clinical Director of Training and Research, Ypsilanti (Michigan) State Hospital. He has recently published a book entitled *Sports and Mental Health.*

Robert E. Neale is Assistant Professor in Psychiatry and Religion at Union Theological Seminary, New York. He was educated at Amherst College, B.A. 1951, and Union Theological Seminary, B.D. 1954, Th.D. 1964. He was ordained by Bennington Association of the Vermont Congregational Conference, and was a pastor at the Federated Church, East Arlington, Vermont, 1954-57.

John S. Oelkers holds a B.Ed. degree from Tulane University, and since 1952 he has been head track coach there. In high school he was All Prep and All State guard and tackle, 1923-25, and he was Prep and State Champion and Record Holder, Southern Shot Record Holder, 1926. At Tulane University he was track captain, 1929, and Southern Conference and Southern Champion and Record Holder Shot and Discus. He has coached over 100 Southeastern Conference and Southern champions, and champions and place winners at all major U.S. track meets. He was Head Coach of the U.S. Track Team in 1962 in meets against the U.S.S.R. and Poland, and in both meets the U.S. won. He is AAU Vice Chairman, U.S. Men's Track and Field, U.S. Long Distance Running, and a member of the U.S. Records AAU National Committee. He was a member of the U.S. Olympic Track and Field Committee, 1965, and the Jury of Appeal U.S. v. U.S.S.R., 1964. On three occasions the City of New Orleans honored him with Award of Merit, and in 1962 he was given an honor of citation by the Mayor of New Orleans, the Governor of Louisiana, and President John F. Kennedy. The Boy Scouts of America has presented him with its Gold Medal Award for outstanding achievement.

Bruce C. Ogilvie is presently Professor at the San Jose State College Department of Psychology. He has taught at San Francisco State College, the University of San Francisco, the College of Notre Dame, City College, San Francisco. He earned a B.A. degree at the University of San Francisco, M.S. at Portland University, and Ph.D. at the University of London, Institute of Psychiatry. He holds Fellowships in the American College of Sports Medicine and the International Society for Sports Psychology. He is Co-director of the Institute for Study of Athletic Motivation, and he is a member of the California Psychological Association and the American Psychological Association. In this volume he is coauthor with Thomas A. Tutko of a paper on the role of the coach in the motivation of athletes; and with him, he has published a series of articles in *Track and Field News and Track Techniques,* and they have presented a number of scientific papers, including "Psychological Profile of Athletes in Three Major Sports," "Profile of a Champion," "Psychological Profile of Successful Football Athletes," "Emotional Problems of Basketball Players," "Effect of Competitive Athletics upon Femininity," "Psychological Profile of Olympic Swimmers," "Handling Emotional Problems of Athletes," and "Psychological Research in Athletics."

Ramon A. Oldenburg is an assistant professor of sociology at Stout State University and was an instructor in sociology at the University of Minnesota where he completed his Masters and is currently completing his work toward the Ph.D. His primary interests lie in the areas of social psychology and social organization.

Barry P. Pariser began fencing as a freshman at Columbia College. As a junior, he was awarded a varsity letter in the sport, and during that year he fenced on the championship Eastern Intercollegiate Fencing Team. He won the silver medal in the Eastern Intercollegiate Individual Sabre Championship. In 1955, his senior year, he was captain of the fencing team, and again repeated his second place ranking in the Easterns. Weeks later he won the NCAA Sabre Championship. He was ranked fourth in the National Amateur Fencers League of America Championship. While attending medical school in Syracuse, he was in 1958 ranked tenth in the country and competed for the USA in the World Championships in Philadelphia. Following graduation from medical school in 1959, he returned to New York City where he interned and then took an Ear, Nose and Throat residency, which he finished in 1964. During this period in New York City, he competed for the New York Athletic Club. He placed second in the Maccabiah Games in Sabre in 1961, and again achieved national ranking in 1963 when he was sixth. He was on the Olympic Squads of 1956, 1960, and 1964. He is currently a Captain in the U.S. Air Force and is practicing his medical specialty.

Thomas A. Petty received his M.D. degree from Indiana University School of Medicine in 1945 and is presently a psychoanalyst in Grosse Pointe, Michigan. He is Trustee and member of the Faculty, Michigan Psychoanalytic Institute; Medical Director, McGregor Center; Clinical Associate Professor of Psychiatry, Wayne State University School of Medicine; consultant to the Detroit-Wayne County Community Mental Health Services Board; Senior Attending Physician, Detroit General Hospital Department of Psychiatry; and consultant, Lafayette clinic. He is a member and officer of various professional societies.

Richard H. Phillips is a graduate of the Baltimore Polytechnic Institute, University of North Carolina, and New York University College of Medicine. He received his psychiatric training at Duke University. He is a Diplomate of the American Board of Psychiatry and Neurology, a member of the American Academy of Psychotherapists and a Fellow of the American Psychiatric Association. He is presently an associate professor of psychiatry at the State University of New York, Upstate Medical Center. Born in 1922, he first learned about games, the subject of his paper, in Demorest, Georgia, where he lived until 1934.

Robert T. Porter is Associate Attending Psychiatrist, Chief of Psychiatric Consultation Services to Pediatrics, Mount Sinai Hospital, New York City. He received his medical degree at the University of California Medical School. He had his internship at St. Elizabeths Hospital in Washington, D.C., and his residency in psychiatry at the New York State Psychiatric Institute. He served as psychiatrist, 1944-46, in Army General Hospitals.

Noman Reider graduated *magna cum laude* from Adelbert College, Western Reserve University, 1929, and he received his M.D. degree from Western Reserve University, 1932, and was awarded the outstanding prize in anatomy. He was a resident in neurology and psychiatry at Mt. Sinai Hospital, New York, 1934-35, and a resident in neuropsychiatry at the Menninger Clinic, Topeka, 1935-36. He was a staff member at the Menninger Clinic from 1936 to 1940. Thereafter, he was in private practice in neurology and psychiatry in Los Angeles, 1940-42, and he served in the Medical Corps, U.S. Army, 1942-46. He is now Senior Chief of the Psychiatric Service, Mt. Zion Hospital, San Francisco. He served as President of the San Francisco Psychoanalytic Institute, 1955-56. He was a member of the Editorial Board of the *Journal of the American Psychoanalytic Association,* 1952-58, and since 1953, he has been a Contributing Editor of the *Psychoanalytic Quarterly*. He is the author of numerous publications. He is an expert on the history of chess and other board games.

Douglas A. Sargent, who collaborates with Viggo W. Jensen on fishing, is a graduate of Brown University and the University of Michigan Medical School. He had his psychiatric training at the Ypsilanti State Hospital and the Detroit Receiving Hospital. He is Clinical Assistant Professor, Department of Psychiatry, Wayne State University Medical School. His major professional interests are psychoanalysis, disturbance in child growth and development, community psychiatry, and film making.

Vernon Scannell was finalist in the Schoolboy Boxing Championships of Great Britain in 1936, captain of boxing, and Northern Universities Champion at welter, middle and cruiserweights, 1946-47. He was a professional boxer, 1947-48. He has published numerous books of poetry and novels. His books of poetry include *A Sense of Danger, The Masks of Love, A Mortal Pitch,* and *Walking Wounded.* He won the Heinemann Award for Literature for *The Masks of Love* in 1961, and was also elected a Fellow of the Royal Society of Literature. His novels include *The Fight, The Face of the Enemy, The Dividing Night,* and *The Big Time*. He is a regular broadcaster and script writer for the British Broadcasting Corporation.

John L. Schimel is a psychoanalyst in New York City, and he is Associate Director of the William Alanson White Institute of Psychiatry, Psychoanalysis and Psychology, as well as the Director of its clinical services. He graduated in medicine *cum laude* from Georgetown University and holds a diploma from the William Alanson White Institute. He has taught at Teachers College, New York University Medical School, and Adelphi College. He is the author of numerous publications, including the books *How to be an Adolescent and Survive, Your Future as a Husband,* and *Your Future as a Wife.*

Margaret Neilson Sidney, born in New Orleans in 1900, was educated in the public schools there and at Newcomb College where she graduated Phi Beta Kappa in 1920. From the first time she saw Pavlova, in 1910, dance has been an essential part of her life. She studied elementary dancing with Lillian Lewis in New Orleans, and the Duncan School method with Elizabeth Lyons and Margot Duncan in Paris; later, she studied modern dance with Phoebe Barr of Dennishawn and with Elizabeth Watters and Hanya Holm, and also at La Meri's Studio of Ethnic Dance in New York, the Irenne Poupart School of Dance in Paris, and Prunella Stack's "League of Health and Beauty" in London. From 1939 to 1955 she taught creative dance for children in her own classes and in summer camps. Besides dancing, her major interests have been civic affairs, mental health, and adult education. At present she is a member of the Academy of Religion and

Mental Health, a member of the Board of the Louisiana Association for Mental Health, and she works with the Great Books groups in New Orleans.

William R. Sorum grew up with no one particular geographical influence. As the son of a regular army officer he lived in the South, the Midwest, the Phillipines, and the Canal Zone. His undergraduate work was done at the University of Alabama followed by medical school at Tulane. An internship at Charity Hospital in New Orleans preceded his years of residency under the auspices of the Tulane University Department of Psychiatry and Neurology. He spent several years on the staff of the Southeast Louisiana Hospital at Mandeville. He is now in private practice and is also on the staff of DePaul Hospital and Touro Infirmary; he is also an assistant clinical professor in the Tulane Department of Psychiatry. His participation in judo began some five years ago, and at present he holds the rank of Brown Belt in the Shufu Yudanshakai. Some two years ago, he developed an interest in karate instruction.

Arthur Sternberg earned his B.A. degree from Syracuse University, where he graduated *cum laude,* and his M.D. degree, in 1961, from the Upstate Medical Center at Syracuse, New York. He had his residency in psychiatry at the Mt. Sinai Hospital in New York City, and he is presently with the U.S. Army in Korea. He says, "Army life is a new (and enjoyable) experience for me, but I find that bridge players are like those in New York and any other part of the country that I have traveled." Bridge "honors" put him into the Life Master status after five years of intensive tournament experience and persistent youthful optimism.

Stonewall Stickney received his B.S. degree in 1944 from the College of Arts and Sciences of Tulane University, where he was elected to Phi Beta Kappa. He attained his M.D. degree in 1947 from the Tulane University School of Medicine. He served his first internship in 1947-48 at Wisconsin General Hospital in Madison, Wisconsin, and then spent a year in a second internship in the American Hospital of Paris, France. In 1950-51 he had his first year of psychiatric residency at Colorado Psychopathic Hospital, Denver, Colorado. The next two years were spent in Japan as a psychiatrist, 1st Lt., Medical Corps, U.S. Army. He returned to New Orleans in 1952 and spent six months as acting director of the Veterans' Administration Mental Hygiene Clinic. From 1953-55 he undertook two more years of psychiatric residency at Western Psychiatric Institute and Clinic, University of Pittsburgh Medical School, and then went into private practice and half-time teaching at Staunton Clinic, University of Pittsburgh Medical School. From 1958 to 1965, he was in training at the Pittsburgh Psychoanalytic Institute. In 1964-65 he began working as a consultant in the Pittsburgh Public Schools, and began full-time in 1965. He is Director, Mental Health Services, Board of Public Education. He has two sons and enjoys hunting, fishing, canoeing, and guitar playing, in reverse order.

Adrian Stokes is a psychoanalyst in London, and he is also painter, historian, connoisseur. In five books — *Michelangelo* (1955), *Greek Culture and the Ego* (1958), *Three Essays on the Painting of Our Time* (1961), *Painting and the Inner World* (1963), *The Invitation in Art* (1965) — written over a ten-year period, he has produced the first comprehensive theory of the nature of art which can claim a firm link to psychoanalysis. His ideas are those of the artist-philosopher who has found in the language of psychoanalysis a means of expressing his insights. His knowledge and experience of art, history, philology and psychoanalysis are wide. He is listed in the English *Who's Who,* and he is Chairman of the Imago society, a group made up of psychoanalysts and some analyzed laymen.

Alan A. Stone graduated from Harvard College *magna cum laude* in 1950, the author of a *summa cum laude* thesis entitled, "A Comparison of Overt and Covert Aggression." He played varsity football at Harvard. He received his M.D. degree from Yale Medical School in 1955, interned at the Grace-New Haven Hospital, Connecticut, and spent two years as a psychiatric resident at McLean Hospital in Belmont, Massachusetts, one year as a National Institute of Mental Health Fellow in Child Psychiatry at the James Jackson Putnam Children's Center in Boston, and two years in the United States Army Medical Corps. Upon completion of his military service, he returned to McLean Hospital as a Special National Institute of Mental Health Research Fellow for one year. In 1962 he was appointed Director of Resident Education at McLean Hospital, a position he currently holds. He also holds appointments as Associate in Psychiatry at the Harvard Medical School and Lecturer on Psychiatry at the Harvard Law School. He is also engaged in the private practice of psychiatry and research. He is president of the Massachusetts Society for Research in Psychiatry and of the Candidates' Council of the Boston Psychoanalytic Society and Institute. He is the author of numerous professional articles and two books, *Longitudinal Studies of Child Personality* with Gloria Onque, and *The Abnormal Personality Through Literature* with Sue Smart Stone.

Gregory P. Stone is a professor of sociology at the University of Minnesota. His primary interests lie in the areas of social psychology, urban sociology, and social stratification. In January, 1965, Professor Stone was the sole United States representative at the first meeting of the International Committee on the Sociology of Sport convened at Warsaw, Poland. The Committee is now a permanent committee sanctioned by the International Council on Sport and Physical Education, UNESCO. In addition to his present position, Professor Stone has taught at Michigan State University, the University of Missouri, and Washington University (St. Louis) . He received his Ph.D. in sociology from the University of Chicago.

Sue Smart Stone is the daughter of Alfred Smart, the late publisher of *Esquire* magazine, and the wife of Alan A. Stone, psychoanalyst, whose paper on football appears in this book. She graduated from Radcliffe in 1952 and is a professional writer. Her poetry has appeared in *The New Yorker* and other magazines. She and her husband have recently published a book, *The Abnormal Personality Through Literature.* Bowling is her hobby. She carries a high average and has bowled in many leagues, including extramural competition representing her local bowling proprietor, as well as city, state, and national tournaments. She lives with her husband and three children in Cambridge, Massachusetts.

Ted Nolan Thompson began earning his own living at age eleven, following the death of his mother and resultant bankruptcy of his father's now reconstructed chemical business. He began weightlifting at age fifteen, inspired out of a tussle with and at the suggestion of one of his father's employees. At age seventeen he enlisted in the USAF, spending three of four years in Germany. He occupied his spare time with interests in expensive German cars-of-old, but became best known for his motorcycling adventures over Europe and North Africa during 1950 and 1951. He enrolled at the University of California at Berkeley as a premedical student but with alternate interests towards the legitimate stage. He was a major participant in the University theatre and a television announcer. He entered U.C. Medical School in 1954, graduated in 1958, returned in 1960 for three years training in neurology, and now practices in Sacramento, California. His competitive weightlifting career began in 1952 and continued through 1962 before retirement. He won the yearly Northern California Senior AAU Championships in the 198-lb. class seven times, the annual Pacific Coast Championships twice, and the Western Division of the Junior National AAU Championships in 1958. In 1959 he won the Outstanding Lifter's Award for Southern California, then in 1961 and 1962 won the same award for Northern California. Applying an idea which works for him – that neither maturity nor happiness nor maximum efficiency can result without energetic diversion of interests – his are athletics, sailing and ship's maintenance, philosophy, acting and writing. He has supervised the weightlifting program for the members of the Balboa Bay Club in Newport, California. Except for very short periods of time, however, he has not placed any interest, including medicine, in a position of more importance than his wife and four children.

Thomas A. Tutko is Assistant Professor of Psychology at San Jose State College. He holds a B.S. degree from Pennsylvania State University and M.A. and Ph.D. degrees from Northwestern University. He is a member of various honorary societies, including Phi Beta Kappa, Kappa Phi Kappa, Sigma Xi, American College Sports Medicine, and International Society for Sports Psychology. He is Co-director of the Institute for Study of Athletic Motivation. He is a member of the Child Research Center, San Jose State College, and the American Psychological Association. He has jointly with Bruce C. Ogilvie published a series of articles in *Track and Field News and Track Techniques,* and they have jointly presented a number of scientific papers on sports before various professional organizations.

Clyde H. Ward is Assistant Professor of Psychiatry at the University of Pennsylvania School of Medicine. He received his undergraduate and medical education at the University of Virginia and took his internship and residency training at the University of Michigan Hospital. His main areas of interest have been those of undergraduate psychiatric teaching, residency training, and psychotherapy research and practice. He is author of numerous articles.

Stephen Daily Ward received his Bachelor of Arts degree in 1950 and his Doctor of Medicine degree in 1954 from the University of Pittsburgh. Following graduation he interned at Mercy Hospital and then served a three-year psychiatric residency at Western Psychiatric Institute and Clinic, Pittsburgh. He was then appointed Clinical Director of Mayview State Hospital, Pennsylvania, and maintained that post from 1958 until 1961 when he became affiliated with the Wheeling Clinic in West Virginia, where he currently has a private practice. He holds membership in the American Medical Association, the American Psychiatric Association, and the West Virginia State Medical Society; and he serves as Chairman of the Public Relations Committee of the Ohio County Medical Society.

Simon I. Wenkart graduated from the University of Vienna Medical School in 1922. He had a four-year rotating residency at the Federal Hospital of Wieden and a one-year psychiatric residency at the Medical Hospital of Vienna. He studied with Freud and Adler for many years. He was engaged in private practice from 1927 to 1938 and in addition was an officer of the public health system of Vienna. During his hospital years he first was team physician of a big league soccer club, then chief consulting physician of the Austrian Amateur Boxing Association, and later chief medical consultant of the Austrian Amateur Soccer Association. He contributed many articles to sport journals. He came to the United States in 1940 and had psychiatric training at the William Alanson White Institute. He is presently psychiatrist and psychoanalyst in New York, and a member of the executive council of the New York Ontoanalytic Association, of which he is a co-founder.

Machiel Zeegers studied medicine in Amsterdam, specializing in psychiatry. His special interests within this field include forensic psychiatry and criminology. He serves regularly as judicial-psychiatric advisor at the Dutch Criminal Courts, and he lectures at the Social Academy of the Hague. In this city he also carries out his private practice. His publications include three books, *Mens en Misdaad* (*Man and Crime*), *De Psychopathologie van de oplichter onder Anthropologisch aspect* (*The Psychopathology of the Swindler, An Anthropological Aspect*), and *Seksuele delinquenten* (*Sexual Delinquents*). He has published articles in Dutch, French, English and German professional magazines and periodicals.

PREFACE

It was an ingenious idea to have this book on the study of play. Some years ago the editors of the *Bulletin of the Menninger Clinic* undertook a similar task on a small scale. A number of psychiatrists were asked to describe their most satisfactory hobbies and explain, if possible, what the hobby meant or did for them. Remembering the difficulties of that pleasant editorial experiment, I can understand why almost nothing of the kind has appeared since then.

This is a much needed scientific contribution. It is the more timely because of the multiplication and expansion of psychiatric treatment programs. Play is a therapy, and now that this fact is better recognized, the number of patients in need of it is far greater. But more than that, it has a prophylactic value.

Once it was held, as some of these essayists recall, that all play was dangerous and destructive, indeed, even an evidence of depravity. "The students (of an American school in 1784) shall be indulged with nothing which the world calls play . . . *for those who play when they are young will play when they are old.*" (Italics mine.)

Over the years this point of view reluctantly yielded to the conclusion that all work and no play made Jack a dull boy, so a little play was permitted Jack while Jack's father might indulge in it only surreptitiously. Even today a business or professional man seen at a baseball game on a week day might cause some eyebrow lifting, although indulgence in such activities as weight lifting, quoits, and even golf can be done in the name of health — (not *mental* health) .

Does play contribute to the strengthening of character and the diminishing of painful inner tensions? Does it indeed favor the improvement of human life and the prevention of mental illness? Some of these essays face up directly to the question — others touch on it transiently or inferentially.

But these are crucial and important questions. For if play is truly a method of self-expression, a communication of goodwill in an inhibited aggression, an important piece in the mosaic of a well-rounded life, then it is, indeed, a *preventive* device and a necessity, not a luxury. This many of us believe, though we have no proof. We know people who play too much, to be sure; but we also know people who do not play enough. We lean to the belief that people should play more — not less, and this in the interests of mental health and the furthering of social good.

Such a justification for the great value of this book might have embarrassed some of the contributors had they known in the beginning that we would suggest it. For most of them the contribution of their particular essay was an expression of the results of self-study and the study of others who shared their preferences. But the results of the joint effort under skillful editorship have been to give this book a strong scientific thrust and dignify the study of why and how we play and are the better for it.

KARL MENNINGER, M.D.

FOREWORD

Man and His Play: A Preliminary Word

WHY DOES MAN PLAY? Why does he engage in games and sports?

The search for the meaning and significance of human events, of one type or another, has a long history, but there is relatively little in psychiatric and other writings on motivations in play, games and sports. Of course, something tremendous is not at stake in every human action, but there is some meaning in the great part of human action, and every action like every object can be viewed from various perspectives. The same reality may be viewed differently. There is an everyday world, for example, in which tables and chairs are solid material things, but in the (equally correct) perspective of physics, they are unstable, moving clusters of atoms.

Viewing play from a psychological perspective, Aristotle proposed a theory which strikingly resembles the present-day psychoanalytic theory of play when he said that in play the emotions "become purified of a great deal of the distasteful and dangerous properties which adhere to them." The theme was neglected until the end of the nineteenth century when it was picked up by Karl Groos in his books *The Play of Animals*[1] and *The Play of Man.*[2] Groos contended that play is an instinct and that play serves as preparatory training for adult life. In 1932 Melanie Klein of London in *Psychoanalysis of Children* pointed out the therapeutic importance of play,[3] and in 1942 Karl Menninger in *Love Against Hate* proposed that play also has prophylactic value against mental disorders.[4]

The importance of play, however, and the discovery of childhood as a distinct phase of life are relatively recent events. Philippe Ariès in *Centuries of Childhood* points out that in the Middle Ages, and for a long time after that in the lower classes, the child was, almost as soon as he was weaned, regarded as a small adult who mingled, competed, and worked with mature adults.[5] Hardly over a century ago American schools, among others, still prohibited play in strongest terms. School rules declared, "The students shall be indulged with nothing which the world calls play. Let this rule be observed with strictest nicety; for those who play when they are young will play when they are old." Nowadays, the useful function of play in the psychological development of children is implicitly recognized by nearly everyone. One noted naturalist recently observed that "perhaps in the future, the playing of children will be recognized as more important than technical developments, wars, and revolutions."[6]

Behavioral scientists following Melanie Klein have all found the role of play in childhood to be filled with significance, but the psychological meaning

Hillside 1846

Order of In-door Duties

for Children.

	Morning		Forenoon		Noon		Afternoon		Evening
5. 6.	Rise, Bathe, Dress. Breakfast Housewifery Recreations. (Chores) in care of Miss Foord	9. 10½ 11.	Studies with Mr Lane. Recreations. Studies with Father	12	Dinner	1. 2. 4.	Rest. Sewing, Conversation, and Reading, with Mother and Miss Ford. Errands and (Chores) Recreations.	6. 8. 8½	Supper. Recreation, Conversation, Music. Bed.
	Bathing Hours 5. 10¾ 5. Study Hours 9 to 10½. 11 to 12		Vigilance, Punctuality, Perseverance. Prompt, Cheerful, Unquestioning, Obedience. Government of Temper, Hands, and Tongue. Gentle Manners, Motions, and Words. Work, Studies, and Play distinct. No interchange of Labors.						Labor Hours 6½ to 8. 2 to 4. Play Hours 8 to 9-10 to 10½.4 to 6 Eating Hours 6 to 6½.12 to 12½. 6 to 6½. Sleeping Hours 8 to 5. 8½ to 5.

Observe Silence and [illegible]

This is the schedule set out in 1846 by Amos B. Alcott (1799-1888) for his now famous daughter, Louisa May Alcott (author of *Little Women*), then 13, and her three sisters. Time for recreation was provided in this rigorous schedule. Applied with affection, and consistency, the structure gave the children a sense of comfort.

of sports in later life has remained relatively unexamined. When we consider the important role that sports occupy in the life of the individual and of the group, it is remarkable how little attention behavioral scientists have given to the subject. People all over the world have read more avidly about miler Jim Ryun of the University of Kansas than about anything else. Sports everywhere are main features of the daily newspaper and weekly magazine, and literally hundreds of narratives have been written on sport events and sport heroes, but little on what psychologically drives man to sport.[7] As an explanation, we may consider that we usually do not ask, "Why do I love that woman?" Only if something hurts, we ask. Sports usually do not constitute a problem for man; hence he does not talk about them in psychotherapy, and psychotherapy is apparently the source of most data nowadays on motivations. The therapist's attention is understandably directed primarily to conflict situations in the patient's life, and that usually involves problems in interpersonal relationships. Psychoanalysis has been aptly described as the science of "human behavior viewed as conflict."[8] Freud wrote in all his published works of clinical conflicts and of the symptoms which they produced. He sought then, as psychoanalysts have since, to identify and unfold intrapsychic conflicts. The role of sports in the patient's life is considered only as conflicts interfere with his capacity to participate or to derive the usual satisfactions from them (as, for example, in the case of a boy with a clubfoot or a boy too modest to undress in the locker room).

There is a child hidden in every man, and this child wants to play. Play does not cease with age. In his book *Homo Ludens* in 1938, Johan Huizinga, historian of culture, pointed out the following:[9]

> A happier age than ours once made bold to call our species by the name of *Homo Sapiens*. In the course of time we have come to realize that we are not so reasonable after all as the Eighteenth Century, with its worship of reason and its naive optimism, thought us; hence modern fashion inclines to designate our species as *Homo Faber*: Man the Maker. But though *faber* may not be quite so dubious as *sapiens* it is, as a name specific of the human being, even less appropriate, seeing that many animals too are makers. There is a third function, however, applicable to both human and animal life, and just as important as reasoning and making — namely, playing. It seems to be that next to *Homo Faber,* and perhaps on the same level as *Homo Sapiens, Homo Ludens,* Man the Player, deserves a place in our nomenclature.

Huizinga in his book set out to answer the questions of what play was in itself and what it meant for the player and "to show that genuine, pure play is one of the main bases of civilization." Huizinga did not identify play with sport, but he did maintain that play was a valuable element in sport, so much so that when sport lost this particular ingredient it became divorced from culture and had little dignity or worth for mankind.

Fairness — playing according to the rules — is an important element of play, games and sports. These promote the development of conscience or super-ego — activity is not their only purpose. They have rules, penalties and limits. They teach discipline and the way to achieve freedom within the limits. The task is to express oneself and at the same time not to jeopardize others. Play, games and sports have no moral doctrine, but they help to develop decent behavior in people.[10] "Unsporting" is "unfair." Poor fortune is taken in stride — "that's the way the ball bounces." The code of good sportsmanship is, indeed, probably the best teacher of decency. "It was on the playing fields," Albert Camus once said, "that I learned my only lessons in moral ethics."[11]

Huizinga defined "play" as follows:[12]

> [P]lay is a voluntary activity or occupation executed within fixed limits of time and place according to rules freely accepted but absolutely binding, having its aim in itself and accompanied by a feeling of tension, joy and the consciousness that it is "different" from "ordinary life."

Huizinga's definition of play lays down three structural conditions: (1) freedom — the player cannot be forced to participate; thus, to run around a track by military order causes the act of running to be no longer play; (2) separateness — the activity must be circumscribed with boundaries of time and space that are precise and fixed in advance; and (3) regulation — conventions and rules of a sport suspend the ordinary rules of life, and for the duration of the sport the new law is the only one which is important. Huizinga maintained that this definition embraced play in animals, children and adults, games of strength and skill, and games of chance as well as exhibitions and performances of all kinds, and that it would embrace dancing and such noncompetitive activities as hunting, plus adventures such as mountaineering and sailing. In psychotherapy the whole world is reduced to the office, and in a quite similar way, the area of the world is reduced in play to the structure of the game. It takes considerable health to be able to participate in play. An individual who is overly rigid, for example, may not be capable of the regression required in play (or in psychoanalysis).

Huizinga's definition of play also sets out a subjective or attitudinal aspect — play has its aim in itself and is accompanied by a feeling of tension, joy and the consciousness that it is different from ordinary life. In work, as usually but apparently inaccurately defined, the (ostensible) end is considered more important than the means, but as this is not the case in play, the latter is considered "aimless." Thus, whitewashing a fence may be play, when the physical exercise is felt to be pleasant and invigorating, but the activity is considered work when it is aimed at accomplishing some utilitarian purpose, as repairing a fence, or when the activity is coerced, as in the case of convict labor. But, as Huizinga and others point out, play has a purpose, a psychologically important one, and it is serious.[13] Athletes take their activity seriously. To quote a common statement, "A lot of sweat went into that trophy."[14] The seriousness of an activity does not preclude its play-quality. Freud said, "The opposite of play is not being serious, but reality."

It is often remarked that play is in itself pleasurable, whereas work is not. "Play has an intrinsic quality of pleasure — it feels good to play." It is said that if there is any pleasure in work, it is an overlay on the drudgery. But for some people, work is pleasurable, and play is drudgery. The term "weekend neurosis" is used to describe the individual unable to tolerate the leisure time of the weekend.[15]

It may be noted that people who grumble about work are often burdened by unconscious emotional conflicts. They are intrapsychically conflicted, and they cannot enjoy play either. A person, for example, who always has to come out on top may enjoy neither work nor play. If one is emotionally conflict-free, work, like play, can be pleasant.[16] Tom Sawyer says, "I turn work into fun." Of course, external reality circumstances are just as important as internal psychic conditions. As Charlie Chaplin depicted in the film *Modern Times,* work on an assembly line, involving machine-like tasks, is drudgery. Work becomes play the more our efforts begin to serve psycho-biological goals. Work like play is dissociated from pleasure to the extent that it is dissociated from individual initiative. But work, unlike play, is directed toward (outer) reality; it aims at changing it. Play has no such mission, but work and play are similar in that both have ego preservative functions.[17]

Recreational activities and sports are intimately associated with the life and thought of man. P. C. McIntosh in his recent book *Sport in Society* observes: "Sport touches human life at many points — so many that it is difficult to define the concept or set limits to sporting activity. *Idrott* in Sweden, *Spiel* in Germany, *athletics* in the United States, admit precise definitions but the word *sport* has a much wider use than these. In origin French, it designates any diversion from the sad or serious side of life. It covers activities ranging from mountaineering to making love, from motor-racing to playing practical jokes. As a noun it can refer to a man, a woman, a game, a pastime, a chase, a hunt, a fight, a joke, or even a botanical freak."[18]

The chapters that follow focus on motivations in play, games and sports. A few chapters have been written as sociological and historical study. The book is large, though not all games and sports could be covered; but the presentation offers a good glimpse of the human spirit.

It must be admitted that each person participating in sports has his own distinctive pleasures and motivations. Sports mean many things to many people. There is no exclusive psychological need which sports serve —

probably that is why they are so popular. Sports may represent man's response to the challenge of nature. Some sports are sublimations of survival activities – hunting, fighting, mountain climbing, or pursuit of the opposite sex. Some persons, sublimating sibling rivalry, engage in sports for competition. Others may resort to sports as a means of dealing with aggressive impulses. The motivations are many, and those that are discussed in this volume in relation to one sport may apply to others. Out of the whole, one may get a feel of motivations in some sports, or perhaps, of some people in some sports.

Admittedly, there is considerable speculation in this book, and we must recall the admonition of Freud himself when he once began a conference by lighting a cigar and saying, "This may be a phallus, gentlemen, but let us remember it is also a cigar." A cigar is a cigar, sport is sport, but it is also something more, and speculation is always the first step in scientific inquiry.

FOOTNOTES

1. Groos, K.: *The Play of Animals.* New York, D. Appleton, 1898.
2. Groos, K.: *The Play of Man.* New York, D. Appleton, 1901.
3. Klein, M.: *The Psychoanalysis of Children.* London, Hogarth Press, 1932. See also Klein, M.: The psycho-analytic play technique: Its history and significance, in Klein, M.; Heimann, P., and Money-Kyrle, R. [Eds.]: *New Directions in Psycho-Analysis.* London, Tavistock Publications Ltd., 1955, p. 3. Lili Peller in one of her early papers, published in 1932 in the *Zeitschrift für Psychoanalytische Pädagogik* in a special issue on "Playing and Games," was concerned with preanalytic attempts to understand the phenomenon of play, based largely on the work of Groot. Peller understood these theories within the context of 19th century psychology, which explained all human play activities as being based on reason and utility. It did not encompass the view that play was in the service of instinctual forces or of unconscious conflict. Roubiczek, L. E. (maiden name): Die wichtigsten theorien des spieles (The most important theories of play). *Ztschr f Psychoanal Paedagogik,* Vienna, *6*:248, 1932. She subsequently created a synthesis between the most progressive educational thinking and the discoveries of psychoanalysis. Peller, L. E.: Libidinal stages, ego development and play. *Psychoanal Study of Child, 9*:178, 1954; Ekstein, R.: Lili E. Peller's psychoanalytic contributions to teaching. *Reiss-Davis Clin Bull, 4*:6, 1967. Robert Waelder in 1933, in a now classic paper, pointed out that play to a large extent is governed by the need or instinct to master. Waelder, R.: The psychoanalytic theory of play. *Psychoanal Quart, 2*:208, 1933. The meaning of play in childhood psychosis is recently discussed in Ekstein, R.: *Children of Time and Space, of Action and Impulse.* New York, Appleton, 1966, p. 207.
4. Menninger, K.: *Love Against Hate.* New York, Harcourt, 1942.
5. Aries, P.: *Centuries of Childhood.* New York, Knopf, 1962.
6. Creative Playthings, Princeton, N.J., in its catalog, 1966, makes the observation: "Would someone like to research an intriguing idea? It would be interesting to ascertain whether the inventiveness and drive of a culture or nation are directly influenced by the type of toys its children play with in the early years. Some toys — like large blocks, people, animals, doll houses, etc. — give children a one-to-one relationship in a child-sized world.

   "Other toys come to a child unstructured so as to challenge a child's creativity.

   "The life-sized preschool toys of Denmark and the United States give their children a manageable toy world which they can direct and experiment with. Can this be the reason for these nations' creativity and driving spirit? Do the miniature toys of German kindergartens build up feeling of world mastery?

"The handcrafted toys of Mexico are for adoring on shelves, not for creating or directing. Does this build insecurity feelings? In Russia, early childhood play and play materials are coming of age, and so is a resurgence of drive and inventiveness.

"In most deprived nations, there are no toys. The absence of good toys in Indian or Arabic cultures has given their children poor self-images and a hesitancy about affecting their environment. India is taking seriously the idea of a massive early childhood education program. In Israel, the introduction of play and nursery education for Yemenite children has brought about greater drive and academic achievement among a heretofore depressed sector of the population. Perhaps our government should include in foreign aid toys which encourage creativity, drive and will-power among deprived people of underdeveloped nations."

See Greenacre, P.: Play in relation to creative imagination. *Psychoanal Stud Child, 14:* 61, 1959.

7. One of few, Robert H. Boyle points out in his recent book that sport can tell us a great deal about ourselves but that its dimensions have not been fully explored. Boyle, R. H.: *Sport—Mirror of American Life.* Boston, Little, 1963. See also Smith, R. [Ed.]: *Sports: The American Scene.* New York, McGraw, 1963. Russell Baker of the *New York Times,* in a review of Dr. Ernest Dichter's "Handbook of Consumer Motivations," protests that psychological explorations into motivations are depressing. He says: "Nobody who wants to know the worst about himself can afford to be without [the book] . . . [It] leaves the reader feeling that life is a drab business . . . [The reader] resents seeing himself so simply exposed as a wretched piece of machinery twitching and jerking before symbolic soup and sausages and razor blades. There must be more to me than this!" Baker, R.: Psychiatry to quit eating by. *New York Times News Serivce,* August 1, 1964. See also Pop-psych. *Time,* October 7, 1966, pp. 38-39. The motivations of a musician in the selection of the instrument that he plays are discussed in Psychic Symphony, *Time,* February 17, 1967, p. 69. Baker and Dichter might wish to consider the motivations underlying the following: "Pencil stubs no longer needed can be sent to the Cow Palace." "Phil Menninger has a friend in Chicago who collects ties. If anyone has ties in their closet that they don't want, please send them to the Development Service." Unofficial Announcements, The Menninger Foundation, February 17, 1967.

   Pollock and Maitland on the opening page of their *History of English Law* (2d ed. 1911) say that "such is the unity of all history that any one who endeavors to tell a piece of it must feel that his first sentence tears a seamless web." The metaphor is peculiarly apt in its application to the study of man. To dissect man, said Nathaniel Hawthorne, is to murder him. A creative writer may indeed do better than a scientist or a psychiatrist in depicting man (compare Shakespeare and Freud), but their goals are different, and the web is so vast that only a small portion of it can occupy one's field of vision at any one time. Necessarily then, the strands which make up the particular portion of the web under scrutiny do not stop at the edge of the field of vision, but extend outward indefinitely and into other fields. Any analysis of man can at best be only a partial analysis, and so it is with this book. We hope, however, that this book does not depress Mr. Baker.

8. Kris, E.: The nature of psychoanalytic propositions and their validation, in Hook, S. and Konvitz, M. R., [Eds.]: *Freedom and Experience.* Ithaca, Cornell, 1947, p. 241.
9. Huizinga, J.: *Homo Ludens: A Study of the Play-Element in Culture.* Boston, Beacon, 1955 (German edition published in Switzerland, 1944).
10. Umminger, W.: *Gods, Heroes and Supermen.* New York, McGraw, 1963.
11. Quoted in Rolo, C.: Albert Camus: A good man. *The Atlantic,* May 1958, p. 27. For a critique of the use of drugs in sports, see *The Listener,* December 6, 1962, p. 955. Faking and deception, too, are learned in play and sports (*e.g.,* faking the ball and decoys in football). In games like hide and seek, if the child wins once, by hiding somewhere, then the next time he hides in the same place, he is taught that that is not a guarantee of success; it is a guarantee of failure. There are games, as in reality, that what works once, the opposite may work next. Games teach flexibility and prepare the child for the varied demands of reality.

Children play many good guy and bad guy games in order to master their good and bad impulses. We are all both Dr. Jekylls and Mr. Hydes, and when Hyde-like qualities are cultivated, what was learned (if anything) may be turned to ill. The adult con game version of the peek-a-boo game may turn out to be, "Now you see it, now you don't." Peek-a-boo becomes hide-and-seek, which may be an antecedent of cops and robbers. In early life, the criminal did not learn basic trust. He has no confidence that the promise will be kept, the rule enforced, and so later in life he does not abide by the rules of the game; anything goes. Coons, J. E.: Legalism in law making and law enforcement. *J of Legal Ed, 19:*65, 1966; Wilmer, H. A.: Good guys and bad guys. *Federal Probation, 30:*8, Sept. 1966; Zeegers, M.: The swindler as a player. *Infra* p. 219. Thinking conceptually, which criminals usually do so poorly, is also learned in play. Shifting categories in play (Ralph bats one inning, Roy the next) teaches that categories are not persons, or that a person has only one category indefinitely. Observation owed to Professor Harvey Sacks, Department of Sociology, University of California, Los Angeles.

12. Huizinga, J.: *op. cit. supra* note 9.
13. See McIntosh, P. C.: *Sport in Society*. London: C. A. Watts, 1963; Klein, M.: *op. cit. supra* note 3. The structural conditions of play provide the ground for psychological effects. For example, freedom in play fosters attitudes that society needs, but conditions in everyday life may not favor them. The differentiation between "play" and "work" is taken to be, respectively, "what *I want* to do" and "what *you want* me to do." Jim Ryun's mother calls him "slowpoke;" he probably is that way when he takes out the garbage. It may be observed that the deprivation of liberty, which so often occurs in work and in education, corrodes and destroys a person's desires and ambitions. Peller, L. E.: Psychoanalysis and public education. *Reiss-Davis Clin Bull, 4:*10, 1967.

The theatre attempts to draw the audience out of reality into the "play." Non-proscenium theatre-in-the-round and other recent theatre productions strive mightily to break down the separation of play and audience. The proscenium, traditionally a "frame" that separates actors and audience, creating a picture of the stage, is virtually eliminated, e.g., in *Marat/Sade,* in an effort more to draw the audience into the play. Tyrone Guthrie commented that realism and the proscenium stage were the killer of Broadway, and he insisted on the involving qualities of the thrust stage. Resnik, H. S.: What Culture? What Boom? *The Atlantic, 219:*51, 1967. The movie version of *Marat/Sade* is framed as a play within a play within a film. A row of bars is set across what was originally the front of the stage and an audience of Parisian notables is placed on the fixed-camera side of it for whom the inmates perform their show of caged hostility in the guise of historical charade. Film critic Robert Hatch observes: "In the theatre, *we* were those Parisian notables, and there were moments when the footlights seemed an all too fragile barrier. Now who are we — an audience behind an audience?" Hatch, R.: Films. *The Nation, 204:*347, 1967.

14. The Englishman particularly has always had the reputation for playing games with an intensity he seldom devotes to real life. *UNESCO Courier,* January 1964.
15. See Baker, R.: Having fun is work nowadays. *New York Times News Service,* July 29, 1964; Bliven, B.: Using our leisure is no easy job. *New York Times Magazine,* April 26, 1964, p. 18; Gunther, M.: How Americans labor in the furious pursuit of leisure. *The National Observer,* July 13, 1964, p. 22; Martin, A. R.: Frustrated aspirations and the tragic use of leisure time, in MacIver, R. M., *Dilemmas of Youth: In America Today*. New York, Harper, 1961; Martin A. R.: The dynamics of insight. *Amer J Psychoanal, 12:*24, 1952; Martin, A. R.: Leisure and the creative process. *Hanover Forum, 6:*3, 1959; Martin, A. R.: Man's leisure and his health. *Bull N Y Acad Med,* 2d Series, *40:*21, 1964; Martin, A. R.: *Mental Health and the Rediscovery of Leisure*. World Federation for Mental Health, August, 1960; Martin, A. R.: Self-alienation and the loss of leisure. *Amer J Psychoanal, 21:*156, 1961; Martin, A. R.: Urgent need for a philosophy of leisure in an aging population. *J Amer Geriat Soc, 10:*215, 1962.

Maria Piers, Dean of the Chicago Institute for Early Education, says that some people play too much, and others not enough. She observes:

"There is a prototype for each extreme. One is the *Playboy*. The other is *Jack* of 'All work and no play makes Jack a dull boy.' Jack is the kind of guy no girl cares to date, even though her mother may urge her to do so, for he is perfectly safe. Playboy (also known as Casanova or Don Juan) is much sought after as a date, but is considered a poor marital risk.

"They are both called 'boy.' This seems to indicate that one who only plays is not a fully developed man. Neither is the one who never plays. He, Jack, has learned to keep out of trouble and to make a living but he misses a great deal. His life is devoid of humor, wrath, a sense of tragedy or exhilaration. In the absence of the entire rich spectrum of emotions, Jack doesn't have what it takes to set the world (or a girl on a date) on fire. While Playboy has never learned to curb his appetite for play, it seems that our boy Jack has forgotten all about it.

"At least a modicum of playful activity is essential to being a fully grown human being. So, once upon a time, even Jack must have known how to play. For if he hadn't played during his infancy, he would not be alive today — a baby cannot survive unless he learns to play. This may sound like a gross exaggeration, but it is literally true."

Piers, M.: Play and mastery. *Reiss-Davis Clin Bull, 4*:51, 1967. See Spitz, R.: Hospitalism. *Psychoanal Study of Child, 1*:53, 1954.

16. "It is the general assumption that one enjoys play more than one enjoys work. This is not always or necessarily true. Many people appear to enjoy work more than they do play, but they are regarded as neurotics, eccentrics or geniuses. I have seen all three, but it is my impression that they most often enjoy work so much just because they cannot enjoy play. On the other hand, it is true that some people are so normal, so to speak — so free from the necessity of retreat from reality and the temporary surrender of repressive efforts — that they can and actually do find almost complete satisfaction in work, and need relatively little play." Menninger, K.: *op. cit. supra* note 4, at p. 170.

17. Hobbies come halfway between play and work. Anna Freud writes: "Halfway between play and work is the place of the hobbies, which have certain aspects in common with both activities. With play they share a number of characteristics: (a) of being undertaken for purposes of pleasure with comparative disregard for external pressures and necessities; (b) of pursuing displaced, i.e., sublimated, aims, but aims which are not too far removed from the gratification of either erotic or aggressive drives; (c) of pursuing these aims with a combination of unmodified drive energies plus energies in various states and degrees of neutralization. . . . [T]he hobbies share [with working attitudes] the important feature of a preconceived plan being undertaken in a reality-adapted way and carried on over a considerable period of time if necessary in the face of external difficulties and frustrations. Hobbies appear for the first time at the beginning of the latency period (collecting, spotting, specializing of interests), undergo any number of changes of content, but may persist as this specific form of activity throughout life." Freud, A.: The concept of developmental lines. *Psychoanal Stud Child, 18*:245, 261, 1963. A symposium on hobbies appears in the *Bull Menninger Clin, 6*:65-102, 1942. See also Menninger, W. C.: Psychological aspects of hobbies: A contribution to civilian morale. *Amer J Psychiat, 99*:122, 1942. William C. Menninger was a great believer in keeping records and in systematic listing and accounting. This found pleasurable expression for him in his stamp collection, and it found clinical expression in the implementation of fine clinical records. Menninger, K., *Memoriam for Doctor Will.* Topeka, Menninger Foundation, 1966.

18. McIntosh, P. C.: *Sport in Society*. London, C. A. Watts, 1963, pp. 10-11.

ACKNOWLEDGMENTS

WITH A FEW EXCEPTIONS, as noted, the authors have specially prepared their material for this volume. Over fifty persons participate. They know privately that we are grateful to them for taking part, but we would like publicly to record our appreciation and indebtedness. This volume was a large undertaking, and it involved much communication and interaction between participants. We have appreciated the wholehearted cooperation that we received every step of the way. And we want to record our thanks to Mrs. Genny Nyman, The Menninger Foundation, Mrs. Lucille Seitzinger, Tulane University School of Medicine, and Mrs. Doris Wolfmeyer, University of Kansas School of Law, for their devoted secretarial assistance.

This book has been a work of love. We are a bit sad that we have come to the end of the journey. We had a lot of fun preparing it. But now it is time to turn it over to you. We hope you have just as much fun reading it.

RALPH SLOVENKO
and
JAMES A. KNIGHT

CONTENTS

MOTIVATIONS
IN
PLAY, GAMES AND SPORTS

PART ONE

PLAY AND HUMAN DEVELOPMENT

INTRODUCTION

IN THE OPENING PAPER in this section, Norman Reider discusses the preanalytic and psychoanalytic theories of play and games.[1] He points out that the preanalytic writers were interested in play and games as biological phenomena, seeing much in play as instinctive, and seeing it physiologically as a device to use excess energy or to conserve it. The psychological theories are most valuable and would fall into that area of present-day psychology which is subsumed under theories of cognition. A consistent developmental theory, however, is missing in the old writers, and their concept of energy is not useful. Nevertheless, important contributions are many, especially the concepts of "playful experimentation" of the sensory and motor apparatuses, later called by Piaget "exploration," and the demonstration that this activity extended into all areas of mental endeavor. Thus, those who hold that all human activity — ranging from sports to politics, science, art and war — is a derivative of play find ample justification for their thesis.

Psychoanalytic theory, Reider says, added a new dimension to the understanding of play and games by showing that what goes on in the play of a child is understandable in terms of previous unsolved conflictual situation. The influence of the biological thinking of the nineteenth century showed itself in some writings. The question of whether some play is functional and not related to problem-solving was also carried over from earlier writers. The sublimatory function of play, especially in regard to aggressive drives, has been stressed. Play has been studied not only as a kind of symptom but also developmentally; content and style change with progressing libidinal phases. Anxieties of different types are the determinants of the different styles of play.

Reider doubts that spontaneous individual play precedes games historically; it may well be that "games" at the breast — or at least rituals in the interaction between mother and child — are the prerequisite for later play and games. The question of the therapeutic value of play and games as such is raised. Likewise the chance of effecting cultural change by introduction of new games is examined briefly.

From the point of view of a natural observer, a game is a strange spectacle. The fun in winning is clearly out of proportion to any apparent real gain. But children's games are frequently attempts to come to terms, to understand, and thereby to organize and absorb their experiences. Martin

D. Capell, in this section of the volume, writes about games and the mastery of helplessness. Examination of a small child's simple game of "Gone!", for example, suggests that the play is an attempt at passively mastering anxiety over a situation of helplessness. Games are not simple regressions; they create the conditions for progress. One naturalist put it this way: "Without a protected childhood in which there is time for play, mankind would probably never have arisen above an animal existence."[2]

In his book *Childhood and Society,* Erik H. Erikson says the following:[3]

> I would look at a play act as, vaguely speaking, a function of the ego, an attempt to bring into synchronization the bodily and the social processes of which one is a part even while one is a self . . . . To hallucinate ego mastery is the purpose of play — but play is the undisputed master of only a very slim margin of existence. What is play — and what is it not? . . . .
>
> When man plays he must intermingle with the laws of things and people in a similarly uninvolved and light fashion. He must do something which he has chosen to do without being compelled by urgent interests or impelled by strong passion; he must feel entertained and free of any fear or hope of serious consequences. He is on vacation from reality — or, as is most commonly emphasized: he *does not work.* It is this opposition to work which gives play a number of connotations. One of these is "mere fun" — whether it is hard to do or not. As Mark Twain commented, "constructing artificial flowers . . . is work, while climbing the Mont Blanc is only amusement." In Puritan times and places, however, mere fun always connoted sin; the Quakers warned that you must "gather the flowers of pleasure in the fields of duty." Men of equally puritan mind could permit play only because they believed that to find "relief from moral activity is in itself a moral necessity." Poets, however, place the emphasis elsewhere: "Man is perfectly human only when he plays," said Schiller. Thus play is a borderline phenomenon to a number of human activities and, in its own playful way, it tries to elude definition.
>
> It is true that even the most strenuous and dangerous play is by definition not work, i.e., does not produce commodities. Where it does, it "goes professional." But this fact, from the start, makes the comparison of adult and child's play somewhat senseless; for the adult is a commodity-producing and commodity-exchanging animal, whereas the child is only preparing to become one. To the working adult, play is recreation. It permits a periodical stepping out from those forms of defined limitation which are his reality . . . .
>
> The playing child, then, poses a problem: whoever does not work shall not play. Therefore, to be tolerant of the child's play the adult must invent theories which show either that childhood play is really work — or that it does not count. The most popular theory and the easiest on the observer is that the child is *nobody yet,* and that the nonsense of his play reflects it. Scientists have tried to find other explanations for the freaks of childish play by considering them representatives of the fact that childhood is neither here nor there. According to Spencer, play uses up *surplus energy* in the young of a number of mammalians who do not need to feed or protect themselves because their parents do it for them. However, Spencer noticed that wherever circumstances permit play, tendencies are "simulated" which are "usually ready to act, unusually ready to have their correlative feelings aroused." Early psychoanalysis added to this the "cathartic" theory, according to

which play has a definite function in the growing being in that it permits him to work off past emotions and to find imaginary relief for past frustrations.

In order to evaluate these theories, let us turn to the game of "Gone!" as described by Sigmund Freud. He observed:[4]

> I availed myself of an opportunity which offered of elucidating the first game invented by himself of a boy eighteen months old. It was more than a casual observation, for I lived for some weeks under the same roof as the child and his parents, and it was a considerable time before the meaning of his puzzling and continually repeated performance became clear to me . . . .
>
> Occasionally, this well-behaved child evinced the troublesome habit of flinging into the corner of the room or under the bed all the little things he could lay his hands on, so that to gather up his toys was often no light task. He accompanied this by an expression of interest and gratification, emitting a loud, long-drawn-out "O-o-o-oh" which in the judgment of the mother (one that coincided with my own) was not an interjection but meant "go away." I saw at last this was a game, and that the child used all his toys only to play "being gone" with them. One day I made an observation that confirmed my view. The child had a wooden reel with a piece of string wound around it. It never occurred to him, for example, to drag this after him on the floor and so play horse and cart with it, but he kept throwing it with considerable skill, held by the string, over the side of his little draped cot, so that the reel disappeared into it, then said his significant "O-o-o-oh" and drew the reel by the string out of the cot again greeting its reappearance with a joyful "Da" [there]. This was therefore the complete game, disappearance and return, the first act being the only one generally observed by the onlookers, and the one untiringly repeated by the child as a game for its own sake, although the greater pleasure unquestionably attached to the second act . . . . This interpretation was fully established by a further observation. One day when the mother had been out for some hours she was greeted on her return by the information "Baby o-o-o-oh" which at first remained unintelligible. It soon proved that during his long lonely hours he had found a method of bringing about his own disappearance. He had discovered his reflection in the long mirror which nearly reached to the ground and had then crouched down in front of it, so that the reflection was "go away."

To appreciate what Freud saw in this game, it is to be noted that at the time he was interested in and writing about the "repetition compulsion" phenomenon — that is, the need to reenact painful experiences in words or acts. As he was writing about this, Freud became aware of the solitary play described and of the fact that the frequency of the main theme (somebody or something disappears and comes back) corresponded to the intensity of the life experience reflected, namely, the mother's leaving in the morning and her return at night.[5]

Commenting on Freud's observations, Erikson says:[6]

> This dramatization takes place in the play sphere. Utilizing his mastery over objects, the child can arrange them in such a way that they permit him to imagine that he is master of his life predicament as well. For when the mother had left

him, she had removed herself from the sphere of his cries and demands; and she had come back only when it happened to suit her. In his game, however, the little boy has the mother by a string. He makes her go away, even throws her away, and then makes her come back at his pleasure. He has, as Freud put it, *turned passivity into activity;* he plays at doing something that was in reality done to him.

Freud mentions three items which may guide us in a further social evaluation of this game. First, the child threw the object away. Freud sees in this a possible expression of revenge — "if you don't want to stay with me, I don't want you" — and thus additional gain in active mastery by an apparent growth of emotional autonomy. In his second play act, however, the child goes further. He abandons the object altogether and, with the use of a full-length mirror, plays "going away" from himself and returning to himself. He is now both the person who is being left and the person who leaves. He has become master by incorporating not only the person who, in life, is beyond his control, but the whole situation, with *both* its partners . . . .

But does the child's play — so a frequent question goes — always "mean" something personal and sinister? What if ten children, in horse-and-buggy days, begin to play with reels on strings, pulling them behind themselves and playing horsie? Must it mean anything to one of them over and beyond what it seems to mean to all? . . . .

Children, if traumatized, choose for their dramatizations play material which is available in their culture and manageable at their age. What is available depends on the cultural circumstances and is therefore common to all children who share these circumstances. Boys today do not play steamboat but use bicycles as more tangible objects of coordination — which does not prevent them from imagining, on the way to school or the grocery, that they are flying through the air and machine-gunning the enemy; or that they are the Lone Ranger himself on a glorious Silver. What is manageable, however, depends on the child's powers of coordination, and therefore is shared only by those who have reached a certain level of maturation. What has a *common meaning* to all the children in a community (i.e., the idea of having a reel and string represent a living thing on a leash) may have a *special meaning* to some (i.e., all those who have just learned to manipulate reel and string and may thus be ready to enter a new sphere of participation and communal symbolization). Yet all of this may have, in addition, a *unique meaning* to individual children who have lost a person or an animal and therefore endow the game with a particular significance. What these children "have by the string" is not just any animal — it is the personification of a particular, a significant, and a lost animal — or person. To evaluate play the observer must, of course, have an idea of what all the children of a given age in a given community are apt to play. Only thus can he decide whether or not the unique meaning transcends the common meaning. To understand the unique meaning itself requires careful observation, not only the play's content and form, but also accompanying words and visible effects . . . .

Child's play, hence, is really serious business. In play a child explores his world, develops his body and its capacities, his mind and its potential. The child is endowed with limitless fantasy and likes to improvise in play. As a result, toys which rigidly re-create the adult world in miniature have limited play value for the young child. Abstract play materials, on the other hand, arouse curiosity and stimulate the child to experimentation. Psychologists and child analysts use abstract toys in a technique called "play therapy," which allows the child to re-create each new insight into the world, relive actual experiences, weave fantasies.

Capell in his paper shows that small children regularly employ magical means of mastery in which they produce pleasurable illusions of power. Play of older children can also be understood from this point of view. The appearance of the Oedipus complex leads to a marked change in the character of games. The boy's relationship with his father is now marked by simultaneous wishes for his protection and envy of his power. Team games incorporate this theme. Traditional games are historically derived from primitive magical and religious rites. These games are a partial concession to reality, in that they express the idea of doubt as to the efficacy of magical works. Winning a game implies a sense of magical participation in power. The creation and success of the game of Monopoly illustrates how helplessness in reality generates a game. As social institutions, games can satisfy a wish for union with an all-powerful being in a variety of ways. Games may be compared with religious systems with respect to the functions of rules and leaders. Numerous survivals of primitive social institutions and magical beliefs can be found in traditional games. Trophies are concrete symbols of participation in power, and may be either awarded or actively secured. Provoking a desired reaction can also be a kind of triumph. The specific anxieties of modern man require new games or old ones tailored to his needs.

Huizinga and Freud both observed that the play of children is a most serious and absorbing activity, consuming most of their waking interest and energy. Nevertheless, as Jacob Levine points out in this volume, laughter and fun are inseparable from their play.[7] Huizinga and Freud pointed out that the opposite of play is not serious activity but reality. It is in this sense that play is recreational because we re-create a real world which is different from the one in which we live. The essential point is that we can play seriously and still have fun and be humorous about it. But, Levine says, humor has little place in our spectator sports. He says that in this day of professionalism, competitiveness, "spectatoritis" and high finance, where joking and laughter are unwelcome intrusions, the childish joy of playing is all but lost.

Many games have been handed down from one generation to another with a degree of care, suggesting some inherent and fundamental value. Although spontaneous play is the primary tool used in exploring the psychology of individual children, traditional games, perhaps because they constitute such an "absolutely normal" activity during childhood, have been virtually overlooked by child psychiatrists and psychologists.

Richard H. Phillips presents a brief review of a number of theories of play, followed by his formulation of a theory of children's games.[8] This theory postulates that children's games have underlying meaning, that by means of symbolic actions children assist each other in reducing some of the universal anxieties of childhood, and that children find no interest in games associated with life situations in which they no longer feel anxious. Four familiar games played at widely varying ages, "peek-a-boo," "drop the handkerchief," "hide-and-seek" and "tag" are analyzed in terms of this theory.

Robert T. Porter, writing on sports and adolescence, says that sports represent an elaboration of play which is not only uniquely human, but which reaches its full potential of complexity at about the onset of adolescence.[9] As with so many highly developed cultural achievements of man, resemblances to behavioral patterns of other higher social animals may help to indicate biological roots of play and sports without lessening our respect for the creative aspects made possible by personality maturation of the child in varied human societies. During adolescence, sports provide much needed outlets for the release of controlled amounts and tolerable forms of aggressive and sexual drive energy, with some relief of tension and some pleasurable integration of aspects of these drives into acceptable patterns. While retaining some of the qualities of play, sports also confront the adolescent forcefully with many realistic aspects of social activities, particularly those related to the problems of coping with aggression. This may assist in recognition of leadership qualities, respect for rules and modes of conduct (sportsmanship) which preserve the team and the basis for competition with a determinable outcome, and testing or establishing one's place in assorted "pecking orders" of various sports. Identification with admired adults and peers is facilitated, which helps in the task of achieving a suitable sense of personal identity. Team sports offer valuable social experience under conditions of stress, and help to establish peer relationships as opposed to parent-child types of dominant-submissive patterns which predominate in childhood. Through intense involvement, instruction may be eagerly accepted, and perseverance in the face of failure and fatigue often leads to such clear gains in strength and skill that self-esteem is measurably enhanced and confidence gained for other tasks of growing up.

Helene Deutsch describes the psychoanalysis of a patient in whom an infantile ball phobia led to a special interest and ability in sports.[10] The patient suffered from an imaginary fear that a ball thrown by himself or somebody else might hit him on the head and either kill him or make him an idiot. The patient turned to playing ball in a successful attempt to assuage a severe castration complex. Getting into games relieved him of his phobia. In her paper, Deutsch illustrates the mechanism of projection as an ego defense, in order to explain the transformation and sublimation of castration and death anxiety into egosyntonic aggressive activities that reestablish the reality relationship between the ego and the outside world. Her paper has clinical character — that is, directness of observation free from far-reaching speculations. She has advised the Editors that the patient whose treatment gave her the opportunity to understand some dynamic factors in sport was her only analytic experience in her years of practice. Patients in psychotherapy do not talk about everything, and while some psychotherapists may present themselves as worldly-wise, their experience with the problems of people is relatively limited. Deutsch would like to emphasize the difference between clinical observations, like her paper, and speculations, respectively pseudo-observations, based on knowledge of analytical concepts, which appear in numerous nonanalytic as well as analytic journals.

Using the sport of swimming, Robert A. Dentler presents in his paper the stages of development in life.[11] Dentler chooses the sport of swimming to demonstrate these stages because, in the American national culture, swimming is an unusually valuable form of play. For developing children, swimming contributes powerfully to motor development, reinforcement of feelings of trust and independence, goal-setting and achievement. For adolescents, swimming supplies occasions rich with competition, body display and sociability. For youthful adults, swimming extends into new modes of release through skiing, diving, water gliding and underwater fishing. Dentler's thesis is that swimming is ideally suited for the realization of age-related maturation and self-realization. He also gives attention to the cultural and technical evolution of the sport.

Dentler follows closely Erik Erikson's stages of psychosocial development. In *Childhood and Society,* it may be noted, Erikson sets out eight hypothetical stages of development, and the characteristic conflicts of these stages: trust versus mistrust, autonomy versus shame, initiative versus guilt, industry versus inferiority, identity versus identity diffusion, intimacy versus isolation, generativity (interest in establishing and guiding the next generation) versus self-absorption, and integrity versus disgust.[12] Erikson regards these eight stages of development as supplementing, not replacing, Freud's theory of periods of development with its emphasis on sexual conflicts and maturation. Erikson relates the eight stages both to chronological age and to Freud's developmental stages, but he does point out the contrast between the stress in Freudian theory on typical danger situations and his own emphasis on maturation of function, and between the Freudian view of the central importance of psychosexual development and his own view of the significance of psychosocial development.

It has been seen how much the theory of play emphasizes the reconstitution of a situation in order that it be mastered. A crude variety of this mechanism is found in wall writing, where the most uncomplicated libidinal and aggressive concerns are externalized, mostly in public toilets. That even such a primitive and transparent play idiom can lend itself to quite complicated and critical group processes is illustrated by Clyde H. Ward in his systematic analysis of the origins of the Kilroy phenomenon. Here a very particular play need becomes widespread, becomes disguised, takes the form of humor, joins the general culture, and develops from the faddistic to the near legendary — all in the service of preserving or restoring a threatened identity.[13]

FOOTNOTES

1. Reider, N.: *Preanalytic and Psychoanalytic Theories of Play and Games.* p. 13.
2. See Capell, M. D.: *Games and the Mastery of Helplessness.* p. 39.
3. Erikson, E. H.: *Childhood and Society.* New York, Norton, 1950, pp. 184, 185, 186, 187, 188. Permission to reprint is kindly acknowledged.
4. Freud, S.: A General Selection, Rickman, J., [Ed.]. London, Hogarth Press, 1937.
5. Erikson, E. H.: *op. cit. supra* note 3, at p. 189.
6. Erikson, E. H.: *op. cit. supra* note 3, at pp. 190, 191, 192.
7. Levine, J.: *Humor in Play and Sports.* p. 55.
8. Phillips, R. H.: *Children's Games.* p. 63.
9. Porter, R. T.: *Sports and Adolescence.* p. 73.
10. Deutsch, H.: *Some Dynamic Factors in Sport.* p. 91.
11. Dentler, R. A.: *Swimming and Personality Development.* p. 95.
12. Erikson, E. H.: *op. cit. supra* note 3. Much has been written recently about individual identity. Many forms of mental disturbance are now being considered as different manifestations of a disturbance of the sense of identity. Erikson extended the psychoanalytic theory of personality development by describing the unfolding of the self as a series of identity achievements and crises in the life of the individual, from infancy through adulthood. Milton Rokeach in his book, *The Three Christs of Ypsilanti* (N. Y., Knopf, 1964), discusses three men in Michigan's state mental hospital — a farmer, a clerk and an electrician — each of whom claimed to be Jesus Christ. What happens when these men come face to face, knowing that three individuals cannot possess the same identity? The author points out that among children the game of "let's pretend" (that he or the parent is someone else) is pleasing only so long as the child can be assured that it is only a game. If the game is persisted in by an adult for more than a few moments, the child's belief system is threatened; he becomes panicky, and he begs that all concerned resume their correct identities. The confrontations of the three Christs at Ypsilanti were upsetting and threatening to the men, and all three responded by a revision and restructuring of their belief system (one may shift to John the Baptist). Peterson, N. M.: What's in a Name? *ETC,* September 1966, p. 387.
13. Ward, C. H.: *Sporting with Language. p.* 104. Wall writing is called "graffiti" by archeologists. Tribune Feature: Graffiti — indoors and out — said to mirror society. *Medical Tribune,* April 22-23, 1967, p. 14.

PREANALYTIC AND PSYCHOANALYTIC THEORIES OF PLAY AND GAMES

NORMAN REIDER

PREANALYTIC THEORIES

THE FUN IN PLAY, a puzzling preoccupation for so many students of the phenomenon, is still not a settled issue. Some authors take it for granted as part of the "nature of the beast," a consoling quasisolution that satisfies some. Any theory which proposes that the pleasure in play lies in doing something for its own sake skirts the edges of the problem, which is quite complicated. Bühler's concept of "functional pleasure" belong to this category;[1] that play gives pleasure in its indulgence adds little except a redescription in sophisticated language. We can accept a child's statement that he plays because it's fun or because he likes it, but we cannot be content that this explains play or even certain kinds of play.

Some prefer to explain the pleasure in play on one variety or another of tension-reduction, a concept which does not explain all the nuances. Another attitude is an extreme one like that of Huizinga,[2] who thought that the fun in play defies analysis or logic. No one knows what logic or analysis would explain the fun in play to someone seeking some transcendental or ultimate essence. But whatever theoretical approach is attempted, all considerations have, with variable emphasis, a strong tendency to allocate play to late infancy and childhood and to evaluate it with laud and envy, on the one hand, or with condemnation and eyeful scorn on the other because of its childish nature. Thus, the genetic aspect is inescapable and leads to developmental theories, best exemplified by the psychonalytic attitude.

Psychoanalytic writers have contributed immensely to the theory of play, especially in explaining the content of play hitherto largely considered "aimless" and in elaborating stages of development of play; but they have often disparaged preanalytic studies as interested in "official games" and play as preparation for the future. As a matter of fact, a large wealth of data and theory existed before Freud and his followers enriched the theory of play by the two general contributions noted above. The preanalytic writers were concerned in their psychological theories with what would now be called ego mechanisms. But they dealt with more than psychological theory, and curiously enough they rarely tried to construct a unified theory of play. As demonstrated by Groos,[3] they did not consider the overlapping of one theoretical aspect with another as methodological obstacles. The following is a summary of what he considered the separate, though connected, main theories:

PHYSIOLOGICAL. (1) Play is a necessary discharge of super-abundant energy, of energy not needed for vital processes. (2) A contrary theory, that play affords relaxation and conservation of energy. (3) Play attempts to recapture a pleasurable stimulus or a pleasurable state of relaxation and exhaustion that follows a reaction to a stimulus.

BIOLOGICAL. (1) Play is instinctual in origin. (2) Play derives out of biological needs to obtain food and sustenance and arises when the vital function is fulfilled.

PSYCHOLOGICAL. (1) Play is a pleasurable activity, a conscious or unconscious copying of useful pursuits, a reproduction of pleasure with a non-serious aim. (2) Playful experimentation precedes play but it is not play; it becomes play when it is repetitive, conscious and accompanied by attention and enjoyment. The joy in being an "active cause," physical or mental, adds to play its creative aspect. (3) Play has a dream quality. (4) The pleasure derived from play comes from the satisfaction of inborn impulses. (5) Some play is not psychological at all; psychological play involves self-deception. (6) The pleasure from play derives from pleasure in the stimulus, agreeableness in the stimulus and in its intensity. (7) The pleasure from play is a feeling of freedom, creativity and mastery.

AESTHETIC. The pleasure of play can lead to aesthetics and art. The skills in artistic endeavor resemble those in games and play.

SOCIOLOGICAL. The cheering and harmonizing effect of play strengthens social ties. Communication is aided.

PEDAGOGIC. Some have held that play weakens character and therefore must be forbidden. Since the time of Plato play has also been held to have high educational value. Play can be a method of instruction, or it can be converted to systematic teaching. The most serious work may include a kind of playfulness, since the highest and noblest forms of work are pleasurable activities which can be learned from play. "Play reveals the breadth or limitations of the child's horizon, the independence of his character, or his need of support and direction."

A detailed examination of these concepts shows that the preanalytic theoretical considerations fit well with modern concepts. The thoughts of the older writers lack only the orderly study of the details of the development of play and the unconscious meaning of play as a means of solution of unconscious conflicts. Although the latter advances are considerable, the early concepts were the fundamental discoveries, later often borrowed without acknowledgment.

First, the quest for primary factors quickly led to the instinctual theory of play; observations of play in higher animals seemed to confirm this theory. Because the nineteenth century behavioral scientists relied on a congenital hereditary factor, a characteristic habit of their thinking, this early beginning, correct or not, furnished a facile causal element to fall back upon. Although playful activity in some animals may not develop without a mother who instructs and is imitated, or secondarily without littermates to play with, the instinct hypothesis may still be valid. Nor does the autoerotic play in children with hospitalism argue for an exclusively social theory of play. Both aspects are necessarily interwoven.

Using different terminology, but still referring to an instinctual source of energy, Schiller[4] and Spencer[5] saw play as a use of "surplus energy," energy left over after vital needs are cared for. Groos saw it as "an impulse to activity." From these initial concepts derives the idea that such impulses lead to "playful experimentation." Though psychoanalytic writers emphasize motor activity as the primary constituent of play in the first two years, Groos correctly begins with the playful experimentation of the sensory apparatus. Of course, sensory and motor systems are intimately bound together; but Groos' emphasis focuses on the receptive helplessness of the infant as a precursor of the motor activity. Thus he demonstrates that antecedents of play lie in the "playful experimentation" with touch, sound, and vision (perception of movement, brightness, color and form). By this he means the repetitive perception that gives familiarity and a sense of easy pleasurable differentiation between self and outside world, welded to a reactive motor responsiveness which continues in the infant a sense of omnipotence. Groos cites the uses of sounds in playful experimentation, dividing them into receptive and productive. Somehow, however, he fails to recognize fully the relation between the two: that the anlage of playful experimentation with sound may truly begin in the repetitive hearing of pleasant voices, like a mother's, or by contrast, of unpleasant noises; but the importance of the experience comes from the infant's recognition that he also can be, and indeed is, the creator of both noises and sweet cooing sounds. In the repetition with pleasure begins play.

Groos thought at first that muscular exercise is the *raison d'être* of motor activity, that it is experienced as pleasurable. This idea is a forerunner of Buhler's concept of "functional pleasure," that is, pleasure experienced in performance without any regard to the success of the activity. But when does such pleasurable activity become play? Surely early sensory and motor experimentation is not play; obviously the factors of repetition and rhythm are necessary conditions for play.

Baldwin wrote that repetition is necessary for development; the infant's explorations of his own body, later extended to others, must be repeated because the infant cannot perceive and master his image of himself at one glance.[6] The unfamiliar has to become familiar, and the infant must realize he is the creator of an act. For example, an infant drops a toy repeatedly out of his clumsy inability to hold on. After repeated tries one day, after he has successfully held on, he throws the toy. After more attempts it dawns on him that he alone did the act. With such a pleasure, play begins. The repetition brings recurrence of the pleasure. Soon the activity extends to other parts of the body, controlled alternate movements of the legs, creeping, turning, walking, climbing, dancing, and hurling; all go through the playful experimentation that is the groundwork for muscular activity in sports and games.

Nowadays, the role of rhythm is widely accepted as a part of the nature of an instinctual biological process. But one hundred years ago opposite views were held as to its role. Spencer noted that passionate excitement naturally manifests itself in rhythmic repetition. But expounding an opposite view also prevalent in the nineteenth century, Minor saw in the "naturalness" of rhythm a sort of prudential instinct to restrain the fury of passionate feeling.[7] Schiller likewise saw the same influence:

> *And like a Nemesis, with the golden veins of rhythm,*
> *Harnesses riotus lust, and tames its madness.*

But taming is not always the result of rhythm. It can also produce wild tumultuous ecstatic conditions, as in some dances which build up to tumultuous frenzy via rhythm. Minor's and Schiller's views of the role of rhythm are understandable, for indeed they recognized that a controlled and steady rhythm bridles excitement. The consistent slow rhythm of being rocked, as by a cradle or a hammock, for example, quiets excitement.

The idea of a development of play from a kind of disorganization to more structured types was certainly obvious to the preanalytic writers,[8] but the relation of such development in play to stages in libidinal development was absent. Therefore, what they frequently hint at are developmental phases in ego structure. For example, Groos describes that once the infant begins to extend his playful experimentation to objects outside his body, any object can become a plaything. Such activity as throwing toys around is already so complex that it is difficult to say whether the goal is the motion of the object, the sounds produced by the throwing, or a combination of both. Then follows a destructive or analytic (as Groos terms it) type of play, which involves examination and tearing to pieces of the objects. Paper is torn up, dolls are dismembered. Lastly, a constructive or synthetic type of play follows, where *le besoin de créer* appears — the arrangement of pebbles, the building with sand, the placing of block upon block. Such a sequence cannot strictly refer to psychosexual stages which undoubtedly play a role.

But the postulation of stages of development of play from only a structural aspect can be deceptive. For instance, the hurling of objects begins toward the end of the second trimester of the first year, long after playful preoccupation with examination by eyes and mouth has begun; but by the age of one year, the play-activity of hurling, examining, destroying and organizing is so interwoven that no predominance can be designated. Patterns of play are so dependent on perceptual and cognitive factors of variable valence. For example, an infant of one year who can grasp the gestalt of a pyramid of discs, one on top of another, already shows inklings of perceptual and conceptual organization. It is interesting and important that such activity has succeeded only if the central stick through which the discs are passed was present. Without the stick, the infant could not arrange the discs. He needed the total gestalt of discs and stick. He could grasp the concept of pyramid made up of discs alone only months later.

The idea of gradual development seemed, nevertheless, occasionally to confuse earlier writers. For example, they tended to jump to the conclusion that, when play becomes task-oriented, such as taking a lid off a can and placing it back on again, activity which infants already do by ten months, a problem-solving instinct also exists. Indeed, Preyer thought that even throwing was instinctual;[9] but such stipulations or designations accomplish little. Another approach is needed to explain the changes that take place in the complexities that give increased pleasure. For example, an infant repeatedly drops an object, which is repeatedly handed back to him; then in the course of his increased development and skill, he picks up the toy without help. Now he is dependent upon another person in his play only when the object falls out of his reach, a significant change. Only after this step can the next one occur — the hurling of the toy. This step is already interwoven with a social element — the presence (or absence) of a person to be part of the play (or to be excluded). Then follows still another step in development. The infant, probably by accident, throws the ball against a wall; the ball comes back to him! He is now sole master of a new play in which he can exclude the parent, who before was a necessity in the game.

Later analytic theory would synthesize the above observations using the concepts of psychosexual development and of object relations. The activity described above is analogous to masturbation. First, the handling of the infant's body by another is pleasurable. Then, the infant's handling of his own body for its own pleasure gives the infant a modicum of independence from adults. After this is accomplished, another person may still be a partner in the bodily pleasure, but already it may be of a different quality. Then shifts to inanimate objects (toys) occur. The game of peek-a-boo is an example of a long series of integration of self-pleasure, experimentation with sight and sound, and of relationship to others. So probably at least a concept of an object, if not an actual one, is necessary for play to change into a game.

Leaving now the earlier sensorimotor background of play for a period when psychic abilities of attention, memory, imagination and discrimination are more developed, we find that all of these are subject to playful experimentation. In these phenomena an object like a toy is not necessary. As a matter of fact, this kind of playful experimentation is of quite a different order of phenomena. To begin with, recognition of a familiar loved object is pleasurable; it is related to the feeling that a loved object is pleasurable and to the feeling that a loved object is not lost. The pleasurable recognition of mother or nurse evokes the shadowy feeling of anticipated warmth and intimacy; play is not experienced, but a game may develop if this way of giving pleasure is repeated again and again, a game at losing and being assured of regaining.

Likewise, acoustic recognition may be for some infants more important. A search for the familiar sounds leads to expectation of hearing them or to an attempt to produce the sounds themselves, again illustrating the turning of passive receptivity into activity. Later this develops into the repetition of rhymes and poetry, or into games of recognition, especially games with blindfold elements, a modern example of which is "What's My Line." Such pleasurable use of memory can become an autonomous function when children obtain satisfaction in the exercise of repetitive nursery rhymes, when recognition itself loses importance and the importance of content yields to the importance of the task of reproduction.

During the third to sixth years, a further extension of the "playful experimentation of the mind" exists in imaginative faculties, the appearance of fantasies. In fever, delirium, hypnosis or psychosis, the appearance of content is not under conscious control and is frightening to all children. To gain a feeling of being in control, they may voluntarily evoke the content; Sourian called this "illusion volontaire."[10] Then they deal with primary process material playfully to gain the illusion of control. Sometimes, schizophrenics or borderline characters play with disorientation, depersonalization, hallucinations, delusions, often giving the aspect that they malinger. As a result, their families and even their psychiatrists accuse many of them of being more in control than they actually are.[11]

The more common and less pathological use of such tendencies is the voluntary distortion of reality in play when a stick is changed into a horse or a knotted handkerchief into a doll. Likewise, distortion of exaggeration and depreciation is indulged in — the fantasies of giants and dwarfs, for example. The saving grace is the constant recognition of the unreality of play.

Even attention, an elementary function which some consider instinctive since it involves lying in wait as if prepared to take flight or to seize a prey, varies with stress and relaxation, which, if controlled intermittently, can give a sense of pleasure. Indeed, some children play with their attentiveness, making a game of it for themselves. In most instances, playing with attention is secondary to the tension of the current activity that demands attention: listening to a play, reading, studying, working, gambling, excitement of one form or another in which a diminution in attention wards off too much tension. Playing with attention may be play, or it may be a game. Thus any of the mental faculties involved may be play or game, depending upon the necessity of another object in reality or in fantasy for the activity. Piaget presents remarkable observations on the growth of attention when a child plays with an object that goes in and out of view.[12] Similarly, even thinking processes can secondarily become the subject of play. As an infant perceives the changes brought about inside and outside by his own activities in his development from unconditional to conditional omnipotence, a shift may take place from the activity (anything may serve the purpose – opening a box, emptying and filling a drawer, etc.) to the pleasure of thinking in a casual way about the activity. Solutions of problems may become a source of pleasure in play just as much as activity. If high value is placed on an intellectual accomplishment, problem-solving can become a play or game, giving even greater pleasure than does muscular activity. This type of play extends to riddles and board games.

Up to this point, Groos deals mainly with the pursuit of pleasure. Without any avowal of a hedonistic principle, Groos realized that when he discussed experimentation with feelings, he had reached an impasse in trying to fit the repetitious search for unpleasant feelings into his scheme. What later became for Freud the paradox in the principle of the repetition-compulsion, Groos largely answered by holding that we commonly enjoy disagreeable sensations because we crave intense impressions. And if our primary search for strong stimuli takes a certain amount of pain along with the rest, we accept it, provided that pleasure predominates over pain and play can continue. For example, in sexual pathology the sexual excitement and pleasure neutralize the pain. But Groos misses the point of the search for unpleasant stimuli and feeling. He does not resort to the concept of repetition as a means of achieving mastery, as he did previously. Nor are Spencer's explorations via the poetic expression of the "luxury of grief" any improvement, as Spencer himself recognized. The fact remains that playing with unpleasant feelings was an observable phenomenon unsatisfactorily explained. The writers of this era might also have returned to instinct as an explanation, since they resorted to it at other times of trouble in their theorizing, but they did not.

Yet, when he discusses the displeasure of playing a game to exhaustion, Groos does resort to a biological theory. Just as there are rhythmic repetitious phenomena in nature (the alternate expansion and contraction of lower animals, breathing, heart activity), Groos believes in inexhaustible tendency to repetition in the sphere of voluntary activity. Baldwin anticipated psychoanalytic theory when he called this tendency of reactors to renew the stimulus a "circular reaction." He emphasized what psychoanalysts now call "stimulus hunger." Yet another explanation for the paradox of play to the point of exhaustion is that the trance-like state resulting from such repetition is the end sought. Although this is close to the modern theory of altered ego-states a more consistent conceptualization had to await the development of psychoanalytic theory.

The voluntary control of play must be emphasized. The pleasure of voluntary control comes from the feeling of mastery over one's self and at least part of one's biological heritage. This may become a contest between one's "will and one's reflective or emotional reactions." When such contests appear in play with suppression of emotional expressions, self-esteem arises in the mastery. For example, children play a game in which they stare ahead without winking. He who winks first when a hand is waved in front of his eyes loses. Here the contest is against the reflex. In another game, two children stare at each other. He who giggles or laughs first loses. Other extensions of such trends use endurance of pain (e.g., holding of lighted matches), but while the initial appearance may seem to be a contest between two opponents, the real antagonist is a part of the self. The reward is primarily the acknowledgment of manliness and mastery over one's own nature, and secondly over another person.

Affects such as love, sadness, or suffering may likewise be suppressed playfully, aiding one in a type of denial. Victory over affects connected with old habits like smoking or drinking is also aided if the habit-breaking is played at. The attempt does not seem so serious, and some thus find it easier; others reserve for themselves the rationalization that they weren't serious, as if it were a game to protect themselves from the blow of failure, especially if others accuse them of not being serious.

Thus we reach the large topic of play and games as a contest. The preanalytic writers missed the point of the antagonist's often being the projection of an internal enemy, as I have indicated above. Emmy Sylvester has called to my attention a play by Nestroy[13] in which Holofernes in a crisis of his strength says, "Now we shall see who is stronger, I or I." A child of six exemplified this by competitive games he played by himself, keeping tally of the scores in two columns, headed, "Me" and "My mind." With the advantage of psychoanalytic theory, the meaning of the social role of the antagonist or partner in play is clearer as a contest with instincts or internalized objects.

The earlier writers dealt with playful exercise of physical contest and physical rivalry. Groos speculates with a rare bit of insight that rivalry in games originates in jealousy for the love of parents, whether it is kite-flying or drinking someone under the table. There are obviously other origins. The aggression in play and games is found in satisfactions of superiority in muscular or intellectual activity. The neutralization of aggression by play can be seen when another person directly threatens an infant with a quick lunge or sharp voice of criticism. The infant may react as if he were actually slapped or physically punished. But what happens if the action of the aggression is mitigated or masked by making a game of the assault? In the latter part of the second year, a child will often burst into gales of laughter if one begins an aggressive movement to the child but switches to hitting himself. Or, if one takes the hand of a child and strikes oneself with it and pretends to be hurt, the child will often react with delight or laughter. Later a child will strike an adult as if it were a game, and the adult is supposed to react by acting hurt. I have seen two-year-olds try to provoke punishment as part of a game. When the adult reacts seriously, it is of course a tragedy. If the adult enters the game, it looks delightfully perverse. All games using physical prowess or skill share this quality with almost infinite variations, from playful tussling, prizefighting, wrestling (which may be very brutal, as in some of the Greek games), games of skill without physical contact (basketball), and those in which contact is necessary (football), to jousting tournaments and contests of confetti throwing. In this simple and incomplete array, the importance and intensity of hostile aggression can be quite variable. Rules of the games temper the hostility, but above all the setting of the hostility in a game gives the infant or child a chance to learn control and thus mitigates the fear of his own impulses with the reminder that he is only dealing with a game.

Just as in individual play, social play can be lifted from the physical plane to the theater of mental contest. Groos holds that mental contests originate in antagonism toward authority, for games can provide the acting out of hostility to parental or any other type of authority and also act as an outlet for sibling rivalry. Huizinga takes a converse position, holding that science, law, war, art and drama derive from games which people play, no matter how seriously or lightly. When intellect is used as a weapon, any sort of achievement is a fair game, from reciting more of a poem or more of the multiplication table than the next one, spelling better, or being awarded a prize for singing or winning a board game.

Many games have varying degrees of chance. Tacitus remarked that the ancient Germans would stake freedom, possessions, and even their lives on the throw of dice. By contrast, many card games have only at the beginning the element of chance in the distribution of the cards. The actual play may require skill and at times high-order problem solving. Chance means that the luckier is more favored by the gods (parents) or is judged right in an open or covert quarrel. How a die is thrown, a spinner set off, or a deck of cards cut signifies who wins, who is favored; the later play may just be a confirmatory ceremonial. Tylor correctly saw that soothsaying and games of chance are closely related.[14] Chance thus enters into the service of the competition. Moreover, different character types vary in their need for confirmation of their victory. Some are content with the victory itself; others need the laurel or the prize and will not play unless, for example, a wager is set so as to make the victory substantial. In some games, primarily poker, chance can be used as a theater for mental contest, where the boldness or cleverness of the bet is a variation of the combat for proof of superiority. Moreover, while most rules provide for the element of fair play in that the beginning of the contest establishes equal conditions for the contestants, some abrogate these rules by bullying or teasing a weaker opponent, since they may need this to fulfill a self-evoked prophecy and also for the practical advantage of whatever may come from the intimidation of the opponent. Teasing itself can be a game and may become in some a part of character structure. Sometimes an audience is necessary for the teasing of a weaker opponent so that the bully may cover up the motivation of self-assurance with the more superficial exhibitionism. Sometimes the spectators simply witness the superiority; sometimes they also act as umpires, as a kind of superego, especially to approve the aggression, or at times to disapprove.

Originally, physical contests may have had the purpose of answering the needs of the crowd and giving vicarious participation. Besides the spectator element, other factors distinguish a sport from a game: seriousness to the extent of professionalism (making a business of it), social status, physical rather than mental contest, the need for special equipment or costumes. Therefore, children are never sportsmen, despite the importance of play to them; nor is the chess player, but for other reasons. However, Ariès holds that children in other times could well be called sportsmen.[15]

Illustrating the fluidity of the boundaries among play, games and sports, in recent years more game activity has taken on spectator quality. Track and field events and golf have become more and more spectator sports, and modern electronic equipment has opened bridge tournaments to the viewing public. Mental contests like chess still attract relatively small crowds in the United States. Only recently the Women's Chess Championship of the United States (1964) often had no spectators during the matches. Five months earlier the United States Chess Championship contest with men only had as many as three hundred spectators in one night. In the Soviet Union, a championship chess match is held in a large auditorium before several thousand spectators, and often the thousand who cannot get into the hall view the play on large boards outside.

In the hunt, a playful pursuit with elements of flight and hiding, the object is not another person but an animal. Since the chase was used early in man's history for sport as well as for food, some postulate a kind of instinctive origin; games based on the chase likewise probably originated early, for example, the game of choosing sides as to roles (the hare and hound), games in which there are safe bases (cities or refuge or "home"), and many board games. The object pursued need not be alive ("who's got the button?"). The earlier writers do not try to bring together such games under deeper motivational scrutiny. Analytic writers identified the unconscious equivalence of the earlier object to be hunted and found (the mother) to the fox or other objects to be hunted in the later social games. Such displacements and distortions hide the hostile aggression as well as the search for a loved object.

While such nuances of the fusion of aggressive and erotic elements of play and games may have generally escaped the preanalytic writers, the fusion in love-play was obvious to them; they wrote on the sensuality of children and emphasized the sexual nature of the belligerent play of boys, "especially when the combattants are on the ground and laughlingly struggle with each other." At times they saw human combat as exciting and attractive to women.[16] But they did not systematically analyze love-play into its division of fore-play and after-play, a surprising omission since the concept of playful experimentation could be so applicable to love-play. Further elaborations, such as stress on the aesthetic nature of play, concern extensions of the above theories into "higher mental and emotional functions." Likewise, these earlier writers recognized that society needed to institutionalize certain games into festivals, circuses, parties and masquerades, and that play and games had social value. But that was the extent of their sociological theory. Finally, the pedagogic theory of play, a kind of extension of Plato and Luther, has assigned a cautious dual role to play: it can help one learn and prepare one for an enjoyable life — "All work and no play makes Jack a dull boy";[17] and yet, on the other hand, "All play and no work perpetuates childhood." This dual role illustrates our ambivalence toward instincts, a paradox solved by the eighteenth and nineteenth century pedagogues by making play and games a part of the school curriculum. If a child had to play, the potentially dangerous aspects of play could be brought under control.[18]

NEWER MEANINGS OF PLAY AND GAMES

Freud had already set forth his theory of psychosexual development before he made cursory interpretations of a child's play in terms of his theory; that little Hans was playing horses and bit his father could be understood as Hans wishing he were the horse (the father).[19] Later while playing with a rubber doll, Hans had pushed a small knife through the opening where the squeaker had been attached and had torn the doll's legs apart so as to let the knife drop out.[20] This symptomatic act in play was Hans' idea of what occurred in childbirth, besides indicating some unclear concept of the feminine genitalia.

"Maybe I'm having span-of-attention trouble, but somewhere along the line here, this playing-in-the-sand bit has turned into just a lotta work!"

Pfeifer propounded the first psychoanalytic theory of play based on the sexual drives of children, relating similarities in the dynamics in fantasies, dreams, neuroses, psychoses, myths and religion.[21] A year later Freud related how a child tried to gain mastery of his mother's going away by substitutive activity in play. The child threw the spool to which a string was tied over the edge of his cot so that the spool disappeared and then pulled it back into sight again, with obvious delight.[22]

These examples show that a new dimension of meaning has been added to play, namely, that play has a specific meaning to the individual which makes sense in terms of the history of the player. Moreover, play viewed clinically is an attempted solution of a conflict, mostly unconscious; it acts out unconscious remnants of the past; it may help recall the past; it enables the player to have the illusion of control of the conflict in its derivative form. Since play may not solve the conflict, it is repeated in order to attempt the mastery. This is the essence of the first psychoanalytic theory of play. Since, to use Erickson's terms,[23] play can be a form of language, it can be the royal road to the child's unconscious and thus serve the basis for therapy in children. Later we shall return to the other chief psychoanalytic aspect, the variations of play in terms of developmental stages.

Yet the older theories still have a magnetic pull on psychoanalytic thinking, and a return to biological concepts is evident. As Peller shows,[24] Darwin's views profoundly influenced psychology, especially since species differences are quantitative in nature and not qualitative. That there "is no fundamental difference between man and higher animals in their mental faculties" appealed to the nineteenth century liberal physiopsychologists. How much animal observation and experimentation can answer questions of motivation, development and learning in humans is another matter.

Darwin's concept of survival as the primal striving of the species, even at the expense of the individual organism, could easily have influenced Freud's classification of instincts into two categories, one serving the individual and the other serving the preservation of the species. As Peller points out, however, Freud clearly differentiated between instincts as applied to animals and his concept of "Trieb" which referred to the psychic representation of drives. Freud was careful not to biologize and even rejected the concept of an instinct to imitate, an idea freely used by preanalytic psychologists, who also used Trieb and instinct interchangeably, as did Groos. If one uses these concepts without distinction and with the easy convenience that comes from a loose theoretical system, the idea of two types of play carries no inherent obstacle. If one type of play serves the individual and another is derived from the drive to maintain the species, all is well. For example, a child may play with a ball for his own muscular satisfaction with pleasure from discharge of tension and a sense of mastery; a kitten may play with anything small which it makes move, like a ball or feather, in preparation for catching its own food. Hide-and-seek, a game played all over the world, may serve both individual pleasures, in reacting to finding what has been lost (for instance, a mother), and the species needs, as a preparation for the hunt.

To Darwin, the play of children and animals posed no problem; all play was "pre-exercise," a preparation for the later tribulations of survival. There was no individual need except as a member of a species. But this concept does not fit the observable play of children who seem to be solving immediate internal problems by play, such as playing with dolls after the birth of a sibling. What theory can combine these two aspects? Alexander proposed that play was "the exercise of surplus libidinal energy not required for the grim task of survival."[25] He thereby went back to the Spencer-Schiller formulations of surplus energy but now stipulated that the energy is libidinal and that all erotic phenomena follow the principle of surplus energy; "energy which is not needed to maintain life, I call surplus energy."[26] This is the source of all sexual activity. In the infant, whose needs are satisfied by adults, the incorporating and retentive vectors outweigh the eliminatory one, hence the rapidity of growth. Despite retention in the form of growth, much surplus is neither stored nor used to maintain existence, but is released in erotic activities. This explains the preponderance of erotic behavior over self-preservative behavior in the child. Expending energy in play, the child discovers new uses for his organs and exercises them until mastery is achieved and their different functions become integrated in a utilitarian fashion for independent existence. The utility of this play is secondary and has no motivational significance. The child does not exercise his faculties in play for an ultimate purpose; playing is an aim in itself. Erotic play for the sake of pleasure is the first phase, and the utilization of the functions acquired during erotic play is the second. This may appear paradoxical, but the prolonged dependence of the child upon the parents permits him the luxury of playful erotic activities. Thus, the energy-saving principles and the creative use of surplus energy are interwoven and combine to maintain life and propagation. Repetition makes useful functions automatic and saves energy which can be used for growth and procreation.[27]

Thus Alexander proposes a theoretical basis to resolve the paradox of the "two types of play." Greenacre objects to Alexander's formulations because they dispense with the unconscious.[28] Glover could not help but wonder whether such formulations of the nature of libidinal energy are not closer to Jung than to Freud, and questions the value of Alexander's instinctual theory.[29] Although Glover's objections may be valid, I object not only to the theoretical aspects but also to what I may call some logical ones. Alexander seemed bent upon pursuing the dichotomy between utilitarian and erotic behavior, an idea he acknowledges having received from Ferenczi's differentiation between the utilitarian and pleasurable functions of all body organs. As an example of the utilitarian function of play, Alexander cites Freud's example of the child with the spool. In distinct contrast, Erikson and Waelder[30] contend that play affords mastery of unresolved conflictual experiences with both external and internal dangers, and Peller argues that the solution of problems is the fundamental function of play.[31] With the weight of evidence that play resolves or at least experiments with conflictual situations, Alexander resorts to the example of a playful colt romping in a field to emphasize that such mastery of problems of locomotion has a pleasurable aim in itself and does not belong to the category of the utilitarian function of play. But why not? Is the differentiation really necessary? Why can't the playfulness of the colt in the field, or that of the sea otter or dolphin be just as utilitarian, resolving some tension or conflict?

The impressive point is the need to believe that somewhere in this wide world a Nirvana exists, a conflict-free area of the ego, an activity purely pleasurable, not involved in trouble of antithetical forces or developmental growth pains; this need expresses itself in the concept of "functional pleasure." It may adequately depict how the play of an animal or a child sometimes appears as if indeed the pleasure is indulged in for its own sake; the description is apt but not sufficiently explanatory. However, the idea is attractive since it continues to exist even in Coser's description of an intellectual:[32] "While earnest practitioners tend to focus on the task at hand, the intellectual delights in the play of the mind and relishes it for its own sake."

Despite the overwhelming evidence supporting the idea that play, no matter how pleasurable, is in the solution of a problem or problems, Waelder still believes that differentiation between functional pleasure and mastery is valid and is best exemplified by children's play, despite the fact that his examples actually provide evidence for the psychoanalytic theories based on resolution of conflict. The latter point of view divides play into phases: the instinct to mastery leads in the direction of developmental growth; wish fulfillment is acted out in play; play permits the child to give himself small doses of overpowering experiences so that he can assimilate them according to the mechanism of the repetition-compulsion; play permits the transformation of passivity to activity; play gives a leave of absence from reality and from the superego; and play permits fantasies about real objects. The content of play and games can have both general and specific meaning, for example, the desire to be big and grown-up. On this last point Waelder quotes Freud: "Every playing child behaves like a poet in that he creates a world of his own, or more accurately expressed, he transposes things into his own world according to a new arrangement which is to his own liking."

Besides this grosser motivation in a child's play, Freud also investigated more microscopic aspects such as the playful use of words.[33] Freud was led to see both the play on words and the childhood pleasure of experimentation with words and nonsense syllables as the ego's attempt to gain control of the primary process. Freud knew Groos' writings well, but significantly he designated more specifically that over which the control and mastery had to be achieved — "the welter of the unconscious," as Gombrich put it in his appreciation of Freud's theory of aesthetics.[34] Seen in this light, there is indeed a kinship between the poet and the punster. Both make their discovery in and through language. Again, the long-recognized connection between art and play comes to the fore, but with newer meaning.

It is now fitting to turn to the relation of play to aggression, one of the finest expositions of which is Karl Menninger's chapter on play.[35] Menninger's thesis, primarily on the nature and fate of aggression, also contributes to other aspects of the problem. For example, he defines play as a pleasurable activity in which the means is more important that the ostensible end. This leaves open more satisfactorily the nature of play than does the concept of "functional pleasure," or that of "pleasure for pleasure's sake." Since the player's "avowed and conscious purposes" may not be as important as the pleasurable activity in play, we can understand play in terms of unconscious motivations. Menninger stresses the somewhat controlled regressive nature of play when it

> enables one to return to those pleasurable intervals of childhood when one could do just as one pleased . . . . He does not have to assume a friendliness, he does not feel or maintain a maturity and dignity that would put some strain on his self-control. He does not have to obey either the time clock or traffic lights. If he wants to take a piece of wood and call it a king and ascribe to it great authority and move it about on a chessboard, he may do so, and he will find others who will make the same assumption and indulge in the same fantasies . . . . Furthermore, play permits the opportunity for many miniature victories in compensation for the injuries inflicted by the daily wear and tear of life. This is a comfort which some egos sorely need. In competitive play there are also defeats, to be sure, but the saving grace of play is that a victory is a victory, and a defeat is not defeat — for, after all, "it was only play" . . . . In play we can fall back upon those principles of magic for which there is an eternal longing in the human heart. Persons and substances take on miraculous powers and virtues . . . by a touch of the hand, the utterance of a single word or the contact with preestablished "base" fundamental changes in states are accomplished. With the aim of magic all the dreams of fairy tales can be realized in play: giants slain, treasures discovered, kingdoms acquired, distances annihilated, dragons destroyed. The laws of the prosaic workaday world are replaced by an entirely new order.[36]

Menninger holds that play's most important value is to relieve repressed aggressions. Any sort of organized play is full of aggression. All physical games, card games, and board games, especially chess, are highly sublimated battles. Even imitative play, like a girl playing with a doll, gives outlet for aggression. Likewise, the "doctor game" described by Simmel under the guise of the curative function, is "the erotic fantasy of being the victim of a powerful man who has access to all parts of the body with a concomitantly acted hostile fantasy directed against the parents' prohibitions."[37] Thus play may be a method of dealing with erotic as well as aggressive problems in a socially accepted form.

Since Aristotle wrote of the emotions becoming purified by play, common experience has attested to that belief. It is generally held that play and games discharge aggression, either as catharsis or sublimation, and Menninger has been a foremost proponent of this view. Yet the question is not so simple.[38] First, I doubt that "repressed" hostility is drained in play; perhaps "suppressed" hostility can easily find partial discharge in play and games. Second, it is uncertain whether all cathexes can be displaced by derivatives and thereby find complete discharge in sublimation. (The same problem applies to an important theoretical question in the psychotherapies.

I believe that our theoretical bases must maintain that not all cathexes can be posited into derivatives.) Moreover, if hostility is discharged via play, it cannot be any complete discharge, or why for one thing, the need for repetition? Why must the play be indulged in over and over if hostility is fully discharged in play?

The possible answers are numerous: hostility is only partly discharged; the genetic (and possibly instinctual) reasons for the hostility are untouched and may continue to generate more hostility, which in turn needs further avenues of release. Granting that partial discharge is better than none, to ascribe to play itself therapeutic function misses the importance of object relations in play and games. Partial discharge which reestablishes an equilibrium is therapy if one decides to define therapy as such.

I doubt that play per se has helped anybody solve anything. Although we are all grateful from time to time that John Smith had his weekly poker game, chess game or his bowling, for otherwise he would be impossible to live with (imagine what he'd be like without this or that outlet for his aggressions), nothing indicates that such activity provides anything but an outlet for this immediate moment. I doubt that it taps the reservoir of aggression at all. I have known hunters, chess players, athletes, orators and great wits, quite proficient in the discharge of their aggressions in their own sublimated ways, whose essential characters are quite untouched, despite years of seemingly effective discharge. I have never known an oedipal problem to be solved over the chessboard. Rather, it seems that play and games provide transient discharge, which is of whatever help it is. Actual solution of problems still depends on play plus other factors operating in concert with developmental ones, or play may be the theatre for working through problems with objects.

Yet the psychoanalytic literature on play therapy repeatedly avows the healing power of play. Erikson illustrates this thesis well with several examples of detailed work with children;[39] but these occurred in a clinical setting with therapeutic intent where, for one thing, transference manifestations could be worked through. It is uncertain whether there exist quantitative and/or qualitative differences in solutions of internal problems when they are "played-through" in individual play in contrast to when they are worked through in play therapy. I believe that a significant difference exists.

However, before any meaningful attempt can be made to answer this question, a developmental theme must be introduced. Pfeifer attempted it years ago, but Peller finally fitted the mass of observational data into a comprehensive conceptual framework.[40] Her main theme stems out of consideration that each libidinal phase has its anxieties and deprivations and that play is instigated by an effort to deny them, to lessen them or to work them through. The general principle of development by turning passive into

TABLE I
SURVEY OF PLAY ACTIVITIES

	Central Theme of Play: Object-Relations	*Deficiencies Anxiety (denied)*	*Compensating Fantasy*	*Formal Elements, Style*	*Social Aspect*	*Play Material*	*Secondary Play Gains*
Group I	Relation to body . . . . Anxieties concerning body	My body is no good I am often helpless	My body (its extensions, replicas, variations) is a perfect instrument for my wishes Imagery of grandeur, of perfect ease	Hallucinations (pos. & neg. rather than fantasies Imagery increases pleasure, persistence	Solitary	Extensions & variations of Body functions & body parts	Increased body skills & mastery Initiation into active search for gratification
Group II	Relation to preoedipal mother . . . . Fear to lose love object	My Mother can— desert me do as she pleases	I can do to others what she did to me I can go on (or quit)	Short fantasies Endless, monotonous repetitions Few variations No risk, no climax, no real plot Tit-for-tat	Solitary or with mother Other children rank with pets, or things—not as co-players Sporadic mirroring play	Maternal play with dolls, stuffed animals, with other children, and mother herself Peek-a-boo Earliest tools	Rage, anxiety mitigated; ability to bear delay, frustration Initiation into lasting object relation
III Group starts about 3 years	Oedipal relations & defenses against them . . . . Fear to lose love of love object	I cannot enjoy what grownups enjoy	I am big I can do as big people are doing Family romance	Spontaneity Infinite variety of emotions, roles, plots, settings Time is telescoped In later times: drama, risk	Early co-play Attempts to share fantasy Fantasy always social Activity may be solitary or social	Dollplay; wide variety of events, of father, mother images: (pilot, nurse, magician, etc.) Creative play, imaginative play Use of emblems, props, insignia	Preparation for adult roles, adult skills Co-play prepares co-work Initiation into adventure, accomplishment
Group IV starts about 6 years	Sibling relations . . . . Fear of superego and superego figures	I am all alone against threatening authority I cannot start all over again	Many of us are united We observed rules conscientiously I can live many lives	Codified plot & roles Importance of rules, program, rituals, formal elements Reciprocity (Piaget)	Organized co-play Fantasy tacitly shared	Team games Board games Organized games Games with token armies	Dissolving oedipal ties Cooperation with brothers, with followers & leaders experienced as gratifying

active applies to play also. Ego and id are on good terms during play, and it may be added that the superego is bribed by the play-like character to disappear or to be rendered inoperative. Play ceases to be play when the child loses his ability to stop when he wants to, when he becomes fixed to a phase and play takes on the nature of phobic defense. Peller organizes a scheme of play as first originating in relationship to one's body.[41]

In the first phase general anxiety results from the feeling that the body is deficient and helpless. The compensating fantasy proposes that the body is a perfect instrument for the child's orders, leading to vague images of grandeur and then to elation. Implements of play are used as substitutes for or improved versions of body parts rather than as tools. Later, this development of accessories to body activities reaches its highest stage in sports. Play at this level, which is inescapably carried forward, is directed against the ego-feeling stemming from the infant's and child's self or helplessness. Peller and Greenacre feel that "functional pleasure," a kind of secondary play gain, brings increased body skill and mastery and is more evident in this phase than in later ones. But in this sense, "functional pleasure" is not "pleasure for pleasure's sake"; fantasies of greater skill of potency are at least original attributes of such play, even though they may become part of an autonomic function or may even become submerged, suggesting that such play has a utilitarian internal function. The concept of utility has been used for centuries to differentiate play from work and has now even been used for different types of play. Each stage of play has its utilitarian function congruent with the capacities, abilities and problems of that phase.

The second phase in development of play is related to the preoedipal mother. The central formula in this type of play is "I can do to you what mother did to me," or "I can leave you as she left me." This style of play contains numerous repetition without many variations; it is serious, sober, business-like and boring to adults. The first displacements of feelings about the mother onto animals occur in this stage. Peller speculates that in the secondary play games of this period the passive turns into the active role, and that by doing unto others what mother has done to him, the child begins to feel the intensity of his anxiety and rage. Although Peller concedes that her generalizations are over-condensed, she stresses that there are no sharp boundaries between these phases; moreover, the child may revert to the play of the first phase at any time for regressive reasons, and play of the first phase becomes woven into the second; these complications also hold for the progressions of the later stages. For example, when a child in a stage of relationship to the pre-oedipal mother plays with a toy dog and has the dog eat everything and make "all gone," play from the first phase has been interlaced with that of the second phase.

However, despite the lack of sharp boundaries between phases, the presence of the pre-oedipal mother is a necessary background for the play of the first phase, play with one's own body. The quality of play with one's own body is quite different in the presence of the mother than when she is not present. The idea of autoerotic play without the background of an object relationship must be abandoned as archaic.[42] So-called spontaneous individual pleasurable play of infants and children is not the first phenomenon which occurs genetically. The game-like activity of infant and mother beginning at the breast is a prerequisite occurrence and is what we later see as individual play. In this sense, mother-child play of infancy games as they are called by some incorrectly, are prerequisites for all subsequent kinds of play.

The next stage is play stemming out of conflicts on the oedipal level. Formally, such play is now ordinarily called games; play activity of the previous phases may also be called games, if another person or image enters in and if there is some semblance of rules, order, or sequence of activity; peek-a-boo is thereby a game. As I stated above, play activity with oneself may be termed a game if the partner or antagonist is only fantasied. Peller further writes that in the oedipal period, the child's play seeks to release him from the painful disappointments of the family attachments. Organized games and identification with playmates offer him reality-adapted goals, more modest now because he has greater abilities. In this phase of play, which may begin at age three, interest and curiosity in riddles, tricky problems, jokes and puns may begin. Social aspects broaden, and children plan their play, communicating their plans and preparations to each other. Greater interest of effort, affect and intelligence develops. The content of the play reveals the attempted solution of oedipal problems.

The last section in Peller's scheme is post-oedipal play, where team games predominate — baseball, football, card and board games. Such games and sports are more reality-adapted than oedipal play and rely on the fantasy of belonging to a group of brothers mutually and jealously guarding the prerogatives or following a chosen leader. Anal sublimations appear on a higher level like collecting, bartering and cheating. Yet sometimes the sublimations are not complete; a preadolescent boy told me of an anal game of his group — to sit on a limb of a tree and shit at a target piece of paper on the ground.

The importance of the group emerges in this phase; cliques, counter-cliques, and secret societies plan deeds of love and hate. Hobbies become important. The underlying anxiety "I have to face authority" is compensated by the games and fantasies of "I am not alone; I belong to a united group." The strict rules of the game give a sense of independence from external superego figures. Peller also emphasizes that these games give the feeling over and over again that a problem may have an attempted solution. For example, in chess one can feel that the king is not killed, because another game can be begun. However, this may also occur in previous phases — the clock can be turned back and a beginning returned to as many times as wished.

It is true, however, that post oedipal play fosters identification more than oedipal play. The play with peers makes the family romance recede, and homosexual strivings are channeled into team games. Cooperation is necessary for the games to go smoothly, and the underlying fantasies are shared with relatively few emotional cathexes. Board games are still one step removed; each player has his pieces, a token army; equality prevails, at least in a formal sense, as long as the rules are observed, both sides can remain friends, and they reestablish identity by the ritual of the handshake after the game.

The principle of equality along with the central theme of rivalry leads to adult characteristics of fair play, an offshoot of the struggle for equality. The culture may value this so highly that chivalry is beginning to be more important than victory. Evans shows that in certain settings honorable defeat may be preferable to inglorious victory, and that instead of victory at any price, the rule may become the narcissistic satisfaction of proving one's own manhood.[43]

In summary, Peller states that the anxiety of one period becomes the favorite play material of the next. Again, I doubt whether this progression really solves anything. For example, an oedipal problem becomes more distant, more hidden, more elaborated and more directed into the formal aspects of the postoedipal games. In a sense, therefore, more successful defenses are added. Certainly, this can lead to "ego-support," as Redl terms it,[44] when games help a player or a group maintain a reasonable balance between impulse and gratification, emergent anxieties, frustrations and excitements on the one hand, and the behavioral demands of the game processes themselves on the other. The moot point is whether such supports carry over into ordinary life behaviors. It is unclear under what conditions the rules of the game, fair play and maintenance of a balance between impulse and gratification can be incorporated into the individual. Possibly some can no longer use such supports once the game situation no longer exists. Likewise, some can probably make the rather easy transference to nongame situations under these conditions: if a style of game-playing continues and is carried into other life situations, if the group situation continues to pertain, if it is fantasied, or if life itself becomes a game. The style of playing games as a way of life certainly characterizes some people, so much so that such a person may be a kind of character type, a variant of the "as-if" character. The success of such playing depends on the necessity of collaborators for which Berne has compiled evidence; his examples indicate that no solution comes from play of the game per se.[45] At most, a very temporary release occurs, and the game has to be played again.

Later concepts of the maturational aspect of play support the thesis of the limited value of play in the solution of central conflicts. Anna Freud traces three development lines that the child goes through:[46] The line from egocentricity to companionship, from the body to the toy, and from play to work. Discussing the function of the game, she points out that since games are governed by inflexible rules to which the individual participant must submit, only a child who has adapted to reality sufficiently to leave egocentricity for loyalty to the group can enter into them. In other words, the maturation has to precede the adherence to the game, and the game does not produce the maturation that makes participation in the group possible.

Likewise, in another context, Greenacre doubts that play thoroughly and generally reduces anxiety.[47] Play may reduce a severe degree of anxiety through the illusory mastery, which in turn permits further maturational development to occur, giving the opportunity to meet similar disturbing experiences in reality later. In the repetitive oscillation between progression and regression, the maturational forces of growth push the organism forward, while the regression to the familiar sets in before the next maturation push. In this light, play and games may be seen to provide a sort of rehearsal of what has to be mastered in a kind of trial maturational push. The real maturation will come with the mastery of the real conflictual situation. If it does not come, the solution will remain on the derivative level, if at all. The apt expression of Phillips on this point is that mastery of anxiety in games is symbolic.[48]

The question of the nature of conflict-free play and play as solution, therefore, has made some advances since 1932.[49] Besides the contributions in regard to development and maturation cited above, Hartmann's concept may be an effective compromise.[50] He writes, "It is possible, and indeed probable that the relationship to reality is learned by way of detours. These are reality adaptations which at first certainly lead away from the real situation. The function of play is an example." So by abandoning the polemic of whether play helps to solve nuclear problems, and by rephrasing the issue in terms of adaptation, we may avoid an impasse. Kardos and Peto make the best contribution to the metapsychology of play, reducing formulations of the disintegrative-integrative process in play to the primary mental processes,[51] a concept with which Ekstein also deals.[52]

Two contributions from social anthropology are also important. First, from the study of about one hundred tribes and their games, Roberts, Arth and Bush classify games as having to do with (1) physical skill, (2) strategy and (3) chance.[53] They conclude that games of strategy are related to social systems, games of chance are related to religious beliefs, and games of physical skill are related to environmental conditions. In general, their studies support the psychoanalytic theory that games are exercises in mastery. In other words, they feel that games of strategy may be related to mastery of the social system, games of chance may be linked with mastery of the supernatural, and games of physical skill are possibly associated with mastery of both self and environment. These opinions are consistent with the concept of ego stages.

"All right! All right! Now it's *my turn! I've* got some hostility left over, *too,* you know!"

The other work, by Maccoby, Modiano and Lander, starts with Huizinga's thesis that play both reflects culture and is "culture-creating."[54] They studied games in a Mexican village to see whether games might reveal character traits consonant with the culture, and they found that the games did indeed reflect character attitudes toward authority, leadership, cooperation and rules. On the other hand, an attempt to introduce new games to observe if their adoption might influence character indicated that character and society were not reformed, but did "support the process of cultural change." The experiment was not convincing, and certainly more similar and sustained experiments are necessary to evaluate the effect of the introductions of new games on a culture.

To orient the problems theoretically: when we study work or play as therapy, we are primarily dealing with the dynamic and economic aspects via concepts of discharge and displacement;[55] when we consider games as a mechanism for ego development in children and adolescents, we deal largely with genetic, structural and adaptational aspects.

Of all of the theoretical data I wish to emphasize the following main points: (1) The concept of functional pleasure is not a useful one since it ignores the unconscious and object relations. (2) The concept of a very early stage of play which is autonomous and concerned only with one's own body will have to be relinquished for a concept that even the earliest play must be considered as social. The earliest play has to take place in the setting of the mother-child relationship. (3) It is doubtful that play helps solve internal problems except in therapeutic situations. Play or games provide at most the vehicle for social interactions which give a rehearsal for mastery at a real level, or give only transient discharge with an illusion of mastery.

NOTE

I wish to acknowledge the assistance of Jonathan P. Reider in the writing of this chapter.

FOOTNOTES

1. Bühler, K., cited by Waelder, R.: The psychoanalytic theory of play. *Psychoanal Quart, 2:* 208, 210, 1933.
2. Huizinga, J.: *Homo Ludens.* Boston, Beacon, 1955.
3. Groos, K.: *The Play of Animals.* New York, D. Appleton, 1898; Groos, K.: *The Play of Man.* New York, D. Appleton, 1901.
4. Schiller, F.: *Essays, Aesthetical and Philosophical.* London, George Bell, 1875.
5. Spencer, H.: *Principles of Psychology.* New York, D. Appleton, 1873.
6. Baldwin, J. M.: *Mental Development in the Child and the Race.* New York, Macmillan, 1895.
7. Minor, J., cited by Groos, K.: *The Play of Man, op. cit. supra* note 3, at p. 89.
8. Lazarus, M.: *Uber die Reize des Spiels.* Berlin, F. Dummler, 1883.
9. Preyer, W., cited by Groos, K.: *The Play of Man, op. cit. supra* note 3, at p. 103.
10. Sourian, W., cited by Groos, K.: *The Play of Man, op. cit. supra* note 3, at p. 131.
11. An exceptionally good clinical paper on this theme, with splendid examples and well-considered dynamics, is by Cain, A. C.: On the meaning of playing crazy in borderline children. *Psychiatry, 27:*278-289, 1964.
12. Piaget, J.: *The Construction of Reality in the Child.* New York, Basic Books, 1954.
13. Nestroy, J.: *Judith and Holofernes, Gesammelte Werke,* Vol. 5. Wien, Verlag von Anton Schroll, 1949, pp. 222-3.

14. Cited by Groos, K.: *The Play of Man, op. cit. supra* note 3, at pp. 207-8.
15. Ariès, P.: *Centuries of Childhood.* New York, Knopf, 1962.
16. See Groos, K.: *The Play of Man, op. cit. supra* note 3, at pp. 252-279.
17. On a recent Candid Camera show, a youngster was asked to complete the saying, "All work and no play makes Jack a . . ." He aptly replied, "A dope."
18. Lehman, H. C., and Witty, P. A.: *The Psychology of Play Activities.* New York, Barnes, A. S., 1927; Mitchel, E. D., and Mason, B. S.: *The Theory of Play.* New York, Barnes A. S., 1934.
19. Freud, S.: *A Phobia in a Five-Year-Old Boy (1909),* Volume 10, Standard Edition. London, Hogarth Press, 1955, p. 52.
20. Freud, S.: *op. cit. supra* note 19, at p. 85.
21. Pfeifer, S.: Ausserungen infantil-erotisaken triebe im spiele. *Imago, 5:*243-283, 1919.
22. Freud, S.: *Beyond the Pleasure Principle (1920),* Volume 18, Standard Edition. London, Hogarth Press, 1955, p. 15.
23. Erikson, E. H.: Studies in the interpretation of play. *Genet Psychol Monogr, 12:*563-564, 1940.
24. Peller, L.: Biological foundations of psychology: Freud vs Darwin. *Bull Phila Assn Psychoanal, 15:*79-96, 1965.
25. Alexander, F.: A contribution to the theory of play. *Psychoanal Quart, 27:*185-193, 1958.
26. Kazantzakis, N.: *Report to Greco.* N. Y., S and S, 1965, p. 168, The surplus-energy theory is beautifully expounded here: "When life has succeeded by dint of daily effort in conquering the enemies around it — natural forces, wild beasts, hunger, thrist, sickness — sometimes it is lucky enough to have abundant strength left over. This strength it seeks to squander in spirit. Civilization begins at the moment sport begins. As long as life struggles for preservation — to protect itself from its enemies, maintain itself on the surface of the earth — civilization cannot be born. It is born the moment that life satisfies its primary needs and begins to enjoy a little leisure.

"How is this leisure to be used, how apportioned among the various classes, how increased and refined to the utmost? According to how each race and epoch solves these problems, the worth and substance of its civilization can be judged."
27. Alexander, F.: *op. cit. supra* note 25.
28. Greenacre, P.: Play in relation to creative imagination. *Psychoanal Stud Child, 14:*61-80, 1959.
29. Glover, E.: Freudian or neofreudian. *Psychoanal Quart, 33:*97-109, 1964.
30. Waelder, R.: The psychoanalytic theory of play. *Psychoanal Quart, 2:*208-224, 1933.
31. Peller, L.: Libidinal phases, ego development and play. *Psychoanal Stud Child, 91:*178-198, 1954.
32. Coser, L. A.: *Men and Idea: A Sociologist's View.* Glencoe, Free Press, 1965.
33. Freud, S.: *Jokes and Their Relation to the Unconscious (1905), Standard Edition,* Volume 8. London, Hogarth Press, 1955, pp. 14, 121, 128, 169-70, 225, 227.
34. Gombrich, E. H.: Freud's aesthetics. *Encounter, 26:*36, 1966.
35. Menninger, K.: *Love Against Hate.* New York, Harcourt, 1942, pp. 167-188.
36. Menninger, K.: *op. cit. supra.*
37. Simmel, E.: The "Doctor Game," illness and the profession of medicine. *Int J Psychoanal, 7:* 470-483, 1926.
38. See Stone, A.: *Football, infra.*
39. Erikson, E.: Toys and reason, in *Childhood and Society.* New York, Norton, 1963, pp. 209-246.
40. Peller, L.: Libidinal phases, ego development and play. *Psychoanal Stud Child, 91:*178-198, 1954.
41. Peller, L.: *op. cit. supra* note 31, at p. 183. Reprinted with permission of International Universities Press.
42. Balint, M.: Love for the mother and mother-love. *Int J Psychoanal, 30:*251-9, 1949.
43. Evans: The passing of the gentleman. *Psychoanal Quart, 18:*19-43, 1949.
44. Redl, F.: The impact of game ingredients on children's play behavior, in Schaffner [Ed.]:

Group Processes. Transactions of Fourth Conference, Josiah Macy Foundation, 1959, pp. 33-81.

45. Berne, E.: *Games People Play*. New York, Grove Press, 1964.
46. Freud, A.: The concept of developmental lines. *Psychoanal Stud Child, 18*:245-265, 1963.
47. Greenacre, P.: Play in relation to creative imagination. *Psychoanal Stud Child, 14*:61-80, 1959.
48. Phillips, R.: The nature and function of children's formal games. *Psychoanl Quart, 29*: 200-207, 1960.
49. Federn, P. [Ed.]: Spielen and spiele. *Z Psa Paedogagik, 6*:173-264, 1932.
50. Hartmann, H.: *Ego Psychology and the Problem of Adaptation*. New York, Int Univs, 1958, p. 18.
51. Kardos and Peto: Contributions to the theory of play. *Brit J Med Psychol, 29*:100-112, 1956.
52. Ekstein, R.: Pleasure and reality, play and work, thought and action. *J Humanistic Psychol*, Fall, 1963, pp. 20-31.
53. Roberts, Arth, and Rush: Games in culture. *Am Anthropologist, 61*:597-602, 1959.
54. Maccoby, M.; Modiano, N., and Lander, P.: Games and social character in a Mexican village. *Psychiatry, 27*:150-162, 1964.
55. Reider, N.: Chess, Oedipus and the Mater Dolorosa. *Int J Psychoanal, 40*:320-333, 1959.

GAMES AND THE MASTERY OF HELPLESSNESS

MARTIN D. CAPELL

IT IS WITH SOME TREPIDATION that I venture on a psychological analysis of games. I hear already the chants of Sophisticated Man: "What, again? Isn't it enough that we have been deprived of our most cherished illusions? Of the innocence of childhood, art, theatre, and literature? Of our mastery over our behavior? Are these High Priests of the Unconscious not yet satisfied with our guilt? Are we also to lose that most elemental pleasure, the fun of a game?"

These mournful pleas need not deter us. Scientific truths are inevitably cast in the role of the Serpent in the Garden of Eden. From a scientific point of view, we need no special justification for wanting to understand such a fundamental human need as game-playing. As there are many roads to knowledge, however, we will follow that one which is paved equally with belief and skepticism. Although our destination is in clear sight, the road winds and turns as if to show its indifference to the demands of time. The scenery ranges from the birth of games in history and human development to the play-contests of today. By the end of our journey, if we have gained nothing but the illusion of mastery over the unknown, our game of psychoanalysis will have been concluded successfully.

First, take one giant step back from the "magic circle" of play of some good (satisfying) game.[1] Really, isn't it a strange spectacle? The players and spectators are utterly absorbed in the action. Play Time proceeds in rhythmic steps, while Real Time passes unheeded. See the tension — and now, the cries, screams, imprecations, flailing of arms and legs. The issue at stake is surely of life-and-death proportions. The participants pit their strength, coordination, craft and faith against each other or against powerful forces of nature, striving desperately to win . . . but what and why? You note the admiration, trophy or money that the winner may receive. But you also know that the inner pleasure of the winner (and corresponding unhappiness of the loser) does not depend upon supplies (or deprivations) from without. Material or interpersonal rewards cannot obscure the fact that games are played basically for their own sake.[2] The fun of a game depends fundamentally on internal satisfaction of some wish, one which is also being represented more or less symbolically in the external reality of the game itself.

"Wait a minute," you remark. "I know people who just don't care about winning the game. To some, playing fairly is all that counts; to others, having emulated their favorite expert is the important thing. One friend of mine just enjoys passing the time. Another one always loses but keeps coming back for more; I almost get the impression that he must want to lose." You are quite right in this. Apparently, there exists games within games.[3]

We observe that the game ends. Real life resumes, and (hopefully) all in reality is as it was before. Only the memory of triumph and defeat remains (which may or may not have further consequences). We carry away our memories, variously glorious or rankling, and remind ourselves of them festively or funereally. Here we see one of the functions of trophies — symbols not only of past triumphs but of triumphs over the past.[4] To carry away a concrete reminder of some event is a victory over time and distance. In our years of declining vitality, we may be very grateful for such souvenirs.

Now, take another giant step back in time to Freud's major commentary on games.[5] He describes for us a boy of one and a half years, very attached to a mother who leaves the home periodically. This child is also an "unusually good little boy." This means that (precociously) he does not permit himself the usual freedom of a small child to protest: to cry, scream, flail his arms and legs about, etc. Separation ordinarily causes anxiety in a small child because he depends on his mother to keep him from being overwhelmed by his own needs. Mastery of the fear of being abandoned is a prerequisite for independence of action.

Freud relates that the boy has a "disturbing habit" of throwing his toys away into corners, under beds, etc., so that picking them up is "quite a business." Although Freud does not say so explicitly, it appears to be disturbing because the mother (or her substitutes) are called upon to retrieve the toys. As the boy throws one away, he exclaims "Gone!" Subsequently, he ties a length of string onto a wooden spool, stands beside his curtained crib, and throws the spool into it, saying "Gone!" Then he pulls it back, hailing its reappearance with "There!" He has constructed a simple game for himself which he plays repeatedly with much apparent pleasure.

Freud interpreted the game as the child's compensation for permitting his mother to go away without a fuss. In the game, the boy has made himself master of comings and goings instead of their passively helpless victim. He has symbolized the departing object (his mother) as a toy and is doing to it what he feels had been done to him. Perhaps he is also denying his real need for her as well, as if to say "Go away, then. I don't need you. I'm even sending you away myself."

These explanations also tell us the reasons for the boy's pleasure . . . or do they? You may object, as did Freud, that while the enjoyment of "There!" was comprehensible, the enjoyment in "Gone!" was not; the associated separations were painful. Yet Freud noted that the little boy often played "Gone!" as a game in itself.

Our road must circle around before we can have an answer to this puzzle. Take one baby step into a nursery, and observe there a hungry infant crying in desperation for some relief of his pangs. His thumb finds its way to his mouth, he sucks, he is calmed for the moment and may even fall asleep before his hunger again asserts itself. In the meanwhile, we have seen what is perhaps the child's first work of magic. The thumb, an object in reality, has been used to bring about a pleasurable illusion of satiety. Even before this, it is thought that the infant simply "wishes up" a picture or sensation of whatever will satisfy him. Thumbs, or later equivalents such as pacifiers, blankets, or dolls sometimes are treated with special reverence, serving as "transitional objects"[6] which have both self and not-self properties (although the distinction in an infant is questionable). We shall have occasion later to point out how a kind of transitional object makes a reappearance in adult games.

The infant is now somewhat older, and his fond mother enjoys playing a game of "peek-a-boo" with him. The child imitates the mother, and a magical effect occurs: she vanishes! Bear in mind that, from his point of view, he has made his mother vanish by his own physical act. He has also begun to master his fear of her absence and to admit, ever so little, that this pleasure-giving mother is separated from him (not a part of him). He accomplishes this in a safe situation; he has merely to drop his hands (another physical act) to reassure himself. These actions in the game are becoming connected with pleasurable memories. It is also thought that imitation is the first step in making an identification with another person; to act like someone else makes you more alike, and thus closer.

More time passes, and we now observe the little boy confined to his crib, high chair, playpen, or toilet seat. He drops one of his toys on the floor, and his loving mother picks it up and gives it back to him. He now repeats his magical gesture; for he has not only brought about the toy's separation from him, and thereby further tested out the boundaries of his inner and outer reality, but he is also making this powerful mother do what he wants. The reality is that he cannot retrieve the desired toy; if he could, he could actively master his helplessness. Instead, he resorts to *passive* mastery.[7]

Perhaps you have already divined by explanation of the pleasure in playing "Gone!" The act of throwing the toy away recalls to mind a memory of passive mastery. The boy masters his anxiety over his present actual helplessness by conjuring up a pleasurable illusion of power, turning defeat into triumph. The word *illusion* comes from Latin roots which mean literally "in play."[8]

This kind of act is similar to other magical acts which explicitly or implicitly are intended to undo prior acts or fantasies. "Knock on wood" is an example of a magical undoing of hostility. Primitive rites are also instances of magical acts of control in which powerful forces are subject to the worshiper's will. An Indian sun dance, for example, obtains its efficacy in warding off famine or evil spirits from the illusory belief that the actions have an influence in reality. This kind of passive mastery of reality is in contrast to empirical (scientific) study of how to improve crop yields. I suggest that such rites, like our little boy's game, arise from anxiety over helplessness at being unable to master the situation actively.

You ask, "What has all this to do with my golf, bowling and bridge? Do you suggest that I enjoy them because I feel anxious over being helpless? A child or savage may be helpless; I am not. In any case, helplessness is a very uncomfortable state, and I wouldn't get any fun out of it." My answer is first to ask you to consider whether or not there are many forces which directly affect your life which are beyond your power to master actively, such as the inevitability of time, of death — and of taxes. Secondly, I must emphasize that it is precisely because awareness of helplessness is so uncomfortable that we seek out illusions with such persistence.

Much is now known about the motivation of children's play. Children are regularly in the position of encountering situations of helplessness which they are unable to master in reality. They are easily stimulated to primitive wishes, the satisfaction of which would be impossible or harmful or forbidden. Adults have learned many ways of warding off awareness of such wishes, but children rely fundamentally on play for this learning. A boy helpless to dispute directly his father's authority can play at being Dick Tracy, who is permitted to control and suppress criminals who oppose lawful authority. This illusion of power, which replaces his awareness of his helplessness, has to do with passive mastery. That the boy is also bulwarking himself against his own unregulated aggression through imitation of a regulatory figure, that he practices and improves his strength, coordination and craft, that he learns how to utilize the resources or abilities of others in achieving a goal — these are all useful self-enhancements whose result is to help relieve the actual helplessness.

Playing doctor is another example of how helplessness in reality promotes a play solution. Being examined or treated by a physician is often a frightening experience for a small child. By turning matters around in play, he is aided in mastering his anxiety over his helplessness and thus is aided in the real situation of having to consult a doctor. Playing doctor (as we all know) is also taken over in the service of children's sexual curiosity. Keep in mind (as we all may not know) that children are sometimes terrified of the physician's curiosity, which leads (in the child's fantasy) to discovery of evidence of the child's forbidden sexual activities. As a game, playing doctor has the virtue of rules, and rules can sanction behaviors which might otherwise be unacceptable; for example, you are permitted and actively encouraged to commit murder during war. However, I think that the fundamental reason that sexual curiosity takes the form of a game for children is that a lack of sexual knowledge is experienced by them as helplessness. The doctor is obviously the person who knows everything in this area. Children do not have the biological competence, if you will, to comprehend sexual activity of a genital kind. To be aware of this incompetence, however, is to feel helplessly left out — therefore a game.

Normal play of children has one overriding virtue for them: they feel that they are seeking it out themselves and that it is not an experience forced upon them. It is as if to say, "It didn't happen to me, I actively brought it about; therefore I am not helpless." Enjoyment of adult play, in which we actively place ourselves into childlike situations, seems to rest on a similar sense of our own control.

In order to bridge the gap between the games of children and those of adults, we will have to invoke that modern fairy tale (or horror story), the Oedipus complex. You have surely encountered the notion that the emotional conflicts of children tend to culminate in their fifth or sixth year and that the focus of these conflicts is in their relationships with their parents (or parental surrogates). At least this appears to be so in Western monogamous families. The child's fantasies may take many forms, but they all derive from a basic wish for exclusive possession of the parent of the opposite sex and simultaneous hostility and competitiveness toward the like-sexed parent who stands in the child's way. All of this is complicated considerably by the coexistence of affectionate and hostile wishes toward both parents and other family members.

We shall deal here only with the aspects of the Oedipus complex which are relevant to boys' games. Games — in this context I mean organized contests played according to rules — are primarily the pastime of boys.[9] The boy's helplessness in reality as compared with his father's power over him is evident, but we must also bear in mind that this same power is also used (hopefully) in the boy's behalf to care for him and to foster his growth toward manhood. How to obtain that same power for himself without losing the protection and security he enjoys under it is the fundamental problem for every son. This problem continues to find a variety of expressions in adult social institutions such as religion and politics, as well as in games.

It is in connection with efforts at resolving Oedipal conflict that an important reorganization of mental functions occurs. A new psychic agency gradually appears: the superego. The child identifies with — incorporates into himself — the ethical and moral aspects of his parents. Ordinarily it is his oedipal rival who is the primary source. The boy now tends to act on behalf of his father's demands, instead of experiencing them as thrust upon him. He has also united himself with his father by "swallowing" his precepts and ideals; if you have something inside of you that belongs to someone else, you are closer to him. In this way, the boys also shares in his father's fantasied power. We are all familiar with the exaggerated extent of this power as seen by the son: "My Dad can lick anybody." Lest you scoff at the connection between oral incorporation and moral precepts, permit me to point out that the word *remorse* comes from the Latin roots of *re-* (back) and *mordeo* (bite). Your conscience "bites" you "back."[10]

Let us be quite clear about the development of children's play by making use of the observations of L. E. Peller, a psychoanalyst of children.[11]. She vividly contrasted the play activity characteristic of oedipal and postoedipal periods of development. She remarked on the vitality and naive urgency of oedipal play, the sense of triumph and invincibility associated with it, and the spontaneous way it comes about. The accent is on the realization of the fantasy rather than on the means by which this is accomplished. Cooperation among peers is relatively unimportant. The predominant theme is that the playing children replace the adults in their fantasy, openly taking over their privileges and enjoying them without guilt.

Postoedipal play (games), in contrast to the earlier individualized and private activities, appears in conventional play-forms. Identification with equals is fostered and further emphasized in the observance of rules and fair play. From this point of view, the essence of a game is a fictional equality of the contestants (the handicap). The fantasies being enacted (which I take to be reactions to the feared loss of parental protection) are somewhat as follows: "I am not alone, there is a group of us and we are all together; I am a good son and have observed the rules to the letter."

Let us take a half-time break in our struggle toward Truth. Perhaps you are irritated. "Child psychology is all very well. But I agreed to come along only because I was interested in adult games. So far the landscape has been singularly devoid of them. What about it?" Please don't be a spoilsport; a whole flock of games is just over the horizon.

You will recall that we pointed out a basic psychological similarity between playing "Gone!" and primitive rites. It should not surprise us, then, to hear that in no sense does a traditional game differ in its origin from a rite. In most cases, in fact, a traditional game is the modern and corrupted form of a rite.[12] The simpler ball and skipping games,[13] all modern games played with bat and ball,[14] the first use of playing cards,[15] gambling,[16] the classical games of Greek antiquity,[17] horse-racing and foot-racing[18] — all of these have been traced to an intimate association or identity with religious or primitive rites. Many primitive peoples engage in solemn rites which we know as games; for example, some Eskimo tribes "play" Cat's Cradle.[19] As late as the fourteenth century, a regular part of the Easter ritual in one part of Europe was for the bishop to kick a ball at the head of a procession.[20]

Even in contemporary games there is a marked formal similarity to ritual.[21] Conversely, it has been observed that there is a partial awareness of "make-believe" in all primitive religions.[22] The opposite of play is not what is serious, but what is real.[23]

Traditional games tend to have ritualistic accompaniments which we consider indispensable to the fun of the game. The baseball ritual of throwing the ball around the infield after a put-out illustrates a common function of all rituals. Apart from its special symbolic implications, the common touching of the ball brings about a communion of purpose among the players in the same way that the seventh-inning stretch accomplishes a sense of team unity among their fans. Religious ritual also serves to further a sense of closeness with a deity; for example, the word *atonement* comes from *at one* – you make a "onement" with God.[24] Apropos of your own favorite game of golf, I seem to recall a flurry of complaints by ministers in recent years that Sunday golf was a serious competitor to church attendance.

We have previously brought out in several instances that a state of passive abandonment is the acme of helplessness. The idea of separation is also tied linguistically to games. The word *game* has been traced to the Old Gothic *gaman,* meaning companion or companionship.[25] We suspect a kinship with the modern French word *gamin,* which means a neglected boy. Our road has again led us back to playing "Gone!"

Consider the process by which a game becomes distinguishable from a ritual. According to Spence,[26] the ancient Mexican game of *tlachtli* – a kind of football – was originally a ritual. The ball, symbolizing the sun in their belief system, was kicked in one direction by priest-worshipers. Through this act of imitative magic, it was thought that the sun's passage through the sky was assured. At some point, a worshiper presumably kicked the ball back. Spence, however, was puzzled by the motivation for doing this; he pointed out that primitive man would naturally benefit from an appropriate position of the sun; indeed, such was the point of the ritual. Why then should he wish (magically) to make the sun helpless, as one "side" at least must have done?

Again we must return to playing "Gone!" You will recall that Freud was similarly puzzled by the pleasure in throwing the toy away. I think that the problem of *tlachtli* is identical; to kick (or cast or hit) an object away in a game is a form of passive mastery, insofar as it conjures up an illusion of control. You will recall that playing "Gone!" was also preceded in time by the disturbing habit of (ritualistically) casting away toys. The development of a game from a ritual is a tacit admission of *doubt* that magical rites alone can "work." The doubt is represented in the "sides" of the game. If the illusion of omnipotence must be given up, at least the possibility of it remains by testing it out in a game. Winning the game is then the equivalent of achieving this omnipotence. The word *magic,* by the way, derives from religious roots: the Magi were early Persian priests who worshipped good and evil gods.[27]

The creation of Monopoly[28] during the Depression of the 1930's is a more recent example of how helplessness in reality leads to a pleasurable illusion of power in a game. Monopoly is a board game in which real estate and properties are bought and traded adaptively for large sums of "money," with the aim of making your opponents helpless. The economic disparities of that era become glaringly reflected in the course of play. The players are required to master concepts like rent, mortgage, bankruptcy, and interest — concepts having much associated anxiety for many Depression people. These terms are defined in a lengthy and detailed document approximating a legal notice of foreclosure or eviction. As in reality, the possibility of sudden economic death on the board exists during play. Active mastery of economic helplessness was simply not possible for most; but passive mastery through the game fantasy of enormous compensatory wealth and power was possible.

As in all board games, the tokens employed to represent the players on the board emphasize the element of control. It seems that the appeal of board games is to that part of us represented by the spectator, who cannot actively master his helplessness on controlling the behavior of the players. One of the widespread illusions that was shattered by the Depression was that it was safe to entrust one's economic life to godlike financial figures and powerful economic interests. This illusion had been implemented in the nationwide stock-market game of the Twenties, in which the sense of participation in power was available by purchasing securities. On a board, previously powerful figures became helpless agents to be manipulated as the player or fate wills.

The creator of Monopoly was an unemployed salesman who turned his enforced idle time toward the construction of a recreation for his family and friends.[29] He reportedly based his game on happier memories of vacations spent in Atlantic City, New Jersey. Those vacations presumably were dictated by his own wishes rather than by the then current reality of lack of work. His fantasy found a responsive chord in the universal anxiety of the times. A good game, like good art, communicates; and like good art, it becomes incorporated into the culture.

In an adult as well as in a child, the wish to win in play refers to the actual helplessness of human beings in feeling and acting and arranging things according to their desires — in short, the unsatisfied longing of man to be heroes.[30] Human beings have only two ways of facing a restrictive power: revolt or else an illusory participation in the power, so that they can bear their suppression.[31] Their hostility or latent revolt still persists, even if not conscious, but it is held in check by the fantasy of having already achieved it. The restrictive power is represented both internally (the superego) and externally (social authority). In a game, it is the fantasy of having won that accomplishes the feeling of union with this power. The universal appeal of games as a social institution lies in the multiple ways in which this wish can be gratified.

Let us first examine those aspects of games in which a submissive attitude is taken toward this power. To a varying extent, a particular kind of game puts emphasis on luck, fate, or some similar godlike principle which can decide the outcome. However this principle is personified,[32] it can be influenced in fantasy to give one what is wanted. Whether favor is granted by virtue of faith or coerced through a magical rite, the basic assumption of an all-powerful fate is essentially maintained. Blind gambling is the epitome of passive mastery, in the sense that you play "Gone!" with reality. Contrast this with chess, in which relatively little room is left to some indeterminate factor.

From the above point of view, the opponent (s) represents for us our latent revolt which we would unconsciously like to disown. This is particularly true for the spectator, since the actual competitors are relatively much more identified with each other than their respective fans. Isn't it always the opponents who are the "dirty" players? This is one reason why we should "root for" (identify with) one side or the other if the game is to be thoroughly enjoyed. We are relieved of guilt about our own rebellious wishes. This is a part of the "good son" aspect of games, which finds expression in our ideal of the good sport.

Perhaps you have already observed the parallel to religious belief. In religion, the hope of participating in godlike power begins by ascribing invulnerability (the denial of helplessness) to a deity.[33] As with fate in a game, the deity is set in place of our superego. By taking a passive and submission attitude, it is prayerfully hoped that this same power will be used according to the wishes of the worshiper. The fantasy of having been granted favor is, in part, by virtue of conscientious observance of specific rules of behavior. The opponents are evil wishes, whether represented as such, as personifications in the mythology of the religion, or as groups of nonbelievers. This is a mechanism underlying prejudice.

Group formation is ordinarily characterized by a leader to whom more or less power over the members is given; in return, he is bound to treat them all with impartial or equal care.[34] This is theoretically true whether the leader is a religious figure, an army general, a president — or an umpire. The equality is maintained through the group identifications. In a game, the opposing players are identified with each other because of common rules, the wearing of uniforms, and the performance of similar acts of play. You know how quickly such identifications can break down if an umpire or referee gives evidence of favoritism. All of these identifications result in a limitation of aggression within the group. By the way, this theoretical understanding of group psychology leads to a practical recommendation: national anthems (since we have no acceptable international ones) might be played more usefully at the conclusion of a game rather than at the beginning, as is the present custom in the United States.

The umpire interprets the rules of the game, and it is the rules which stand in place of the omnipotent group leader. The rules of a traditional game are typically handed down from generation to generation. They tend to be experienced by some as ancestral pronouncements and, as such, are most resistant to change. Those who must play "by the book" uphold the sacred and inviolate quality of rules. In general, younger children take this point of view, while older ones (and adults) tend to experience them as socially defined; the more dependent the relationship of an adult to others (whether individuals or groups), the more his game-playing attitudes will resemble those of children.[35]

As the laws of a game, rules are essentially prohibitions or restrictions on behavior, and thus parallel morality. They are *verbal* statements; similarly, it is the actual words of parents that are incorporated in the process of forming the superego. Hasn't Hoyle been called the "Bible of Play"?

In the above context, a trophy is a voluntary yielding up by authority of a concrete symbol which authorizes the participation in power.[36] It is equivalent to fulfilling an ideal passively (although it may be very aggressive manifestly). Corresponding kinds of trophies would be a fetish given to a faithful religious adherent, a medal in the military, a certificate of appreciation in a bureaucracy, and a diploma in education.

"Nonsense!" you cry. "There is nothing passive about *my* enjoyment of games. Give me a good heavyweight fight anytime. And that stag head over my mantel — it wasn't given to me. I went out and took it from its previous owner. In fact, I play best when I'm out for blood. How do you account for that?" I shall do so shortly (for we see our scoreboard clock ticking on); but if we are to understand your lust for blood, we shall have to backtrack again to primitive man.

Let us then turn to *Totem and Taboo,* a work by Freud on totemism,[37] the earliest known form of human social and religious organization, and taboo, the most ancient unwritten code of laws. And because time is running out, we ask you to be content with a cursory survey of a complex and controversial subject. Please feel free to anticipate our remarks as to the survivals of these primitive attitudes and customs in our modern games.

As a rule, a totem is a kind of animal, more rarely a plant or a natural phenomenon such as rain, which stands in a peculiar relation to a clan. The totem animal is considered to be the common ancestor of the clan. It is also their guardian spirit and helper. (Teams in sports commonly adopt the name of an animal as their identity.) The clansmen are under a sacred obligation, subject to automatic sanctions, not to kill or destroy their totem and to avoid eating its flesh. However, there was some evidence to suggest that the totem animal was sacrificed and eaten by the whole clan on certain set ceremonial occasions: the disputed "totem feast." From time to time, festivals are celebrated at which the clansmen represent or imitate the motions and attributes of their totems in ceremonial dances. The totem bond is stronger than the bond of blood by family in the modern sense. (The true game player or fan permits no other ties to interfere with his game.) The totem is not attached to one particular place, so that clansmen live peacefully side by side with members of other totem clans.

Taboo restrictions are a seemingly unrelated and illogical set of prohibitions. The word *taboo* implies both "sacred" and "dangerous" or "forbidden," somewhat in the sense of "holy dread." The source of it is attributed to a peculiar magical power, *mana,* which is inherent in persons and spirits and can be conveyed by them through the medium of inanimate objects. An analogy would be an electric charge capable of transmission through contact. This power is attached to all special individuals, such as kings, priests or newborn babies, and to all exceptional or uncanny states, such as menstruation, puberty, birth, death and sickness. The violation of a taboo often engendered death or serious illness, imposed "automatically" or by the community if necessary.

Freud reasoned that taboo was originally a primeval prohibition forcibly imposed by some authority from the outside and directed against the most powerful longings to which human beings are subject. This conclusion follows from the argument and clinical observation that a prohibition exists only in proportion to the strength of a wish, however disguised or displaced that wish might be. The desire to violate the prohibition persists unconsciously; thus, those who obey the taboo have an *ambivalent* attitude toward it. (I have earlier indicated how this same ambivalence characterizes the individual's attitude toward his own superego and toward social authority.) The prohibited act is dangerous in others because it arouses temptation; a bad example is contagious — consider the consequences of "foul play" in a game. Renunciation of some possession or freedom may atone in part for the violation of a taboo; compare this with the treatment accorded an infraction of rules in a game.

The prohibitions in taboo particularly involve touching; and touching, as a social phenomenon, is to be understood in the sense of attacking, of getting control and of asserting oneself. In short, the prohibitions were directed against murderous or exploitative wishes that might be aroused by special states of helplessness in others and by envied possessions or power.

For example, the fear of evil spirits and the taboos associated with the dead can be traced to the hostility of the mourners. The dead person has somehow turned into a wicked demon eager to kill, so that defensive measures must be taken.

I must interject here that the origins of athletic events are almost invariably connected with funeral rites.[38] For example, the classical Greek games, such as wrestling, running, throwing the discus and chariot-racing, arose in this way.[39] If we apply Freud's reasoning, these events become instances of hypocrisy by the mourners. Behind the guise of enhancing the honor of the deceased by celebrating in his name, we cannot mistake the agility of the contestants for other than an invidious comparison with the helplessness of the dead hero. What better proof of vitality can there be? And by the way, when you hear of the death of someone with whom you feel identified, do you ever find your thoughts straying to the stadium or golf course?

"Foul!" you cry in outrage. "I see your game now. You intend to convict me of the most primitive motives there are — naked envy, taking advantage of the helpless, satisfaction in someone's death. I am not a savage. I am a civilized and reasonably moral person."

I suggest that we call time-out to discuss the issue. You must understand that it is precisely those "primitive" motives which persist more or less unconsciously from your own childhood. Perhaps you have observed small children who were not aware of your presence; you would then have ample evidence of the open wish for property of others and for frustrating persons to be out of the way. Further evidence for this — and time prohibits me from illustrating it — comes not only from psychoanalytic treatment of so-called emotionally disturbed people, but from dreams, slips of the tongue, art, etc., of quite "normal" and civilized persons. Be honest with yourself: haven't you ever taken advantage of a card inadvertently exposed by someone else in a game? Haven't you ever wished that the star player on the other team or your opponent were "disabled"? The hallmark of civilization is behavior in reality, not wishes transiently enacted in the magic circle of play.

Time-in! We will mention only in outline Freud's discussion of the totem feast, the function of which was to unite the sacrificial animal, the totem clan, and the god in a bond of kinship. The animal was treated ambivalently: it was first mourned by the clan, who then gave way to a mood of holiday excess. The slaying of the totem animal was permissible only because the whole clan takes an active part. Relying on a theory of Charles Darwin as to the earliest state of human society, Freud developed the notion of a primal group composed of a jealous and violent father whose females he kept for himself and whose sons he drove away as they grew up. Freud proposed that these exiled brothers finally banded together, killed and then (being cannibals) devoured their father, thus bringing an end to the patriarchal group. The guilt at the deed persisted, however; social organization, moral restrictions and religion arose from it. In this first totem feast, the brothers each acquired a portion of the father's strength and strengthened their identification with him, for he was both feared and hated. Because no single brother was strong enough to assume his father's role, they all renounced this wish in the interest of self-preservation. (Does the play-contest also trace its origin to such a feast? Are the brothers still fighting over the spoils?)

Primitive peoples eat the conquered enemy whose qualities they admire and wish to acquire for themselves.[40] This is basically what being "at one" with an ambivalently regarded object implies; a trophy represents such an object. No doubt you have seen slapstick comedy movies, where the animal head on the wall "comes alive" and bites. By the way, you did eat the previous owner of your own stag trophy, didn't you?

Now you can begin to see how transitional objects return in adult games: as trophies. In particular, the object which is being contested, such as the ball, will serve this purpose. It is an appropriate trophy because both you and your opponent (s) *handle* it; this magically infuses it with both your *mana*. It is the current custom for footballs to serve in this way. The early custom in baseball was also to have the winning team appropriate the ball used in the game for their trophy case. You know that the most prized trophies in games are those which show signs of use or damage from the contest. If they are autographed, so much the better; savages believe that possession of a man's name gives you power over him. Books "borrowed" (but not voluntarily returned) have a similar function.

Active devouring is apparently not the only way to "participate in power." Another executive mechanism underlying identification is thought to be that of being passively swallowed up by an omnipotent being.[41] It seems that this latter method of gaining power is the equivalent of a passive mastery. To a greater or lesser extent, any organized group demands a loss of personal identity, offering as a substitute a union with some greater ideal. Passive mastery is also the basis of those games or game-strategies which emphasize *control* of the players or their representations, as in board games which utilize tokens, pieces, etc. Provoking or eliciting certain desired behaviors or "moves" by your opponent can also be experienced as a triumph, even though the manifest game is lost. If you can feel that you made it happen, rather than having it happen to you, you have won "something."

In recent years it has been found that games not only make an excellent model for understanding the interpersonal aspects of behavior,[42] but that a plethora of actual interpersonal games go on among us all. "Gamesmanship" is perhaps the most widely known.[43] More recently, Berne has described a variety of such activities, in which people (more or less unconsciously) assume complementary learned roles with each other, hoping for a "payoff" by eliciting specific social responses by the other "players."[44]

The homestretch is here. Look about you at the contemporary American game scene, as we prepare to enter the Age of Leisure. The trends are obvious: the rising tide of violence in organized athletics; the material rewards associated with winning; the dehumanization of the individual player, so that roles supersede the person; and the premium on the show offered, ostensibly because of the influence of television. In my opinion, all of these characteristics reflect the qualities of our culture to which we are helplessly subject and which we strive to master in our game-playing. Organized games have become more and more like board games, just as "real" life is tending toward increasing regulation, impersonalizing of relationships among individuals and lack of personal identity.

Three major wars and a monumental depression in this century have punctured a series of precious illusions among Americans, illusions which formerly warded off one's awareness of helplessness. Take the threat of atomic annihilation, for example; if we cannot believe that God would prevent it, or even that the UN (with all its human failings) would prevent it, we can at least play the grand stategy game of mentally trading 60 million (lives) for 150 million. How do you compete with a machine? One way to deal with automation anxiety might be to master complex power accessories in the car, home or workshop. Does your helplessness with Big Government disturb you? Perhaps you play the traditional American game of Income Tax with Uncle Sam: you can win either by depriving him of a few "legitimate" dollars or successfully provoke an audit so that you *make* him take your money. Is fear of sudden death on the highway a problem? A recent innovation, the Demolition Derby, may be helpful; after the other competing automobiles have smashed each other up, a live winner emerges. How do you keep other people from getting in your hair? Try one-upmanship: at least you can be successful in provoking them, and not be just the passive victim of their envy.

The final whistle sounds. I trust that you have enjoyed playing *my* game. And if you do not see truth as I do, it doesn't matter; what counts is that you enjoyed the play. Perhaps I can play *your* game some day. When we have done the volume, we must each return to reality . . . or should I say, to the Game of Life.[45]

For now, though, play ball!

NOTE

I wish to express my appreciation to Dr. Jean Rosenbaum for his many helpful suggestions and to Miss Linda Ganley, Chief Librarian of the Veterans Administration Hospital, Dearborn, Michigan, for her diligence in securing obscure references. The views presented are entirely the author's and do not necessarily represent those held by any other persons or organizations.

"Spooky won't cooperate in our mastery over helplessness — he won't let us take his tonsils out!"

FOOTNOTES

1. Huizinga, J.: *Homo Ludens: A Study of the Play-Element in Culture.* Boston, Beacon, 1962.
2. Huizinga, J.: *op. cit. supra.*
3. Szasz, T. S.: *The Myth of Mental Illness.* New York, Hoeber-Harper, 1961.
4. Fenichel, O.: Trophy and triumph, in *Collected Papers of Fenichel* (2d Series). New York, Norton, 1954, pp. 141-162.
5. Freud, S.: *Beyond the Pleasure Principle (1920),* Standard Edition, Volume 18. London, Hogarth Press, 1955, p. 1.
6. Winnicott, D. W.: Transitional objects and transitional phenomena. *Int J Psychoanal, 34:* 89, 1953.
7. For a fuller discussion of this concept, see Fenichel, O.: *The Psychoanalytic Theory of Neurosis.* New York, Norton, 1945.
8. Huizinga, J.: *op. cit. supra* note 1.
9. Peller, L. E.: Libidinal phases, ego development, and play. *Psychoanal Stud Child, 9:*178, 1954.

10. Funk, W.: *Word Origins and Their Romantic Stories.* New York, Grosset, 1950.
11. *Supra* note 9.
12. Spence, L.: *Myth and Ritual in Dance, Game, and Rhyme.* London, Watts & Co., 1947.
13. Children's Games. *Encyclopaedia Britanica,* Vol. 5. Chicago, Banton, 1959.
14. Fenichel, O.: *op. cit. supra* note 4.
15. Card Playing. *Encyclopaedia Britanica,* Vol. 4. Chicago, Banton, 1959.
16. Gambling. *Encyclopaedia Britanica,* Vol. 9. Chicago, Banton, 1959.
17. Games. *Encyclopaedia Britanica,* Vol. 10. Chicago, Banton, 1959; Spence, L.: *Myth and Ritual in Dance, Game, and Rhyme.* London, Watts & Co., 1947.
18. Spence, L.: *op. cit. supra* note 17.
19. Frazer, J. G.: *The Golden Bough: A Study in Magic and Religion,* pt. 3. New York, Macmillan, 1935.
20. Henderson, R. W.: *Ball, Bat and Bishop: The Origin of Ball Games.* New York, Rockport Press, 1947.
21. Grespi, I.: Card playing as mass culture, in Rosenberg, B., and White, D. M. [Eds.]: *Mass Culture: The Popular Arts in America.* Glencoe, Free Press, 1957, pp. 418-421; Greenson, R. R.: On gambling. *American Imago, 4:*61, 1947; Huizinga, J.: *op. cit. supra* note 1; Peller, L. E.: *op. cit. supra* note 9.
22. Huizinga, J.: *op. cit. supra* note 1.
23. Freud, S.: *Creative Writers and Daydreaming (1908),* Standard Edition, Volume 9. London, Hogarth Press, 1959, p. 143.
24. Funk, W.: *op. cit. supra* note 10.
25. Games. *Encyclopaedia Britanica,* Vol. 10. Chicago, Banton, 1959.
26. *Supra* note 12.
27. Funk, W.: *op. cit. supra* note 10.
28. Bongartz, R.: Pass go and retire. *Sat. Eve. Post,* April 11, 1964; Wilkinson, J. F.: The play-money game that made millions. *Sports Illustrated,* Dec. 2, 1963.
29. *Supra* note 28.
30. Freud, S.: *Psychopathic Characters on the Stage (1905),* Standard Edition, Volume 7. London, Hogarth Press, 1953, p. 303.
31. Fenichel, O.: *op. cit. supra* note 4.
32. Greenson, R. R.: *op. cit. supra* note 21.
33. Freud, S.: *Group Psychology and the Analysis of the Ego (1921),* Standard Edition, Volume 18. London, Hogarth Press, 1955, p. 65.
34. Freud, S.: *op. cit. supra.*
35. Szasz, T. S.: *op. cit. supra* note 3.
36. Fenichel, O.: *op. cit. supra* note 4.
37. Freud, S.: *Totem and Taboo (1913),* Standard Edition, Volume 13. London, Hogarth Press, 1955, p. 1.
38. Spence, L.: *op. cit. supra* note 12.
39. Games. *Encyclopaedia Britanica,* Volume 10. Chicago, Banton, 1959.
40. Fenichel, O.: *op. cit. supra* note 4.
41. Fenichel, O.: *op. cit. supra* note 4.
42. Szasz, T. S.: *op. cit. supra* note 3.
43. Potter, S.: *The Theory and Practice of Gamesmanship.* New York, Holt, Rinehart and Winston.
44. Berne, E.: *Games People Play.* New York, Grove, 1964.
45. *Tis all a Chequer-board of Nights and Days*
Where Destiny with Men for Pieces plays:
Hither and thither moves, and mates, and slays,
And one by one back in the Closet lays.
Fitzgerald, E., *Rubaiyat of Omar Khayyam,* Quatrain LX IX (1937), Garden City, N. Y., Garden City Publishing Co.

HUMOR IN PLAY AND SPORTS

JACOB LEVINE

It was the 1929 Rose Bowl game between California and Georgia when Roy Riegels, captain and center of California, grabbed a fumbled football and ran for a touchdown. The crowd roared with laughter, for Riegels was running in the wrong direction towards his own goal. He was stopped by his teammates at the two yard line. In another hilarious incident, as Red Smith recalled it, Walter Johnson, the great big-league pitcher, "threw a nothing ball to Ken Williams, who hit a triple. Joe Gedeon tripped Williams at second, fell on him, hollered for the ball, and tagged him. But Billy Evans (the umpire) sent Williams on to third for interference and he scored on a fly."

In the annals of organized sports, many comic incidents have occurred which interrupted the impassioned rivalries of the game by the crowd's laughter. But these episodes, funny as they were, were nothing but accidental, unexpected and momentary digressions from the business at hand. Humor has little place in our spectator sports. Doubtless, the grimness of our major sports is not inherent to them but perhaps reflects the expectations and attitudes with which we participate in them. Most evident, however, is our difficulty in being "in humor" even when we are supposed to be having fun.

There is really a lamentable lack of fun and humor in our strenuous pursuit of organized sports. It seems indeed an odd quirk of man's nature that the more zealously he pursues a sport the less fun he has doing it. In this day of professionalism, competitiveness, "spectatoritis" and high finance, where joking and laughter are unwelcome intrusions, the childish joy of playing is all but lost. With the commercialization of most adult sports, dominated as they are by the profit and competitive motives, the game is no longer played for fun but by paid performers as exhibitions, and participants are made into spectators. The only fun left to the adult in America's favorite sports of baseball or football is to get into the cheering section of the stadium.

It may seem that humor is a trivial component of sports, and there are some who would maintain that humor does not belong in a sport which is properly pursued, that it is not only superfluous but even debasing. To the sportsman who takes himself and his sport seriously, humor is both irrelevant and irreverent. Yet, in laughter we have the deepest and clearest expression of the fact that the basic aim of a sport is being achieved. After all, the primary goal of all sports is to have fun, and laughter is the best proof that we are having fun.

The sports of adults are clearly extensions of children's play. But unlike adults, children play spontaneously with few rules and little organization. Animals play like children do, with much fun in teasing, horseplay and competition. As Huizinga pointed out in his classic *Homo Ludens*, "We can safely assert that human civilization has added no essential feature to the general idea of play. Animals play just like man." He stated further, "Really to play, man must play like a child." As both he and Freud have observed, the play of children is taken by them as a most serious and absorbing activity, consuming most of their waking interest and energy; but laughter and fun are inseparable from their play. It can safely be said that one cannot be truly playful without laughter, nor can one be humorous without being playful.

Much of the fun of animals and children at play takes the form of competitive teasing. Though carried out in the context of some contest or game, the teasing is an invitation to be playful, and the mild aggression is not "for real." The fighting, the growling, the nipping, the slaps, the kicks and even the name calling are carried out in the play. It is the metacommunication of playfulness between playmates which creates the "game illusion," where even pain is endured as part of the fun. In the world of play, the child is freed from the restraints and prohibitions of the real world, and he can enjoy the license of aggression with immunity. A father scolded his young son, "I'm ashamed of you, Robert; I saw you kick your little friend while you were playing together. Why did you do that?" "Oh, I was tired of playing with him and wanted him to go home." "Why didn't you ask him to go home?" asked the father. "Why, Daddy," cried the boy, "that wouldn't have been polite!"

Then what is a humorous approach to sport? Freud provided the answer to this question by pointing out that the opposite of play is not serious activity but reality.[1] To play is to detach oneself from reality and create one's own reality. Both the "game illusion" and the "comic illusion" are expressions of this voluntary withdrawal from the real world into a world where the rules and the procedures are of one's own choosing and making. It is in this sense that play is recreational because we re-create a real world which is different from the one in which we live. Thus both play and humor express a freedom from the realistic cares and problems of reality. It is humor that also frees one from rational thought and natural law. The essential point is that we can play seriously and still be humorous about it. It is not because we take the game so seriously that robs it of the fun. Rather it is that we take ourselves so seriously.

To be able to assume a humorous attitude requires not only a freedom from reality but a freedom to laugh at oneself. It has often been maintained that a sense of humor depends almost entirely upon the ability to laugh at oneself, not to take oneself so seriously that he cannot take a joke at his own expense. Many of our modern writers have deplored the fact that America has lost its sense of humor by taking itself so seriously that it cannot laugh at itself nor poke fun at its foibles. In this country, with our wisecracks, gags and glib comebacks, our humor seems to suffer from superficiality and an unwillingness to acknowledge weakness or to tolerate being laughed at. Thus, if we are too serious about ourselves and take our successes and accomplishments to be so important that failures are shameful, then our sports become merely extensions of our real life and not recreations.

The rejection of humor in any activity reflects an unwillingness to take a chance and expose oneself to the laughter of others. In our culture we seem to have a definite need to be appreciated and accepted, and sports very often serve as the vehicle. Moses from his heavenly perch once saw an orthodox rabbi playing golf on the Sabbath. Irate, he reported this sinful act to the Lord. "I'll fix him," said the Lord, and on the next hole the rabbi made a four-hundred-yard hole in one. "Is that how you fix him?" asked Moses, aghast. "Yes," replied the Lord. "Whom is he going to be able to tell?"

It appears then that because we take ourselves so seriously in our sports that we are not willing to take a chance that we might be laughed at. Though we are perfectly willing to laugh, we cannot take a joke — if it is at our expense. Malcolm Muggeridge, former editor of *Punch,* had the perfect solution when he suggested that perhaps our scientists might develop a serum the injection of which would induce laughter from a so-called laugh serum. Thus, we would be doing away with humor altogether. Imagine what a market it would have — every supermarket could carry it in one-a-day tablet form and thus save us all the trouble of risking exposure. The point is that humor implies ability to be self-critical, and if we cannot do this we cannot assume a humorous attitude.

In many of our popular sports, like golf and tennis, the consuming passion is to win. We practice and seek perfection only to beat the other fellow. After a long day of absorbing competition, a golfer came home from the golf links; his wife greeted him and remarked that their young son Henry had just come in before him. "He says he's been caddying all day for you," she said. "Is that so," said the golfer. "Somehow I thought that boy seemed mighty familiar." This preoccupation with winning is obviously an extension of the compelling force which motivates us in real life. It thus has become a serious activity little different from our everyday life, where humor has little place. Because losing is too painful, confronting us as it does with our own inadequacies, we cannot tolerate joking about it. The intensity of our need to win is clearly not the cause of the lack of humor in our sports, but it is rather symptomatic of our conflicted motivations and the consequent solemnity with which we pursue them. An avid golfer was just about to make a putt at the eighteenth green in a closely contested match when he stopped suddenly, took off his hat and stood respectfully while a funeral cortege passed slowly by on the road nearby. After it had passed, he carefully and skillfully sank a fifteen-foot putt and won the match. His defeated opponent, though disappointed, congratulated him and remarked, "You must have had iron nerve not to let that funeral procession fluster you into missing that putt." "It wasn't easy," admitted the victor. "On Saturday we would have been married twenty-five years!"

The striking weakening of our morality and ethical standards in sports is no doubt one of the consequences of this drive to be a winner. What is now popularly known as Durocher's Law illustrates this importance of winning. When Leo Durocher managed the New York Giants, his players were known as the dirtiest players in the big leagues; no trick or dirty tactic was overlooked, even to injuring key players of the opposing team. When asked by sports writers why his players played so dirty, he replied, "Nice guys finish last!" D. W. Brogan has characterized the situation well: "In the United States being a good loser is not nearly as good as being a winner, good or bad." The sad and fatal degradation of boxing perhaps illustrates the depths to which ethical standards will decline in this hot pursuit of the champion's belt. And it is probably no accident that boxing is the sport so recognized, with destructive aggression so nakedly expressed.

According to psychoanalytic theory, humor is one of a number of psychological activities which are functionally adaptive modes of withdrawal from reality into a self-made world. The importance to adaptive functioning of the capacity to withdraw voluntarily from reality into an imaginary world can be seen in such eagerly pursued pleasures as plays, sports, humor, sleep, intoxicated states and literature. Psychodynamically, neuroses and psychoses reflect similar regression detachments from reality, but they are pathological and not voluntary or adaptive; that is, they do not function for ego gratification or pleasure but are attempts to cope with conflict and anxiety. By participating in an illusion, play and humor express to others the communication "this is for fun"; as a form of metacommunication, this gives license and freedom to share in the disregard for reality, propriety and rationality. Others are then free to join us in this adaptive withdrawal. In the context of this playful illusion, nonsense, mild aggression and teasing are permissible. Furthermore, by sharing in the comic illusion, participants in the play are liberated from the procrustean demands of reality and can achieve heights of perfection and freedom only the imagination can attain.

Freud pointed out, "Humor has something liberating about it . . . the grandeur in it clearly lies in the triumph of narcissism, the victorious assertion of the ego's invulnerability. The ego refuses to be distressed by the provocations of reality, to let itself be compelled to suffer. It insists that it cannot be affected by the traumas of the external world, in fact, that such traumas are no more than occasions for it to gain pleasure. This last feature is quite an essential element of humor."[2] Thus joking even in an important contest expresses the victory of the individual — not necessarily over his opponents but over reality. "The world has not mastered us," says the joker. This is best illustrated in the so-called gallows humor, as for example in the story about the man who was about to be shot. He was offered a last cigarette. He refused, declaring, "No thanks, I'm trying to give up smoking." Another example is given by the two Jews who were about to be shot by the Nazis. As they were being put up against the wall, one Jew cried, "I want a blindfold. I must have a blindfold." The other Jew became upset over this outcry, and exclaimed, "Sh! sh! stop stirring up trouble."

But the man who finds losing too distressing, who feels vulnerable when he makes a mistake or does not win is not able to assume the humor attitude; he is not even able to be playful. To be able to laugh at one's defeat, one cannot be overwhelmed by it or discouraged or resigned; humor is never resigned. On the contrary, it constantly reasserts the superiority of the ego over the real world. It emphasizes that the individual can gain pleasure even in defeat. Freud further emphasized in this connection that the person who assumes a humorous attitude toward himself in order to ward off possible suffering is in a sense looking upon himself as a child.[3] It is in this context that the individual by assuming the humorous attitude of a superior adult looking down on a child is actually participating in an illusion. It is in this way that humor is both liberating and elevating. As Freud put it, it means, "Look! Here is the world which seems so dangerous! It is nothing but a game for children — just worth making a jest about!"

The fact that man has the great need to indulge in sports reflects among other things his great need for a periodic relief from the real world. He can do this not only by going to sleep but also when he is awake. He uses a variety of devices for doing this: drinking, reading novels, listening to music and indulging in sports. This universal need to escape from the oppressive force of the real world with its frustrations and conflict, the troubled interpersonal relationships and the loneliness is relieved by the sharing and the playfulness of sports. To be able to joke about one's defective playing is to be able to recognize man's imperfection and accept it, yet feel above it — it's only a game.

But we have motives for pursuing sports so avidly other than that of the sheer fun of it. A preacher in a backwoods fundamentalist parish had to ice-skate down the river to church one Sunday morning because the roads were impassibly snowbound. For this he was called before the presbytery for breaking the Sabbath. The young man naturally defended himself by saying that this was the only way he could get to church that day. The elder replied to this, "Young man, there's just one question, did ye or did ye not enjoy the skatin'?"

Kris has pointed out that we can appreciate situations as funny only after we ourselves have mastered them.[4] "A feeling of anxiety over our own powers of mastery, or more accurately, the memory of an averted, superfluous anxiety, seems to accompany the comic." According to him, an important function of play in the development of the child is to help the child master some source of anxiety as experienced in the plaything, his own body or perhaps some previously experienced anxiety situation which has been passively experienced. In a sense, play may help us to overcome the many anxieties which the real world engenders. The preoccupation with winning and the grim humorlessness of our national sports may well be symptomatic of these anxieties, for it is understandable that joking is not tolerated where anxiety is too great. We have some clues as to the anxieties we are trying to master in our sports activities.

A college football team was being badly beaten. It was the break between halves when the coach usually tries to arouse and lecture the players to increased efforts to win the game. During this half the coach said nothing, and the silence conveyed the gloom and lack of spirit. At last when the time was up and the team prepared to go back on the field, the coach looked around carefully and very deliberately remarked, "Well, girls, shall we go?" They won the game.

The need to prove over and over again the reality of one's prowess and masculinity in a sport seems clearly demonstrated by the importance we attach to winning. We are repeatedly confronted with the heartbreaking scene of the merciless defeat of the aging hero-athlete by the aggressive youngster. The universal themes of the young displacing the old, the waning of one's powers and its denial, the dangers of physical contests, are dramatically expressed in sports. These collective anxieties and needs have created the hero-athlete who is perhaps more acclaimed than any other public figure. Identification and reassurance sustain the sports fans who endow their hero with all the manly attributes and prowess of the ideal male. The myth of the sports hero grows as he continues to win, even though he may be a vicious corrupt competitor, immoral, feebleminded or alcoholic. The captain of a great college football team suddenly burst into tears after winning the last game of a very successful year. The coach was aghast. "What on earth have you got to cry about?" he asked. "You're the captain of the best team we've had in years. You're the most popular guy in college, you're handsome and rich. What's wrong, man?" "Oh, Coach," sobbed the player, "if I could only read and write!"

It is easy to understand how a man becomes an avid sportsman, for not only does the sport provide a recreational release from the cares of real life, but it also serves as a talisman of manliness, constantly to be tested. In the sport, we are perpetually testing and proving ourselves, never acknowledging defeat nor fully enjoying victory. It develops into a compelling drive. The situation is like that of the racetrack fan who remarked, "I hope I break even today. I need the money." Our success at the sport thus comes to define our worth. Winning is important not only because we enjoy the feeling of mastery and competence, but because by winning we can say, "I'm a better man than you are." It is perhaps a matter of basic integrity where the person puts the definition of himself on the line of the score card. He lets the game define him. The fact that a person can joke about the game, winning or losing, points to his own feelings of integrity, that as a person he does not depend upon the confirmation of this integrity by proving he is a better man. Win or lose, his relation to his competitor is unchanged, both as a man and as a person.

In essence, the fact that humor does not appear in our American sports suggests that other strong emotions do not permit it to arise. Freud has amply demonstrated that there can be no comic pleasure where the individual feels threatened, overly anxious or uncertain about himself. As with children, the adult plays at the sport as a way of mastering these anxieties. On the other hand, when we can appreciate humor in sports, the game and the humor express the mastery we feel over all our uncertainties. This orientation frees us to laugh at mistakes and defeats, for even the unpleasant becomes a source of pleasure if we can laugh at it. Freud related how "a rogue . . . being led out to execution on a Monday remarked, 'Well, this week's beginning nicely.' "[5] In short, when we can assume a humorous attitude, we are not taking ourselves too seriously, and it is the sport itself which is giving us the gratification and not some overriding needs like applause or success. We are then able to enjoy the contest as a sharing experience between friendly rivals rather than enemies. Yet this still permits us to take delight in winning the contest, in getting the better of our opponent. There is much pleasure, too, in playing the game skillfully. In this context, humor becomes an indispensable, not an incidental, ingredient.

SUMMARY

Humor is important to the full enjoyment of any sport. By assuming a playful, humorous attitude, we are not taking ourselves or our performance too seriously. Whether we win or lose, our sense of humor expresses our victory over reality and our mastery over what might have been feared earlier. The sport, like life itself, is only a game, and winning really proves nothing. "In humor" we can fully enjoy the satisfaction of playing the game with competence.

"Another one of my troubles is that I find that my work is a hell of a lot more fun than playing."

FOOTNOTES

1. Freud, S.: *Jokes and Their Relation to the Unconscious,* Standard Edition, Volume 8. London, Hogarth Press, 1960.
2. Freud, S.: *Humour,* Standard Edition, Volume 21. London, Hogarth Press, 1961, pp. 159-166.
3. Freud, S.: *op. cit. supra* note 2.
4. Kris, E.: *Psychoanalytic Explorations in Art.* New York, Int Univs, 1952.
5. Freud, S.: *op. cit. supra* note 2.

CHILDREN'S GAMES

RICHARD H. PHILLIPS

THE ORIGIN OF THE WORD "game" is somewhat obscure, but there is some indication that it comes from the Gothic *gaman,* a term combining the prefix *ga,* meaning together, with the root word of "man."[1] This sounds reasonable enough, since games, as surely as any activity one can imagine, bring people together and sustain them for a time in relationship to each other. In fact, in America an activity which does not combine the efforts of two or more people is not ordinarily called a "game" regardless of how intricate and diversionary it may be.[2]

In this chapter, as when I first considered the games of childhood,[3] I want to highlight such play experiences as "hide-and-seek" and "drop-the-handkerchief." In these activities there is so much emphasis on rules and specific objectives that I feel the term "formal games" is appropriate. Formal games are a kind of subdivision of the more general category of children's play. They have, however, held little interest for child psychiatrists and psychoanalysts, who have focused their attention on free play, or play that takes place spontaneously in the absence of rules or of any predetermined plan of action. It is the analysis of free play, centering around the common toys and equipment of the nursery, which constitutes the most basic tool for both diagnosis and treatment in child psychiatry. The study of a child's patterns and idiosyncrasies of play provide insights regarding his personality and his problems, much as the understanding of an adult is derived from an analysis of the patterns of association of ideas, from the interpretation of dreams and phantasies and from the study of persistent nonadaptive or neurotic behavior.

In an attempt to understand the meaning of play, students of child psychology have, during the past century, devised some theories. Kanner has summarized and classified a number of these as follows:[4]

> The *surplus energy theory* postulates that in play the child "blows off steam." There is an "aimless expenditure of energy" (Schiller, 1875). A view closely related to this states that play is an expression of energy left over after the necessities of life have been satisfied (Spencer, 1873).
>
> The *instinct practice theory* holds that man does not play because he is young, but because he is required by nature to go through a period of childhood so that he may play and thus prepare himself for adult activities (Groos, 1896).
>
> The *recreation theory* assumes that play is a necessary means of satisfying a physiological need for relaxation; after work we require rest which accomplishes

recuperation (Lazarus, 1883). Expressed somewhat differently, the idea is that at the present stage of human evolution, there is a greater exercise of mental powers than previously; hence there is greater mental fatigue. Play avoids such fatigue by reverting to phylogenetically older, more deeply rooted racial habits which involve the relaxing use of muscles (Patrick, 1916).

The *recapitulation theory* of G. Stanley Hall (1906) is based upon the idea that play can be explained by the history of the human race. The child goes through stages which recapitulate "cultural epochs" in the evolution of the human race: animal, savage, nomadic, agricultural and tribal. Hall regarded play as "the motor habits and spirit of the past race persisting in the present as rudimentary functions . . . . This is why the heart of youth goes out to play, as into nothing else, as if in it man remembered a lost paradise."

With this somewhat mystical and quite poetic phylogenetic explanation of play proposed by Hall, I shall turn to some more recent theoretical contributions from the field of psychoanalysis. In 1933, Waelder made some suggestions regarding psychoanalytic insights into the nature of play.[5] Let me attempt to paraphrase and to parenthetically illustrate Waelder's statements as follows:

1. In play there is evidence of an instinct on the part of all children toward a higher level of mastery. In play, the child challenges his own intellectual, emotional and physical capacities, both testing and perfecting his skills at progressively higher levels. (A child having learned to skip rope standing on two feet may then proceed to skipping on the right foot only, then the left foot only, then back to two feet but crossing the hands on alternate swings of the rope, etc.)

2. Play may represent the simultaneous statement and symbolic fulfillment of a wish on the part of an individual child. (A small boy having neither a horse nor the ability to ride, but desiring both, gallops himself off down the sidewalk or across the lawn slapping himself smartly on the rump and yelling "giddap," obviously expressing both a wish for something and its attainment.)

3. At times play represents an attempt to come to terms with some overpowering emotional event by symbolically repeating it in some way. (Following the assassination of the late President Kennedy, the author noted among neighborhood children a brief but sharp increase in the amount of play with toy guns, the capturing of "baddies" and tying them up, converting "dangerous men" into harmless prisoners.)

4. A child who has in reality been forced to take an unwelcome, passive role may, during play, represent himself as the active controlling agent in a similar situation. (A young child having undergone the frightening experience of hospitalization and surgery may for some time after he arrives home play at putting his younger brother, his dog or his teddy bear to sleep in preparation for an operation.)

5. In his play the child may take a leave of absence from reality and from his inner negative dictates. (Imagining himself a robber, a little boy pretends to be stealing enough money from the bank to buy all the ice cream and all the candy at the corner store.)

6. By means of play, the child may center his phantasies around real objects. (A boy of five stalks his own cat from behind a hedge or tree, professing the animal a tiger in need of being caught for the circus.)

These then are some of the theories which have been proposed regarding the origins, meaning and function of play conceived of generally. If we focus specific attention on formal games, there are a number of special observations which can be made:

1. There are a number of games which have been played for a remarkably long time. More than 350 years ago the little Dauphin (later to become Louis XIII of France) is known to have played "hide-and-seek," "charades," and "prisoner's base."[6] Roman children also played "hide-and-seek" along with "blindman's bluff" and "hopscotch."[7] There is considerable variation in the names applied to certain formal games;[8] but even some of their names have proved highly durable. Both "London Bridge is falling down" and the "farmer in the dell," for example, have a strong flavor of the Old English about them.

2. Certain games seem to be virtually universal. Chinese children play a form of tag.[9] French children play a game very similar to "here we go round the mulberry bush" while singing a song called "On The Bridge at Avignon";[10] and Ethiopian children play a game called "cock-a-loo," a variant of "hide-and-seek."[11]

3. Within a given culture, particular games are played by children within certain age brackets; and parental approval of a game, freely given to a child at one point, may be sharply curtailed and then replaced by disapproval if the game continues past a particular age.

4. In relationship to the formal games of children, spectator-participation is virtually nonexistent. The *Encyclopaedia Britannica* article on "Classical Games" refers to children's formal games under the heading of "private games" to distinguish them from "public games" such as the Olympian and Pythian games, forerunners of today's spectator sports.

5. Children are extremely inventive in regard to games. One does not generally have to watch a group of children playing very long before he will note that they are making up new games. Objectives are established, rules are formulated, participants are selected, penalties are agreed upon and an original game, fully equipped with structural components, is under way. However, few, extremely few, of these games last, even in the memories of the children who create them. It is indeed striking that thousands of games die the day they are born while a certain game born thousands of years ago is still played with as much enthusiasm as ever. And the game which disappears quickly is not necessarily either less or more challenging physically or intellectually in terms of its general makeup than the game which has lasted for centuries.

Each time I have considered some of the immediately preceding observations, my thoughts have moved in the direction of a rather obvious idea. It is this: if a child likes a game, plays it over and over and passes it on to younger brothers, sisters and neighbors as faithfully as it was passed along to him, then that particular game must do something quite special in his behalf. It must do even more than provide him with a sense of group identity. It must do more than offer him a scaffold for relating to other children, thereby allaying the uneasiness associated with lack of structure and threatened chaos in the social situation. It must do more than allow the child to demonstrate skill and mastery by performing correctly and well, the component parts of the game.

In the course of considering the special value of those games that have found their way into the "permanent" folklore of childhood culture, I have constructed a theory specifically applicable to games. Briefly stated, it is as follows:

1. In their formal games children attempt to master, by means of group activity, anxieties associated with specific kinds of life situations.

2. The reduction of anxiety is brought about by the use of symbolic acts within the games.

3. Both children and adults perceive unconsciously the underlying meaning of games.

4. A child is allowed to continue playing a particular game without adult or peer censure if, in a person of his age, anxiety seems a reasonable response to the situation with which the game is associated.

5. A child will of his own volition discontinue a game when he has mastered his anxiety regarding the related life experience.[12]

There is, of course, a group of games which children play before they have learned to speak. Even though the children cannot talk, these games require their full participation and an apparent knowledge of what is going on. Among these preverbal games are "this little piggy," "peek-a-boo," and a game I shall call "bumble bee," although I have never really heard a name for it.[13]

Although these three games are quite different, I must limit myself to looking closely at only one of them, "peek-a-boo" or "bo peep," as it is sometimes called in England.

"Peek-a-boo" is a rudimentary or primitive game in which a familiar older person, classically a child's mother, hides herself, or more likely hides her face, or at times only hides her eyes from the very young child. This having been done, the mother reappears, saying "peek-a-boo!" There are of course no stated rules for this game. There are, however, some quite definite "requirements." Mother must not stay hidden for more than a few seconds; some part of her should usually be showing; the words "peek-a-boo" must be said in a rather soft, nonfrightening voice; and the repetitions of the hiding and reappearing must be performed in a quite similar way. "Peek-a-boo" is the game which offers great assistance to the very young child in mastering his separation anxiety. Again and again mother disappears, and the child shows an increase in his level of tension. This tension is then dispelled and replaced with a sensation of pleasure and gratification when mother reappears.

When a child's sense of reality has developed to the point that he knows other people are not simply swallowed up, that they do not disappear arbitrarily; when he understands that a person whom he cannot see nonetheless continues to exist; when he feels ties of affection which even in absence connect him with a separated person — at this point a child no longer has any need to play "peek-a-boo," and the activity disappears from his repertoire of games. This usually happens when he is about two years of age. An attempt at "peek-a-boo" with a three- or four-year-old is usually sufficient to prove this point.

By the time a child is five, he has developed the capacity to play a fairly intricate game. He can understand rules which involve contingencies (i.e., "If this happens, I must do that; if not, I must do something else"). He can use equipment. He can restrain many of his aggressive impulses. He can await his turn and accept other kinds of frustration.[14]

An especially interesting game of this kindergarten age is "drop-the-handkerchief." In this very familiar game, one child is selected as "It," and the others form a circle facing each other. "It" is then given a handkerchief. With the handkerchief in his possession, he begins to move around the outside of the group. As he does so, he selects as a culprit one of the children in the circle and drops the handkerchief behind him or between his legs. As soon as the culprit discovers he has been given the handkerchief, he must pick it up and chase "the dropper" around the circle trying to catch him before he can get back into the open space left in the circle when he himself pulled out to give pursuit. If the culprit is successful, the child who is "It" must take the handkerchief back and try again. If not, he becomes "It" for another round of the game.

The essence of "drop-the-handkerchief" lies in the fact that one of the children is marked or stigmatized by his association with a symbolic object, the handkerchief. He rids himself of the stigma by stealthily placing it behind or between the legs of another child, or (after the first round of the game) by attempting to restigmatize the person who has placed responsibility for the object on him. This is a preschool and first-grade game which assists the young child in managing the anxiety associated with the thought that he may not be able to control excretory functions, a matter of considerable though unmentionable concern to children when they are first away from their homes and mothers for any length of time. But should stigmatization occur, even within the symbolic framework of "drop-the-handkerchief," social exclusion may be avoided by shuffling the blame off onto someone else. Children rarely play "drop-the-handkerchief" after the age of six, nor need to.[15]

One of the truly ingenious games of childhood, and certainly one of the best known, is "hide-and-seek." This game provides children an opportunity to master a very important anxiety about being lost.[16] "Hide-and-seek" has many minor variations (for example, "cock-a-loo," the Ethiopian children's game previously noted, in which interestingly enough the concept of an all-seeing, all-knowing madonna is introduced to supervise certain important aspects of the game). The essence of "hide-and-seek," however, is essentially this: one child who has been selected as "It" closes or covers his eyes while the others run away and hide. The child who is "It" sets about the task of finding his playmates. Symbolically, in "hide-and-seek" a child is lost; that is, his location is unknown to "It," who in this case is a surrogate for the searching parent. In the game there is no intention that a child should remain undiscovered. Instead, he should be *almost* undiscovered and then found, or at times he should be passed by, whereupon he runs "home-free," or unpunished. The penalty prescribed for the first child of the hidden group to be found or "caught" is that he himself becomes "It" — the anxious, searching, angry, exasperated parent.[17]

Perhaps the most ingenious part of "hide-and-seek" is that it cannot fail. It cannot leave unresolved anxiety created within the game. The ability of the hidden or lost child to run "home-free" provides this assurance. The lost child will *always* reach "home." If he is not found, he can, in terms of the game, find himself.

Under ordinary circumstances children stop playing "hide-and-seek" at about the onset of puberty.[18] This coincides with the time when they are allowed to leave home alone by train, bus or airplane, or when they are permitted to go on long hikes without adult surveillance, confident of their ability to find their own way to a destination and to return home again safely.

Evidence regarding the time of cessation of this game can be obtained by a brief conversation with almost any child who is in his early teens. Once I recall speaking to a thirteen-year-old girl who told me it had been about a year since she had played "hide-and-seek." Her reasons for discontinuing the game were simple enough and cast vivid light on this subject: "Because nobody plays it anymore," she said. "And because all the old hiding places are gone."

The last game I should like to discuss is the game of "Tag." Basically it is about the simplest game imaginable: One child touches another and says either, "Tag!" or "You're it!" At this point one cycle of the game has been completed, although it is possible for the game to continue for a considerably longer time. In "tag" there is an attempt to master anxiety associated with physical contact. Just as in "drop-the-handkerchief," a noxious stigma is involved which must be disposed of. This is accomplished in a ritualistic manner with the assistance of some magical thinking. By means of a mere touch, one child places his stigma onto another child and magically relieves himself of the burden. Since nothing is actually passed between them, the "tag" may symbolically represent a variety of things: disease, weakness, ignorance, stupidity, bad luck, a curse, or even in some mystical way, all the evil residues of a day or of a lifetime. Perhaps because of the very vagueness of what is transmitted during "tag," the game may be used in an attempt to master anxiety associated with a wide variety of personal exchange situations which extend well past preadolescence. Certainly "tag," unlike the other games discussed, is played with enthusiasm by many adolescents and even at times by some young adults.

In thinking about children's games, it is not only conceivable but quite likely that certain games have more than one "meaning." This is to say that a single game may assist children in mastering anxiety regarding several life situations. To the extent that this is true of a game, the more valuable that game will be, and the greater will be the likelihood of its survival as a part of childhood culture.

At this time I must turn you back to your own laboratories for the study of children's games: the school yard, the backyard, the back alley, the park, the porch, the sidewalk. The only real requirements for a game are more than one child and a bit of freedom. As I noted earlier, children's games are not spectator sports; and frequently, if an adult attempts a direct observation of a particular game, that game simply dissolves and disappears. However, some day soon, you may hear children's voices, and one of them will begin to chant something like: "Engine — engine — number — nine — running — on — Chicago — line — when — she's — polished — how — she — shines. Engine — engine — number — nine. You're It!!!" If you hear something like that, watch carefully out of the corner of your eye. Something important is going on.

FOOTNOTES

1. *Oxford University Dictionary*, 3d ed., 1955, p. 773.
2. An exception to this general rule is the card "game" of "solitaire." However, in this case the name of the game has by custom been converted into an imaginary adversary called "solitaire" or "sol" who is the person the player tries to beat. He is also the one who arranges the deck so there are enough cards in the wrong places to insure a loss but enough in the right places to call for another try at the game.

   In regard to Yo-Yoing, I would not call it a game per se, although it can be converted into a game by the introduction of rules, competition, etc. Freud described a child who repeatedly tossed away a spool attached to a string and retrieved it, representing his desire and ability to bring his mother back. The spool and string is rather like a Yo-Yo, but in the context that Freud described it, I personally would use the classification of individual spontaneous play. If on the other hand one turns to the street, and I think there is a lot of information to be found there, Yo-Yoing is often considered by boys to be a masturbatory substitute; and, at least in my neighborhood, the expression "Johnny is playing with his Yo-Yo" frequently had this double meaning.

3. Phillips, R.: The nature and function of children's formal games. *Psychoanal Quart, 29:* 200, 1960.
4. Kanner, L.: *Child Psychiatry,* 2nd Ed. Springfield, Thomas, 1955, pp. 228-229.
5. Waelder, R.: The psychoanalytic theory of play. *Psychoanal Quart, 2:*208, 1933.
6. Ariès, P.: *Centuries of Childhood,* tr. Baldick, P. New York, Knopf, 1962, pp. 62-99.
7. *Encyclopaedia Britannica,* Vol. 10. Chicago, Banton, 1957, pp. 2-5.
8. In many instances the local or regional name for a particular game is derived from minor variations in the standard procedure. For example, "hide-and-seek" is in some places called:
   a. "Red light" — since the person who is "It" sends the other players off with a series of counts which go "One," "two," etc. to "ten" — "Red LIGHT!"
   b. "Tappy on the ice box" — when this is the phrase, the person who is "It" is requested to say so after he has spotted another player and also before that player has reached home base.
   c. "Beckon" — where those who have been caught may be released to hide again by a signal from some player who has not yet been discovered.
9. *World Book Encyclopedia,* Vol. 7. Chicago, Field Enterprises, 1961, pp. 20-3.
10. *Ibid.*
11. Keene, F. W.: *Fun Around the World.* New York, McGraw, 1955, p. 50. In "cock-a-loo" one child is chosen to be the "madonna." Another is chosen to be "It." "It" hides his eyes in the madonna's lap while the rest of the children run and hide. While they are hiding, "It" says to the madonna, "cock-a-loo?" He answers, "No, it is not yet dawn." "It" keeps on crowing and the madonna keeps answering "no" until all the children are hidden. Then he says, "Yes, it is dawn now," and "It" goes to look for the children. As he finds them they race back to the madonna. The first ones to touch him may hide again.
12. I do not wish to indicate a belief that specific situational anxiety is ever mastered exclusively by means of a game. All of those factors which foster ego development play a role in diminishing the anxieties of childhood (e.g., factors such as the improvement of mental and physical skills through growth, training and practice; the enhancement of judgment by means of experience and increasing knowledge of the world; and the formation of a social personality with the sense of protection provided by cohesive group relationships).
13. This is the game in which an older person says, to a quite young child, something like this: "The bumble bee came out of the barn and went buzz, buzz, buzz." And with each "buzz" the older person darts in with his index finger at the child's ribs, his tummy or the area of his neck beneath his chin.
14. A game which is at times urged upon five- and six-year-olds but involves more frustration than some of them can tolerate, is musical chairs. This is hardly surprising when one remembers that this is an activity in which the individual child is precipitously, permanently and often quite roughly excluded from the playing group; and following which exclusion he is usually left alone to contemplate his misfortune while the game goes merrily on.
15. There are a variety of games in which children commence by forming a circle, but which have widely varying meanings. I am indebted to Dr. Alvin B. Blaustein of New York City who recently called the following to my attention: "The 'ring around a rosy' game dates from the Black Plague. Its ring-dancing form originated in the dancing mania of the times; and the words 'pocket full of posies' refers to the custom (common) then of trying to ward off contagion by filling the pockets with flowers and other strong smells. Its persistence suggests the child's attempt to master anxiety about death by falling down and getting up." (Dr. Blaustein's statement regarding the significance of this game is entirely in keeping with the theoretical formulation presented earlier in this

chapter. The stability of "ring around a rosy" within childhood culture attests to the ubiquitous nature of death anxiety in young children of all times.)

16. A large painting by Pavel Tchelitchew owned by the Museum of Modern Art in New York and entitled "Hide and Seek" shows a central, lonely figure with his back to the viewer. In front of him is a tree which suggests an entire forest, dark and ominous in nature. Surrounding this person, and primarily fitted into the inter-spaces of the branches, are countless faces, feet, heads, hands and entire figures of concealed children. The painting is fantastic, fascinating, frightening and strangely grotesque. It suggests the game of "hide-and-seek," with all the fun and reassurance stripped away, or perhaps it suggests only a frozen, early moment in the game before any of the inherent anxieties of the symbolic situation have been resolved.
17. In his games the child does not merely reverse the roles of reality, as initially suggested by Waelder, but provides himself with the opportunity to play all roles; e.g., exhibitor and spectator, chaser and chased, seeker and sought, laugher and fool, aggressor and passive recipient. The classical expression: "Turn about is fair play" obviously derives from the concept of role switching in games.
18. An interesting exception to this was related to me by a colleague who informed me that at an orphan's home where he spent some time as a child, a variant of hide-and-seek involving tackling and called "ring a leave io" was played by both boys and girls well into adolescence but never when outsiders were watching. It seems to me that in such a setting one might reasonably postulate an extension of the usual period of childhood anxiety about the experience of being lost, along with a need for the continuation of measures designed to alleviate such uneasiness.

"After retiring, my Stanley had to learn to play all over again. First it was peek-a-boo, then we played tag, and now its boats, boats, boats!"

SPORTS AND ADOLESCENCE

ROBERT T. PORTER

PLAY IS OBSERVED IN THE YOUNG of nearly all the higher animals, and it persists into adult life in a relatively few species, including man. For thousands of years, and in all known societies, man has developed the impulse to play into fairly elaborate games and sports with well-defined rules and wide social acceptance and participation. Practicing and training for such specialized activities must have depended in some degree on the level of prosperity of a society, but certainly as early as the original Greek Olympian games (776 B.C.), youths were coached and practiced diligently to become proficient in sports.

This chapter focuses on the role of sports during adolescence, with emphasis on how they serve the special needs of this period of life for the individual and for society. In describing the psychology of adolescence, many observers include the years of prepuberty, so that adolescence is defined as extending from the end of the latency period (about age ten and a half) to adulthood.[1] With reactivation of the instinctual drives, which marks the end of latency, the youngster enters upon a phase of development which is often described as fateful, since many fairly final choices of role and character pattern are to be made. Among the serious tasks which must be successfully undertaken if the individual is to emerge as an adequately organized adult, none is more crucial than that of achieving a stable and appropriate sense of personal identity – and this usually is an accomplishment of late adolescence, dependent in no small degree on having met the challenge of other principal adolescent tasks. Perhaps the most widely recognized of these is the achievement of ego mastery over the intensified sexual and aggressive drives, so that they will neither run wild nor be permanently shackled by excessive defenses. Equally important is the attainment of a realistic independence from parents, through the acquisition of occupational skills and of the capacity to form new object relationships which will meet the basic social and sexual needs of adult life.

Much has been written on the complex steps of personality maturation from infancy through childhood and adolescence; and this has included some detailed consideration of play activity, which is so much a part of the child's exploration of himself and his environment and of his role in relationship to his environment. Sports are perhaps the most prominent form of play during adolescence, and particularly for boys they seem to provide opportunities for meeting many of the developmental needs of this period. In tracing the development of earlier play patterns which lead toward those of adolescence, some observations about the play patterns of small children and of the young of some of the higher animals will be included.

A striking scene from *Seal Island,* one of the first Disney films of actual wild animals, was that in which the young (adolescent) male seals, in "bachelor colonies" apart from the harem territories, engage in seemingly endless mock battles with one another. The quality of the sparring appears clearly playful, with no indications of serious attempts to injure one another — yet it also strongly resembles the serious fighting for territory by the enormous adult bulls. Peterson has intensively studied these same northern fur seals (*Callorhinus ursinus*).[2] He reports that the pups begin playing within a week after birth. There are frequent interchanges with their mothers, especially nipping of the maternal abdomen or neck. Pups also often spend long periods in tidal pools or near shore on calm days, bobbing about and catching crustacea or tugging at bits of kelp and pebbles. Another individual play pattern is darting about, tossing of the head from side to side, flopping down on the chest, or merely "rocking" from side to side by jumping up and down on the foreflippers. It occurs in pups but is most noticeable in bachelors (age 2 to 5 years) when they first haul out or have been on land only a few hours.

Peterson speculates that such play might be a reaction to land locomotion, a temperature adaptation, or some reaction to the crowds of seals after a year of near-solitary life at sea. The social play appears to Peterson to be practicing of adult male-male and male-female interaction patterns. Almost every movement can be identified in adult behavior. One interesting point is that male and female roles seem to be quite interchangeable, even in one individual, from one mock fight to the next. Such social play occurs without the usual stimuli for the patterns in adults, or "out of context" with the physical and social environment. There are really no territories being defended, no serious efforts at copulation, and no harems being rounded together. Among females, this play disappears to a large extent after weaning, although it may continue until about three years of age. Among males, the behavior continues from infancy until it becomes exaggerated at three to five years of age and then seems to graduate toward adult display by the age of seven. Females begin to bear young at three to four years, and males' testes are known to begin spermatogenesis at the same age — but the males are prevented from participating in the reproductive life of the colonies for several years more. (A mature female may weigh from 95-110 lb; a mature bull, 400-600 lb. An average 4-year-old male would weigh only 78 lb — and hence would not yet have much chance with a full-grown bull in a serious struggle for territory.) Full-grown bulls do not "play" even when congregated in bachelor groups; their interchanges resemble the more serious, damaging fights of adults.

These seals spend all but a few weeks in summer in the open sea, where they can sleep and feed adequately; in fact, they seem to be tied to land simply for reproduction. The pups leave for sea at weaning age (about 4 months after birth), and many do not return for the next two years. They live singly or in small groups at sea. There are some accounts of playful behavior at sea; Peterson points out that, as might be expected, most of the prereproductive behavior on land seems to be related to the reproductive behavior of adults. That the social play of the females stops when they are old enough to engage in actual reproduction, whereas the social play of the males increases at adolescence (which is for them a period when they remain barred from actual reproductive behavior), does suggest that the play patterns of mock battles, courtship display and brief attempts to mount may represent both practicing and discharging of tensions. Surely it would take skill and practice, as well as adult size, to undertake an encounter with an experienced harem bull. Also, as the bachelors approach adult size, perhaps even the playful jousting can give indications of some sort of dominance ranking among themselves which could allow a few of them to feel ready to challenge some of the older or less dominant harem bulls.

Play behavior has also been carefully observed in animals which have more enduring group relationships and are biologically closer to man. Harlow has conducted extensive studies on the development of play behavior in rhesus monkeys.[3] On the basis of his studies and field studies which have been reported, he concludes that social play evolves automatically as long as infant monkeys have easy access to age-mates. He states that if groups of perhaps four monkeys grow up together, "they develop friendship through play, and this tends to ameliorate their later maturing aggressive responses to their playmates. (In the monkey, aggression begins to take on adult-like forms at about 1 year of age.) Furthermore, if monkeys develop affection for playmates early in life, they will subsequently cooperate and aggress against any member or members of the out-group, whether these happen to be other monkeys, people, leopards or alligators." He adds that there can be no question whatsoever but that play provides practice for necessary adult skills, including social skills.

It is worth mentioning that not only Harlow but other observers of primates have noted that they engage in a great deal of sexual play even during infancy and adolescence. Harlow's work has been particularly illuminating in this regard, for as a by-product of the experiments where young rhesus monkeys were raised with only inanimate "dummy" surrogate mothers and no age-mates, one of the unanticipated findings was the tremendous later lack of social, and particularly of sexual, capability. The males were never able to learn to function as sexually adequate adults, and the females were incredibly inept mothers with at least their firstborn infants. However, when raised without mothers but with access to other motherless age-mates, there was much social playing, including all the usual forms of sexual play, and these monkeys appear to Harlow to be essentially normal as adults.[4]

Lorenz states that "whenever there is playful activity in the developing behavior of a young animal, we may safely assume that it contains variable acquired elements."[5] Since it is generally accepted that man is the animal least bound by invariable patterns of response or instinct, we might anticipate that play would find a correspondingly greater role in the development of the human child — and certainly this appears to be true. Extra dimensions are provided by man's capacity for evolving cultures (as opposed to the more fixed patterning of group behavior of animal species), by man's consciousness of past and future, and by the tremendous variety of possible experiences, actual or imaginary, of other individuals which is made available to even the young child through the medium of language. We are therefore not surprised at the developing complexity of play as the child matures and gradually develops the capacity for object relationships with other individuals, and finally at age eleven or twelve the capacity for formal thought and logical assumptions.

Play is one form of experiencing and experimenting which is active from infancy. Erikson, in distinguishing between the play of adults and that of children, says, "The playing adult steps sideward into another reality; the playing child advances forward to new steps of mastery. I propose the theory that the child's play is the infantile form of the human ability to deal with experience by creating model situations and to master reality by experiment and planning."[6]

Stone and Church describe the various forms of play which develop during infancy and childhood.[7] According to their classification, probably the first form of play in infancy could be called *sense-pleasure play.* This kind of play continues throughout life, usually in increasingly complex and patterned forms. Even during infancy, sense-pleasure play branches out into a somewhat less self-contained *skill play,* the exercise of one's capacities for action. Early in toddler-hood, the first signs emerge of *dramatic play,* initially consisting of enactment of scenes from everyday life. In dramatic play the child tries out concretely (by identification) what it feels like to be in the roles of other people and other things. Also, considering play in relation to the presence of others, there is by the toddler stage the possibility for *solitary play* or *parallel play,* and by the age of five, there is the capacity for *cooperative group play,* in which several children can coordinate their activities in sustained group projects.

Other observers, too, have reported that social participation with peers increases in versatility and complexity between the second and fifth years, as shown by the more cooperative nature of their participation and the tendency to play in larger groups of up to five or more. That is, the size of the play group increases with age during the preschool years. Competition, too, becomes more evident in the preschool period. Using several criteria of rivalry, Greenberg found no competitive responses for children aged two to three, 43 per cent for children aged three to four, 69 per cent for children aged four to five, 75 per cent for children aged five to six, and 86 per cent for children six to seven. Stone and Church found that with regard to quarreling, before age three there is no noticeable difference between boys and girls, but thereafter girls show a decline in frequency of quarreling, while boys become increasingly combative up to age five, when they quickly become more self-contained.

In our attempt to observe the evolution of the forms of play toward those we may call sports, it may be of interest to note the stages of thinking of the child as described by Piaget.[10] He states that "thought's most spontaneous manifestation is play, or at any rate the quasi-hallucinatory form of imagination which allows us to regard desires as realized as soon as they are born." He also concludes that

> there may be several realities for the child, and these realities may be equally real in turn instead of being arranged in a hierarchy as with us. It may be, moreover, that the disharmony resulting from this fact is in no way a source of discomfort to the child. The facts show this very clearly. Four stages can be picked out in the evolution of modality. This first lasts till the age of 2-3, the second extends from 2-3 to 7-8, the third from 7-8 to 11-12, and the fourth begins at this age. During the first stage, reality may be said to be simply and solely what is desired. Freud's "pleasure principle" deforms and refashions the world to its liking. The second stage marks the appearance of two heterogeneous but equal realities — the world of play and the world of observation. The third marks the beginning of hierarchical arrangement, and the fourth marks the completion of this hierarchy, thanks to the introduction of a new plane — that of formal thought and logical assumptions.

Piaget notes that the advances in logic (at age 7-8) are connected with the definite diminution of egocentrism at that age, and that at this same age, certain changes take place in the modality of childish judgment which are in close relation to the appearance of a desire for a system and noncontradiction. At about 11-12, the various planes of reality — play, verbal reality, observation — are set in a hierarchy that is defined in relation to a single criterion: experience. Piaget relates the development of logical thought to the social need to share the thought of others and to communicate our own with success: "Proof is the outcome of argument. . . . Argument is, therefore, the backbone of verification. Logical reasoning is an argument which we have with ourselves, and which reproduces internally the features of a real argument."

Stone and Church mention the "ancient tribal rituals of middle childhood," pointing out that it has been possible to trace many still-common children's games and chants back to the Middle Ages and beyond to Roman and Druid sources.[11] These have been handed down from generation to generation not by adults, but from generations of almost-adolescent children to generations of younger brothers and sisters whom they initiate. They observe that "this remarkable durability depends in large part on children's love of ritual for its own sake and on their (mostly unspoken) sense of magical power in the literal repetition of forms which share the character of rites and incantations," and "young schoolchildren play their games, just as they recite their sayings and perform their rituals, according to ironclad formulas that permit of no variation."

In another work, Piaget investigated children's concepts of rules and morals and found definite changes with age in the way rules are conceived.[12] At first, in the early school years, children have rigid and decidedly ritualistic attitudes toward rules. Later, in the middle years of grammar school, minor changes in the rules are permitted, provided everyone agrees. Finally, late in childhood, there is a capacity to grasp the fact that rules are arrived at by consensus and serve merely to define the conduct and purpose of the game in an orderly way. Stone and Church note that "this development in the conception of rules runs parallel to a change in the kind of games children play. Increasingly, during the middle years, children engage in competitive games, games which do not simply run their course like London Bridge and Farmer in the Dell, but have an outcome."

In discussing sports, our topic will most closely correspond to the phase of play where competitive interests have developed, where there is a growing awareness of the purpose and use of rules and where there is a conscious interest in attainment of skills. The active pursuit of organized sports seems to come into its own at about the beginning of adolescence as defined by Pearson,[13] or as the adult mode of thinking is attained according to Piaget. This would appear to correlate with the increasing need to achieve a sense of identity compatible with the goals of the impending sexual maturing (which would increasingly demand social contacts with meaningful communication — a precondition for the "argument" which Piaget considers the backbone of verification) and to find channeled outlets for the drive energy which emerges with such growing intensity at puberty. Spiegel has noted that the early adolescent "often feels sexual tension as an external force — not as part of himself. . . . Sexuality at first appears to act *on* the individual rather than to *express* the individual. . . . but it is also during adolescence that the gradual integration of sexuality into the self takes place."[14] The need to find ways of integration of the sexual drives and of ego mastery of the aggressive drives is too pressing not to be felt in most of the activities of this period of life.

The importance of the aggressive drive was recognized by Freud much later than was that of the sexual drive[15] – but most subsequent psychoanalytic consideration of these two major drives has not found the first less important in its social consequences or in its impact on the developing personality organization. There is a good deal of data to indicate that the struggle with aggression is greater in the male – and that this is correlated with the greater muscular strength, especially that of the extremities and shoulder girdle, of the male throughout childhood as well as after puberty. Thus the equipment for what Greenacre calls centrifugal motor aggression is available from infancy.[16]

Numerous observers have reported that by nursery school age, boys are definitely more quarrelsome than girls, and that boys are more angered by interference with their toys and possessions and show greater anger outbursts. It seems reasonable to recall that greater physical aggressiveness of the male is typical of nearly all higher animal species, suggesting that at least a significant part of the apparent greater aggressiveness of the human male is a feature of our biological endowment. At the same time, while aggressiveness appears to be less in girls, it is by no means absent. It may be that the changing customs which seem to define social roles for male and female less distinctly than in the past also affect the ways in which aggressiveness may find expression in both sexes. In the past, the sports in which girls and women traditionally participated were those which had a minimum of body contact and which involved grace and rhythm (such as tennis, swimming and riding). Today, the number of sports in which women participate is greatly expanded, although the body contact sports (football, boxing, ice hockey) are still generally avoided. Where they are strongly motivated, girls appear to train as strenuously as boys in such sports as swimming – and often outperform boys who have not trained as well. Nonetheless, there is probably little doubt that sports still play a more important role in the childhood and adolescence of boys than of girls – especially strenuously competitive sports. In discussing some of the functions sports serve for the growing individual, boys may be referred to at times where it seems that what is being said applies more particularly to them, but the same functions may well be served for girls who engage actively in the same sports.

Particularly in the area of learning how to deal with the aggressive drive, sports may well play their most significant role – both for the individual and for society. To the extent that aggression could really lead to danger, and to the much greater extent that it appears overwhelmingly dangerous in the limited understanding of the child with his persisting belief in the magic omnipotence of his thoughts, then to a corresponding extent the child's effort to cope with his aggressive impulses is of tremendous importance to him. Much of the early play and many of the early childhood games (especially those without rules) reveal the preoccupation with aggressive fantasies. With boys in particular there is a period when a most favored game, with or without playmates, is being a man with a gun who can dispatch any or all of those about him by aiming and saying "Bang, bang – you're dead!" To again quote Erikson, "to hallucinate ego mastery and yet also practice it in an intermediate reality between fantasy and actuality is the purpose of play."[17] In the example given above, the child finds a release for his fantasy of needing to be able to eliminate those who for any reason appear to him to represent obstacles to gratification – and yet, he also observes that the victims of his imaginary shooting do not actually fall mortally wounded.

Preoccupation with how the longed-for goals of adult fulfillment may be attained can scarcely fail to evoke fantasies of competition in even very young children. For example, if he is to obtain the most desirable girl in the whole world, the young boy imagines he must inevitably contend with the efforts of all other boys and men (who would of course also want her). He must further expect that, to win her, he must be the most desirable of all those males seeking her love. This is the theme of endless stories of the prince trying to win the princess – stories enjoyed by quite young children for many centuries. Thus, on the basis of the child's own desires, there is the need to become outstanding and to excel in whatever is perceived, correctly or incorrectly, to be important in the competition for approval and love. All this must be seen in relationship to the child's level of development.

In early childhood, the social relationships within the family and then with playmates and schoolmates confront the child with many critical tasks and generally provide opportunities for identifications, for increasing ego mastery of the drives and for a growing sense of objective reality. Play and – in later childhood and adolescence – games and sports are among the social activities that permit practice in channeled and controlled release of sexual and aggressive strivings, frequently in symbolic form. During some developmental stages and particularly during latency, many of the most important fantasies and life goals may be largely unconscious or so disguised as to be hard to recognize. Thus, unless we keep in mind the main theme of the child's romantic fantasies of competing for the most desirable mate imaginable with an intensity of desire which would indeed claim "all's fair in love and war," it is easy to overlook the continuity of purpose beneath nearly all of the child's efforts to grow up and to hold his own in at least some of the important areas of endeavor.

"Now that I've won the Druid Princess, all I have to say is 'Ugh!' "

If the child shared the normal goals of the oedipal period of development (approximately $2\frac{1}{2}$ to 6 years of age), then nearly all subsequent attainments or failures have significance to him in terms of whether he is becoming the kind of person who may achieve the important goals of those early romantic fantasies. These goals are undergoing continual revision in keeping with reality as he increasingly comes to understand it. Thus later it need no longer be only mother who is the most desirable girl in the world, and he may be more and more able to realize that not all boys will compete for the girl he will want, and that not all girls will be won by the same kinds of excellence. Still, for many years most boys will be uneasy if they do not feel they can keep up in most of the areas of competition to which their society pays tribute in one way or another. "Competent" and "compete" both derive from the Latin *competere* (*com-*, together + *petere,* to seek). So even etymologically, being well qualified (competent) is clearly associated with one's ability to contend with others (compete).

As mentioned earlier, Spiegel has emphasized that while some of the sexual tensions of early adolescence may be experiencd as alien, still it is one of the important tasks of this phase of development to integrate these feelings into the personality.[18] The social experiences – friendships, parties, dances and dates — provide most important practical opportunities for gaining ego mastery of the sexual strivings and for combining them with the capacity to form increasingly stable affectionate relationships. During early adolescence, however, many youngsters are still apprehensive about some aspects of these intensified feelings and unsure about their control of them and of their capacity to fulfill what are often still childishly perfectionistic ego-ideals. Yet tensions may mount which not only need some outlet, but if possible one that is acceptable to the individual and his society. In general, it is not acceptable in our society for younger adolescents to have complete heterosexual experiences — and this means that the release for these tensions must be largely in the realm of fantasy, including symbolic expressions which may be part of unconscious fantasies. Adatto states that unconscious drama is present in all play, whether of adult or child.[19] While the aggressive elements are readily recognized in competitive sports, there is more reluctance to see in these same sports the many possible expressions of sexual goals. If we return to our model of the small child's richly enjoyed fairy story, once the hero overcomes the obstacles, he wins the princess and "they live happily ever after." Thus the old persisting ambitions of the oedipal period, together with the rich array of symbolic attributes of many games, would readily allow such games to represent sexual fulfillment on the level of the unconscious drama, and with as much social approbation as was present earlier in the fairy stories eagerly offered to the child by the parents.

Even while the aggressive aspects of sports are more readily recognized, it may hardly be overemphasized that since aggression is the most threatening human propensity, its free and direct expression is curbed not only by society but by the child's own fears of serious consequences. Since it is felt that there is a considerable increase in aggressive drive energy in adolescence — and we can note the clear association of aggressiveness with sexual maturation in other animals, and the impressive difference in tractability of bulls and steers, or stallions and geldings — then there is clearly need for an outlet for aggression, too, and again one which will be acceptable to the adolescent and to society. While many such outlets do exist, including competition in sophistication, mode of dress, even scholastic achievement, still sports probably offer the outlet combining the largest number of elements which are close to the modes of drive expression observed in other higher animals. Thus the aspects of display, motor discharge and direct expression of competition in terms of physical strength, skill, and determination or courage are all present in many sports. The strong competitive urges may be expressed in forms about as strenuous as anyone could wish, with the clear determination of the opponent to strive just as strenuously; and yet in victory there can be exhilaration without guilt, and in defeat generally quite tolerable disappointment without shame or rage, since no real injury has been dealt or received. Thus sports can offer acceptable forms of release — safety valves of a sort — for the intensified drives of adolescence, providing at the same time many additional personal and social values.

From earliest childhood, the process of identification is of great importance in the developing sense of identity. Jacobson discusses how the selectivity of identifications, which is noted already in early childhood, increasingly expresses the child's rebellious struggle for the development and maintenance of his own independent identity.[20] She notes during adolescence the increase of ego identifications with realistic images of the adults, even while concomitantly the role of identifications is receding in favor of autonomous thought processes; and she believes that during this phase the ego-ideal gradually bridges the superego and ego systems and may ultimately be claimed by both. She also states that the ultimate identity formation rests on successful modification, stabilization and integration of the relations and identifications with persons of the past, and on the resulting capacity for the establishment of sound, new selective personal and group relations and identifications.

Another comment on the problem of the ego-ideal and past identifications is made by Josselyn.[21] "Because of his strong urge to mature, his childhood ego-ideal creates a problem for him in itself. It was molded from two major components: identification with the parent of the same sex and acceptance of the conceptualization of a desirable person as revealed by the parent of the opposite sex. To the adolescent, therefore, his ego-ideal of the past often fails as a model of what he, as an individual, would like to be, since to attain individuality he must be different from those who were the source of his original idea of himself." She points out that the adolescent eases this conflict by shifting the major authority to whom to conform. The important authority becomes his own peer group. Thus the group superego provides standards which the individual accepts while his own are in turmoil.

Most authors indicate that the ego is enriched by the many identifications the normal child makes in the course of growing up. At certain stages, there is a quite conscious seeking for heroes or figures who will serve as ideals with whom to identify. Pearson mentions that with the onset of adolescence, the individual may fall back on the use of the early mechanisms of imitation, introjection and identification to strengthen his ego, but with different objects: not his parents, but adults outside the family, and not the adults as objects, but their habits and points of view.[22] Josselyn, too, emphasizes that commonly in adolescence, the conscious identification is with the feelings of the hero, whereas earlier it was with the hero's actual struggle against real and external dangers and frustrations.[23]

In essence, then, identifications in early adolescence tend to be increasingly selective, to turn to persons other than the key figures of childhood and to seek more realistic aspects compatible with the need for development of more mature ego-ideals and ego goals. Acceptable for hero worship and practical ego-ideal identifications are many openly admired teachers, athletes, coaches and even older adolescents whose performance realistically warrants admiration. Particularly in sports, the efforts to attain similar qualities and skills can be quite well defined in functional, objective terms. In choosing a hero or ego-ideal figure consciously, the child usually is able to find a useful model for helping consolidate role and body-image in gender-appropriate ways, and often too, his ideal is someone approved by others and thus may reflect values of his peers, family or society. In the event the child has less conformist ego strivings, his need for some actual model may be even more urgent.

The great variety of sports, constantly increasing as man has access to new devices (such as the parachute and scuba), offers almost endless opportunity for an adolescent to find challenges which are emotionally meaningful to him. Once a thrilling or daring feat has been performed by someone, many adolescents will then be stimulated to fantasy what this experience might be for them. The wish to be free of childhood fears usually influences the ego-ideal, and the performance of a feat which represents mastery of fear bolsters self-esteem and may generally strengthen confidence that other fears may be similarly overcome. While the choice of challenge may often be based on unconscious symbolism, still some fairly common sports seem to have such a meaning for many adolescents. Thus, to dive from a high board is initially sufficiently frightening to most boys so that it may be regarded by them as a personal test of the ability to overcome their fear. In *The Adolescent Through Fiction,* Kiell includes several fine excerpts from novels which convey the intense meaningfulness of such challenges to the adolescent.[24]

Sports can also help some adolescents to find more positive attitudes toward instruction and work. Where toilet and habit training was either badly timed or too anxiously insistent, a stubbornly negativistic attitude may have become established whereby much of the subsequent instruction offered at home or school is experienced as oppressive and stifling rather than helpful. Sports may offer a fresh opportunity to find instruction a desired rather than an imposed experience, especially where coaching is received as part of team membership, generally welcomed by the peer group and offered by an older boy or man who may be much admired for his skills and his willingness to share these. To gain special skills, to develop form and to build muscular strength and endurance, the athlete must be able to persevere in the face of frequent failure and fatigue. Thus, without giving it such a label, the adolescent who engages seriously in sports is also practicing stretching his frustration tolerance. The resemblance of such intense efforts to those usually regarded as "work" is worth observing. The self-chosen aspect of the sport activity and the related pleasurable expectations may be the only factors that distinguish some of the more complex adolescent sports from work as we usually think of it. People who are fortunate enough to be able to earn their living by pursuing activities that they chose for positive pleasure (and this group includes many scientists, writers, artists and musicians, as well as professional athletes) may indeed blur the boundaries between work and play for themselves as well as for anyone trying to devise hard and fast definitions. In any event, because of the intense personal motivation of some devotees of sport, remarkable accomplishments of coordination, strength, stamina and even memory are often seen. Boys who may block or balk at spelling or arithmetic tables will often memorize many times as much information about baseball records. The boys in *Tom Sawyer* vigorously painted the fence when it was considered play.

There are many ways, too, in which sports serve the global need of the adolescent to face and accept realities of the kind with which he must deal as an adult — particularly those in which he will come into possible competition with other men. Whatever the fantasy or unconscious drama, a sports competitor usually wins, loses or ties in terms that can be validated by others. There are also successes or failures which are quite clear and definite even in sports where the individual performs alone. In noncompetitive skiing, for example one descends without falling, makes turns as intended and keeps control — or one falls, or clearly has poor control and cannot accomplish what he has in mind. Team sports offer many opportunities for realistic self-appraisal, partly through the awareness of the appraisal of others. Many team games are often played informally in "choose-up" fashion, and the judgment of the others as to the skill or team value of each player is soon clear in the order in which each is chosen — painfully clear to those chosen last.

Leadership qualities, which do not necessarily depend on athletic prowess, may also often be recognized in play and sports situations, and certain games clearly offer practice in leadership skills and responsibilities (as with the quarterback in football). Such team sports not only offer an opportunity for the confirmation of leadership capacity for those who already have such skills, but they may also offer comprehensible and tangible models for other team members, possibly younger or less experienced, who aspire to develop such skills themselves.

On the basis of family experience, many children see all important relationships as based on the parent-child model, with one individual consistently dominant, the other submissive. Team sports and group activities where a common effort is required may demonstrate an alternative way of relating —

where leadership may shift on the basis of special skills or knowledge, with realization of the mutual benefit of making the best use of each individual's special abilities, rather than having a complete monopolization of all the most desired roles on the basis of simple domination. A sports team often has a clearer basis for cooperative effort than clubs of various kinds where there may be a mutuality of interests but still largely individual pursuit of those interests (as with hobbies).

Another major problem which every individual must face in order to take a responsible role in adult society has to do with bridging the gulf between the society of the family group in early childhood and the society of larger groups on which we are all in some degree dependent today, whether or not we choose to be. Portmann regards man as a social being "whose natural abilities are appropriate to life in a small group where clearly defined relations can exist between its members."[25] Artiss reports recent studies based on military and industrial experience which indicate that "small face-to-face units of six to twelve persons . . . appear to maintain the greatest effectiveness in terms of output and stability over time."[26] An established order, a clear basis for hierarchy within the group, appears to be necessary — but even in animal groups, an actual physical contest is not always required to secure this. It appears that all sorts of testing of relative confidence and aggressiveness are possible through various kinds of display or greeting rituals. When it does come to an actual physical encounter, both with animals and small boys, a fight is not usually to the death but to the point of clear decision. Without real contests — actual competitive striving with strong affect — either in fights or in sports, many individuals may retain exaggerated fears and may remain passive or avoid challenges; or they may develop passive-aggressive patterns with swings to unwarranted antagonistic or overbearing behavior when they can no longer tolerate feeling so fearful and submissive. Only with actually experiencing the outcome of such contests do most boys come to realize fully that even in angry fights, when the outcome becomes clear, usually the loser "gives up" and the victor seems to have lost his rage and his determination to destroy his opponent. The relief which comes with this realization can be immense.

Practical methods have evolved for establishing hierarchies within groups without bloodshed. Rules, or laws as they are called in certain larger social groups, are among these methods — and may define the conditions under which roles may be attained and how such roles may be employed. Much of the law under which groups operate is taken for granted, since it is understood in principle from other situations where similar rules prevail. Just as schools provide an early social experience which may help to compensate for deficiencies in individual families, so do sports offer intensely experienced contests with individuals from other family backgrounds, in a setting where group attitudes become very important and where traditional, well-tested techniques for dealing with problems of aggression may be learned from contemporaries.

Several of the widely accepted techniques are clustered in the concept of sportsmanship — an ability to abide by rules of the game ("play fairly") so that the outcome can be determined, and to accept defeat or victory in a manner which maintains a sense of perspective and considers the feelings of others. These are abilities which, within the group, help preserve it as a functioning unit; and this is clearly important in team sports where the team could be incapacitated if several of its members walked off the field or refused to cooperate. In the relationships between individual contestants or between teams, good sportsmanship helps to insure that rivalries can continue to be expressed in sporting contests. The practice of such sportsmanly modes of behavior in groups outside the family helps to reinforce and extend the concepts of fairness, respect for rules and respect for the feelings of others which must have had their origins in the family; and surely it helps to modify these so that they may be applied to larger and less intimately known groups, which might ultimately include groups of strangers. It would certainly appear easier to learn these attitudes where the competition is in play rather than where it might be for a mate or literally for life or death.

Having emphasized such attributes of sports as their provisions for group activity, tests of skill and courage, competitiveness and symbolic gratification of sexual and aggressive strivings, it may be worth observing that such activities of adolescents and preadolescents as truancy, vandalism, pilfering and various other delinquent or unlawful pursuits may also satisfy these particular criteria. Some particularly hair-raising adolescent outlets, such as the driving contests labeled "chicken" (one version of which has two cars speed together each straddling the center line, the first to turn aside being "chicken"), violate the quality of play whereby the release of aggression should not result in actual death or mutilation. In evaluating such contests, it is not easy to ascertain whether there is a real breakthrough of unmodulated aggressiveness toward others or self, or whether there is inadequate reality testing or failure to be able to anticipate an actual violent outcome. In this respect, it is a little more like sport than Russian roulette — since the drivers may both believe that they have the skill to turn aside in time to avoid a collision. The same may be true of some gang fights which, like the one depicted in *West Side Story,* may in the planning stage be visualized as rough but not lethal contests, but where only in the heat of battle, with recourse to weapons, does it become clear that rules are not established or enforceable which could avert actual killing or serious injuries.

In *Under the Mountain Wall,* a fascinating account of a Stone Age culture in present-day New Guinea, Matthiessen describes the continuing tribal wars which are an important and rather ritualized part of the way of life.[27]

> . . . for display and panoply were part of war, which was less war than ceremonial sport, a wild, fierce festival. Territorial conquest was unknown . . .; there was land enough for all, and at the end of the day the warriors would go home across the fields to supper. Should rain come to chill them, spoil their feathers, both sides would retire. A day of war was dangerous and splendid, regardless of its outcome; it was a war of individuals and gallantry, quite innocent of tactics and cold slaughter. A single death on either side would mean victory or defeat.

Certain aspects of war have been experienced as sporting contests down through the ages. The Trojan War, as described by Homer, had much of this quality. So did the dogfights of the combat pilots of World War I. Again the distinction between actual fighting to the death and contests in which losing may symbolize death is a very important one. Sublimations often fail, and the breakthrough of the repressed drives always threatens. Many factors are necessary to keep aggressive drives within appropriate boundaries for the good of the individual in his society, and some of the most important of these are characteristics of the society itself. In the delinquent "sports" such as vandalism, there is no effort to "match" opponents or teams; instead there seems to be a pitting of the "oppressed" young against the "tyrannical" or "rich" adults or privileged "others," and the "rules" are not mutually agreed upon. Where such activity has any organized, purposeful quality, the fantasy would appear to be that there can be no bargaining with tyrants, and there is no need to "match" teams since the whole of adult society may be imagined to be the other team, against which the assault of a small delinquent band has the heroic quality of a David against Goliath, or Robin Hood against all the representatives of the King and the rich nobles. In smaller, tribal-size units, breakdowns of social controls corresponding to what we call "juvenile delinquency" seem to be uncommon, and one could surmise that communication is more reliable in the smaller group and that dissatisfactions are more quickly perceived and dealt with in some way. "Cultures of poverty" in the sense of Oscar Lewis,[28] discontinuity in role between child and adult, and lack of a meaningful social role for the adolescent (as commented upon by such authors as Slavson or Erikson) are not features of small tribal societies.

Even where there is partial breakdown of social organization, as in slum areas of large cities, sports would still be one of the outlets which might offer to individual adolescents some experience with small groups organized around principles which could help bridge the gap to participation in a more organized adult society. However, it would be well to remember that sports have not been a "magic" answer to all of our social problems. PAL (Police

Athletic League), Boys Clubs, and other such programs recommended as measures to reduce delinquency undoubtedly have value to the community and to most boys, but it is also true that some boys will participate actively in such sports programs and either concurrently or later become actively delinquent anyway. Others may be too impaired even to participate in sports. The impact of many other factors from earliest childhood, some of great intensity and occurring at critical phases of development, has much to do with the choices an adolescent will make when faced with severe conflicts. Notwithstanding these limitations, sports do appear to provide many adolescents with practice for adult roles, just as does the play described for the young seals and monkeys.

Sports appeal to adolescents the world over and thus lend themselves to potential sharing by all segments of the world's population. They provide group activities where there is intense emotional involvement and where there is a basis for an aggressive contest with another group which can lead to a mutually accepted decision. As international matches become more widespread and more games and sports are shared by all nations, sports may provide one important basis for empathy and understanding between individuals of different societies. Providing comprehensible experience with the problems of aggression and the modes of conduct and the rules which settle contests and leadership conflicts without disrupting team organization, and offering a basis for understanding members of other groups engaging in similar activities, sports would seem a particularly suitable training for adolescents who will soon be facing the critical challenge of how to extend the concepts of law and the control of aggression to the international level. Today's adolescents face the possibility of annihilation, and at least some of them demonstrate appropriate concern about this most urgent of world problems. From about the same age that such problems may begin to concern them, and at a period of life when their social attitudes are still in flux, sports evoke strong involvement and provide intense actual interpersonal experiences closely paralleling those with which adult society must cope in social organizations ranging from those concerned with small villages to states and nations. The wide flexibility and range of sports, with varying degrees of actual physical contact and varying team sizes, and with established rules such that outcome of encounters can be determined, provide one important potential training ground for adolescents who may soon need to assume responsibilities as productive citizens and leaders.

FOOTNOTES

1. Pearson, G.: *Adolescence and the Conflict of Generations.* New York, Norton, 1958, pp. 78-79.
2. Peterson, R.: Personal communication.
3. Harlow, H.: Personal communication.

4. Harlow, H., and Harlow, M.: Social deprivation in monkeys. *Scientific American,* Nov. 1962, p. 10.
5. Lorenz, K.: in *Instinctive Behavior,* 1st Ed. trans. and ed. by Schiller, C., New York, Int Univs, 1957, p. 99.
6. Erikson, E.: *Childhood and Society,* 2d Ed. New York, Norton, 1963, pp. 212-222.
7. Stone, L., and Church, J.: *Childhood and Adolescence.* New York, Random, 1957, pp. 110, 148, 150, 209-213.
8. Greenberg, P.: Competition in children: an experimental study. *Amer J Psychol, 44*:221-248, 1932.
9. Stone and Church: *op. cit. supra.*
10. Piaget, J.: *Judgment and Reasoning in the Child.* London, Routledge, 1928, pp. 205-253.
11. Stone and Church: *op. cit. supra.*
12. Piaget, J.: *Moral Judgment of the Child.* London, Routledge, 1932.
13. *Supra* note 1.
14. Spiegel, L.: in *Adolescents: Psychoanalytic Approach to Problems and Therapy,* Lorand, S. and Schneer, H. [Eds.]. New York, Hoeber, 1961, p. 13.
15. Freud, S.: *Beyond the Pleasure Principle,* trans. by Strachey, J. New York, Liveright, 1950.
16. Greenacre, P.: *Trauma, Growth and Personality.* New York, Norton, 1952, pp. 161-163.
17. Erikson: *supra* note 6.
18. Spiegel: *supra* note 14.
19. Adatto, C.: *Golf,* appearing herein at p. 458.
20. Jacobson, E.: *The Self and the Object World.* New York, Int Univs, 1964, pp. 161-195.
21. Josselyn, I.: in *Readings in Psychoanalytic Psychology,* Levitt, M. [Ed.]. New York, Appleton, 1959, pp. 74-79.
22. Pearson: *supra* note 1.
23. Josselyn: *supra* note 21.
24. Kiell, N.: *The Adolescent Through Fiction.* New York, Int Univs, 1959, pp. 27-38.
25. Portmann, A.: *Animals as Social Beings.* New York, Viking, 1961, pp. 70-76.
26. Artiss, K.: Human behavior under stress. II.: Small group process. Lecture, Forest Hospital, Des Plaines, Illinois, Oct. 14, 1964.
27. Matthiessen, P.: *Under the Mountain Wall.* New York, Viking, 1962, pp. 10-11.
28. Lewis, O.: *Five Families.* New York, Basic Books, 1959, p. 2.

SOME DYNAMIC FACTORS IN SPORT

HELENE DEUTSCH

THE OBSERVATIONS WHICH FORM the material of this communication are derived from the analysis of a patient suffering from impotence, together with anxiety states and depression. Owing to his feelings of inferiority, he is almost incapable of accomplishing anything in his profession or entering into any social relations. There is only one way in which he can temporarily feel "full power" and completely master the inner attitude which has its origin in his complexes. He does this by eagerly engaging in every possible kind of sport. During his analysis we have often been able to discover the relations between his interest in sport and his symptoms and to determine what were the impulses thus desexualized or sublimated and how he had succeeded in overcoming his castration complex, that is to say, in making his activities in sport compensate for the inferiority feelings in which that complex expressed itself. Though such an investigation does not present anything new to the analyst, I think the material obtained is worth reporting because the patient's early infantile experiences give us an insight into the mechanism of which the complexes made use in order to relieve the psychic apparatus through this particular outlet. This mechanism, in itself nothing new, does seem to me noteworthy in this connection, and I think it exhibits something of fundamental importance for the psychology of sport.[1]

During the analysis, we had occasion more than once to deal with a dream which appeared in various forms and which had recurred since earliest childhood, always with the same content accompanied by the most intense anxiety. A round object, a ball, a balloon, a circular building, a Roman column, a cloud of a round shape, a strange bird or something of the sort was hovering above his head and threatening to fall down and destroy him. In the dream the patient sought in vain for help and awoke with anxiety.

The analysis of this dream helped us to track down the symptoms to their sources. We found the patient's infantile neurosis in his fourth year manifesting itself at first in the typical childish fear of darkness and solitude. At that time the phantasy with which the anxiety was connected was that of a hand extended menacingly towards him. Dread of this hand was the content of his fears. At this time the patient was engaged in severe struggles against masturbation, accompanied by masochistic-sadistic fantasies. The hand which menaced him in the darkness was the hand of his father, punishing him by castration; hence his anxiety was the dread of castration.

In his eighth year these first anxiety states were succeeded by a fully developed phobia. The latter had the same content as the anxiety-dreams; the memory of the phobia belonged to material which had been wholly buried and came into discussion only at a late phase of the analysis. His condition at that time exhibited a kind of agoraphobia with a sharply defined content: he was afraid that a ball with which he himself was playing or which someone else might throw would fall on his head and either mortally injure him or so hurt his head as to make him an idiot. This anxiety restricted his freedom of movement, for wherever he went he dreaded this sinister event. This phobia, like the first anxiety state, proved to embody the dread of castration, the threatening hand of the father being replaced by the ball. To explain how the hand came to be transformed into a round object would take us too far from our subject; I can only briefly indicate that the genital organ of the father, perceived by the child as "round," and the rounded organs of the mother had something to do with the transformation.

The phobia lasted for a short time and was then succeeded by diffused feelings of anxiety, slight obsessional symptoms, etc. A short time after the phobia disappeared (perhaps immediately afterwards), the patient developed his first keenness for sport. Curiously enough, it was sport with balls which so strongly attracted his interest — first playing at ball, then football and tennis; and from these beginnings his athletic tendencies continued to develop. We see that the whole pleasure-giving play situation which the patient created for himself was identical with the situation of his phobia. In both, the patient awaited the ball in a state of tension. The difference between the two situations is this: in the phobia he ineffectually took to flight, while in games he endeavored effectually to master the situation. We have already seen that the phobia was a continuation of the dread of the threatening hand, the ball corresponding to the anxiety-object which had been projected further off — the castrating hand of the father, who in that phase was the object at one and the same time of libidinal desire and hate.

If we take as a starting point for further discussion the fact that the sport situation repeated in its content that of the phobia, we must suppose that from the economic point of view it had also the same aim — to free the psychic apparatus from its inner burden by displacing the danger, which really arose from the subject's instincts, into the outer world and by avoiding it through suitable defense reactions.

However, we know that the anxiety can never be wholly "bound" in a phobia, for it is not possible in actual fact to displace the inner danger outwards. Moreover, this process takes place only at the cost of self-imposed prohibitions and renunciations; that is to say, it is a painful process. It is a different matter in sport. Here it is perfectly possible to displace the danger threatening from within to the outside world and so to convert neurotic into real anxiety and, by observing certain conditions, to create for oneself the pleasurable situation of a game instead of the painful situation of a phobia.

When a certain amount of castration dread (the amount will vary with the individual) has passed into "justified anxiety," the sport situation provides the most ideal conditions for release from fear, namely, expectant readiness, contempt of the danger which threatens, a trial of the subject's own powers and rational attack and defense.

I speak of "justified anxiety" in the sport situation, although in actual fact the anxiety developed does not reach any degree of intensity. Nevertheless, the feeling of excitement and tension differs only quantitatively, and not qualitatively, from anxiety. There are, too, differences of degree in this, and even people well accustomed to sport tell us of states of excitement with which we are familiar as anxiety-equivalents. The anxiety-object (now located in the outside world) towards which the tendencies to mastery are directed is either the opponent in the game or the element which has to be mastered, e.g., mountains, water, air, etc.

There are other libidinal tendencies as well which find outlet here, but to discuss them in greater detail is outside the scope of this communication. In particular, homosexual propensities and the aggressive tendencies connected with them, as well as masochistic punishment-wishes, are here discharged in a desexualized, egosyntonic form. In our particular connection it is a matter of indifference whether we are dealing with an unrepressed part of the libidinal impulses, that is to say with genuine sublimations, or with reaction-formations.

The possibility of discharge in an egosyntonic form lessens the conflict between ego-tendencies and sexual instincts, and the harmonious operation of the two leads to an increase of feelings of power within the ego.

Another motive from which the ego derives satisfaction is to be found in the self-exhibition which is so outstanding a feature of sport and in the sense of one's own physical power which it gives. Hárnik has already pointed out the connection of the latter with the castration complex.[2]

Thanks to the egosyntonic nature of the discharge and the accompanying reinforcement of the narcissistic feelings, the whole process here assumed to afford the subject a partial relief from castration-dread has a highly pleasurable tone, in contrast to the "pain" of the phobia. The explanation suggested in this case may be extended into a general assumption that, even in a person who is not markedly neurotic, the mechanism in the pursuit of sport is the same: projection of a source of anxiety into the outside world and discharge of the anxiety. For even in normal people, situations arise in which the binding of anxiety, which has hitherto been perfectly satisfactorily effected, suddenly fails, the whole proud structure of narcissism collapses, and the athletic Hercules plainly sees the hand appear once more out of the dark and trembles and is afraid.

It is in such moments that the athlete is suddenly overcome with feelings of anxiety which have no rational foundation. This anxiety makes its appearance either just as he is about to engage in some athletic performance (as a sort of stage fright), or it surprises him suddenly on the trapeze, on a lonely mountain path or in some other sphere of athletics. It is of the nature of neurotic anxiety and indicates a breaking through, a failure of the apparently successful mastery. Thus we see in sport one of those precautionary measures or safety valves by which the harassed human being tries to ward off at least a tiny part of his fear of the threatening hand.

This helps us also to understand why the foolhardy tourist risks the uncertain event, at the utmost peril to his life; he is trying to rid himself of part of his fear of death by daring the contest with the threatening hand (God – father – nature). For he has succeeded in locating or projecting into the outside world the forces dominating him within and so converting his anxiety of conscience into a real "justified" anxiety. The original situation between ego and external world is thus restored; the whole battle is no longer waged between the institutions of the ego, but between the ego and the external world. The social value of sport, too, from the point of view of psychology, lies partly in the fact that, through this process of displacing the battlefield, aggressive tendencies are discharged in a manner consonant with the ego. By the increase in narcissistic gratification, the wound inflicted by the castration complex is assuaged, and above all, the subject is afforded a possibility of getting rid of part of the dread of castration or the fear of death which is common to all mankind.

NOTE

This paper is reprinted with permission from the author's article, "A Contribution to the Psychology of Sport," appearing in the *International Journal of Psycho-analysis, 7*:223, 1926.

FOOTNOTES

1. In her paper entitled "Infant Analysis" in the International Journal of Psycho-Analysis, vol. 7, p. 31, 1926, Melanie Klein attempted to elucidate this problem.
2. Harnik, J.: The various developments undergone by narcissism in men and in women. *Int J Psychoanal, 5*:66, 1924.

SWIMMING AND PERSONALITY DEVELOPMENT

ROBERT A. DENTLER

In the world of the child, play is often the most important thing there is. It amounts to primary life reality. It is what you plan to do, dream about, scheme toward and, most of all, spend your waking hours on. Moreover, good play is not easy for the child; psychologist Roger Barker has pointed out that good play entails risks. It involves a balance of drama, danger and challenge. Because it requires courage, skill and power to undertake, children choose each other first on their ability to play. As children move through the years from four to fifteen, their play becomes increasingly more intricate and demanding. There are more elaborate rules, and these are more strictly enforced. Play comes to involve the regulation of ends — the goals of the play — as well as means and to involve the aesthetics of form, or how one should look while playing. In play, the whole child may become involved rather than some special aspect of his mind or body. When it is very good, play totally motivates the child as well.

Here I want to apply this general theory of the meaning of play in childhood to the special, practical case of swimming. Before getting at the psychology of the question, however, let us make sure of the facts of the American situation. Some of the play of children anywhere is universal. The forms, the rules, the pleasure spring from the nature of being built a certain way and of having certain energies. This might amount to 5 per cent of the play of children; The other 95 depends on what is *available* to play with.

For example, in 1906 a swimming pool was a concrete tank equipped with inlets and outlets for filling and emptying it. Before the twentieth century, Americans seldom had a place of any kind in which to swim. In one sense, beaches for swimming in America were discovered after children learned to swim in pools. The modern well-planned pool is efficient, functional, designed for health, safety and comfort; but most of all it is built for good play. In 1946, the United States had 8,000 permanent pools. New construction in 1956 alone more than tripled this number. By 1957, the nation had more than 56,000 permanent pools of fifteen by thirty feet or larger. Three out of five were private residential pools, available to no more children in a community per generation than two dozen bicycles. However, one eighth were community pools, and another one pool in six was institutional or commercial but somehow fairly public. The community average remains well below that for New Zealand or Australia, but it is large and growing. The time is very near when most children, even regardless of color, may have a chance to play in a swimming pool and to do so regularly.

The statistics emphasize that swimming becomes more important for children as pools become more widely available. Boys long ago discovered for themselves the glories of play in the old mud hole, but until very recently most American boys, lacking a north forty to explore, did not know what they were missing.

In this matter of opportunity, consider Cleveland for example. In 1955, Cleveland opened ten new ultramodern neighborhood swimming pools at a cost of one million dollars. This is particularly fascinating when we note that Cleveland lies on the shores of Lake Erie. But as Cleveland Recreation Commissioner John S. Nagy observed, little children cannot walk to the beach. Besides, near Cleveland Lake Erie is polluted, and when the contamination count is low, the weather is apt to be 90° in the shade.

The sixteen pools of Cleveland in 1956 served over 600,000 swimmers, most of them children. More than 50,000 were taught to swim in free classes. According to a reliable source, the pools were especially appreciated by the mothers who could stop worrying about where junior was and whether he would be home for lunch. The pools closed from noon to one. "If we didn't close," a guard said, "most of the kids wouldn't even go home to eat." Most significantly, the pools were located with care within walking distance of highly populated family sectors. There is nothing like the boon of availability, then, to make a form of children's play important.

Toward the close of the summer, Commissioner Nagy said, "It is obvious the pools are the answer to one of the most pressing problems every large city faces — how to keep children off the streets when school's out." However right Nagy may be, however imaginative his program, he seems not to have said the whole of it. For there are valuable ways of keeping children off the streets, and there are worthless ways.

What makes swimming such a good form of children's play? What makes swimming of special value for children? To approach these questions, consider the special growth problems of children during different life stages. Swimming has different values for each life phase. The idea here is not to suggest that swimming is more valuable than any other type of play, but to look at some values peculiar to swimming.

THE PRESCHOOLER

How four- and five-year-olds will respond to water play depends largely on how their parents handled bathing and water toddling when the child was one, two and three years. But one might concentrate on the behavior of four- and five-year-olds, however, because functions such as running and swimming cannot be exercised heavily before the age of four.

Part of the motor development of four-year-olds is intrinsic or maturational. That is, it depends upon what happens genetically from within the child. Most research on motor development, however, emphasizes the external factor of *learning*. By age four, most children have the stamina, the musculature and the bone structure necessary for sustained swimming activity. Whether they will swim depends chiefly upon whether they have a chance to learn.

Learning to swim depends first upon proper motivation. Swimming provides an ideal motivating condition for motor development for the advanced preschooler because of three very fundamental factors: personal initiative, trust and autonomy. First, the four- or five-year-old is psychologically most concerned with the problem of personal initiative. If he has developed soundly as a two- and three-year-old, he has begun to solve two earlier psychological problems, those of trust and autonomy.

Trust is a matter of the younger child's realizing that his parents and indeed the world around him as a whole are there to stay, that they hold no threat of withdrawing support; it is also a matter of sensing that one can trust one's own responses to this world. Water play is important to this development problem because it involves risks and danger in the view of the child. Through experimentation, one more area of threat surrenders to a sense of trust. Part of the motivation of the four-year-old toward water play and swimming comes from a reliving of the achievement of trust.

The key psychological problem for most two- and three-year-olds might be said to be that of autonomy, the problem of whether the child can realize he is someone set apart, independent of parents and other people and things generally. Autonomy involves also the challenge of control, for it is hard to be *somebody* apart from others until you can make your body behave as you wish.

One often sees one- and two-year-old children having more fun in a pool than three-year-olds. The three-year-olds are more fearful and more frustrated. They are coping with the question of whether they can "handle themselves" safely and successfully in the water, a question that seldom occurs to the two-year-old. Part of the motivation toward swimming for the four-year-old, then, is a reliving of his sense of being somebody set independently apart from adults.

For the five-year-old who has achieved a sense of trust and a sense of autonomy, the prime challenge is one of active initiative. The four-year-old is self-activated. He has a high surplus of energy to pour into play. He can forget failures quickly, and he can aim his efforts at mastery of skills. Play becomes less and less random for him. Activity gets focused and disciplined.

Splashing and running in the water, for example, are transformed into efforts to hold one's breath under water, to go out where it is deeper, to dog-paddle and, most of all, to swim like the bigger children.

The preschooler of five knows he can walk and run effectively; indeed, he is interested in what else he can do with his arms and legs. He is no longer self-conscious about his basic motor activities. He does not have to think about walking. Swimming for this child is more novel than any other leg or arm exercise. It seems like another sort of basic achievement, a way of getting your body to do what you want under completely changed conditions. As a challenge for the child wrapped up in the question of initiative, it is ideal.

THE YOUNG SCHOOL-AGE CHILD

The limitation on the five-year-old is that he tires quickly of sustained effort. He likes to initiate, but he seldom follows through. If the chance at trying to swim or to water slide is missed during this period, they become that much harder later on, for no confidence has been built up. They are untried activities, and four and five are the best years for *trying*. They are not the best years for motor learning, however. Fatigue, boredom and distraction are quick prohibitors; concentration is short, and the child turns quickly toward distractions.

Water play for the preschool child is not merely a siphon for excess energy. It is not simply a good substitute for baby-sitting. Nor is it nonsense. Rather, it is a road toward mastery of the self, the body and the world through experimenting, sharing and trying out the body. For the eight-year-old, it is all these things, too. Water play and swimming are *not* merely exercises toward mastery for the eight-year-old. Rather, they are ways of becoming part of the adult world. Erik Erikson says that the key psychological challenge for the eight-year-old is the problem of industry or skill.

The child from seven through twelve sees the swimming pool as a miniature world, socially as well as physically. Everything about the pool area and its operation becomes important. Lifeguards are men and women to be identified with. They represent the serious business of adult life. Locker-room transactions, dressing, undressing, showering, being inspected, are significant procedures for the school-age child, procedures he sees as part of the industrious, busy world of rules, skills and achievements. The same principles hold for beach experiences.

The big danger in this elementary school period is the psychological danger of inferiority. Learning to swim and to do it well, learning to dive, to stay under water, to play complicated games of tag and water-hide — all are vital resources for achieving a sense of physical and social adequacy. If the child has had a chance at the water before he is seven or eight, this adequacy and the confidence it brings are easier to achieve.

If a child's color of skin or his parent's income prevents him from joining his friends at the swimming pool or beach during these years, the effects will begin to appear in early adolescence. A sense of earned worth is impossible to achieve if social or economic barriers prevent any opportunity for trying out what can be accomplished.

Incidentally, school-age children are the hardest hit group when pool administrators place sharp restrictions on the games and forms of play that are permitted in the swimming area. These rules are often necessary. Often they result from poor design of the plant. Where conditions are ideal — where the diving area is widely separated from other sections, where a sloping wading section is available, where the decks are thirty feet wide or wider — rules against diverse play can be held to a minimum, and younger children can become skilled in rapid order. Some risk and some danger are inherent in all good play.

That learning to swim has very high priority on any list of elementary school age children's interests is clear from a variety of studies of play preferences. It is also clear from the record of what happens whenever a swimming program opens up in a community, that is, a well-planned program. We have already mentioned the experience in Cleveland. We might add the more sensational story of swimming classes for rural children in Simcoe County, Ontario.

> In 1946, The Simcoe County Recreation Service began a single swimming class at a township park. Thirty children enrolled. Eight years later the program had developed, under spontaneous pressure from children and their parents, to the point where about fourteen hundred children from twenty-seven towns in the county came in cars, busses and trucks to take swimming lessons in eleven town pools. All of this called for local committees of volunteers, adequate facilities for dressing, instruction and so on, transportation planning, membership fees, paid instructors and the like.
>
> The important point is that unlike the common response to programmed recreation, where a few children are sure to enroll but the program seldom grows beyond its second-year level, the Simcoe County program boomed without advertising or promotion. The children themselves and their parents were seriously concerned with joining in.

Programs of instruction, supervision, transportation and water play that reveal to children the possibilities for fun and learning are a necessary part of pool and beach operations. But it is doubtful whether competitive swimming and diving are sound features of such pool programming for school-age children; there are two reasons for this opinion. First, American school-age children are exposed year-round, at home, at school and in their peer groups, to routines of competition. Research investigations suggest that eight- and nine-year-old children have learned to be more competitively oriented than cooperative. They will work harder to make a good individual or team showing than to cooperate with others. Competitive swimming of the organized sort simply adds to this exaggerated condition. When overdone, organized competition can become just one more among dozens of competitive situations confronting the child. Where organized competition is de-emphasized, swimming takes on a novelty and uniqueness not shared by other child activities.

Secondly, competition strikes deep at the key function of swimming and water play for the school-age child. This function is, we believe, to provide a learning experience that increases the sense of *adequacy*. In competition, few are good enough even to get into the running — and they are always the least inferior among the children. Most children must find themselves too inferior even to "get in the swim" when organized competition is the theme. This hardly makes pool life the place where confidence-building play can be engaged in openly. Competitive swimming puts most of the children out of the pool and on the deck, where they do not really want to be.

THE ADOLESCENT

Competitive swimming for teen-agers is an entirely different matter. Psychologically the concern of the adolescent is aimed not at answering the problem of learning skills and adequacy, but at estimating identity. The questions for the sixteen-year-old are "Who Am I?" and "What do they think about me?"

Much fear of inferiority may be built into the asking of these questions for youth who did not gain enough confidence earlier. But the distinctive interest is centered on the question "How do I look — to others and to myself?"

For this and other reasons, pool life becomes for the teenager a blend of self-display and spectatorship. The fifteen-year-old is showing himself off and is watching others show themselves off. Organized competition is one ideal vehicle for constructive channeling of these impulses. It gives the teen-agers a chance to work toward a good display of self under fair, or adult-supervised, conditions. And it gives them a chance to watch, review and appreciate each other as audiences.

Excluding commercial pools for the moment, without organizing something for teen-agers, life around the pool is apt to move toward its silliest level among teen-age youth. In trying to give the world of the pool the appearance of glamour and excitement — in trying to build up a setting in which they can "see themselves" and others most impressively — adolescents are very apt to settle for suntan lotions, cokes and nervous flirting, combined with blaring radio or phonograph music. These features are essential to this world – in proper degree. But if this is all the pool has to offer, it gives nothing more than the roller rink, the sock hop or the drive-in and therefore becomes a bore.

The three best techniques for fulfilling adolescent needs constructively in the world of the pool or beach may be these: First, teen-agers should have a part in the operating of the plant as lifeguards or other employees or helpers. This tells them as an age group that the world of the pool is partly theirs. Since the best youth may be chosen as workers, models are provided for the Big Watching Activity that is part of the search for identity.

Secondly, organized competition is ideal for teen-agers. Thirdly, there must be some tolerance for the junk of their special world – the lousy music, the sex byplay, the lounge-lizardry of lazy kids – to prove that the pool is a place where they can find themselves. But this third feature must be limited. If the pool becomes only a place for them, it offers nothing of special value. It must be controlled by adults and operated for little as well as big children.

THE ADULT

Adolescents grouped about any American pool on a summer day may share substantial fragments of a common culture, but there is for adults *no* such context. Americans born before World War I, for example, are generally ignorant of the craft and accoutrements of recreational swimming. Even if they once learned to swim, which is unlikely, they may not have learned to enjoy it. If they have spent time at pools or on the beach, it has usually been given to managing the very young or to strolling and sunning and resting. Swimming as a pleasure, as exercise and most of all as an extension of self into nature could perhaps become a part of the geriatrics and group work for the aged of the future, but this is hypothetical.

Adults from twenty to fifty, in striking contrast, take the lead in *elaborating* the sport. For reasons of maturity as well as money and business, Americans reared during and since the twenties know how to swim and how to enhance the art. They have added the paraphernalia for skiing, diving, flying, gliding and fishing while swimming. A marvelous proliferation of modes of expression through swimming is now available. These are not all vulgarized forces, for some purists have perfected the ancient strokes, simplified the apparatus and heightened the quality of swimming for its own sake.

Young and middle-aged adults today can make of swimming a vehicle for whatever drives they have acquired. Competition, conspicuous consumption, rehabilitation, and extension of personal boundaries are but a few of the more obvious impulses gratified through the current fashions in swimming. More elementary needs carried over from childhood may also continue to be met: pool, bath and beach clubs flourish *nearly* as much for parents as for their children, for example.

Yet, there is evidence that swimming for adults has personal or social importance only to the extent that it was learned early in life and had some special significance then. There are vital exceptions worth searching out, no doubt, but the great spread of participation in all water sports is, I believe, associated at base with the radical change in access to "swimming opportunities" between 1910 and 1950 and with the changes in cultural meanings attached to the sport at the same time.

"Jenkins wanted his kids to enjoy learning swimming like he did, so he rejected the conventional pool and installed a chlorinated mud-hole."

CONCLUDING COMMENT

Nearly every community in New Zealand has a public swimming pool, even the remote rural towns. This will come to be the case for the United States, where it is already becoming commonplace for every new public high school and most high-priced homes to include a good pool.

The implication is that future generations of adults will have the *option* of enjoying swimming and related water sports throughout a lifetime. A larger and larger proportion of people of all ages will thus find meaning in swimming. As an ever more elaborate technology builds up around water sports, then we should see the American character changed as it is enhanced by a new culture of swimming and water recreation.

Swimming can resonate with deep and intrinsic psychological trends in the life history of individuals. This durable fact may soon begin to ramify out into the vaster domain of man's changing relation to nature. The leading edge is perhaps reflected in the nature-mystique of the surfer and the skin diver, both of whom deserve serious and respectful study.

NOTE

This paper is revised and enlarged from an article published in Recreation, Journal of the National Recreation Association, June 1962.

SPORTING WITH LANGUAGE

CLYDE H. WARD

RECREATION AS RENEWING LIFE is common to all sports in all times. There are moments, however, when the need for recreating goes beyond that of replenishing a physical state, restoring a visceral balance or redressing an affective insult. There are times when play is called on to help preserve or re-create an identity. Such identity crisis times, in contrast to more usual recreational needs, are fleeting but critical. With them play becomes more particular and more disguised as to purpose. Here play is apt to take the form of humor.

There are moments in time, too, when crises of identity confront not only individuals but groups, even generations. Then the most successful humor joins the general culture, at least transiently as a fad. If the crisis is enough prolonged or recurrent and if the humor has sufficient meaning, then the fad may take further substance and enter the folklore of a people. The comical may then become the legendary or the mythical.

These beguiling generalizations are valid at least to the degree that the lessons from one fad-become-folklore sequence may be extrapolated. The reconstruction of this sequence can engage us in a fascinating exercise in deduction, a pursuit which is in itself sport.

Kilroy was Here — but When? and Why?

The cryptic character, Kilroy, despite his inelegant and banal nature, would seem to have won a lasting niche in the popular awareness of our times.

Among the emotion-charged comments in the guest books at a recent Russian cultural exhibit in New York, one comment appeared in nearly every book, "Kilroy was here."[1] From the first of the satellite rivalry, it was the fond wish of a prominent American scientist to put by rocket a marker on the moon to show "at least — that Kilroy got there first."[2] When the Suez Canal was being cleared of sunken ships, one vessel was found when raised to have the inscription "Kilroy was here" lettered in the silt on its side.[3] At the outbreak of the Korean War, Kilroy again greeted the American military in Japan.[4] Kilroy has been cited by a scholarly historian.[5] He was recently featured in a cartoon series and a television advertisement sketch.[6] He has been the hero and his existence the main theme in a recent biographical novel.[7] He has been harkened to in a current best-selling mystery.[8]

But of course it was in the mid 1940's that Kilroy had his heyday, and the impression is nearly universal that this was during World War II. "During the second World War, this inscription ('Kilroy was here') or the crude drawing of Kilroy appeared everywhere. His bald head, his staring eyes, his long drooping nose could be seen where they were least expected and where they were certainly not supposed to be. Like the private eye of the detective story, Kilroy had always been there, had already looked, had violated the secret. His talent for reaching the most remarkable places was amazing."[9]

KILROY WAS HERE!

PREVIOUS INTERPRETATIONS

How can we understand the scope and longevity of this elfin enigma? The poet and philosopher first approached the unconscious significance of Kilroy. Their allusions are astonishingly serious and difficult to grasp immediately. Later, I think, we shall find them not without meaning.

In verse, Griffin struck chords of death, of rebirth, of disguised desire and intense ambivalence.[10]

Kilroy . . . you descended into hell and then you died,
With a thirty M-one in your hands,
You rose from the dead . . .
. . . giant of ourselves . . . the epic wish . . .
Dogface; ciphered identity . . .
A sacred name . . .
What act too low to be attributed to you?
To rise to this high point, ...

The Harvard classicist, Finley, then likened Kilroy to Odysseus.[11] The ancient hero, like the modern, "attached folk-tale [to do with permanent and representative attitudes] to legend [telling of history]." Each was "a traveller not in random experience but . . . in representative male experience" and concerned "a kind of search into the future by uniting it with the past; . . . had two sides — *a desire for travel and for homecoming*" (italics added). Finley's pupil, the poet Vierick, next took up the theme with a more ominous note of guilt and dangerous homecoming.[12]

> Orestes — guilty *of what crime? for whom the furies*
> *still are searching . . .*
> *. . . the G.I.* Faustus *who was everywhere . . .*
> *Kilroy* beware. Home is the final trap
> *that lurks for you in many a wily shape . . .*
> *. . . thus home becomes that sea*
> *where you were always drowned.*

After this, psychological theory gave articulate reason to part of the poets' intuition when it deciphered the unconsciously contrived cryptogram of the name itself[13] — *Kilroy:* Kill Royalty (*le roi*) — Killer of the King. Thus the hero of the mid 40's, World War II's best-known G.I., was revealed as the timeless oedipal hero, the killer of the paternal tyrant. With this, many of Kilroy's symbolic aspects became illuminated. We see his oedipal nature in his provocative defiance — the little one with the big nose, the victorious peeping Tom. The paternal rivalry relates itself in legends which have him striking in dangerous and forbidden places (to Stalin's disconcertment, e.g., in the exclusive toilets of "The Big Four" at the Potsdam Conference) and (the mother image) in intimate or unlikely places (off-limits areas, unexplored territory and, always, the lavatory).

Thus a puzzling behavioral phenomenon became more comprehensible, and we are helped to see just why this character became so intensely popular, so hardy and ubiquitous and why, typically American, he was so much associated with a time of American opposition to tyrants. Still, this understanding focuses only on the aggressive father-son conflicts stirred up by wartime demands for both violence and discipline. We see in this humor the impudent, triumphant son. But what of the grief an Oedipus must bear? What of the tragedy at which the poets hint? Where is Ulysses of the difficult homecoming, or Faustus who after his excesses must keep a fateful bargain, or Orestes who is cursed after his violence with long, guilt-wracked wandering?

ANOTHER DIMENSION

A lengthy search for the origin of this mythical soldier-hero has suggested another level of meaning to the Kilroy phenomenon, a meaning which further helps to explain how this particular G.I. caricature, at first apparently a mere fad, endured to become something of a legend and a part of our folklore in the years since the war. In this new meaning we may see again how much intelligence is compressed, in a disguised and over-determined manner, into such unconsciously derived constructions. We may see, too, how playful humor which appears to be only obscure whimsy can reflect the deepest levels of psychic integration at a time when historical exigence poses problems of identity challenge and identity change.

The deeper meaning hinges around the time sense conveyed and hidden in the Kilroy slogan. As the mystery of the name itself may be better understood by an analysis of its component parts, so also more meaning may be gained from a literal scrutiny of the rest of the expression "Kilroy was here." Why the past tense? Let us set ourselves the question: *when was Kilroy here?*

If we date the quaint hero's presence not by retrospective anecdote but by those printed dates on which someone actually recorded his appearance, we come upon a surprising fact. Although virtually all previous thought has placed Kilroy as a phenomenon of World War II, *in print Kilroy was never here before the end of that war.* In other words, neither in the popular press nor apparently anywhere else are there printed references to Kilroy during World War II, and there are a large number of such references immediately thereafter.

After an exhaustive search, all conceivable sources having been negatively explored, I am compelled to conclude that Kilroy was a postwar phenomenon, and indeed to wonder if anyone will ever find a printed reference to Kilroy's being here that is dated prior to mid 1945. It seems highly unlikely that as striking a character as Kilroy would have been overlooked had he actually been much around.

FURTHER SUBSTANTIATION FROM THE LITERATURE SEARCH

If we accept this hypothesis, what might be the meaning of this development? The data insists that Kilroy's appearance was only postwar, and yet popular memory insists that his was a wartime career. We are led to a heightened appreciation of the word *"was"* in the slogan "Kilroy was here." Usually when the human psyche both seeks and resists an awareness, a compromise product results which simultaneously expresses and disguises. It is suggested that "was" is the nodal point of this mechanism in the Kilroy slogan. "Was" affords the clue to a meaning which is both post war and present-times, in essence; yet "was" simultaneously furnishes the distortion whereby the meaning can be kept hidden and whereby only the more superficial, retrospective wartime meaning is first perceived.

Before further considering the applications of the conclusion, it will be best to see how, in more detail, some of the literature findings give substance to it. For it is remarkable how, when this postulate is entertained, the evidence itself, in so many ramifications, adds confirmation.

Was the Phenomenon Simply Too Trivial?

Although these findings lend substance to the conclusion that Kilroy might actually be a postwar phenomenon, one must still consider the possibility that such a character was present but was just too trivial to be focused on during the momentous years of the war itself. While previously appealing, this is an argument which, after the search described above, has altogether lost meaning for the writer. In fact, as I have grown more acquainted with the popular press of the wartime years, this very point has seemed to weigh more and more against the possibility of Kilroy's having actually been prominent during the war itself. The amount of unimportant slang and the large number of evanescent comic characters and insignificant happenings to be found in the popular press during the War are incredible, and it is difficult to believe that such a character as Kilroy could have been missed; to illustrate: the columns of Ernie Pyle are full of slang sayings. Such characters as "Sad Sack" and "Artie Greengroin" abound in *Yank*. Columns in *Yank* and the *Stars and Stripes* are full of "snafu," "yardbird," "gremlins," "whammies," "womgats," "latrine orderlies" and so on. Feature articles treat of G.I. nicknames given to airplanes and roadsigns in various zones of the war. Contests were run for alternate names for G.I. Joes – and in all of these there was no Kilroy!

The Striking Change from Kilroy-Absent to Kilroy-Present in the Most Definitive Literature Sources

Another convincing point as to postwar origin is the pattern of how consistently just after World War II Kilroy appeared in the same reference sources where one looks vainly for him during the wartime period itself. This is noteworthy in the standard reference sources. It is reiterated impressively in the news wire files, in the *Stars and Stripes* and *Yank,* but is perhaps most convincing in those exhaustively thorough special language studies which describe the variations of language as they develop in the general idiom. In *American Notes and Queries,* Kilroy does not appear in the 1943, 1944 or 1945 editions but does appear in the January, 1946, edition[14] and thereafter. In Partridges' *Dictionary of Forces Slang, 1939-1945,*[15] there is no Kilroy; but he appears in that author's *A Dictionary of Slang and Unconventional English* in 1949.[16] In Wood's *American Sayings*[17] there is no Kilroy in 1945, but he is recorded in the next edition of 1949. And in Mencken's *American Language,* Kilroy does not appear in the 1945 edition or the 1946 supplement but does occur in the next standard edition of 1948.[18]

Other Observers' Opinions

At least three other writers support the notion of the greater frequency of Kilroy's appearance after the war, although most have retrospectively placed it during the war itself.

Sterba wrote: "It is my impression that the Kilroy stories and inscriptions, although they may have started earlier, became numerous and ubiquitous only after the middle of 1945. They spread like wildfire from then on, and have continued to do so until the present time — (1947)."[19]

The novelist Schmidt, writing much later, intuitively associates Kilroy with the end of the war. "As World War II came to a close, the phrase [Kilroy was here] became a slogan to millions of war-weary, lonely servicemen homeward bound at last — reassuring the soldier that he too was going home — back to those he loved."[20]

The Associated Press literary files note the expression as "current in 1945 and 1946."[21]

Kilroy's Earliest Appearances

If an important part of Kilroy's *raison d'être* has suffered disguise, then one might anticipate that the closer one approached his true origin the less distorted this hidden significance might appear. The disguise might have required some time to become fully developed. The closer to the time of origin, the more Kilroy might be referred to in the present tense.

The very earliest established record of Kilroy's appearance is curiously enigmatic as to time, and it gives another significant clue — it conveys a theme of wry mourning and of demobilization.

On June 26, 1945 (6 weeks after VE Day), in an obscure camp newspaper at Fort Kearns, Utah,[22] a full page cartoon appeared which proposed some memorials to the war. Three statues were sketched. One was of a long queue of G.I.'s waiting patiently in line; it was entitled "To the Men Who Stood at the Battle of Fort Kearns." The second statue pictured a miskept PFC saluting a pompous officer who is scolding the soldier; it was captioned "To the G.I. — Last of the Enslaved Peoples." The central statue depicted only a bucket and cleaning mop beside a toilet bowl; these were atop a marble slab, representing a tomb stone, and the stone's inscription read "To the Unknown Soldier — Kilroy *Sleeps* Here."

The second earliest record of Kilroy was from the Pacific theater and expressed a note of wonderment at the *new* arrival. "Who the Hell is Kilroy?" asked the August 19, 1945, mid-Pacific *Stars and Stripes*,[23] and then discussed his origins (possibly at Camp Meade, Maryland). There followed during the next month a series of exchanges of letters in which various servicemen discussed the problem.[24] Three of these writers ascribed his place of origin to the same Fort Kearns which was the locus of the first reference yet discovered. Four thought he had recently originated in the Hawaiian Islands. The remaining three said Kilroy started at various other places within the continental United States. The tone of these letters indicated that Kilroy was a recent comer to the scene. In October this same

newspaper carried the next reference to Kilroy;[25] this was of a mock funeral for him and maintained thus the note of humorous melancholy struck by the earliest appearance, that at Fort Kearns.

Another of the earliest references to Kilroy very strongly associated him with the end of the War and with homecoming. The December 28, 1945, edition of *Yank* carried a feature article which treated Kilroy as a newcomer and stated:[26] "The signs at Kwajalein *eight months ago* used to read 'Welcome, you lucky people!' *Kilroy and the peace* [italics added] have changed all that." The article went on to relate the rumor that Kilroy had just arrived from Washington, D.C., with new orders whereby enlisted men only were to be immediately towed home on barges fashioned from the Japanese Home Islands.

INTERPRETATION OF THE NEW DIMENSION

There remains, then, the fact that from all available evidence Kilroy was here in fad intensity only at the close of World War II. It is extremely unlikely that this reflects simply the relative triviality of the subject; the most definitive sources indicate just the opposite. It is likely that there has taken place a retrospective distortion in the popular memory as to the time of Kilroy's origin. The earliest valid references treat Kilroy as a relative newcomer and carry also the associated themes of the war's ending, of return home, and even of sadness, dejection and death. In the face of these findings, the popular insistence that Kilroy was not postwar takes on sharper significance. We have postulated that the distortion of time would be central to the fad's further meaning. What might this meaning be?

At the end of the war, Kilroy was here. At that moment in time when Kilroy's existence, by the victorious course of the War, is drawing inevitably to a close, the gremlin's existence is first insisted upon with enough energy for the slogan to find its way into the popular press.

Pondering the significance of this, our interest is increased by the discovery that the incidence curve of Kilroy's life in print closely parallels the period and patterning of the demobilization of the American Armed Forces. The process of demobilization was biphasic. It began in April of 1945, moved to a sharp peak in November of that year and fell to a low level in mid-1946.[27] This is the first phase. Kilroy appeared in print two months after demobilization began (i.e., June, 1945), reached his peak in September-November of that year (identical with demobilization) and dwindled off to a low in the summer of 1946, just as did the demobilization curve. The second phase of demobilization began with accelerating discharges in October of 1946, peaked in November and fell until its completion in March of 1947. Kilroy's recrudescence was likewise in the fall of 1946, with its peak in December, and (except for language studies and review articles) had its end in April, 1947. A more exact time parallel for two separate phenomena could hardly be imagined.

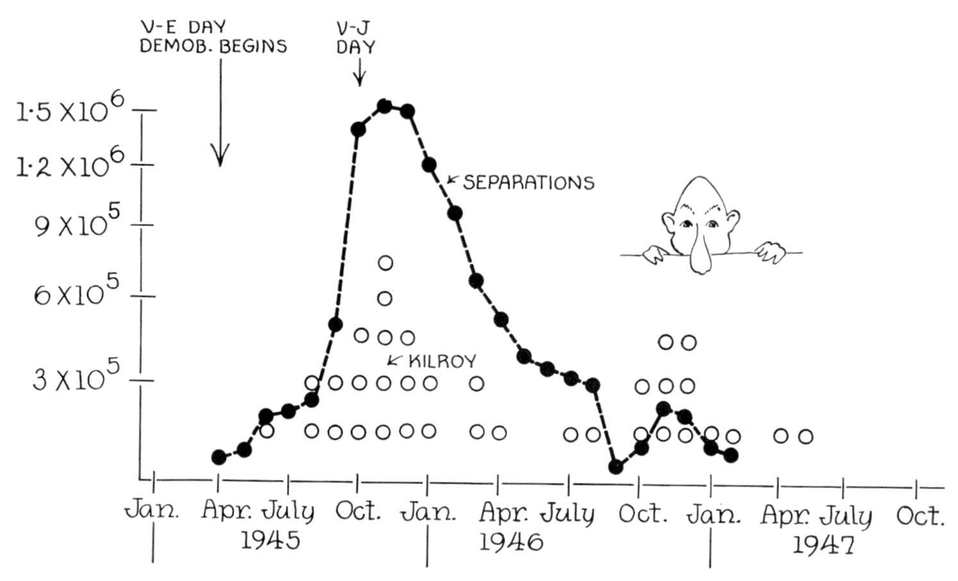

Kilroy and Demobilization

○ Popular press Kilroy references (single or related series).

● Separations from all U.S. armed service per month (ordinate scale).

So Kilroy is a demobilization phenomenon. This finding may be correlated with the often made and often forgotten psychiatric observation that the greatest adjustment difficulties (and therefore the time of greatest need for humor) were very often associated, not with the conditions of wartime service, but with the return to civilian adjustment after the war. The problem was described as follows: "Every soldier has a problem,"[28] "The Veteran is like an immigrant in his relationship to society."[29] "Civilian readjustment may put the exhausted adaptability of the individual under a new stress. . . . Every veteran struggles unconsciously for integration of his army experience. In many ways readjustment to civilian life may be more difficult than adjustment to the Army. Jealous civilians, no preparation, unable to love family again — civilian life not as pictured — confused between two worlds."[30] "The cessation of hostilities is an emotional shock. The veteran is labile, unpredictable, disorganized, and uncertain — he has been taught to hate. Wives have been more independent and both have gone separate ways. Job changes — family changes — previous dependence on the military — lost individuality — drabness and dullness of civilian life. . . . They will be changed — they will have to learn how to adjust themselves to peace — to reassemble the broken world into a pattern."[31]

The veteran struggles to rechannel his aggression, to accept his disarming, to shift his identity. Kilroy was here. He stills his anxiety for the future (personal and national) with memories of past triumphs (personal and national). The soldier becoming veteran turns homeward. Kilroy was here.

OTHER GLEANINGS – CONTIGUOUS LANGUAGE FADS

The coded message in the name Kilroy – oedipal triumph, defeat to tyrants – and Kilroy's disguised temporal context – reassurance and redirection at a time of disorganization and uncertainty – afford a uniquely witty comment on the events of the mid 1940's, especially the period of demobilization. There is inescapably a sense of history in the Kilroy fad.

A library search of this magnitude affords secondary findings which amplify the concept of historical sense in language fads. There were a number of other caricature fads comparable to and chronologically contiguous to Kilroy. The evidence here is less detailed, but the impressions which result are interesting.

In the British press during World War II, there was a series of popular characters which caught the public fancy. They were, like Kilroy, little elfin men whose sketches with accompanying slogans appeared in public places. They had the following sequence. There was first "Doomie," an RAF character who warned fledgling pilots of the dire results of carelessness or the lack of preparation.[32] Then came "Chad" or "Mr. Chad," another British military product who was accompanied by an expression referring to some item missing or in short supply because of the wartime shortages – "That comical figure peering over the top of a wall, whose long pendulous proboscis and single hair in the form of a question mark have been found scrawled on the walls of passages, guard rooms, railway stations and other public places. His eternal question "Wot, no ——— [beer, potatoes, etc.]" has become both a challenge and a commentary upon the times in which we live."[33]

There then followed, or was simultaneous with Chad, a popular character, "Flywheel," usually encountered in the saying "Flywheel is coming" and again associated with the British Air Force.[34] Next in the chronology was Kilroy, and then followed briefly in the metropolitan New York area and in the separation camps a more plaintive and possessive fad embodying the character "Clem." "Clem had chow here," "Clem sweated out his last queue here" are typical comments accompanying the appearance of the "wall peeper."[35] Then, according to H. L. Mencken, there followed in America the popular expression, "Open the door, Richard."[36]

The name "Doomie" would seem self-explanatory. "Chad" may be less obvious. The word Chad is an obsolete spelling for the fish, shad, and is etymologically related to the meanings "little twig," "little child," a "fragment" and (slang) "small potatoes" — the themes of inadequacy and dependent attachment. "Flywheel," again, has an apparent meaning: central force, unifying motion. (Kilroy is a braggart; Flywheel, a thinker, an English observer said.) "Clem" (clemency, clam, clamp) is etymologically related to such meanings as the following: to starve, to pinch as with hunger or cold, to confine, press together, urgency, call for relief.[37] As for "Open the door, Richard," if we follow the usual principles of symbolic interpretation, this would seem a reference to homecoming and reunion, including the sexual connotations.

To order these fads again in their chronological sequence, we have the following themes: first, "Doomie" — the threat of doom that hung over the British Isles in the first part of the war? "Chad" — inadequacy, dependency — England's turning to help from a stronger ally? "Flywheel" — the healing realization that, nevertheless, the British are central to the war's means and goals? Enter "Kilroy" — the American tyrant killer and his subsequent confrontation with demobilization, "Clem" — the clinging, urgent reaction at the point of actual separation from the service, and then, "Open the door, Richard" — the imperative, climactic note of reunion.

As one last addition to these historical grace notes, we come to the fascinating observation that the American character Kilroy was apparently assimilated into the German language where it became the equivalent of the American "Oscar,"[38] the title given to statuettes awarded annually to those persons and productions judged most excellent in the cinematographic arts.[39] What might it mean that the *Herrenvolk* incorporate the proud-sad image of their American adversary? What history is sensed in this vicissitude of our fad?

SUMMARY

An exhaustive search for the origin of one of the heartiest of modern caricature fads has reaffirmed old lessons and offered us new ones regarding the Kilroy phenomenon and the import of such fads more generally. It was the philosophic and poetic mind which first approached the meaning of the cryptic fad, likening Kilroy to Ulysses, to Orestes and to Faust — to accursed heroes charged by fate with wandering, with difficult homecoming, with revenge, estrangement and atonement.

Systematic inquiry articulates this intuition when it makes most tenable the view that the popular conception of Kilroy as a mythical wartime character is essentially misplaced in time. This distortion disguises the fact that Kilroy was a postwar occurrence. His earliest discernible origins are just after victory and are concerned with themes of wry humor, of the end of the war and of homecoming.

The emphasis thereby added to the *was* of the saying "Kilroy was here" is further substantiated by the discovery that the pattern of Kilroy's popularity closely follows the life pattern of the demobilization process. The cryptogram may thus be rendered – this hero is no more; he is being disarmed. The popular psyche is grappling with the problems of lost identity and difficult returning.

That an unconscious sense of history may reside in such language fads is further suggested by the occurrence of some other sayings, accompanied by imaginary characters who are related in chronology and in historical context to Kilroy. And thus, perhaps, from a sportive language fad, from a humorous character incorporated into our modern folklore, a deeply recreational, identity re-creating aspect of play may be deciphered.

NOTE

This paper is adapted, with revision, from the author's paper "Kilroy Was Here," appearing in the *Psychoanalytic Quarterly, 31*:80, 1962. Acknowledgment is kindly made.

FOOTNOTES

1. Associated Press Wire Release, New York City, July 6, 1959.
2. Pearson, D., *Washington Merry-Go-Round*. October 9, 1957.
3. *Life:* April 8, 1957, p. 44.
4. *Detroit News:* July 1, 1950, p. 1.
5. Street, J. H.: *The Civil War*. New York, Dial, 1943.
6. Smith, Capt. J.: Personal communication.
7. Schmitz, R. J.: *God's Wayward Son*. Minneapolis, Morris, 1954.
8. Travers, R.: *The Anatomy of a Murder*. New York, St. Martins, 1958.
9. Grotjahn, M.: *Beyond Laughter*. New York, McGraw, 1957.
10. *Saturday Review of Literature,* March 23, 1946, p. 26.
11. Finley, J. H., Jr.: Personal communication.
12. *Atlantic Monthly,* April 1947, pp. 70-71.
13. Sterba, R.: Kilroy was here. *American Imago, 5*:3, 1948.
14. *American Notes and Queries,* January 1946, p. 152.
15. Partridge, R. A.: *Dictionary of Forces Slang, 1939-45*. London, Secker & Warburg, 1948.
16. Partridge, R. A.: *A Dictionary of Slang and Unconventional English*. London, Routledge, 1949.
17. Woods, H. F.: *American Sayings*. New York, Duell, Sloan & Pierce, 1945, 1949.
18. Mencken, H. L.: *The American Language,* Supplement 2. New York, Knopf, 1948.
19. Sterba, R.: *op. cit. supra* note 13.
20. Schmitz, R. J.: *op. cit. supra* note 7.
21. Gould, A., Exec. Ed., The Associated Press: Personal Communication, Jan. 31, 1956.
22. *Kearns Air Force Post Review,* June 26, 1945, p. 5.
23. *Stars and Stripes, Pacific Edition,* August 19, 1945, p. 1.
24. *Stars and Stripes, Pacific Edition,* August 26, 1945, p. 2; August 28, 1945, p. 2; August 30, 1945, p. 2; September 5, 1945, p. 2; September 11, 1945, p. 2; September 15, 1945, p. 2; September 17, 1945, p. 2; September 18, 1945, p. 3; September 28, 1945, p. 2.
25. *Stars and Stripes, Pacific Edition,* October 13, 1945, p. 5.
26. *Yank Magazine,* New York Edition, December 28, 1945, p. 10.
27. United States Selective Service: Fourth Report of Director, 1944-1945, Supplement 1946-1947. Washington, U. S. Government Printing Office, 1948.

28. Strecker, E. A., and Appel, K. E.: *Psychiatry in Modern Warfare.* New York, Macmillan, 1945.
29. Walker, W.: *The Veteran Comes Back.* New York, Dryden, 1944.
30. Chisholm, G. B.: Emotional problems of demobilization, in military psychiatry. *Proceedings of the Assn. for Research in Nervous and Mental Diseases,* Dec. 15-16, 1944. Published in Vol. XXV, pp. 63-69, Baltimore, Md.
31. Benedek, T.: *Insight and Personality Adjustment. A Study of the Psychological Effects of War.* New York, Ronald, 1946.
32. *Yorkshire Post,* January 31, 1945.
33. *Ibid.*
34. *Toronto Illustrated Saturday News,* October 26, 1946, p. 7.
35. *New York Times,* January 6, 1946, p. 18; Feb. 10, 1946, p. 6; February 24, 1946, p. 16: March 17, 1946, p. 42; *New York Times Magazine,* December 9, 1945, p. 40.
36. Mencken, H. L.: *op. cit. supra* note 18.
37. Whitney, E. D. [Ed.]: *The Century Dictionary and Cyclopedia.* New York, Century, 1911; Wyld, H. C. K. [Ed.]: *Universal Dictionary of the English Language.* London, Routledge, 1932.
38. This, in turn, leads us to consider the origin of the title, "Oscar," as applied to these six-inch-long statuettes. As might be expected, there was no apparent logic for the usage. It originated spontaneously in the mind of a new secretary in the office of the American Academy of Motion Pictures and "spread like wildfire thereafter." A symbolic analysis of the word Oscar, breaking it into its two phonetic parts, leaves us again with crudely obvious phallic symbolism.
39. Ramsaye, R. [Ed.]: *International Motion Picture Almanac,* Volume 1. New York, Quigley, 1956.

PART TWO
PLAY AND THE HOLY

INTRODUCTION

In the twentieth century American Protestantism has been forced to grapple with the question of what attitudes it should take toward sports and their spectacles. The story of the changes in the attitudes held by most older Protestant denominations is largely one of grudging but accelerating accommodation, a contrast indeed to the nineteenth-century practice of attaching the label "sinful" to each new sports innovation, as well as to the dance, the theatre, the opera, the saloon and the novel. Sports at one time were an anathema to religious denominations devoted to preparation for the afterlife in man's all-too-brief span on earth. They were time-wasting in a nation committed to the Gospel of Work; they were to be avoided because they were attractive to rowdy and gambling unbelievers. Thereafter, Protestants, Catholic and Jews alike responded to an urge to seek common ground with the insatiable sports hungers of people rapidly removing themselves from the farms. In the initial decades of the twentieth century's uneasy Leisure Revolution, sports were included in ever-widening church and church-college recreation programs designed to give outlets, under proper supervision, to the now nonsinful play instincts of the faithful.[1]

In his essay on "Sin and Sports," Professor William R. Hogan describes church accommodation to the changing American environment.[2] He offers a variety of illustrations of modern interaction between sports and organized religion, and he includes an analysis of the program of the Fellowship of Christian Athletes.

Actually, early Christians (e.g., Paul) called themselves athletes of Christ. The idea of asceticism goes back to the Greek practice of discipline or exercise (*askesis*) as a means of achieving excellence in athletic as well as intellectual pursuits. Then came the influence of the heretic Gnostics who claimed to be in possession of supreme knowledge (*gnosis*), the essence of which rested in the belief that the body and its senses are evil and in opposition with the light of the soul and the rest of the spiritual world. Self-discipline became mortification of the body and its senses for the perfection and glorification of the soul. The Socratic maxim "know thyself," popular among the intellectuals of the time, likely enhanced self-conscious tendencies, which soon developed into a tradition among monks of extreme individualism and self-absorption. According to the monastic ideal, as thus evolved, the concerns of the world had to be renounced totally so that union with God might be achieved. Those who followed the monastic ideal removed themselves from the concerns and temptations of family and social life.

In the next essay, on "Play and the Sacred," Robert E. Neale suggests both a theory of play and a theory of religion as play.[3] His thesis is as follows: Man's basic urges toward sensation and organization may exist in conflict or in harmony. Continued conflict creates a "work self" which experiences a minimum of energy and uses this for the work of resolving inner conflict. Continued harmony creates a "play self" which experiences new energy and uses this for any activity not motivated by the need to resolve conflict. One outcome of the play self is the life of adventure which entails chance, risk and remarkable events and may be characterized as a narrative life. Maturation allows for an increase in the breadth of play; full play for the adult would include all the fundamental concerns of the mature human being. Such play is traditionally known as religion. The sacred is defined as the new energy released by the harmony of the two basic urges. Man responds to this new power ambivalently with both fascination and awe. Release from the ambivalence occurs in three ways — the religious, the magical and the profane. The religious is the total acceptance of, and appropriately playful response to, the sacred. The magical is the ambivalent and inappropriate work response to the sacred. The profane is the denial of the sacred and adherence to the world of work. The three responses are illustrated by consideration of adventure as myth. The religious response to myth is that of make-believe, the magical response that of belief, and the profane response that of disbelief. The magician tries to make myth effective in daily life, the profane person unhappily accepts this as impossible, and the religious individual rejoices in myth for its own sake.

FOOTNOTES

1. The history of morality plays has been well documented, but it is interesting to observe the present rapidly developing use of the theatre in the church. Ellison, J.: Churches take up show business. *Saturday Evening Post,* Sept. 22, 1962, p. 60.
2. P. 121.
3. P. 148.

SIN AND SPORTS

WILLIAM R. HOGAN

In the twentieth century, sports have become an increasingly conspicuous part of the recreation programs of thousands of churches and church colleges. In an earlier era, however, church recreation activities were confined to sociables in some towns and cities and to neighborly visiting in connection with "dinner on the ground" following preaching in rural areas; and sports were widely regarded by Protestants as snares of the Devil himself.

THE NINETEENTH CENTURY

. . . and exercise thyself rather unto godliness. For bodily exercise profiteth little: but godliness is profitable unto all things (I Timothy 4:7-8).

During the initial decades of our national life, the small Protestant religious groups that later were to come close to dominating the nineteenth-century religious scene in the United States found plenty of "sin" to shun and combat. By 1830 their remedy was a commitment to a set of propositions that called for the faithful to practice an asceticism even more rigorous than that advocated by the "moral athletes" in the Puritan Oligarchy of the seventeenth century:[1] "Indolence leads to amusement, amusement to dissipation, and dissipation to ruin," and "Be not conformed to the world," especially "worldly amusements." Accordingly, in the pre-Civil War period, Presbyterians, Baptists, Disciples of Christ, Methodists and even certain Protestant Episcopal bishops struggled to keep the saints "unspotted from the world" by repeatedly assailing major sins, some of which – such as moderate drinking and lotteries – had been approved by Puritans in earlier years. Most of the Protestant denominations also condemned horse-racing and the few minor sports that appeared before 1850.

Methodists and Presbyterians fired much of the heavy artillery directed against amusements and play. Whatever differences of opinion existed between John Wesley in England and his early American Methodist disciples regarding other matters, there was none concerning recreation. Wesley had written: "Thou fool! dost thou imagine because thou dost not see God, that God doth not see thee? Laugh on; play on; sing on; dance on; but 'for all these things God will bring you to judgment!' " The American Methodists incorporated into their General Rules of the 1790's the Wesleyan admonition that forbade "such diversions as cannot be used in the name of the

Lord Jesus."[2] These were apparently almost nonexistent by modern standards. The opening, for example, of a preparatory school for boys called Cokesbury College at Abingdon, Maryland, in 1787 was "marked by an ominous sermon by Bishop Francis Asbury from the foreboding text, 'O, thou man of God, there is death in the pot'." The spirit of this text and of Wesley's dictum, "He who plays as a boy will play as a man," was carried out in the stringent Cokesbury regulations that required students to live austerely and made no provision for group or sportive play.[3]

Methodist leaders maintained this theoretical position for at least a century. As one Texas preacher wrote as late as 1890 in a book published by the Southern Methodist Publishing House: "Life is short, and no time is to be lost in youth's valuable years. . . . Sport, fun, and frolic, have no chapter in youth's Book of Life in our day; *learning* and *doing* fill up the entire volume."[4]

Meanwhile Protestant churches had been confronted with many disturbing "sinful" diversions, both old and new. With the sole exception of novel-reading, certain old amusements were condemned almost as forcibly in 1900 as in 1800. Each new one received its share of word-lashing, at least for a time, either because of its supposed inherent sinfulness, because of its association with sin (as in the association of baseball with gambling and misuse of the Sabbath), because a strong Christian should heed St. Paul's admonition to avoid any practice that might cause a weaker brother to stumble, or because *all* of a true Christian's time and much of his money belong to the Lord and not to the World.

In the application of these principles, pre-Civil War Disciples of Christ periodical editors followed the advice of their leader, Alexander Campbell, in disapproving all games that lent themselves to betting — even checkers and pitching quoits, a "sport of gentlemen" similar to horseshoe pitching. Another admonition in the same spirit appeared in 1840 in Georgia's leading Baptist periodical. A reader had inquired whether professing Christians could rightfully "mingle with the world in playing marbles, ball, &c.?" Editor Jesse Mercer replied:

> . . . we think the injunction of the Apostle quite sufficient — *Abstain from all appearance of evil.* Now can it be a compliance with this requisition to be seen playing ball, marbles, backgammon or any such thing? Surely no. The parties may say indeed, "We don't bet anything, we intend no harm, it is only pastime." Very well, and the card player and horse-racer may say the same. — But how would it look for Baptists or Methodists to be seen playing cards and running horses?
>
> Again, many brethren are stumbled by such conduct. And for this reason it should not be indulged in . . . . Can the *ball-playing, marble-playing brother go from his* [prayer] *closet into such exercises?* Or can he very well go from these scenes to his closet? How does the backgammon box look by the Bible? True, it has been fashioned after the similitude of a book, but such similitudes are *painted lies.*[5]

Nineteenth-century Protestant keepers of their brothers' consciences considered their major enemies in the realm of conduct to be the "promiscuous" social dance (especially the seductive waltz), the theater, the gaming table, the saloon (but not before 1820) and fiction (but not *in toto* after 1880). However, a mere listing of the *additional* proscribed sports and social practices suggests that the churches were fighting a prolonged but losing war. Among those denounced at some point were frivolous conversation; telling a child a story "because of its having a laugh in it"; chess; checkers; card-playing of any kind; backgammon; *bowling; croquet; pool; billiards; marble-shooting; roller-skating at public rinks; bicycling; baseball; football, prizefights,* and *cockfights* because of their brutality; *horse races;* fairs and picnics, even under church auspices; fashionable parties; puppet shows; the "vulgar entertainments of jugglers, mountebanks, street-music grinders, and circus exhibitions" ("No Christian can follow Jesus, and then be found in a circus," cried a Georgia Baptist periodical in 1892); public musical exhibitions; minstrel shows; public lectures; the use of tobacco not only because it was a filthy habit that defiled the human body in an unchristian manner, but because medical evidence allegedly had demonstrated that smoking and chewing led to a craving for strong drink and to a great variety of serious ailments, and even to loss of virility, imbecility and insanity; *boating* and *fishing* because they "lead to vice in some of its more alluring forms"; *"mixed bathing";* nonreligious Sunday visiting; the invasion of family privacy by newspaper society pages; newspaper *sports pages* and the daily newspapers that had become "questionable guests at the firesides on account of their frightful powers of suggestion." In the first quarter of the twentieth century, the list was expanded to include Sunday newspapers and their colored comic sections that were evidence of "The [Current] Plague of Jocularity" and "the over-emphasis on the comic [that] is the prolific breeder of irreverence."

This massive, century-long onslaught provoked conscience-searching by innumerable individuals and opposition both within and without the congregations. In 1848, for example, a thoughtful boy named Washington Gladden began the pondering that was to last for many months as to how he could "unite" with the Presbyterian church in Owego, New York. This twelve-year-old had been a constant attendant at its services, and he yearned to become a member. He faced two problems, however. He had been given to believe that in order to be "converted" he must undergo some sort of overwhelming "emotional or ecstatic experience," and this he was unable to accomplish; and the sermons had left him with a strong "impression" that "the change" would involve "giving up all my boyish sports — ball-playing, coasting, fishing; and I was more than ready to make that sacrifice" in order to find "the peace of God" and thereby escape "his wrath and curse." His impression as to sports was theoretically correct, although some members of the evangelical Protestant churches gingerly engaged "to some extent in sport and merriment, but . . . with the feeling that the indulgence was a charge against their piety."[6]

The "ideal Christian" reserved his enjoyment for the rapturous "awful mirth" of true sanctity described in the hymns of Dr. Isaac Watts composed in the eighteenth century. As Edward Everett Hale, the Boston Unitarian clergyman soon to become famous as author of "The Man Without a Country," stated in public lectures and sermons in 1855-1857: "I may dig in my garden, because there is a pretense of usefulness; though the crop I raise is not worth a hundredth part of the money it cost me. But if I spend a tenth part of the same time in playing ball, or in skating, or in rowing, my reputation as a man of industry, or even of sense, under our artificial canons, would be gone."

Hale was one of a dozen or more prominent eastern Unitarian, Congregationalist and Presbyterian preachers of the period 1845-1870 who boldly (for that period) supported such laymen as Dr. Oliver Wendell Holmes and author Frederic W. Sawyer in pleas to provide the thousands of new city workers with recreation and facilities for "athletic exercises." "When we choose to bring people into crowded towns," wrote Hale, "to substitute pavement for the meadows, and mains six feet under ground for the trout-brooks, we must substitute something for the relaxation and amusement we have taken away." He insisted that it was the duty of Christian men to undertake the management of the people's entertainment and sports — preferably with city government support.[7]

Such "advanced" talk was an anathema indeed to the vast majority of American religionists, but it was probably well received by a goodly number of well-informed New Englanders. A noted modern scholar observes that "Reading the biographies of New Englanders active before 1850, one expects to find in them a chronicle of family ill-health (tuberculosis among the Emersons is a case in point) ; but the drive for exercise . . . stemmed largely from New England in the fifties and sixties."[8] Even so, the startling idea that sports should be actively promoted by Christian leaders did not go unchallenged. In 1851 the staid Congregationalist magazine, the *New Englander,* printed a fifteen-page attack on the break with the past urged in Frederic W. Sawyer's 1847 *A Plea for Amusements.* After deriding Sawyer's view that Christians could and should reform amusements and sports — who ever heard of a "reformed bowling alley?" — the article concluded with a call to retread "the old paths" that would have delighted Asbury and Wesley:

> Let our readers, one and all, remember that we were sent into this world, not for sport and amusement, but for *labor;* not to enjoy and please ourselves, but to

> serve and glorify God, and be useful to our fellow men. That is the great object and end of life. In pursuing this end, God has indeed permitted us all needful diversion and recreation. . . . But the great end of life after all is *work*. . . . The Christian fathers have a tradition that John Baptist, when a boy — being requested by some other boys to join them in play — replied, *"I came into this world, not for sport."* Whether the Baptist ever said this, we are unable to decide. But whether he did or not, it is a remarkable saying. It is a true saying — however cutting may be the reproof which it carries to not a few of our fellow men. It is a saying which we may all with propriety adopt: *"We came into this world, not for sport."* We were sent here for a higher and nobler object.[9]

Fifteen years later, however, this conservative religious periodical announced that among its plans for improvement would be one for fresh consideration of "grave questions relating to Christian Life, to the subject of Amusements, for example." In 1867, the *New Englander* turned aside from "deep investigation in Theology, aroused by the war" and began to carry out its improvement plan by printing a twenty-five page review of seven recently printed sermons and two secular magazine articles on the subject of the proper Christian stance toward amusements. The review noted that several of the sermons, which had been given at Young Men's Christian Association meetings, took a very liberal view of the role of athletics as a part of Christian amusements. One of them, delivered by a Congregationalist minister at the annual meeting of the YMCA of Saint Paul, declared flatly that Christians should "take the lead in entertainments and recreations" and spoke favorably of light gymnastics, outdoor skating, baseball, college athletics and the new Yale gymnasium, "the Seminary for 'Muscular Christianity.'" He also recounted the astonishment of a Yale alumnus who had recently returned to the campus to find the "venerable President, dignified Professors, learned Tutors and College boys" bowling at the six new alleys. "Roll ten pins!" he said in astonishment. "Why, thirty years ago I was expelled from the College for rolling ten pins."

Another of the clerical discourses reviewed in the *New Englander* had been delivered to a Massachusetts congregation by Rev. Washington Gladden, now a young Congregationalist minister who later was to become famous as "the father of the Social Gospel." He, too, took a sanguine view of bowling conducted under proper auspices. Nearby Williams College, "always wisely conservative of morals," had encouraged its students to use new alleys on the campus without "any alarming increase of vice . . . [or] serious falling off in religious activity" in Williamstown. "Now if Williams College can christianize a bowling alley, I submit that it is not absurd to suppose Christian people anywhere if they took the matter in hand might christianize a billiard room." In more general terms, Gladden stated, "I wish to speak earnestly in approval of the various athletic sports, which are so useful in cultivating the physical nature. . . . The day is not far distant when physical culture will be enjoined as a Christian duty." To this end, he urged that the religious education of young people should include a dictum that "sport, glee, fun, not the dismal, repressed, shame-faced variety, but the real hilarious, exuberant sort, is their lawful inheritance; and that there is by divine appointment, 'a time to laugh,' as truly as a time to pray. Then their consciences will not be constantly tormented with the thought that it is wicked to do that which they are all the while longing to do."[10]

"This doctrine," Gladden admitted, "is not yet universally received" by Protestant churchmen. This was an understatement of huge proportions. A Disciples of Christ writer in 1883 was much more typical in denouncing a proposal to reform certain sports as being a good deal like an attempt to engage in "purifying a lump of total depravity."

Even if the lump was not 100 per cent depraved, it still could be very dangerous. Even such a mild sport as croquet came under the Disciples of

"In my view, all of your hellishly, fiendishly clever — but fun — innovations for starting nice girls like me down the skids to perdition, croquet and the bicycle built for two are the greatest!"

Christ ban in the 1870's. The editor of the "Missouri Department" page in the Cincinnati *American Christian Review* was especially vehement in his opposition to this game, which swept over the country "like an epidemic" after its introduction from England in 1866. "Croquet is to most persons a most fascinating game [wrote the editor], and the desire to engage in it increases rapidly. When young Christians should be reading the Bible, meditating, conversing about religious matters, praying or attending to some important religious duty, they are often found playing croquet. We have in our mind the history of two interesting young ladies who were in the habit of playing croquet by moonlight, frequently until past twelve and even until two o'clock. The result of their dissipation was consumption from cold, a very sad and untimely death, without that preparation which consists in holiness, without which no one shall see the Lord."[11]

The same editor, in an attack on "the dancing fever," which "like the yellow fever of the South" numbered "thousands among its victims," believed that croquet-playing often was an integral step on this road to perdition. He wrote that the following was "the general rule":

1. A social party
2. Social and play party
3. Croquet party
4. Picnic and croquet party
5. Picnic, croquet and dance
6. Absence from church
7. Imprudent or immoral conduct
8. Exclusion from the church
9. A runaway-match
10. Poverty and discontent
11. Shame and disgrace
12. Ruin[12]

The recreation movement of the late 1860's and the 1870's met with its readiest response in the colleges. William Dallman — later a Lutheran church leader, but about 1880 a young German immigrant and a ministerial candidate at Concordia College — engaged in gymnastics there, played baseball and later testified in his autobiography that he had been inspired to introduce football by reading *Tom Brown at Rugby*. Intercollegiate rowing regattas and the rising new American game of baseball were quickly adopted by college students almost before the faculties and administrators could recognize that the new "gospel of the body" was in the process of creating a serious educational problem.

Early intercollegiate rowing contests in particular received the adverse attention of portions of the eastern religious press. In 1867 the Boston *Congregationalist and Recorder* headed its lead editorial against intercollegiate regattas with a question, "Has It Not Gone About Far Enough?" — especially in view of the amount of prerace betting and postrace drunken carousing in which the losers joined "just to show they are not 'spoopsey' enough to be beaten without good grace." The Protestant Episcopal New York *Churchman* inquired in 1875 whether the regatta was the "highest aim of college education," and whether spring training was not developing more "bull necks" than "superior gifts in literary culture." In particular, it objected to the publicity attendant upon the spectacle. "When the glory of the college is not so much in the classic or scientific race, as that Cornell or Columbia has the best stroke oar; when our papers are crowded with portraits of the young argonauts of the day, the exact number of inches on the chest, and the style of the flannel shirt; when we read of grave Presidents flinging up their hats and saying, 'This is the proudest moment of our history,' the mania becomes a little ridiculous." Later, a northern Methodist editor commented that "Athletic sports are like eating, too much is as pernicious as too little, and sometimes more so."[13]

As early as the late 1860's, the Northern Methodists took the offensive against the rising popularity of baseball in two books published by the official denominational press. In one, Rev. Hiram Mattison, D.D., wrote that bowling, ball-playing and pitching quoits probably were healthful in a few cases, but "not as usually practiced. The exercise is *too violent and irregular* to be of any essential service. This is taught by both physiology and experience."[14] In the other, Rev. J. T. Crane, D.D., devoted whole chapters to the evils of theater attendance, dancing and novel-reading, and equal space to horse-racing and baseball, and in addition paid his respects to billiards, which he damned by describing as shooting "big marbles."

Dr. Crane chiefly objected to professional baseball on the grounds that the players were recruited from the "idle, shiftless, and yet ambitious class of mortals," that their pay was "ridiculously high," that injuries and fights occurred at games, that the winners and losers engaged in "wine-bibbing" at suppers following games, that the newspapers so featured this "overgrown piece of folly" as to relieve it of "a single feature of real recreation" – and, worst of all, that large sums of money were bet on the outcomes of the games. Crane's prediction that "the modern bubble" of baseball would soon collapse may have been a product of prayer, but it was oversanguine, for professional baseball was barely in its promising infancy. Nevertheless, opposition to "the idea of having to hire the flower of our youth to run, jump, and play ball" continued for half a century to be parroted by some religionists who regarded professionalism as "degrading" and "absurd."[15]

In the period 1870-1900, professional baseball expanded and grew in popularity, and literally thousands of amateur teams were also organized. Churchly opposition to professionalism in the sport gradually subsided except in the South, where the attack shifted to a denunciation based on the rowdy nature of the spectator crowds and on the unquestioned fact that both professionals and amateurs played on Sunday. All of the Protestant denominations were opposed to this violation of the sanctity of the Sabbath, but there was a difference of opinion as to whether baseball on weekdays should be tolerated. The Disciples of Christ and the Southern Baptists demonstrated the most extreme animosity. One of the Disciples cried out in 1885: " 'Our national game,' one of our national curses! Does not every watchman on the wall cry the alarm? . . . Speak out. Keep the boys away from it. Don't allow them to become fascinated with it. Treat it as an enemy. Base ball playing is apt to lead to Sunday base ball playing. . . . My voice is against it. Cry with me." In 1891 an Arkansas Baptist editor asserted that baseball was the chief evil of the day, one of the reasons being that players could "execute more deviltry, use more profanity, and make idiots of themselves in more ways" than any other segment of society.[16]

In the 1890's college football spread from its original base in the older eastern colleges to educational institutions in other sections. Its "strong streak of brutality" was condemned by the secular press, but the southern religious press was even more vehemently opposed. In 1897 the Richmond (Va.) *Religious Herald,* a Baptist journal, could not understand the appeal of "that dirtily clad, bare and frowsy headed, rough-and-tumble, shoving, pushing, crushing, pounding, kicking, ground-wallowing, mixed-up mass of players, any of whom might come out with broken limbs, or be left on the ground writhing with ruptured vitals." A Texas Southern Methodist journal decried "this barbarous amusement . . . this savage and brutal performance" in which a Texas lad recently had been killed in an intracollege game in North Carolina. "All the amusement gotten out of the foot ball craze during the next 100 years will not be able to compensate for the loss of this noble young life." In 1903 a Mississippi Baptist editor delineated this "murderous" sport as "more brutal than a bull-fight, more reprehensible than a prize-fight, and more deadly than modern warfare."[17]

Meanwhile archery, tennis and bicycling accelerated the process begun by croquet of "bring the women out of stuffy living rooms and parlors to participate in outdoor exercises with men."[18] But in the mid-eighties an indoor play "craze" aroused the ire of religionists.

Roller-skating in especially constructed rinks had been an eastern society pastime in the 1860's, but after the patent rights expired, the religious press discovered in 1885 that rinks in many sections of the country were being erected not only in cities but in towns and villages. Northern and Southern Methodists, Northern Presbyterians, Cumberland Presbyterians, Disciples of Christ, Congregationalists and some Catholics denounced "the rapid growth of this epidemic" in which "the worst of passions are inflamed and virtue is slain on the crowded arena."[19] Several church magazines presented frightful accounts of formerly sober persons squandering their grocery money at the rinks, of some individuals borrowing or stealing in order to obtain funds to skate, of elopements with disreputable "professors" who taught skating, of broken homes and even suicides. In a representative statement, an Ohio Presbyterian referred to "this social cyclone" as "our greatest national evil."[20]

The two most elaborate attacks on roller-skating rinks, both printed in 1885 in religious journals and later reprinted as tracts, were written by Mrs. C. A. Richardson, wife of the editor of the *Congregationalist,* and by James M. Buckley, a Methodist preacher and the vigorous editor of the New York *Christian Advocate.* Both deplored the mingling of respectable religious folk with "bar-room loafers," "libertines" and prostitutes on the rinks' floors. Both cited cases of young girls, "once gentle and obedient," who became wild and unmanageable "under the excitement of the rink." Mrs. Richardson told of three "young girls dear to their parents" who had encountered married men at the rinks, yielded to their "persuasions" and run off with them; and Buckley later asserted that he "could easily fill this column every week with authenticated cases of health injured, of serious accidents, of young girls ruined, and of indecent masquerades and balls held in rinks." Both authors presented evidence from "leading physicians" that young women had suffered serious respiratory and spinal injuries, one becoming "insane from spinal disease, the result of several severe falls." But the most harrowing medical testimony was printed by Buckley in one of his numerous follow-ups to his tract. He quoted a woman doctor who attacked roller-skating in the *Medical Record* as productive of "no good, moral, mental, or physical. . . . All sorts of latent tendencies are developed. It aggravates all cases of heart, kidney, and other organic troubles, and causes anaemia of the most intractable sort. Leucorrhoea is both caused and greatly aggravated by skating."[21]

Roller-skating nevertheless remained immensely popular throughout the 1880's, after which bicycling became "the most spectacular craze of all," particularly after the invention of the safety bicycle, the drop frame for women and the pneumatic tire. Bicycle clubs, often affiliated with the League of American Wheelmen, were organized in almost every town and city and sponsored professional and amateur races, hill-climbing contests and bicycle parades, one of which in Chicago was led by the mayor and a bugle corps on *Sunday* morning.

This sporting miracle which placed millions of Americans of all ages and both sexes on their individual wheels was the subject of many thousands of words that appeared in both the secular and religious press. But James M. Buckley, who was so influential that he was facetiously called "the pope of the Methodist Church," probably wrote the most all-encompassing religionist discourse in his six-part series, "Psychology, Hygiene, and Morality of the Bicycle," in his New York *Christian Advocate.* The Reverend Buckley, obviously fascinated by the bicycle and its "psychology" but repelled by the effects of some of its uses, learned to ride at age sixty-two: "I took many lessons, and tried in vain to mount; sometimes I leaped over the machine and lighted on the handle bars, again upon the rear wheel. One day I discharged the instructor and devoted myself to mastering the machine. On the twenty-seventh effort I mounted and rode away for seven miles. I should still be trying to mount had I not broken the spell." Although he claimed that bicyclists frequently suffered "hallucinations, imperative conceptions, and other forms of functional nervous and mental disorders," with not a few resulting tragic deaths, he believed that "the bicycle used in moderation is an excellent means of exercise." This was testimony from an authority, because he had engaged in outdoor exercise for a half century as a means of warding off the consumption that had almost sent him to his death as a very young man.

In his last three articles, Buckley summed up the religionists' case against bicycling, but before concluding returned again to its salutary results.

> A heavy charge must be made against it for depraving the manners of young women. Many of good family become bold in feature, bearing, and gesture, and indulge freely in road badinage and slang. They sit in indelicate attitudes on curbstones, roadsides, and under trees, with young men; they drink and joke at drugstore counters; not a few have become typical hoydens and, when not riding, parade the streets in bicycle costume.
>
> The bicycle has inflicted untold evils upon many by relieving young people of surveillance by day and night. Children and youth cannot stray far from home on foot, but fifteen minutes on the wheel may put them miles away. . . .
>
> Many parents who have had a pardonable ambition for their children, find to their horror that the bicycle has been a medium of communication with those whose lack of morality or cultivation has been so manifest as to restrict all relations to formal requirements or neighborly recognition. . . .
>
> Wives have taken to the wheel against the expressed wishes of their husbands, and have neglected their family duties. . . . The bicycle has figured in divorce cases without number. Bicycle acquaintances are far too easily made. . . .
>
> Many things have contributed to popularizing Sunday bicycling. Club runs have been set for Sunday. Red Cross corps have been founded to give prompt succor to injured cyclists. . . . Hundreds of Christian Endeavorers have been caught in this snare. . . .
>
> [Nevertheless] it is entitled to great credit for developing courage, self-possession, and determination. It is especially beneficial to young and middle-aged women without an aim in life, who have no special business to take them away from home, and who from lack of company are not able to pedestrianize except to walk in the ordinary streets, but who by means of the wheel can have a constant change of air and scenery. To low-spirited people it is a boon, and it prevents or ends many family quarrels. The wheel absorbs attention; the air freshens the blood. . . . A man [on a wheel] forgets his cares and troubles.[22]

Although many clergymen harangued the faithful about the sin of bicycle-riding on Sunday, the religious press as a whole was surprisingly quiet about many of the evils that Buckley enumerated in 1898. In the same year, a prominent Disciples of Christ leader advocated long bicycle tours as vacations for able-bodied men or women. The following year Dr. H. Clay Trumbull, the editor of the conservative *Sunday School Times,* published *Border Lines in the Field of Doubtful Practices,* in which he recommended bicycling, golfing and tennis — along with art study and fashionable handiwork — to young women as "sensible occupations" to replace the sinful social dance. The Boston *Congregationalist* even reprinted a long newspaper article "New Conditions of Love-Making," which praised this "new fad for athletics for women" for enabling courting couples to appraise each other more realistically than in earlier days when, attired in their best clothes, they had sat in the parlor and talked about "soulful things."

> The girl who goes out a-wheeling with her beau and takes the rain and sun and dust and wind and tan may not be a divinity to him like the parlor maiden, but . . . if she still appears beautiful to him and he is still in love with her, she has nothing to fear from fading good looks or wearing curl papers and wrappers to breakfast; while if he still appears heroic to her in knickerbockers and with a sunburnt nose, she may rest satisfied that her love is founded on a rock that nothing can shake. . . . It is one thing to spring to pick up a lady's handkerchief in a parlor. It is another to stay his pace all day to keep near a woman who is a poor rider. That is the real chivalry a woman may trust to protect her in the days of sickness and misfortune, and to be patient and forbearing with her weakness.[23]

American young women would have been the first to agree with the Census Bureau expert who praised the bicycle in 1900 for being the means of "bringing out for exercise in the open air millions of persons, men and women, young and old, who otherwise would have confined themselves to homes, stores, and offices." If he could have foreseen the future social effects of another invention which had not been perfected — the "horseless carriage" — perhaps he would have tempered the principal generalization in his report: "It is safe to say that few articles ever used by man have created so great a revolution in social conditions as the bicycle."[24] At the end of the nineteenth century, however, young people of all ages, their parents and the clergy gave a full-voiced "amen" to the expert's sentiment.

THE TWENTIETH CENTURY

The continuously mounting popularity of sports in the present century has caused observers in several of its decades to view their own periods as surpassing all others in the past. The 1920's were called "The Golden Age of Sports." A widely read sports journal recently declared that the golden age is now — the 1960's. But many sober observers of the American scene in the first decade of the twentieth century were certain that "the sporting mania" was already "rampant." In 1904 an *Atlantic Monthly* writer compared it to the compulsion to join the Crusades in the Middle Ages and the tulip mania of Holland in the seventeenth century; he offered for proof the increasing scope of intercollegiate athletics and international sports contests and the money that "poured out like water on race-horses, motor-cars, dirigible balloons and what-not," including golf.[25] In 1905, when Lord James Bryce revisited America, he noted "the passion for looking at and reading about athletic sports. . . . It occupies the minds not only of the youth at the universities, but also of their parents and of the general public. Baseball matches and football matches excite an interest greater than any other public events except the Presidential election, and that comes only once in four years."[26]

During the subsequent sixty years, American churches have been confronted with all the problems of a society "on wheels" growing more and more mechanized, industrialized, urbanized and affluent. The Gospel of Work has grown gradually less pertinent to a populace presented with "the provoking gift of increasing leisure" in which sports have played a major role. American Protestantism has had to grapple with the question of what attitudes it should take toward sports and their spectacles, which have reached such incredibly gigantic proportions. The story of the changes in those attitudes held by most older Protestant denominations is largely one of accelerating accommodation, a contrast indeed to the nineteenth-century practice of attaching the label "sinful" to each new sports innovation.

The accommodation to "the city problem" had already begun in the North before 1900. For the Catholics, Jews and Germans, no great about-face or psychological wrench in regard to sports was involved. In fact, the German Jews who dominated American Jewry from 1820 to 1880 were exponents of gymnastics; and Young Men's Hebrew Associations organized in more than a dozen cities by 1880 had gymnasiums. Other German immigrants organized many *Turnvereins* (literal meaning: "associations of gymnasts and athletes").[27] In addition to their support of the YMCA movement, the Episcopalians and Congregationalists, and afterward the Northern Presbyterians and Northern Methodists, established, in the 1880's and 1890's, a number of mission churches and huge "institutional church" enterprises that included gymnasiums and athletics in their programs, often specifically designed to enrich the lives of poverty-blighted young people in the cities.

The editor of the leading Disciples of Christ journal helped bring in the new century with a story about a recent international yacht race. When a reader objected to the inclusion of such material in a religious periodical, the editor replied: "The Christian attitude toward sport consists not in ignoring them; it is scarcely possible to do that; . . . but rather in taking from it the preeminence which the frivolous mind gives to it; reducing it to its proper place as a matter of mere momentary interest and rebuking those phases of it which may be immoral." The editor's position, however, was much less advanced than that of the Southern *Methodist Review* writer who claimed that "puritanical notions of propriety are entirely out of date," or that of the rector of Holy Trinity Church in Brooklyn who believed that since 1880 the "curious shamefacedness about taking pleasure" had been broken down "nearly everywhere," and invited Sunday golfers to stop at a church en route to the links and utter their prayers there. In 1907 the *Michigan Christian Advocate* predicted that a Northern Methodist bishop's recent treatment of the "agitating topic" of amusements would be "sure to set the tongues a-wagging," for he could find no New Testament authority for his denomination's ban of certain specific amusements. "Does the spirit of Christianity enjoin total abstinence from amusements?" the bishop inquired. "If not, how far may one use time or money on innocent sports?"[28]

After a half-century of vexatious argument, the bishop's own denomination waited until 1924 before it took a formal step in the direction of approving his position, but in the intervening period there were many indications that much of Protestant America was beginning to view sport as a positive force for good and even as an effective tool to promote the Lord's work. In 1908 the Boston *Congregationalist* published a piece entitled "Football as a Study," in which it asserted that football trained "young men to self-control and readiness in the tremendous emergencies which men must meet in the busy, struggling life of these times," and that it was "as real a study as mathematics" in cultivating "mental discipline." To illustrate this startling message, it printed Walter Camp's stirring account of the recent Yale game with Princeton in which he praised the Yalemen even in their loss because they had withstood a bone-chilling and bloody battering with admirable fortitude. Camp, a powerful propagandist for "hard-nosed" but clean football, often published essays in the religious press. His "Honor in Athletics," which appeared in a prominent Southern Presbyterian periodical in 1912, stressed two of his favorite themes: (1) taking *money to play* involves a loss of honor; and (2) cheering should be reserved for the opposition's good plays. The same year, however, the same magazine printed a message from Christy Mathewson, the great *professional* pitcher, to the Boy Scouts, asking them to play "Clean Baseball"; and the *Amethyst,* "Official Temperance Organ of the [Northern] Presbyterian Church," soon reinforced this theme with an account of "What Baseball Men Think of Cigarettes." Clark Griffith, Branch Rickey and "Home Run" Baker were opposed to smoking; Walter Johnson, "the world's greatest pitcher, does not drink, smoke, nor chew, and goes to bed early"; and Connie Mack, manager of three world's championship teams since 1910, was quoted as saying,

"There is very little cigaret smoking among our baseball boys. We find that those who smoke never amount to much in the profession."[29]

The catalog of the Southern Methodist Publishing House in 1914 reveals a rather startling use of athletic literature for boys. The namby-pamby juvenile fiction that had been issued by Methodist and Presbyterian publishing houses in the late nineteenth century, with the invariable moralistic preachment at the end of each book, now had been replaced largely by books by Horatio Alger, G. A. Henty, Edward S. Ellis (a former dime novelist) and other adventure authors and a number of writers who portrayed athletics as a boost to morality. Ralph Henry Barbour's *Winning His "Y"* (fourteenth in his series of college athletic fiction) dealt with characters "such as all right thinking parents would desire their children to take as models of manly, active, and honest youthfulness." A champion sprinter's novel showed "the proper relation between physical, mental, and moral excellence" – an echo, perhaps, of the nineteenth-century statement attributed to Harvard's President Charles W. Eliot: "Football supplies a new and effective motive for resisting all sins that weaken and corrupt the body."[30]

After World War I, reconciliation between sports and organized religion approached finality. Intercollegiate athletic competition now became a virtually unchallenged part of the activities of church-controlled colleges. Occasional sports stories and advice-from-champions pieces appeared in the church youth magazines; and in 1929 the Southern Baptist Sunday School Board published *Faith Lambert* and her fictional relationship with "Big Jed Carlton, upper classman and gridiron hero." More typically, church publishing houses and magazines published learned homilies on the theory, philosophy and morality of "the people's play" (as opposed to professional baseball) and often quoted Dr. Richard C. Cabot's statement that "Play is just as much a part of our proper life as is love, or work, or worship. . . . [We should] make games and sports a part of our recreational program."[31] Implementation of this last sentiment had already begun in New York and Chicago around 1910; and in the twenties, many Baptist, Methodist and Presbyterian churches – large and small, north and south – organized athletic, and especially baseball, leagues. "Don't fail to capture some of the summer athletics for your church. We need to keep play wholesome, clean and Christian, just as much as we need to keep civic or industrial life Christian," the New York *Christian Advocate* advised Northern Methodists.[32]

The symbolic relationship of the connection between sport and religion was best exemplified in the dedication in 1929 of a Sports Bay in the awe-inspiring Cathedral of St. John the Divine in New York. Bishop William T. Manning averred in the ceremony: "A well-played game of polo or of football is in its own place and in its own way as pleasing to God as a beautiful service of worship in the Cathedral. . . . True sport and true religion should be in the closest touch and sympathy."[33]

Six years later, in the middle of the Great Depression, a Presbyterian professor of religion and Christian ethics at a leading seminary was certain that "closest touch and sympathy" had not been achieved. He declared that "Protestantism has tardily and grudgingly adopted recreational activities into its program"; he called on "the Protestant Church" to "repent," "to recognize fully the values of recreation and to integrate them with all other values which are basic to the abundant life," and finally to develop both "a philosophy of play" and "a recreational conscience."[34] This was by no means an original notion. Congregationalists and Episcopalians had been preaching this doctrine for a number of years. In 1915, for example, Henry A. Atkinson, Social Service Secretary for the Congregational Churches of the United States, had published *The Church and the People's Play* (with a perceptive introduction by Washington Gladden) which also called for a change: "The weakness in the prevailing attitude of the church is that it fails to recognize the insistence of social demands. . . . 'If eating meat' – said St. Paul – 'makes my brother to offend, I will eat no meat while the world stands.' This position was heroic and splendid in Paul's day; interpreted today, it might be put in these words as expressive of the ideal attitude of each church member: 'If failure to provide for the play of the people by means of playgrounds, social centers and other recreational facilities makes my brother to offend, I will exert myself to favor and to work for the establishment of these things.'"[35]

Atkinson's chief hope, however, was never realized. He urged all the churches in a given community to lead and educate in a program to make recreation available to all citizens. In the post-World War II years, most of the large denominations have established or greatly expanded their own recreation programs, published their own recreation guides by the score and established their own large summer encampments – all parallel to the public recreational programs and facilities provided by government agencies.

As an example of the interpenetration of Christian activities and athletics, a comparison of the Southern Baptists in the 1920's and 1960's is most instructive. For the earlier period, the files of the *Baptist Student*, primarily read by Southern Baptist college students, are invaluable. Although it reprinted an editorial from the *Baptist Record* pointing to "athletic carnivals" as the "diseased spot in all our educational institutions," the *Baptist Student* made it clearly evident that sports were no longer sinful to this denomination and even strongly endorsed "clean" athletics. It reprinted two sermonettes that used football terminology. One of them began with this proposition: "With apologies to Shakespeare, all the world is a football game, and we are the players." Both of them pictured the game as between Christians and anti-Christians. One discourse named the Devil as fullback and Sin as quarterback on the opposing team, and the other concluded that "God rewards the men who play on His team with eternal life." The periodical also featured pictures of both Baptist women's and men's athletic teams. Among the individual students praised were Miss Inez Hardin, co-president of the state Baptist Student Union in Mississippi, who had been voted "the healthiest girl in the United States, Cuba, and the Hawaiian Islands"; the all-Southern football player, "Goat" Hale; and All-American Gene McEver, "the Bristol Blizzard" of the University of Tennessee, the highest football scorer in the nation and "a clean Christian athlete" who taught a Sunday-school class for boys and abhorred dancing.[36]

The athletic policies of several small Baptist colleges were also extolled by the *Baptist Student*. Georgetown College in Kentucky, the readers were informed in 1923, "has always stood among the leading institutions in the South. . . . But it is not in an intellectual field that Georgetown has led all other colleges in the South. Georgetown's real leadership is in the field of athletics" — the result of a three-point system: (1) placing the athletes under faculty supervision, thus enabling the college to keep its accreditation and eliminate "any crooked work" on the part of overzealous students, "so-called friends of the college" or professional gamblers; (2) the efforts of the football coach to produce a "thinking team" by trying "to cover every possible play that could come up"; and (3) installing "a compulsory course in athletic coaching" for *nonathletes* who had been "missing one of the biggest things in their college lives." At Mars Hill College in North Carolina, the football and basketball teams organized the "Fearless Fighters," a Sunday-school class that won the efficiency banner and took individual Bibles with them on all athletic trips. "The athletes of Mars Hill College," this article informed the Baptist college sporting world, "therefore challenge athletes of all other colleges to fear nothing in playing the game fair, to be up and doing in the Master's work."[37]

The *Baptist Student*'s longest series in this period was an exchange of letters (in 1925-26) entitled "Confessions of a Four-Letter Man" and "Confessions of a Three-Letter Lady." These fictional athletes were seniors (in different colleges) who deplored "rolling your own," bare knees, freak skirts and "form-fitting, flapper one-piece dresses," "the high-heel wiggle," cosmetics, petting, dancing (it was "deadly to a wholesome soul") and drinking. Both were avid believers in becoming superior athletes, presumably to release their abundant physical energies in a "clean" manner and thus avoid immodesties — and "worse" practices. At the end of the series, Billy and Caroline agreed to marry, both being happy that their only physical lovemaking in four years had been his once kissing her hand "under the blooming laurels." The anonymous author was finally revealed to be a

Macon, Georgia, preacher who had obtained most of his "material" from actual student confessions, he said.[38]

Since the 1920's no other denomination has surpassed the Southern Baptists in growth of the size and scope of recreation and sports programs.

Church Accommodation to Sports. Mrs. Andrew Hall, wife of the pastor of the First Baptist Church in Fayetteville, poses with a sign in the churchyard that expresses the feelings of folks in Arkansas. Nationally ranked no. 3 Arkansas upset no. 1 ranked Texas in the last minute of play, 27-24. Courtesy World Wide Photos.

The Sunday School Board of the Southern Baptist Convention now has a fully staffed Church Recreation Department which furnishes counsel, including sports advice, to local churches and seminaries, and publishes the lively periodical, *Church Recreation.* Its many articles on sports during the 1960's have included "Fly-Tying," for fishermen; "Coaching Church Basketball," which advises that all church athletic contests should begin with the teams engaging in a simple prayer that "all will be Christlike in victory or defeat"; and "The Sky Pilots Roll 'Em," an account of the Baptist Preachers Bowling League of Paducah, Kentucky. At the local church level the recreation programs, headed by "ministers of recreation" or "recreation directors," grow more extensive each year. Many churches either have or are planning complete recreation buildings which include gymnasiums, volleyball and badminton courts and facilities for bowling, skating, weight lifting and table tennis. The First Baptist Church of Greensboro, North Carolina, for example, has a $335,000 plant, a picnic shelter and a ball field.

At the same time, Southern Baptists lead other denominations in their use of sports in diverse and interesting ways. *The Game of Life,* a long-playing record in football terms with God as the referee, has sold thousands of copies. It was the first disc released by Word Records, founded by a young Baptist divinity student to issue religious material.[39] In the early 1960's Southern Baptist periodicals for teen-agers and college students carried numerous sports stories (each with a moralistic teaching), articles on how-to-improve-techniques in given sports and accounts of sports stars who were dedicated Baptists.

Although Southern Baptists have embraced athletics — once regarded as a "worldly" waste of time that could be better used in preparing for the afterlife — their use of sports is one means of keeping congregations apart from the snares of this wicked world by providing for congregational play as well as worship. It is true that Baptists such as Baylor football coach John Bridgers and professional baseball players Alvin Dark and Bobby Richardson participate in the program of the Fellowship of Christian Athletes, but the ministerial leadership in this unique amalgamation of sports and religion is provided chiefly by former athletes who are now Presbyterian and Methodist divines.

Among the cofounders of the Fellowship of Christian Athletes in 1954 were the eminent pulpit orator Louis H. Evans, minister-at-large of the Northern Presbyterian church, and Branch Rickey of baseball fame, who announced in the keynote address at the FCA's first annual conference in 1956: "I have never faced a program which is so full of promise for so many young men in terms of service to God."[40] In subsequent years the FCA has held numerous summer conferences attended by ministers, college coaches, and high school, college and professional athletes. Announcements are always made that the conferences will be primarily spiritual, but that athletic activities will be an important secondary concern. One prominent Presbyterian pastor describes the purposes of the FCA as an attempt to combat juvenile delinquency, to elevate the moral and spiritual standards of sports "in an unprincipled secular culture," to challenge Americans "to stand up and be counted for or against God" and to appeal to sports enthusiasts and American youth through "hero worship harnessed."[41] The conferences always feature religious "witness" by star athletes such as professional quarterbacks Otto Graham, Bill Wade, and Fran Tarkenton and basketball luminaries Bill Bradley and Bob Pettit. Pettit's testimony is to the effect that the greatest team of all is that of "Jesus Christ which is playing for a lasting victory." One of the most indefatigable lecturers, both at the conferences and elsewhere, is Rev. Donn Moomaw, former All-American football player, whose message usually includes a variation of the Pettit statement, with the additional identification of Christ as "the greatest coach of all."

The Fellowship also casts its net widely by arranging special events. A professional athletes' religious retreat, held in a Tampa motel in 1964, was partly underwritten by *Guideposts,* the magazine of all-purpose inspiration for all faiths and all ages edited by Dr. Norman Vincent Peale. In 1957, at Nashville, Tennessee, the FCA sponsored a typical three-day rally at which twenty-five famous athletes "related their faith to crucial sports events" at a youth rally, assembly programs in twenty-five schools, Vanderbilt Stadium and the Tennessee State Prison. An unusual twist to the use of religious testimony by athletes occurred on the beaches of a Florida seacoast town when public appearances by FCA members were alternated with performances by a dixieland jazz band in a highly successful attempt to avoid rioting by college students during the Easter holidays.[42]

This organization's "Muscular Boost for Christian Doctrine" uses a variety of additional methods to spread the message: two books of religious testimony by star athletes, *The Goal and the Glory* (1962) and *Play Ball* (1965), tape recordings of these and other "dynamic messages" furnished free for local performances, movie films, and a high-fidelity record, *Under the Master Coach.* In 1962 the FCA estimated that each year its speakers and films were reaching more than one million persons and that it was sending out nearly 300,000 pieces of free items of printed matter to churches, schools and individuals. The thousands of members receive the *Christian Athlete,* a periodical containing such diverse fare as the following: "The Huddle" (a Bible study outline series); a paragraph that describes "THE CHURCH" as "a sanctuary for worship" which "adds to the attractions of the country club the power of religion and the generous sympathies of the altruistic impulse"; inspirational and often maudlin poems; "Football Player's Prayer"; "A Trainer's Prayer"; suggestions for coaches' bulletin boards and short discourses on athletic techniques in different sports. The chief articles in the *Christian Athlete* are contributed by ministers and coaches. In "I Pastor the Packers," a Methodist minister asserted that in 1962 their coach fined them "heavily for unethical rough house tactics on the playing field. I have observed (sometimes to my deep personal chagrin) players 'turning the other cheek' again and again in games this fall" — an observation that the opponents of Packer fullback Jim Taylor must have considered ludicrous. Other articles include "A Man on His Knees Is Close to God," by a college wrestling coach, and "Not Always a Winner — But Never a Loser" and "Christian Obligations as a Coach" by a college football coach.[43]

In the 1960's a number of well-known coaches have been seriously involved in the FCA program. Among those who are *not* is Paul "Bear" Bryant of Alabama, who is quoted as using a slogan that never would have appeared in the *Christian Athlete*: "A moral victory is like kissing your sister."[44] Another football coach in the same athletic conference, Charlie Bradshaw of the University of Kentucky, imitates Bryant's technique of dismissing all players not prepared and willing to play hard-nosed football, but insists that those hardy souls remaining on the Kentucky squad "form and join a Christian athletic chapter," presumably of the FCA.[45] Paul Dietzel, named Coach-of-the-Year in 1958 after leading the Louisiana State University football team to the national championship, is apparently the coach who has served most "untiringly and faithfully" to further the FCA cause. In 1964 Dietzel, while president of the FCA, stated in a speech: "Out on the football field I feel so infinitesimal — just one coach and one big stadium, one large city, one great nation, one large world, one vast universe before one all-present God. Being a Christian and a top athlete or coach is a challenge but it is also one of the most thrilling experiences in my life. I find it means a great deal to God how I act as His tool." This was the same coach who in the year of his greatest success (1958) had given this estimate of what happened to the opposition when it encountered his star player: "When he blocks, or even when people tackle him, [Billy] Cannon hurts people, he caves them in. They carried a Mississippi State boy off the field last Saturday after he tackled Cannon. He buckles them." According to Dietzel, he did not make his own full "personal commitment to Christ" until he attended an FCA conference as a speaker in the summer of 1959;[46] and soon thereafter he was viewed by a television audience, with his handsome profile fixed at the most advantageous angle and his eyes looking upward as if toward heaven, as he gave a postgame statement to an interviewer that a victory over the arch rival University of Mississippi team had been followed immediately by his leading his Christian athletes in prayer in their dressing room.[47] Dietzel had arrived – apparently in all sincerity – at the position taken by Amos Alonzo Stagg who, in his letter accepting an offer to coach football at the University of Chicago in the 1890's, declared: "After much thought and prayer I feel decided that my life can best be used for my Master's service in the position which you [the president] have offered."[48]

In our generation the clergy as well as the coaches have a part in the stylized rites that introduce many amateur football spectacles in the autumn. Innumerable college and high school pregame ceremonies include a prayer delivered by a minister over a public-address system, a convergence of religious approbation and emotional frenzy preceding a kickoff that brings to mind the ancient Greeks and their belief in the symbolic relationships between sports and their gods. A modern parallel to the pagan concept has been suggested by Thomas Hornsby Ferril, the Denver poet and publisher:

> Obviously, football is a syndrome of religious rites symbolizing the struggle to preserve the egg of life through the rigors of impending winter. The rites begin at the autumn equinox and culminate on the first day of the New Year with great festivals identified with bowls of plenty; the festivals are associated with flowers such as roses, fruits such as oranges, farm crops such as cotton, and even sun-worship and appeasement of great reptiles such as alligators.
>
> In these rites the egg of life is symbolized by what is called "the oval," an inflated bladder covered with hog skin. The convention of "the oval" is repeated in the architectural oval-shaped design of the vast outdoor churches in which the services are held. . . . These enormous roofless churches dominate every college campus . . . and bear witness to the high spiritual development of the culture that produced them. Literally millions of worshipers attend. . . .
>
> Subconsciously, these hordes of worshipers are seeking an outlet from sex-frustration in anticipation of violent masochism and sadism about to be enacted by a highly trained priesthood of young men. Football obviously arises out of the Oedipus complex. Love of mother dominates the entire ritual. The churches, without exception, are dedicated to Alma Mater. . . .
>
> The rites are performed on a rectangular area of green grass oriented to the four directions. The grass, symbolizing summer, is striped with ominous white lines representing the knifing snows of winter. . . .
>
> The ceremony begins with colorful processions of musicians and semi-nude virgins who move in and out of ritualized patterns. This excites the thousands of worshipers to rise from their seats, shout frenzied poetry in unison and chant ecstatic anthems through which runs the Oedipus theme of willingness to die for love of Mother.
>
> The actual rites, performed by twenty-two young priests of perfect physique, might appear to the uninitiated as a chaotic conflict. . . . However the procedure is highly stylized. . . . The group in so-called "possession" of the oval first arrange themselves in an egg-shaped "huddle," as it is called, for a moment of prayerful meditation and whispering of secret numbers to each other.
>
> Then they rearrange themselves with relation to the position of the egg. In a typical "formation" there are seven priests "on the line," seven being a mystical

number associated not, as Jung purists might contend, with the "seven last words" but actually with the sublimation of the "seven deadly sins" into "the seven cardinal principles of education."

The central priest crouches over the egg, protecting it with his hands while over his back quarters hovers the "quarterback." . . . To the layman the curious posture assumed by the "quarterback" . . . immediately suggests the Cretan origins of Mycenaean animal art, but this popular view is untenable. Actually, of course, the "quarterback" symbolizes the libido. . . . Behind him are three priests representing the male triad.

At a given signal the egg is passed by sleight-of-hand to one of the members of the triad, who endeavors to move it by bodily force across the white lines of winter. . . . At the end of the second quarter, implying the summer solstice, the processions of musicians and semi-nude virgins are resumed. . . . The virgins perform a most curious rite requiring far more dexterity than the earlier phallic Maypole rituals from which it seems to be derived. Each of the virgins carries a wand of shining metal which she spins on her fingertips, tosses playfully into the air, and with which she interweaves her body in most intricate gyrations. . . .

The foregoing, I confess, scarcely scratches the surface. Space does not permit interpretation of football as related to dreams, or discussion of the great subconscious reservoirs of thwarted American energy that weekly seek expression through vicarious enjoyment of ritualized violence and infliction of pain. To relate football to the Oedipus complex alone would require, as it well deserves, years of patient research by scholarly men.[49]

This psychological-religious analysis is, of course, facetious and satirical, but its avowal of interaction between modern sports and organized religion is by no means entirely farfetched. In the spring of 1965, Pope Paul VI addressed the International Congress of Psychology of Sport in Rome; and in the following summer more than three hundred priests, nuns and seminarians were "helping take city children off the streets" at thirty-five centers in the Archdiocese of New York.[50] The coach of the Brigham Young University football team is reported to be able to move a Mormon student pep rally to tears with a talk about the power of prayer. The American Tract Society, publishers of Christian literature since 1825, is now distributing *A Purpose in Life,* a small pamphlet by Bobby Richardson, second baseman of the New York Yankees. Photographs of sports figures occasionally adorn the covers and pages of periodicals for young people issued by Lutherans and other denominations. Just as prominent politicians have used religious terminology in their public addresses, churches now form "teams" for various purposes, including fund-raising. A Methodist minister — now a bishop and his denomination's outstanding thinker and personality — once announced that "God is an amateur" and that "Christianity is the philosophy of the amateur"; and in early 1964 one of his denomination's periodicals commissioned the South's leading sports editor to select "The 1963 Methodist University and College All-American Elevens."[51] Jewish and Catholic young people's organizations encourage participation in sports. The Bible-oriented Churches of Christ oppose organized congregational recreation, but their colleges engage in intercollegiate competition. A Fundamentalist educational institution, Wheaton College in Illinois, requires each student and faculty member to abstain from dancing and attending theaters, including the movies, but the Wheaton Crusaders consistently field strong small-college athletic teams in a number of sports.[52]

Most of the rapidly growing Pentecostal, Holiness, and Church of God church bodies espouse intraschool sports. Some of them believe that viewing and participating in high school and intercollegiate sports are harmless; but a substantial number of the numerous small sects condemn interest in both intercollegiate and professional sports, "since there is practically as much gambling, drinking, and sin carried on in connection with collegiate sports as in professional circles."[53] The most explicit reminiscent note of this type was struck when a recent general assembly of the Church of God of Prophecy in Tennessee proclaimed that "dabbling with worldly amusements such as professional ball games, horse races, stock car races, wrestling arenas, skating rinks, bowling alleys, and 'mixed bathing,' " will "give the devil a foothold or place in your life."[54] Jehovah's Witnesses hold that some sports are "wholesome" and some are not. "Those depending upon skill are; those depending upon violence are not."[55]

In recent years even many of the "Plain People" known as Mennonites gradually have accepted intracongregational sports and a limited amount of intercollegiate competition among Mennonite colleges. An ultraconservative branch of the "Plain People," the Amish, are grimly determined to preserve intact a farming culture they transplanted from Switzerland and Germany more than two centuries ago, and to this end they discourage the use of automobiles that might lead to attendance at sporting events and other types of urban entertainment; but occasionally they have found time to play baseball.[56]

In the beginning, there was the Protestant compulsion to separate from "the world" and especially "worldly amusements" — the dance, the theater and the opera, the saloon and the novel. Later there appeared sports that were another anathema to religious denominations devoted to preparation for the hereafter in man's all-too-brief span on earth — sports that were time-wasting in a nation committed to the Gospel of Work, and sports that were attractive to rowdy and gambling unbelievers. Thereafter Protestants, Catholics and Jews alike responded to an urge to seek common ground with the insatiable sports hungers of a people rapidly removing themselves from the farms. In the initial decades of the twentieth century's uneasy Leisure Revolution, sports were included in the ever-widening church and church college recreation programs designed to give outlets, under proper supervision, to the now nonsinful play instincts of the faithful. In the end, all major churches have affiliated with "the world" of sports even though the ghost of nineteenth-century "puritanism," I dare say, continues to haunt the dreams of millions of adult Americans.

FOOTNOTES

1. Degler, C. N.: *Out of Our Past.* New York, Harper, 1962, pp. 8-15; Marty, M. E.: *New Shape of American Religion.* New York, Harper, 1958, p. 88; Smith, C. P.: *Yankees and* God. New York, Hermitage, 1954, pp. 10-17; Chase, G.: *America's Music: From the Pilgrims to the Present.* New York, McGraw, 1955, pp. 3, 7, 9.
2. Martin, J. B.: History of the Attitudes of the Methodist Church in the United States of America toward Recreation. Ph.D. dissertation, Univ. of So. Calif., 1944, pp. 90, 93. Modern Methodists are fond of recalling Wesley's admonitions to women correspondents and his preachers that their physical and mental health would deteriorate unless they walked or rode in the open air. *Together, 8:*25, 1964; Telford, J. [Ed.]: *Letters of the Rev. John Wesley,* London, Epworth Press, 1931, vols. 1, 5-8, *passim.* But Wesley attacked horseracing, hawking, and cudgeling, and the cruel pastimes of bear-baiting, bull-baiting and cockfighting. As to "sports of the field," he wrote, "Let those who have nothing better to do, still run foxes and hares out of breath." *Works of John Wesley,* Grand Rapids, Michigan, Zondervan Publishing House, 1958-59, reprint of London, 1872, edition, vol. 7, p. 34; Edwards, M.: *After Wesley,* London, Epworth Press, 1935, p. 134.
3. Posey, W. B.: *Development of Methodism in the Old Southwest, 1783-1824.* Tuscaloosa, Weatherford Printing Co., 1933, pp. 66-67; Curts, L. [Ed.]: *General Conferences of the Methodist Episcopal Church from 1872 to 1896.* Cincinnati, Curts & Jennings, 1900, p. 56.
4. Graves, H. A.: *Andrew Jackson Potter: The Noted Parson of the Texan Frontier.* Nashville, Southern Methodist Publishing House, 1890, copyright 1881, p. 448. See also, for a representative treatment of a favorite Wesleyan subject, Allen, J. W.: Outline of a sermon on self-denial. *Nashville Christian Advocate,* Sept. 21, 1849.
5. Queries: *Washington, Ga. Christian Index,* July 30, 1840.
6. Gladden, W.: Christianity and popular amusements. *Century Mag., 29:*385-86, 1885; Gladden: *Applied Christianity.* Boston, Houghton-Mifflin, 1886, p. 253; Gladden: *Recollections.* Boston, Houghton-Mifflin, 1909, p. 35.
7. Hale, E. E.: *Public Amusements for Poor and Rich.* Boston, Phillips, Sampson, & Co., 1857, pp. i, 13, 21, 23. The following year Dr. Oliver Wendell Holmes recommended rowing, walking and riding for both old and young. He himself for the past nine years had greatly enjoyed rowing. He deplored Boston's paucity of skilled amateur boatmen, horsemen and cricket players, "and for any great athletic feat, performed by a gentleman in these latitudes, society would drop a man who would run round the Commons in five minutes." The autocrat of the breakfast table. *Atlantic Monthly, 1:*878-81, 1858.
8. Jones, H. M.: The recovery of New England. *Atlantic, 185:*51, 1950.
9. Amusements. *New Englander, 9:*358, 1851.
10. Gilman, E. W.: Amusements. *New Englander, 26:*399, 1867; Williams, E. S.: *Christian Amusements.* St. Paul, Davidson & Hall, 1866, pp. 17, 27; Gladden, Washington: *Amusements: Their Uses and Abuses.* North Adams, James T. Robinson & Co., 1866, pp. 7, 9-10, 20-21.
11. Headington, J. R.: Base-ball — croquet — dancing, etc. *Cincinnati American Christian Rev.,* Oct. 19, 1875. If the Reverend Mr. Headington had been privy to one of the findings of modern psychoanalysis, his opposition to croquet doubtless would have been even more obdurate: "Our games serve to reflect the emotional alternations which are typical of the adolescent in the process of controlling and directing the rush of genital feelings: the quick change, for instance, from active to passive, from attack to defense, from feelings of omnipotence to those of lurid disaster. They reflect also the huge patience to be learned in our civilization for the attainment of propitious genital satisfaction. Thus,

the rather eccentric game of croquet provides for the strict hierophant a sado-masochistic alternation, now as the son prevented by the father from passing even one hoop." Stokes, A.: Psycho-analytic reflections on the development of ball games. *Int J Psychoanal, 37*:185, 1956, appearing herein, p. 387. See also Natan, A. [Ed.]: *Sport and Society*. London; Bowes & Bowes, 1958, p. 167.

12. Headington: *American Christian Rev.*, Sept. 24, 1878, quoted in Harrell, D. E.: A Decade of Disciples of Christ Social Thought, 1875-1885. M.A. thesis, Vanderbilt Univ., 1958, p. 193.
13. *Boston Congregationalist and Recorder,* July 26, Aug. 19, 1867; *N. Y. Churchman,* June 12, Aug. 21, 1875; *N. Y. Christian Advocate,* Mar. 10, 1898.
14. Mattison, H.: *Popular Amusements: An Appeal to Methodists.* New York, Carlton & Porter, 1869, p. 81.
15. Crane, J. T.: *Popular Amusements.* New York, Carlton & Lanahan, 1869, pp. 80-85; Hough, J. W.: *The Amusement Question.* Jackson, Mich., no pub., p. 5; Sargent, A. D.: Physico-medical education. *N. Y. Christian Advocate,* Aug. 13, 1885.
16. Frazier, E. L.: Base Ball. *Cincinnati Christian Standard,* Aug. 22, 1885; *Little Rock, Arkansas Baptist,* Sept. 10, 1891, quoted in English, C. D.: Ethical Emphases of the Editors of Baptist Journals Published in the Southeastern Region of the United States, 1865-1915. Th.D. thesis, So. Baptist Theological Seminary, 1948, p. 70.
17. *Richmond Religious Herald,* Feb. 25, 1897, quoted in Spain, R. B.: Attitudes and Reactions of Southern Baptists to Certain Problems of Society, 1865-1900. Ph.D. dissertation, Vanderbilt Univ., 1961, p. 327; Football once more. *Dallas, Tex. Christian Advocate,* Oct. 25, 1900; *Jackson, Miss. Baptist,* Jan. 8, 1903, quoted in English: ethical emphases, p. 96.
18. Krout, J. A.: Rise of American sport, in Krout: *American Themes.* New York, Columbia, 1963, p. 122.
19. *Philadelphia Presbyterian,* Mar. 28, 1885.
20. Northern Ohio roller-skating rink craze. *Philadelphia Presbyterian,* Feb. 28, 1885. See also Western New York prevailing crazes, *ibid.,* Mar. 14, 1885; Religion and skating, *ibid.,* Apr. 18, 1885; Garrison, James H.: Boston miscellany. *St. Louis Christian-Evangelist,* Mar. 26, 1885; The roller-skating rinks. *Nashville Christian Advocate,* Jan. 17, 1885.
21. Richardson, C. A.: *The Skating Rink.* Boston, W. L. Greene & Co., 1885; Buckley, J. M.: The roller-skating rink craze. *N. Y. Christian Advocate,* Jan. 8, July 23, 1885.
22. *N. Y. Christian Advocate,* July 7, 14, 21, 28, Aug. 4, 11, 1898.
23. *New Orleans Picayune,* reprinted in *Boston Congregationalist,* Aug. 4, 1898. But for a typical Northern Methodist attack on *Sunday* cycling, see *Western Christian Advocate,* quoted in Presbyterian, U. S. A. (Northern), *San Francisco Occident,* Oct. 19, 1898.
24. 10 U. S. Twelfth Census (1900), Pt. 4, p. 329.
25. Haultain, A.: Mystery of golf. *Atlantic Monthly, 94*:88, 1904.
26. Bryce, J.: America revisited: The changes of a quarter-century, Pt. 1. *Outlook,* Mar. 25, 1905.
27. Postal, B.: YMHA's and Jewish community centers, in Postal, Silver, J., and Silver, R.: *Encyclopedia of Jews in Sports.* New York, Bloch, in press.
28. Sport: A criticism. *Saint Louis Christian-Evangelist,* Oct. 31, 1901; Hawley, J. M.: The twentieth century Protestant outlook. *Methodist Review, 49*:317, 1900; McConnell, S. D.: Moral side of golf. *Outlook,* June 2, 1900; *Michigan Christian Advocate,* quoted in A Methodist bishop on amusements. *Literary Digest,* Aug. 24, 1907.
29. Football as a study. *Boston Congregationalist,* Nov. 24, 1908, including a Camp, W., article reprinted from *Yale Alumni Weekly;* Camp, W.: Honor in athletics. *Louisville Christian Observer,* Oct. 23, 1912; Mathewson, C.: Clean baseball, *ibid.,* Sept. 4, 1912, reprinted from *Boy Scouts Magazine*; What baseball men think of cigarettes. *Amethyst, 5*:8, 1914.
30. *Smith and Lamar's Classified Catalog of Books.* Nashville, Smith & Lamar, 1914, pp. 94-118; for Eliot quotation, see Meigs, J.: Some aspects of physical training and athletics for boys. *Philadelphia Sunday School Times,* July 28, 1900.
31. Burton, M. S.: Play: Effects of leisure time on personality and the Christian life. *Adult Leader, 5*:492, 1930; Cadwell, L. R.: Piety at play. *Chicago Baptist,* Sept. 7, 1929. In the

1920's and 30's both Northern and Southern Methodists and Northern Baptists published numerous books designed both to stimulate and to regulate Christian recreation. See especially Richardson, N. E.: *Church at Play*. New York, Abingdon Press, 1922.

32. *N. Y. Christian Advocate,* July 10, 1924.
33. Modern sport symbolized. *Sportsmanship, 1*:9, 1929; quoted in Cozens, F. W., and Stumpf, F. S.: *Sports in American Life,* Chicago, Univ. of Chicago, 1953, p. 104.
34. Frank, R. W.: Protestantism and play. *Social Progress, 26*:24, 26, 1935.
35. Atkinson, H. A.: *The Church and the People's Play.* Boston, Pilgrim Press, *c.* 1915, p. 28.
36. In order quoted: *Baptist Student, 3*:2-3, 1925; *ibid., 9*:12, 1930; *ibid., 5*:21, 1926; *ibid., 1: passim,* 1922; *ibid., 8*:7, 1930.
37. *Ibid., 1*:9, 1923; *ibid., 8*:24, 1929.
38. *Baptist Student, 4*: p. 4 of each of nine issues, Sept.-Oct. through June, 1925-26, and p. 5, June, 1926.
39. Hamill, K.: The record business — "it's murder." *Fortune, 63*:149-50, 1961.
40. Christians in sport. *Newsweek,* Sept. 3, 1956; Hero worship harnessed. *Sports Illustrated,* Feb. 6, 1956; Muscular boost for Christian doctrine. *Life,* Sept. 17, 1956; *Fellowship of Christian Athletes: Five-Year Report of a Dream Come True.* Kansas City, Mo., *c.* 1960; Shoemaker, S. M.: *Fellowship of Christian Athletes: Answer to America's Youth.* Kansas City, FCA reprint of sermon, 1959; Armstrong, R. S.: *More than Champions.* Kansas City, FCA reprint of article in *Presbyterian Life,* 1959.
41. Armstrong, R. S.: A movement, force and program, *Christian Athlete, 4*:5, 1961. See also *F.C.A. Summer Conference Guides,* Kansas City, Mo., 1961-64.
42. Professional athletes' retreat. *Christian Athlete, 7*:6-7, 1964; Carty, J. W.: Christian mission to athletes. *Saint Louis Christian-Evangelist,* Jan. 13, 1958; interview with band leader James W. "Knocky" Parker, 1963; *Lexington, Ky. Leader,* Mar. 30, 1966; *New Orleans Times-Picayune,* Apr. 8, 1966.
43. *Christian Athlete, 5*:10, 1962; *ibid., 5*:6-8, 1962; Bourland, R.: I pastor the Packers. *ibid., 6*:5-6, 1963; *ibid., 6*: cover, 11-12, 1963; *ibid., 6*:20, 1963; *ibid., 7*:7, 1964; *ibid., 8*:1, 1964.
44. *Time,* Nov. 17, 1961.
45. *Lexington, Ky. Herald-Leader,* Feb. 7, 1965.
46. Dietzel, P.: To be a champion in life. *Christian Athlete, 4*:10, 1961; F.C.A. personality you should know. *ibid., 6*:4, 1963; *ibid., 7*:5, 1964; Dietzel, P.: Football is my field. *Collegiate Challenge Mag., 3*:7, 1964; *New Orleans Times-Picayune,* Nov. 19, 1958.
47. Compare with Marciniak, R.: Your dressing room can also be your chapel. *Christian Athlete, 5*:8, 1962, which states that the University of Arizona football team was led in prayer both before and after each game.
48. Hoobing, B.: Stagg's contributions immense. *New Orleans States-Item,* Mar. 18, 1965.
49. *Denver Rocky Mountain Herald,* Sept. 10, 1955; Dec. 28, 1957. Used by permission of the author, Thomas Hornsby Ferril.
50. *Sports Illustrated,* May 10, 1965; *New Orleans Times-Picayune,* July 27, 1965. Fullman, R. B.: *The Popes on Youth.* New York, McKay, 1965, contains more than a dozen pronouncements on sports.
51. Kennedy, G. H.: The decline of the amateur. *N. Y. Christian Advocate,* Dec. 26, 1940; Russell, F.: 1963 Methodist . . . All-American elevens. *Together, 8*:29, 1964.
52. *Bulletin of Wheaton Coll., 1961-62.* Wheaton, 1961, pp. 11, 13; Wheaton Coll., 1860-1963. *Collegiate Challenge Mag., 2*:13, 1963; Wallace, W. E.: Beyond the horizons. *Lufkin, Tex. Gospel Guardian,* Mar. 17, 1960.
53. *Pentecostal Holiness Church Discipline.* Franklin Springs, Ga., 1961, p. 65; Long, A. M. [Ed.], *Franklin Springs Pentecostal Holiness Advocate*: to writer, July 1, 1964.
54. *Minutes of the 56th Annual Assembly of the Church of God of Prophecy.* Cleveland, Tennessee, 1961, p. 153.
55. *Awake,* Dec. 8, 1960.
56. Oswald, C. E.: History of Sports in the Mennonite Church of North America since 1900. M.S., in Ph.Ed. thesis, University of Illinois, 1956, pp. 52-62; Kephart, W. M.: *The Family, Society, and Individual.* Philadelphia, Houghton-Mifflin, 1961, p. 203; Newswanger, K. and C.: *Amishland.* New York, Hastings, 1954, pp. 9-10, 126.

PLAY AND THE SACRED

ROBERT E. NEALE

"PLAY" IS A TERM WHICH HAS BEEN applied to many of the affairs of nature, man and God. We speak of a piston rod playing in its cylinder, a fountain playing streams of water, the play of wind on fields of grain, and the play of otters who fashion slides out of mudbanks and slip on their backs into the water. We see ourselves as players of games and musical instruments, participants in love-play, and players of both ends against the middle. It has even been asserted that existence itself is the play of the gods and that to be in tune with these gods is to be in play. This essay responds to our obvious concern with the phenomenon of play by suggesting both a theory of play and a theory of religion as play.[1]

The basic premise is that man has a dualistic nature and is subject both to inner conflict and resolution of this conflict into inner harmony. The two poles of the duality are inherent urges toward sensation and organization.[2] There is a sensuous urge which drives us toward the concreteness of the moment of time and of the object of space, which enslaves us to the accidental. There is an organizational urge toward permanency and universality which seeks to maintain our personality in spite of change and diversity, to produce laws rather than accidents. By this urge, the permanent personhood of the individual is assured; but by following this urge alone, man is cut off from the material world and loses his personhood, becoming an abstract member of a species. It is possible to demonstrate that this dualism underlies both the instinctual theories of Freud and his division of personality into id and ego.[3]

Conflict between these two fundamental urges seems inevitable but not necessary. Conflict occurs because one or the other transgresses its own nature and ignores its limits. Harmony occurs when each accepts its limits and excites the other. Continued conflict leads to formation of the work self. The basic characteristic of this self is the tying up of energy in inner conflict. The two urges expend themselves in battle. Consequently, the individual experiences an absence of energy. What energy he does experience is used to try to resolve inner conflict; this activity may be defined as work. Thus, continued inner conflict leads to formation of a self devoted to psychological work.

The existence of continued harmony leads to formation of the play self. With inner conflict being resolved, the energy of both urges is freed and experienced as new power by the individual. Moreover, since conflict is eliminated, this energy need not be used for work, but for play. Play is defined as any activity not motivated by the need to resolve psychic conflict. It should be understood that such total conflict or harmony is a theoretical abstraction and not found in the concrete individual. Some harmony must be present in the work self, or it would not be motivated to continue existence. Some conflict must be present in the play self, or it would not be able to assure existence. While "All work and no play makes Jack a dull boy," it is equally true that "All play and no work makes no Jack." So the conflicted self differs in degree from the harmonious self, being ruled, however incompletely, by conflict, whereas the harmonious self is ruled, just as incompletely, by harmony.

Phenomenological descriptions of play abound in the literature.[4] It is sufficient here to suggest one fundamental outcome of the play self. This self participates in adventure. According to the dictionary, the noun "adventure" refers to happenings that are by chance, involve risk and are striking or remarkable in nature. These three elements are a part of any play activity. From the conscious point of view, play happens suddenly by chance. Its occurrence is an occasion for surprise and wonder. The adventures of King Arthur's knights, the adventures of Sherlock Holmes and the adventures of small boys all reveal the thrill of the unexpected. The factors of risk, hazard and danger are equally apparent; these are the sources of the basic suspense of play where there is no predictable outcome. Whether the contest is with oneself, as in learning to spin a top, with others, as in a game of soccer, or with nature, as in climbing a mountain, the results are uncertain and the play is challenging. Even in that form of play which is largely representational, as in the wearing of a mask or participation in a drama, there is the challenge of the attempt to reveal someone other than oneself with the risk of losing one's work identity. Also, the phenomenon of play is deemed remarkable by the participant. It is important to note that the player never loses consciousness of the fact that he is playing, always remaining aware of the difference between the two worlds. If this were not so, there could be no attitude of adventure, no sense of an unusual experience. Thus, to play is to participate in an event which takes place by chance, entails risk and is of remarkable purport: it is to have an adventure.

The attitude of adventure is a result of the harmony of the basic urges toward sensation and organization. In the world of conflict there can be no delight in chance, risk and striking events. The work of the conflicted self is so crucial that events must be made as normal as possible, the strategy carefully planned and the future predictable. Spontaneity, surprise and novelty upset the careful controls of the work self and produce the response of dread. Curiosity and experimentation are limited by reliance on the results of previous work and by fear of failing at something new. The attitude of adventure is quite different. The harmony of the urges provides confidence in the individual's inner and outer environments. Emboldened by trust, the shock of chance, fear of danger and suspicion of novelty are overcome. Moreover, success is not an issue. As countless observers have pointed out, what is crucial is to play the game and be a "good sport." The kite may become caught in and torn by a tree; in a formal contest, one side will usually lose; and in the climbing of a mountain, a life may be lost. The adventurer knows this full well. His trust is not in a naïve promise of successful outcome but in the value of an adventure for its own sake. Having found fulfillment in the harmony of the two urges, he has no need other than to allow them full play in adventure.

To claim that the attitude of the player is adventuresome is to say that he lives and communicates a narrative life. To play is to be an actor in a drama. The most developed form of the play attitude leads to participation in a story by listening, telling, or, at best, living the story. Whatever the mode of participation, the story is accepted as sufficient unto itself. It is not shrouded with morals and dogmas. It is not beseiged with such questions as "Is the story true?" "Is there only one story?" or "Who creates the story?" Nor is the story told to convince or convert someone to a particular point of view or to suggest a specific action. If such things occur, the story has fallen into the world of work and is no longer a true tale of adventure. The person who leads a narrative life and has a story to tell is ruled by the spirit of play and has no need to justify his adventures to himself or others.

The discussion thus far may be seen as both narrowing and broadening the application of the term "play" to human activities. Much of what is commonly known as play does not necessarily fit the definition at all, and much of what is not commonly associated with play may be exemplary. The remainder of this essay will serve to illustrate the point by considering the experience of the sacred and the religious, magical and profane responses to it.

Maturation of the individual allows for an increase in the breadth of play. The infant, if indeed he does play, is limited to activity with his body and the nipple of the breast which feeds him. As the child develops, play may come to involve other objects, feelings and thoughts. While it begins as a private activity, it may become "parallel" play and then group play with social rules. However, the early ways of play are not necessarily left behind, for the adult can return to the simple forms of a child's play or incorporate them into his more advanced play. It is useful to speak of partial play and full play. Full play for the infant is physical only; the adolescent whose play is only physical is only partially playing, for the other possibilities offered by maturation are absent. So the game of football may be closer to full play than the stunt of juggling three oranges if the individual has reached the adolescent stage of development. Full play is that which uses all the potentials offered at the particular developmental stage of the individual's growth.

Many discussions of play development end with the stage of adolescence and the addition of a few remarks to the effect that the adult also plays. The implicit suggestion is that the adult does not play very much, that his play is unimportant, and that when he does play, the activity is similar to that of the child. But the adolescent discovers new realms of human activity, the areas of sex, vocation and philosophy of life. These new possibilities are commonly seen as matters of work, but they present potentialities for play as well. There is no category of adult behavior that cannot be play as well as work; whatever can be experienced as conflict between the two basic urges can be experienced as resolution of conflict. The limiting of adult play to such activities as golf and amateur theatricals is artificial obscurantism. What is commonly understood as adult play is only partial play. Full adult play would include all the fundamental concerns of the mature human being. Obviously, such an experience is quite rare. The adult remains on the work level for the most part, and his entries into the world of play are partial, relating only to certain aspects of his life. But the ultimate experience of full play does occur. And when it does, although it is similar to all the partial experiences of play which have preceded it, it is of such greater breadth as to seem entirely different in nature. So it is no wonder that the participant responds in terms of religion.

The basic theory of religion as play concerns the definition of the sacred, religious, magical and profane. The sacred is defined as new energy, the religious as the appropriately playful response to the sacred, the magical as the inappropriate work response, and the profane as the world of work.

Perhaps the most fundamental characteristic of man's experience of the sacred is the awareness of power. The distinction between the sacred and the profane is commonly made in terms of the former's force, energy and urgency.[5] This understanding is in accord with the psychological theory of conflict and harmony, the transformation of conflict into harmony enabling the energy of the basic urges to appear suddenly for new activities. But it is the reaction to this experience which complicates understanding of the sacred. Man responds ambivalently to sacred power: on the one hand, the sacred appears as awful, an object of dread and horror; on the other, it appears as fascinating, an object of comfort, love and bliss.[6] Man responds to the sacred with both the negative taboo and the positive festival.

This fundamental ambivalence between awe and fascination is a result of man's psychic situation. The sacred is fascinating because its appearance is necessary for the psychological fulfillment of the individual. Equilibrium is the inherent goal of an organism, and in the human being this includes that psychic harmony which creates the potentiality for adventure. The desire for a play self is innate. But the ingrained longing for a new self is matched and frequently conquered by the fear of loss and desire to preserve the old and conflicted self. The sacred appears as awful for two reasons. First, the work self is dedicated to the goal of minimizing risk and fostering routine. Its basic reaction to new experience is anxiety, for the breaking up of rigidity appears as chaos to the individual. Second, the work self misinterprets the sacred. It does not know the active peace of harmony, but the inactive peace which is stalemate. It does not know the creativeness of pretending, but the pretensions which corrupt society. The conflicted self knows the perversions of play and can interpret the potentialities of the sacred only in this vein. Consequently, anything new is seen as more dangerous than what already is, and any possible change is construed as a change for the worse. Thus, the sacred is the experience of power which appears as fascinating to man because it is the sign of human fulfillment, and it almost inevitably appears as awful because it is interpreted profanely as the sign of human destruction.

Such a fundamental ambivalence toward the sacred cannot be maintained by the individual. The tension it creates is unbearable, and release must be found; there are three possible "solutions": entrance into sacred life in religion; flight into profane life in daily work; and mingling of sacred and profane life in magic.

When the response of fascination rules over awe, the individual fully surrenders his work self. As a religious man, he is a different person who lives in a different world, receiving a new name, and considered as being "not of this world." He becomes a player with the playtime and playspace of the play world. However, he does not forever abandon, but continually returns to, the work world. He returns to labor for those who know nothing but labor. The religious man alternates between play for its own sake and work for the sake of his fellowmen. Thus, in the religious response, there is full acceptance of sacred power and yet acknowledgment and consideration of the profane world. This is the only viable solution to ambivalence toward the sacred.

When the response of awe rules over fascination, the result is a retreat to the profane in an attempt to ignore and forget the sacred. For primitive man, the sacred is then experienced more as taboo than as festival. Modern man seems to have gained more facility in this attempt and has created such effective taboos on the sacred that one can refer to desacralization. Rather than merely limit the sacred, he has attempted to ignore it as completely as possible. It can be said that, contrary to the common assertion that religion is born out of fear, it is the profane life that is born out of fear — fear of the sacred.

It is important to realize that this "solution" to the problem of ambivalence cannot be successful. Just as primitive man's daily adherence to taboo was periodically broken into by the festival which energetically sanctioned the breaking of sacred prohibitions, so modern man is continually plagued by a religious response in spite of himself. No longer knowing that he fundamentally desires awareness and acceptance of the sacred, he falls into minor forms of worship. The modern adult tends to play as a child plays, racing speedboats and playing cards. The denial of the sacred is the denial of the opportunity for full play and the result is regression into partial play. Religion appears in an immature form, and the modern trend away from the sacred is matched by increased participation in leisure time activities. The conclusion is that fascination for the sacred is intrinsic to man and cannot be abolished. If the attempt is made to live profanely, the sacred will become manifest as religion, although in a partial and regressive form. As rare as the saint who fully plays is the one who leads a profane life which is not implicitly and partially a religious response to the sacred.

The third possible outcome of the initial ambivalence toward the sacred is the response of magic. This is the most common and yet least viable "solution," for it is the attempt to mingle the sacred and the profane. The ambivalence is maintained with fascination, preventing flight to the profane, and awe, preventing participation in religion. The only possible outcome is that profane use of sacred power which is magic. The magician can neither deny nor accept the power; he is compelled to work with it. But this mingling of the sacred and profane is impossible, for the two realms are antagonistic.[7] On the one hand, the profane may weaken and eventually destroy the energy of the sacred. Magical practices become profane routine which vaguely recall the sacred rite. On the other hand, the sacred may eventually destroy the profane world. The magical practices may reduce the organization of the society or individual to chaos. The magician is quite right to fear and protect himself against the sacred. He is exposed to the possibility of having his profane world destroyed and at the same time is incapable of allowing a new religious world to be created. To live in such a state has been known as damnation and is now known as mental illness. Magic is an attempt at an impossibility and must necessarily end in the chronic dying of profane man or in the cataclysmic death of psychosis. It is only the religious response to the sacred which recognizes the distinction and antagonism between the sacred and the profane and yet allows them to be complementary.

It should be noted that none of the three possible responses to the sacred is easily identifiable. He who is labeled by modern man as a primitive sorcerer might well be more concerned about sheer participation in the sacred than the attempt to manipulate it, and the seemingly religious person might well be devoutly intent on seizing divine power for his own use. Further, primitive man is no longer considered to have been completely captured by the magico-religious response as was once thought by historians of religion, and modern man is surely not so profane as he may like to imagine. Thus, an understanding of the basic dynamics of play and work as revealed in the sacred and the profane is not sufficient for analyzing specific responses.

The sacred is rarely experienced purely as power but usually appears as a powerful form. In the phrase of Schiller, the sacred is "living form."[8] To explore the meaning of the religious, the magical and the profane more concretely, the understanding of play as the living form of adventure can be used. Religious tradition acknowledges the role of adventure in terms of myth. The sacred is the world of the story, and the profane is the world without a story. A story has a beginning and an end, and the two are always related. A story is, by definition, significant; for significance to a human being is precisely the awareness of beginnings and endings and the relations between them. The conflicted world of the profane is without a beginning or an end, consisting only of disconnected, unending events. Primitive man describes it as chaos. The best possible response to it is to attempt to routinize it. It is only in play that a story emerges which eliminates the chaos by revealing the source and future and, therefore, the identity of the individual. The sacred prompts anticipation of adventure, and the profane elicits the retreat to routine.

Since it can be said that the sacred is never manifest as pure power but always as a powerful story, man has no choice but to respond to the story in terms of the religious, the magical or the profane. Of the many elements pertaining to these responses, one of the most illuminating concerns the term "believe." The theory is that the religious response is that of make-believe, the magical response that of belief, and the profane response that of disbelief.

The religious response to the sacred is complete acceptance, that is, a primal recognition that something has happened. The mythical story is neither doubted nor buttressed by belief simply because it is there. To judge is to stand outside of the story in the profane world, and this is precisely what the religious person does not do. Perhaps even the term "make-believe" is inadequate and reflects the point of view of the outsider. The player is not really making-believe or deliberately making anything. He is simply participating in a story, and nothing else is required. Questions of truth and falsity remain irrelevant. Unless belief and disbelief are transcended, the life of adventure in the partial play of the immature or the full play of the religious adult does not occur.

It follows from the above conclusion that when an individual becomes concerned about the validity of a story, he has entered into the realm of the profane. The magical mingling of the sacred and the profane issues in the promotion of belief. Belief is the acknowledgment of the sacred for the sake of the profane, a work reaction to the manifestation of new energy. The statement "I believe" is always incomplete. One always believes "because." So the primitive magician affirms, "If I pronounce the sacred words over the sacred animal, I will catch my fish"; and the modern magician states, "If I say my prayers, I will receive strength for tomorrow." Even such seemingly benign statements as "I believe because of what God has done for me," or "I believe because I have received meaning for my life," represent the attempt to make the sacred useful for profane life. Consquently, the call to believe is usually accompanied by promise of benefit or threat of harm, and these promises and threats refer to the struggles of profane living. The magician is a pragmatist who believes the sacred story is true because it works. Thus, belief is the result of an inappropriate work response to what offers the potentiality for play. The sacred is purposeless, and the attempt to use it is antireligious.

The profane response to myth is disbelief. Whereas belief is the conviction that the individual can receive what he desires, disbelief is the acknowledgment that this is impossible. This can occur in two circumstances. First, the profane individual may actually hear the pure myth. In such an event, no promises are given, so the worker hears nothing which will assist him. Moreover, since the sacred appears threatening to the profane world, he may conclude that the myth not only fails to aid his struggles but even interrupts and destroys them. There is no choice but to disbelieve as emphatically as possible. Second, the worker may hear more concerning dogmas and creeds than about the story itself. On the one hand, he may practice them to attain what he desires and fail, so he disbelieves because the story does not work for him. On the other hand, he may correctly realize that the dogmas and creeds really have nothing to do with the profane world and respond by ignoring them. Thus, there is a similarity between the religious and profane responses, for it is only the magician who believes that myth will work in the profane world. The distinction between the two is that the one reacts negatively and the other positively. The magical person tries to make myth effective in daily life, the profane person unhappily accepts this as impossible, and the religious person rejoices in myth for its own sake.

This paper, while presented as a summary and not as a fully developed theory of play and the sacred, may be sufficient to indicate new ways of looking at traditional problems. For example, the Christian church has frequently criticized the leisure time activities of society. This is reasonable because such activities may be only profane work, a magical use of the sacred, or at best, immature religion. However, the modern gamester or sportsman may reply that immature religion is better than no religion, for the church is comprised of profane social routines and magical rites, manifesting an almost complete lack of the spirit of play. Consequently, the task of the church should be to encourage play on all levels. The task of the average person should be to continue his true playing and to allow the spirit of play to enter into all areas of his adult life. Thus the church may assist the culture and the culture assist the church, so that the idolatrous attachment to the work would be diminished and the playful response to the sacred be enhanced.

"It's jerks like you, Gessler, that knock all the fun out of sports like archery!"

FOOTNOTES

1. For an expanded discussion of the theories, see Neale, R. E.: *Play and the Sacred: Toward a Theory of Religion as Play*. New York, Union Theological Seminary, unpub. dissertation, 1964. For representative theories of play, see Alexander, F.: A contribution to the theory of play. *Psychoanal Quart, 27*:175, 1958; Appleton, L. E.: *A Comparative Study*

of the Play Activities of Adult Savages and Civilized Children. Chicago, Univ. of Chicago, 1910; Caillois, R.: *Man, Play, and Games,* trans. by Barash, M. New York, Free Press of Glencoe, 1961; Erikson, E. H.: *Childhood and Society.* New York, Norton, 1950; Freud, S.: The relation of the poet to daydreaming, trans. by Grant Duff, I. F., *Delusion and Dream and Other Essays,* Rieff, P. [ed.], Boston, Beacon, 1956, pp. 122-33; Freud, S.: *Beyond the Pleasure Principle,* trans. by Strachey, J. New York, Bantam, 1959; Groos, K.: *The Play of Animals,* trans. by Baldwin, E. L., New York, D. Appleton, 1898; Groos, K.: *The Play of Man,* trans. by Baldwin, E. L., New York, D. Appleton, 1901; Hall, G. S.: *Youth: Its Education, Regimen, and Hygiene.* New York, D. Appleton, 1907; Hendrick, I.: Work and the pleasure principle. *Psychoanal Quart, 12*:311, 1943; Lantos, B.: Metapsychological considerations on the concept of work. *Int J Psychoanal, 33*:439, 1952; McDougall, W.: *An Introduction to Social Psychology.* Boston, Luce, John W., 1926; Patrick, G. T. W.: *The Psychology of Relaxation.* Boston & New York, Houghton-Mifflin, 1916; Piaget, J.: *Play, Dreams and Imitation in Childhood,* trans. Gattengo, C., and Hodgson, F. M. New York, Norton, 1962; von Schiller, J. C. F.: Letters upon the aesthetic education of man. *Literary and Philosophical Essays, The Harvard Classics,* Volume 32, Eliot, G. W. [Ed.]. New York, P. F. Collier & Son, 1910, pp. 221-313; Spencer, H.: *The Principles of Psychology,* 2 Vols. New York, D. Appleton 1873; Waelder, R.: The psychoanalytic theory of play, trans. by Bennett, S. A. *Psychoanal Quart, 2*:208, 1933.

For representative theories of religion and play, see Brown, N. O.: *Life Against Death: The Psychoanalytical Meaning of History.* New York, Vintage, Knopf, Random, 1961; Caillois, R.: *Man and the Sacred,* trans. by Barash, M. Glencoe, Free Press, 1959; Huizinga, J.: *Homo Ludens: A Study of the Play-Element in Culture.* Boston, Beacon, 1955; Schorsch, R. S.: *The Psychology of Play.* Notre Dame, U of Notre Dame, 1942.

2. See von Schiller, J. C. F.: Letters upon the aesthetic education of man. *Literary and Philosophical Essays, The Harvard Classics,* Volume 32, Eliot, C. W. [Ed.]. New York, P. F. Collier & Son, 1910.
3. See Neale, R. E.: *Play and the Sacred: Toward a Theory of Religion as Play.* New York, Union Theological Seminary, unpub. dissertation, 1964.
4. See Caillois, R.: *Man and the Sacred,* trans. by Barash, M. Glencoe, Free Press, 1959; Groos, K.: *The Play of Man,* trans. by Baldwin, E. L. New York, D. Appleton, 1901; Huizinga, J.: *Homo Ludens: A Study of the Play-Element in Culture.* Boston, Beacon, 1955; Schorsch, R. S.: *The Psychology of Play.* Notre Dame, U of Notre Dame, 1942.
5. See Caillois, R.: *Man and the Sacred;* Eliade, M.: *Patterns in Comparative Religion: A Study of the Element of the Sacred in the History of Religious Phenomena,* trans. by Sheed, R. New York, Sheed & Ward, 1958; Otto, R.: *The Idea of the Holy: An Inquiry into the Non-rational Factor in the Idea of the Divine and Its Relation to the Rational,* 2d ed., trans, by Harvey, J. W. London, Oxford, 1950; Van Der Leeuw, G.: *Religion in Essence and Manifestation,* 2 vols., trans. by Turner, J. E. New York, Harper Torchbooks, Harper, 1963.
6. *Supra.*
7. Caillois, R.: *Man and the Sacred.*
8. von Schiller, J. C. F.: *op. cit. supra* note 2.

PART THREE
SPORTS, GAME PLAYING AND HUMANKIND

INTRODUCTION

THE HUSTLING, EVER BUSY American in a work-conscious and work-oriented society is an almost cliché representation of America. But there is an "other America." Work and play are related ("people who work hard need and deserve relaxation"), and indeed one may make out a strong case that the dominant principle of American life is play. Historians are apt to forget this, as Sir Arnold Lunn points out in his book *The Story of Ski-ing*: "The historian is apt to forget that sport in some form or another is the main object of most lives, that most men work in order to play, and that games which bulk so largely in the life of the individual cannot be neglected in studying the life of the nation."[1]

Americans have been enthusiastic about sports since the 1890's, and in the mid-twentieth century, sport in America and throughout the world is assuming far more importance than it has before. The World Series of 1964 tied the 1960 election for the largest audience ever to be attracted to a television show.

Sport touches life at many points — different patterns of sport are related to different levels of economic development. Robert Boyle in his recent book *Sport — Mirror of American Life* observes that "sport permeates any number of levels of contemporary society, and it touches upon and deeply influences such disparate elements as status, race relations, business life, automotive design, clothing styles, the concept of the hero, language, and ethical values. For better or worse, it gives form and substance to much in American life."[2]

Sports provide an insight into a nation's basic attitudes. A generation ago, A. A. Brill, one of Sigmund Freud's enthusiastic disciples in America, observed: "That the contestant in a game or sport can forego an accidental advantage and the spectators cheer him for it — that the loser can smile and congratulate his vanquisher — these are among the major achievements of the human race."[3] Fairness and playing by the rules have always been regarded as basic elements of sports, and they set the model for other activities in the life of man. For example, when law enforcement is carried out according to humane rules, the system is called the "sporting theory of justice"; when the rules are not observed, it is persecution. The adversary system on which U.S. trials are based is a legal contest — it is often called a game, a battle carried out under civilized rules, and these is a winner and a loser. In theory, if the system is working well, the winner more often than not closely approximates the proper party. James Reston of the New York *Times* suggests that politics too could learn something from sports. He says: "On the baseball diamond, a foul ball is a foul ball and no argument, or anyway not much. Stealing is legal in baseball, and if you're caught you're out. Hits are rewarded; errors and wild pitches are punished, and a man's record means something specific. Maybe politics has something to learn from sports."[4]

In his paper on "Sports and Contemporary Man,"[5] Simon Wenkart points out that man has always attempted to counter the forces of gravity; to rid himself of the weight of his body; to master his medium, whatever it may be; to experience his body and extend its efficiency by the use of various tools; to develop muscular prowess, dexterity and physical fitness — a matter of strength, coordination and integration, both physical and emotional. On a deeper level, sports may help to build up a person's self-confidence, to gratify his desire for achievement, to develop his ability to share instead of being isolated. Conversely, spectator sports exemplify participation by derived involvement and also a means of identification. Sports may be an expression of neurotic needs — to outdo everyone else, to assert and prove oneself. Not infrequently they serve as expression for aggressive impulses against society or an imagined foe. On the other hand, sports may be a truly existential experience taking place in time and space and giving the individual the feeling of being-in-the-world. Wenkart in his paper tries to illuminate a myriad of facets that underlie motivation in sports from a historical, ontogenetic, phylogenetic, emotional and intellectual point of view. The goal may be physical perfection or the urge to become the standard bearer of one's country, as in the Olympic games, or it may be a wish for self-aggrandizement at the expense of others. The crucial problem is whether sports are being used as a hazard or a boon in the furtherance of physical fitness and mental health.

In this volume Margaret N. Sidney writes about dancing,[6] which is one of the most popular forms of active recreation, though it is not usually thought of as a sport. However, a closer look shows it to be a game based upon primitive instincts (the ballet evolved out of fencing); and it is socially useful, like all of the major sports. The arts constitute the highest form of play, but of course there are primitive and aggressive uses of music and ways of dancing.[7] Edward Greenwood, a member of the staff of the Menninger Foundation, has said:[8]

> Dancing is an art as old as man himself. Through this highly adaptable medium, one can express widely variable feelings and meanings. The earliest dances perhaps reflected the simple rhythmics of Nature; unable to propound a theory which would satisfy his eagerness to understand the mechanisms of life, primitive man may have sought to re-enact similar rhythmical schemes. With his

> dancing he appealed to his gods, by movement imitative of those things which he desired. He prayed for rain, good crops and safety by dancing; he also gave thanks at the time of birth, marriage and victory, by dancing; he gave up his dead with dancing. Dancing was a part of his daily life, like eating and sleeping. Down through the ages, the dance has continued to express many things; sheer physical exuberance, sexual attraction, religious consecration; simple joy at the times of birth, marriage and victory. . . . In modern times there has been an evolutionary series of more individualized dancing. . . . At the present, dancing, for many, has fallen into a rather idle shuffling of feet to music, or energetic jitterbug antics which serve some complex usefulness for the younger set.

Sense of movement is inherent in every human activity. The arts of movement are the foundation for the learning which takes place under the broad heading of "physical education." The program of instruction in this field is ordinarily centered around individual and team sports and gymnastic activities, with the dance being at most one among many options. Margaret Sidney says that the basic motivation for dance is our need for rhythm and our response to it. The grace and joy of body movement, expressed in sports of all types, finds its epitome in dancing.

Dance itself may be most simply defined as rhythmic movement that is not work; the rhythmic movement is a necessary part of life. It expresses and communicates feelings, but at the same time it can create and intensify feelings and profoundly affect and alter the emotions and physical condition of the dancer. Dancing is a sort of oil for the human machine. In highly civilized societies, more primitive movements are constantly imported to relieve the tension that people feel from the necessary restraints of living together. Dancing is a natural means of expression for both the aggressive and the cooperative components in human nature, satisfying our need to be individuals and our need to be part of a group, our competitive desire to excel and our striving for social approval.

Dance is also a means of expressing and controlling erotic desires and is used by society to teach its approved attitudes and behavior between the sexes. The conventions of the dance floor mirror the surrounding culture.[9] Social or ballroom dancing is the modernized "game of courtship" and stands in the same connection to intersexual relations and family life (and the family side of community life) as team sports do to the relations between individuals in the competitive, acquisitive "outside" world. Both give opportunity for the expression of energy and emotion largely repressed in civilized living, and both train the individual in acceptable attitudes and behavior.

Part of the present boom in dancing in the United States is due to financial interests that have discovered that dance is a money-maker. However, people do seem to be getting what they pay for — dancing does make them happier at the same time that it makes billions for industry. Adolescents are taken by rock 'n' roll: "This music makes us go." "It's not music to listen to — it's to move by." Dancing is more varied and popular than ever, but people still dance for the same old reasons — to feel the joy of rhythmic movement, to express feeling, to promote courtship and sociability, and, at the prereason level, to integrate the individual with himself, his fellow man and the eternal. It is a path to ecstasy.

John L. Schimel, author of "Sports Games and Love" in this volume,[10] advised the Editors in the preliminary planning stages of the volume that "you have left out of the oldest, noblest, grandest, most engrossing and engaging sports known to man, a sport that has involved the best talents, energies and fortunes of mankind since recorded history, namely, the sport, art or game of WAR. Many of the sports you cover are certainly subsidiary or preparatory for this sport. I think it is a tribute to your goodness that you have overlooked this key human sport. I believe it is also undemocratic to look at war as anything but a horror and something to be prevented. Nevertheless, I suspect you might be neglecting an important area, maybe a central tie, if you do not deal with this subject."[11]

Schimel may be absolutely right in calling war a sport, or in terming many sports as preparatory for war. Huizinga says, "Ever since words existed for fighting and playing, men have been wont to call war a game."[12] Bill Maudlin, famous World War II cartoonist, has called war "man's most ancient and robust sport." The Duke of Wellington declared that the Battle of Waterloo was won on the playing fields of Eton. When General MacArthur was superintendent of the U.S. Military Academy at West Point, he had inscribed over the gates of the stadium: "On the Fields of Friendly Strife Are Sown the Seeds that on Other Days and Other Fields Will Bear the Fruits of Victory."[13] In ancient days, the Olympian games were held every four years (starting about 776 B.C.), and during the games a truce was observed and warfare was suspended. Greek mythology seems to claim that the contests began as religious celebrations and games in commemoration of Zeus' having defeated Kronos in a mighty wrestling match of the gods for possession of the earth. At first only pure Greeks could compete in the games. Running with full military equipment, including shields, and jumping were features of the earlier games. Today, however, the world looks to peace and cooperation and "good will to man" through the Olympic games. Adrian Stokes, in his paper in this volume, sees games as a substitute for warfare.[10]

It is interesting to note that, assigned the subject of love games, Schimel was reminded about warfare. Hemingway in *The Sun Also Rises* presents an interplay between sex and sport, in *To Have and Have Not,* one between sex and crime; and it may be said that in Hemingway's vision, war is a climactic experience that is the combination of sport and crime.[15] Nearly two thousand years ago, Ovid in his *Art of Love* sensed the similarity between love and warfare. He said:[16]

> Aye, believe me, Atticus, every lover is a soldier. The age which suiteth war is also favorable to Venus. A fig for an elderly soldier! A fig for an elderly lover! The age which generals demand in a brave soldier is the age which a fair young woman demands in the possessor of her charms. Soldier and lover have, each, their vigil to keep; both couch upon the hard ground; both have their watch to keep, the one at the door of his mistress, the other at the door of his general. What a weary way the soldier hath to march! And the lover, when his mistress is exiled, will follow her, with a stout heart, to the uttermost limits of the world. He will fare over the loftiest mountains and over rivers swollen with rains; he will cleave his way through the snowdrifts. Is he compelled to cross the seas? He will not plead that the tempests are let loose; nor will he wait till the weather be propitious for setting sail. Who but a soldier or a lover will brave the chill nights and the torrents of mingled snow and rain? The one is sent forward as a scout towards the enemy; the other keepeth watch upon his rival as upon a foe. The one lays seige to warlike cities, the other to the dwelling of his inexorable mistress. One beats down gates, the other doors.
>
> Oftentimes it hath brought victory to catch the foe asleep, and to slaughter, sword in hand, an unarmed host. Thus did the fierce battalions of Thracian Rhesus fall and you, ye captured steeds, forsook your lord. So, too, a lover oft is able to profit by the husband's slumbers and to turn his arms against the sleeping foe. To elude the vigilance of watchmen and sentinels is ever the perilous task alike of the soldier and the lover.
>
> Mars is uncertain and in Venus there is nothing sure. The conquered rise up again, and those you would deem could never be o'erthrown, fall in their turn. . . .
>
> Love is like warfare. "Faint heart never won fair lady"; poltroons are useless in Love's service. The night, winter, long marches, cruel suffering, painful toil, all these things have to be borned by those who fight in Love's campaigns. Apollo, when he tended the herds of Admetus, dwelt, so 'tis said, in a humble cottage. Who would blush to do as Apollo did? If you would love long and well, you must put away pride. If the ordinary, safe route to your mistress is denied you, if her door is shut against you, climb up on to the roof and let yourself down by the chimney, or the skylight. How it will please her to know the risks you've run for her sake!

Naked aggression may be expressed in some sports (e.g., boxing),[17] but so much here for warfare. In this section of the volume, we concentrate on the sport of love, i.e., erotized aggression.

The Olympics may have started in Greece in the service of war, but today the great "sport" in Greece (and around the world) is sitting outside a coffee shop or on university steps watching all the pretty girls go by. Boy chasing girl (or the other way round) is often called man's favorite sport.[18] One individual has quipped that while announcement of a first marriage may belong on the society page, the announcement of subsequent marriages ought to appear on the sports page. Jacques Casanova, the renowned indoor sportsman, made love to women as a gymnast does his daily exercises. Box-scores or census figures are not kept today, but statistically-inclined Casanovists have counted 116 romances in his *Memoirs.* To some women he was the Knight of the Golden Swindle, but to others he was Prince Charming and Fairy Godfather.

The related subject (related to everything) that is not included in this volume is game theory. This is a highly technical mathematical concept, the implications of which are profoundly influencing the field of psychiatry and many others, including warfare. It is implicit in Nobert Wiener's work on cybernetics and in the work of Ruesch, Sullivan and, more recently, Bateson, Haley, Masserman, Spiegel and Jackson.[19] Military-technological theorists (Herman Kahn, Henry Kissinger, Edward Teller, Walter Marseille, T. C. Schelling and others) attempt to apply "game theory" to the problem of nuclear war. A so-called "Rand Hymn," an anti-Rand folksong by a San Francisco writer, Malvina Reynolds, concludes:

> Oh, the Rand corporation is the boon of the world.
> They think all day long for a fee.
> They sit and play games about going up in flames.
> For counters, they use you and me,
> Honey Bee,
> For counters, they use you and me.

The theory of games is enjoying special fashion these days in the social sciences. Eric Berne has used somewhat crude models of transactional systems based consciously or otherwise on game theory and related theories, such as the various system theories. When someone creates a commonplace social disturbance in order to gain some secret relief or satisfaction, Berne calls it a game. In his popular book *Games People Play,* Berne sketches 101 games, jassily named "Kick me," "If It Weren't For You," "I'm Only Trying to Help You," "You're Uncommonly Perceptive," "Wooden Leg," "Schlemiel," "Let's Pull a Fast One on Joey." Berne pays homage to Stephen Potter (Gamesmanship, Lifemanship, etc.) as a pioneer in the field.[20]

Thomas Szasz in *The Ethics of Psychoanalysis* compares psychoanalysis to contract bridge:[21]

> Bridge and psychoanalysis are two-phase games. In each, the players have a proximal and a distal goal, the former being a means to the latter. In each, the character of the first period of the game – bidding bridge and the trial period in psychotherapy – will depend on whether bridge is auction or contract and whether psychotherapy is psychodynamic or autonomous. . . . If an agreement can be reached, there will be a contract and hence commitment to a pure common-interest game. . . . Overbidding is severely penalized . . . underbidding is also costly. . . . If the contract has been correctly negotiated, that is, if the bidding was proper, a competent player can usually fulfill it.

Even before "game theory," of course, contests of every type furnished metaphors for the disclosure of virtue and vice in human affairs, and present game theory likewise may be an effective device in some cases for describing human entanglements; but Berne and Szasz apparently have gone overboard and have fallen captive to the analogy. Leaving aside the repugnance one may feel to the semantics employed, to say that a homosexual is playing a game is perhaps to lose sight of the individual's psychic conflict and to ignore his suffering.[22] Games are a reflection of the human condition, its contests and struggles, and not vice versa — that is to say, the human condition is not a reflection of games, as some game theorists seem to postulate.

Moreover, serious objections to their logic arise in the assumptions that are made. For example, military-technological theorist Kissinger wrote of an explicit assumption that "the opponent must be rational, i.e., he must respond to his self-interest in a manner which is predictable," to allow one to use logic or game theory. If such an assumption is necessary, it lifts the remainder of the arguments out of the realm of logic. Computer techniques may be flawless, but nothing ever comes out of mathematics that is any more reliable than that which was put in as assumptions and raw data. The musical revue, *"Oh, What a Lovely War,"* a satire on World War I, notes: "In 1960 an American military team fed all the facts of World War I into the computers they used to plan World War III. They reached the conclusion that the 1914-18 war was impossible and couldn't have happened. There could not have been so many blunders nor so many casualties."

Probably the most sophisticated adventurer working in the field of systems theory in psychiatry is Kenneth Mark Colby, who is a mathematician as well as a psychoanalyst. His most recent work has been computerizing patient models. John Schimel's paper in this volume is in part at least based on this concept.[23]

As Schimel reminds us, Arthur Miller has suggested that a great play cannot concern itself solely with the problems of the bed or living room. A theme of broader significance must be exposed. Our bed and living rooms echo and even resound to the furor of transcendental issues being knocked about. There is little genuine pleasure in the fleshpots. Such simple marital exercises as sexual intercourse and its timing and outcome embody, exemplify or violate such sacred tenets as equality and dignity, not to mention success and failure. The examination and reporting of such data ineluctably lead to the satirical. Nevertheless, there is much genuine suffering in the interpersonal pleasures of the privileged.

The inner clash is no less resounding. The hedonic urge is stimulated and encouraged as is its contrary, the moral ascetic. The result is a compromise — the resolve to be earnest and do a good job in pleasurable activities. The earnest lover is a contradiction in terms. Such contradictions tend to take the sport out of sport, gaming out of games and laughter out of love.

Schimel says that the modern psychiatrist is hedonistically oriented. His empirical knowledge is necessarily opposed to the weight of the older moral imperatives. He observes that perfectionists are migranous; the righteous suffer ulcers; art is despairing; the Good Man is gloomy; but happy children are curious and learn. He longs for a more compassionate morality.

Machiel Zeegers in his study of the "swindler as a player" brings us into contact with fundamental human problems.[24] The swindler's behavior, he points out, has many characteristics similar to those of the play sphere. Play takes place in a world of concrete objects which are used as playthings. These things have a symbolic function for the swindler. He attempts to be something by that which he possesses and portrays. He is induced by his objects of play and by the victim's behavior toward him.

The swindler is a false-player, a cheat – he only pretends to be playing. He also is a spoilsport, not respecting his part in social role-playing. Yet he is a player. He is bent on proving himself superior; he is out for escape and revenge. Even his hostile and aggressive conduct shows play elements, though it be play in deterioration. The swindler's victim has to some extent the same features. In fact, all men have something in common with the swindler, for in his playing way of existence the swindler reflects general human problems.

At all times the swindler remains an ambiguous figure, attracting us because he reflects human problems and because he shows fascinating solutions. The swindler is worshiped as a hero and a god in mythology. In literature and in history, fraud and deception are frequently dealt with as ever-fascinating phenomena.

We can identify with the swindler in many respects. This is why he can always find his victims and why he can be sure of some kind of sympathy. But at all times we recognize in him the other, the hostile element. His existence shows man's wealth as well as man's void, his possibilities of transcendence and of deterioration, the expectation of salvation and its unattainability.

FOOTNOTES

1. Lunn, A. H. M.: *The Story of Ski-ing*. Toronto, Collins 1952.
2. Boyle, R. H.: *Sport—Mirror of American Life*. Boston, Little, 1963. See also Menninger, K.: Human needs in urban society. *Architectural Record,* July 1959, p. 197; Spectators and sports. *This Week,* November 15, 1964. "Nobody in America has really analyzed the positive effects of sports on the remarkable growth and development of state university education in America. No doubt state university sport has been professionalized and corrupted, but it has produced football teams which have become symbols of state pride. It has kept the alumni in touch with the university. More important it has held the interest and the allegiance of legislators in the state capitols, and has in the process helped produce educational appropriations for all these land-grant institutions on a scale that would never have been possible without the attraction and the pride engendered by these sporting events at the universities on autumn Saturday afternoons." Sports: Therapy with our fun. *New York Times News Service,* October 10, 1966.

3. *North American Review,* October 1929.
4. Reston, J.: Politics could use some rough umpires. *New York Times News Service,* September 23, 1964.
5. P. 171.
6. P. 184.
7. Karl Menninger says that dancing, art and music are the most refined and stylized forms of play. He writes: "These modalities have both active and passive aspects. One can enjoy them by participation or by seeing or hearing them. That they constitute play in the sense that they enable people to live out unsatisfied, instinctual urges in a way not hampered or restricted by reality considerations is obvious. . . . We ought [also] to consider the pleasure derived from smooth, rapid movement through space such as is experienced in skating, skiing, tobogganing, airplaning and even automobiling. . . . I suspect that some of them, such as skating, combine elements of erotic pleasure with athletic satisfactions related to the pleasure of activity and a sense of power in the overcoming of gravity, air resistance, etc. There are also, of course, the elements of novelty and rhythm. Some psychoanalysts have emphasized the relationship of these pleasures to the pleasures obtained earlier by the child in being carried or moved by his parents in a way vastly transcending his own feeble powers of locomotion.

   "As for the idea that sublimations represent the fate of certain highly transformed aggressive impulses, we must admit quite frankly that the aggressive element in art and in the forms of sport I have just mentioned is usually difficult to recognize, the erotic (creative) elements greatly predominating. This is why I have postulated that the arts must constitute the highest form of play." Menninger, K.: *Love Against Hate.* New York, Harcourt, 1942, pp. 183-4.
8. Greenwood, E.: Dancing. *Bull Menninger Clin, 6:*78, 1942.
9. Recreational dancing, for example, shows the changes in contemporary American culture. Particularly, the new equality between men and women shows in the popularity of "free" dances — like the twist, in which the man is not the obvious leader. In her paper Margaret Sidney explores the influence of Negro culture, where there is no "subjection of women," such as there has been for centuries in European culture. The tendency in upper-class American conservative culture to prefer couple dances where the man obviously protects and leads may be based upon a desire to cling to male dominance.

   Margaret Mead once said that a major problem of civilized societies is to convince the young male that it is worthwhile to give up his freedom for family life. And it would seem that the dependence of women builds up the male ego and makes men more responsible. Perhaps the dance preferences in different strata of society reflect this.

   Spanish dancing (really stemming from Gypsy culture) is very popular today (José Greco and his dance group make more money than any other independent dance performer), and might point the way to a solution of the relative position of the sexes. Spanish dancing represents the sexes as different and independent. It gives full expression to feeling but always with superb control and integrity, a most moving expression of individuality in creative cooperation.
10. P. 204.
11. Personal communication.
12. Huizinga, J.: *Homo Ludens.* Boston, Beacon, 1955.
13. Toward the game of life. *Kansas City Star,* June 28, 1964.
14. P. 387. See also comments in Boyle, R. H.: *op cit. supra* note 2, at p. 76.
15. Jovanovich, W.: Sex, crime, and, to a lesser extent, sports. *Saturday Review,* July 18, 1964, p. 14.
16. Ovid: *Art of Love.* New York, Grosset & Dunlap, Inc. (Universal Library).
17. Coach Vince Lombardi of the Green Bay Packers recently commented that "football is becoming the dominant sport in the United States because it is a game of violence. Football is a game of violence, and people like violence." But he added, "There is nothing wrong with violence if it is controlled." AP News-release, July 12, 1966. See Team Sports, *infra* at part 8, p. 373.

18. Recall, e.g., the recent Howard Hawks' film, *Man's Favorite Sport?,* starring Rock Hudson. "Girls are good at it too," a subtitle added.
19. See Wiener, N.: *Cybernetics.* 2nd Ed. Cambridge, M.I.T., 1961.
20. Berne, E.: *Games People Play.* New York, Grove, 1964. Quite rightly, Berne points out that every person is actually three — child, adult and parent. Whenever you relate to someone, you may be relating to the child, adult or parent aspect of him. Thus, in a room of eight people, there are actually twenty-four persons present, and Berne says, it is important to recognize the stance that is taken. Persons can communicate only when they interrelate on parallel lines. These aspects are ego states, and are not to be confused with Freud's conception of id, ego and superego. Berne's book, *Games People Play,* explains in popular language the stance that people may take, and his book has been on the best seller list for over a year. He maintains that humor is an appropriate attitude in psychotherapy. It need not be solemn (like a courtroom hearing), but as might be expected, his contention has alienated many solemn psychotherapists. However, with his ironic humor, Berne teases, and one may wonder what game he is playing on the public.
21. Szasz, T. S.: *The Ethics of Psychoanalysis.* New York, Basic Books, p. 125.
22. See Farber, L. H.: Psychoanalysis and morality. *Commentary,* November 1965, p. 69.
23. P. 204. See also Schimel, J.: Parents vs. children. *Redbook,* August, 1966, p. 46.
24. P. 219.

SPORTS AND CONTEMPORARY MAN

SIMON WENKART

"WHAT A PIECE OF WORK IS MAN!" exclaimed Hamlet.[1] "How noble in reason; how infinite in faculty! in form and moving how express and admirable! in action how like an angel! in apprehension how like a god!" These words came vividly to mind some time ago as I gazed at the "Discus Thrower" in the Vatican and later admired the "Wrestlers" in Florence. Both statues are striking examples of the consummate skill of the artist in giving shape to the absolute in beauty and capturing high moments of action in sport. Sports have always had momentous significance for man and have served as a source of great inspiration.

Let us examine what has made sports so meaningful to humankind. Man's first struggle was to defend himself against the dangers of his environment and the vicissitudes of life. Self-defense against wild animals, inclement weather and dearth of the means of sustenance posed a tremendous dilemma. Physical fitness and mental adaptation were certainly the primary prerequisites for meeting that challenge.

Down through the ages these two basic premises, so vital for man's survival, have been developed and refined to the point where they can be used not only to prevent danger but also to afford pleasure. When it became possible for man to set aside some time for play, sports were developed and became a rich source of enjoyment. Thus the culmination of physical fitness and mental health has found expression in the pursuit of athletic activity.

The history of sports mirrors the historical development of a nation and bears witness to the contemporaneous image of man in regard to his body as well as to his position in the world.[2] Greek mythology offers keen insight into the Hellenic ideal of body development and its aesthetic value: *Aner kalos kai agathos,* the man with the beautiful body and spirit is the man loved by the gods.

Physical fitness was stressed by the ancient Greeks who originated the Olympian games. Education for physical fitness in the gymnasium was the only type of instruction given during the first few years of life. A strong belief was prevalent that building up the body would of necessity build up the mind. While sport and play were then obligatory and looked on as a career, Plato felt that mere athletics and gymnastics would make man too one-sided. He did not relish the thought of a nation of prizefighters and weight lifters; it did not fit in with his idea of the universal man. Although calisthenic and agonistic endeavors were indispensable as stepping-stones in a person's development, aesthetc and philosophical contemplation as well as the development of will and cognition should complete the man.

To one from the East, philosophy of life is also closely linked to body development. The emphasis, however, is placed on mastery of oneself. As Herrigel points out,[3] the great achievement in archery lies not in mastery of technique but in mastery of oneself. Only the utter congruity and spontaneity of body, mind and spirit enable the archer in one perfect stroke to encounter the world of objects and become one with them. With this attainment the releasing of tension at the moment of the shot goes by itself. This immediacy of experience with the full measure of physical strength, coordination and will comes into play in that one active encounter with the target.

A similar phenomenon is what has been called "The Moment of Truth" in a bullfight. Here the training, mobility and versatility all converge to achieve a degree of attention that eliminates all extraneous perception and pinpoints one decisive movement. The climactic lunge at the beast symbolizes the triumphat finale of human courage.

When we approach present-day sports, we start with the Golden Age of Sports some forty years ago. This was a great era, with Babe Ruth on the American scene breaking records with his home runs, Paavo Nurmi winning his Olympic honors for long distance running and in Vienna the soccer club Hakoah working its way to world fame.

Man's phylogenetic development lay the groundwork for the human ambition to master the elements and spar with his fellow man. The transition from Greek mythology to current views is portrayed by Icarus, who wished to lift himself against the force of gravity and rise above the earth, and the contemporary flyer who tries to rid himself of the weight of his body and enter outer space.

In all phases of human development, from infancy to adulthood, from disorientation in the physical world of objects to orientation, one has to start with the upright posture which distinguishes the human being from all other creatures.[4] The emancipation from the soil takes place as the child emerges from a supine position into upright posture. He fulfills the exquisitely human task of opposing gravity and encountering objects and people in his world. Upright posture brings man into distance from the ground, from things, from his fellow man, on the one hand, and into closer contact with him, on the other.

The problem of gravity plays an important role in sports. The center of gravity in the human physique is the sacroiliac region. Upright man has to support his weight by the two pillars of his lower extremities. This means that we have to use our legs alternately for two different functions — as a moving pendulum and for resting. Therefore we have to shift the main support of our center of gravity from the left side to the right and vice versa. This puts us into a constant struggle for our precarious position but also affords us more variety of movement and greater expansion and choice in space. Confidence and timidity, elation and depression, stability and insecurity — all are expressed in gait.

Sports entail a growing experience of one's own body. Among other things, this experience involves strength, skill and gracefulness. The gait becomes more elastic and swinging, less heavy or stiff. Subjectively, the feeling for movement, for kinesthetics, improves. Balance and skill augment each other.

Nowadays, kinesthetics or the development of the sense of movement is more important than ever, if only because the automation in our daily lives threatens us with a complete loss of a sense of being, a sense of our own physical existence. Modern man is desperately trying to counteract what threatens to make of him a puppet rather than a self-directing, self-regulating, active organism.

The performing of physical activities brings with it satisfaction for many reasons. For one thing there is the intrinsic value of body movement and its proper coordination. Then there is the visible and concrete evidence of one's ability to move within the medium, whether water or air, within the dimensions of the external world. In addition to these pleasurable feelings, there is the gratification derived from the proper handling of the tools, the sports equipment, which gradually become an extension of one's own body.

Throughout all the stages of the individual's development, physical and emotional conditions coincide. In one way or another, most adolescents in the early stages of rapid growth and change indicate uncertainty with respect to their bodies through self-conscious eccentricities of posture, gait and general behavior. A key to the popularity of the Beatles may be that this musical group effectively mirrors the eccentricities of teen-agers.

In an organized form of bodily expression, such as the school's physical education program, and elsewhere through hiking, bicycling, skating or skiing, boys and girls can express their attitudes toward their bodies more freely. The satisfaction that comes from such use of the body not infrequently forms a sound basis on which the adolescent may arrive at an acceptance of himself in the course of his physical changes. Emotional security is derived from the body's adequacy.

The baby in the family catches the greatest attention as he reaches out toward the world of objects and first falteringly then more and more steadily starts his exploits in walking, climbing and dancing. The whole family shares in the baby's zest and delight, and he goes on to greater feats. With the development of muscular prowess and physical fitness, youngsters go on sparring with their partners and develop attitudes of sharing, competing or fighting with others. In sports a growing person experiences his own body in joint participation with others. If exaggerated, the spirit of togetherness is distorted, and sharing degenerates into neurotic competitiveness.

If ambition and competitiveness run rampant with a sportsman, he loses sight of any fairness essential to the game. He does not regard his opponents as coexisting partners but is obsessed by his wild need to win. The neurotic need to win is liable to hamper even the very ambitious person. The boxer who takes a terrific roundhouse swing and grunts with the effort of his punch is not able to knock out his opponent. He cannot aim his blows, and even if he does, he doesn't have his weight behind them.

Nowadays the need for physical fitness is being stressed more than ever in governmental high places and halls of science. We are reminded of the late President Kennedy's words: "Let's not just be watchers . . . let's be doers in athletics . . . to keep our country strong and vital against the great challenges we must face."[5] This advice comes from a man who himself suffered intense pain and coped with it very well.

The whole concept of fitness comes down to a question of fitness for what. Is the aim to reach a condition that enables a person to deal with all the details of daily living, including proper care of one's body, appropriate response to time schedules, necessary endurance of inclement weather, commuting exigencies and the like? Many people, torn by inner struggles, feel exhausted before they even begin in the morning. They are not able to apply themselves to the daily routine of taking a shower or shaving or grooming their hair. Some are so slowed down in their reflexes that they spend an inordinate amount of time getting ready for the day's work.

Fitness is a matter of strength, coordination and integration of all the aspects of one's physical and emotional state. Muscular innervation and awareness of coordinating ability both contribute to the subjective experience of fitness. A depressive sluggishness of movement prevents a person from feeling fit, even though the general psychobiological prerequisites may be fulfilled.

To comprehend man's being in the world, that is, the person *and* his environment, we have to consider fitness also in terms of another dimension — namely that of time. Fitness as a preparation refers to past conditioning; fitness as far as the present is concerned conveys an immediate sense of preparedness with all the faculties present and instantly available. Fitness as a goal to strive for and train for is directed towards the future when the elements of dexterity, strength and alertness come into full play.

There are two phases of body fitness and body relaxation which are important to the goal of accomplishment: one is a certain body tension and mental alertness; the other is the relaxation of both. The one leads within a time element from a plateau to a peak, the other from the peak to the plateau. The time element involved in the second phase is reserved for leisure. It is the diastolic state of effortlessness which puts one into the proper mental and physical frame for the alertness and strain to come. In addition to that, it is an experience of rhythmicity within the element of time, the ebb and flow of strain. It is the ability to change from one state into another that predisposes one to accomplishment.

Sports medicine developed greatly and became a speciality around the Golden Age of Sports. It was the physiologist, in the first place, who tried to gain insight into the body's functioning under special circumstances such as stress, physical exhaustion or frustrated ambition. Very soon other specialties followed suit. Organizations of sports-interested physicians were formed and sports clinics set up. One athletic stadium after another was built. When Konrad Adenauer, then Mayor of Cologne, inaugurated the stadium there, he declared, "Sports are the physician at the sickbed of the German people."

Intensive research in Europe produced such early books as *Sport and the Heart* by Deutsch and Kauf and *Surgery of Sport Accidents* by Felix Mandl. Doctors observed the athletes during training, and a body of knowledge was added to sports medicine. The thresholds of endurance and efficiency became known. Setbacks and pathological development were weighed against the background of physiology. It became widely known that an individual would eventually have to suffer a setback if he recklessly continued his heavy training. This setback is now known to be characterized by a number of symptoms, such as headache, dizziness, general lassitude, nervous irritability, loss of weight and the like; the condition is known as overtraining. Some boxers or wrestlers deliberately overtrain so that they will lose weight and get into a lower weight class, thereby becoming eligible to compete with lighter partners.

Good advice in regard to the extent and intensity of training is expressed in the saying, "Tire yourself often, overfatigue rarely, exhaust yourself never." The case of the man who ran from Marathon to Athens to bring news of victory to his people is an early historical example of death brought on by exhaustion and collapse.

In sports activities, time is another cycle — from the experience of free time at hand to the feeling of leisure, to the filled-in time, to the highest crescendo of immediacy in achievement. There is but one cycle from apartness to oneness with the elements of nature. In the transition from subject to object, there is a complete elimination of schism and an existential experience of oneness. The development of a philosophy of life congruent with the contemporary image of man leads to that existential experience of oneness.

The conquest of nature or the physical world around us really consists of many existential acts that are not so much directed towards a triumphant conquest as they are an expression of the natural desire to be familiar with any medium in this world. Analyzing different facets of existential activity, Sartre speaks of appropriation through sport.[6] The initial feeling of enterprise, the fulfillment of fitness and the subsequent fatigue belong to one cycle of the full measure of corporeal existence or (*leibhaftige Erfahrung*) of being-in-the-world. Concomitant ingredients are emotional curiosity, the peak of satisfaction and the plane of quiet exhaustion concluding the cycle.

A well-known anecdote about the runner Paolo Nurmi bears repetition.[7] When he set his record 4:10 mile mark in Sweden, word was flashed to every continent. American fans could hardly believe it. A wild-eyed student burst into a philosophy class and blurted out, "Sir, Nurmi has just knocked two seconds off the mile record! Two whole seconds!" The professor fixed a cold eye on him. "And how," he asked, "does the distinguished Finnish gentleman propose to employ the time he has saved?"

Experienced time runs the gamut from fullness to sheer emptiness. This is true both in mental health and illness. Fullness experienced because of healthy activity points to personal involvement and is a self-determined task. Fullness experienced on account of pressures and obligations seems to the individual to be put upon him by the world outside.

Time experienced is time being used. It is also a consciousness of a certain limit set aside for a specific accomplishment. The experience of really free time is spread out in front of us. Here the individual feels free, prepared and adequate for any satisfactory occupation. In contrast, when we are coerced by pressures, time seems to drag with the weight of boredom. Time then does not move but has a density, a heaviness of an object lying across our path, and is construed as an impediment. This time cannot be entered. It feels as if it were hanging over us. Sometimes it feels like a hopeless vacuum that can never be filled. This vacuum or horror of a vacuum forces a person to defy and obstinately protest any prospect of occupying time. Catatonic passivity is a dramatic example. Edward Munch depicts man oppressed by his outer world as a child screaming in horror in front of a tunnel to be entered.

Time is lived, spent or shoved aside. Time is a privilege or a blessing, a danger or a horror. A sportsman is in his time, enjoying his leisure and spending it satisfactorily in his chosen activity. Many neurotic individuals engage in sports to build up their bodies which they regard as faulty instruments in need of improvement. They use a certain apportioned time which they feel they have to fill with physical activity because they cannot manage to enter their time but rather cling to the margin between present and future. The disorganization of their poorly attached limbs is their constant threat.

Truth is an important component. While science is obedience to facts, truth is also served by art and the humanities. In the psychological sense, it amounts to being true to oneself. The pursuit of science is based on necessity, the pursuit of humanities on freedom. Through scientific obedience to facts, the individual may orient himself in the world and toward the objects of his world. He becomes part of his world and expands in it. Here not even the sky is the limit, as we know from our fledgling space exploration. Man transcends the orbit, and when he is outside the orbit he permits himself a comprehensive objective view of our planet.

Alas, this transcendence also creates an existential monstrosity. The transgression of limits threatens the wholeness of existence. The act of freedom is not confined to limits or transgression of limits. It belongs to quite another category — that of no limit whatever.

We may regard as existential the human activity which calls on the integration of thought, will, decision and the act. All the inner processes that come into play when man reveals himself become manifest in the world of deeds. The time sequence, the congruence and the confluence of all the steps we take depends on the synthesis of all activities. The dynamic expression of man's being hinges upon his activity. A creative act which is based on freedom is also found by the rigorousness of synthesis in order to make this act or any act a singular whole.[8]

Albert Camus said of his student days, "Sport was the main occupation of all of us, and continued to be mine for a long time. That is where I had my only lessons in ethics. . . ."[9] Cruikshank tells us about Camus' continued enthusiasm for sports — he was a regular club goalkeeper — and at the same time for the theater.[10] Clamence, the main character in Camus' novel *La Chute* seems to reflect very faithfully Camus' attitude. When Clamence says, "I was really sincere and enthusiastic during the period when I played games, and also in the army when I acted in plays which we put on for enjoyment. . . . Even today, the stadium crammed full of spectators for a Sunday match, and the theatre which I loved with unequalled intensity, are the only places in the world where I feel innocent."

Many persons who suffer from severe alienation and inner fragmentation are either unaware of their body or perceive their body as limp and inert, and are plagued by feelings of self-consciousness. Often we are told by a schizophrenic person that he exercises, does pushups, headstands and the like to regain a sense of his own body. He claims he has to perform headstands so that the blood will flow into his brain. He feels the natural physiological phenomenon of blood distribution needs special help. He is convinced that the vitality or strength of his heart is lacking or insufficient and that his own blood can reach his extremities only if he does something about it. This shows a lack of body sense and body perception, as well as the wish to develop a full-bodied organism.

As to body image, a normally developing individual gains a proper orientation in the world, connected with a true sense of his physical faculties. Awkwardness is significant of an improper adjustment to the outer world. Self-consciousness is the feeling that one's appearance and movements are being observed and found inadequate by other people. The individual does not sense a physical connectedness with the world but rather his own apartness from the world. Small wonder that those individuals have to exploit physical activity to gain the feeling of being-in-the-world.

The critical point of the limit of expenditure varies. The workout for the sake of training is meant to increase endurance, prolong fitness and accelerate replenishment after an exhausting encounter. Toughness is endurance plus stamina. People who experience their split as a numbness of body and sluggishness of movement will repeat a certain pattern of exercises to counteract their deadness and lack of vitality. It is interesting to note that such people hardly ever arrive at a degree of facility necessary for achievement in sports.

Weight and weightlessness are very important phenomena in the experience of corporeality. Dancers like Nijinsky were reported to have had no feeling of weight, but were able to soar effortlessly into the air. Just the reverse is true of the person who not only feels his own weight but also has great difficulty lifting it from the base of his action.

Julius Caesar had a point when he told Anthony he wanted men about him that were well fed and sleek, men who slept through the night, not men like Cassius with his lean and hungry look;[11] "He thinks too much. Such men are dangerous." Obviously, Caesar perferred well-built fellows to those who deny their physical existence, neglect their bodies and are given to thinking, scheming and speculating. Shakespeare, great philosopher that he was, saw human existence as the intermingling of physical being and body activity with all other human faculties.

Under pathological conditions, withdrawal from the world, apathy or fear of the world manifest themselves in restricted physical activity, hesitant movements and a whole range of characteristics from sluggishness to utter stupor. Frequently, fear of the world is expressed as fear of inclement weather. Wind, rain, change of season seem to threaten the fearful patient to whom the world seems inimical. In contrast, those who brave the weather take delight in rhythmic and cyclic changes.

Other external conditions connected with strain also contribute to bodily withdrawal. The healthy individual wishes to participate fully in being-in-the-world by means of his physical activity. In sickness, physical activity is often used to bring about a balance between emotional tension and physical strain. Anxious people often have a sense of physical strain which helps them overcome or forget their emotional tension. Another aspect of physical strain is the effort to adapt the tempo of one's physical activity to conform with the intensity of one's mental activity.

When the body is in action, as in sports, we can regard it as a human existence open to the world. Man can become deeply involved in an external situation, but he always keeps a certain distance from his world. That is why we may say that man not only is his body but he has his body. Man's adaptive reactions are based on his physiology and also on his emotional state. Much in his conduct in sports will depend on his affectivity. It makes a great difference if the athlete is joyous, angry, irritable, rested or fatigued.

There are different feeling types of people in training. Some sportsmen show a good measure of equanimity. They are steady in their active feelings; they are always optimistic, courageous, patient and convinced that their self-disciplinary activities will bear fruit. Others in training show labile feelings. They vascillate from fortitude to anxiety, from optimism to pessimism for no good reason. This sort of thing can lead to bitter disappointments.

Bob Richard, a world champion vault jumper, was once asked in an interview how he started the day when he was scheduled to defend his championship. "I pray to the Lord," he answered. "Lord, let me do my best today." Obviously, Bob Richards does not pray, "Let me be better than everyone else." The creative act is always liberation and conquest. However, egotistic and self-conceited concentration on oneself indicate a morbid separation between man and the world.

Exercise and drill, when imposed forcibly on individuals, can have devastating effects. The humiliation of having one's body used as a mechanical instrument is aggravated by the abuse of one's free will, unless of course the meaning of the drill is to foster *esprit de corps* and have men join in a common enterprise.

Achievement in sports has a unique place. In other struggles for achievement, the person is not necessarily faced with the criteria of evaluation. In sports one cannot help but be aware of the measure of success or failure. This is compounded in those situations created by the highest acumen as with participants in a baseball series or the Olympic games. Here personal achievement is heightened by the strong feeling of being on a mission for one's country. The individual is not only motivated to do his best, but he is also the symbolic standard bearer and representative of the ambitions and dreams of millions of other people.

Motivation is the driving force behind any deed or act determining the path taken and influencing the ultimate goal. If this driving force is unconscious and of a compelling nature, it may be so overwhelming that the individual has to follow blindly the compulsion, though his reason and experience dictate otherwise.

Where there is inner freedom, the individual experiences long-term motivational inclinations or even spurts of short duration as his own conviction. It leaves him the possibility of a choice. Genuine motivation can only start from within. All wishes, drives and needs arising out of social situation alone may be considered secondary and somehow extraneous. The question of where motivation starts can only be answered by a topographical reflection which posits that man has a divine spark originating within him.

Insight into human motivation involves the problem of victory or defeat. As far as victory is concerned, we have to distinguish the basic attitude of a constructive wish to win victory over oneself from the destructive victory which only supports the false pride of the winner over the vanquished, satisfies deep feelings of revenge against the opponent and feeds the hate of a man possessed by inferiority in comparison with his assumed foe.

True victory contributes to the self-satisfaction derived from real achievement. It creates the mood of greatness and may even invoke a spirit of elation in the defeated partner. It is not the simple counting up of points which finally proves the superiority of one against the other; it may be just a hair's breadth distinction, a nose length, and still contain uplifting moments. Conversely, defeat in real sportsmanship ought not to bring humiliation to the defeated one. He might be saddened by the fact that he did not measure up to his own expectations, but a real sportsman though defeated should come out of his fight unscathed and unbroken. Defeat might make the victim admire his conqueror. It might instill in him a determination for greater perseverance.

Hand in hand with perserverance goes patience: the capacity to tolerate suffering quietly and not be overwhelmed by it. Two sides of the coin are seen in patience. One is the passive patience which tolerates all pain and annoyance without griping and resisting, and the other is the active, expanding force of the spirit that enables man to roll with the punches, take things in his stride, rise again after defeat, disappointment or loss and start living again without inhibition. Of the two sexes, patience seems to be more the province of woman. Her capacity for suffering and her fortitude are part of her natural endowment. A man, however, has to get used to the idea. Eventually, he acquires patience through higher cognition.

A 250-pound quarterback may not only experience himself as an able and efficient person, he is also cognizant of the weight he carries, the role he is assigned and his mastery of the space in relation to the others and in view of the goal that the whole team has to reach. The space experience in sports activities has this special feature of the *Mitwelt* shared with others.

Awkwardness is the expression of painful self-consciousness on the part of an individual who feels that he does not share the common space of the *Mitwelt* with others and that his movements do not contain a purposefulness in their direction. Such a person is constantly afraid that he is about to fail in the common purpose shared by others.

Motivation as seen in sports can be pursued in general observation of young and old. Like other people, teen-agers who feel deprived and abused are apt to nurse their desires for revenge. In sports they keep picturing their moment of triumph as a physical knockout of their enemy. Persistence in training and endurance of adverse circumstances add up to a storehouse of pent-up energies ready to be unleashed on the day of reckoning. In such instances, of course, a sport lacks the flavor of sparring. It becomes a bitter fight for victory, a battle against an enemy, a triumph over the indignity of frustration.

In other instances, people can be observed struggling to overcome timidity or give vent to the expression of aggression. In the case of a man paralyzed by fear, for instance, he might be under the impression that his milieu demands an ever present fitness for violent outbreak. Such aberrations, however, do not apply to the average wholesome view of natural fitness. A person's life history and course of development are reliable indicators of his individual fitness or lack of it.

Biographical notes on some prizefighters, for instance Floyd Patterson, confirm the motivation of vengefulness. Patterson often speaks in interviews of the explosive energy he once wanted to direct against society. In his case, a kindly teacher and director of a reform school succeeded in winning him over to more socially acceptable ways. Nevertheless, even in the dream of victory this is given added impetus. Deprivation and humiliating discomfort are actually overcome when the crowd reaffirms a champion's superiority. With no audience present to roar its approval of him, what lonely champion could consider himself victorious?

Plato's idea of universal man is still as valid as ever. However, in today's cultures we are far from realizing the ideal epressed by Goethe, who towards the end of his life wished to be whole. Cassius Clay is a case in point. This handsome, seemingly bright young man revealed an unfortunate affliction of inner split and segmentation, a blight that is so prevalent in the man of our day. At the peak of physical fitness, masterful control of space, orientation and relationship of objects, this self-aggrandizing maker of rhymes failed in army mental tests. His unbalanced, disproportionate integrative power is quite significant.

The crucial question of whether sports are a hazard or an asset in the development of mental health can be answered only in the context of the human condition of today. The physiology and pathology of the observer also throw light on our present state of affairs. The growing crowd of spectators provides telltale glimpses of our society. The spectators are frequently engaged in their pleasure of killing time. They participate indirectly by physical gesticulation and cheering, by emotional tension and thrills. Also, there is the added incentive of the pot of gold at the end of the rainbow for those who place bets.

Spectators, as well as active participants, are all out for the same purpose of sharing an experience. People try to progress from the sidelines to the center of the arena, transcend the role of spectator into the one of actor, break through from a tertiary witness to a secondary observing participant to land finally in "primary spontaneity." Such experience, even if only derived, is preferred to a state of isolation, to the feeling of being an outsider.

An interesting phenomenon having to do with participation is the *espontaneo*.[12] In Spain they give this name to a man who on sudden impulse tries to get down into the bull arena in order to steal the show, to draw the attention of the matador, the bull and all the spectators. This sort of exhibitionism is rare in America. It leads to a need to catch the limelight in sports and can be found in some sports writers who believe one has to try it out for himself to know just how it feels to play in the big league or to box with the champion, and so forth. They try to get a semblance of a quasi-primary spontaneous experience by divining situations where they are thrown together with members of a successful league or rub shoulders with champions. Paul Gallico, the famous American writer, wrote about such experiences in *Farewell to Sport.*

The natural use of leisure time as a safety valve for tensions and the healthy identification with the sports hero undergo decisive changes in the pathological aspects of any of the aforementioned experiences. Not only are the rules of the game corrupted, but outstanding athletes are exploited for financial profit as well as for questionable social purposes.

What about the future of sports? We may look at it from the standpoint of census figures. Surely, many more millions of people will be involved in it, whether actively or as spectators. We hope that an ideal of man's fitness, skill, courage and alertness will be achieved. Man will become more and more open to actualize that which is his natural endowment. Despite technical advances, despite the dangers of the dehumanizing effects of some aspects of contemporary attitudes toward sports, the wish remains to have sports take their proper place in human existence and enhance human naturalness.

FOOTNOTES

1. Shakespeare: *Hamlet.*
2. Wenkart, S.: The Meaning of sports for contemporary man. *J Existential Psychiatry, 3*:397, 1963. See also Boyle, R. H.: *Sport—Mirror of American Life.* Boston, Little, 1963; McIntosh, P. C.: *Sport in Society.* London, C. A. Watts, 1964.
3. Herrigel, E.: *Zen in the Art of Archery.* New York, Pantheon, 1953.
4. Straus, E. W.: The upright posture. *Psychiat Quart, 26*:529, 1952.
5. *Seagram's Sports Almanac.* New York, Masthead Corp., 1962, p. 7.
6. Sartre, J. P.: *Existential Psychoanalysis.* New York, Philosophical Library, 1953, pp. 117-118.
7. Masin, H. L.: *Sports Laughs.* Englewood Cliffs, Prentice-Hall, 1956, p. 133.
8. Berdyaev, N.: *Meaning of the Creative Act.* New York, Collier, 1962, p. 144.
9. Cruickshank, J.: *Albert Camus and the Literature of Revolt.* New York, Oxford U P, 1959.
10. *Ibid.*
11. Shakespeare: *Julius Caesar.*
12. Plimpton, G.: *Out of My League.* New York, Harper, 1961.

DANCING

MARGARET N. SIDNEY

In spite of our Puritan beginnings and the disapproval still expressed by some Protestant groups, dance flourishes in the United States. On Friday and Saturday nights especially, millions of Americans are to be found dancing in night clubs, corner bars, country clubs and homes. In a word, dancing would seem to be our most popular form of active recreation.

Most people do not ordinarily think of dancing as a sport – nor, for that matter, do they so consider chess or cards. Webster defines sport, in part, as "that which diverts and makes mirth . . . a diversion of the field, as hunting, fishing, racing, games, especially athletic games, etc." and similar games played indoors. To the man in the street, the word "sport" usually refers to competitive games and to many outdoor diversions that are not primarily contests, such as skating, swimming, hunting and fishing. Of these, the first two are in essence merely effective forms of locomotion, and the second two, man's first means of earning a living! Even today, hunting and fishing done for the purpose of food-getting become work rather than sport.

What is sport and what is not seem to be largely a matter of purpose. So we might conclude that any activity (especially those involving the use of the larger muscles) is "sport" when engaged in for the purposes of play.

Why then the seriousness with which children and adults alike take their play? Apparently, human beings have not only a physical need for vigorous muscular move, but also an emotional need for conflict and struggle, and overcoming far beyond what is required or even possible in daily life. We long for the elation that comes with the mastery of the self and the non-self; and the greater the obstacle, the more skill required, the greater the elation.

All popular sports satisfy these needs to some extent and at the same time are a means of training the individual for his place in society. In organized team games such as basketball, football, baseball, etc., the player is being prepared for the role of soldier-citizen, whether military, industrial or political (compare President Eisenhower's constant references to "team spirit"). Sports such as tennis and golf inculcate the skills and attitudes needed by those who would rise to the top in our competitive world.

And where does dancing fit into this picture?

In the first place, what sport gives more scope for active play and mastery than dancing? The delight of the dancer in successfully performing a difficult movement is very much akin to that of the fisherman skillfully landing his "adversary," or that of the fielder catching a "fly," or that of the pitcher making the ball behave exactly as he wants it to. The dancing of partners, especially when they face each other as in the latest teen-age and college fashion, is very like the back-and-forth play of the ball in tennis, where each player tries to outdo the other in his control of the external object. For music and the beat is to the dancer what the ball is to the ball-player: the "other" which is the measure of self-discipline and control. The ball-player must adjust his movements to the nature of the ball in order to control it, and the dancer dominates the music by conforming to it and surpassing it. Partners delight in tossing rhythmic responses back and forth to each other with increasing virtuosity. And if their performance is so much above the ordinary that others stop to watch, so much the better. It is as though tennis players decided that their purpose was to keep the ball going between them, rather than to force the failure of the opponent – and the longer the volley, the greater the public admiration and applause. In the game of dance, the opponent is seldom another human being, but instead the limitations of gravity and the flesh, the conquest of the self and the admiration of others.

In the second place, I would suggest that social dancing holds the same position in regard to intersex relationships and the life of home and family that other sports hold in regard to the relationship of individuals to each other in the outside world. Both are games played for the double purpose of releasing natural energies and feelings that cannot be fully expressed in our culture and of training the individual in attitudes that are socially acceptable. Social or ballroom dancing is the ancient game of courtship, well-regulated to suit our society, giving expression to erotic emotion and training in the proper attitudes between the sexes – a very useful form of play!

But this hardly explains the popularity of dancing. We do not play because we *ought,* but because we *like.*

Of the many reasons why we love to dance, the most basic is our need for rhythm and our response to it. This we share with all living things. Whereever we look, within or without, we find rhythmic movement – from the alternation of day and night and the varied procession of the seasons to the steady beat of the heart and the rise and fall of the breath. We seem to be embedded in constantly changing, very recurring motion. Like fish in the swaying waters of the sea, we float in a rhythmic world and are easily swept up in any current to which we are exposed.

It is this tendency to which Aldous Huxley refers in the *Devils of Loudun* when he says, "If exposed long enough to the tom-toms and the singing, every one of our philosophers would end by capering and howling with the savages."[1] And in the recent best-seller *Lord of the Flies,* William Golding makes dramatic use of the power of rhythm to produce mass hysteria in his castaway boys. According to Curt Sachs in his *World History of the Dance,* the pygmoid bushmen of Africa "are so transported in the dance that during the Boer War they could be surrounded and shot down in droves while dancing."[2] And the recent reports in our daily papers of teen-age rioting after rock 'n' roll sessions, or at performances of the "Beatles," are further reminders of the power of rhythm.

This hypnotic effect is so well known that an example of rhythm overpowering reason is often used on the Jackie Gleason television Show. One of the characters, "Crazy," begins to tell a tale to Joe, the bartender. His phrases gradually fall into a sing-song. Soon he is chanting doggerel such as:

> I went to the house and I saw the bride
> Cutting the cake and the groom beside . . .

and both he and his listener are swaying and beating time, until the nonsense goes too far, and Joe wakes up with a roar that breaks the spell — to the delight of the audience who were getting a bit "hooked" too.

Dance may be defined as organized rhythmic movement or, even more simply, as rhythmic movement that is not work.[3] It is amusing to note that this might also include walking, swimming, skating, skiing or riding "just for fun"! Like music and language and other forms of movement, dance is both a means of expressing and communicating feelings, and also of altering or intensifying them. It is important to remember that dance is always a two-way street, it not only expresses and communicates feelings to others, but at the same time it intensifies or even creates these feelings and profoundly affects and alters the emotions, thoughts and physical condition of the dancer. This is true of every form of movement to some extent, but rhythm intensifies the effect. This is why the depressed man who deliberately straightens his back, lifts his chest and swings off into a long walk to the imagined accompaniment of the Soldiers' Chorus from *Faust* cannot possibly remain depressed. And this is why it is a thousand pities that we so often allow people to sit quietly in hospitals waiting for shock treatment.

Dance has always been used by both the individual and the community for its effect upon the dancer, for the release of dammed-up emotion and for the creation of moods of joy, anger or calm. In pre-Civil War New Orleans, the slaves were encouraged to dance in Congo Square as a means of relieving tensions and hostilities[4] — the sort of emotional purgation that our teenagers find in rock 'n' roll.[5] And in primitive societies, warriors who performed the war dance not only expressed and increased their rage against the enemy, but by so doing prepared their minds and bodies for action.[6] A modified version of this is to be seen today in bayonet practice, where there is not only training in skill but also in expressing and feeling fury, thus preparing the body for combat. In the same way a football squad practicing is not only acquiring muscular strength and agility and a knowledge of the "plays" of the game, but, most important of all, the team spirit. They work together as one man, and each feels himself supported, his confidence increased, his ability magnified by the actions of the others. Marching has a similar effect. Nothing expresses and increases group feeling and confidence like marching, with its steady, exhilarating beat and the immediate response to orders, the whole group acting as one person. Seeing a marching column approach a wall, who doubts for a moment that it would march straight through were it not for that last-minute command to turn aside! The feeling of invincibility is there — for observer and participant alike.

The dance is also used for release from the personal will and the attainment of selfless ecstasy. Thus we see the young couple of Victorian days floating, gliding, twirling to the strains of the Viennese waltz, losing all sense of separation, feeling completely at one with each other. Thus, too, the whirling dervish of the Middle East, losing all sense of self as he spins, becomes a receptacle of Divine Will.[7]

Here we must note that authorities on the dance agree that the transcendence of the self, or ecstasy, is always present in some measure in all forms of dancing.[8] And it is this ecstasy, this loss of self in something more inclusive that is the ultimate reason why we love to dance.

Karl Menninger has emphasized the importance of sports as a safety valve for the destructive forces in human nature. In the *Bulletin of the Menninger Clinic,* in an article "Recreation for Morale," Karl and Jeanetta Menninger say:[9]

> Hobbies may be divided into those which are primarily constructive, creative or preservative and might therefore be said to relate to the erotic or reproductive impulses of life, and those which are primarily aggressive in purpose, or even actually destructive, such as fencing, boxing, chess, bridge, games and sports. We believe that a case could be made for these that the most important contribution which recreation makes to moral or human welfare is the diversion of antagonisms and hatred and frustration into healthy aggressive outlets such as competitive sport. It is also true that much daily work does not permit satisfaction to the creative impulse. . . .

From what has already been said, dancing would seem to qualify as a healthy outlet for both the aggressive and the cooperative components in human nature. In the same publication, Edward Greenwood says about dancing:[11]

> The most important value of dancing as a hobby is that it brings great emotional release for primitive impulses which are not given adequate expression in daily life. . . . Throughout the ages, it has been a universal mode of expression. It seems more logical to ask why everyone does not dance than to try to explain why some people do!

> Group dancing permits the individual to keep his own minor variations of style and rhythm and at the same time to be a part of a larger moving whole which is tending to establish a single impression or mood.
>
> In some specialized forms of concert dance the individual must undergo training. The classic thinker would probably turn to the highly technical ballet, while the emotionalist would find a better outlet in modern dance. Those who choose dancing as a hobby because of the opportunities offered for group activities would join one of the social groups for ballroom dancing or square dancing.

Besides the pleasure of both belonging and being free, to many the great joy of dancing is the conquest of skill and self-mastery. As in competitive sports the athlete ultimately competes against himself,[12] so too, the dancer in acquiring greater skill rejoices in surpassing himself. This may explain why the enthusiastic dancer is always eager to learn new dances and to outdo himself in each performance; his great joy is in adding more and more complicated variations of his own, while never missing a beat of the music. Even for the average dancer, some of this sense of self-surpassing is experienced. As he acquires skill in keeping time with the music, he feels at one with it and as though he were himself its creator. It is for this reason that dance music needs to be simple enough to be easily followed, but enough beyond the inventive power of the average dancer to hold his interest and give him a sense of expanded ego as he identifies with it. Jazz is a brilliant example of this.

There are also those who go to the dance floor to prove their social know-how. Dancing, like golf and tennis, is considered the proper way in which members of the upper class enjoy themselves. It is a status symbol and shows, "I have arrived; my appearance and behavior and that of my partner show my good judgment; others envy me; and this makes me more valuable to myself. I delight in the admiration of those about me, and the warm glow of public approval." And this, plus the reward of permissiveness to erotic feelings when properly expressed, is the source of the strong, molding influence of the dance floor situation.

As the young boy in England learned on the playing fields of Eton how to become an English gentleman, subject of the Queen and soldier of empire, so in our courtship dance-game erotic feelings are aroused, controlled and guided. Each partner takes the role that our culture expects of him in regard to the opposite sex; the man leads, the woman follows, seeming to have no other wish than his will; the man chooses, she accepts or refuses; he is pleased by her acceptance, she is flattered by his choice; he embraces her (many men insist that this is the best part of the dance), and she accepts the embrace with every show of pleasure. Although the embrace has public approval, a certain amount of decorum must be observed on the dance floor. But no doubt many couples find an evening of dancing a pleasant prelude to lovemaking. The man must be polite and courteous to other men as well as to his partner. And he must stay with his partner, whether she is a good dancer or not, or however much she bores him, until the end of the music or until some other man breaks in and asks to take his place.

At the turn of the century, to make sure that erotic feeling was kept within bounds, there was usually careful chaperonage and, although there were occasional mishaps, on the whole young ladies remained intact until after marriage. Young men, on the other hand, when the ball was over, might go, with social permission, to houses of prostitution.

This double standard for the sexes, so faithfully mirrored in dance etiquette, was a major motivation in the battle for equal rights for women and their revolt against the man-made customs that divided womankind into "good" women – suitable as wives and mothers, respected, dull – and the "other kind" – mistresses, courtesans and prostitutes, not respected, not suitable as wives and mothers, but necessary for "passion" and oh-so-much fun! As the suffraget marched and carried her banner "Votes for Women," the cry in her heart was, as perhaps it has always been, "Why does my man need these others? What have they got that I cannot supply?" And she set out to correct the omission. The dance floor echoed woman's change of heart. Jazz became popular, along with its dances, the Onestep and the Foxtrot, straight from the old "Boarding Houses" (Negro euphuism for baudy houses) of New Orleans[13] – the music untouched, the dances toned down a bit, but still giving a new, freer movement of the hips, the close embrace and the cheek-to-cheek.

After World War I and the experience of thousands of women in work outside the home and in the Red Cross overseas, it not only became evident that woman could be financially independent and do valuable work in a man's world, but also that premarital sex experience did not make her less desirable as a wife. This, added to increasing knowledge of birth control, encouraged women to try to be "both kinds of woman" – with, perhaps, a little emphasis on the role of the "others," as this had the charm of novelty – and produced the "Roaring Twenties" with its "Flapper" – the eternal, irresponsible little girl – wild parties and, on the dance floor, the Charleston, the Bunny Hug and the Black Bottom, all lifted from the Negro cabin or the brothel, and the Big Apple and the Little Apple from the "poor white trash" of the Carolinas. The chief attraction of these dances seemed to be their demonstration of complete absence of the corset – for body or mind! – a visible declaration of "Let joy be unconfined!" Since then it has not been possible to get back into the old restrictions, although a slight trend toward formality may be developing at the present time, judging by the revival of formal English ballroom dancing in some dancing schools and with a small but enthusiastic segment of the public.

Since the Twenties, dancing has continued to increase in popularity, and the age span of participants has broadened. The elderly no longer hesitate to appear on the dance floor. A woman of fifty-five, interviewed in the dressing room between dances at the ballroom of the Roosevelt Hotel in New Orleans admitted, "We just love to dance, my husband and I! It is more fun than anything else we do!" She was sparkling and gay, radiating joy, and the washroom attendant, her face glowing with reflected happiness, exclaimed, "We just love to see you two dancing! Does us all good. You sure do keep young!"

There is great freedom, too, in the choice of dances. There is a steady flow of "new" dances from South America and the West Indies, and there are several of American (and recently, African) Negro origin. But old forms and dances are still with us, and the embrace position persists, both on the ballroom floor and in the dim twilight of cocktail lounges and bars where the failures in the love-game hope to console themselves. Here the dance of the close embrace, slow and cheek-to-cheek, is perfect for creating

This scene from the Inaugural Ball, Washington, D.C., January 20, 1965, shows the great variety and freedom to be found on the modern dance floor. As in our description of "Dance Night" at the Country Club; couples are dancing as they please, some old-fashioned, some new. Wide World Photos.

the right mood. The identity of the partner is of no consequence; it is enough to be human. The jukebox expresses desire at the simplest common denominator, and the bodies follow.

At country clubs, no longer for the wealthy only but centers of social life for the whole family in the middle income groups,[14] "Dance Night" is popular with everyone, and the dances are as varied as the ages.

An enterprising young grandmother of forty-seven, a dentist's assistant, tells of her vacation spent with her married daughter in Houston. The high spot was "Dance Night" at the Country Club. She relates, "First we had a 'smorgasbord' supper and an hour of Bingo; then the dancing – 'til 2 A.M.! We had a wonderful time! It was mostly Foxtrots and Waltzes, and quite a few 'Mixers,' so we all got to know each other. A few of the young ones now and then would do the Twist, or something of the sort, but mostly people just danced what they liked to the music."

Not all ballroom dancing is as informal as this. Dances and balls for adults – those beyond the college age – are often very elegant affairs where correct manners, clothes and dancing are all very important. Those who take their dancing seriously like to brush up or keep in training and learn the latest steps in dancing classes – just as golfers like to have a few lessons with the "pro."

There are many schools of ballroom dancing in every city, but perhaps the most famous are the Arthur Murray studios, with 275 branches in the United States and twenty-five in foreign countries. It is interesting to note their character. They appeal to a "status conscious" group and teach the kind of dancing that is acceptable in the "highest echelons of society." The average age of students is forty. They put great emphasis upon skill, good form and correct dress. Everything is well done and in good taste. They have a system of grading achievement – a very definite opportunity for the competitive spirit! And twice a year medals are awarded signifying that the dancer has achieved the bronze, silver or gold degree of skill and experience. This system follows the English method, and it is not surprising to find that English ballroom dancing is the highest accomplishment of the gold medal class.

These dances, based chiefly on the Foxtrot, the Quickstep, the Slow Waltz and the Tango, are most popular with a small, highly sophisticated group, mostly in their late twenties or early thirties, who look with disdain upon the formless, mannerless exuberance of rock 'n' roll, the Twist, the Frug, the Jerk, etc., and remark, "They really seem to be missing something" – exactly as the Twisters might say of them!

As to what dances are most popular at present, teachers at the Arthur Murray studios say this depends upon the group, especially upon age. Older people still prefer variations of the Slow Waltz and the Foxtrot; middle-aged people like the Cha-Cha, the Rumba and the Tango. The Mambo is popular with everyone who is young enough to do it. Almost exclusively, the teen-agers and the college set go in for the Twist, the Watusi, the Swing, the Frug, the Jerk, etc. Perhaps this is because the young marrieds are apt to be too busy with their home work to have time for dancing. There is quite a drop in dancing participation in the twenty-two to thirty-two year bracket.

A moment showing the restraint and dignity of the "new" English ballroom dances as taught by the Arthur Murray Studios.

Watching an Arthur Murray ball, it was plain to see that the women delighted in the opportunity to display their evening dresses, enjoying the feeling of being beautiful and admired; and all the dancers, men and women, seemed very pleased with their skill and their partner's appreciation of it. With each succeeding dance, they loosened up, giving themselves more fully to the music, weaving in more complicated steps as they kept the rhythm going, particularly in the Mambo — than which nothing could be gayer! The English dances which came later were much more controlled, sedate and even serious.

Like all ballroom dancers, Arthur Murray students seem to be motivated by the joy of movement, interest in the opposite sex, the satisfaction of acquiring a skill and being part of a group and making friends. They seemed to be especially pleased to be among the "best people" and to be enjoying themselves in the manner of ladies and gentlemen.

Picture of Bob Dewar and Maureen Alexander dancing in the ballroom division of the Northeast Coast Modern and Old-Time Amateur Championship Competition held at Whitley Bay, England, Sept. 1963. Photo by Dance News Ltd.

Square dancing is another form that has become very popular with the young marrieds and the middle-aged, especially those of rather independent, democratic character. A fifty-five-year-old devotee of square dancing told me with glowing eyes of the wonderful holiday he and his wife had spent at a "dude ranch" many miles from his home state.

> We had heard about the dancing and we went mostly for that — and the people! You always meet the nicest people in these groups. It turned out just perfect! We danced every night and learned a lot of Folk Dances, too. We had a wonderful experience on the way home, too. We stopped at a place where we heard they did a lot of this kind of dancing, and when they played the music for one of the dances we had just learned, we got up and danced it. And everybody stopped to watch! It was a bit of an ordeal for my wife, but she didn't miss a beat! Lots of people came and shook hands with us afterwards. And then they got all fired up to do some more dancing themselves! It was a great evening!

Obviously, to the very real joy of rhythmic movement and skill was added the delight of seeing himself and his wife reflected in admiring eyes.

Square dancing has become so popular that there are square dance clubs in all the big cities and in many small towns. New Orleans has the largest

Partners swing lively at the New Orleans Annual Square Dance Festival held at Municipal Auditorium. With the "Rhythm Outlaws" furnishing the music, some 2,000 people swirled and stomped through the evening. The event was sponsored by the Greater New Orleans Square Dance Association. Photograph by Terry Friedman, *The Times-Picayune*.

club in the country, the "Barn and Ranch" club run by Chuck Goodman, with a membership of 240; and there are thirty smaller clubs in the area. There are also clubs in Baton Rouge, Gulfport, Mobile, Pensacola, etc., and there are similar developments in other regions. Each area plans to hold a square dance festival once a year, and dancers from clubs all over the country try to attend. In the summer of 1964, two thousand dancers attended such a festival in New Orleans.

The picture shows the dancers' dress to be simple but attractive and festive, uniform in general effect but allowing for minor variations. Longer and fuller skirts and the obvious emphasis on twirling suggest conservative leanings. These dances are typical of the early stages of democracy[15] and have an old-fashioned appeal for those who value independence and "grass roots" government. They avoid the "sexy" close embrace and are less objectionable to Protestant religious groups than are the descendants of jazz. Perhaps the ecstacy of the twirl is at a higher level than the hip-wiggle!

At a college fraternity dance today, the scene is quite different. There the popular dances are the Swing, the Watusi and the Jerk – nothing done in the embrace position. There is no "stag line." Each man brings his own girl and expects to dance with her all evening. Turning the lights low seems to be a necessary part of the fun, although "necking" can hardly be the purpose of this as the partners dance a foot or more apart most of the time.[16]

The importance of the dim lighting and the character of the dances themselves puzzled the chaperones, a dance-loving couple in their late forties. The wife mused:

> They don't dress up at all. They wear slacks or blue-jeans – nothing like evening dress – and the dancing isn't beautiful or graceful either. Yet I think I would have to describe it as a kind of showing off of vitality and know-how. The men dance with as much gusto and enjoyment as the girls, and the married students come and bring their wives, however pregnant. They all seem to enjoy the dancing, but there is no form to it. I think they miss a lot, especially the 'stag line.' To me that was the most exhilarating part of the dance.

"Killer" Joe Perro, famous New York dancer (who got his nickname in dance competitions where he "killed" all rivals by his vitality, virtuosity and staying power), says that young men are very nervous about touching a girl, and that the old embrace position made them feel anxious and self-conscious. In the new "no-touch" dances they are free to dance with as much enjoyment and abandon as the girls.

As to how the very young feel about their dancing, Jeremy Larner writes:[17]

> Rock 'n' Roll endures because it answers a need rooted in strong feelings, a need fulfilled by the one ingredient in all Rock 'n' Roll: its steady, heavy, simple

> beat. . . . When the listener submits himself to the beat, he loosens his mind from its moorings in time and space; no longer does he feel a separation between himself and his surroundings. The difficult world of external objects is blurred and unreal; only the inner pulse is real, the beat its outer projection. Earthly worries are submerged in a rising tide of exaltation. Dream and dreamer blend, object and feeling jell; the whole universe is compressed into the medium of the beat, where all things unite and pound forward, rhythmic, regular, not to be denied. . . . Rock 'n' Roll dulls the capacity for attention; the steady beat creates instead a kind of hypnotic monotony. Seen in this light Rock 'n' Roll is only the latest in a series of rituals which have existed in many societies for the purpose of inducing mystic ecstasy, usually in connection with religion. . . . Rock 'n' Roll is always doing two things at once. If it seems to be encouraging riot and destruction, note that it is also dissipating destructive impulses before they can be turned into action. If its lyrics seem to purvey a "wholesome" message, the orgiastic thump of the beat will carry along with it the wildest fantasies. In short, through exposure to Rock 'n' Roll teen-agers learn to handle their aggressions and discontents – not through understanding, criticism and conscious social rebellion but through surrendering them to a manufactured purgative . . . [thus] the lyrics generally capitulate to the concept of "'True Love," but the music itself expresses the unspoken desire to smash it to pieces and run amuk. . . . Though the lyrics [of the former hit song, "Bye Bye Love"] portray the familiar broken heart who cannot go on living without his True Love, the jouncing rhythm of the song conveys another emotion altogether; the desire to thump straight on through all broken hearts and difficulties. . . . That many adults resent Rock 'n' Roll is only another of its many advantages from the teen-age point of view. . . . Teenagers want to challenge the adult world . . . [but] their challenge is competitive rather than rebellious. And that is just the trouble with Rock 'n' Roll; it simultaneously accepts and rejects the values of our society without passing through the stages of questioning. It makes no attempt to confront reality. Rock 'n' Roll is the music of young people who are alternately sullen rebels and organization men; or, perhaps, sullen rebels on their way to becoming organization men.

However, in evaluating rock 'n' roll it must be remembered that the older generation has always thought the "new" dances of the young "outrageous," "disgusting" and dangerously "undisciplined." All these adjectives were used to describe the waltz when it first appeared! Besides, there is always a vast difference between the point of view of the observer and the participant. Typically, Dr. Johnson, the onlooker, insisted that the only good in dancing was that it made one appreciate the comfort of sitting down![19] On the other hand, Mozart gladly danced all night whenever he had the opportunity and wrote much of his most beautiful music for dancing, regarding it as one of the greatest of human delights.[20]

Perhaps, too, there is more than a touch of jealousy on the part of older people who complain of the dancing of the young. It is so very difficult, even impossible, for the older, more rigid body to learn new movements that require pliability and the absence of resistance. Besides this, the old, remembering the joys of their youth, long to hand these same joys on to their children, forgetting that, though the river flows forever, it is never quite the same. Each generation must discover its own joy — in its own way!

Dance is such a universal activity that it is strange to find that in our society it has been considered the special domain of women.[21] Even the editors of this book initially planned to place dancing under the general heading of "Games and Pastimes of the American Woman."[22] And Paul Nettl in his recent book *The Dance in Classical Music* quotes from the "Reminiscences" of Mozart's friend Michael Kelly, writing in 1826:[23]

> The propensity of the Vienna ladies for dancing and going to carnival masquerades was so determined that nothing was permitted to interfere with the enjoyment of their favorite amusement — nay, so notorious was it, that, for the sake of the ladies in the family way, who could not be persuaded to stay at home, there were apartments prepared, with every convenience for their accouchement, should they be, unfortunately, required. . . . The ladies of Vienna are particularly celebrated for their grace and movements in waltzing, of which they never tire. For my part, I thought waltzing from ten at night until seven in the morning, a continual whirligig; most tiresome to the eye and ear — to say nothing of any worse consequences.

And yet, then as now, all forms of social dancing were based on the couple, one man and one woman!

Obviously, as many men as women dance, but in talking about the matter, men usually give the impression that they dance to please women, that for them the important part of the dance is the embrace and the cheek-to-cheek, or, for the younger generation, the dim lights and the "necking" of the intermission. A successful young designing engineer (35, married and with several children) gives a typical point of view:

> I like to dance well enough, but we never have time. Actually, what I used to enjoy most was getting to put my arms around a pretty girl and dancing cheek-to-cheek. . . . I can't imagine what the teen-agers today see in these new dances, the Twist, Watusi and all that! They don't even hardly touch each other's hands!

It seems that many men do not admit to any special joy in rhythmic movement. For them "Life is real, life is earnest." To move without a tangible purpose would be "silly." To play they must have an objective — they must hit or kick a ball, catch or kill an animal, knock a man down or win a prize. They measure self transcendence in terms of overcoming the external; elation and victory come only from defeat of the "other." And so for them dancing is merely a means of pleasing a woman and making her more receptive to their advances. A young mother of two, divorced and working in business, agrees:

> I think most women care a lot more about dancing than men do. I think men dance to please their dates and put them in a receptive mood. Really, I guess that's why I don't like to dance!

Yet, in most primitive cultures, dancing has been predominately masculine and purposeful. *Men* danced – not only to express their feelings or to attain ecstasy, as in the case of the whirling dervish[24] or the arrow dance of the Vedda of Ceylon,[25] but to exert power upon the forces of nature and the world about them. As with the primitive huntsman or fisherman, dance was no sportive game but serious work. Ruth Benedict, writing of the Zuni in her book, *Patterns of Culture,* says:[26]

> Their dance . . . is a monotonous compulsion of natural forces by reiteration. The tireless pounding of their feet draws together the mist in the sky and heaps it into the piled rain clouds. It forces out the rain upon the earth. They are bent not at all upon an ecstatic experience, but upon so thorough-going an identification with nature that the forces of nature will swing to their purposes. . . . It is the cumulative force of the rhythm, the perfection of forty men moving as one, that makes them effective.

In the same spirit, men danced to insure the fertility of the fields or successful hunting, or to drive away winter and bring in the summer. The Maypole dance and the performance of the Morris dancers as late as Elizabethan times are survivals of this attitude. But as science has replaced magic and our early myths have faded, men have switched their energies from the dance floor to laboratories and offices. They worship reason and wealth as the means to power and look upon dancing as feminine frivolity or childish play without purpose and beneath their dignity.

Pierrepont gives the practical man's view:[27]

> You may be invited to a ball or a dinner because you dance or tell a good story; but no one, since the time of Queen Elizabeth, has been made a cabinet minister, or a lord chancelor for such reasons!

The one admitted valid reason for dancing, from the masculine point of view, is to please a woman; and for the purposes of courtship the good-natured man is willing to humor the childish, emotional creature. Tennyson sums up this leftover nineteenth-century view in *The Princess:*

> *Man for the field and woman for the hearth*
> *He for the world, and for the needle, she;*
> *Man with the head and woman with the heart,*
> *Man to command and woman to obey;*
> *All else confusion. . . .*

But before we accept this appealing division of the race into heads and hearts, let us take another look at the ballroom scene. All is not so cooperative as at first appears, and it is a little difficult to say who is "humoring" whom! Man may be a born hunter of everything and anything, but woman has become a skillful hunter of man. In the ballroom situation, she prepares a "tender trap." She builds up man's ego; *he* asks, *he* leads, etc. She appears quite dependent upon him for the pleasure of dancing, although every woman knows that she could thoroughly enjoy dancing with anyone — man, woman or child, or even alone, rather than sitting still and unresponsive to the enticing music. (In girls' schools and camps throughout the country, ordinary ballroom dancing is one of the most popular evening recreations, although there are no men available.) But she does sit still and wait, pretending that she could not possibly enjoy the dance without a man for a partner. Women are very disapproving of any of their number who betray this secret. The rules of the game must be maintained — and it pays for good hunters to work together, especially when their strategy is based upon skill rather than force. There are no frontal attacks; everything is done by indirection. The snare is baited, the apple polished; the man's desire is stimulated by sight, sound and touch, and by sweet permissiveness up to that final barrier that is to be crossed only at a price — commitment for life![28]

Perhaps this aggressive undercurrent has had something to do with holding men back from full enjoyment of the dance. Bulwer-Lytton expresses how some men feel about this when he says:[29]

> A ballroom is nothing more than a great market place of beauty. For my part, were I a buyer, I should like to make my purchases in a less public mart.

A present-day college professor presents a similar reaction:

> I didn't learn young enough to dance well. I come from a family that disapproved of dancing. My mother used to say, "Why do you want to stand up in public and embrace a girl when you would get a slap in the face for doing the same thing in private."

An enthusiastic student at Arthur Murray's, a man of about fifty, agreed that women love dancing more than men do. "I enjoy dancing," he said, "but what I really like most about dancing is the women! Of course, you understand, my wife is the one woman for me, but I do like women. I like being with them." Later this same man was heard explaining to a new student how "dances come and go, fashions change, but in the ballroom one thing remains the same: *the man leads and the woman follows* — and don't you ever forget it! When a woman forgets that, her dancing days are over!" Certainly this suggests that he feels some anxiety about the dominance of women. It also suggests that under the depreciating pressures of the modern world, men need the ego buildup they get from this last relic of the "subjection of women" — dance-floor etiquette.

A young employed mother (about 28 years old) who meets many South American men in her work was surprised to find that they frankly enjoy dancing as much as women do. "They have often asked me," she said, "why, at a dance, so many men here just stand around and watch. Perhaps," she wondered, "American men are self-conscious. They don't like to be conspicuous. They seem to dance in the quietest way, with the least amount of movement. Lively waltzes they simply do not want to do — and that is what I love best. Are they afraid to enjoy themselves?"

Are they afraid? Of women? Of close contact with them as "Killer" Joe Perro suggests? Of falling from the pedestal where women have placed them? Of *not* dancing with the most attractive woman in the room and so *not* being superior to all others? Or of themselves, their own suspected inadequacies? Or of what inner emotional sea, unknown and treacherous?

Perhaps the dim lights, so dear to the very young and becoming more usual in modern ballrooms, are important because they make the dancers, especially the men, feel less conspicuous and better able to shed their anxieties. Under cover of semidarkness, without the necessity of guiding a partner, encouraged by the music and the socially approved occasion, they can forget their supposed devotion to reason and fact. The outer world fades, public opinion ceases to matter. They can drop their manly dignity and let themselves go!

Irving Berlin knew what he was about back in 1936 when he wrote his famous hit song for the "tired business man":

> Let yourself go! Relax!
> You got yourself tied up in a knot!
> The night is cold — but the music's hot!
> Relax! Let yourself go!

In the new no-touch dances of today, American men *are* at last letting themselves go — and enjoying the game of the courtship dance with full freedom of movement, even to the hip-wiggle, once reserved exclusively for women. And as they free themselves, they seem to accept more freedom for their partners. In the new dancing exact following of the man's lead is no longer required. And, although at college dances girls do not go unless a man invites them, at some public "discotheque" sessions women attend unescorted. When the music starts, they get up and dance, and any man who fancies them or their dancing may come and dance with them or, more exactly, *opposite* them — a return to a very ancient form.

In fact, our new no-touch dances call to mind an old Gnostic hymn of the second century in which Jesus is described as dancing with his disciples in solemn farewell after the Last Supper. As they circle about him he faces each in turn, exclaiming, "Now answer thou unto my dancing and behold thyself in me"[30] — which sums up the ultimate meaning of the dance.

But besides the inner motivations already discussed, there is another force that impels us to dance. Behind today's explosion of dance activity lies the will to power of our acquisitive society. Dance has been found to be a money-maker, and financial interests have moved in. All the advertising media are brought to bear – newspapers, magazines, radio and especially television. Our supposed secret longings are stirred and promised fulfillment.

Are you a teen-ager, rebellious, yet longing for acceptance? Tune in on the "Saturday Hop" and get with the latest. Here are your rock 'n' roll and your "Beatles." Your nearest music store will supply you with a steady stream of records – to the tune of ten billion dollars a year!

Are you a little older? Is the dream in your heart "Forever will I love and she be fair"? Well, there are plenty of records for that, too. Or what about taking your date to dance at the "Diamond Slipper" or the "Fountain Hall," open from when – 'til?

Is time running out? Would you like to turn the clock back a bit? Recapture the joy of youth? No trouble at all! There is lots of gold in Ponce de Leon's fountain! At holiday resorts and country clubs, on ocean cruises and in dance clubs throughout the country, the courtship dance, that affirmation of eternal youth, has become, hopefully, a means to hold back the strange cold dawn we dread!

Or are you lonely? Would you like to make friends with the "best people," be popular, enjoy life? All this can be had for a fee – ridiculously small, considering the benefits, as can be seen from dance club advertisements in any paper.

No wonder so many people are dancing!

And strange as it may seem to critics of our "materialist" society, people apparently do get pretty much what they pay for. Group dancing does renew the zest for living and bring new friends. It does make people happier, at the same time that it makes billions for the industries that supply the service. That delightful maxim – "the customer is always right" – pays off again, for both parties.

To sum it all up, the more things change, the more they remain the same – only, perhaps, bigger and better. People love to dance, as always, for the joy of movement, the exhilaration of skill and self-control, and for ecstasy, that glorious freedom of release from reason and the individual will. Social dancing continues to be a conscious means of promoting courtship and sociability, and a prereason means of integrating the individual with himself, his fellow men and that totality from which he feels separated and with which he longs to be reunited. Reason may leave us pessimistic, but the dancer knows that life and all it implies is well worthwhile. Not to dance is to be only half alive.

And if all this seems stupidly confusing – forget it! Just find yourself a partner and go out dancing. You'll have a wonderful time!

"Thinking back on tonight – in your opinion, was it the waltz, the samba, the watusi or frug that sent us a bit overboard with ecstasy?"

FOOTNOTES

1. Quoted from Huxley, Aldous: *Devils of Loudun,* by Sargant, W., in *Battle for the Mind.* London, Pan Books, 1959, p. 142.
2. Sachs, C.: *World History of the Dance.* New York, Norton, 1937, p. 16.
3. Sachs, C.: *op. cit. supra* note 2, at p. 6.
4. Quoted from information on display at the Jazz Museum, 917 Dumaine St., New Orleans, La. An AP news story recently reported: "Eight women, three of them housewives, are starting a new hobby. They are learning the art of Mid-East belly dancing. All said they were doing it just for fun and that they would be afraid to perform in public. . . . 'I'm doing it for personal satisfaction,' said one student, the mother of three children. Her sister-in-law, also the mother of three children, said, 'I'm doing it for release'." AP new-release, June 17, 1965.
5. Larner, J.: What do they get from rock'n' roll?, *Reader's Digest,* Nov. 1964, pp. 181-187, reprinted from *Atlantic Monthly,* Aug. 1964.
6. Seton, J. M. B.: *The Rhythm of the Redman.* New York, Barnes, A. S., 1937, p. 3.
7. Sachs, C.: *op. cit. supra* note 2, at p. 41.
8. Sachs, C.: *op. cit. supra* note 2, at p. 251.
9. Menninger, K., and Menninger, J.: Recreation and morale — some tentative conclusions. *Bull Menninger Clin, 6:*100, 1942.
10. *The Bulletin of the Menninger Clinic, vol. 6,* no. 3, May 1942, contains psychological studies of various hobbies.
11. Greenwood, E.: Dancing. *Bull Menninger Clin, 6:*78, 1942.
12. Boyle, R.: *Sport, Mirror of American Life.* Boston, Little, 1963, p. 61.
13. Quoted from display at the Jazz Museum, 917 Dumaine St., New Orleans, La.

14. Boyle, R.: *op. cit. supra* note 12, at p. 180.
15. Sachs, C.: *op. cit. supra* note 2, at p. 428; Nettl, P.: *The Dance in Classical Music.* New York, Philosophical Library, 1963, p. 93.
16. Those afraid and shy of the opposite sex find relief in dancing apart. This group at one time stood on the sidelines (a "wall flower"), but they now dance.
17. Larner, J.: What do they get from rock 'n' roll? *Reader's Digest,* Nov. 1964, p. 181, reprinted from *Atlantic Monthly,* Aug. 1964.
18. This should be compared with the dancing of slaves in Congo Square in New Orleans, or to the function of religious ritual in reconciling man to his world.
19. Edwards, T.: *New Dictionary of Thoughts.* New York, Standard Book, 1944, p. 114.
20. Nettl, P.: *op. cit. supra* note 15, at p. 62.
21. Yet how beautiful it is to watch a man dance! Consider the ballet (in the USSR); and dancers like Fred Astaire, Gene Kelly, Paul Robeson and Sammy Davis, Jr.
22. Editors' note: We relented.
23. Nettl, P.: *op. cit. supra* note 15, at p. 103.
24. Edwards, T.: *op. cit. supra* note 19, at p. 114.
25. Sachs, C.: *op. cit. supra* note 2, at pp. 12, 41.
26. Benedict, R.: *Patterns of Culture.* New York, Mentor Books, 1946, p. 90.
27. Edwards, T.: *op. cit. supra* note 19, at p. 114.
28. Schimel, J.: *Your Future as a Husband.* New York, Rosen Press, 1964, p. 11.
29. Edwards, T.: *op. cit. supra* note 19, at p. 114.
30. Sachs, C.: *op. cit. supra* note 2, at p. 57.

SPORTS GAMES AND LOVE

JOHN L. SCHIMEL

JOSEPH WOOD KRUTCH HAS WRITTEN, "One of the advantages – perhaps there are not many – of having lived a long time is the fact that it inevitably makes one something of a square. We know by experience what those who know the past only through history can never believe, namely, that those 'eternal truths' which have been newly discovered turn out to be mere fashions after all."[1] Since my profession as a psychoanalyst has required interminable listening to an exposition and a search for the verities of love and lovemaking, I have become an expert – not on the verities of love and lovemaking, but rather on what people say they are.[2]

My scientific training prepared me for a career of cataloguing and analyzing facts and the patterns into which they fall, as in chemistry, physics and pathology. It did not prepare me for cataloguing and analyzing the patterns into which opinions and attitudes fall, although I had vaguely perceived that this was the terrain surveyed in the so-called field of psychopathology. I learned that the psychotic surveyed self and surroundings in language and concept that was "autistic," "not related to reality," "symbolic," "primitive" and "primordial." These were more or less imprecise terms utilized to delineate striking differences from the elusive and even evanescent "normal" modes. The neurotic also surveyed self and surroundings through a distorting lens, but his "difference" was less different – an uneasy semantic state of affairs for an "expert."

My colleagues and I clutched and tend to clutch such solid concepts as ego, libido and self-system with some degree of desperation, drowning men barely afloat in a sea of relativity. We tittered when the libido was "discovered" to have its anatomical location in the hypothalamus, Freud's profligate arrow, his high level abstraction, fallen to earth indeed. It was a nervous titter, however. We avidly clutched psychic economy, bisexuality and homeostasis, with their promise of measurability and allure of scientific respectability.

Alas! Except for psychoanalysts in training and other candidates for the laudable and fashionable state of engagé (psychotics, the other seriously ill and degagé psychoanalysts[3] also fit rather neatly into this group), my patients (not to mention friends and colleagues) over the years have been increasingly more than committed, involved, engagé, dedicated to and, if you will, enmeshed in the skeins of living situations with others. It is true enough that the beginning psychoanalyst is generally referred the more seriously disturbed, the anomic, the socially disoriented and unskilled. It is sometimes said within the profession that a lifetime of service to this group indicates the analyst's failure to develop.[4] Be this as it may, workers in the field of both child and adult schizophrenia have made a disproportionate and perhaps in some ways misleading contribution to the field of psychological inquiry. An evaluation of Freud's case histories in the light of modern clinical sophistication would suggest that some of the "neurotic" men and women he studied would be considered to be psychotic today. Psychiatry has tended to proceed from a study of serious maladaptation within a particular human context to an implicit codification (often explicitly denied) of the normative. This is necessarily circular since the study of the maladaptive presumes normative criteria.[5] This is reflected in the frequent predictive statements of the hospitalized. One told me: "When we outnumber you, we will have the keys, and you will have the benefits."

The above considerations seem far from the field of "sports and love." Their import for man seems more apocalyptic than hedonic. I subscribe to the notion that psychiatric theory is far from competent in the realm of love. In our theories love is no laughing matter, nor is sex. Sex can be counterfeit, perverted, polymorphic, pregenital, sadistic, masochistic, excessive, deviate, autoerotic, homoerotic and bi-. Its execution can reveal frigidity, impotence, premature ejaculation, anesthesia of the erogenous zones, dyspareunia and psychosomatic manifestations such as itching, smarting, swellings and rashes, all true, as I can testify from my clinical experience. It *should* be genital, orgastic, mutual, loving, productive, egosyntonic and fulfilling, and I suppose it should be. It does suggest, however, the subordination of the pleasure principle to the reality principle, with a vengeance. I wonder if it could be easier. The laughter is offstage, not in the bedroom.

Little boys, as well as little girls, play many games — some gay, some serious. They play games of violence (with or without stimulation by television) presumably to cope with current anxieties as well as to prepare for future contingencies. They play with gaiety presumably in response to the hedonic impulse, as long as they are not rendered incapable by training, fate and circumstance. I do not know how to prove the existence of the hedonic impulse[6] any better than I know how to demonstrate the need to overcome anxiety as a basic and primary fact of life and development, although the volumes attesting to the latter are far weightier. There are, however, indications that the dominant mores, ideologies and theologies which rigorously define acceptable pleasures produce anhedonic populations, psychiatrists and psychiatric theory alike, despite more or less universal strivings to be "happy."[7] Here I do not equate the hedonic with the irresponsible, although this has a hoary tradition, any more than I equate the gloomy with the serious. The latter two are often confounded in our time. "He is a serious man" is a designation often used for men who are gloomy, empty, misanthropic, opportunistic, bitter or flatulent. For the hedonic man who is serious, see Benjamin Franklin's ribald and pornographic writings as well as references to his forgeries and practical jokes.

Gaiety is often a quality of great men, geniuses, and certainly of pleasant companions, though woe to the politician or statesman who does not conceal this inclination. The games of children often deal gaily with themes that our current adults deem undemocratic or sadistic.[8] I have dealt with the seriously disturbed offspring of pacifists who have denied their youngsters the opportunity to play with guns and other toys symbolic of "man's inhumanity to man." I found no dearth of irrational hostility whatsoever in these youngsters or their parents. Perhaps, as Freud suggested, denial and suppression do not eliminate but augment. Perhaps the denial of the hedonic in the aggressive will lead sooner to the apocalypse. Perhaps the Pollyanna practitioners are really agents of the Devil clothed in the raiment of the Reformer.

And what of love? And what of sports and love? Thoreau wrote: "The mass of men lead lives of quiet desperation. What is called resignation is confirmed desperation. A stereotyped but unconscious despair is concealed even under what are called the *games and amusements* of mankind. There is no play in them." Much of man's written record is concerned with the problem of conflict of interest in human affairs. It has been, and continues to be, a vital subject for dramatic vehicles. Edward Albee's play, *Who's Afraid of Virginia Woolf,* is such a vehicle. It is appropriate that the first act is entitled "Fun and Games," a study of repetitious, although destructive, patterns of behavior between people. Albee graphically represents the "how" of games and leaves the "why" up to the audience and critics.

The psychiatrist is heavily involved in such questions. He is consulted because of the pain or destructive aspects of the games that people play with each other. The psychiatrist is not an expert on love, although his patient will often be. The psychiatrist will know, however, the repetitive patterns of behavior that make up human experience. Pastimes and games are patterns of repetitive human behavior or engagements between people. Pastimes are the more straightforward engagements where no particular conflict of interest arises. These include, for women, such conversational interchanges as those involving clothing, groceries and other details of life. Games have the added component of dissimulation. A common game is that of "Alcoholic." The alcoholic is a dependent person who is currently considered to be ill and who finds a "mothering" woman or group like Alcoholics Anonymous to attend to him. The game aspect was caught in the play

Brigadoon.[9] Two friends are wandering in an enchanted wood where a lost city appears on one night each one hundred years. They pause to rest, and a conversation ensues:

Jeff: Maybe we took the high road instead of the low road. (Takes a flask from his inside pocket.) Would you like a drink?

Tommy: No, thanks.

Jeff: Good. That leaves more for me. (He unscrews the top.)

Tommy: Didn't you tell me you were going to cut down on that stuff?

Jeff: Yes, I did. But I'm a terrible liar. Besides, it doesn't pay. I remember one time I was going with a wonderful girl and she used to plead with me and plead with me to give it up. So one day I did. Then we discovered we had nothing more to talk about so we broke up.

The game was over, the game that supplied him with care and attention and her with a maternal gratification without the problems of intimacy. It has been noted that chapters of AA may fail when the supply of new members dries up. Both roles, rescuer and rescued, are required for the game of "Alcoholic." It is perhaps unfortunate that the word "games" may conjure up only an image of children having fun. On the other hand, it must be kept in mind that there are gratifications of some kind for all the players, as in the game of "Alcoholic." We must keep in mind, too, that games are repeated, they have rules, there are penalties for infractions of the rules, there are signals for the beginning of a game, there is a scoring system, there is a winner or a loser or a draw. All the players must know all the roles. Some cheat. The behavior I am describing is not necessarily deliberate behavior. It is largely unnoticed by the players themselves. They suffer a great deal. I believe that their goal is the human one of getting and receiving love and achieving intimacy. Instead, many have reached a despairing or fragile equilibrium. There is, however, always an equilibrium in ongoing human affairs even if the appearance is chaos.

Example of a Nightly Game

A young woman had recently failed in college. She had been depressed and apathetic for some time. There were nightly games and occasional weekend matinees, that is:

Mother offers a helpful hint, such as how to study better (get along better with her boy friend, etc.)

Daughter becomes incensed.

Mother is deeply wounded.

Daughter claims unfair treatment.

Mother becomes indignant.

Father enters. Joins mother.

Daughter feels betrayed. Claims unfair treatment by father.

Uproar.

Dissolve in tears.

In our discussion, this youngster was surprised to realize that it was the same basic game each night. It always started differently. Each episode had been judged on its own merits. Important values seemed at stake: independence, respect, considerateness, honesty and integrity. She was pleased that she could begin to predict what would happen next in the chain of plays that made up the game. We discussed ways of breaking the chain. She felt most keenly the betrayal by father. We devised a strategem to counter his involvement. That very evening, when he entered the game, daughter was ready. With some qualms and a dreadful feeling of hypocrisy, instead of an angry rejoinder, she smiled and said, "All right, Daddy, *you* are always so sensible. If *you* say so."[10] The game ended in a love fest, and exchange of compliments between father and daughter, with mother anxiously joining in with her reassurances.

The change in the young woman was remarkable. She blossomed, felt love for her parents and compassion as well. She entered a constructive and hedonic relationship with an appropriate young man. While in the thrall of this all too common family game, the player feels (and is) in the control of dark forces which he cannot regulate. Self esteem suffers. School and other situations tend to deteriorate. There is a feeling of hopelessness and impotence. There seems to be no way out. There may be some awareness of being sucked into something against one's wishes, but with no way out, except perhaps a forcible or violent one. As Thoreau put it, "There is no play in them."

In the following material, there may seem to be an overemphasis on the gory aspects of human relationships. It is not the whole story or perhaps even the major aspect of human behavior. It must be told, however. I hope further that the reader will not be misled by an irreverent attitude toward clinical material into believing that this is not a serious treatment of an important subject. Although the material I am using has its amusing aspects, it does have serious consequences.

I am consulted by a mother who is distraught about the problem of Strontium-90 (which she identifies as Strontium-92) in the milk which she gives her child. She implores me to tell her what to do. I suggest joining "Women Strike for Peace," to which she responds, "That's a Communist organization." I then suggest "Turn Towards Peace," to which she replies, "That would take too long." The last answer clearly indicates that I can help her solve the problem in a shorter time. Since I am not mindful of the fact that the world's greatest statesmen have been working on this problem, it appears that I am being tendered a great compliment.

On the other hand, I am somewhat regretfully aware that very little of the advice of psychiatrists (or for that matter, other physicians) is accepted or acted upon. I am also aware that in this clinical situation, my two rather humble suggestions were turned aside quite brusquely. This does not anger me nor surprise me, since I recognize the opening steps of a game which this woman plays in practically all situations with practically all people. It operates at the pastime level when there is no particular conflict of interest involved, and at the game level when my patient is characteristically "dreadfully concerned" about something.

Since the use of the notion of games is one that refers to a process in which there may be many steps or many interchanges between one person and another, the name of a game may have to be correspondingly lengthy. This particular game may be called, "You are the only one who can help me and I can prove that you can't."[11] This game is often mistaken to indicate such things as indecisiveness, compulsive doubt or a castrating attitude. It may also be misunderstood to indicate sincere concern or intelligent conversation — which it is not. Many six-year-olds have mastered this game to perfection. It is true enough that a game is often played to be won, and that frustration and rage frequently appear in such discourses.

Let us now approach the subject of games in another direction, namely, that of the function of reciprocal roles in game playing. The psychiatrist, of course, attempts to analyze the game, although often enough he becomes a player. A game takes two players and at least one observer, if it is to be realized that a game has been played. A player can be an observer as well as a participant. It is as though there is an unwritten script to cover most situations in life, which takes into account the varying circumstances that may obtain. When two people with complementary scripts meet, the game is on.[12] The game may not be pleasant, but it is always engrossing. The woman who has complained about her husband, say, for the last twenty years is a woman who has not left him. The woman who is annoyed by her husband or disgusted by him has been prepared for exactly this role by her earlier experiences. This is often evidenced by the woman who has one unhappy affair after another, or a series of marriages with "very different men," but in all of which the game is more or less identical.[13]

The preparation starts very early and includes learning the appropriate emotional responses. A mother is consulting me about her six-year-old. She wants him out of the room while she tells me something. She suggests to him that he go to the corner drugstore and buy a nickel bar of candy. She gives him a quarter. He returns in a few moments without any change. She immediately berates him; he hangs his head in shame; his face expresses guilt and remorse. However, at that moment, mother and son are facing me, as they are side by side. Mother can see his repentant face and dejected figure and begins to wind up her lecture on honesty, truth, morality and the virtues of virtue. However, while this is going on, I can see that the boy is giving me a long, slow wink, which seems to say "I know the price of that extra

20¢ worth of candy." He has learned the game and learned to give the appropriate emotional concomitants. Unfortunately, he will forget that he has learned a game and will become sincere, which means that having achieved this prerequisite for game playing, sincerity will take the place of reason. He will thenceforth feel remorse each time he cheats.[14]

Let us turn now to another example of game playing, this time in an adolescent boy. As you read portions of his letter about experiences in a house of prostitution, I hope you will be thinking about the kind of girl he will "fall in love with" – What games will she play? What will she "believe" in? What will she be sincere about?

> I bought her a drink. She placed a hand on my thigh, and I responded by kissing her neck and ear. I seemed unable to treat this girl like anything else than one of my regular dates. I insisted on talking to her in typical making-an-impression fashion. I felt as though I had demonstrated my great ability at picking up girls. I even recall asking her if we were going to her room, although it was only too clear that the row of one-room apartments was the "business establishment." I even vaguely hoped that I had gotten lucky and picked a "hot number." Once inside the room, it seemed like an extremely successful date experience. I kissed her and fondled her for a long time. She played my game quite well and seemed surprised and aroused by my adolescent ardor. We undressed each other and fell onto her bed. I was simply unable to do anything other than to caress and kiss her to exactly the same extent as I have my most promiscuous dates at home. I tried to discuss my ridiculous plight, but she sensibly answered she had no idea what was happening. She redoubled her efforts to improve matters. I finally felt so helpless and comical in my impotence that I got up. I helped her get dressed. I felt like apologizing to her and I did – several times.

This is a not uncommon and even poignant scene. It illustrates the compulsion with which game playing may be carried into entirely inappropriate situations. When this same game, however, is brought into an appropriate situation, the fraternity house or an automobile, with an appropriately conditioned girl, very often "love is born." This youngster did not wish primarily for sexual gratification. That was available. He wanted a "hot number," which meant in his own words, "a passionate girl, not an excitable whore."

It would seem from the above example that it really takes only one to play a game. In some ways, this is true. The letter from the young man indicates that. He was also aware that his behavior was inappropriate and that he was assigning roles to his partner which were not relevant to the actual situation. Such a game could not continue indefinitely with the prostitute – a game in which he had to make advances, make an impression, then fail, discuss it with his girl, agree on his shortcomings,[15] have a disappointed woman on his hands, and resolve to do better in the future. Incidentally, as he left, he heard some laughter and concluded that they were laughing at his failure, which may or may not have been the case. Although he could not play this game indefinitely with a prostitute, it is very likely that he can and will play this game for the rest of his life with some lovely woman who is already conditioned to play the complementary role. Perhaps they have already met. Perhaps they will meet next week or next month or next year, and the game will commence.

I must say that I have at times been surprised, and even entranced, when a shy and frightened young woman or her Helen Hokinson elder blushingly confesses herself to be a sexually dissatisfied "hot number." I review in my mind her lack of experience, except that with the unsatisfactory spouse. I wonder, "How could she know?" I may wonder out loud, "But you were a virgin when you married and you have told me that sex was *always* unsatisfactory with your husband."

"If it weren't for him, things would have been different with me," says she, quoting the name of the most common game played between spouses. The warm, outgoing wife of the cold, withdrawn husband is practically an American cliché. She gives "love." He rejects it. Sex life dwindles to nothing. She accuses him of coldness. Her sexual longings and approaches increase as the probability of his response diminishes. "If it weren't for you . . ." goes on and on. It conceals the fact that the wife has a sexual problem and one of social grace. In her dream life, she is the belle of the ball, or would be, "if it weren't for him." He wins in this game, too. He is "safely" married, without the threat of the intimacy he could not tolerate. How does she know she's a "hot number"? Well, she isn't; but it doesn't matter. It's the role she plays with her spouse. He has been conditioned to play the same complementary role as our adolescent played with the prostitute. His father played it with his mother.

This game of "If It Weren't For You" has been with us for a long time. Around the turn of the century, it sounded like this, in a song entitled "The Curse of an Aching Heart":[16]

> *You made me what I am today,*
> *I hope you're satisfied,*
> *You dragged and dragged me down until*
> *My soul within me died . . . .*
> *And though you're not true, may God bless you,*
> *That's the curse of an aching heart.*

Nowadays, the love game often starts with a preliminary game which we call "psychiatry." The psychiatric game consists in the exchange of rather detailed case histories, increasingly frank in terms of both sex and disappointment in one's personal achievements. In this game, possessing understanding parents is a great disadvantage, and the youngster who admires his parents feels distinctly left out. During the exploratory game, the young lovers reveal themselves as having very high aspirations which are often dashed. This is a very important clue and is in conformity with the dominant social ethic of aiming high. It also sets the stage for the subsequent disappointments in self and in the other. Being disappointed, hurt, wounded, unfairly put upon, taken advantage of and betrayed by self and others are essential ingredients and, of course, could not exist without the opposite numbers: lofty ideals, high aspirations and expectations. "Sensitive" is a crucial word. The young woman is clear-eyed, dedicated, noble, idealistic, and falls unselfishly, completely, and one might add madly, in love. The idealistic man can do no less.

You will note that the utmost gravity is required for this particular game, which keeps me and my psychiatric brethren quite busy with the second phase of the game, which is the disappointment — and with the idealistic and disappointed offspring of such players. Our current generation has been described as serious, thoughtful, dedicated and sincere. I believe this is an attempt to describe the gloomy, humorless approach to life which this national pastime requires. The American who brings his disappointments to the psychiatrist is a very serious person, if one accepts his definition of the word. As a word, it seems to be more and more reserved for a state of mind in which despair, hurt and betrayal are the important ingredients. I have come to the regretful conclusion that if my patient tells me he is a very serious person, I must interpret this to mean, from an objective standpoint, that he is probably a very frivolous person indeed. Paying attention to the course of people's lives has forced me to the conclusion that gloom, sorrow, tears and despair do not have to be serious emotions, but are likely to be maneuvers in the game of being a good but letdown child.

Sincerity, too, is a very highly valued "commodity" in our lives. It is taught our young children and our young doctors equally. Sincerity is a form of being identified with what one believes and says, and hence often functions as a lack of openness and insight.[17] Most people, however, treasure their sincerity and are enraged if their sincere statements or attitudes are challenged. In games, sincerity is a very potent ploy. I know only one antidote to sincerity, and that is humor. I do not mean "antidote" in the sense of using it to cure or reverse the sincerity in the other person. However, if you are exposed to a great deal of sincerity, humor may save your *own* life. Humor, I must say however, enrages the serious and sincere denizens of our communities if applied to their personal problems and games. Erich Fromm has suggested that if a silent film were taken of the usual psychoanalytic session, the viewer would necessarily conclude that some great tragedy were being discussed.

You may be getting the idea that, in the strict sense of the word, serious game playing may be very serious indeed. With very sincere players, the game may include such consequential activities as homicide and suicide. I agree with Sullivan that suicide can be considered to be a stratagem in an interpersonal situation in which a person has been resorting to more and more desperate strategies to continue a game on a level approximating the wishes of the player. Sullivan refers to suicide as the outcome of an incompleted fantasy.[18] The suicide occurs at the point of the fantasy in which the stratagem of suicide "evens the score," as it were. If the fantasy were completed, the person would realize that he would be dead, that life would go on and that his personal game would be over. The fact is that the malignant effects of suicide may continue the game *ad infinitum*. In a way, it is the ultimate in the game of "You Made Me What I Am Today" or perhaps "Now You See How Much You Have Disappointed Me."

It is no accident that most suicides do not quite come off, since it is a rash player indeed who pushes all his chips into the center of the table. Nevertheless, many suicides are completed by inadvertence, as it were. It is not inappropriate to hold the notion that the suicide attempt is an appeal for help. This is deduced from the fact that many suicides give clues as to their intention. Indeed, as in the case of Marilyn Monroe and many others, the suicide calls or attempts to call some significant person. The plea for help might perhaps be considered to be a plea for help "on the terms" of the player. I was consulted after the death of a less than prominent actress by her distraught husband. In essence, his story was that she had made several suicide attempts, each in the late afternoon. He would discover them and "save" her. This was followed by a period of making amends, resolutions to be a more thoughtful husband, etc. On the day of her death, she had apparently turned on the gas at approximately 5:00 P.M. He usually returned home at about 5:15. On that day, however, he was delayed by a business conference. He wondered whether the "business conference," which he could have declined or deferred, was a way of terminating the game. I wonder, too.

Indeed, I wonder about a great many things. Psychiatrists, for example, are becoming more and more aware of the role of their own values and ethics in evaluating human behavior. The older notion was that the psychiatrist either made no judgments insofar as the patient's dilemmas were concerned or was able to suspend such judgments. A newer notion is that the psychiatrist, too, is a product of his culture and that rather than denying his values, he must needs become quite familiar with them and the role they play in how he sees and treats his patients. This certainly seems to be a most valid concern. On the other hand, in game playing, as I have implied in the foregoing, ethical principles generally occupy the central role. Struggles between woman and man center about moral issues, in a manner akin to the old morality plays. The serious (and humorless) players hold up nobly inscribed banners. They fight for justice, equality, thrift, loyalty, fidelity, honor and the freedom of the individual.

I am always convinced of the good intentions, integrity and rightness of her position by an embattled wife. This was not so bad in the old days, when technical considerations precluded seeing the spouse. However, these days, it is not uncommon to see both parties. I must tell you that when I see the other spouse, I am also convinced of his good intentions, integrity and the rightness of his position. This has complicated my life. Indeed, I may say that when I first started in practice, I saw mostly women, and I concluded that men were a pretty unfair and generally corrupt lot. However, some years later, I had a run of male patients, who convinced me that women were an unfair and corrupt lot. It could be that both are. There is another possible inference, however, which is that ethical principles are the very stuff of games. In effect, this means that what the psychiatrist observes is a misapplication of ethical principles — indeed, a corruption of them. The indictment and defense on the one hand, as well as the hortatory on the other, are substituted for the communicative. Indeed, the manipulations of virtues oppose communication. A paradigm is that of our legal system. It is commonly called "the sporting theory of justice." It postulates that even in such matters as divorce, one party is the plaintiff and the other the defendant; the winner is precisely the one who demonstrates that the other has violated some rule or principle. Conversely, the winner may be the one who successfully defends himself against such a charge. In Eric Berne's groups, such marital exercises are referred to as "Courtroom," which many couples play interminably. By and large in such games, each player knows both roles, which may be used reciprocally. When children come along, they soon enough learn the rules of the game.[19] The situation then becomes somewhat more complicated. Alliances are formed — the child joins one team or the other and may shift back and forth in a more or less opportunistic fashion. "Democracy" may then become the important game.

It is important to note that the inferior, abused or weak role is simply one of the roles in the game, and not without certain functional aspects. It may be used in the form of, "You're right. I am weaker," or "helpless" or "inferior" or whatever. "How can you expect so much of me?" — this aspect of game playing is a powerful inducement and reinforcement to infantalism, invalidism and neurosis.[20] It is not all bad to be the underdog or loser. This insight is shown in the Israeli joke: A suggestion is made in the Parliament that the Israeli Government declare war on the United States. It is reasoned that Israel will certainly lose such a war and that afterwards, the United States will rehabilitate Israel to a state of security and prosperity which they couldn't achieve on their own. The debate ends when one thoughtful man wonders aloud, "But what if we win?"

The role of the hedonic in games sports and love is one of the best-kept secrets of our time. The psychiatrist talks of anxiety and dreams of his country home or yacht. His face lights up as he speaks of the pleasures of man. It darkens as he discusses humanity. In 1962, Americans spent $20,-470,000 on powder puffs, $113,750,000 on toilet water and cologne, $27,-970,000 on playing cards and $347,280,00 on chewing gum – all to allay anxiety and feelings of inferiority, no doubt. Further proof lies in the fact that they spent $11,628,260,000 on alcoholic beverages. Grim. Grim. Grim. Yet who is kidding whom? Could it be that nervousness resulted in the $3,377,000,000 spent on foreign travel? Perhaps with a more open attitude toward pleasure, this lonely chapter on "Sports Games and Love" might have been included, in whole or in part, under such chapter headings as "Team Sports," "Great Outdoor Sports," "Family Sports," or "Body Building Sports."

In the analysis of games and game playing, a crucial phase occurs when the prospect of giving up games arises. "What will I do instead?" is a not infrequent puzzled question. Indeed, some who have given up game playing have initially reported that life has become dull and without flavor for

"This is the 50th anniversary of my winning the National Gigolo Championship. Then I decided to turn in my suit, quit while I was on top and take a crack at the World Celibacy record."

them. It is true enough that the arts of peace are more subtle, sensitive and, I believe, less tangible in an emotional sense than the arts of strategy and war. They require more sensitivity, cultivation and dedication. They require more insight, delicacy and consideration of the other person's role as an individual. A poem is less substantial than a punch, more elusive and beyond the reach of many.

FOOTNOTES

1. *Playboy,* Dec. 1964.
2. Dr. Joseph Jaffe, Director of Research of the William Alanson White Institute and a psychoanalyst armed with a computer, has calculated that a psychoanalyst listens to twenty million words a year, a staggering and, to me, frightening figure.
3. See Farber, L. e.g., in "I'm Sorry Dear" in *Commentary,* Nov. 1964, for a lamentation bewailing research into the physiology of sexual responses.
4. The so-called organic and, to a large extent, the social psychiatrists are more or less restricted to the disenfranchised and psychologically primitive members of our society. The National Mental Health Act and the Community Mental Health programs are providing powerful ideological incentives to psychiatrists to invent and practice the primitive psychotherapies which may alleviate the sufferings of the many. Research into societal sources of emotional disorders is not so generously endowed. Irving Kristal has noted that "though democracy is the political system which encourages the greatest freedom of speech and the widest margin of opinion, it is nevertheless curiously invulnerable to self-criticism." New York *Times Magazine,* Dec. 20, 1964.
5. See Wheelis, A.: To be a god. Commentary, August 1963, for an explication of the circularity of the "free will" which the psychotherapeutic method strengthens by the application of the theory of "psychic determinism." See also Szasz, T. S.: *The Myth of Mental Illness. New York,* Hoeber-Harper, 1961, in which he hypothecates that psychotherapy which has the goal of increasing the patient's ability to behave responsibly is based on a metapsychology which has progressively robbed man of the responsibility for his own behavior by defining irresponsible behavior as illness. I am not sure I understand what he advocates. His work seems to fall into the group of "Golden Age" theories. These have been defined as those advocating a return to a better time in man's history, which never existed.
6. See Schactel, E.: *Metamorphosis.* New York, Basic Books, 1959, for an elucidation of the "reaching out" ("activity affect") propensities of the human as well as the more attended-to phenomena of ego defenses (Anna Freud) and security operations (Sullivan). See also Silverberg, W. V.: *Childhood Experience and Personal Destiny.* New York, Springer, 1952, for a prior study couched in terms of "heroic" and "non-heroic" life solutions.
7. I do not recommend asking the usual seeker for happiness to define either the means by which or the ends for which he strives. Patient listening on my part to such seekers tends to thrust me into a state of hopelessness and deep despair, which on balance, however, seems preferable to "happiness."
8. The editors of this volume failed to find a writer who would "seriously" do a chapter on the hedonic gaming or sporting aspects of war, although it is clear that many of the sports considered are or were subsidiary and preparatory for that ancient art. See newspaper accounts of bomber pilots over North Viet Nam reporting, "It was a ten strike" (bowling), "It was like shooting fish in a barrel" (fishing and hunting), and "It was a bullseye" (target shooting, archery), indicating the origins, or at least the relatedness of sports and war. Recall also the British dictum that the British Empire was forged (through warfare) on the playing fields of Eton. "Fallout makes war a whole new ball game," says *Life,* May 28, 1965, p. 91.

Machiel Zeegers in his paper in this volume, "The Swindler As A Player," p. 219, points out: "Huizinga [in *Homo Ludens*] emphasized the closeness of the notions of play and fight. In many languages the word play means fight, deadly struggle. He also recalls the play factor of warfare through the ages." See also Reider, N.: *Preanalytic and Psychoanalytic Theories of Play and Games, supra* at p. 13.

9. Copyright 1947, Alan Jay Lerner.
10. There is more to this situation and its outcome than can be dealt with in this paper.
11. Note the frustrating paradox offered, in the form of a double-bind (Bateson, G., Jackson, D. D., *et al.*). See also Haley, J.: *Strategies of Psychotherapy*. New York, Grune, 1963, for an exposition of the paradoxes of difficulty in living with others as well as the coercive (toward health) paradoxes forced on the patient by the psychotherapist, regardless of school or persuasion.
12. For an explication of "game" playing in groups and in pairs, see the work of Eric Berne. His work, stemming from and applied to group therapy, is relevant here. See *Games People Play*. New York, Grove, 1964 and *Transactional Analysis in Psychotherapy*. New York, Grove, 1961. For prior studies see Sullivan, Harry Stack: *The Psychiatric Interview*. New York, Norton, 1954. Sullivan, psychoanalyst and American pragmatist, originated the concept of interpersonal psychiatry and pioneered interactional and transactional hypotheses to conceptualize processes that go on *between* people in contrast to the prior (and continuing) preoccupation with inner phenomena and content analysis. As with modern physics and modern art, he attempted to transcend the form-content dichotomy and anticipated the present "form *is* content" world view.
13. An early and obviously premature attempt to cope with these data are the extremely interesting speculations by Edmund Bergler on repetitive and destructive marital couplings in his *Divorce Won't Help*. New York, Harper, 1948.
14. A mother recently told me that she pleads with her six-year-old not to look so pleased when he hits his younger brother and makes him cry. "At least, try to look sorry," she instructs. See also Bierce, Ambrose: *The Devil's Dictionary*. New York, Dover, 1958, "Apologize, v.i. To lay the foundation for a future offence."
15. For the less sublimated, more socially disoriented prostitutes are available who wear boots and whip the male a la the Marquis de Sade. Although available in New York, the great center for this game and variations was Havana, Cuba. The sincerity of reformers and revolutionaries is not compatible with "certain" games. I am told that the brothels (as well as the well-appointed and hygienic facilities for aborting American females) have been taken over for more "serious" activities. Restrictions in permissible sexual practices are equated with prowess in warfare, i.e., "one dedicated (ascetic) Cuban can lick six Norteamericanos," and also, "one good American can lick any six Cubans."
16. Words by Henry Fink; music by Al Piantadosi; copyright 1913, copyright renewal 1941, Leo Feist, Inc., New York, N. Y. Used by permission copyright owner.
17. When I listen to the "justified" punishments or neglects my patients perpetrate on their opposite numbers (and vice versa), I am reminded of the W. C. Fields dictum, "You can't trust an honest man." In a similar vein, Harry Stack Sullivan commented: "Rationalizing is the technical word for this misuse of reasoning which, in some people, amounts to their major nuisance value in society. All the things they do that don't happen to receive just the right response from the other fellow are 'explained,' and they are always explained plausibly, although few indeed of us know why we make particular social mistakes. If I were asked at a moment of weariness, 'What is the outstanding characteristic of the human being?' I believe I would say 'His plausibility'." See *Conceptions of Modern Psychiatry*, Washington, D.C., Wm. Alanson White Psychiatric Foundation, 1940 and 1945, p. 26.

I consider any psychotherapist who is unfamiliar with the works of Stephen Potter to be ill-informed in an important area. See *Three-upmanship* (*The Theory & Practice of Gamesmanship, Some Notes on Lifemanship, One-upmanship*). New York, Holt, Rinehart & Winston, 1962. See also Parkinson, C. Northcote: *In-Laws and Outlaws, Parkinson's Law*, etc. Boston, Houghton-Mifflin. These British writers deal with the repetitious abrasive activities that go on between people. To the charge that their work is superficial and certainly not psychiatry, I can only console myself with the fact that they offer more reliable and predictive tools in anticipating human behavior than much "deep" psychological theorizing.

18. Sullivan, H. S.: *Conceptions of Modern Psychiatry*. New York, Norton, 1940, pp. 12-13.
19. Here as elsewhere in this paper, analogies to the computer suggest themselves. The child is fed "bits" of information: factual, emotional and operational. He is gradually "programmed" for transactions within a particular field or context.
20. See Szasz, T. S.: *The Myth of Mental Illness*. New York, Hoeber—Harper, 1961.

THE SWINDLER AS A PLAYER

MACHIEL ZEEGERS

IT SEEMS THAT A GREAT MANY human activities are aimed at stimulating negative feelings. We visit tragedies, we look at thrillers, we enjoy our reading or theater visits with trembling lips and weeping eyes, with palpitations of the heart and with all signs of anxious sorrow. On our holiday trips, many of us take part in activities that require extreme efforts and cause us muscle pains, utmost fatigue and worse. A play center, where children enjoy themselves, is full of instruments apt to make them dizzy and sick. Many sports, too, bring us to the verge of exhaustion or of vertigo. Thrilling experiences, dangers, emotions — that's what we want for our diversion and amusement.

We like being dazed, dizzy, giddy. Note that each of these words has at least two meanings. Dizzy, giddy, and dazed mean, in the first place: suffering from vertigo. They are also synonyms of "being bewildered." The same holds true for the word swindling, which has the original meaning of "being dizzy."

I am not playing upon the word when I connect swindling in the sense of being dizzy with the criminal actions of the swindler who deceives people. Etymologically the word swindle is derived from the German *schwindeln.* In the English language this word received a secondary meaning of fraudulent practices, a meaning that was then adopted in German. Indeed the acts of the swindler have something bewildering, something that makes us dizzy. His unstable equilibrium, his shrewd maneuvering on the brink of ruin, his dangerous play, his reckless bravura — for the spectator they rouse emotions like a trapeze performer or a rope-walker do.

Here we are confronted with a kind of action which itself is called swindling; we might say: "with swindle for swindle's sake." This must be an action which appeals to many of us. Is this not the purest and the most perfect sport on record? Shakespeare, in *The Tempest,* has given us a precise description of the pathological liar, who gradually tends to believe his own fraudulent role:

Like one,
Who having, unto truth, by telling of it,
Made such a sinner of his memory,
To credit his own lie, — He did believe
He was the Duke; out of the substitution,

> *And executing the outward face of royalty,*
> *With all prerogative: — Hence his ambition*
> *Growing.*

In fact, it is the outward scenery of the role-playing that leads the liar on and makes his ambition grow. The real swindler is induced by his victims as well as he induces them. He has much in common with the playing child and with the actor.

It has often been said that the pathological trait of the swindler is a belief in his own lies. The combination of conscious lying and self-deception has been called *pseudologia phantastica.* In a more modern conception, we will try to see the swindler's behavior in connection with general human problems. His playing way of existence reflects man's possibilities and man's failures.

PLAY, LYING AND FANTASY IN PSYCHOANALYSIS

Freud has connected lying and fantasy with play.[1] Fantasy, like the games of children and the work of the artist, is aimed at satiating the feelings of pleasure and avoiding displeasure. Likewise, the fantasies of the daydreamer tend to sate his desires. In another work Freud calls fantasy a split-off kind of thinking.[2] With the entry of the reality principle, this way of thinking has been kept free from comparison with reality, and it has such remained subordinated to the pleasure principle.

Later, Freud introduced the term repetition compulsion.[3] He remarks that in their playing, children repeat all that makes a great impression on them; by repeating they achieve a belated mastery of the situation; from undergoing events passively they proceed to evoke them actively. Denial of unpleasant reality by means of play and fantasy is one of the defense mechanisms described by Anna Freud.[4] Other authors emphasize the possibility of escape from reality and of avoiding fear by means of fantasy. Feshbach showed in experiments that a decrease in the hostile attitude occurred when the person had occasion to express his aggressiveness in fantasies.[5]

In these analytical observations, it is of the greatest value to recognize that both play and fantasy are very useful and even necessary human activities. This also applies to the swindler.

THE SWINDLER: PROTOTYPE OF THE "HOMO LUDENS"

To what extent may swindling be characterized as play? Huizinga indicates the central position of play as an element of culture.[6] As regards the form, he calls play a voluntary act or occupation which is performed in certain fixed limits of time and place according to a self-imposed but absolutely binding rule, with its purpose in itself, accompanied by a sense of tension and joy and by a notion of being different from common life. He mentions two aspects of the function of play: it is a battle *for* something or a show *of* something.

The notion that it is only play may be pushed into the background but is never missing. The difference between what is believed and what is faked gets lost in the notion of play. We would say that the savage who plays at being a kangaroo is in his own idea a kangaroo. But here our ability to express ourselves fails; the savage is not aware of any distinction between the notion of being and playing; he knows nothing of identity, image or symbol.

A play community, Huizinga remarks, likes to shroud itself in mystery or to accentuate itself, by disguise, as different from the ordinary world. The mask, to us seemingly beautiful, terrifying and mysterious, takes us into an uncommon world, into the domain of the savage, the child and the poet, into the sphere of play.

In play there is always an element of suspense and uncertainty. Something is "at stake"—not the material results but the idea of succeeding. Even in the solitary game, such as patience, we observe that success satisfies the player. It is essential, however, that the player can boast of his success to others. Winning means proving one's superiority, not only in the game but in a more general sense of prestige and honor.

One fights not only with power, weapons, ingenuity or display, but sometimes also with tricks and deceit. Outwitting one's opponent becomes in itself a play figure. Mythological heroes such as Pelops, Jason, Gunther and Fria succeed through deceit or help from without. The false player is a player as yet.

Here, again, we remark that Huizinga's description fits the swindler.

BREAKING THE RULES OF THE GAME: THE FALSE PLAYER

Huizinga's definition of play has a strong sociological color. We certainly cannot say that playing originally relied upon an agreement to keep the rules. In animals we see play as a primitive activity without any agreement in a sociological norm-giving sense. It remains to be seen whether this holds good for human activity as well, or whether play becomes human only after a norm has been given. In erotic play, for example, there is hardly any agreement, but there is limitation. That limit is found in human existence itself, but it also depends on individual and social factors.

Playing cannot be confined to an intrinsically serious aim; it is rather one of the most essential human traits that man can be "unserious," that he can, even must, play. The relation to reality is not given up. But it is not the rules that matter, but what is possible within the rules. When respecting the rules, one tries to escape from limitations by exploring possible variations. So does the false player, in whose play the nature of play is not fully lost. But breaking through the rules, he loses sight of reality and his play becomes unacceptable.

The falseness of a swindler's play has different levels. First of all there is the moral level. The intent to benefit is a tacit agreement in every transaction. This becomes morally unacceptable when the opponent does not expect it and when he need not expect it. The second form of falsity lies in the social and juridical field. This conception of falsity is more restricted than the moral one. The law cannot cover all forms of falsity.

In a psychological sense, there is a third form of falseness; it is very distinct in the confrontation with the swindler. His behavior, his speech, his attitudes toward his victim are false. His affective contact is not genuine. He devaluates conversation, denatures suggestive communication and perverts words. This "lifting up" of objects to a false and untruthful level is typical of the swindler.

SOCIAL ROLE PLAYING: THE SPOILSPORT

The question remains how the falseness, the "role" of the swindler, differs from the role everybody plays in social intercourse. More than we realize, our behavior is influenced by what is expected of us. An actor may play the part of a king, doctor or vagabond because a definite classical image of "the" king, doctor or vagabond exists. He cannot be ordered to play the part of a megalomaniac when he does not know what a megalomaniac is. Nor can he play the part of an inhabitant of Mars as long as he has no example of one. We may go further and agree with Binswanger that the actor would not be able to play a part, and the poet would not be able to create one, if the role were not the base of human intercourse.[7]

In daily life a role is forced upon us: the part of a doctor, family man or chairman at a meeting. All those parts one man can play in succession. He does not stand on the stage in despair, like one who does not know his part. Before he becomes a doctor or chairman, he has been able to learn by watching how to play that part. Look how children imitate their parent's attitude, how the assistant unconsciously behaves and speaks as his professor does.

The famous German novelist Thomas Mann called character "a mythical role played in the illusion of being unique and original, as it were out of one's own invention."[8] The player of this role can act with certainty and dignity only because something timeless comes to light in him: the myth, the timeless scheme. Usually he does not realize this. Ancient man consciously lived in myth. He searched for an example in the past to tackle a problem of the present. Alexander followed in the footsteps of Miltiades, and Caesar identified himself with Alexander. Napoleon declared: "I am Charlemagne." He did not say that he was like Charlemagne, but that he was. That is the formulation of myth, according to Mann. Here we may subjoin Malinkowski's description of myth in primitive psychology: Myth is not meant as a symbol, but just expresses what is meant.[9]

Mann speaks of "the celebration of myth." In his novel *Joseph,* he used this motive: life as an imitation, a following-in-footsteps, an identification. This celebration of life, this playing and mythical identification, approaches swindling very nearly. Perhaps we may turn it around and say: Swindling is very close to the human need of playing a part, of celebrating a myth, of following-in-footsteps.[10] The swindler is in urgent need of clinging to an example. He plays to be what he is not and because he is tired of being what he is, as Sartre put it.[11]

However, a closer differentiation is necessary to show the specific quality of deceit as play. The swindler wears a mask: this he has in common with every human being. Jung distinguishes between persona and anima.[12] The anima only reaches the fellowman by sounding through the mask (*per-sonare*). Now it is evident that the social role is part of a highly organized and regulated game. In social life the roles are attuned to each other. They are complimentary. The salesman cannot do without the buyer's part. The pivot of a football team can only play his part when the other parties play, and he must rely on them.

This is not the swindler's way of playing. His goal is other than that of his fellows, but they do not know it. The swindler makes a show of cooperating, and he is even very adept in making pretenses. He skillfully answers to what people expect him to be. But suddenly he proves a spoilsport. He does not stand to his role. He drops his mask or he changes his role without giving notice.

THE SWINDLER'S MOTIVATION

He is a queer player indeed, this swindler. He is a false player, and he is a spoilsport who breaks the rules of society. He plays with things that do not belong to the world of play. Without their knowledge he plays with other people's money and goods. He plays with words and promises that are taken seriously by others. He plays with his own good reputation and honor, with notions such as guilt and responsibility. Everything is approached in a playful fashion and turned into a toy. The world of others is his playground.

Yet we say that he is a player. His mode of existence is playful, and his motivations lie in the sphere of sporting. Huizinga speaks of the desire to be praised and honored on account of superiority. Play and competition are aimed at proving oneself superior. The same holds true for crime, especially for swindling. This playing form of crime is clearly connected with personal achievement, with the desire for honor and fame. We should not forget that the swindler always has to gain the victory over his victim in a personal meeting.

There are swindlers who clearly show the tendency of proving themselves superior. They enjoy their roles and boast about their victim's stupidity. There are others who came to their fraudulent actions out of some bitter need. Many swindlers are neurotics. They fail in their personal relationships. The combination of swindling and sexual abnormalities is a frequent one.

Psychoanalytical authors, for example, Fenichel, have stressed frustration in youth as a condition which leads to swindling.[13] Abraham pointed out how an imposter time and again in his delicts took revenge for having been wronged by his parents.[14] A case described by Bromberg and Keizer gives a good example of swindling connected with sexual abnormalities as a consequence of lack of care in the youth.[15]

Also in these cases where swindling is a pathological symptom, we may maintain that the swindler is playing. As Huizinga proved, play may be very serious. In literature the "hero" has to fulfill a difficult task, which seems impossible. That is the agonal form of play. He also has to conceal his identity, which reminds of the secret elements of the sacred play. In the swindler we recognize the same motives of the agonal play and of disguise.

In every game one's own existence is at stake. Play is an attempt to conquer fear. As psychoanalysis shows, play and phantasy are means of mastering an otherwise unbearable situation. So when a man living at high pressure escapes into the game of swindling, he falls back on an original human mode of existence. There he obtains honor and adventure, there he can live in the sphere of festivity and exaltation, he can join the child and the poet.

Huizinga remarks that in archaic society, virtue had as yet no moral purport. Virtue implies being good, in the sense of being suitable for something. Then comes pride in one's own virtue and disdain of the opponent. Again we see how important these elements are in the swindler's game. He wants to show that he is "good" — for establishing contacts, obtaining prestige, love and confidence, which were denied him previously. The swindler, having proved himself to be more clever than his victim, does himself credit.

Modern man does not have many possibilities for escape. For wanderers and adventurers there is little room. Franz Alexander remarks how the desire for prestige and adventure may lead to crime in America.[16] "The land of the free and the home of the brave" has become a country of order. Where a short time ago pioneering spirit and courage were highly esteemed at the frontier of culture, adaptation to an extremely ordered society is now required. The sons of Buffalo Bill have to subject themselves to the routine of factory and office. Swindling, that play of imagination, is still left as a playground for those who are unfit to play their parts in society or who are tired of being what they are.

PLAY AND AGGRESSION

But, we may ask, does not the swindler fall out of the playing sphere, where his delicts cause serious harm and where his motives are hostile? The play element is indeed sometimes far removed. There has to remain an ethos in human play.

On the other hand, Huizinga emphasized the closeness of the notions of play and fight. In many languages the word play means fight, deadly struggle. He also recalls the play factor of warfare through the ages. It is this aspect of play that we find in psychoanalytical conceptions.

In the swindler a hostile and aggressive attitude can be stated. There is always some viciousness in his play. He is out to revenge himself, he wants to get the other person down. Some aim especially at women, others at the rich or the conceited, at the established order of society.

Aggressive behavior takes place in the scope of human encounter. Van der Horst shows how the specifically human aggressiveness arises from the encounter with a fellow-being.[17] One man "does" something to the other. Just by "being" we influence each other. Here the central problem of anthropology is approached: man as an individual and yet in communication, alone and member of a community. The encounter with the other always includes a challenge, an appeal for response. Also in play the encounter raises an aggressive attitude. But healthy man finds a response to a new appeal. Then encounter and play proceed harmoniously. Fighting spirit, competing spirit, ambition are forms of aggressiveness that need not be vicious.

Aggressiveness becomes malevolent when it is a reaction to experienced resistance and frustrations. Man lapses into aggressiveness when he cannot find the right response to the invitation in the encounter, says Van der Horst. This aggression arises from unbearable inferiority and isolation of the individual. In the same way the swindler's play becomes aggressive in the malevolent sense. When his encounter and his communication fail, he denatures play.

THE VICTIM

In many sports there are two parties playing the game. It is not to be expected that there will be any difference between the motivation of the two. Both are playing the game on equal terms, with the same intention. On this point, however, swindling makes an exception.

The swindler's opposite party is his victim. This victim does not accept his role as such. On the contrary, he expects somehow a benefit. The swindler promises him something of importance. This may be financial profit, esteem, adventure. Coming into connection with a duke, taking share in an inheritance of millions, being mixed up with military secrets or, in some cases, being considered a benefactor, that is satisfying to the victim's vanity. Sometimes the victim as well is somewhat treacherous. He is the man who is susceptible to flattery, open to dubious affairs, impressionable to the suggestion of the bogus title, the uniform or the clerical garment so often used by the swindler who knows his customers.

In Maurer's study we learn of many cooperating victims, they too fascinated by the allurement of money, fame, hero-worship.[18] We read the same in the revealing book of Sutherland:[19] "In the confidence games the principle is the same — beat a man who is trying to do something dishonest. It is impossible to beat an honest man in a confidence game." And further on: "Con mobs in England are compelled to confine their efforts to American visitors, whose sense of larceny has not been affected by the ocean voyage or the British environment. Even when abroad the average American will not pass up an opportunity to show how smart he is." To pour balm into the wound of his American readers, the author willingly admits that in his own case histories he meets the same traits in his countrymen.

As Bromberg remarks, the wish to acquire wealth is a normal tendency in everyone.[20] "The victim believes what the swindler tells him only because it coincides with his own inner wishes. In common language, the swindler succeeds in 'reading the mind' of the victim and in correctly interpreting his wishes. At the same time the swindler offers a target for ridicule, a scapegoat to beguile the victim into exposing his greedy wishes." This last remark refers to some confidence games where an accomplice of the swindler serves as an apparent stupid man who is deceived by the victim. So Bromberg concludes: "The study of the swindler's victims reveals the presence of similar unconscious tendencies within themselves, namely the wish for unlimited bounty and, second, the feeling of personal infallibility. The strategy of the total swindler relationship is that of a shrewd use of victim psychology by the criminal."

It is clear that here it is a question of mutual induction. The swindler, in his turn, needs his victim. He needs objects of play to support him in his role. The big car, the fine coat which makes the fine gentleman, impressive letterheads — all serve him as symbols. A uniform with distinctions, even false, gives him the rank and prestige that make him feel important. His victim's attitude toward him, though he knows that he does not deserve it, confirms his self-esteem. Being called an officer and being treated like an officer, he feels inspired in his role-playing.

So did the famous captain of Köpenick in one of Berlin's suburbs in the year 1906. So did the false brother who temporarily replaced the duke in Shakespeare's drama, *The Tempest.* The bogus titles and distinctions serve as symbols. For a symbol is not only a sign, it creates a new reality.

People clinging to symbols have visiting cards and letterheads printed immediately after a promotion or an examination. They arrange their desks according to their new position, with stamps, telephone and air-conditioning, not because they are needed but out of a craving to be what they are as soon as possible, that is, to express it symbolically. This leaning toward externals is observed in most swindlers. One of my patients, intending to write a book, had bought especially for this purpose an expensive scrap-book, beautiful portfolios for the illustrations, a typewriter and other properties which he showed proudly, even though he had hardly put pen to paper. Such imposing externals belong to the swindler's way of life; they are the side scenes he needs for his part. In the same way he needs his victim, whose attitude inspires him.

". . . and successfully to play topnotch swindling, one secret is the proper selection of a worthy opponent – commonly called a mark, or sucker."

THE SPECTATOR

There always has been and ever will be a peculiar interest in crime, especially in the swindler's shrewd actions. Nearly always we observe that the spectator entertains mixed feelings toward the swindler. A certain amount of admiration and envy are mingled with our indignation for his fraud. For he appeals to our own feelings. He transgresses the conventions, he proves that fairy tales can be true, he fulfills what we should like to do.

Swindler's stories are read like novels. For what interests us is the transgression, that is, stepping across the boundaries. People who travel, who become rich, who find happiness and love, the hero of the story, science-fiction — these are the themes that bring us into contact with romantic worlds. There are not many people who are able to lead a romantic life in reality. The swindler is one of the few who succeed in that performance.

The swindler's victim, who also tried to take his chance and to come in for a windfall, failed. He listened to the voice of the charmer and was mislead. The spectator, feeling inclined to the same game, establishes with malicious joy that such illusions cannot be real. He regrets this fact, and he calls himself happy that he could learn this lesson to someone else's cost. The swindler, the victim and the spectator all have the same human problems. So are all of us captivated and fascinated by the enchanting possibilities which are conjured up by the swindler.

THE SWINDLER AND THE PROBLEMS OF HUMAN EXISTENCE

We have observed in the foregoing how much we have in common with the swindler. It can be said of man in general that he plays. The swindler attracts our interest because he reflects human problems and because he shows fascinating solutions. The swindler-figure is worshiped as a hero and a god in mythology. Radin describes him as a trickster.[21] The trickster is a source of pleasure and mockery, but he has superhuman traits, too. We hear of disguise and deceit at all times. The Bible describes to us the serpent's deception in the beginning; and even the patriarchs Abram and Jacob used deception when they were in need. The mythological Trojan horse is an example of a subtle trick which has often been imitated in history.

Some animals have fallen into disrepute as deceivers. The spider allures the fly. In some primitive myths, it is also the spider who impersonates the deceiver. The Dakota Indians call the trickster by the name used for the spider. In other stories the wolf and the fox appear as deceivers.

Picaresque novels have been written by many great authors. The Spanish word *picaro* means rascal. The rascal is always a cunning and deceitful figure who nevertheless is the hero of the story. So Rabelais described Pantagruel, de Coster Till Eulenspiegel, Daudet Tartarin de Tarascon, Thomas Mann Felix Krull. Corneille adapted a Spanish play in *Le Menteur.* Goethe wrote his *Gross-Cophta,* referring to the historical impostor Cagliostro and the notorious affair in which Marie Antoinette's necklace was involved. Chaucer gave a description of clerical swindlers who sold pig's knuckle bones as relics. Wells, in his *Tono-Bungay,* described a swindling druggist, and Dickens, in his *Pickwick Papers,* the fraudulent lawyers Dodson and Fogg. Literature is thus full of swindler-figures, admirable for their playful behavior, with which they break through the limits of our delimited human existence. What is living deep in our hearts is reflected in these ambiguous figures of the godlike trickster, the worshiped and derided deceiver. He reveals our needs and problems, our want to escape from everyday reality, our tendency to cross the limit, to transgress.

Kerényi, in his essay on the trickster, compares him with Prometheus and even with Hermes.[22] As the Greek god, the trickster is an enemy of boundaries. Every man may perceive how his own feelings are the same. We want an escape, all of us. This means not only a flight, it also implicates unfolding, development, giving full scope to human possibilities; it also leads to culture. In play, in fantasy, in travelling, in scientific research, man is always in search of new worlds.

Huxley, who described our need for "doors in the wall," used the term self-transcendence.[23] Indeed, escape may be a form of transcendence. It is clear that Huxley did not think that human problems were solved when all suffering had been eliminated. Therefore his *Brave New World* is too gloomy, too inhuman. In the tendency to escape, we may recognize an effort to set ourselves at liberty. H. G. Wells in his autobiography speaks of his need for freedom of mind, of "escape from individual immediacies" and of a "powerful desire for disentanglement."[24] In this context, escape does not mean a retreat from the world, but an existential desire for reflection and independence in order to live in the world. It is the same tendency for transcendence that we find in the sphere of sacrifice, as Gusdorf described it:[25] *Le sacrifice consomme le dépassement d'un univers et l'institution d'un univers nouveau.*

Sometimes people seek escape in intoxication. This also may be a means for reaching contact with the other world, with the Holy. Everywhere we meet the image of Hermes, who is the messenger, the intermediary between gods and men, the hero who transgresses the boundaries. It is worthwhile to note that he is also the god of the thieves.

Are we not going too far in our attempts to connect crime with sacred things? Van der Horst has discussed human problems caused by the loss of Messianic expectations.[26] He describes how in the past there was always hope for the better, hope for salvation. Then he mentions "precriminological problems," since crime is connected with this topic. Indeed, the central problems of human existence come under discussion where crime is concerned. Every crime must be considered as a failed anticipation of salvation. The swindler sets salvation tangibly before his victim's and spectator's eyes. But the crime never fulfills the actual hope. Lindner, too, points out that crime has an aim, that it is "an alternate form of adjustment, responsive to basic needs and appetites, an avenue for the release of accumulated tensions and frustrations, designed to restore the integrity of the person. . . ."[27]

In the swindler these elements are obviously present. His crime seeks a solution for his needs, which are not in the first place financial needs but, however obscure even to himself, human problems. He anticipates salvation. Imagination, hope and transcendence are evident in this sort of crime. Playing, the swindler's central characteristic, is related to the notions of salvation and holiness. Huizinga remarks that human nature always strives after higher things, whether these are worldly honor and superiority or a conquest of all earthly things. The inborn function by which man activates these strivings is play, he says. "The notions of play and holiness touch," a trend of thought that Huizinga cites from Plato. So indeed our study of the swindler brings us into contact with fundamental human problems. Worshiped as a god, derided and prosecuted as a rascal, as a trickster a source of pleasure, as a criminal an example of human needs and strivings, the swindler remains an ambiguous figure to the last.

FOOTNOTES

1. Freud, S.: *The Relation of the Poet to Daydreaming,* in Collected Papers, Volume 4. London, Hogarth Press, 1924.
2. Freud, S.: *Formulations Regarding the Two Principles in Mental Functioning,* in Collected Papers, Volume 4. London, Hogarth Press, 1924.
3. Freud, S.: *Beyond the Pleasure Principle.* London, International Psychoanalytic Press, 1922.
4. Freud, A.: *The Ego and the Mechanisms of Defence.* London, Hogarth Press, 1937.
5. Feshbach, S.: The drive-reducing function of fantasy behavior. *J Abnorm Soc Psychol,* 1955.
6. Huizinga, J.: *Homo Ludens.* Boston, Beacon, 1955.
7. Binswanger, L.: *Grundformen und Erkenntniss menschlichen Daseins,* 2. Aufl. Zürich, Max Niehans, 1953, p. 355.
8. Mann, Th.: *Freud und die Zukunft,* in *Adel des Geistes.* Stockholm, Bermann-Fischer, 1943, p. 592.
9. Malinowski, B.: *Myth in Primitive Psychology,* in *Magic, Science and Religion and other Essays.* Glencoe, Free Press, 1948, p. 79.
10. Deutsch, H.: The impostor: Contribution to ego psychology of a type of psychopath. *Psychoanal Quart, 24:*483, 1955; reprinted in Deutsch, H.: *Neuroses and Character Types.* New York, Int Univs, 1965, p. 319.
11. Sartre, J.-P.: *Kean, par Alexandre Dumas. Adaptation de Jean-Paul Sartre.* Paris, Gallimard, 1954, p. 81.
12. Jung, C. G.: *Die Beziehungen zwischen dem Ich und dem Unbewussten.* Zürich, Rascher, 1939.
13. Fenichel, O.: *The Psychoanalytic Theory of Neurosis.* London, Routledge, 1946, p. 529.
14. Abraham, K.: The history of an impostor in the light of psychoanalytical knowledge. *Psychoanal Quart, 4:*570-587, 1935.

15. Bromberg, W., and Keizer, S.: A psychologic study of the swindler. *Amer J Psychiat, 94:* 1441, 1938.
16. Alexander, F.: *Our Age of Unreason.* Philadelphia, Lippincott, 1951.
17. Horst, L. can der: Agressivité et délire. *L'évolution psychiatrique, 4:*591, 1950.
18. Maurer, D. W.: *The Big Con. The Story of the Confidence Man and the Confidence Game.* New York, Bobbs-Merril, 1949.
19. Sutherland, E. H.: *The Professional Thief.* Chicago, U of Chicago, 1937, pp. 69, 71.
20. Bromberg, W.: *Crime and the Mind.* Philadelphia, Lippincott, 1948, pp. 23, 24, 75.
21. Radin, P.: *The Trickster. A Study in Indian Mythology.* With Commentaries by K. Kerényi and C. G. Jung. London, Routledge, 1956.
22. Kerényi, K.: in Radin, *op. cit. supra.*
23. Huxley, A.: *The Doors of Perception.* London, Chatto & Windus, 1954.
24. Wells, H. G.: *An Experiment in Autobiography.* New York, 1934.
25. Gusdorf, G.: *L'expérience humaine du sacrifice.* Paris, Presses universitaires de France, 1948, p. 249.
26. Horst, L. van der: Precriminological problems. *J Soc Ther, 2* (No. 4) , 1956.
27. Lindner, R. M.: *Stone Walls and Men.* New York, Odyssey Press, 1946, p. 39.

PART FOUR
PHYSIQUE AND PERSONALITY

INTRODUCTION

MIND AND BODY ARE INTERRELATED — the body influences the mind, and the mind influences the body. Man is not separable into parts. Descartes in his *Discourse on Method* advised those who sought the truth about man (or other subjects) to divide the subject into as many parts as are necessary in order to make a complete inventory of each, but that it should be clearly understood that such a division is only a methodological expedient created by ourselves, and that man remains indivisible. The word "and," in speaking of "mind and body," is only a grammatical conjunction and not a term designating an existential conjunction. Our body shows the appearance of age, as a glance in a mirror should readily reveal, but our spirit or soul may seem ageless or immortal. Bifurcation of the two is comforting. Mind-body or soul-body, however, is a relation or organization; the human being is a unity.

Hippocrates postulated the *habitus phthisicus* and the *habitus apoplecticus*,[1] and ever since then at various times studies have been made on the possible relation between the shape of a person's body and his behavior. Most notably, in 1925, Kretschmer postulated the asthenic, athletic and pyknic body types.[2] In 1942 Sheldon produced a study on physique and temperament, substituting ectomorph, endomorph and mesomorph for Kretschmer's trio.[3] These and other studies have suggested that the relationship between body shape and behavior is not artifactual.[4]

Although there is considerable disagreement over the significance of an association between physique and behavior, the evidence suggests slight positive associations between a build that is short and broad with traits resembling friendliness, moodiness, aggression and impulsivity, or between a build that is tall and narrow with the traits of introversion, inhibition and obsession. In a recent study Kagan of Harvard University favors an interpretation based on the assumption of the establishment of attitudes toward the self as a function of body build, but he adds that it is not possible to rule out completely the possible influence of complex physiological factors that are antecedent to both body build and the behavioral variables.

Yet the body-mind relationship is not a one-way street. The body affects the mind, and the mind also affects the body. Embarrassment, for example, causes blushing. To his monumental credit, Freud demonstrated the formation of symptoms as one of the possible consequences of internal psychic conflict.[5] But the chicken-egg dilemma of which comes first is invariably raised about the body-mind relationship. Thus, it has been observed, for example, that people who have a tendency toward depressive mood states have an increased incidence of upper-respiratory infections at the times of their depressions; and it is asked, does the upper-respiratory infection trigger the depression, or vice versa? Is the question a moot one?[6] When a question is asked over and over again, through the centuries, it is usually a meaningless question, and the problem might be better approached differently.

It is generally agreed, in medical circles, that mind and body are on a two-way street. A curved spine and a curved personality may go together. So too with ulcers and tension, acne and hostility, etc. The emptiness of ages appears in the face of "The Man with the Hoe."[7] The ancients wisely said, *Vultus est index animus.* The shape of one's body is a result, to a considerable degree, of the way one thinks and of one's experience.[8] We may say that the face of a child may not be his determination, but the face of an old man comes from what he has done with himself as well as what has been done to him. "God has given you one face, and you make yourself another."[9]

Like other forms of expression, body movement and posture reflect state of mind.[10] Although physically small, a person who moves with grace and assurance is majestic. How a person exercises provides a clue to his character. Gymnastics, for example, requires attention. One who cannot mobilize his energies or direct his physical movements may also be unable to organize his work; another who tenses every muscle and expends too much effort for good results may do the same in human relations. Too much or too little effort, fear of floor or other special exercises, a rhythm of movement unsuited to one's size, weight and age — all these reveal personality traits. So does one's manner of walking. The rapid "dog-trotter" may have a one-track mind; the large strider may be driven by high ambitions; and the irregular short-stepper may be emotionally insecure.

Physical exercises help in changing physical patterns which in turn influence inner attitudes. Good physique and overall coordination make for improved self-esteem. Athletics and gymnastics improve physique and coordination, and with such improvement, the individual usually makes progress in intellectual and other endeavors. Physical exercises may help a person become more keenly aware of some of the hampering unconscious factors in his personality structure. This awareness may stimulate him to change. Furthermore, the use of regular exercises, successfully performed, may give a feeling of physical and psychological well-being, which in turn may contribute to the solution of other problems of living. Movement, especially for the child, is the royal road to body image and self-identity.

Gertrud Lederer-Eckardt has a paper in this volume on gymnastics and personality. She worked with many of Karen Horney's patients, and in a preliminary statement, Horney has observed:[11]

Most neurotic persons have one or the other disturbance in their muscular systems — spasms, backaches, neckaches, arthritic propensities, weakness in moving this or that part of the body, poor coordination in gait and posture, shaky bodily balance.

Some of these are secondary adaptations or organic deficiencies such as deformed feet, or a curvature of the spine. But the ailments under which the patient suffers are often less due to the original deficiency than to the secondary faulty use of muscles. These can be corrected by competent gymnastics.

What is of special interest to the analyst is the fact that many muscular disorders are the expression of psychological difficulties. Thus general or localized muscular tension can be the expression of psychic tension engendered by the necessity to suppress an explosive hostility. Cramps in the neck or legs of an acute nature may indicate a spell of a destructive self-condemnation. A gait in which only the legs move forward while the trunk leans back may express a conflict between aggressiveness and self-effacement — and so on. The analyst may observe at least some of such psychosomatic parallels; or he may be aware that complaints about muscular pains occur at a time when certain conflicts become more acute in the analysis. But here he tends to be over-confident. Since the faulty movements or posture are determined by psychic factors, he expects them to disappear automatically when the particular neurotic difficulties are straightened out. To some extent such changes actually do take place spontaneously. The patient's physical balance, for instance, will improve as soon as his psychic equilibrium is stabilized. But often such expectations are not borne out by facts, the reason being the same as mentioned before in the case of an originally organic defect. The faulty movements or posture, however determined, do not remain static; other muscle groups are set in motion in order to compensate for the first wrong attitude; and these adaptive changes in turn influence other parts. The secondary changes, then, are no more psychological; they are due to physical necessities. This is why they do not yield to psychotherapy. It would be better, therefore, to encourage the patient to get expert help for his bodily difficulties. To do so will benefit him also in two other ways: To do gymnastics requires active and consistent effort on the patient's part because it means not only to take lessons but also to do regular exercises on his own. And here he runs up against frequent difficulties: knowing full well that exercises are in his own interest, he just cannot get himself to do them. He is faced, thereby, more unequivocally than in analysis with his resistance against doing something for himself constructively.

The other benefit lies in the observations of an intelligent gym-teacher. The analyst may be an astute observer; yet he would not see in handwriting what a graphologist sees. Similarly, concerning bodily movements and attitudes, he will fail to observe many peculiarities which would strike the trained gymnastic teacher. The latter's observations will frequently coincide with factors discussed in analysis. For instance, the patient may have recognized in analysis how alienated he is from himself. The gym-teacher will observe that the patient, complaining about a pain in his foot, is unable to indicate the exact spot which hurts. This means that he is not directly related to his foot and must interpolate a period of thinking before he is able to find out the source of his discomfort. If this is discussed with the patient, his alienation from self is demonstrated to him on a basis that is different from analysis. Experiences of this kind carry quite some conviction, particularly for those patients who tend to regard psychological findings as a matter of purely intellectual interest.

Finally these observations dispel an illusion which many patients cherish. Not having much real regard for themselves, they often discard their own neurotic suffering as unimportant. What counts is to maintain an impregnable facade. Their pride would be wounded if others would be cognizant of their inner difficulties. They like to believe, therefore, that their disturbances are invisible to others. Being presented with evidence to the contrary may come to them as an unpleasant surprise but also gives them an additional incentive to overcome their predicaments.

Intelligent gymnastic work, then, has psychological value. It calls the person's attention to his pecularities in gait or posture which he has not observed on his own. It points out to him possible connections with psychic difficulties. It makes him aware that these latter are noticeable to others. It gives him, last but not least, a feeling of the unity between body and soul.

Crawling on all fours is certainly not an heroic posture. For example, the snake, crawling on its belly, offends the sensibilities (a worthless or treacherous fellow is called a snake), whereas the peacock, strutting vaingloriously, represents royalty. The more erect an individual stands — the more he gets off the ground — the more we admire him. A speaker who leans on a lectern is not as compelling as a speaker who stands erect, unsupported by the lectern. And going underground is unbecoming to man. The attributes of a bird are more appealing than those of the worm. Going into a subway or a bomb shelter lowers the dignity of man. The coal miner — and even the man who went "20,000 Leagues Under the Sea" (as Jules Verne fantasied it) — are not hero-ideals. On the other hand, Icarus while a fool is an ancient hero, and nowadays spacemen are idolized.

Being a "man" means being "up." Sexually, he must have the power of erection. In life generally, you have to call a person *up* before you can call him *down*. You do not hit a person who is down. While being up has its perils, it usually brings rewards. Michael Balint in his paper on "Philobatism and Ocnophilia" reminds us that in the circus the trapeze artist is admired and received back to the ground by an attractive young girl.[12] Elsewhere in this volume,[13] Dennis Farrell and Samuel Z. Klausner discuss the adventures of sky sports. (We do not expect a woman to get off the ground — perhaps because women, especially those called "dizzy," are often considered to be already out in space.)

Ted Nolan Thompson discusses the "whys" of weightlifting along with a description of bodybuilding, Olympic-styled competition and power-lifting.[14] Weightlifting requires efforts which are measured objectively, and physical measurement helps one gain inner security. Weightlifting, an individual enterprise, fits the needs of persons who want to be alone, and through the activity one *really* changes physically. The change may help one's self-image. Thus, as one individual said, "I'm three inches taller and thirty pounds heavier, and I feel I have become a man." Thompson considers that the motivational force in weightlifting is basically the desire to increase strength and improve bodily shape (some persons, however, say they weightlift to "let frustrations out, not to bodybuild").

We are all familiar with the recurring illustrated advertisements showing a pathetically skinny young fellow who through a muscle-building program changed into a big, powerful-looking, supremely confident man. One individual known as Charles Atlas apparently had been a ninety-seven pound weakling and developed a magnificently muscled body through a process he called "dynamic tension." One young man, concerned about "body worshiping," recently inquired of the Editor of the *Christian Science Monitor:* "I am sure you have seen 'muscle men' at the beaches where they perform. Is such body worshiping wrong? I would like such muscles but this I feel is obviously a material goal not to be conquered by spiritual means. Am I correct?" The Editor replied: "The 'muscle men' business at certain beaches seems to have become a kind of cult or affectation with a highly materialistic basis. But of course there is nothing wrong with your desire to be fit and vigorous, indeed to excel in physical sports. You can strive for such excellence through a mental attitude which does not make little false gods of muscles, but takes the proper human steps — notably hard work and skillful training — to achieve dominion over the body and its ever-increasing potentialities. It's interesting that so many new records in sports are being set lately, doubtless the result of an increasing awareness of the possibilities of dominion."[15]

Thompson has been critical of the sideshow aspects that he says the Amateur Athletic Union has allowed to come into the sport, and he participated in a lawsuit to restrain the Union from letting body-building displays accompany lifting contests. It is a kind of show, he says, that features male "beefcake" rather than female "cheesecake." The bodybuilders are photographed, almost nude, biceps and pectorals oiled and distended, in magazines that compete with "girlie" picture magazines at newstands. He feels that bodybuilding is tolerated by the AAU as a feature of its weightlifting competitions apparently because it increases attendance.

According to Thompson, some myths surrounding weightlifting have kept physicians and laymen alike from deriving full benefit from the sport. Many persons, he says, believe that weightlifting makes an athlete musclebound; that "dynamic tension," as taught by Charles Atlas, produces what schoolboy athletes call "eggshell" muscles; and, in general, that weightlifting is too strenuous to fit into most medical regimens. With most of this, Thompson emphatically disagrees. Weightlifting does not stiffen an athlete's muscles. It can be and is a valuable part of training for many other sports.

Those so-called eggshell muscles developed by Atlas products cannot make a champion out of an ordinary performer, but much the same system of muscle development, under the name of isometric contraction, has been studied systematically and is a useful part of physical medicine today. As for strenuousness in a medical regimen, no form of exercise, if exercise is tolerable at all, can be so carefully graduated and adjusted, and none gives so quick a return for time invested.

Is there any truth to the before-and-after magazine and newspaper advertisements of muscle-building courses? One weightlifter observed: "Sure, I've seen a 135-pound man transformed into a 175-pound 'giant' in comparison, by working out with weights. But," he sadly added, "it doesn't happen overnight, and I'm not sure about the guarantee that the 'after guy' always gets a beautiful girl."[16]

FOOTNOTES

1. Hippocrates: *Genuine Works,* tr. by Adams, F. Baltimore, Williams & Wilkins.
2. See generally, Kretschmer, E.: *A Textbook of Medical Psychology.* London, 1934.
3. Sheldon, W. H.: *Varieties of Temperament.* New York, Harper, 1942.
4. See Gleuck, S. and E.: *Predicting Delinquency and Crime.* Cambridge, Harvard U Pr, 1959.
5. So many people asking for surgical and medical assistance are in fact suffering from emotional problems. The conversion of neurotic or emotional suffering into organic illness (psychosomatic or conversion symptoms) has been called that "mysterious leap into the organic," but while a mystery, it is one of the fundamental concepts in psychoanalysis. An individual thus may speak with his body as well as with words. Most often, he is by his symptom saying that he is starved for kindness and affection.
6. The philosopher Hegel (1770-1831) would object to trying to trace back the chain of causes to a First Cause. He broke with the sort of logic which deduces one proposition from another. The philosophy of Hegel is the philosophy of the dialectic. Poet Yevgeny Yevtushenko comments as follows on the mind-body interaction: "Pushkin was short, poorly proportioned, ugly. But he overcame his own ugliness, both through his awareness of the strength of a trained mind and through his awareness of the strength of his body, a physical strength cultivated by his mind . . . The feeling of one's own disharmony makes a person suspicious, jealous and spiteful, and such malevolence crushes a person's inner capabilities. Often physically strong people behave unpleasantly because of a feeling of mental inadequacy and, conversely, people whose minds are well educated sometimes behave unpleasantly because of a feeling of physical inadequacy. Only a harmony of the two elements leads to kindness, and kindness is the fullest expression of one's humanity." Yevtushenko, Y.: A Poet Against the Destroyers. *Sports Illustrated,* December 19, 1966, p. 105.
7. Millet's painting.
8. The outstanding physician, Alexis Carrel, put it thus: "Our outward form expresses the qualities, the powers, of our body and our mind." Carrel, A.: *Man, The Unknown.* New York, Harper, 1939, p. 62.
9. Shakespeare: *Hamlet.* Act III, Sc. 1, Line 150.
10. To go from the sublime to the ridiculous, one commentator has said that the best characterization of a man is how he wears his hat: "If he wears it perpendicular, he is honest, pedantic and boresome. If he wears it tipped slightly, he belongs to the best and most interesting people, is nimble-witted and pleasant. A deeply tipped hat indicates frivolity and obstinate, imperious nature. A hat worn on the back of the head signifies improvidence, easiness, conceit, sensuality and extravagance; the further back the more

dangerous is the position of the wearer. The man who presses his hat against his temple complains, is melancholy and in a bad way." Gerstacker, F., quoted in Gross, H.: *Criminal Psychology*. Boston, Little, 1915. Dr. Ralph Gerard, Director of Special Studies at the University of California, has reported that schizophrenics drink less coffee than other people. (Lecture, The Nosology of Schizophrenia, presented at the Menninger Foundation, Topeka, Kansas, September 21, 1966.) Bernard Shaw once observed that we judge an artist by his highest moments and the criminal by his lowest. Of course, though, the human personality, both normal and abnormal, is full of paradox. Carl Sandburg said that Abraham Lincoln, for example, was as hard as rock and as soft as drifting fog. See Macdonald, J. M.: The prompt diagnosis of psychopathic personality. *Amer J Psychiat (Supp), 122*:65, 1966.

11. Horney, K.: Preliminary statement of Lederer-Eckardt, G.: Gymnastics and personality. *Amer J Psychoanal, 7,* 1947, reprinted with permission.
12. P. 243.
13. Farrell, D.: *Infra* at p. 661; Klausner, S. Z.: *Infra* at p. 670.
14. P. 254. It is also to be noted that the process of reducing involves "putting on a new face" or developing a "divine posture." See Bruch, H.: The psychology of reducing. *Quart J Child Behav, 3*:350, 1951.
15. Consider Alexander, F.: Concerning the genesis of the castration complex. *Psychoanal Rev, 22*:49, 1935.
16. Quoted in *New Orleans Times- Picayune,* May 23, 1965.

"Mummery, Old Man, I know what a shock those dirty dogs at KanineKix dealt us when they cancelled their account. But where are you going now? Would you mind growling once if you're off to tackle the Seamless Shoe people or growl twice if you're heading for your psychiatrist?"

PHILOBATISM AND OCNOPHILIA

MICHAEL BALINT

THE INTRODUCTION OF NEW WORDS calls for justification; their usefulness has to be proved. I propose to do this in two ways. I intend to show, first, that by using these two terms we can discuss certain human experiences more easily than without them; and, secondly, that in this way we can better understand these experiences and their dynamism. Let us therefore briefly survey what we already know about thrills; that is, philobatism and ocnophilia. This will help us at the same time to clear our way for the next step, since this survey will bring us to the point which our theory of these phenomena has reached.

Let us start with the children's games. As I have said, the zone of security is always called either "home" or "house," which points to its being a symbol for the safe mother. We have seen also that all thrills entail the *leaving* and *rejoining* of security. The pleasures experienced in either of these two phases – that is, either when staying in security or when leaving it in order to return to it – are very primitive, self-evident, and apparently in no need of explanation, although it must be stated that not every adult can enjoy them equally. True, some adults seem to be at ease only when in the state of stable security; others, on the contrary, enjoy leaving it in search of adventures and thrills and show signs of boredom and irritation if they have to forgo them for any length of time. Somehow, however, correctly or incorrectly, one gets the impression that ocnophilia might be the older and more primitive of the two attitudes. Later we shall have to examine more closely how far this impression is misleading.

One's relation to security – that is to say, one's behavior in the state of security – appears *prima facie* to be simple, uncomplicated, practically unstructured, whereas one's relation to the intervening state, while enjoying the thrill, seems very complicated and involved indeed. A readily available parallel is the way the infant clings to his mother before leaving her, before walking away. This is undoubtedly true, but it should not be forgotten that this difference might be caused merely by the unequal rate of maturation of the various systems of motility and not necessarily by those of the mind; that is to say, because the nerve centers and musculature of the mouth and arms involved in clinging mature earlier than those concerned with walking and maintaining equilibrium. It would be wise to be cautious in our inference from these observations about the existence of certain mental attitudes; as, for instance, taking the nipple and sucking it appears in a full-time baby at about the same time as pushing the nipple out of the mouth and turning the head away. It is even possible that the pushing out might be the earlier function, as premature babies often have to be taught to take the nipple, although they can already swallow faultlessly. What we can say at this moment is that the relative chronology of philobatism and ocnophilia is uncertain, although it is certain that they are both very primitive.

Nevertheless, ocnophilia impresses us as the more spontaneous, almost reflex-like attitude, whereas one cannot state with certainty where philobatism really belongs. In addition, the appearance of ocnophilic tendencies in seemingly purely philobatic situations suggests a kind of regressive trend and, conversely, a more primitive nature on the part of ocnophilia. To quote a few examples: the tight-rope walker holds a pole in his hands, the lion tamer a whip, the conductor of an orchestra a baton, and so on. Moreover, the car driver has to learn not to grip the wheel and the skier not to press his sticks; similarly a boxer, a weightlifter, an oarsman, in fact every athlete, has to be taught not to tense up his neck and jaw muscles when making a supreme effort. As already mentioned, the performance of an acrobat is valued more highly if he does *not* use his hands; if he hangs from the trapeze by his feet or his teeth, lets go the handlebars of the bicycle, drops the reins of his horse when standing on its back, enters the lion's cage without a whip or, to come down to the level of ordinary human beings, rides on the round-abouts standing up, without leaning on or holding on to anything. A traditional trick often used by acrobats which always increases the excitement, the thrill, is to get rid of and throw away parts of their equipment in an already exposed situation or before entering into a still more exposed one. We may even add that the transitional objects of young children and toddlers described by Winnicott[1] are nearly always clutched, pressed or cuddled; furthermore, all artists must have something in their hands: a brush, a chisel and mallet, a baton, a bow, a drawing pencil and ruler, a pen and so on. In general, even statues tend to hold something fast, no matter whether they represent soldiers, scientists, artists, politicians or martyrs, and even the Virgin and the Infant Jesus apparently must have something in their hands. So it seems that to hold on to something, to have something in one's hand, is more primitive and more general than being independent, being completely on one's own, with hands empty. The things that we cling to — the ocnophilic objects — appear in the first instance to be symbols of security, that is, the safe, loving mother.

After this digression, let us turn to the behavior in the philobatic state. The first feature that impresses itself upon us is that the individual is on his own, away from every support, relying on his own resources. The outward expression of this attitude is a brave, erect stance; crawling on all fours, as we all know, is not an heroic posture, whereas walking, and especially stalking and strutting, usually is. In this respect it should not be forgotten that walking in an erect position means being fairly well away from the safe earth, the only contact with it being through the soles of the feet. We understand now why the thrill is the greater the farther we dare get away from safety — in distance, in speed or in exposure — that is to say, the more we can prove our independence. A further relevant factor is the duration of this independent state, the length of time we can hold out in it. This explains why it is so attractive for some people to undertake crossings of the ocean in small boats, in one-man dinghies or on rafts, as in the famous Kon-Tiki expedition or to remain in the air in a glider for hours or even longer than a day.

These observations suggest that philobatism is symbolically related to erection and potency, although it is difficult to decide whether philobatism should be considered as an early, primitive stage of genitality or the other way round, as a retrospective, secondary genitalisation in adult age of an originally nongenital function. In any case, this interrelation explains the other aspect of the objects the philobat clings to, which we called ocnophilic objects. The whip of the lion-tamer, the pole of the tightrope walker, the sticks of the skier, the baton of the conductor, the sword or rifle of the soldier, the artist's tools and the pilot's joy-stick are undoubtedly symbols of the erect, potent penis. Having an ocnophilic object with us means also being in possession of a powerful, never-flagging penis, magically reinforcing our own potency, our own confidence. From this we can understand the special affection people have for their particular ocnophilic objects. The skier must have his own particular sticks, the lion-tamer his favorite whip, the tennis player his special racket, the cricketer his favorite bat, the conductor his baton, the artist his brush and so on. Possessing these well-proved ocnophilic objects, he feels himself in possession of almost magic powers and is much more confident in braving the hazards of the philobatic state.

Seen from this angle, we may say that the philobatic thrills represent in a way the primal scene in symbolic form. A powerful and highly skilled man produces on his own a powerful erection, lifting him far away from security, performing in his lofty state incredible feats of valor and daring, after which, in spite of untold dangers, he returns unhurt to the safe mother earth. In this connection the earth has a double aspect corresponding to the ambivalent situation; she is dangerous because of her irresistible attraction which, if unconditionally surrendered to, may cause mortal damage; but at the same time she is loving and forgiving, offering her embracing safety to the defiant hero on his skillful return. It is traditional in the circus for the hero-acrobat while performing high up in the air to be assisted, admired and finally received back to the gound by an attractive young girl.

Acrobatics, therefore, are one special form of shows all of which symbolically represent the primal scene. Funfairs also offer primitive shows of various kinds. One type of showpiece is either beautiful, attractive women or frightening, odd and strange females; the other type is powerful, boasting, challenging men. Simplified to the bare essentials, practically all stage plays or novels, however highbrow, are still concerned with these three kinds of human ingredients.

The specific difference between shows in general and philobatic shows and feats is the presence of *real external danger*. In classical times the real danger was, in fact, naked cruel death and not merely a threatening possibility of it. People were killed in reality by wild beasts, in gladiator fights, mock battles and so on. As civilization progressed, this real death was replaced gradually by illusions, as in the theater (the last scene of *Hamlet* ends with about *half a dozen corpses* on the stage), or by threatening presence of real danger of death as in the modern circus. However, both in the circus and in the theatre, the performers are professionals who have inherited from the ancient heroes all the highly powered and ambivalent emotional tributes of the general public, such as awe, envy, contempt, admiration and so on. The dynamic reason for this ambivalent respect is that acrobats and actors are allowed and dare to perform publicly philobatic acts symbolizing primal scenes. The community, however, is allowed to participate in the form of passive spectators only, thrilled by identification.

The question of what happened, mainly during the nineteenth century, that turned the spectators into actors is an interesting problem and worth a proper study. It is possible that this change is only one symptom of a general tendency of that epoch, perhaps best expressed by Nietzsche, "to live dangerously."

Why do some people expose themselves unnecessarily to real dangers in search of thrills, while others cannot even bear the thought of exposing themselves to dangers? In others words, what are the relevant mechanisms involved in these two — apparently equally irrational — attitudes? The essays in this volume suggest answers to the question.

NOTE

This essay, slightly modified, is reprinted with permission of the International Universities Press from Michael Balint's book, *Thrills and Regressions*.

FOOTNOTES

1. Winnicott, D. W.: Transitional Objects and Transitional Phenomena. *Int J of Psycho-Anal, 34*:89, 1953.

"Surprise! I know that gorgeous doll, Georgia, always receives you back to terra firma. But she's mad at you and asked for volunteers from the bookkeeping department!"

GYMNASTICS AND PERSONALITY

GERTRUD LEDERER-ECKARDT

WE HAVE MANY WAYS of expressing ourselves. In whatever we do, we display traits which are our very own and part of our whole personality. There is an intimate relationship between our movements and posture and our mood, state of tension or relaxation. One reflects the other, and each is part of our whole self. Most people are unaware of this connection. They pay little attention to their bodies unless there is some disturbance. And then they become indignant. They show more respect for the little signs of car trouble and take better care of their cars generally than of their bodies.

This neglect of our bodies is particularly unnecessary since the body responds so readily and gratefully to even small attentions regularly given. Regular exercises help to increase our relaxation, flexibility in movement and general health. By doing exercises, we can also learn about, or at least become aware of, our inner selves. How we perform the exercises, what difficulties we have, and how we walk and carry ourselves — all of these reveal much about ourselves. A trained gym teacher can be helpful in bringing some of these points to our attention.

Here are some examples of what we can learn about ourselves and others from exercising:

When you hear adults remark: "No wonder I am fat. In my profession I must sit all day. I never get a chance to move. I can never find the time to do anything for myself. Anyhow, why should I bother at my age?" Such people certainly neglect themselves and are inclined to blame other factors for their extra fat when they are really personally responsible for it.

When we observe a person trying to do an exercise, we get a clue to his character. One person, for instance, when asked to swing his leg backward and forward began frantically to wave both arms and legs and twist his body. He could not seem to mobilize his energies or direct his movements. On better acquaintance, he told me that he could not get organized in his work. Another person, when asked to put her hands on the floor without bending her knees, said, even before she made any attempt: "Oh, no, I could never do that." After further work we both found that she had to avoid all situations where she might appear awkward or did not show up well in her own eyes or the eyes of others. Every challenge frightened her because she lacked self-confidence.

Another person stiffened his body, tensed every muscle and tried to do the bending exercise. Naturally he could not do it. You need a flexible back and a relaxed state to reach the floor without bending your knees. When he could not do it, he looked at me with silent reproaches and seemed to say, "I am brave and willing, but this will kill me. It is not my fault; you expect the impossible of me." He later admitted that he often felt the same way and acted the same way at work and with people.

You will no doubt recognize the person who is just too relaxed to do exercises and generally seems unable to "pull himself together." And, by contrast, you probably know the kind of person who approaches his exercises with a "hammer and tongs" attitude. He drives himself ruthlessly, never takes a rest and only stops when he is near collapse. No pace is too fast for him, and whether it be in exercise or elsewhere, he makes enormous demands on himself and expects the impossible of himself.

EXERCISE AND EFFORT

There are people who complain quickly and openly about the effort required of them in exercising, although they want to achieve the results. We can be sure that these people guard themselves against exertion in other fields, pamper themselves and feel very hurt if they do not get great returns for their efforts. Other people put out effort willingly but do not even take reasonable precautions against injury. They bump into everything in their paths, and do not seem to see obstacles, nor do they feel their bodies as real and subject to pain and injury.

Floor exercises bring out other personality traits. Some people are enthusiastic about them and say they are reminded of childhood pleasures and games. Others prefer floor exercises because they eliminate the dangers of falling and stumbling and also allow for greater concentration on one exercise. Mrs. B., however, detested floor exercises despite her need for them. She was a woman who "lived in the clouds." As she "came down to earth" and got greater insight into her personality problems, these exercises became less objectionable to her. Personality difficulties often interfere with a person's ability to relax enough and yet to maintain the control of muscles needed to fall without injury to himself.

INDIVIDUAL RHYTHM

In the course of exercising, we watch our bodies and discover our own individual rhythm. Two factors determine our rhythm. One is the biological factor, which is dependent on the person's size, weight and age; the other is the psychological factor. Both influence a person's speed of performance. People vary considerably in their innate rhythms. A better understanding of these factors and testing of them can help a person to get more pleasure from effort, to conserve his energy and to use it more effectively. Working against the rhythm best suited to our biological and psychological needs may produce tensions. Disturbance in our natural rhythm may express itself in many ways.

Mr. A., for example, could not sleep. His wife suggested exercise as a way of tiring himself out so he would get some rest. He began to do the exercises in a hurried fashion. I brought this to his attention and told him that he moved much more quickly than was natural for his body length. Tall people need more energy to move as fast as shorter ones, and if they move too fast they tire more easily. Tall people get better results if they move more slowly. Mr. A. said that he was always forcing himself to move more quickly to complete what he felt was expected of him. He complained that he never accomplished enough. When he recognized the general need to push himself, he began to consider his need for psychological help. Moving against his natural rhythm was probably one of the factors which contributed to his insomnia.

Some people need a breathing-spell more often than others. This need for a creative pause shows up in exercise, in work, in walking and in thinking. Other people begin slowly and increase their speed as they near the goal. Still others maintain the same steady, even pace from start to finish.

It is possible to learn about a person not only from his attitudes to physical exercise but from the manner in which he walks. There is the person who rushes past you, his neck outstretched, his head forward, trotting doggedly ahead without turning to right or left. He often turns out to be a person with a "one-track" mind, who is so driven by his inner pressures that he has no consideration for others. And there is the person, who although he is walking forward, bent at the waist, seems to be pulling himself away from his own legs or at least following them reluctantly. He certainly appears to be devoted to maintaining distance between himself and people. And the short man who takes tremendous strides may be driven by excessive ambition to fantastic goals, whereas the irregular short steps of another may indicate a deep inner insecurity and uncertainty.

Popular figures of speech also reveal a recognition of the relationship between personality, posture and walk. Some of these are "he looks as if he is carrying the world on his shoulders," "keep your chin up," "pull yourself together," "he is a jellyfish," "he needs to be straightened out" and "he lacks backbone." It would be fallacious to regard every defect in posture, walk or exercising as an index of deep-seated personality difficulties. However, it would benefit a person at least to recognize a small physical defect and try to correct it before greater bodily harm ensues.

EXERCISE AND INNER CONFLICTS

Physical exercises assist in changing physical patterns which in turn help to influence inner attitudes. Some successful achievement, small though it may be, with regular, steady physical exercise, often encourages a person sufficiently to use the same approach to other problems, like dieting, or other changes he may have not had enough confidence to attempt previously.

Physical exercises in conjunction with psychological treatment often help a person to become more keenly aware of some of the underlying unconscious factors in the personality structure which contribute to his difficulties. The following examples will serve to illustrate this point.

Miss C. was very willing and eager to practice moving her body in all forward directions but bluntly refused to do any backward movements. She even confessed fear of the latter movements. She feared everything which was "behind" her. On my suggestion, she started watching her movements in a big mirror which enabled her to observe what she was doing while moving backward. Eventually she tried to look at the mirror less frequently. She finally conquered her fear. At the same time she also had overcome a deadlock in analysis which was related to a fear of facing her past realistically. From this instance we see that gymnastics can bring an individual to an awareness of the influence of unconscious factors on bodily movements. This awareness may stimulate an interest in change.

A young man was sent to me by his analyst because he did not know what to do with himself. Everything bored him, and he entertained ideas of suicide. He was brilliant, good-looking and wealthy. He had every external advantage. When he came to me, he made it quite clear that he did not think I could teach him anything at all. He had come to prove his good will to his analyst. Also, he had nothing better to do. I gave him a thoroughly exhausting workout. Steaming with perspiration and breathing heavily, he admitted smilingly, "Oh, that was fun." I smiled back and said, "You might have more fun if you made efforts more often." This started him thinking. Real satisfaction can be achieved only with the output of honest effort.

The use of regular exercises gives a feeling of physical and psychological well-being as well as the satisfaction which always accompanies effort and achievement. Exercising is one of the ways of becoming more aware of oneself, and a physical education instructor, oriented towards people and their problems, may be of considerable assistance. The characteristics which show up in exercising often point to extensive personality difficulties. When an individual becomes aware of the connection between what is revealed by exercise and his personal and social problems, he may begin to take his entire welfare more seriously.

It is never too late to begin to pay attention to our long-neglected bodies. The results are usually gratifying and lead to greater hope for oneself and increased self-confidence. The success an individual achieves in exercise may encourage him to make renewed efforts for development in other directions and give him convincing evidence of untapped resources. When we have learned to coordinate our bodily movements, we gain in satisfaction, hope and pleasure. These gains contribute actively to a pervasive feeling of well-being.

NOTE

This paper is reprinted with permission from the *Amer J Psychoanal,* 7:48, 1947.

"Just what's eating you, Igor?"

WEIGHTLIFTING

TED NOLAN THOMPSON

THERE IS MORE WORK THAN enjoyment in weightlifting (as in some other individual sports). Essentially, weightlifting is a lonely sport. Progress in weightlifting may lead to competition — further stress and strain!

Why work at a sport? Why not rest? Why become involved in what at first may appear to be the grunt and sweat of a dreary life? Why lift a weight? Why run a race? Why climb a mountain?

Those who climb mountains often are at a loss for words when asked, "why?" A natural impulse is felt, but puzzlement for the precise answer is masked by a fashionable smile and the words "because it's there!"

In 1964, a young Californian surfboarded four hundred nautical miles from San Francisco to Newport Beach. Why? Amusingly, newspapers quoted a psychiatrist who, while looking at the fierce Pacific from the vantage point of Carmel, remarked, "because he's insane!" Of course, this was not seriously intended.

But one may challenge those who respond by saying that man has death wishes. To risk one's life need not imply any wish of death. A greater purpose must be defined.

When Socrates posed so many "whys," he provided beginnings for many answers. He spoke of the unexamined life as not worth living. One of man's natural impulses, when followed, is to search for measures of objectivity about himself. For this to be rewarding, objective measures of progress must be examined and recorded by organized means. While a mathematician may fulfill his search through theoretical equations and examined proofs, gifted and less gifted minds alike may find physical measures of objectivity through a medium of athletics.

Measured objectivity fosters inner security. Since most of life's successes and failures are often the results of subjective appraisals, a nidus of objectivity is virtually essential for one to realize where he stands with fellow man and environment, especially when security is threatened and the depressing aspects of surrounding confusion and misunderstanding harass the individual.

So, join with me while we lift a weight! In this friendly tussle with measures constant and gravity virtually the same the world around, we have just one variable . . . ourself. Let's examine our progress and come forward to be measured. Let's help ourselves acquire inner security.

Progressive resistance training distinguishes itself by providing one with rewards of long-lasting physical achievement. Its ultimate value exceeds units-of-effort spent. Mountain climbing contrasts with weightlifting in that energy spent in the former exceeds physical benefits derived. Individual sports like weightlifting and mountain climbing are often more work than pleasure; therefore motivational forces must be stronger, or at least different than in basketball, skiing and other team or individual socio-athletic activities.

Easily understood motivational factors prompting one to lift barbells are the desire to improve bodily shape and the wish to increase strength. When either or both are accomplished, there results a durable effect on one's personality, more noticeable and perhaps, at times, more useful the higher the intellectual level.

Desired goals from weightlifting take considerable time, persistence and self-discipline. Training principles and methods need to be learned, especially to surmount the inevitable plateaus which discourage progress; there are no successful gimmicks, no short-cuts. Improvement is slow for everyone, some more so than others. But the only basic physical requisite for assured gains is the ability to move one's bodily parts.

Beware though of the isolated, socially motivated workout. It rewards one with sore, aching muscles as well as transient slowness of limb movement. Possibly this is the reason many are dissuaded and acquire the completely erroneous fear of becoming "muscle bound." On the other hand, many years of training result in a measure of strength which often exceeds one's fondest imagination, together with increased speed and agility of more all-around value than that achieved through any other systematic means.

One's motives should not be hindered by the mistaken concept that cessation of training automatically means that muscles turn to fat. Those who reduce and improve their build with barbells gradually may, upon retirement, become heavy again. A former "ectomorph" likely loses muscle bulk and overall body size upon quitting, though seldom does he return to his pretrained weight.

BODYBUILDING

Bodybuilding usually stems from a phase of adolescence when body appearance is a primary influencing factor. The "V-shape" has an important competitive value among teen-agers. However, while most appreciate a naturally broad-shouldered, small-waisted build in the male, unfortunately many who strive for it through barbells become so prepossessed with the importance of their acquired form, with its implications as to physical ability, that they defeat their real purpose. They become less attractive! Reacting defensively, many understandably withdraw too far into the mystic world of cults and fads, where in addition, compounded sets of repetitions of barbell and dumbell exercises are questionably overdone to achieve "bulk" (weight and mass) and "cuts" (definition of muscle through reduction of subcutaneous fatty tissue). Mirror (subjective) judging of oneself becomes habitual and exaggerated weight-gain programs arise from impatience in desire to change shape and gain power.

However, there are hierarchies of involvement. Most ultimately continue because they discover that barbell training renders practical physical benefits, makes them feel better, helps them with their jobs, especially manual labor. This takes very little time. But some perservere in a mammoth attempt to acquire objectivity out of the subjective – they may spend fifteen to thirty or more hours per week for a period of years, finally to reach statuesque, herculean proportions sufficient to compete for honors on posing platforms. Those who succeed often make their living in gymnasium businesses, professional wrestling or the motion picture industry.

As in all sports, there are those involved in bodybuilding who act out of other than healthy motives. Such examples must never be permitted to detract seriously from a sport but should serve to illustrate the need for outside interest in the athlete.

In the past decade, with acceptance of the values of weight training, new motives have been created. Most vital has been the impetus through worldwide recognition by coaches that barbell training is an ideal and productive means of conditioning athletes for various types of competition. In track and field, football, swimming, boxing, basketball and other sports, the barbell has become the recommended off-seasonal conditioner. Some of the world's best high-jumpers have attributed additional leg-power and spring to heavy deep-knee-bends. Strenuous progressive resistance exercises have been most important in boosting records in the shotput, discus and hammer, as well as other well-known events. Thus, weightlifting has gradually become an integrated part of the athletic world.

Gains are achieved with relative rapidity when the naturally fast, strong and well-coordinated take to lifting. Some try it simply because friends recommend it; others because their competitor already has! It is something new, or it is something their dad did years ago. It provides speculative change-of-pace and hopes of improving one's particular event through other means than exhaustive repetitions. Nevertheless, it is doubtful that anyone using barbells for any length of time is not further motivated by his changing body image, even though this factor usually remains secondary among successful competing champions.

COMPETITIVE WEIGHTLIFTING

Competitive weightlifting has two categories. The first is Olympic games-fashioned and consists of three arms-length overhead lifts. The first lift is the press to demonstrate strength; in recent years the press has become controversial in that covert speed assisting movements have escaped the notice of judges. The second lift is the snatch, demonstrating speed, balance and agility; the third, the clean-and-jerk, is a somewhat less precise combination of all aspects of lifting and the style which permits the heaviest lifted poundages.

Another category is "power lifting," which essentially involves extraordinary ability in deep-knee-bending (the squat) and bench-pressing (supine press with both arms). Heavy training of this kind requires maximum strength but minimum speed and agility. These two lifts are popular, however, not just because they are less precarious competitively and provoke less anxiety, but because they represent two of the most beneficial and overall muscle-encompassing exercises. Competitively speaking, they permit considerable leverage advantages.

Olympic games weightlifting remains a sport with considerable interest on all continents. A most important reason is that winning is based on highest *total* poundages achieved from the best of each overhead lift. Nine attempts are allowed each competitor, three presses, three snatches, three clean-and-jerks. The total of the best of each provides a score in kilos or pounds for seven world-recognized weight classes. Since leverage advantages possessed by short-statured athletes for pressing become disadvantageous for snatching, tall and short of similar bodyweight compete for total score with relative equality.

In contrast to boxing, where heavier classes have most crowd appeal, advanced bantam and featherweight lifters are frequently the most amazing to watch! Disbelief arises when a world caliber lifter weighing less than 132 pounds hoists and supports 330 or more pounds overhead in a clean-and-jerk. Thus, men of any size and shape are able to excel in weightlifting as well as enjoy spectator appreciation.

Commonly wondered is what motivates some contestants to become so large that they appear "restricted." Practical advantages of gained weight and limb girth lie in the fact that increased mass improves fixed stability. And even fat-enlarged limbs decrease one's active range of motion. In performing a squat, a very stout lifter may have a comfortable resting-position with tops of thighs parallel to the platform (the officially required low-point), whereas thinner-legged competitors struggle with antagonistic muscles to prevent buttocks from nearly touching the floor, a position with gluteal and thigh muscles well beyond resting-length thus difficult for recovery. And in unlimited class competition, there is no handicap for being heavier.

Speed is important for championship lifting; power depends upon speed. Experiences teach one to exert suddenly, but with chest full of air. This affords secure back protection since the spinal column then becomes a relatively small part of a rapid, tightly muscled upper body with diaphragm pushing down to pressure strong abdominal muscles supporting viscera. A resultant Valsalva maneuver sometimes provokes mild light-headedess or visual experiences similar to heat-waves, but rarely among the experienced does loss of control occur as a result of vertigo or momentary blackout.

The Olympic Standard Barbell Shaft was thoughtfully determined as seven feet in length, and the barbell "plates" which form the basic "wheels" are eighteen inches in diameter, and each weighs forty-five pounds. Actually, a competitor is quite safe from being struck or pinned to the platform should he slip with poundage coming down upon him. In snatching, shoulder and elbow dislocations have been known, but they are sufficiently unlikely, as are other serious injuries, so as to be practically disregardable. Injuries are not likely to curb motives for weightlifting since, aside from temporary aches and strains, they are quite rare. Gravity plus inhibition usually succeed in preventing the novice from lifting more than he can handle. Fatigue precludes excessive repetitions. As lifting ability develops, so do protective reflexes.

Compared to men with similar years of training, rarely do women succeed with more than half the poundages. But weightlifting is just as beneficial for the fairer sex. Indeed, it is a rare exception for a woman to develop masculine-appearing musculature if she is not already so inclined. In the vast majority, endowed subcutaneous tissue precludes appearance of muscular definition. Motivational factors applicable to men apply to women as well, although in numerous instances they participate essentially because their husbands or boy-friends want them to, and other factors need not play any appropriate role.

At what age does one reach his competitive peak? The answer must be so long as enthusiasm and the will-to-win prevails! Uncle Sam's greatest prospects in two divisions for the 1964 Tokyo games are now just under and just over forty years of age.

Nowadays, champion discus throwers stand over six feet, weigh between 220 and 270 pounds, are fast and superbly coordinated. Without natural attributes of being tall and long-armed, success is nearly hopeless. However, Olympic weightlifting provides a chance, if one stays with it for the years needed to reach interesting and challenging competitive levels. When these levels are reached and goals are realized, a psychophysiological dependency results. Unless effective substitutes are found, tapering from training, especially a competitive pattern, becomes very difficult. The years of effort are sufficiently gratifying so as to make the price of quitting the self-inducement of multiple conflicts, or a state of psychoneurosis with variable levels of compensation. A most happy alternative exists, however, and that is to "push on!" Weightlifting is a worthwhile lifetime habit.

"You were right, darling – we should have brought your barbells along on our honeymoon!"

NOTE

This paper is dedicated to Bob Hoffman – he paved the way.

PART FIVE
BOARD GAMES

INTRODUCTION

BOARD GAMES, PLAYED FIRST on the ground, go back to prerecorded history. They were derived from divination and were in ancient times almost entirely games of chance; however, mancala, one of the oldest games, was a game of skill. Board games have become more games of skill in recent years. Many games are combinations of skill and chance. Chess, probably not as exacting strategically as the Japanese game go, has a high order of symbolism relating to the family romance. Dice, dominoes and cards may be considered as board games. The psychological factors in board games are the same and as varied as those that pertain to all games — the competition for victory, the need for an external or internal adversary or partner, the displacement of conflict to the game situation, the attempt to master the displaced conflict and the outlet for sublimation and creativity.

How educative or therapeutic board games or games of strategy are in overcoming conflicts, or in teaching logic, cooperation or mastery which can be carried over to life-situations, is an unsettled question. Norman Reider, in the opening paper in this section,[1] makes the suggestion that if players can remain intact as a group or if the game situation can be carried over into life-situations, the games may be ego-strengthening. Otherwise, their effect is isolated and not carried over.

Probably no game is so full of possibilities for psychoanalytic study as that of chess. Man in society, it is said, is like a chess-player writ large. Norman Reider once observed: "Chess is the royal game for many reasons. It crystallizes within its elaborate structure the family romance, is replete with symbolism, has rich potentialities for granting satisfactions and for sublimation of drives. Not without reason is it the one game that, since its invention around A.D. 600, has been played in most of the world, has captivated the imagination and interest of millions, and has been the source of great sorrows and great pleasures."[2]

Although chess has a long history and a large literature, it cannot be said to be a popular form of recreation. Karl Menninger, wondering why this is so, says: "The game is not difficult to learn, much less so, for example, than bridge; it is very inexpensive (in contrast to poker, golf and backgammon); it requires less time than many games and it is not, as many people think, a slow, dull game. The pictures of two individuals sitting peacefully regarding a piece-studded board before them are exceedingly misleading. Silently they are plotting (and attempting to execute) murderous campaigns of patricide, matricide, fraticide, regicide and mayhem."[3]

It has been reported that the game of chess developed in India among the Buddhists, who believe that war and the slaying of one's fellowmen for any purposes whatever are criminal, and who thus invented chess as a substitute for war.[4] However, in his study of the psychology of chess, Ernest Jones, the biographer and student of Freud, says that " it is plain that the subconscious motive actuating the players is not the mere love of pugnacity characteristic of all competitive games, but the grimmer one of father murder."[5] The goal of the game is the capture (immobilization) of the king, the father-figure. Chess has frequently been prohibited by kings, bishops and others because of its warlike import. "In attacking the father," Jones says, "the most potent assistance is offered by the mother (queen)." Jones goes on to say that the game is anal-sadistic in nature, "adapted to gratify at the same time both the homosexual and the antagonistic aspects of the son-father contest."

Reuben Fine, one of the world's great players in the 1930's and now a psychoanalyst in New York, is inclined to agree in his chapter on chess in this volume.[6] He finds the king a symbol of castration anxiety – of rivalry with one's father. The pawns symbolize children, especially little boys. The entire game, according to Fine, is one of profuse phallic symbolism, and the chessboard represents the entire family situation wherein the player can work out in fantasy what he has never been able to do in reality.

But whatever the reason for the appeal of chess – whether it be father murder, combative release, joy in combinations or a necessity for escape or for a creative outlet, it generally strikes between the age of fifteen and twenty. Harold C. Schonberg has pointed out that chess, with its four-hundred-year history in its present form, has had only four supreme prodigies (four males – Paul Morphy, Samuel Reshevsky, José Capablanca and Bobby Fischer), whereas music and mathematics are full of prodigies.[7] There are over fifteen thousand books on chess, starting with Jean de Vignay's *Solacium Ludi Schacchorum* (c. 1480), but a handbook is not enough. Chess is an activity that for greatness requires a combination of egomania and a ferocious will to win, plus memory, visualization, organization and imagination.

Arthur Sternberg in this volume explores the motivations of bridge players.[8] For the unacquainted reader, he gives a brief description of the game and its history. Special emphasis is placed on the tournament aspects of bridge, the chief interest of the author for over seven years.

Contract bridge is one of the most rapidly growing sports of the past thirty years. It boasts about 35,000,000 adherents in the United States, ranging from the Saturday night "Party-Bridger" to the more serious tournament fan. Novice classes have sprung up in almost every city and hamlet in the United States. The game is popular worldwide too, and has even made inroads into the Soviet satellite nations, which are now sending representatives to international competition. Over one hundred major tournaments are held monthly in the United States alone, and it is a rare community that does not have a Duplicate Bridge Club. Thus, it does not appear so surprising that more books and journals have been published about the game than any other pastime, including chess.

Some time ago, Robert P. Knight in an article on contract bridge in the *Bulletin of the Menninger Clinic* said:

> Those critics of the game who regard it as a highly transient, ephemeral and largely aimless tossing around of cards in hand after hand monotonously dealt and played, have no conception of the planning, strategy, safety plays against danger, and the dozens of possibilities that must be taken into account while the declarer works out the play of the hand against all the obstacles thrown up by the defense and finally brings the contract home. Such a hand is remembered and cherished, with every card placed just as it was, and the sequence of plays exactly remembered, all to be recounted to another addict who also will appreciate it, just as one collector of old coins might cherish an especially rare item and show it to another numismastist. . . . One might conclude an apologia for bridge by speaking of its social values — the fact that a minimum of four people is required for a game, so that it is necessary to invite someone in and be invited back. Conviviality is promoted, and in spite of raucous comments from the poker players in the next room to the effect that everyone must be dead in the bridge room, and from the cultural, "no card sense" critics to the effect that bridge is a regressive substitute for intelligent conversation, bridge players *do* converse. Too much, to suit me.[9]

FOOTNOTES

1. P. 266.
2. Reider, N.: Chess, Oedipus, and the Mater Dolorosa. *Int J Psychoanal, 40*:320, 1959.
3. Menninger, K.: Chess. *Bull Menninger Clin, 6*:80, 1942.
4. See Menninger, K.: *Love Against Hate.* New York, Harcourt, 1942, p. 175.
5. Jones, E.: The problem of Paul Morphy; a contribution to the psychoanalysis of chess. *Int J Psychoanal, 12*:1, 1931. See also Coriat, I.: The unconscious motives of interest in chess. *Psychoanal Rev, 28*:30, 1941; Fine, R.: Chess and chess masters. *Psychoanalysis, 4*: 32, 1956; Karpman, B.: The psychology of chess. *Psychoanal Rev, 24*:54, 1937; Schonberg, H. C.: A nice and abstruse game. . . . *Horizon, 4*:14, 1962.
6. P. 274.
7. Schonberg, H. C.: The chess nut is a helpless pawn. *New York Times Magazine,* Nov. 29, 1964, p. 67.
8. P. 282.
9. Knight, R. P.: Contract bridge. *Bull Menninger Clin, 6*:68, 1942.

BOARD GAMES IN GENERAL

NORMAN REIDER

THE ORIGINS OF BOARD GAMES is lost in antiquity and probably belong to prehistory.[1] Murray believes that they go back four thousand years.[2] Culin speculates that they have their origin in arrow divination.[3] Religious practices and magic are often cited as the origins of board play, as are all early games in man's history.

To describe all board games, their rules and their psychological factors would be an impossible encyclopedic task; so I must be content here with some general remarks. Murray classifies board games into (1) games of configuration and alignment, (2) war games, (3) hunt games, (4) race games and (5) mancala.[4] Games of configuration and alignment are played on lined boards by two players who hold their men in their hand and enter them alternately on the points of the board. The aim is to align three men on three contiguous points of a marked line of the board. Three-in-a-row games have been played for over twenty centuries in both Europe and Asia on boards of various types, called merels or muehle. Five-in-a-row games (pegity) are undergoing a kind of revival. It is significant that a child (or adult) often discovers the game for himself if he indulges in spontaneous play on a lined board with pieces.

War games are (1) battle games in which the players either capture or immobolize the opponent's men, like chess and checkers; (2) battles for territory in which the player tries to gain control of the larger portion of the board, like the Japanese go; (3) blockade games in which no captures are made and the aim is immobilization of the opponent's men; and (4) clearance games in which the only moves are captures, and the aim is to make the greatest number of captures.

Hunt games are a variety of war games often played on the board as war games. Sometimes special boards are made for each game. Two people usually play, one with many pieces and the other with less, usually not more than four; and the player with the larger pieces tries to take his opponent's pieces or to hem them in: the larger party is the hunter and the smaller the quarry. The typical European game of this type is fox and geese. But these are only variations on the names in each country — coyote and chicken, sheep and wolves, tigers and goats, etc.

Race games consist of teams of equal size which race one another along a given track; the first player to complete the course with his team wins.

The moves are controlled by the throws of the dice or other implements of chance, like cowries, marked staves or spinning arrows. The typical English games of this type are backgammon, ludo and the games of goose. Race games are among the earliest played of which there are records.

Mancala games are played with boards consisting of two, three or four rows of cup-like depressions, each of which is large enough to contain a number of beans. The method of play is to lift the beans out of one cup and deal or sow them one by one into the following cups. Today it is played all over the tropical and subtropical regions of Asia and Africa and in other parts of the world which dealt in slaves. It can be played on boards marked out on the ground, and Murray quotes Leaky, who believes that one mancala board in Kenya dates back to neolithic times. As happens with many old games, it has been reintroduced in this country as "Wari," which is the Ashanti name for it.[5] (The varieties and rules are numerous. Murray gives the details of this ancient and simple but intriguing game.) Bell says that it is still possible to trace the ancestral origin of some West Indian Negroes by their style of mancala-play.[6]

CHESS

Among board games, chess is so rich in symbolism, so varied in nuances of unconscious significance, and so structured a combination of intellect and art that it deserves special treatment. No other board game offers the opportunity of reenactment of the elements of the family romance, with all of its displacements of attack upon and protection of the family (king, queen, etc.) and the possibility of the lowly pawn becoming the most powerful piece; no other game approaches in its having so unique a history, language, literature, strategy, beauty and influence.[7] Since its invention around 600 A.D., it has been played in most parts of the world and has captivated the imagination and interest of millions and has been the source of great sorrows and pleasures.

Chess has been praised as "the art of the intellect" and has had attributed to it pragmatic, educational and therapeutic values. It has also been damned by devotees who have become addicted to it. It has been encouraged as a model for learning strategy, patience, coping with adversity and politics; it has also been forbidden as sinful, wasteful of time and energy. Pope Innocent III wrote a morality on chess, and Caxton's second book in English, published in 1474, was likewise a morality on chess. Once its play was restricted to the royalty — hence part of the derivation of its description as the "royal game"; now its democratization, along with much of political life — has made it a game for all classes. Once in medieval times it was the vehicle and geography for lovemaking for allegories and love poems in its own language; now its association with love is anachronistic and humorous.

In ancient days it was a game of violence; murders were committed over the board; castration is reported as a sequel to one chess game; lives and great material possessions were once the stakes for its play; now it has settled down to a sublimated, mildly homosexual preoccupation, controlled and scientific.

These and other themes, especially the myths of the origin of the game, I have elaborated elsewhere.[8] I deal there briefly with three trends in the psychological studies on chess. First are the "philosophical" studies, mainly extensions of the old allegorical moralities on chess which compare the game to the struggle of life. Second, the academic studies, the classic of which is Binet's work on blindfold play. Examine the nature of the thinking process in chess; the most recent and best of the studies on decision-making, aside from the work on computers, is de Groot's.[9] The third group are the psychoanalytic works, the classic of which is Jones' study on Morphy, which demonstrates how the motive of father-murder distinguishes chess from all other board games. Correlatory studies on women in chess, wherein father-murder may or may not be as important as with men were made by Kavka[10] and Reider.[11] Waelder uses the chess game and problem as an example of aesthetics and beauty from the psychoanalytic point of view.[12]

The chess problem is rivaled in its aesthetics and strategies by mathematical puzzles and games. Many of the latter are really varieties of board games in their formal characteristics. At present I wish to mention only one of the complicated psychological factors. In the chess problem or mathematical puzzle, who is the adversary? The problem itself may superficially be considered the antagonist; but deeper and subtler antagonisms exist. In the chess problem, the composer is often the adversary with whom one matches wits. In the mathematical game, as Williams puts it, the adversary is likely to be Nature.[13] "One-person games (including solitaire) may be regarded as a special kind of two-person game in which you are one of the players and Nature is the other. This may be a useful view even if you don't believe that Nature is a malignant being who seeks to undo you." I wish to add that the adversary may also be part of oneself like one's mind, one's own stupidity as a kind of "alter ego," or an internalized object. Aesthetically the chess problem has an advantage over mathematical games in that the element of sacrifice of material may be a part of the solution, as in the chess game itself, and the victory which may be achieved by a lowly pawn or by weaker forces, thereby giving an illusion of mastery of mind over matter.

But chess did not always have such spiritual primacy. Once it was a gambling game like dice. Its present rules are only a little over a hundred years old. Over a hundred varieties of the game exist;[14] and most of these retain the central theme of capture of the kind. The first of these varieties is Wieckhmann's in 1664, a curious reversion to four-handed chess, from which the game was originally derived.[15] New varieties of the game appear frequently as games mostly for children, but very few are original. What motivates these changes? Aside from the commercial aspects, the motivations are many and complicated: to increase the pieces and the symbolism, to make the game more difficult, to make it more a game of team-play; contrarily, other variations go in the direction of making chess more like other board-games: less symbolic, more impersonal, more dependent on chance and less strategic.

GENERAL DISCUSSION OF PSYCHOLOGICAL FACTORS

All that I have written about psychological factors in play and games in a previous section in this volume pertains to board games. The competition is foremost and the aggression bound by rules; but board games usually are also distinguished by the factors of skill and chance. Many games are pure skill, many are determined by chance, some are mixtures. All card games are combinations, requiring varying degrees of skill.[16] Board games may be wholly games of skill, like chess and go; some advantage in some games accrue to the first player; yet some games have persisted for centuries (like some varieties of three-in-a-row, tic-tat-toe), despite the fact that the first player has at least a draw.

A consideration of psychological factors in gambling is not germane here, since gambling belongs more to treatises on psychopathology, even though Cardano four hundred years ago[17] and many students and practitioners of gambling have tried to make it a science. But even Cardano, the father of the science of gambling, stated, "Even if gambling were altogether an evil, on account of the very large number of people who play, it would seem to be a natural evil. For that very reason it ought to be discussed by a medical doctor like one of the incurable diseases." Being addicted to all games from dice to chess, Cardano knew well the obsessional nature of his incurable disease, as have also his followers.

The depth psychology of the gambler is examined in the psychoanalytic studies. Here I shall merely discuss some clinical features of the role and use of chance in board games where gambling is not a factor. It was once said, "There are two classes of men: those who are content to yield to circumstance, who play whist; and those who aim to control circumstance, who play chess."[18] True as this may be as a superficial typology, it misses the point that games with important elements of chance may also be attempts to control circumstances. Magical thinking and its derivatives are never forsaken as devices to control the outside world. And, despite our cultural heritage of magic and its potent influence on our methods of coping, individual factors often make the use of chance an attractive way to give satisfaction. Besides the use of magic and chance to determine if one is loved or to regain a lost omnipotence, chance can aid the adaptation of children playing. In the play of small children attempting to master a skill, I have observed a sense of conviction of their inadequacy; then a sudden unexpected success, like hitting a target after many failures, appears to them to have been not only a triumph of skill but also one of luck. I do not know if the child actually feels "lucky." I have seen, however, that the fascination of these "chance" successes can lead to the future enjoyment of games of chance. To control circumstance by chance may become a style of approach to problems.

On the other hand, chance is too anxiety-laden for some children. They prefer the controlled, structured situation of board games. A colleague told me of an obsessional six-year-old of superior intelligence who walked into the office for his first appointment, glanced at the various toys, dolls and therapeutic equipment of the play-room, and then said to his therapist, "Hello. Let's play chess."

Since the symbolism of many board games other than chess is much less, they provide greater distance from internal personal problems than does chess. Most board games have counters or pieces which are all alike and have no special names, or they may frequently be those of animals, as examples cited previously. It is surprising to find a race game cited by Murray,[19] a Sudanese game played by children on a twelve-by-twelve board where one piece is called "the mother," who may be "eaten" by the "hyena," another piece. This game is the only one I have encountered with the designation of a piece in a board game called "mother." Otherwise, symbolism is limited, as has been mentioned. But Brewster has argued that symbolism is present not only in cards, an obvious point, but also in apparently impersonal board games, like three-in-a-row.[20]

More leisure time has increased the interest in board games among children and adults, especially war games that attempt to reproduce the present chaotic world situation.[21] Just as centuries ago chess was taught to princes with the conviction to prepare them for regency and the use of strategy in politics and war, so even today the Defense Department commissions studies in military colleges to aid in preparation of strategies, for "counter-insurgency techniques and problems of pre-revolutionary activity in under-developed countries."[22] Thus, the belief persists that games are a preexercise, as Darwin put it, for life situations; Waterloos are still won on the playing-fields of Eton and Harrow, it seems.

The conviction that such preparatory games influence real-life tasks is obviously shared but with apprehension by the enraged parents of a segment of our population who decry the booming business in war games and toys, fearing that children will be warped by such social acceptance of aggression and war. But the reverse is also true; some believe that games can prepare for peaceful uses, for cooperative enterprise, for assumption of responsibility and for logical thinking. So parents, teachers, group workers and therapists encourage games which hopefully teach modes of coping with hostility, cooperative coexistence and creativity. Playing at "normal" family life is encouraged (provided that it does not include sex or assault).

However, the creators and users of life-career games,[23] community planning games and games of strategy are usually more cautious about their expectations.[24] They are primarily interested in studying the effects of such games on those who learn them and to see how learning of the advantages of cooperative effort are nullified by previous patterns of behavior or by irrational emotional factors. Research interest in such areas is rising rapidly.

Such efforts may be successful in teaching logical thinking or cooperative advantages if the game situation closely resembles the life situation or if many elements of the game situation can be kept intact in the life situation by maintenance of the group, which will continue to play the game in life. Clinically, we already know that exposure to games with alternating moves may help a child learn to wait until it is "his turn." But we also know that some children never learn to wait. Let me cite another example: a little girl "learns" to take care of children in playing with her dolls, playing out an identification with her mother, among other mechanisms. Such play activity may serve her well in later life. But we also have seen that such a girl, when later a mother, gets along fine with her children only as long as they behave like infant-dolls. When they begin to show independence from the doll-playing role, the mother has trouble. It takes two to tango; it takes two to play a game under either explicit or implicit rules.

The moot points are, therefore, the genetic background and the conditions under which game situations may be extrapolated into later life. Only historical studies with the focus on styles of play will help unravel the complexities. We are still a long way from making true Callois' quotation, *Dis-moi a quoi tu joues; je te dirai qui tu es.*[25]

FOOTNOTES

1. Falkener, E.: *Games Ancient and Oriental.* London, Longmans, Green and Co., 1892; Fouquieres, L. A.: *Les Jeux des Anciens.* Paris, Didier et Cie., 1873.
2. Murray, H. J. R.: *A History of Board Games Other Than Chess.* Oxford Press, 1952.
3. Culin, S.: *Chess and Playing Cards.* Washington, D. C., U. S. Government Printing Office, 1898; Culin, S.: *Games of the Orient.* Tokyo, Charles E. Tuttle Co., 1958 (reprint of 1895).
4. Bell differs from Murray in his classification of board games, preferring to list them as (a) race games, best represented now by parchisi, cribbage and backgammon; (b) war games (chess, draughts); (c) games of position: Go, halma; (d) mancala; (e) dice games; and (f) domino games. Bell, R. C.: *Board and Table Games from Many Civilizations.* London, Oxford, 1960.
5. The modern commercial version "Kalah" is obviously derived from "mancala."
6. Bell, R. C.: *Board and Table Games from Many Civilizations.* London, Oxford, 1960.

7. Murray, H. J. R.: *A History of Chess.* Oxford, Clarendon Press, 1913.
8. Reider, N.: Chess, Oedipus and the Mater Dolorosa. *Int J Psychoanal, 40:*320-333, 1959.
9. de Groot, A. D.: *Thought and Choice in Chess.* The Hague, Mouton and Co., 1965.
10. Kavka, J.: The theme of Parricide in a female chess player. *Amer Image, 20:*149-159, 1963.
11. Reider, N.: The natural inferiority of women chess players. *Chessworld, 1:*12-19, 1964.
12. Waelder, R.: *Psychoanalytic Avenues to Art.* New York, Int Univ, 1965, pp. 46-47.
13. Williams, J. D.: *The Compleat Strategyst.* New York, McGraw, 1954, p. 13.
14. Boyer, J.: *Les Jeux d'Eschecs Non-Orthodox.* Paris, 1954; Boyer, J.: *Neuveaux Jeux d'Eschecs Non-Orthodox.* Paris, 1954.
15. Wieckhmann, C.: *Des Grossen Koenigs-Spiels.* Ulm., 1664.
16. Lasker, E.: *Das Verstandige Kartenspiel.* Berlin, August Scherl, 1931; Lasker E.: *Das Verstandige Kartenspiel.* Berlin: August Scherl, 1929.
17. Ore, O.: *Cardano, The Gambling Scholar.* Princeton, Princeton, 1953.
18. Collins, quoted in Reider, N.: Chess, Oedipus and the Mater Dolorosa. *Int J Psychoanal, 40:*320, 1959.
19. Murray, H. J. R.: *op. cit. supra* note 2, at p. 143.
20. Brewster, P. G.: Symbolism and allegory in card and board games. *Southern Folklore Quart, 23:*196-202, 1959; Brewster, P. G.: Some notes on the Slovenian game volka. *Bilten Instituta za Proucavanje Folklara, 3:*143-149, 1955; Brewster, P. G.: Malomjatek and related three-in-a-row games. *Acta Ethnographica,* 225-232, 1957.
21. Carlson, E.: Games for grownups. *Wall Street Journal,* December 22, 1965, p. 1.
22. A. P. Dispatch: War on war toys rages. *San Francisco Examiner,* March 13, 1966.
23. Those who think life-career games are a new development out of our highly competitive society may be surprised to learn that Chinese, Japanese, Korean and Tibetan race games of promotion to higher status existed centuries ago. Murray, H. J. R.: *A History of Board Games Other Than Chess.* 1952, pp. 144-146.
24. Rapaport, A. and Chammah, A. M.: *The Prisoner's Dilemma: A Study in Conflict and Cooperation.* Ann Arbor, U. of Mich. 1965.
25. Callois, R.: *Les Jeux et Les Hommes.* Paris. Gallimard. 1958.

"They were trying to resolve their inter-service squabble by playing a game of parchesi. Now it looks like a duel in the offing – they've accused each other of cheating!"

CHESS

REUBEN FINE

FOR SEVERAL CENTURIES chess has been the most popular game in western civilization. It is played in substantially the same form in all countries. Tournaments to decide champions of local, national and international caliber are held regularly. An enormous literature has grown up which is said to surpass the literature of all other games combined.[1]

Although chess has become so universally popular, it is still primarily a man's game. While no exact statistics are available, it would appear that there are at least a hundred men to every woman among the devotees of the game. Even in countries such as the Soviet Union, where it is officially promoted by the state, the number of women who engage in chess is still quite small.

Chess has always been accorded a special place in men's minds. It is referred to as "the royal game." Some people have said that it is too difficult to be a game and yet not difficult enough to be a science. In England's Parliament, the only game permitted on the premises is chess. The tradition among Orthodox Jews is that on Saturday, the day set aside for the Lord, the only activity permitted is to play chess. Somehow, skill at chess is regarded as a sign of tremendous intellectual power, somewhat akin to skill in mathematics.

Chess is a game in which two men fight with one another about intellectual problems similar to those encountered in mathematics. The motives which drive men to play chess must be sought first in the fact that it is a battle between two men, and secondly in the fact that it is an intellectual battle rather than a physical one.

The aggressive element is obvious to any psychologist, but chess players by and large are reluctant to admit that they express any aggression in the game. Their emphasis, consciously, is rather on the intellectual aspects, the puzzle, the mathematical problems which are created with every move. This leads one to add another motive: chess is not only a game in which there is some release for the aggressive impulses, but also one in which it is easy to deny that any aggression has been let loose.

Norman Reider has collected a number of interesting legends about the origins of chess which very clearly bring out the aggressive factor.[2] In one European legend by Jacob Cessolis, about 1275, the story goes that an eastern philosopher invented the game in the reign of Evil-Merodach, who is presented regularly in medieval works as a monster of cruelty. Evil-Merodach chopped up the body of his father, Nebuchadnezzar, into three hundred pieces and threw them to three hundred vultures. The sages then invented chess in order to cure him of his madness. In another legend told by al-Adli, it is said that the game was invented to assist in the military education of a young prince who pleaded that he was incompetent to lead his armies into war, owing to his want of experience.

Legends frequently relate how chess was invented to be a substitute for war. In one, a certain king of India who was peaceably inclined procured the invention of the game in order that his fellow monarchs might settle their disputes over the board without effusion of blood. In another, a king who was passionately fond of war had overcome all his enemies and was bored and ill. He instructed a sage to distract him, whereupon chess was invented and he was shown how to manipulate forces and devise tactics. The king tried the game, ascertained that the philosopher had spoken truly, and found distraction and health in playing chess. Still another legend, related by Firdawsi, told of a queen who had two sons, each by a separate marriage, who quarreled and finally resorted to war. One died in battle, though not through being slain, and when the news came to the queen, she accused the brother of murder. He could not satisfactorily explain to his mother how the death happened, and so he called together the wise men of his kingdom and laid his case before them. They invented the game of chess and made clear how a king can fall in battle without having been slain. The son then took his game of chess to his mother and thus explained the death of his brother. She continued to study the board all that day and night without desiring food, until death released her from her sorrow, and from that time the chess board has remained in the knowledge of mankind.

A frequently repeated story is that of the reward to the philosopher who is supposed to have invented chess. When the king invites him to choose a reward for the invention of such a charming game, he is said to have asked for a quantity of corn to be placed on the chess board in a special way: the first square is to hold one grain, the second double, the third double that, the fourth double that, and so on. At first the king gladly agrees, but then he realizes that there is not enough corn in his kingdom to comply with the request. Someone has taken the trouble to compute that the amount of corn asked for, a total of $2^{64} - 1$, is enough to cover England to a uniform depth of more than thirty-eight feet. In this legend the close connection of chess with mathematics is readily brought out.

In going from legends to present-day reality, it may be observed that the aggressive element recedes more and more into the background. In the game itself, the king is no longer killed; he is "checkmated," a word which derives from kill but no longer has any meaning outside of chess. Players give check to the enemy king; they do not attack him. In fact, as the game is played, the enemy king is not captured at all; he is only mated. Pieces are captured, but the ultimate goal is always kept from the player.

As players become more expert, their aggression has to be held back more and more. Beginners still say "check" when they attack the enemy king; experts no longer do so. Beginners may laugh and joke in the course of the game; the expert does not. A German wit, in fact, once wrote a book entitled, *Instructions to Spectators at Chess Tournaments.* The book consisted of three hundred blank pages and one other page on which was written: KEEP QUIET.

Most often, chess is learned by boys somewhere between the ages of ten and fourteen, that is, around the time of pubertal development. In this period the boy is especially concerned with his identification with his father and with his identity crisis, with what kind of a man he will become, either in his own right or in contrast to his father. In this process chess is an excellent medium for working out the numerous conflicts which arise.

Unlike other board games, chess has pieces with a variety of different names. In English they are the king, the queen, the rook, the bishop, the knight and the pawn. The king is a universal figure; the names of the pieces in other languages vary all over the lot. This variability allows for the projection of all kinds of symbolism into the pieces, a projection which is not possible in a simpler game such as checkers.[3]

It cannot be said that there is any one type of personality which lends itself to chess. Among chess players one finds men from all ages, all countries, all walks of life. What is common to them is rather that while they have mastered their aggression more than most men, they still feel the need to find some outlet for it in the form of a game.[4]

To the player, the game of chess is completely absorbing. It takes him away from all his everyday cares into another world of sheer enjoyment. As a great chess master, Siegbert Tarrasch, once wrote: "Chess, like music, like love, has the power to make men happy."

In most contests there is some kind of physical contact between the two men. Sometimes, as in boxing or wrestling, the physical contact is the primary element. Sometimes, as in tennis or golf or other ball games, the only physical contact is via an inanimate ball. Chess has less of this physical contact than any other game.

Psychologically we know that when two men engage in physical combat, there is frequently a repressed element of homosexuality. Athletes, though they may be greatly admired by women, are frequently rather poor sexual partners. Often enough, boxers, wrestlers, even tennis players are overt homosexuals.

In chess it is rare to find a devotee who is an overt homosexual. It is almost as though these two kinds of men were at opposite ends of the pole. If a chess player becomes conscious of his homosexual wishes, he finds it very difficult, if not impossible, to control the excitement aroused by the game, in which he is face to face with another man over a long period of time. Contrariwise, the homosexual has poor control over his aggression. Either he represses it entirely, in such a way that he lets the other man do with him what he will, or he becomes very aggressive and has to engage the other man physically in one way or another.

Studies have tended to confirm the popular impression that chess players are, on the whole, rather intelligent people. Barendraegt of the Netherlands has stated that chess players whom he has studied have an average IQ of about 125. This seems rather high, and may be the result of a special sample which he chose. However, while it requires relatively little intelligence to learn to play the game, it does seem to require a fair amount to become competent at it.

On the whole, chess players are competent in other areas of living as well. In terms of intellectual abilities, what the game calls for above everything else is organization and foresight. These same qualities are those that enable men to succeed in other areas of life as well.

PERSONALITY OF THE CHESS PLAYER

A number of interesting points can be raised with regard to the personality of the chess player. Three questions particularly can be approached: First, is there some core personality constellation common to all chess players? Second, what role does chess play in the life of any particular individual? And third, what connection, if any, is there between personality and chess style?[5]

In order to answer these questions, the writer some years ago undertook a detailed analysis of the lives of the world champions of the present century (excluding Petrosian, who has been champion for only a few years). It could of course be objected that these men are not representative of the average chess player. To a certain extent this objection may be valid. At best it can be only partially valid with respect to certain traits, but not for all. We would expect that many of the differences between a champion and an ordinary player lie in native skill, and that the personality structure is in many respects the same. This holds true for creative artists in other fields, so that a study of eminent painters such as Leonardo, van Gogh or Picasso would shed much light on the character structure of their less celebrated colleagues. That there is always a connection between style and personality, regardless of talent or training, is a general psychological assumption.

For roughly somewhat more than a century, the chess world has been sufficiently organized to speak of a world champion; the title itself has been in use since 1870, when Steinitz claimed it on the basis of his many successes. Before Steinitz the champions were, unofficially, Staunton (1844-1851), Anderssen (1851-1858 and again 1859-1866) and Morphy (1858-1859). Since Steinitz (1866-1894) the champions have officially been Lasker (1894-1921), Capablanca (1921-1927), Alekhine (1927-1935 and 1937-1946), Euwe (1935-1937), Botvinnik (1948-1963) and Petrosian (1963-present).

The occupations from which the champions came show some similarities and some differences. Anderssen and Lasker were mathematicians, as is Euwe; Botvinnik is an engineer. Capablanca began to study engineering but abandoned it in favor of chess. Thus about half came from mathematical-scientific fields. This agrees fairly well with the tabulation of de Groot, who collected data on the forty leading masters of modern times.[6]

However, many other professions are represented among the chess masters. While perhaps half come from scientific fields allied with mathematics, the other half do not. Ruy Lopez was an ecclesiastic; Philidor was a musician; Deschapelles was a soldier; Lewis, M'Donnell and Saint-Amant were businessmen; Kolisch a banker; Zukertort and Tarrasch physicians; Buckle a historian; Tartakower a poet. The young Russian master Taimaoov is a concert pianist. There was a chess master named Harmonist who danced at the Opera House in Vienna. There was even one who was a professional strong man. There was a serf on an Indian estate, Sultan Khan, who was almost illiterate; he comes closest to the chess champion of Stefan Zweig's novelette *The Royal Game,* who is depicted as a kind of idiot savant.

The personality structures of the champions show some marked similarities if we divide them in two groups. In one we have Morphy, Steinitz, Capablanca and Alekhine, who devoted themselves almost exclusively to chess. Let us call these, for the sake of convenience, the heroes. The others, who also pursue interests apart from chess, would then be the non-heroes.

The hero group has been given this designation because myths have been built up about each of its members. Morphy is popularly looked upon as "the greatest chess player of all time," Steinitz as "the father of modern chess." Capablanca was known as the "chess machine" and publicly announced that he had mastered the game once and for all. Alekhine came to be talked about as "the greatest attacking player of all time."

Needless to say, all these superlatives derive from the chess player's need to find some hero whom he can worship. But the champions themselves played into the hands of their worshipers and obtained some of their most profound unconscious satisfactions from the idolatrous groups which grew up around them. Even Morphy's withdrawal after a little more than one year of international competition is perhaps most simply explained by saying that he knew that if he went back the illusion of his invincibility would be destroyed.

All these men showed considerable emotional disturbance. Morphy's illness was the most profound. He became deeply paranoid at an early age, which led him to give up chess altogether. Steinitz and Alekhine both had harmless megalomanic ideas toward the end of their lives. Capablanca suffered from extreme tension.[7]

All four display in marked degree the character traits of aggression and narcissism which theoretical analysis indicated could so readily be brought out by the game. Underneath, they all had fantasies of omnipotence; to some extent they literally identified themselves with the king of the chess board. With Steinitz the regression to a more omnipotent fantasy state (he boasted that he could give God Pawn and move) came after he lost the world championship.

In order to accomplish what they did, all four had to work very hard. The grandiose wishes could not be satisfied by simple daydreaming. Their successes could be achieved only after long and careful preparation. For this, much ego strength is needed, which again fits in with the theoretical analysis. Some of them, like Steinitz and Capablanca, would have seemed more or less normal by customary standards. Only a more refined analysis serves to bring out the neurotic conflicts which troubled them.

All four were well-endowed men who did not care to use their abilities outside of chess. Particularly striking is their gift for languages, which fits in with the capacity to master the symbolic meanings of chess.

The role which chess played in the lives of these men is clear enough: it served as a vehicle for the gratification of their omnipotence fantasies. As time went on, these fantasies, which were originally under control, became more and more open and suffused an increasing portion of the personality.

In almost every respect, the other group, the non-heroes, show exactly opposite tendencies. They had no myths built up about them, although they could easily have done so. Staunton and Anderssen both could have claimed the title of champion of the world, but they had other satisfactions in life and did not have to do so. When Lasker was alive, the critics liked to say that he won because he was lucky or because he blew smoke into the eyes of his opponent. He did not bother to refute these fairy-tales.

All of these non-heroes except Anderssen have substantial achievements to their credit outside of chess. Lasker, Euwe and Botvinnik have all held positions equivalent in rank to that of an American college professor, while Staunton was an eminent Shakespearean scholar.

For them, again in contrast to the hero group, chess was one of several intellectual pursuits in which they showed varied degrees of competence. Penetration underneath the surface showed that chess provided a libidinal outlet, especially for aggression, which the other intellectual areas did not.

These observations can be generalized to the average player. Some play chess because it is a vehicle for fantasies of omnipotence; they too identify with the king. Others see it as merely another recreational outlet. Intellectuals particularly value it because it provides libidinal satisfactions which otherwise rigorous work does not permit.

With regard to the connection between personality and chess style, in every case in which this is examined carefully some clear bond can be seen between life experience and behavior on the board. But the connection is not a simple one. The aggressive player may be compensating for his timidity in everyday life, like the traditional Caspar Milquetoast, or he may be releasing the excess of aggression which he carries over from other activities. Thus lawyers, whose sadism is often quite obvious, frequently find chess a gratifying means of getting rid of more aggression. Research workers, whose work isolates them from their colleagues, may use chess as a way of making human contacts. In other cases research workers who have many contacts may find chess a more exciting one than their ordinary everyday work. In many others the connections are far more complex, but can always be located.

Psychoanalysis has stressed the fact that one of the major attractions of artistic productions is their capacity to arouse multiple projections on the part of the spectators. Both the excellence and the durability of any work

"I resent your jeering unsportsmanlike conduct every time I get checkmated!"

of art depend very heavily on this capacity to stimulate the audience to different reactions.

A similar dynamic underlies the continuing popularity of chess. It is based on a universal conflict, that surrounding aggression. It is learned most commonly in the period from ten to fourteen, when the boy is concerned with mastering the identification crisis with his father, again a universal conflict.

But the conflict is handled in a variety of ways. Some deny it by insisting that chess is merely a mathematical pastime. Others revel in it day and night. Some, probably the majority, pursue it intensively for a short time, months or perhaps years, then go on to some other stage in development. Some lean heavily on the multiple sexual symbolism inherent in the game; some are totally oblivious of it.

With such a variety of motivations to choose from, it is no wonder that chess has such a broad appeal. Added to this appeal is its enormous complexity, which still defies the efforts of many ingenious minds at precise resolution. So everything suggests that chess will be sought after as a diversion for many years to come.[8]

FOOTNOTES

1. See Murray, H. J. R.: *A History of Chess.* Oxford, Clarendon Press, 1913.
2. Reider, N.: Chess, Oedipus and the Mater Dolorosa, *Int J Psychoanal, 40:*320, 1959.
3. Colby, K. M.: "Gentlemen, the Queen!" *Psychoanal Rev, 40:*144, 1953; Coriat, I. H.: Unconscious motives of interest in chess. *Psychoanal Rev, 28:*30, 1941; Djakow, J. N.; Petrowski, N. V., and Rudik, P. A.: *Psychologie des Schachspiels.* Berlin, Walter de Gruyter and Co., 1927; Horowitz, I. A., and Rothenberg, P. L.: *The Personality of Chess.* New York, Macmillan, 1963; Menninger, K.: Chess. *Bull Menninger Clin, 6:*80, 1942.
4. Fleming, J., and Strong, S. M.: Observations on the use of chess in the therapy of an adolescent boy. *Psychoanal Rev, 30:*399, 1943.
5. Binet, A.: *Psychologie des Grands Calculateurs et des Joueurs d'Echecs.* Paris, Hachette, 1894.
6. de Groot, A.: *Het Denken van den Schaker.* Amsterdam, Noordhollandsche Uitgeversmaatschapping, 1946.
7. Jones, E.: The problem of Paul Morphy: A contribution to the psychology of chess. *Int J Psychoanal, 12:*1, 1931.
8. Fine, R.: *The World's Great Chess Games.* New York, Crown, 1951; *The Psychology of Chess.* New York, Dover, 1965; The psychology of blindfold chess. *Acta Psychol (Amst.),* 1965.

BRIDGE

ARTHUR STERNBERG

TO THE 35,000,000 OR MORE PLAYERS in the United States, bridge is the only true scientific card game. People in all walks of life indulge in it. Some play weekly or less, with friends. Others play for varying stakes, while the rest seek the status of the tournament awards.[1]

The invention of modern or contract bridge is generally credited to Harold Vanderbilt. The game is actually a derivative of whist and auction bridge. Previous to 1925, the four players would choose arbitrarily a suit as trumps, and a set number of plays, or "tricks," had to be won. Vanderbilt's idea was to have each of the players, in two opposing partnerships, bid for the suit and the number of tricks the hands might produce. A scoring system was devised with bonuses when a desired contract was reached and fulfilled. Penalties were assessed per trick when the contract was not fulfilled or "made."

Thus modern bridge came into being. For many, the game is a blessing, as one can change a life of boredom into a pleasant social outlet and relax from the worries of daily life. Others find it a compulsion to which they are enslaved and cannot escape. As dim as this latter situation sounds, one rarely finds, if ever, a bridge player anxious to give up his addiction to the game.

The bridge table is a battlefield of human emotions transferred into fierce card combat. In what other sport can one "smother an opponent's Queen," "belt him with a penalty double," or "squeeze him mercilessly"? The more skillful declarer can actually "double squeeze" both opponents in an awesome display of intellect combined with brute force. This is bridge as the late, voluble expert Ely Culbertson probably would have described it in his usual enthusiastic effort to recruit neophytes. However, to an astute observer, the jargon of the plays, maneuvers and gambits are quite appropriate, despite the apparent violence of the terminology.

The excitement following a well-played hand is found with all the devotees. It is easy to detect another bridge buff by the inevitable greeting, "Hi, Art. How are you? Let me tell you about a hand I played last week. I held etc., etc. and etc., and the bidding went. . . ." At least twenty minutes later, you smile wearily and agree your friend did well (although you would have done better undoubtedly) and attempt to escape from him before he gets started on the next hand he played.

However, devotion and enthusiasm of the bridge multitude is universal.

Indeed, most players look forward to their moment of glory when, perhaps if only briefly, they triumph over better adversaries or make a financial "killing" in one session. Motivation in bridge, therefore, stems from one key intrapsychic source — a strong desire for mastery of a given situation, usually expressed aggressively, on both conscious and subconscious levels.

There is a corollary to the above statement, to which most experts will agree. Nobody plays bridge strictly for relaxation. The desire to win makes it impossible. Marshall Miles, in the introductory chapter of his excellent book on strategy, *How to Win at Duplicate Bridge,* addresses himself to the player who wants to win and not just play "for fun." His book was not meant for the latter type of reader. A fine player whom I know told me seriously before a New York regional tourney, "I want to win so much that I concentrate on the game and nothing else. During the play, my opponents become personal enemies and I hate them because they want to win as much as I do. Yet, once the game is over, everything goes back to normal and I am not angry at anyone."

A friend and occasional partner of this writer possesses a more whimsical view; yet the feeling is quite apparent, "I am really a nice fellow. I was once a boy scout, and on occasion, I still help old ladies cross the street. But if I ever meet them at the bridge table, they'll have to cross the street themselves."

There have been few attempts in psychiatric literature to explore the motivation and emotional makeup of bridge players. A review of the past twenty years of monthly and periodic journals proves nonproductive. However, Jack Olsen, in his *Mad World of Bridge* finds an interesting quotation of the late Alfred Adler dating back at least thirty or forty years. He stated, "Bridge players are usually suffering an inferiority complex and find in the game an easy way to satisfy their striving for superiority. . . . A little of it is relaxation, but a lot becomes a mental habit; an attempt to satisfy a striving for superiority. It offers an opportunity to conquer things."

There is still validity to much of what Adler said. Players recognize a desire for superiority and many try a lifetime to achieve it. Terms such as "card sense," "killer instinct" and a "feel for the game" refer to those who have succeeded above the average level. As one improves, he becomes increasingly aware of his ability and often becomes assertively confident of himself. Perhaps this is the sublimation of the "inferiority complex" as Adler saw it.

Take one of the greats — John Crawford, for example. He was once asked of the toughest game he could think of. Partner? "John Crawford." Opponents? "Two other John Crawfords." Would that be the toughest game? "Yes. But I wouldn't play in it. It would be too tough." In the New York *Times,*[2] columnist Alan Truscott offers a formula for a budding bridge expert. This would include intelligence, absorbability of knowledge, self-confidence ("perhaps unfortunately loudly confident"), fanaticism and a passionate interest in analyzing one's own mistakes. It is this last criterion that separates the true experts from the multitude of ordinary competitors. This constitutes insight, certainly an important attribute even in daily life.

Often, a player's actions during the game contrast similarly to his usual behavior. Sometimes they assume a fantasied existence. I have wondered what many of my adversaries are really like outside the Bridge Club. In my mind, there marches a long procession of card-slappers, questioning bidders (*e.g.*, "Two clubs?"), growling doublers, sad passers, etc., etc. One fellow once cashed the setting trick of a contract so forcefully that his thumb went through the table. (No, he was not a lion-tamer, but actually a quite successful salesman.)

Sadomasochistic relationships appear at all levels of bridge. Unfortunately, they are exceedingly prevalent in husband and wife partnerships, with the husband usually the aggressor. Verbal abuse is most common, and the players' shafts are often witty as well as sarcastic. For example, there was Somerset Maugham's classic, "When did you learn how to play this game? Oh, I know it was today, but what time?" Many partnerships are thus temporary; yet others last for years as the observer shrugs his shoulders in amazement at what he sees. The female half of a loud but longlasting partnership once told me, "Sure, (A.) makes a lot of noise. But I'm accustomed to it by now. My husband is much worse at home. As long as we do well at the tournaments I let my partner make as much growling as he wants."

Alvin Landy, Executive Secretary of the American Contract Bridge League (ACBL), feels that arguments are detrimental and do not often occur in the highest circles. "Most experts analyze their mistakes and feel that they were at least partly responsible for disasters that occur. Besides, it takes something out of your partner when you are rough to him. To me, the desire to win is more important than the destruction of a partnership."

Perhaps more representative of the vast majority of players (of whom less than 1% of all competitors are considered expert) is a type described by Ed Pinner, who serves as assistant manager of the Mayfair Bridge Club in New York City. "I know of a good 'house player,' who fills in on an occasional rubber bridge game. He's an argumentative guy who never made much in life. The others in the game are usually doctors, lawyers, dentists, etc. He is always complaining, 'Why are they so bad they don't even know how to take a finesse? I'm not half as well off as those guys and yet I can play much better.' He then ends up by giving Hell to some poor fellow."

Bridge players often find the game a welcome and a convenient time passer. This form of diversion holds a definite therapeutic effect for people with free time on their hands, especially the retired. For others, it can be the opposite. Harry Fishbein, a well-known expert and manager of the Mayfair Club, states, "You can see the same faces at my club all the time. The cards become the masters of many, and a lot of people who play this game are sick. They use it as an outlet for their inhibitions and they get little pleasure out of it anymore."

A different view comes from Mrs. Flora Munroe, an eighty-year-old denizen of New York's Grand Slam Duplicate Club. "Without bridge, I would have nothing to do. There would be few people I could maintain contact with. At least, now I spend my evenings at the Club, where I have many friends. This, to me, is a lot more important than winning or losing." Mrs. Munroe's comments are typical of older players to whom I have spoken. For them, the game is most important because of its social nature. Yet it is common for many to wish to learn to improve their skills, and they often succeed.

To those who think bridge is strictly a young man's game, there are active experts such as Waldemar von Zedwitz, Oswald Jacoby, B. J. Becker, Olive Peterson and Stella Rebner, each with more than thirty years successful tournament experience, and each of whom still wins regularly. One could not omit George Beynon, a pioneer of modern bridge, who frequented Florida tournaments at the age of one hundred!

As previously mentioned, a desire to escape from outside worries, even if for only a short time, brings many enthusiasts to the bridge table. Here one finds an opportunity to utilize new-found skills and exercise deceptive tactics that can bring him into the winners' circle. A typical response was offered by a Florida friend of mine who is a retired teacher in his sixties. "I find it a wonderful outlet. It takes my mind off problems and presents a new intellectual challenge. I feel happy if I have played well, and sometimes I even win first place at a tournament. It's the diversion that counts, and at my stage of life, being occupied is the most important thing for me."

Of course, indulgence in the game is often overdone. At times, it becomes the opiate of the college student, the smalltime gambler, and the Bridge Widow's mate (that is, one who prefers a grand slam to his wife's kiss). It has even been known to lead to marital disaster when husband and wife are regular partners. One famous partnership had to break up after numerous complaints that the flying cards and coffee cups were becoming a grave menace to life and limb at the tournaments.

The most famous explosion occurred in Kansas City in 1929. Following the misplay of a four-spade contract by a Mr. J. Bennett, a loud argument ensued with his wife. It was suddenly terminated when she fatally shot him with a pistol. It actually became a national issue of the day as people tried to figure out whether Mr. Bennett could have won the hand and thus saved his life, while his wife was later acquitted of homicide.

Married pairs play together for two main reasons: to share a mutual interest in the game and, it is assumed, because regular partnerships have a better chance of winning due to deeper understanding. Often this succeeds. A famous West Coast couple, for example, the Morris Portugals of Los Angeles, recently won the right to compete in the team trials for the 1965 International championships. However, when mistakes occur, it is not easy to remain silent over them. For married couples, arguments tend to take on a more personal meaning, and deep underlying resentments come out into the open. Often, these partnerships take their misgivings home with them, where the battle rages on late into the night. It may, therefore, sound paradoxical when they reappear on time for the next game, pleasant and outwardly calm as usual, until their first mishap of the night.

However, these are the accepted mores of the society of bridge. Sporadically, since its inception, various psychologists, clergymen and even statesmen have decried its evils. Yet nothing short of natural disaster can shake a devotee from his game — of course, it has to be a large disaster. For example, in 1962, while a large regional tourney was being held in Albany, New York, one of the curtains in the playing room caught on fire. Play continued uninterrupted while firemen battled the flames, and many of the players did not even seem aware that anything unusual occurred at the time.

A brief discussion of rubber and tournament (duplicate) bridge seems in order at this point. Rubber bridge constitutes the competition of two pairs of partnerships against each other. The game is played with or without the involvement of stakes, and the partnerships often change several times during the course of an evening. There is no set limit to the amount of games or "rubbers" that are to be played.

In tournaments, the setup is totally different. Events may differ in the types of partners eligible to play (*e.g.*, men's pairs, mixed pairs, and open pairs). A national organization coordinates all the events, from the local or club level to the larger regional and national Tourneys. Thus one may compete in his home-town unit for first-place against five to fifteen pairs. Or, if he has the time, he can attend one of three nationals and fight it out among thousands of participants.

In rubber bridge, each hand is played, the cards are tossed together into the center of the table, reshuffled and redealt. In duplicate, all the hands are predealt. As the cards are played, they are not tossed into the center of the table, but individually kept before the player. At the conclusion of the deal, each player's hand is reinserted into a small metal rack (or "board") and sent to another table to be replayed, by other partnerships in the room.

Match points are then used to compare the best scores per pair for the given hands. After approximately twenty-four to twenty-eight boards are played by everyone, all the scores are tallied. The pair with the highest total of match points is declared winner.

The monetary prizes are usually insignificant, if any, as the ACBL has tried to discourage gambling. A cleverly devised form of status symbol, the master point award, is allotted to the highest finishers in any event. The lure of these awards is great to all tournament goers. The bigger the match, the greater are the number of points given out. When a novice wins his first point, he automatically becomes a junior master. An ascending scale symbolizes increasing proficiency: senior master (20) , national master (50), advanced senior master (200) , and life master.

The latter is the most coveted status for a player to achieve. This involves the winning of at least three hundred points, fifty of which were won at regional or national tournaments. It has been estimated that over 250,000 play duplicate events regularly in North America. Bridge is also popular on an International level. The 1964 "Olympiad" held in New York City had participants from countries such as the United Arab Republic, Thailand, South Africa, Poland, Japan, Argentina and twenty-three other nations. The strongest team in international competition for the past five years has been from Italy, with its supremacy annually being challenged by Great Britain, the United States, Canada and France.

The motivation of rubber players often parallels the interest seen in duplicate competition. However, here the impact of chance and gambling becomes increasingly felt. Big-time gamblers are not regularly addicted to bridge for stakes. Landy says, "The game is too slow to gamble for money. The better card players go to Las Vegas, where they find more action for their money. According to Fishbein, "In rubber bridge, it is difficult for gamblers to earn a living. They need people willing to play and the crowd they frequent is often smart and shrewd. The games are cut-throat, but the players usually know what they are getting into."

Most players in big "money" games are relatively sophisticated. They can detect a cheat or hustler quickly and will exclude him. Fishbein says he has no use for either at his club. He states, "Hustlers are hard people, with no feelings toward the others at the table. At least, the gamblers have to win to get by. The hustler is cynical and challenges his opponents. When he gets the upper hand, he chides them for their inferiority."

What happens at the smaller-staked games? There are rubber bridge addicts at all levels of caliber and livelihood. They play almost daily, at homes or in clubs, with the game preying constantly upon their minds. Luck carries a more significant role for two probable reasons — the deal for the cards, and the limited skill of many of the players frequently putting the bid and the play up to chance. Many of these competitors whom I have interviewed readily admit they play the game for its excitement. They find a thrill from the uncertainty of each deal of the cards and most of the bidding situations, something that does not happen often to them while under tournament pressure. This declarer (the one that plays the hand out) usually feels an increase in tension as his partner's hand ("dummy") is exposed into view and he contemplates his approach. This sense of anticipation and thrill is described in almost erotic terms, with the likely significance that the game acts as a form of sexual substitute for them. Many of the "regulars" readily admit that their social and marital lives have been affected greatly by their devotion to the cards over a long period of time.

Thus, with a modicum of good luck, anyone can be a winner for a given session. When the cards run sour and errors of judgment occur, the game separates the better players from the regular losers. Everyone consciously strives to win; yet it is amazing how many are unable to succeed. Edmund Bergler, in his *Psychology of Gambling*, attempted to explain this by describing a phenomenon he called "psychic masochism." By this mechanism the gambler, being unable to deal with unconscious conflicts while at play, actually punishes himself by losing often, although he has no idea he is doing it.

The gambler at bridge is no different from the race-track tout, the number's player or the roulette habitué. He will be quick to deny that he might be responsible for his own losing, but blames it on extrinsic factors. A census of bridge-losers following the game usually results in the following comments: "I never got any good card cards," or "Boy, did my partner play lousy." It is rare indeed that someone in this group will admit he played badly.

Pinner recognizes this at his club, where he is frequently asked to fill in when needed. "I see a lot of bad players who seem to play to lose. They bid on junk and always get into bad situations. These fellows are born losers and will never learn." This temperament also exists in the tournament circuit and keeps many players from ever being successful since they do not believe in their own miscues or try to correct them.

A discussion of motivation in bridge could not be complete without mentioning the type known as the kibitzer. This is the spectator privileged to watch the game, theoretically in silence. Some even prefer kibitzing to playing and rarely take an active part.

Many of this breed to whom I have spoken say they watch to learn or just to pass idle time. Others spoke quite candidly in admitting they kibitz just to see how much more they know than the players in the game. Their unsolicited comments have often provoked warfare with the participants, but this is an accepted part of the combat. Thus the kibitzer can be likened to the voyeur, who, after observing an amorous liaison, helpfully says to the couple, "But you did it all wrong."

"This is the only time I detect any *verve* in Harry – when he makes a damned slam!"

Jack Olsen in his *Mad World of Bridge* has an amusing classification to offer. "The full-fledged kibitzer . . . has received permission from all players to kibitz the game; he may comment at will and may be called into the game as a consultant, or a relief-station fourth. A Dorbitzer has received permission from the Kibitzer to watch the game. He may speak to the Kibitzer, but not to the players. A Tsitser has received nobody's permission to do anything. He may only linger in the background, commenting on the play by saying, 'Ts! Ts! Ts!"

In the foregoing discussion, I have tried to demonstrate that bridge has a wide range of appeal and much to offer in the way of personal satisfaction. Perhaps in no other sport can an amateur have his moment of glory by beating the experts on any given day. In the hierarchy of the tournament circles, the Life Master status is coveted and can be attained by anyone with competence and perseverance.

Surely, bridge can be possessed by unhealthy motivations, and many have fallen slave to it by playing compulsively day after day. Yet, if this pastime were not chosen as a neurotic outlet to escape from realistic daily pressures, some other form of activity would likely be distorted. This writer believes he is therapeutically addicted to the game and will discuss it with whoever is interested. It is likely that he may be found at the next major tournament that comes to town.

NOTE

Special thanks are offered to Messrs. Alvin Landy and Harry Fishbein for their assistance and ideas in contribution to this paper. The author is also grateful to his many partners and adversaries, who (paraphrasing a Yogi Berra remark) "helped make this paper necessary."

FOOTNOTES

1. See generally Miles, M.: *How to Win at Duplicate Bridge.* New York, Collier, 1957; Olsen, J.: *The Mad World of Bridge.* New York, Holt, Reinhart & Winston, 1960; Ostrow, A. A.: *The Bridge Player's Bedside Companion.* Englewood Cliffs, Prentice-Hall, 1956; Bergler, E.: *Psychology of Gambling.* London, Bernard Banison, Ltd., 1958; Landy, A., and Frey, R.: *Easy Guide to Duplicate Bridge.* New York, American Contract Bridge League, 1964.
2. Dec. 16, 1964.

PART SIX

SPORTS AND THE FAMILY

INTRODUCTION

IN THE PREVIOUS SECTION ON "Board Games," we saw that "man in society is like a chess-player writ large." Here we shall look more directly at the family.

In his paper in this section, Stephen D. Ward, psychiatrist and former college football star, studies the motivation of the superior athlete.[1] Why does the superior athlete subject himself to pain and suffering and hard work? Is this peculiar to him, or are his motivating forces the same as those of a doctor, engineer or other professions and occupations? Certainly the athlete's body image is different. He is much more "body" oriented in an almost dissociated way.

Mental defense mechanisms (e.g., denial, repression) serve to protect against overwhelming anxiety. The athlete uses his body as a mechanism of defense by performing feats of daring, strength and agility. When he fails in these feats, severe anxiety often results. To avoid failing, he will go to extremes of aggression and viciousness.

Mothers may be very important determinants in the child's desire to excel in athletics. Does she reward physical activity or inactivity? Does she take great pride in his motor ability? It would appear, Ward says, that superior athletes have a very intense relationship with their mothers. While they try to please mother by their prowess, inevitably they are going to get hurt and bruised, then mother is blamed. They get mother's approval, but there is a price tag. The principal is never paid up, which makes further athletic endeavors necessary.[2]

Imitating or identifying with a parent is a well-known psychological process. The little boy who does things the way father does them so as "to be like Daddy" is a conspicuous example of imitation. A boy patterning himself after his father acquires the characteristically masculine traits; the girl in patterning herself after mother acquires feminine traits (of course, the boy or girl often cannot make an adequate identication respectively with father or mother). The parents have the responsibility of helping the child move forward on the road from babyhood to adulthood. The parent has to "grow" with the child; he has to change many of his ways of thinking and acting. He has to decide whether he wants the child to be an independent personality or a dependent facsimile of himself. He has to decide whether he will try to live his life over again (as he may have liked to have lived it) through his child, and whether he will try to achieve potency not through himself but rather through his child.

Studying certain psychological factors in athletic injuries affords us an additional view of motivations in sports. While other factors such as conditioning and equipment may be more vital, the emotional meanings of injury in sports also should be considered. Robert A. Moore in his paper lists nine possible indicators of a psychological need for injury:[3] (1) gross disproportion between athletic ability and willingness to be aggressive; (2) disproportion between father and son as to athletic ability and expression of aggression; (3) lack of adequate control of aggression; (4) fear of injury; (5) history of multiple injuries; (6) concealment of minor injuries; (7) exaggeration of injuries; (8) inability to tolerate success; and (9) omnipotent feelings of invulnerability.

Our present view of the nature of man emphasizes the basic impulses and their control by increasing layers of civilization. Too rigid control results in guilt when impulses are stimulated; and when there is too little control, anxiety and self-destructive behavior result. Competitive sports is an exception where aggressiveness is demanded with resultant defeat of the opponent. For some, this shift from the usual controls firmly incorporated in the unconscious to such overt expression results in severe psychic conflict.

If this conflict is too intense, the athlete may resort to injury, which provides both the escape from the conflict and also his excuse for the escape. Others, abnormally afraid of injury, may resort to counter-phobic courting of danger until their luck runs out. For some, injury is both a punishment sorely needed and a protest of weakness to avoid a much greater danger.

Parent-child interaction in sports is depicted in that delightful film *That's My Boy!* where Jerry Lewis plays a puny son who is beseeched by an aggressive father into playing football. Try as he will, the father could not make a football player out of him — and the coercion caused the boy considerable psychic pain. In this volume, Joseph Lupo describes the case of a weakling father who seeks potency through the accomplishments of an athletic son.[4] Anna Freud in her book, *The Ego and the Mechanisms of Defense,* points out:

> We know that parents sometimes delegate to their children their projects for their own lives, in a manner at once altruistic and egoistic. It is as if they hoped through the child, whom they regard as better qualified for the purpose than themselves, to wrest from life the fulfilment of the ambitions which they themselves have failed to realize. Perhaps even the purely altruistic relation of a mother to her son is largely determined by such a surrender of her own wishes to the object whose sex makes him 'better qualified' to carry them out. A man's success in life does, indeed, go far to compensate the women of his family for the renunciation of their own ambitions.

An individual's interest in sports is often increased when he has a son or daughter who is engaged in competitive athletics. In the opening paper in this section of the volume, Joseph P. Dolan observes the interplay of personality factors involving the expression or control of frustration, or the joy and dejection associated with failure or success during games. The vicarious association of parents – through their children – can tell us much about a nation's culture regarding the importance of children's efforts. Among other things, Dolan describes parental frustration of young athletes.[5]

Parents are not bound by team discipline or the psychology of "covering" frustration. The athlete, on the other hand, must control egotistic selfishness, greed and those very normal human traits that organized religions have tried to govern from earliest times. The parent, not a part of team or coaching control, does not possess in many cases the emotional control demanded of the athlete son or daughter; thus we observe what coaches call the "over syndrome" – over-affection, over-anxiety, over-authority, over-indulgence, over-protection, over-responsibility, over-restriction and over-perfectionism – displayed by parents who otherwise are paragons of community behavior.

And a child wants to measure up to his parent (as well as vice versa). The son of one of America's greatest poets, to take one example, wanted to be a great poet like his father. He could not and, frustrated by the impossibility of ever achieving his parent's stature, he became despondent. He ended up in an early grave by his own hands. Other sons in one way or another throughout life fight their fathers – secret grudges held from childhood often motivate such crimes as check forging, which often occurs among children of financially solid citizens. Others turn to alcohol, narcotics or other disordered mental conditions. The neurotic parent especially will treat his children after his own precepts, and just as he spoils his own life, he will create difficulties for his children. Earl Nightingale once put it thus:[6]

> The neuroses which so plague our civilization are created by mothers and fathers who don't know what they're doing. For example, parents try to make their children meek and obedient in the family, but want them to be strong and competitive when thy're grown. It's an interesting study of opposites, isn't it? Thousands of parents spend years making the kids toe the line at home, becoming little yes-men and women, letting their parents do all their thinking for them, being protected and ordered around – and then, when they finish school, the parents sit back and expect these poor kids to go out and whip the world. It's like spending eighteen years training a person to play golf and then tossing him in the water and expecting him to swim the English Channel. . . . Sometimes training in docility and meekness is so strong that the child is never able to hold its own later in the world outside the family. In other cases, the children are forced to become so rebellious against training they know to be unfair and unintelligent that they develop a grudge against the world and all authority and go out into the world as real, full-grown problems. . . . Occasionally the parents themselves may be infantile, selfish, lazy, obsessed or timid. In one way or another they compete with their children, overtrain them, underlove them or fail to make the vigorous

> demands required to force children up the inclined plane of culture. Something to think about, isn't it? . . . . There is one rule of thumb that can be applied in all human relationships that works like a charm. It's one of the world's oldest rules: the golden rule. Whenever a situation comes up which involves a decision with regard to a youngster, the experts suggest that you stand in your youngster's shoes. How would you want to be treated if the positions were reversed and knowing what you now know? What would be best for your parent to say or do to you that would make you wiser, or better or happier? . . . . Yes, it's still the best rule for getting along with other people, young or old.

Instead of or in addition to a child, a person may inflict his frustration upon a cockfighter, a jumping horse, a greyhound racer or other animal. The boss balks at his employee, and in turn he takes it out on his wife, she takes it out on the child, and the child takes it out on the dog. The process of displacement gives meaning to the expression, "It's a dog's life."

No child regards a pet as an inanimate object. In some quarters, however, a pet is regarded as an object of property rather than as a person. For example, a trial court judge in San Diego, California, recently ruled, according to law, that a writ of habeas corpus does not apply to a canine and rejected a petitioner's demand that a dog be released from "illegal custody." The petitioner felt that the dog was wrongfully held in a pound, but as he was not the owner he could not bring a property action. He also could not, as the court ruled, bring a writ of habeas corpus, which protect personal liberty. The judge said that writs of habeas corpus apply only to human beings. Animal "lovers" protest the classification; they say that an animal ought to be regarded as a subject, not as an object.

Marcel Heiman in this volume points out the highly complex relationship between man and his pet.[7] People choose pets that not only resemble their outer image but also mirror their inner characteristics. A person may choose an animal to fill a deep personal need for companionship, love or self-esteem, or because it resembles his own self-image. The pet may represent the person himself, the child who was or the child who never came into being. The pet may represent the deepest and highest aspirations in the life of his owner.[8] For example, a cat is for the lonely person whose need is for independence — the cat's independence gives him strength. A dog has remarkable ability to imitate his owner, but this is as much based on the dog's own tendency as it is fostered by the owner's need to have the dog comply and obey (what would an old woman do with a dog that only wants to romp and play?).[9]

When an owner talks about his pet, he is often really talking about himself — remember, the owner often identifies with his pet. A pet owner might look askance at being asked to see a psychiatrist on the basis of his pet's neurotic problems, but in emotional or mental disorder, the roles of the individual, the family and their pets may be intimately interlocked. In one family, for example, the mother had a phobia against leaving the house. This spread to her daughter and, to a lesser degree, to her husband and son. The family dog and cat also were frightened of leaving the house. In another family, the pet bird – a cocatiel – was very sensitive to increases in tension within the family. Whenever the family became noisy and fought, the bird would become excited. And in another family, a canary (named "Pretty Bird") would never sing when the little girl was away. We can try to understand what life is about through our experiences with pets.[10]

People may unconsciously train their pets to be what they would like to be themselves: obedient or defiant, barking or quiet. They then can identify with them. Heiman sees today's pet as a direct descendant from a totem animal used by man in his development and useful to him in the process of civilization. In primitive man, totemism was a device used to control and conceal sexual and aggressive drives within the family. The pet is for civilized man what the totem animal was for the primitive. The pet represents a protector, a talisman against the fear of death.

FOOTNOTES

1. P. 307.
2. The myths of the stupid athlete and the benefits derived by all boys from participating in sports are refuted. Most superior athletes are also superior in other fields unrelated to athletics. The participation in athletics for the boy who does not have the desire, the interest or the ability is really cheating him. Life is a game, too, and the rules are clear — you must be able to compete. The "planners" have observed this and, in fact, may be threatened by the individual confidence, spirit of enterprise and independence nurtured on our playing field. Ward, S. D.: *Infra* p. 307.
3. P. 315.
4. P. 325. Harvard anthropologist John W. Whiting says, "I've noticed that many of the best professional athletes have grown up without fathers — either the father died or they came from broken homes." Quoted in Cope, M.: Mama makes them champs. *This Week,* Oct. 14, 1962. See Freud, A.: *The Ego and the Mechanisms of Defence.* New York, International Universities Press, 1946, p. 142.
5. P. 299.
6. The Earl Nightingale Program, copyright Earl Nightingale, Chicago, Ill.
7. P. 329.
8. Ralph Slovenko's father loved guinea hens.
9. Senator George Vest, in his famous eulogy to the dog delivered in 1870, said: "The one absolutely unselfish friend that a man can have in this selfish world, the one that never deserts him and the one that never proves ungrateful or treacherous is his dog. . . . A man's dog stands by him in prosperity and in poverty, in health and in sickness. He will sleep on the cold ground, where the wintry winds blow and the snow drives fiercely, if only he may be near his master's side. He will kiss the hand that has no food to offer, he will lick the wounds and sores that come in encounters with the roughness of the world. He guards the sleep of his pauper master as if he were a prince. When all other friends desert, he remains. When riches take wings and reputation falls to pieces, he is as constant in his love as the sun in its journey through the heavens." That eulogy now has been translated into more than 200 languages and spread throughout the world. *Kansas City Times,* September 24, 1966, p. 16C.

10. Ernest Dichter, president of the Institute for Motivational Research, reminds us that objects — things which we own — are also our links with life. In his book *Handbook of Consumer Motivations,* Dichter points out that objects are far more than the simple inanimate things they may seem to be. They are little mirrors of ourselves; they reflect our image; they are our anchors. The child clutches his teddy bear or blanket, and adults find substitutes for them. Nightingale, E.: The World of Things, *The Earl Nightingale Program,* no. 1341, 1966.

PARENTS OF ATHLETES

JOSEPH P. DOLAN

WATCHING ATHLETES IN COMPETITION establishes psychological identification with youthful attitudes (and attributes) and helps to create a climate of vitality and ebullience. In any human activity where more than a single person is involved — in industry, in the military, in the professions, in trades or in sports — we constantly see an interplay of personality factors involving the expresson or control of frustration or the joy or dejection associated with failure or success. We see a reaction to projection on the part of one man and a defensive denial on the part of another. We see symbolization and identification on every side — to an even greater degree with parents. We see feelings displaced and converted. In observing these reactions when they are associated with athletic competition, we have the opportunity to learn a great deal about human nature and how it reacts when placed rather close to its biological frontier. Athletic competition can often remove the veneer of "culture" rather quickly if the personal or association stakes are high enough.

Unless an individual is actually participating in an athletic event, chances are that his enthusiasm for the events involved are through a vicarious involvement. The degree of vicariousness is usually in relation to the spectator's personality index for "getting involved." The involvement of the college and university alumni takes a distant back seat to the involvement of the parent of an athlete, if the particular parent chooses to become involved in the athlete's activities.

Hanging on the wall in this writer's office is a picture painted by a graduate student many years ago of a Little League baseball game between eleven- and twelve-year-olds. The picture shows an eleven-year-old batter talking to a twelve-year-old catcher while in the near background four umbrella-wielding mothers are beating the umpire over the head. The picture's caption shows the batter saying to the catcher, "Ya know, I'd give up this darned game if it wasn't such a healthy outlet for my parent's frustrations and protective instincts."[1]

The profession of medicine realized back in the 1920's that the care and management of the athletic injury — both emotional and physical — represented a special task for which a special series of experiences in postgraduate medical preparation is demanded. Dr. S. J. Miller, former athletic team physician at Purdue University, had the following advice for externs, interns and young general practitioners when he discussed athletics and medicine: Those who would understand the problem of medical treatment of athletics must first understand the psychosomatic drives which lead a man to make a career of sports. Miller would conclude, "The neophyte physician will quickly learn there is a fundamental difference between the practice of general medicine and that of sports medicine."

The practice of sports medicine is quite often prolonged pediatrics, and some old-timers who have cared for ball clubs during their medical careers will hasten to warn a physician that the practice of sports medicine is the "public practice" of medicine. This writer, when interviewing a surgeon who had recently operated on a famous baseball player's elbow, was told that he felt as if he had twenty millions sets of eyes peering down his instruments throughout the surgical procedure.

Any analysis of the behavior of parents of athletes must consider the environmental and emotional aspects of the game in which the athlete is playing. Our society does not think of an athlete as a normal human being with stress to overcome. Every occupation has tensions predisposing its members to certain attitudes, and these often interfere with the task at hand. The athlete, in addition to having such tensions, is subjected to mob pressures, be it a small community or New York City (or national or international, as in the Olympics).

The nonathlete might be able to hide or at least become inconspicuous during a period of depression, but the athlete cannot "goof off." There is no place to run; he is on display; the mob watches. The mob in athletics, like any mob, is determined by its lowest common denominator. The sports audience is total and absolute . . . ; it possesses no shades of adequacy; its reaction is total acceptance or total rejection. Since the athlete performs before such an evaluation board, his own evaluations — and those of his parents, his wife and extremely close friends — are not realistic. Normal anxieties are exaggerated.

One associated with athletes soon realizes that athletes are body-oriented. With this body orientation is associated a vicarious body orientation of the boy's parent, if the parent is the type who experiences "through the lad" the attributes and reflexes of athletic endeavors. If the athlete is injured, and if his index of body orientation is high, there may be a tendency for a concern for the injury to be expressed psychophysiologically by the parent. These conversion symptoms felt by a parent are complex when one takes into consideration that the United States is "star oriented." That is, our sports programs tend to produce star athletes, and often these same programs (or games) may well produce a "goat" or the chap who "blew the big one."

As a result of feelings of association and certain projection reflexes, his immediate family is also "branded" by the act or the failure to act. All too often, journalists contribute to the "goat" stories. Frequently the pressure to "star," and above all to avoid the play that might contribute to the title of "goat," comes from a boy's parents. Such a constant pressure from within the home, running counter to the coach's desire to create a "balanced team," creates a high degree of conflict within the athlete. One must remember that the athlete is an oridnary person, and therefore, when playing on a well-coached team in front of classmates, friends and hostile opposition, he is called upon to lead a life of fiction. He must win rather than play for play's sake. For instance, in a high school football game during the first quarter of a 0-0 game, with the game situation reading "fourth down and one yard to go," the quarterback is signaled "from the bench" to punt. The player (quarterback) does not want to punt; instead, he desires to try for the first down. Here is conflict between expressing oneself and playing the coaching percentages. The coach wins. The parent of the well-disciplined quarterback is frustrated by the coach's lack of "confidence" in the lad's "ability" to make a sound choice.

In addition to the "star mentality" of the American sports audience, there exists an intra-team conflict in the mind of the athlete. This refers to the expressed philosophy in all coaching and team play that the team shall take precedence and demand the whole effort of the individual. No individual athlete should try to excel personally. If the athlete is sensitive to roles, he might find himself in a moral and ethical state of stress because of his continued attention to team play instead of individual stardom . . . or his unsung contribution to another's individual stardom.

His parents, not bound and controlled by team effort coaching, school spirit and adolescent ideals, might very well create conflict for the lad by reminding the boy of the market value of personality through constant superiority in athletics. Many well-meaning fathers, motivated by society's market value of public accomplishments, have created resentments within the psyche of fine athletes until these same athletes perform far below their potential. This is especially applicable to fathers of high school seniors who might be "athletic scholarship" material . . . and the "pro contract" duplicates the problem for the college senior, and a fine team becomes mediocre.

The process of sublimation of personal goals to team goals is an old story to those associated with positive athletic effort. Often the process of sublimation is viewed by a parent as the loss of a son's identity for a vague purpose. However, sublimation of personal desires to group effort actually comes rather easy for the average athlete. These lads possess certain character traits that control egotistical selfishness.

Bruce C. Ogilvie and Thomas A. Tutko in their study "Motivational Patterns of Athletes" show an emotional profile of the "well-defined" athlete.[2] In this study, covering a two-year period, more than one thousand athletes were evaluated on 150 different personality dimensions. These investigators used athletes from four sports — football, basketball, track and baseball. One wonders if the fathers of athletes would reveal the same personality traits as their sons regarding athletic competition and life in general.

The Ogilvie-Tutko study indicated the following athletic profile:

1. Greater achievement orientation.
2. Greater aggressive tendencies.
3. More willingness to pay the physical and emotional price for success.
4. More in touch with the reality demands of life.
5. More open and trusting.
6. Warmer and socially conforming.
7. Definite lack of extroversion in the form of "showboating."

Certainly items (4) to (7) of these findings indicate that an athlete conforms easily to the demands of competition and the preparation for competition. If a parent does not have the high index of plasticity or psychological resiliency of the trained athlete, a fundamental part of the mental repertoire of the schoolboy athlete, there may be conflict in the home. This creates two sets of demands for the athlete — those from without and those from within. All guidance is strained through an emotional screen, and often a family's demands upon a son's team-oriented philosophy causes nothing more than frustration. This frustration arises from unresolved conflict. But the opportunity to handle frustration with logic and reason is one of the educational aspects of school athletics. Coaches teach that the degree to which a youngster can handle frustrations is the athletic maturity index. This can be applied to any human endeavor. Maturity is a fundamental prerequisite for expressing effective judgment, or enlightened self-interest must often be ignored for long-range benefits to the organization (the team).

The index of athletic maturity is such a part of the total picture of human effort in athletics that coaches cannot discuss sports effort without referring to the role of maturity and the final result of effort in sports. For instance, at any level of development, there is a tendency to fall back upon previous levels of development. This occurs because there is more security here than in facing the present stress. Here is a clear example of regression. Since adolescence is an intense period of feeling that tends to drown out logic, an over-protective parent might add to the athlete's regressive tendencies by encouraging low goals for the particular athlete. There may be reverse dangers here, too, and these come from the parent who creates demands far and above the potential of the lad.

If the aspiration level is higher than the achievement level — and in athletics, the aspiration level is often the projection of a father's desires, not the boy's — chronic frustration may result that can cause a distinct lack of mental hygiene at a later hour in life. If a parent can control the normal desire to see his child excel, and channel (or repress) such desires to support of the total athletic effort of the son's team, a dangerous culmination of frustration can be avoided.

In industrial psychology and in professional athletics, one hears of the "Plimsoll Point."[3] In athletics this refers to the condition which a person reaches when he can no longer tolerate more frustration, motivation and outside stimulation. The anxiety that is present in modern society in almost epidemic proportions is often projected by a parent into an athlete's career when a deep-felt threat to personality security is indicated by a hostile press, crowd or community. An athlete is bombarded with constant reminders that "there are no complacent champions," "reputations are never established — they are a continuous responsibility," "there exists no plateau in sports — you either get better or worse."

Maybe a constant home and school "coaching program" contributes to a Plimsoll Point for what had been a balanced athlete. It is a wise and experienced coach who recognizes the early symptoms of "Plimsoll." Often a mature teammate can tip off a coach regarding this, and coaches put much faith in such observations of some athletes.

Parents, especially fathers, often have to call upon quite a few of the better-known mechanisms of adjustment in order to control what is termed by some college health physicians as the "Good Family Syndrome." This refers to the normal desire of a parent to shield his children from those experiences through which the father achieved his own development. But the same father substitutes the laboratory of human behavior called the athletic field for his own lower socioeconomic background of work during a less technological era. Let us observe some of these mechanisms of adjustment as observed in some parents of athletes.

Projection of blame to other members of the team is an old escape for parents who would rather ignore their son's contribution to team failure. Unable to accept blame for mistakes by their son, these parents will condemn the referee who was "picking on my boy." The coach can be brought into projection, too, because as far as the father is concerned, his son is being played "out of position," is "warming the bench too long," or the lad's teammates "won't throw him the ball," "won't block for him, but he blocks for them," etc.

Displacement is seen throughout athletic endeavor. Feelings are transferred to another. Quite often, a lad who has been reared by an autocratic father will transfer an anti-father feeling to his coach and all supervisory personnel. The other side of the coin finds the father who does not appreciate his own supervisor, thus transferring his anti-leadership attitude to the coach and referee.

A valuable tool that enables most fathers to enjoy athletic participation by their sons is the process of repression. This serves a useful purpose in a normal pattern of everyday living; it removes thoughts, desires, impulses and strivings that are incompatible with social mores. Here, the well-adjusted father buries in his mind the protective urge of parents, and if he must, he rationalizes.

It is a wise father who recognizes that his son may be a poor ball carrier and motivates him toward a career as a defensive specialist or as a blocker or in some aspect other than the "glamor" of always being the focal point.

The process of denial creates a problem for those who direct athletic activity. For instance, we realize that in most sports there is a chance that injury may occur. When such an injury causes the physician, following his examination, to preclude athletic activity for a period that may find the son "missing the big game," it is acceptable moral responsibility for a "reasonable" parent to follow the physician's advice. Not so for a small percentage of fathers; they have been known to take their son "medically shopping" to seek a physician who "understands the importance of playing the big game." Here is denial that has frustrated many a fine physician who is thinking of a boy's future, not just of a particular Friday night or Saturday afternoon. Papa denies that the injury exists. The attitude of an athlete's parents toward his participation in athletics is of great importance not only in the behavior of the parents but in the development of the athlete's own personality. Often athletes will experience emotional and performance regression. A survey of his parents' personalities as these relate to the boy's athletic career is of first importance. The feelings of the overzealous father who uses athletic results and performance as the reference point from which anything is measured will usually reflect a mixture of affection rejection, hostility and guilt. A small percentage of parents spend their lives reacting to the results of athletic performances by their children.

The devotion of fathers to sons who are athletes is usually intense. When calibrated along a scale of values by parents, the small group of over-affectionate, overprotecting fathers of athletes will be matched by a similar group of rather indifferent or rejecting fathers at the other end of the scale. High school and college coaches refer to the "over-syndrome" as the tendency of some fathers to exhibit degrees of over affection, over-anxiety, over-authority, over-indulgence, over-protection, over-responsibility, over-restriction, and perfectionism.

Coaches and team physicians who have associated with athletic team events in the twentieth century tend to agree with the Bulgarian-born author Elias Canetti's description of the "baiting crowd."[4] The crowd is an immediate report card involving the athlete's performance, and the boy's father can hear and see if his son is accepted, approved and accorded authority. Canetti writes:

> One important reason for the rapid growth of the baiting crowd is that there is no risk involved because the crowd has immense authority and superiority on its side. The victim can do nothing to it. His permitted murder stands for all the murders people have to deny themselves for fear of the penalties for the perpetration. A murder shared with many others, which is not only safe and permitted, but indeed recommended, is irresistible to the great majority of men.

A sports fan, especially if he has paid admission, feels that he has a vested interest in the performance of athletes. His attitude, whether expressed or controlled, is a conscious or unconscious pressure on the overtly interested father of an athlete. Such a parent remains intuitively and instinctively alert until such alertness reaches the point of habitual excess.

The aggressive parent of the athlete can contribute inescapably to an entire team's mediocrity if the particular parent's anxieties are continually registered in expressed frustration mechanisms. If the boy becomes a professional athlete, the professional team's manager or coach finds the same problem with a few player's wives, but this is another story.

"Just think of it, Mama — that's our boy!"

FOOTNOTES

1. Compare children who commit delinquencies as an acting out of the parent's conscious or unconscious wishes. Johnson, A. M., and Szurek, S. A.: Etiology of antisocial behavior in delinquents and psychopaths. *JAMA, 154:*814, 1954.
2. Ogilive, B. C., and Tutko, T. A.: Motivational patterns of athletes. Paper presented to the American College of Sports Medicine, Los Angeles, Calif., April, 1964; reported in *Medical Times,* June, 1964.
3. The Plimsoll Point is a term from the field of aviation. It refers to the weight-carry ability (load capacity) of an airplane, and if this load is exceeded, the airplane cannot get off the ground. See Murphy, G.: *An Introduction to Psychology.* New York, Harper, 1951, p. 90.
4. Canetti, E.: *Crowds and Power.* New York, Viking Press, 1962.

THE SUPERIOR ATHLETE

STEPHEN D. WARD

To define what constitutes a superior athlete is a hopeless task. I shall not attempt it. Each year a new crop of superior athletes appears in grade schools, high schools, colleges and the rosters of professional teams — in every sport. Generally, however, it is obvious and even inevitable that the purest examples of superior athletes are the pros — in every sport.

To my knowledge, no worthwhile scientific study of motivation in sports has ever been accomplished or even attempted. Certainly this chapter cannot be considered such a study. The views and opinions expressed here are based on a number of years of personal observation of athletes and coaches, diligent reading of sports pages and sports magazines and many hours of reflection on the problems and enigmas which were thus presented.

Many people play golf or tennis well, swim well, ski — even play baseball or football well. They have mastered the game, know all the rules, all the moves, have been able to make their bodies perform — at times — but not consistently. Even Arnold Palmer hits bad shots. He just does not hit as many as others do.

What is the indefinable something that makes a good physical specimen, who has studied and become skilled, add something more and maintain an intense almost excruciating consistency about his particular physical skill or prowess?

Actually the problem of motivation as it applies to any endeavor is a primary field of interest in psychiatry today. It is of interest not only from an academic standpoint but also from its pragmatic aspects as it might apply to education, politics, criminology, advertising, selling. This list could be continued almost indefinitely.

The big question, of course, is why does the athlete do it? Why does he subject himself to the physical pain of a training regimen in order that he might endure the mental anguish and further abuse of his body in a competitive sport? It does not seem to make much sense. The only answer to this seems to be a rather simple one — the athlete does this because he has to. In superior athletes there is an urgent need to play, almost a compulsion to play.

Looking at it from the standpoint of the pleasure principle which holds that all activity stems from efforts to gain pleasure and avoid pain, it is quite obvious that there must be something hidden or secret, something very personal, leading to a quite basic form of pleasure which induces an athlete to undergo all of this.

An immediate and startling thing that quickly catches the eye is the manner in which an athlete tends to look at his body. It is difficult to come up with a good simile to describe this but in some ways it is very similar to the regard some men have for pieces of machinery such as sports cars. They will pamper them, worry about them, tinker with them, tune them up, shine them up and repeatedly test them out. In his training regimen the athlete does much the same thing with his body. The sports car buff has the advantage, however, in that he can purchase replacement parts for defective material.

The high regard in which an athlete holds his body is sometimes best seen after a defeat. It is difficult for him to accept the fact that his body has failed in its requirements, so he chooses one small area of his body and singles it out for attention and disapproval. He will come to the training room with an innocuous bruise or abrasion and seek treatment for the specific area. He may at the same time ignore bruises and abrasions on other areas of his body of equal or greater severity. He displaces dissatisfaction from the whole to a part.

Experienced trainers following the defeat of a team always expect a greatly increased volume of business over that which occurs following a victory. This is not really a mass attempt to alibi a defeat, for the wounds are rarely disabling, and few aside from the trainer and other teammates seeking similar attention are even aware of such treatment. It is not unusual to hear an athlete refer to an injured member as "the leg," "the hand," "the arm," "the foot" and so on. This attitude reflects a psychic detachment of the injured part from the remaining uninjured portion.

Actually, defeat is viewed as a narcissistic injury to our self-concept or body image. It is a function of our ego defenses to protect our self-concept. Our self-concept is always a very fragile thing which must be protected at any cost. Failure to protect it adequately results in severe anxiety — a feeling that we are helpless and unprotected in frightening surroundings. The manner in which we defend our ego and protect our self-concept accounts in large measure for the differences in personality among all of us.

A bit of very brief and simplified theoretical background is probably in order. A commonly accepted psychoanalytic theory of the derivation of the ego holds that it is an offshoot of the id. The ego is the more civilized part of our psychic apparatus; the id is the very primitive, savage, selfish and even murderous part. Id impulses are bred into all of us through our animal heritage, while ego controls over these impulses are learned, hopefully, during childhood and our early adult period. In primitive man (if we may jump from ontogeny to phylogeny) we can picture the ego as being at one time indistinguishable from the id. The id freely expressed needs no defense. Its mode of expression is action. It is only as the ego becomes distinguishable that defenses appear. The body is the instrument of the id-ego and assures it of both continued gratification and continued existence. Thus, skillful and accomplished use of the body in a primitive society is not only a most necessary defense of life itself, but also a most primitive ego defense.

Use of the body expressively or ego-defensively is not restricted to athletes. We all use body and hand gestures in communicating with one another. We use many muscles in smiling, frowning, furrowing the brow, winking, blinking, crying, shrugging the shoulders and so on. All of these have protective as well as expressive characteristics.

In my view the athlete uses his body, in particular his musculoskeletal system, to a far greater extent in defending his ego than a nonathlete. I say musculoskeletal system to make the point that it is the body in motion that counts. It must be able to perform feats of strength, agility and daring. I am reminded of one coach I know whose favorite expression of encouragement to his players is "You've got to be daring." Risks must be taken for rewards to accrue. Businessmen as well as athletes understand this, and successful businessmen in their own way are just as aggressive and daring as the successful athlete.

It is not the body beautiful that is important. I do not classify physical culturists along with athletes. In my mind they fall into the field of psychopathology.

If this use of the body by an athlete is accepted, it can be seen that athletic failure or defeat could precipitate extreme anxiety. To avoid this anxiety, the superior athlete will go to extremes of viciousness and savagery in order to win.

None of the foregoing, however, could adequately explain how the whole process is set in motion. An answer, satisfying at least to me, came from an unexpected source – a friend who had been crippled as an infant by polio. His own experiences in growing up were so completely different from what one is normally accustomed to see that the contrast provided an illuminating bit of insight. His childhood was spent with mother discouraging efforts at physical activity, which would have and frequently did result in falls and other major and minor accidents and injuries. As a result, his childhood was spent with encouragement and reward for lack of physical activity but with a corresponding emphasis on intellectual activity and skill.

It occurred to me at about this time that mothers, as the primary teachers, could be the chief agents for determining who might and who might not achieve athletic excellence. It has long been known and even confirmed by scientific experiments that a mother's love and approval are essential to an infant's normal growth and behavior. Infants will even die without them in spite of adequate nutrition and medical care. As an infant reaches the crawling and toddling stages and starts holding his own bottle and feeding himself, mother's love and attention must be gained from sources other than her holding, fondling and feeding him, which initially served this purpose.

Most parents are proud when their infant son starts pushing or dragging himself to an erect position and eagerly look forward to a child's taking his first few steps. In some mothers, however, this period produces tremendous anxiety because of the fear that the child will fall down and hurt himself, climb up on a piece of furniture and fall off, stumble down the steps or some such thing. Consequently, she spends a great deal of time watching the child, keeping him from putting himself into dangerous places. Such a child, I feel, will find little satisfaction out of sports or athletics. To begin with, the child very quickly learns that physical or athletic endeavor not only does not please mother but causes her great anxiety. I am not about to postulate that such mothers in diverting their children by playing intellectual games thereby produce budding intellectuals.

But there are other mothers. These take great pride in their child's agility, ability to climb, move about and perform physically in spite of the fact that the child occasionally falls down and hurts himself. Every new physical achievement is greeted with obvious expressions of approval and love on the mother's part. The child recognizes this and will outdo himself to get more of it, and then simply continues repetitively for the rest of his life. These children are more than likely to be athletes of one sort or another depending on their size and physical makeup.

Whether superior athletes are subjected to such situations in a more intense or exaggerated manner is difficult to determine. There is little doubt, however, that top athletes have a peculiarly intense relationship with their mothers. This one can confirm simply by reading interviews with athletes appearing in sports publications. Personal interviews or even casual chats with athletes quite often are startling in the easy flood of material and comments relating to maternal relationships.

A difficult thing to reconcile with maternal influence is the anger which is so obviously present in any athletic contest. Those who do not believe it is present are simply naive. Players capable of becoming enraged and staying that way are the superior performers. The old call to "give all for dear old Alma Mater" becomes a little too obvious to miss — or perhaps even to cite. Pep talks are meant to get players angry and keep them that way. Various techniques are employed, but the most common and probably the most effective is the use of shame.

An athletic field is no place for a gentleman. He can be, and usually is, a gentleman off the field, but not on it. The origin of these angry feelings became clear to me one day as I watched a little boy showing off in front of his mother by walking along a bench pretending it was a tightrope. The bench tipped over and he fell bumping his knee. Leaping up he rushed at his mother and furiously started beating at her legs. The message was very clear. It was her fault. She had made him hurt himself.

In spite of this, however, I do not feel that an athlete out on the field is just assaulting his mother in some unconscious way. He is out there in a dangerous and vulnerable situation. He can be hurt physically, or he can be hurt ego-wise through losing. Both are to be avoided, and it is quite clear that the instrument potentially inflicting these hurts is that other contesting body across the way. Under such circumstances, rage is a fairly understandable and natural phenomenon.

I find it much more difficult to understand or to accept pacifists or practitioners of nonviolence as honest and honorable men. The reason, of course, is that pacifism and nonviolence are disguised or an underhand form of aggression — passive aggression. These are always difficult people to like — or even to tolerate. It is interesting to note that our current campus marchers are usually from the intellectual group. Athletes rarely involve themselves in such movements.

I once tried comparing superior athletes with practitioners of yoga. A yogi says that he masters his body, but it appears that all he does is make it quit complaining by mastering some sort of hypnotic trick of the mind. Athletes make their bodies do things, accomplish things — extraordinary things — and endure the pain.

At any rate, the child and the athlete do what is expected and yet can be enraged at the necessity of it — the necessity of risking or suffering injury and pain. It does hurt physically to be good enough to receive recognition or acclaim. These, however, do little to relieve the hurt, and at times it does not seem worth it all. Athletes frequently talk about quitting or retiring. Why does the athlete endure the suffering? Just to get some love. He does it in the same way he learned as a little child.

Someone is bound to ask: "What about female athletes?" Female athletes, no less than female nonathletes, present special problems in evaluation. I am aware of no one who claims any special competence in assessing either group. In my view, however, the same general dynamic structure motivating males would have to be the basis of the female athletic motivation. The real enigma is in the reconciliation of the soft, physiologically, socially and culturally determined maternal inclinations with the harsh phallic requisites of competitive sports at a superior level. Rather strangely, in my estimation, I have seen this same constellation of conflict with ensuing difficulties in several professional female dancers. In these instances the mothers were strong, pathologically ambitious women when it came to their daughters' careers. Many ramifications for speculation are available, but I am unequipped with experience enough to pursue these.

All of us have heard many platitudes about the benefits to be derived from participating in sports, and we have heard a corresponding number of tales about the ox-like stupidity of athletes. I personally have many doubts about both. To begin with, I have known many athletes and have found few of them stupid. They are rarely intellectually clever or witty. They do not use either words or wit to assault an opponent or to defend themselves. To them, direct action always seems much more effective than talk; actions have always spoken louder than words. And it really is not surprising to find that in a study of varsity lettermen at one major university, more than a third had gone on to receive graduate degrees.

Participation in sports is of value to boys. Learning to be a good sport and a gracious loser is neither good nor desirable. Among superior athletes, good sports and gracious losers are probably nonexistent — at least the variety of these generally recognized by some sports reporters, most spectators, and every playground and youth center organizer, boy scout leader and the like. Good athletes do respect and admire skill, strength and aggressiveness in opponents, and even occasionally can admire dirty play, if it is done with some degree of finesse. Strong objection, however, is always taken to dirty play aimed at producing physical damage.

Some last-ditch ego-saving devices are available to athletes involved in losing causes. In a team sport even though the team might lose, the individual player can be quite comfortable and free of anxiety providing he has the conviction that he personally performed well. If it is inescapable that he has done poorly, fantasy will frequently come to his aid. He will defeat his opponent in another endeavor. A very common fantasy in a defeated football player is that he will meet his opposite number or the whole opposing team, singly or in groups outside the dressing room and literally mutilate them in hand-to-hand combat. Occasionally the fantasy does not suffice; it must be acted out, and the crowd is treated to an added attraction. The late Jim Tatum, former head football coach at Maryland and before that at North Carolina, was pretty close to the spirit of things when he said, "Winning is not the most important thing — it is the *only* thing."

It takes a brand of courage to take your chances in a contest before a crowd. Courage is what is learned in any competitive sport. It is a necessary ingredient for success in any field. Courage is not a gift given freely to a few by some lucky chance of heritage or genetics. It must be learned; it must be acquired, for we are all basically cowards.

Should participation in sports be encouraged? Even egghead intellectuals will agree that it should, or at least they will pay lip service to this with the provision that everything should be regulated and controlled. There is room for disagreement on how this should be done and at what age body-contact sports should be encouraged.

I am not a believer in the Little League philosophy that everyone who shows up should get to play, regardless of who wins. Athletic contests are the relics and vestiges of what in former times were tribe and life-preserving struggles. I think it is not too farfetched to parallel our present international political no-win philosophy with our Little League philosophy for juvenile sports. It is somehow or other not very nice any more to win. Leo Durocher summed it all up very neatly several years ago when he said, "Nice guys finish last." We are certainly very busy trying to be nice guys.

One hears claims that this or that number or percentage of professional baseball players got their first start in the Little League. I am inclined to feel that they made it to the big leagues in spite of, rather than because of, their experience in the Little League. Why delude a child into the belief that success can be achieved by merely presenting himslf as an aspiring candidate for the rewards of life? Will his first employer have as gentle a regard as did his Little League manager for the possible psychic trauma that might be done by firing him?

The Little League philosophy fosters security-seeking dependency, acceptance of weakness and goals of mediocrity. It does not breed superior athletes or enterprising citizens.

It has been said that the British Empire was won on the playing fields of Eton. There are many today who would therefore curse those playing

"My success as a field goal kicker, including today's 53-yard championship-winning field goal, I have to attribute to my mother. She always gave me a lollipop whenever I kicked my father!"

fields for having nurtured imperialism and all of its much maligned concomitants. Perhaps, too, a similar hypothesis could account for the disdain with which intellectuals in general hold athletes and athletics. Perhaps the individual confidence, spirit of enterprise and independence nurtured on our playing fields constitute a threat to our current crop of social, economic and philosophical planners.

If such be the case, let's get on with the game!

INJURY IN ATHLETICS

ROBERT A. MOORE

In a book devoted to studying motivations in sports, it is necessary also to consider how these motivations may work to the disadvantage of the participant. In this chapter we will review certain psychological conflicts that may be resolved through injury or which result indirectly in injury in an attempt to find a solution.

We are concerned with the unconscious and do not suggest that some athletes may be injured "on purpose." The need to underscore this was brought to my attention a few years ago after presenting some of these ideas at a professional meeting. An enterprising sports writer polled a professional football team to find how many of them actually wanted to be injured. Unfortunately, their responses were not printable, but the impression was quite plain that psychiatry had struck out again or, to keep the metaphor more appropriate, was guilty of a personal foul.

When consideration is given to athletic injuries, it is quite appropriate that the major emphasis be given to proper physical conditioning, protective equipment and rules of safety. Unfortunately, there has been a tendency only to think of the athlete as a biochemical repository for unwelcome stimulant drugs, an anthropologically measured body on which to put protective devices or a prepubertal Little Leaguer with unclosed epiphyses. We must remember also that the athlete has a mind and in an attempt to reach a compromise between certain desires and prohibitions may conduct himself in such a way to increase the likelihood of injury.

First, a brief review of the nature of man is indicated. For most of the intelligent history of man, an infant has been assumed to be interested only in food and warmth. Children have alternately been viewed as miniature adults with the same legal responsibilities or as innocent and happy lambs with nothing more important than play and school to consider. An unfortunate revolution in thought has disrupted this comfortable fantasy during the twentieth century, and we have been dismayed to learn of some of the unpleasant wishes possessed by little children.

The baby is born with certain biologically determined drives that are more readily identified in retrospect. Lack of better terms has left us no alternative other than to name these drives as the sexual and aggressive drives, though these terms have caused much misunderstanding. We are referring to an innate feeling of uneasiness and anticipation which moves the individual to certain activities which give a sense of relief, satisfaction, even satiation. These drives vary in their intensity from individual to individual. If you watch a row of newborn infants in a nursery, you are struck by the unevenness of activity; some babies are moving about violently, others are resting passively and only periodically thrusting their fists about and crying when hungry. Some babies seem to be born more kinetic, more aggressive if you wish, than others.

The infant, in its omnipotence, believes it has only to make certain magical gestures and satiation will follow. It learns in time this is not so, that someone other than itself is required, when its magical gesture is not immediately followed by satiation. It becomes angry, screams, flails about, and when the breast or bottle appears, may hit it with a vengeance reminding one of a shark hitting a bait. It moves toward the object of supply hungrily. With the appearance of teeth, it bites and chews, as any nursing mother can testify.

The aggressive urge at this point consists of an active movement toward the object with the intent to bite and swallow, but as the object becomes more clear it also fears retailiation in the form of being bitten or swallowed. Gradually the baby shifts its expression of aggression to a more passive and obstructive form, particularly as parental prohibitions of natural wishes cause him increasing resentment. He must in some way defy the adult world for fear he will otherwise lose his separateness in complete submission.

New dangers occur as his wishes for greater closeness with his mother place him, in fantasy, more and more in direct competition with his father. He would displace and defeat this powerful figure, but he fears his puny self would be mutilated or destroyed in the process, so he withdraws till a day he is better prepared.

After several years of relative calm while he invests his assertive, active strivings for motor expression in play and school outlets, he reaches puberty with its biochemical storms. The release of aggression again is connected in fantasy with competition with the adult male and with concomitant strivings to continue as a helpless child but also with a wish to be rid of any dependent ties on the adult world. Eventually, the youth survives adolescence, and some balance is reached with the adult pattern of aggressive display assumed.

We understand that by aggression we are referring to a sense of anticipation, a desire to move towards another, to be assertive yet to remain a separate individual. A sense of satisfaction follows a display of aggression for some, but others become uneasy or feel guilty that they have done something wrong and now will be punished. Aggression is not hostility, anger, nor assault. However, aggression is now in the service of the desire to attack a competing or disappointing object; that is, it furnishes the power or energy for such an attack. Aggression is also involved in adult sexual activity, giving the sexual act the urgency and force it requires for complete gratification.

To be aggressive, then, is to bring closer the intense conflicts over ambivalent feelings towards loved (and hated) parents and the fears of retaliation for wicked sexual urges. No wonder so much conflict is to be found over expression of aggression. This is intensified by the process of symbolically taking within oneself the stern prohibitions of one's parents against aggressive and sexual strivings. As a result, even thinking of such things, oftentimes where the thought is unconscious, causes guilt as intense as if one had committed the act.

Social limitations intensify the very personal conflicts over display of aggression. These social taboos were minimal in cave-dwelling times since failure to be aggressive meant early extinction. Today it is different, and society will punish uncontrolled aggression. A mature modern man is supposed to be calm and composed and would think it uncouth to be overtly aggressive motor-wise. He has adopted better techniques of discharging these urges. He has learned to channel the energies from direct motor expression to a useful assertiveness in his business, social, and creative life. We call this sublimation.

Another problem intensified by social changes is the increasing blurring of the distinction between sexes in the allowable expression of aggression. It seems, today, that women are increasingly assuming male prerogatives and that men are becoming more passive and woman-like in their family behavior. There is a very serious question of what the long-range effect will be on children when mothers work like men and men wash dishes, help with housework and change diapers like women. It is possible that the modern way increases the child's confusion over what is acceptable aggressive behavior for a male as contrasted to a female, at least in comparison with the old world tradition of how man and wife differ.

In summary, we see that aggressive urges become invested with conflicts in expression of hatred or anger and with conflicts over manliness.

THE DEMAND TO BE AGGRESSIVE

There are two areas of behavior where the expression of aggression is sanctioned, in fact demanded: in wartime military service and in competitive sports. A lack of ability to be aggressive may mean a short survival in either. Unfortunately, it is not possible for everyone to shift from an existence where aggressive display is dangerous to one where it is demanded without arousing many old conflicts.

A young man is taken from a peaceful world and placed in military service. He is told he must kill his enemy without hesitation. Fortunately, modern warfare makes less such demands for personal or direct killing. Nevertheless, careful observations of American ground forces in World War II revealed they often failed to fire their weapons at enemy forces, even passively accepting death as an alternative. Medical facilities were overwhelmed by psychiatric disabilities from such situations, not just as a result of the fear of being killed but of the fear of killing. Many casualties came from training camps where men could not tolerate even the aggression demanded in bayonet drill against straw dummies.

In competitive athletics, where participation is voluntary, we might not expect to find such conflict over aggressive display. A high premium is placed on aggressiveness, not only in team sports, but in individual sports, too. However, we realize participation is not entirely voluntary as there are external and internal pressures which may push one to participation and at the same time increase his feelings of danger.

The athlete will give top performance as long as he is willing to try and beat his opponent. But if a shift in the struggle occurs and he feels fearful now of his opponent, he begins to falter, lose his momentum, guard himself against retaliatory blows and probably loses. Before, he had an omnipotent belief in his safety in being aggressive, but now old unconscious fears of overwhelming retaliation for aggression cause him to hesitate. The phenomena of upsets in sports may well be related to this problem as well as the ebb and tide of success in a particular contest.

INJURY AS AN ESCAPE

The inward struggle over the wish to and fear of displaying aggression and the desire to be reassured of manliness has a decided effect on certain athletic participants. Two brief case references will illustrate this.

Case 1. A young high school boy with little athletic ability but tremendous desire tried out for the baseball team. This boy had led a rather sheltered life and was not too confident of his manliness nor was he particularly an aggressive person. He had entertained phantasies of being an athlete as long as he could remember as this would give him proof he was a manly and worthwhile person. His phantasies were never realized; instead he was the perpeutal benchwarmer, good enough to make the team due to his tremendous push, but with so little real ability that he made the ideal batting practice catcher. This particular spring it was apparent to him that, though he had been a substitute the two years preceding, he would probably not make the team at all this year because there were some promising newcomers trying out as catchers. Twice that spring he suffered painful bruises on his fingers for failing to keep his right hand closed till the ball was in the mitt. He gritted his teeth, however, and just tried harder. One day in an intra-squad practice game, the same thing happened, this time resulting in a severe fracture of the right index finger. His season was over.

Was he bitterly disappointed? Not in the least. His response was one of relief as he could now leave the field of combat with banners flying high.

He had escaped defeat and inescapable proof of his unmanliness. His splinted finger was a badge of manly combat. Was his injury incurred on purpose? The boy would deny this, of course, and yet three times in a span of several days he suffered an injury, the prevention of which was well-known to him, that he had not suffered in the previous years he had played baseball.

Case 2. This is a case of a much more successful athlete. He was an outstanding high school football player, much sought after by several colleges before he enrolled at a large university. Despite his great success, he never felt he achieved sufficient acclaim from his father. His father was a rather distant, nondemonstrative man who emphasized the gloomy side of life with the central theme being that their family wasn't meant for big things. Overt demonstrations of anger were not tolerated, and an overall picture of passivity pervaded the family with only the patient not fitting the pattern. The much less successful and much less aggressive siblings were given considerably more praise by the father. So the message began to get across to this athlete — the more successfully aggressive he was, the more alien and nonunderstandable he became to his family. He started off his sophomore year in college by running with the first string before the opening game. Unfortunately, he suffered an injury to his leg and missed the opening game. Somehow, the leg didn't respond to treatment though the team physician and trainer pronounced him fit for duty and the discouraged athlete limped through drills with the scrubs, no longer noticed by the coaches, until he finally quit the team.

While the injury itself may or may not have had a purposeful reason behind it, certainly the recovery from the injury was prolonged as a solution to the problem. He was now safe from further straying from his family's demand to remain passive.

From these illustrative cases, we see how athletic injuries or slow recovery from the same may result from psychological conflict between passivity and aggressivity. In one, the young athlete wants to prove himself by being more aggressive than his ability allows, so must extricate himself by injury before defeat gives him the final proof of what he feels others will perceive as his unmanliness. In the other, a boy with great athletic potential must not allow it to be manifest as the aggressive component of this would cause a loss of love from his passivity-demanding parents. Again injury is the ideal way out.

COUNTER-PHOBIA AS A SOLUTION

A somewhat more subtle solution to conflict over expression of basic urges is the development of what is termed a counter-phobic reaction. Because of fear of retaliation for the wish to express these aggressive urges when very young, the boy anticipates with terror some form of body mutilation. As a protection against this, he develops a pattern of "whistling in the dark," by feeling himself totally unafraid, invulnerable to injury. He tests and retests himself to prove magically he cannot be seriously hurt by daring and even dangerous activities. Typically, he feels very keyed up before facing danger, experienced often as an exhilarating anticipation. After the danger has been challenged successfully, he feels satisfied, often powerful for a short period of time. This is not a real solution, however, and he must repeat this experience over and over. Because this individual must take so many risks, it is only a matter of time before some injury results. This type of reaction may lead men to daredevil circus activities, auto-racing, stunt-driving, direct combat sports such as boxing, etc. Two examples follow:

Case 3. A young man became a professional motorcycle and auto racer and stunt flier on the county fair level. He had a reputation for foolhardy courage, actually deriving pleasure in watching other drivers spin off the track. He felt a real thrill when this occurred to him, suffering only minor injuries from which he would return with renewed enthusiasm. His background revealed his father was killed in an auto accident when he was six weeks old. On the way to the funeral one of his brothers, his uncle and grandmother were killed in an auto accident. From his earliest memories the patient recalls this gruesome story being retold many times by his mother. His oldest brother many years his senior became a substitute father and treated him very harshly. One day, this brother and the brother's son were killed in an auto accident, and the patient shortly after quit racing and flying, saying he was tired of it. Actually he had become too nervous to continue since his brother's death. His symptoms worsened considerably, and he had to enter a psychiatric hospital because of his terror of being injured. He repetitively dreamed of seeing his brother's mutilated body in the morgue which he had to identify.

From early life, this man felt a terrible vulnerability to injury. If such a horrible fate could befall a powerful person like a father, a puny figure like himself had no chance. He anticipated mutilation as a consequence of the most minor expressions of aggression. His constant danger-defying activities were of a counter-phobic type, a magical attempt to undo his vulnerability by constantly conquering danger. This tenuous defense crumbled when his hated older brother was killed, combined with the added blow of the death of the brother's son, proving finally that not only fathers but sons too are destined to be killed. As a result of his brother's demise, the patient unconsciously felt that his death wishes for his brother were now known and retaliation must surely follow. While his counter-phobic activities were intact, however, this man had many accidents in racing with numerous injuries, most of which were fortunately minor. The law of averages would probably have caught up with him if his brother's and nephew's deaths had not intervened to disrupt his "brinksmanship" way of life.

Case 4. This revealing vignette unfolded in a hospital emergency suite. An auto accident victim was such a problem for the surgeons that the services of a psychiatrist were required. Although the man had painful injuries, they were not life-threatening. Nevertheless, he was so terrified he was dying that he refused to allow the surgeons to touch him. The typical accident victim, while frightened, is passive and submits to almost any indignity. Thus this man's behavior was unusual in the extreme, and no one present could recall such a terrorized person. Only with great reassurance and much hand-holding was it possible to proceed with his care.

Surprisingly, the man's name and his scarred face revealed him to be a professional hockey goalie with many a grueling battle to his credit. A few days after the accident when he was nearly recovered he was quoted in the papers as saying the accident was nothing as he'd been hurt much worse many times in hockey games.

This episode suggests partially why this man is a professional hockey goalie who makes his livelihood facing flying pucks that have frequently smashed into his face making it look as if a macabre game of tic-tac-toe had been played on it. Few of us would be able to face such danger; yet he thrived on it. It was a danger he anticipated, planning the time and place, so that he would not be surprised and could maintain magic control over all the world's dangers. Danger must be very real to him to have to undo it by such risky activity. His real terror of injury was revealed when an injury he had not planned surprised him and destroyed his counter-phobic omnipotence.

SUBMISSION TO INJURY

Because of much greater than usual guilt over unconscious hostile or sexual wishes, some individuals must suffer failure and pain. Their lives are filled with repetitive sabotage or chances for success and sometimes with frequent self-induced physical harm. This inability to tolerate success, in fact to seek out failure, is one of the more common symptoms seen in psychiatric practice and is certainly one of the most resistant to treat since even success in treatment cannot be tolerated.

Case 5. A college track-man was the top sprint man on the team in his junior year. He had the top times in the conference but at the conference meet fouled and was disqualified. In his senior year, he again had the top times but developed a "charley horse." Despite efforts of the coach and trainer to restrain him, he insisted on coming back too soon and developed a more severe quadriceps muscle tear, ending his running career.

This boy had had a very conflicted relationship with his father who was quite competitive with his son. Unfortunately, the father had not been too successful in his life and made it quite clear to the boy that this was one competition he expected to win.

Actively seeking out physical harm may have two meanings. Guilt over wrong wishes can be expiated by punishment in the form of bodily injury. A more passive and submissive seeking of injury has the following meaning: A boy is in terror of mutilation for his transgressions. He allows himself to be hurt or actively seeks injury. He now unconsciously says, "See, father, I am injured, you don't have to hurt me" or "I am injured and helpless, thus I am no danger to you." These mechanisms can sometimes lead to rather gruesome and permanently disabling injuries.

PREDICTION OF POTENTIAL DANGERS

If only we could know when we are faced with one of the prospects covered above, we could help boys avoid injury. Unfortunately, prediction of the future is risky and uncertain, and our wisdom is greatest in hindsight. Perhaps, though, knowledge of basic mechanisms may help us be alert for certain situations of potential danger. A few such situations can be listed.

1. Gross Disproportion Between Athletic Ability and Willingness To Be Aggressive. Included are boys who want so badly to play and be aggressive, but have so little ability, and boys with great athletic potential who are hesitant to be aggressive. The first and second cases illustrate this.

2. Disproportion Between Father and Son as to Athletic Ability and Expression of Aggression. Every coach has been plagued by the athletically successful father who pushes ambitiously his not-too-capable and not-too-aggressive son into sports, forcing the boy into competition for which he is unprepared. The fifth case illustrates the opposite danger. For the son to be more capable or aggressive than his father arouses old terrors over urges long ago to displace his father. One young man of better than average athletic ability refused to participate in athletics despite his father's urging. His father had been a varsity football player in college and was now a high-ranking business executive. The boy dreamed of athletes who would beat him regularly and in college decided to be an English teacher. By his defiant passivity he was able to avoid injury as a way out.

3. Lack of Adequate Control of Aggression. The too-aggressive athlete who lacks sufficient control of himself may rush blindly into the battle with injury resulting to himself and an opponent. Movies of some football injuries suggest that certain players have "tunnel vision" and in their mad charge fail to see blockers not in their immediate line of vision.

4. Fear of Injury. The over-timid athlete who hesitates just before being tackled loses his momentum and is more likely to be injured. He would better confine his competitiveness to noncontact sports.

5. A History of Multiple Injuries. The accident-prone athlete can be expected to be injured again sooner or later, and the next injury may be serious.

6. Concealment of Minor Injuries. A frequently-voiced complaint is that, contrary to exaggerating their injuries or prolonging their recoveries, many athletes make light of their injuries and want to return to action too soon, even concealing rather serious hurts. Such bravery and devotion is

commendable within limits, but one should watch carefully when an athlete carries this to extremes. Is he, by overdoing it, trying to prove he isn't afraid because he is afraid? Is he actually seeking to be seriously injured as a just punishment for some deep feeling of guilt, perhaps over his previous conflicted expression of aggression?

7. EXAGGERATION OF INJURIES. At the opposite extreme is the cry-baby whose every little bruise needs immediate attention. He's scared and perhaps would be better out of the game before he has to take himself out with a more serious injury.

8. INABILITY TO TOLERATE SUCCESS. Sometimes an athlete with considerable ability starts out like a world-beater but then begins to slip and finds himself more frequently on the bench. Perhaps his dwindling skill represents his inability to allow himself the success he did and could continue to experience. Maybe when he seems to be trying so hard to regain his position he will solve the conflict through injury, this having the double meaning of preventing intolerable success and providing welcome punishment for previous success. This is demonstrated in the fifth case.

9. OMNIPOTENT FEELINGS OF INVULNERABILITY. The athlete who seems to relish danger to an unusual degree and has an omnipotent sense that he cannot be hurt may be demonstrating a counter-phobic reaction which will

"Just between us girls, Coach, I think that, down deep, our hitherto superb bare-footed kicker *hates* the game. This is the third time this season that he's let the enemy severely bite his kicking foot!"

require his taking unnecessary risks till he is finally injured. The third and fourth cases demonstrate this.

These situations may be found among boys trying out for every high school, college and professional team, or those engaged in various individual sports. These boys do not give evidence of psychiatric illness and may seem quite similar to the other team members except for one or more of the above situations. Nevertheless, it behooves all who work with athletes to be sensitive to these possibilities as a means of reducing injuries. As to the general subject of motivation, we find some meaning in this area for what pushes us to competitive athletics.

NOTE

There is some similarity in certain parts with an article by the author published in the *Journal of the Michigan State Medical Society,* December 1960, vol. 59, pp. 1805-1808, under the title "Psychological Factors in Athletic Injuries." Acknowledgment is kindly made.

CASE STUDY OF A FATHER OF AN ATHLETE

JOSEPH LUPO

FATHERING IS COMPLEX and is influenced by many factors. There are intrinsic characteristics of all relationships which have special significance in the father-son relationship. In fathers of sons in sports, some of these factors and characteristics are spotlighted and may give rise to conflicts. In the main, most fathers and sons get through these conflicts smoothly, sometimes without notice. On the other hand, in some fathers these factors can become so intense that the forces that motivate fathering take various forms.

Behavior in emotionally disturbed persons can be viewed for our purposes as an exaggerated or inappropriate expression of "normal" needs and tensions. We may turn to an actual case of an emotionally disturbed father of an outstanding high school athlete to see what features stand out that are reflections of characteristics of the ordinary father-son relationship. In this case the symptoms and behavior which brought the father into psychotherapy were intimately related to his relationship to his son and were triggered off by the son's becoming a sports hero in high school.

Case. Louis is a thirty-eight-year-old man who was referred to the clinic because he was unable to control his rage toward his sixteen-year-old son, Richard. The son was in his junior year of high school when the father first came to the clinic. Richard was an outstanding athlete and a popular football star in the state. For two years, since the boy began to excel in sports, Louis began to have outbursts of rage and assaultive behavior toward Richard.

The outbursts were inappropriate and were triggered off by such minor incidents as the son coming in fifteen minutes late from a date. After two of the episodes Louis was jailed. One was running up and down the sidelines in a hotly contested high school football game before thousands of spectators, and yelling obscenities toward the field at his son. This was because the son had made a bad play in a game in which he otherwise starred.

Existing side by side with this extreme and inappropriate behavior was a sort of "hero worship" that Louis had for his son. He would go out of his way to do favors for Richard and to try to get Richard to share the glory with him. Louis expressed a keen interest in the son's development, especially in sports. The father would wear the son's football jersey and would spend hours pouring over newspaper clippings of the son's achievements. He wanted to share the intimacies of Richard's life, getting excited over his fantasies of the son's sexual life and wanting to double date with the son. He would organize his seven other children into cheering sections to greet Richard when he came home from games. When rebuffed by the son who wanted to live his own life, the father would become depressed and rageful. He concluded that Richard was thankless of the sacrifices that he had made. Louis would confront Richard with such improbable choices as "would you prefer to be with me or with your girl friend." He attempted in subtle ways to sabotage the son's relationship to the girl friend.

The involvement with the son, then, was very intense. During this time, Louis' sexual desire for his wife began to wax and wane. He resorted to masturbation, during which he often had thoughts of Richard and the girl friend. He became very jealous when the son danced with the mother. At the same time, he began leaving himself out of family affairs and turning more and more of the responsibility over to Richard. When Richard finally went away to college, Louis moved into his room and intensified his identification with Richard. He began to have fantasies of Richard winning the Heisman trophy as outstanding football star of the country. The presentation of honors would spotlight Louis in the fantasies, as the father of the winner. In spite of these inappropriate feelings and behavior, Louis was able to maintain a good job and do excellent work.

Of course, this is an example of extreme involvement between father and son. There are important aspects of Louis' personality that caused him to react this intensely. These aspects stem from his childhood. For our purposes there is no need to go into these. The focus will be on the characteristics of the father-son relationship with which Louis could not cope. In varying degrees these are present in all father-son relationships, and how they are dealt with of course depends upon the psychological makeup of the individual father and son.

The first and perhaps most significant feature in the relationship is identification. That is, the father sees the son as himself, as living proof of the father's potency, maleness and success. This can be carried to the point of the son's being an "extension" of the father. The son is not really allowed to be a separate being. We see how Louis vicariously experienced the "glory" as if it were really he earning it. The son acts out the father's wishes, both in sports and in the sexual power and freedom that he himself wishes. According to Ackerman, "Historically the role of the father, especially the American father has changed. He is no longer the unquestioned ruler of the family, to be feared. His power has been undercut. The contemporary father may be regarded as weak, frightened and continuously in dread of defeat in competitive struggle with other men."[1] No wonder then, that many men push this vicarious power and glory through their sons to extremes. The son is not allowed to be a separate being, but a pawn for the release of the father's own emotional needs. In Louis we see this identification over and over again. He wore Richard's jersey, wanted to be included in his intimate activities and finally moved into Richard's room when Richard went away to college.

A second feature of the relationship is the rivalry between father and son. The most obvious example in ordinary relationships is that as an infant the son gains some of the affection that the mother has for the father. Later, as the son becomes stronger and more independent, he may challenge, in the father's mind, his image as head of the household and provider. Also, the son may be viewed as a brother for whom the father had hostile and rival feelings. These are then displaced on the son. The father begins to fear in the son feelings that he had toward his own father. Louis took some pleasure at competing with Richard at all levels. He compared himself to Richard in strength, intelligence and sexual abilities. At the same time he felt threatened when Richard danced too close to his mother. As Richard became a hero, the younger children vied for Richard's attention and would even go to him for advice.

An important factor which reinforces this rivalry is that it is a universal and healthy aspect of adolescents that they begin to detach themselves from childhood dependency and search for their own independence and identity.[2] This often takes the form of rebellion, but it is necessary if the person is going to mature into an adult. Louis however, took this as a challenge to his role as father. Richard's being a sports hero intensified the challenge in Louis' mind.

The last feature that we can examine is the homosexual aspect. As well as serving as a proof of the father's maleness and power, the son who excels in sports and is assertive will inadvertently show up the father's sense of

"Freddie, my boy, you're not acting like a very nice extension of myself!"

masculine deficiency. This, coupled with pleasure in seeing physical strength develop in the son's body, can be confused by the father as homosexual feelings; or they may uncover previously unknown homosexual feelings in the father. To cope with this, fathers assume an attitude of hostile rejection. In Louis, the raising of doubts about his sexual identification was the chief feature of the relationship with which he could not cope. His erratic, push-pull attitudes toward Richard are expressions of a wish and a fear of the sexual feelings. Louis would attempt to seduce Richard's time and attention. He would describe at length how handsome Richard was and what a powerful body he had. He would hero-worship Richard, as if he had a crush on him. When the threat of closeness became too great, the violent behavior began. As the intensity of the involvement with Richard increased, his sexual feelings for his wife waned.

Although aspects of these features of the relationship between Louis and his son overlapped, the three were also distinct in their own ways and served as determinants of Louis' behavior. Although Louis had many positive feelings toward Richard, these were mainly overshadowed by his need to use Richard for vicarious release of his own emotional needs.

Ackerman's general description of the good father certainly can apply to fathers of sons in sports: "A man whose primary incentive is the thing itself; the development and welfare of the child rather than a spurious glorification of his maleness in the eyes of other people."

FOOTNOTES

1. Ackerman, N.: *The Psychodynamics of Family Life*. New York, Basic Books, 1958.
2. Johnson, A.: Juvenile delinquency, in Arieti, S. [Ed.]: *Handbook of American Psychiatry*. New York, Basic Books, 1958, p. 840.

MAN AND HIS PET

MARCEL HEIMAN

Some years ago, on the basis of clinical observations, I demonstrated the important needs that are served by pets in our society. In my paper on "The Relationship Between Man and Dog,"[1] I stated that "Pets may be considered as a descendant from a totem animal used by man in his development and useful to him in the process of civilization."

"In primitive man," I continued, "totemism was a device used to control and conceal sexual and aggressive drives within the family. The pet is for civilized man what the totem animal was for the primitive. The pet represents a protector, a talisman against the fear of death." Indeed, by the mechanisms of displacement, projection and identification, a dog or other pet may serve as a major factor in the maintenance of psychological equilibrium.

While in most instances among grownups the identification with and displacement and projection onto the pet are unconscious, among children they are conscious processes. As we know, the pet often serves as a good companion, a pal, a confidante. The absence of barriers between child and animal allows for an easy exchange between the two. Here it may be noted that the relationship between parent and child also takes place to a great extent on a nonverbal level (and earlier on a preverbal level), despite the fact that verbal communication does exist and is used.

We know of many instances where a dog who once held the position of an only child in a household showed signs of jealousy when a baby was born into the family. In some cases, the dog will attack the infant viciously. However, it should be pointed out that jealousy and sibling rivalry show up just as violently at times among children who are confronted by a new baby, and later on, more often than not, the older child and the dog do an about-face and become the baby's protectors.

Since our remote heritage stems from the animal kingdom, it is not unreasonable to suppose that the small child finds the pet, especially the dog, closer to himself than the adult. There is certainly no better way for a child to learn about the so-called "animal" nature of man than by growing up with pets and observing them in their grooming, their play and their sexual actions, as well as watching them perform their bodily functions.

There are times, however, when the closeness between child and pet goes beyond this point, and the child moves from the position of observer to that of participant. I have had several accounts from patients who recalled indulging in sexual play with their dogs when they were children. Such sexual activities in adults would of course fall into the category of perversions.

Just as we hear of pets being treated like children—with the addition of beauty parlors and exotic ways of sleeping and eating—so we know of children who in their lively imagination take the role of an animal. Once in a while a child has to face such overwhelming problems within its family that it does not stop at the fantasy of being an animal. Instead, the child attempts to make it real—which is a sure sign of serious mental disturbance. A sad example is the little girl who became increasingly unhappy and began to emulate her dog in every way. She stopped speaking and would only bark. She crawled around on all fours and adopted the dog's eating habits, even allowing her mother to lead her about on a leash.

But it is not enough to speak of the neurotic pet and the neurotic owners as if we were dealing with an overall condition. We are faced with special individual problems and conflicts pertaining to the owner or the family into which the pet has been drawn. It is quite true that the dog is not an inanimate object, a mere plaything or toy. The dog "is capable of entering into human emotional relationships which seem almost as complicated bilaterally."[2] For the most part, however, the dog reacts and responds to the actions of the person.

Of all the animals, the dog is the only one accustomed to living in close proximity to man and with the psychic equipment to play whatever role is required of him by his master. I am not alluding here to any of the utilitarian functions that might be assigned to the dog. Rather, I am referring to that complex interrelationship between man and dog wherein man, reenacting his own conflicts of the past, uses the animal in place of a human object.

VETERINARIAN AND PSYCHIATRIST

When Barton approached me some years ago and suggested that veterinarian and psychiatrist work together, I agreed to the idea but was then not yet ready to participate. I can still see some practical obstacles. When a child manifests evidence of psychological disturbance and the parents are advised to seek psychiatric consultation and treatment, the advice very often falls on deaf ears. Imagine how much deafer the ears would be in the case of a pet owner. It seems very unlikely that many pet owners seeking consultation on behalf of their pet will be advised to get psychiatric help for themselves.

The psychiatrist is in a good position, provided he is alerted to it, to observe and understand from his patients the nature of the interaction between man and pet. The veterinary physician, on the other hand, is at a disadvantage. Not only is his client none too communicative, but the owner might not take too well to the advice that he see a psychiatrist about his pet's neurotic problems.

The veterinary physician cannot be expected to diagnose the mental state of his client's owner. He cannot tell where normalcy leaves off and neuroticism begins and where the symptomatology is indicative of psychosis. I have the impression that the veterinary physician is inclined to think in terms of neurosis where a psychiatrist would regard the state as psychotic.

According to my observations, a psychotic individual is more apt to be engaged in the kind of intense relationship with a pet in which the pet is used to play a part in his owner's emotional life, and consequently such a pet is more apt to reflect its owner's psychopathology.

This brings us to another serious consideration. The animal that comes to the attention of the veterinary physician might be the last and only animate object with which his owner is able to establish and maintain contact. In such a case, even a careful study of both pet and owner might leave us with no alternative but to allow the status quo to remain. In other words neither would the owner be treatable nor would we be in a position to suggest a substitute for his pet—some other object better equipped to serve that particular purpose.

The danger of anthropomorphizing in discussing these matters is evident. We have to bear in mind, however, that what we are after here is not scientific proof of a pet's motivations for his actions. We are trying to enable the veterinarian to deal more adequately with this client by helping him to understand the complex interrelation between man and animal.

The situation is not too dissimilar from that of the child psychiatrist. When parents bring him a child with somatic and emotional problems, it is essential that he understand the particular relationship that exists between the parental figures in that family. It has been said that a child is closer to the family pet than to the world of grownups. In other words, dog and child understand each other without words better than child and parents at times with words. How often have we heard from a patient, recalling his childhood and the inevitable unhappiness he suffered, that he could not tell anyone about it, neither family or friend. There was no one to whom he could pour out his heart—no one except the family pet.

One of the main things the dog and the young child have in common is their inability to communicate through language. In trying to understand what is bothering the child, a psychiatrist has to rely on information supplied by the parents and his own observations of the youngster at play.

Eventually, however, the time comes when the child is able to speak about what is troubling him, and therein lies the big difference between coping with a child and a dog.

There are some important matters that I can only mention in passing. For instance, what is the nature of the dog's psychic apparatus? Is the dog able to conceive an object in the absence of that object? In other words, is the dog capable of symbol formation? To what degree are precursors of a superego developed in the dog?

Moreover, what are we to think of a dog who lies next to his master watching television? According to the *New York World Telegram*,[3] the dog was watching another dog on the screen which was mad with rabies, and "it promptly turned away and vomited its dinner. Since that time the dog's interest in TV has greatly diminished." In human terms we would consider this a traumatic event in the dog's life.

DOG OR CAT AS PET

Comparing the relationship of man and his dog and man and his cat, there are some interesting differences. Generally speaking, I would say that between man and dog the tie is more or less a symbiotic one, and that between man and cat a parasitic one. The former is mutually beneficial to both parties, while the latter means that one derives benefit at the expense of the other.

The terms symbiotic and parasitic were originally applied to describe those levels in biology referring to physiological aspects only. The meaning becomes more complicated when we use these words in regard to man in his relationship with others, whether human or animal.

For instance, is has been said that the fetus lives parasitically on its host —the mother. There is no doubt that this is true. But when we consider the emotional aspect as well, we find that a woman often obtains as much emotional gain from the fetus as the fetus derives physiological benefit from the mother. Thus the mother feeds the fetus physiologically and, in turn, is fed by it emotionally. Here we are dealing with a complex symbiotic-parasitic bond, a concept that seems useful in answering some questions as to what benefits man derives from his pet.

There is another psychological phenomenon to be considered whenever man and man or man and animal enter into a relationship. To some extent we all put ourselves in the place of the other object. This is called identification. The mother who derives emotional succor from being pregnant, from the fetus, does so because to some degree she is unconsciously putting herself in the place of the fetus and is able to achieve a feeling of Nirvana, or utter bliss. Playing the role of the fetus, she feels completely taken care of with no demands made on her.

Now we may better understand why some people want the closeness of a dog and others the aloofness of a cat. A lonely woman who is unable to get married or even live with a friend uses the cat the same way women use their unborn children. She puts herself in place of her cat and then feels completely taken care of, with no worries that any demands will be made on her.

The woman who is afraid to be close to another person, fearful not only that her needs will not be met but that too many demands will be made on her—such a woman has no choice at times but to live without human company. The pet she is likely to choose as her companion will be a cat—an animal which by nature lives an independent sort of life. Some people may decry this quality in the cat, but the woman I am describing likes and even fosters it. The cat's independence lends strength to her own.

PURPOSE SERVED BY PET

It is said that for every problem pet there is a problem owner. On this score, Barton pointed out that the most neurotic pets are those which are kept without serving any practical purpose for the owner, but which instead satisfy a psychological need. As soon as we include the psychological factor, we can see that any pet serving such a purpose is just as important, if not more so, than the so-called practical pet.

I agree with Barton that much may be learned about the emotional problems of a person who is a pet owner if the psychiatrist allows him and even encourages him to talk about his pet. Every so often, the owner identifies with his pet without being aware of it, of course, so when he talks about the animal he is really giving himself away.

The pet serves a variety of functions for a variety of people. The single woman's cat plays a different role from the homosexual man's dog; the childless couple's lap dog a different one from the pet in a family of many children who may have a dog, cat, bird, fish, and other assorted animals living with them.

Besides, the pet represents more than a single object to one and the same person. The pet may be the person himself (identification) and also the person's mother, father and himself as a child—the child that was or the child that never came to be. Furthermore, the pet may represent one particular aspect of a person, one characteristic or a part of his body. Also, the pet may stand for the meanness of the father or the shyness of the mother. In some instances, a person may even notice similarities in facial expression between the pet and a dead parent.

A patient of mine used her dog in an unusal way. Her relationship with her mother, who had apparently been as psychotic as the patient, was a most difficult one. There was good reason to believe that the patient was the fruit of one of her mother's many love affairs. A few years before she died, the mother had a stroke which left her paralyzed on one side of her face and body. Later on, the patient took her dog, which was getting along in years, to the veterinarian. She was in a state of panic, absolutely convinced that one side of the animal's face was paralyzed. As we can see, she was repeating with her dog what she had gone through with her mother.

Of course, it is possible that in this day of weakening family ties, the role of the pet for the lonely deserves our special attention. As we have seen, the woman who is afraid of her own dependency needs, not to mention the demands that might be made upon her by others, can find a compromise solution by living alone with a cat whose independence mirrors her own.

Zoo-therapy

Some of my experiences with patients, either neurotic borderline or ambulatory psychotic, have shown me that the dog, the cat and at times the bird were of the utmost importance to them. Like the "seeing eye" dog for the blind, these animals constitute the only lifeline for these persons. So there are times in my office or hospital when I practice what I like to call zoo-therapy. In other words, I advise people who are unable to live with another human being and at the same time are too full of anxiety to be alone, yet who are self-supporting, that they take an animal to live with them. It might be a fish or a bird or a cat or a dog, depending on the person.

To illustrate, I would like to go into some detail about a patient I saw intermittently over a period of many years. She had been unable to marry and was also not able to live with any woman friend for any length of time. Finally, she resigned herself to living alone, while holding down a newspaper job. Miss R's symptoms included a morbid fear of death, a horror of being alone, a fear of losing control and either killing herself or doing harm to others, a feeling at times of being outside her own body and a sense of unreality.

All her life she had made a very poor social adjustment. Her demands for attention were extreme, exaggerated and highly unrealistic. There had been a great need for dependency, without her being able to give in to it. Off and on, she lived with a conscious fear of impending insanity. At times when her anxiety mounted to panic Miss R. was able to keep a grip on herself only by a continuous shifting back and forth from reality to unreality. Over the years the periods during which she was lucid and free of panic became shorter, and the times when she lived in a semipsychotic state grew longer and more frequent. Miss R. was extremely articulate about the whole thing.

> I think some part of my anger and belligerence arose from the realization later that to some extent what you call complaining is actually an attempt, involuntarily almost, to convey the basic inner fear that I find at times impossible to hold at bay — the kind of fear a person might feel clinging to a raft on the high seas for a protracted time, wondering if help would come before endurance ran out, or if help would come at all. I seem enmeshed in fear from all sides, and there are brief intervals of acute intensity when there seems no island to stand on, no way to escape or hold on.
>
> When one gravitates daily between acute fear of being alone, fear on the street, fear of strange feelings that sometimes arise when I am with people, fear of falling asleep, acute tension when I awaken in the morning, the strain, stress and enervation that are engendered are considerable and I would be less than human if at times I didn't temporarily lose faith in being able to hold on to my present way of life until I find my way out of this bewildering maze that has built up. When this sort of hopelessness sets in, it is almost impossible to think constructively, and for brief moments it sometimes seems that I would welcome any altered way of life that would bring relief from this never-ending battle against fear, fear, fear. When I complain or dwell on the grim side of things, I now believe it is a sort of desperate "cry in the wilderness" for something to reassure me that I can muster up the courage and hope that will enable me to maintain a hold on some normal way of life.

In this patient's case, everything known at the time short of hospitalization was tried. Finally, because of her feeling that she never had anything she could call her own—her father belonged to her mother, her brother to his wife, her lover to his wife—I suggested that she should get something that would belong to her and to her alone. In that way she need not borrow it, she need not feel that all she could get out of life were crumbs.

When I mentioned to her the possibility of having a dog, she showed relief and said she had been thinking of it for some time but had been ashamed to mention it to me. However, she objected to the idea of having a dog because of the responsibility it would place on her. As a compromise, she expressed the wish to buy a bird, feeling she could meet its demands.

So she purchased a parakeet. Aside from weekends, she would leave her apartment in the morning and return in the evening. Soon a routine was established: she would open the cage when she came home and then go to the kitchen to prepare her dinner, while "Putzi" walked after her just like a dog. Dinner over, Miss R. would sit down to read her paper. One evening an "argument" developed with Putzi. Miss R. was tired and irritable. The parakeet, as usual, was perched on her shoulder. She was trying to read the paper but he kept plucking at it. She yelled at him and the bird yelled back. She grew more and more angry and so did the bird. Then to punish him she put him back in his cage. He really got angry and let it out at a little plastic parakeet in the cage, yelling and pecking at it. By this time Miss R. was feeling very badly and guilty, and as a gesture of conciliation poked her finger into the cage. Whereupon Putzi, perhaps not quite ready to make up, pecked it severely.

It was after this incident that Miss R. became aware of how demanding she really was. It was her strong reaction to the demands of the bird that helped her to see the light about herself. Two or three weeks later, she told me rather candidly that she realized that what she expected of other people, whether a roommate or the brother or an office associate, was utterly unreasonable, and she now understood that these demands were apt to arouse in them feelings which led to friction and arguments.

She also realized that the severe phobic states she experienced, whether on a bus or in a taxi or just walking along the street, might be relieved by her recognition that these states were the expression of her feeling of helplessness and rage at not having anyone at her side to take care of her at such times. So with the help of her parakeet, Miss R. was able to go on living in her apartment by herself without suffering intolerable anxiety, and before long she was able to dispense with her therapy.

The situation is quite different when it comes to people who do have a need for a close relationship with another person. Where this need assumes exaggerated proportions, we know we are dealing with childish needs that were never outgrown or resolved.

Take the case of a woman who has an intense desire to be close to her mother. There are a variety of physical and mental symptoms that crop up when such a woman is separated from her mother, whether by the mother's death or the daughter's getting married and moving away or the mother's going on vacation. I have found two ways of helping such women cope with the crisis: one is to unite them if possible with the person they need to be with, and the other, where reunion is not possible, is to suggest a substitute, namely that they get a pet — *Ceteris paribus* — a cat, as was previously mentioned, for persons whose greater need is for independence, a dog for those who require closeness.

Loss, Separation and Substitution

People who have experienced separations of traumatic proportions, especially during early childhood, may be seen in later life to react almost invariably to situations of separation with regression: that is, they return to functioning and feelings on a level compatible with their early childhood. One of these levels of infantile functioning, and perhaps the most important, has to do with the mouth. The loss of a person is felt as a loss of food, or as a loss of security in regard to obtaining nourishment.

The need to eat is a common accompaniment whenever a loss is experienced — witness the eating and drinking that goes on at a wake. What is more, the wish to eat refers to the same object that was lost. Think of the baby who has lost a nipple or a pacifier and does not stop crying until it is put back in his mouth.

As mentioned previously, I have found that the loss of a human object can be made up by substituting an animal object.[4] The ready acceptance of such substitutes may be understood in the light of the child's closeness to the pet. The interchangeability between dog and human, as well as the central position of orality, is vividly dramatized in *Come Back, Little Sheba.* Shown in flashback in the play is the story of a woman who becomes pregnant illegitimately. The man marries her, but she loses the baby and has no other children of the marriage. Then the woman acts out her own oral need by projecting it onto her alcoholic husband. Some of the more subtle nuances of the play come up in connection with the little dog Sheba which got lost. This dog represents the baby as well as the mother.

The same symbolism may be found in a well-known nursery tune, "Oh, Where oh Where Has My Little Dog Gone?" based on "Der Deitcher's Dog" which goes like this:

Oh where, of where ish mine lit-tle dog gone
Oh where, oh where can he be
His ears cut short und his tail cut long
Oh where, oh where ish he

I loves mine la-ger 'tish ve-ry goot beer
Oh where, oh where can he be
But mit no mon-ey I can-not drink here
Oh where, oh where ish he

A-cross the o-cean is Ger-man-nie
Oh where, oh where can he be
Der deitch-ers dog ish der best com-pan-ie
Oh where, oh where ish he

Un sas-age ish goot, bo-lo-nie of course,
Oh where, oh where can he be
Dey makes un mit dog and dey makes em mit horse
I guess dey makes em mit he

Need For an Animal

The dog's aptitude for pleasing his master is of course expressed most readily where the dog enjoys what the master wants him to do. Those who advise people to let the dog lead its own life rather than the man's life fail to understand what I believe is one of the main reasons for this peculiar relationship between man and pet; namely, that the pet is needed to satisfy some of his master's needs. A person who wants a watchdog, a dog that spends the night outside the house, has quite a different relationship with the animal and different needs than someone who wants his dog next to him in bed at night.

The first dog leads a dog's life, the second a man's life. The same holds true for the kind of food for the pet and the manner of feeding. From filet mignon — with mushrooms of course — to ice-cream cones, the dog has learned to live his master's life to the enjoyment, it seems to me, of both. A famous novelist takes her tiny dog riding in a taxi at feeding time because the little creature only enjoys eating while in motion.

For children, pets serve many special purposes.[5] In view of the closeness between children and pets, I would certainly encourage every family whose living conditions permit it to keep a pet. During the trying years of childhood, especially in the latency period between the age of four and the beginning of puberty, the company of a dog is a fine thing. If ever there is a need for a "seeing eye" dog, it is then — to lead the child through the labyrinth of the oedipal phase and help him find a secure identity.

An example of how much a dog meant to a child was described to me by a girl, then fifteen. She had been raised in a family with one brother fifteen years her senior, so that actually the parents had raised a single child twice in their lifetime. Until the girl was nine years old, she slept in the parents' bedroom. Then her brother married and moved out of the house, and the girl moved into the vacant room. She promptly took sick and had to have psychiatric attention. But her problems were held more or less in abeyance by her dog, which was her companion and slept with her. It was unbearable for her to be alone, to be separated from her parents.

For one year, until she was ten, the dog was her substitute for the brother who had left and the parents who had kept her close to them until the other room became available. Then the dog died and she was all alone. This forced the family to make some changes. The girl moved back into her parents' bedroom, but with one difference — this time the mother moved into the vacant room and surrendered her place to her daughter.

The need of the adolescent is illustrated by a girl of fourteen, a lonely shy child who told me how she feels about her pet. Her mother had bought her a dachshund, a male named Wolfi. When the girl feels lonely and cries, she tells her troubles to him and he licks the tears off her face. She feels he is the only friend she has. Of course, he cannot go to the movies with her and cannot accompany her to school (shades of Mary and her little lamb): but he sleeps at the foot of her bed or right beside her. No dog-type food for him — he eats only "people food," and in the morning his mistress fixes scrambled eggs for him. If left alone, he whimpers like a baby or wets the floor. Then she beats him for it the way her father beats her. It was her decision to have a male dog and not a female one because father is the only male in a house with a mother and two daughters. When she was younger, she wanted to be a boy, much more so than now.

The Pet as a Mirror

If people choose their pets not only because they resemble the person's outer image but his inner traits as well, it follows by the same token that the person will reflect his pet. But the picture is even more complicated than that. It is a matter of observation that individuals are constantly attempting to mold their children and marital partner into a pattern which best suits their own taste.

Now, it happens that dogs are so sensitive to the conscious and unconscious expectations of their masters that they will do anything to please them. A dog will be obedient, soil, bark, be vicious and, as I recently saw on a television program, even try to speak. Then, after a man has succeeded in making of his pet what he wants him to be — which is something the man himself aspires to be without his knowing it — the master identifies with his product and becomes what his pet is. To that extent the man reflects his pet, but only because he chose to make the pet into what he himself wanted to be in the first place.

Besides psychiatrists, psychologists, ecologists and veterinary physicians, there is a group of gifted observers and writers who have contributed as much or more than the so-called scientific community. Among them are Konrad Lorenz and the Papashvilys who have made very keen observations and from whose writings a great deal may be learned.[6]

A dog's ability to imitate his master as soon as he is taken under the family roof is truly remarkable. The Papashvilys show us how the dog in particular takes on the color of his environment. This is as much based on the dog's own tendency as it is fostered by man's need to have the dog comply and obey.

What would an old couple do with a dog that only wanted to romp and play ball? Or how would the youngsters in the family like it if their dog wanted to lie around and sleep all day long? It is as if the dog were promising, "I shall try to be what you'd like me to be." For instance, a man who habitually visits the doctor might very well have a dog that is taken to the veterinarian quite often.

The very selection of a pet in itself reveals a great deal about the climate within a family. Once I came across a couple whose two children were both bed wetters. Intent on purchasing a pet, the couple visited a kennel where they were shown several dogs. Which did they choose? With uncanny accuracy they went straight for the only dog that was not housebroken and never would be. It fit in very well with the family.

We have to understand that having a pet which continues to soil is as significant of one person's particular needs as in other instances where a pet's fastidious training bespeaks his master's need for control — that is, control of his own instinctual wishes. A patient I treated some years ago kept two dogs. During the day when the master was out they used the apartment freely to urinate and defecate. No arrangements were made for them to be taken out, they were never trained to use one particular place in the house and never disciplined or punished. Soon it became apparent that the dog's behavior had their master's approval, although unconsciously.

As we have noted, some of us require an independent cat for our particular needs, just as there are those who need an obedient dog, and others a dog that is not housebroken. We come now to the case of a man whose training of his dog backfired, so that he was compelled to follow the same rules he taught his dog. According to an item in the *New York Times,*[7] the man planned on going hunting, but first he got himself a setter puppy and set to work training her "out of a book." The four-month-old setter took to the training rather well. His master was particularly fussy about hand signals in the event the dog should not be able to hear him when they were out hunting.

"Before the dog was six months old," the news story read, "she would stop when he held up his hand, palm outward, and come when he dropped his hand quickly." And then something happened which was not in the plans. The man himself developed a tendency to stop whenever he saw an upraised hand. "If somebody said the word 'Stay' in an ordinary conversation, he got a strange urge to freeze in any position that he happened to be in at the moment." And who do you think was the first in the family to guess what was happening and take advantage of it? None other than the man's four-year-old daughter, who one day ordered her father to "sit" when he was standing over her toy fire engine. "He sat compulsively."

The last straw was the morning he was trying to catch his usual train for New York. He had just reached the station as the local pulled in. Then it happened — "the conductor jumped off, threw up a hand, palm outward, to signal the engineer. He froze." As we see, the training in this instance really took hold of the man as well as the beast.

Aggression

Some of our requirements are potentially more dangerous than others. A story I was unable to confirm appeared in the *World Telegram and Sun.*[8] It was about a woman who owned two Doberman pinschers, a male and a female. While walking her dogs on the beach near her home, she was attacked by them and killed. According to the newspaper account, "She was found lying on the beach, her face and body covered with bites and her left arm and shoulder almost torn off. The dogs were racing madly around the body. Blood covered the male dog's face and mouth." When the police arrived, however, the dogs "made no effort to attack them. In fact, they seemed friendly."

Fortunately, there is a brighter side to the picture. Some people, with the help of an animal, are able to sidetrack their own conflicts, hates, sins and guilt and make the animal the scapegoat. This is strikingly illustrated by a patient observed by Flanders Dunbar[9] who had a need to hurt cats. She simply could not live without cats in the house: "I guess I was lucky I have a cat or I would be doing all these things to my child, even worse things than I do now." One day, while sitting alone in the house, she heard faint footsteps. She did not know if it was her son stealing downstairs or the cat: "If it would have been him, I would have jumped at his throat."

Parenthetically, regarding cruelty to animals, it seems to me highly ironic, and I hope some day it will be placed in its proper perspective, that our society has for some time established laws for the prevention of cruelty to animals but has only recently awakened to the fact that little children are left more or less at the mercy of their parents' viciousness and neglect. How often has the innocent family pet been used as a scapegoat for the uncontrolled fury and hatred which might otherwise be vented at the equally innocent child? Fraser devotes a whole volume to the use of an animal as a scapegoat.

The sacrificial custom of *Capuroth* among Orthodox Jews takes the form of atoning with fowl on the morning before the Day of Atonement. Male persons take a rooster, females a hen, and a pregnant woman both a rooster and a hen. The idea is to pass along one's sins and guilt to the chicken. The person chants, "This is my redemption. The rooster is going to be killed, and I shall be permitted a long, happy, peaceful life." Alas, all too often I have had occasion to observe a child being made the *Capore* for his parents.

The Pet as Talisman

Of course, we have to bear in mind that while the animal may take the place of a hated human being, positive feelings are also directed at the pet. After all, we are dealing with ambivalent feelings which are transferred from a parental figure to the family pet. A moving account of how her dog took the place of her mother and later her nurse in shielding her from anxiety and fear of death is given by Marie Bonaparte in a little volume about her dog Topsy.

Marie had once saved her dog's life when it was ill with cancer by having the dog treated with radiation: "Topsy," she wrote, "when I am ill you stay at the foot of my bed. . . . I remember, when I was small, days of illness like these. I was no more ill than I am now and yet I had to stay in bed. Then Mimau, my darling nurse, would not go out, and that alone was enough to reconcile me to my sickness. She stayed then, caressing me with loving hands and eyes, stroking me, giving me food and drink. And her presence alone told me — a child who feared death, the same death that had taken away my mother — her presence there in the room assured me that death would not enter."

Now that her nurse is dead, her own children grown up and her husband busy, there is only Topsy to stay with Marie. "And as in bygone times from Mimau, a power seems to emanate from Topsy, as a talisman of life. Topsy who, thanks to me, has probably recovered from a terrible ailment. Topsy, who has reconquered life, is for me a talisman that conjures away death. A simple dog, lying there by me, just like Mimau by the child that I was, she guards me, and by her presence alone must bar the entrance of my room to a worse ill, and even to death."

The Pet and Sex

As we know, certain aspects of human behavior are strictly controlled in our civilization. Among the strongest pillars of our society is control of the child's sexual and aggressive wishes toward his parents. To my mind, it would be a big step forward if we could establish that the pet, particularly the dog, is of assistance to man in protecting him against and helping to ward off those instinctual wishes which are basic to mankind yet incompatible with his civilized state.

The defenses which the dog serves so well, as previously mentioned, are displacement, projection and identification. In my aforementioned paper on this subject, I used clinical material to illustrate how the pet (primarily the dog, but the cat as well) was used to ward off mainly pregenital aggressive drives. The following will illustrate how the pet may be used in dealing with sexual curiosity and sexual drives.

A woman, single, mostly homosexual but at times engaging in heterosexual sex usually short of intercourse, had a schnauzer, a bitch she referred to as her "baby" but at times also as if referring to herself. In discussing the dog's frequent pseudopregnancies, she said, "I'm rather ashamed to admit it but if she *is* [meaning pseudopregnant], it's my fault. I let her be present while I had sex with B. [her girlfriend], and with C. [her boyfriend]. She gets very excited watching us."

I have pointed out elsewhere[10] that "the experience of pseudocyesis may be observed not only in man but in a number of other mammals; in some animals, for example the rat, stimulation of the vagina with a glass rod produces pseudocyesis (as do a number of other stimuli). On the other hand, pseudocyesis in the human is the result of a purely psychological process. But betwixt the rat and the man we find the dog. In addition to physiological factors (hormonal) we find that psychological factors can already be observed."

From our patient's point of view her dog's pseudocyesis was brought on by witnessing sexual relations – what psychoanalysts call the "primal scene." The patient was actually saying (using her dog to give expression to her own childhood fantasies and experience) that watching the intercourse of grown-ups stirs up sexual excitement and leads to the wish or fantasy of being pregnant.

The patient's remarks about her dog's pseudocyesis left no doubt as to the person in her life by whom she wished to become pregnant. She described a recent encounter with a man twenty years her senior with whom she had sex – both of them in the nude, he on top of her with his penis between their bellies – and her dog present. Then she recalled how her father behaved toward her soon after her mother died. First he was so upset that he asked her to come to bed with him, and then he was so jealous of her going out with a boyfriend that when she came home he slapped her.

A fairy tale I came across from Greenland illustrates how fantasies of sexual relations between daughter and father make use of a dog to circumvent the carrying out of the sexual wish for each other. The story is called "The Maiden and the Dog":[11]

> A maiden was ripe for marriage but laughed at all the fellows who came to her father seeking her hand. Finally, her father lost his temper and shouted to his dog, "Come in! You take her!" The dog bounded into the hut, sprang at the maiden, tore her clothing and clung fast to her, the way dogs do at times. She struggled and grew faint. Dragging her between his jaws, the hound pulled her out of the house. She managed to climb up on a large walrus bone out of his reach. There she crouched until she fell asleep. But the dog gnawed away at the bone until it tilted over and the girl slipped down.
>
> The dog began to maul her again and this lasted all that day and into the next. At last the father took pity on the girl. He called off the dog and rowed his daughter far out to an island. However, the dog sniffed the tracks and dived into the water. The father caught the dog, brought him back and tied him to the skin of a seal which he had filled with stones. He thought this would keep the dog on land. But wonder of wonders! Dragging the skin and stones and all, with only his mouth above water, the dog swam out to the island and the maiden. Again, the father took pity and started bringing them food.
>
> The maiden became pregnant and gave birth to twins. And very peculiar creatures they were – half dog, half man. They had the bodies of dogs with human faces. The descendants of these creatures and others the woman bore were also half dog, half man. So it came to pass that a completely new species – with no language but with great strength – sprang up on the island. To this very day one can find many graves there containing the bones of men and dogs. So I guess the story must be true.

This tale, apart from illustrating how the dog is used to displace and project onto it the sexual wish of man, also tells us something about the fears pregnant women are apt to have — namely, fear of giving birth to a monster. Studies of this problem have brought to light the fact that the unconscious fear hiding beneath the conscious one is that her wish to have a baby by her father will result in the birth of a creature which is part human and part animal. Thus we see that the feared monster is a reflection of the woman's "monstrous" desires.

The following case illustrates how helpful the pet is in maintaining the psychological balance within a family by draining off to itself some of the harmful acts intended either as self-destruction or meant for a member of the family. Another patient of mine had one child, a daughter of eleven, and a dog, a bitch boxer. The dog was used by the patient to represent her daughter. Recalling her own sexual experiences, she was worried that her daughter might misbehave sexually and perhaps get pregnant. Anxious to learn whether or not the girl had started menstruating, the patient expressed her curiosity this way. She had just blown her nose with a tissue, and while the dog was eating, she used the tissue to wipe the dog's vagina "to see if she was still in heat."

Her further comments left no doubt as to what she was concerned about. She related that a few days before, her daughter, on reading of the early age girls marry in India, asked her whether a girl of eleven (her own age) could have a baby. The patient, too, had become preoccupied with pregnancy fantasies, again not admitting them as her own but displacing them to her dog. She recalled that there were times when her dog would go through its "period" and not become impregnated but after six or eight weeks would go about preparing a place to whelp. "I expect her," said the patient, "to have pregnancy fantasies." As we see, the patient has scrambled into one entity herself as a young girl, her daughter and her dog. A short while later, the patient was able to recognize that she was using her daughter and her dog to act out her own fantasies of becoming pregnant by her father.

Castration Anxiety

There is another significant aspect of the oedipal conflict to be considered here. As a result of the incestuous wish, the person is fearful of punishment, that is, castration. A patient of mine at one time had a pair of dogs, a mother and son. He reported how the male, not yet fully grown, testicles not yet descended and therefore unable to ejaculate, mounted his mother. The patient was extremely concerned and watched carefully to make sure the mother would not pull away after they were "locked." He was afraid if she did the son would be badly hurt, that is, castrated. Here we have the complete oedipal situation between the patient and his own mother acted out through his pets.

Not only does the pulling away of the mother dog imply castration of the son dog, but the threatened injury caused by the pulling away is a composite one, consisting of all kinds of deprivations a child suffers at the hands of his mother. It starts at birth and continues with the process of weaning, encompassing all the many vicissitudes in an individual's life, with the extreme of separation being, of course, the death of the parent.

I have spoken earlier of the degree to which identification between man and pet takes place, especially during childhood. We can imagine what a strong impression it must make on a child when he sees animals locked in sexual intercourse. What an impact it must have on a child when he hears about his beloved pet being "spayed" — filling in with fantasy what his little mind is unable to grasp accurately. Also, we can imagine the child's reaction when exposed to artificial insemination of farm animals as patients have been telling me more and more often in recent years.

The following is a case in point. A young woman, the youngest of three sisters, whose father lived for years with a mistress, came for analysis a few years after she married because she found herself following in her father's footsteps. Sex with her husband never failed to have a certain quality of the forbidden, which only added to her uneasiness. Yet her few extramarital escapades brought her little happiness. She found herself falling back again and again on daydreaming, just as she had when she was little and took refuge from her misery in fantasies.

One time she experimented with her husband by having intercourse "dog fashion" and enjoyed it so much that it frightened her. Then she had a dream about her little boy coming into bed with her and pressing his body against her breasts while she shouted "No, no." This dream recalled nightmares she had as a girl, finding herself in bed between mother and father, with a terrible fear of father coming close to her while her back was turned. She felt that having sex like an animal was degrading and degenerate. Yet there is little doubt that such a feeling was the result of her sexual desires for her father. Her stomach felt upset, and she wondered whether she was pregnant, and then she was overcome with a feeling of wanting to go back and be a child again.

Then she remembered about Bobby, her dog of childhood days, and how she wanted to *be* Bobby because the bitch got away with everything. Suddenly, she recalled one particular time when Mother had Bobby spayed, and how she wondered then, "What did they do to her? Why did Mother do it to her?" Then came the realization, "Mother punished her by spaying her so that she couldn't have babies because Bobby had intercourse." As a child, she thought that by Bobby's being spayed she would be prevented from having intercourse as well as having babies. It was only in this light that a memory of her childhood could be understood. When she was little and woke up in the hospital after a tonsillectomy, she remembered seeing her mother's huge body looming over her and was seized with fear that mother had done something to her hymen, that mother had taken her hymen, that mother had destroyed it.

As for children being exposed to artificial insemination of farm animals, I have been told about it but have not had anyone in treatment who had such an experience in his own childhood. However, it is not too difficult to surmise what kind of distortion regarding sexual activities might take hold in the mind of a child who is told that the man he sees putting his arm way inside the animal from behind is helping the female to have a baby.

DOGS AMONG DOGS

Some observations of kennel owners on the behavior of dogs among dogs rather than among men may be in order here. Following the birth of pups to her kennel mate Lori, a five-year-old Collie bitch named Copy went in among the pups and wanted to nurse them. Copy had had pups of her own about a year earlier, but she had not been in heat or shown any signs of false pregnancy prior to the birth of Lori's pups. Although she had witnessed the birth of the puppies, she had shown no interest in either the birth or the pups until they were cleaned up by the mother. The owner of the kennel didn't permit Copy to nurse the puppies when she caught her at it, but the dog continued to have milk and did some nursing on the sly until the puppies were weaned from their mother.

Another kennel owner who also breeds collies had a similar experience. The mother of a litter of seven died and the puppies were being bottle-fed when another collie bitch, three or four years old, voluntarily began to nurse them. This collie, too, showed no signs of being in heat or false pregnancy prior to that moment. She had had several litters of her own but not immediately before undertaking to nurse the seven pups. Alas, the owner says she did not have enough milk to go around and the feedings had to be supplemented.

DEATH OF A PET

Finally, as we know, one of the most moving events in a man's life is the death of his pet. One such incident involving a patient took place before vacation time. There had been a lot of talk about what the patient was to do with his dogs (toy poodles), especially "Alice." Nobody wanted to take her. She was such a "bitch," so "jealous," and "bites" if the patient paid any attention to any of his other three dogs. Clearly describing himself, he said, "I wonder why nobody wants Alice. I won't put her in a kennel. I'm almost sure she would die there because she wouldn't eat." This was one of his own problems whenever someone close to him left, which was the case now since I was leaving on vacation. At the same time, he was going abroad himself and leaving his dogs. Whenever he was being left, he would develop severe depression and loss of appetite.

Upon his return he found Alice very sick and felt quite gravely about not taking her to the hospital because he was afraid she would die there. To him she was very special and couldn't be replaced by another dog. She was highstrung, sensitive, bitchy, aggressive — and feminine. "I see myself as a child," he said.

His guilt about not having taken proper care of the dog brought on a wave of resentment against his mother: "She never took care of me the way I wanted her to — she had to work [his father had died when the boy was five]. I behaved toward Alice the way I felt Mother behaved toward me. In addition I took out on the dog a feeling of vindictiveness against Mother. I must have been an uncompromising child."

Alice was getting sicker, showing choreiform movements, probably due to encephalitis after distemper. "She is so pathetic, tiny, scrawny, sad — pleading looking — just like my mother," he moaned. "I thought I loved Alice — and how I *not* loved my mother. How can I love this dog — this is a *dog* — more than my mother? How can I have such feelings towards a dog?" Yet the patient was like the dog, the dog was like the patient's mother, so he was like mother.

"How much like my mother am I? We both have tremendous amounts of anger. It is eating away on her. I remember when I entered the army and felt lost and anxious, I felt myself getting angry at my mother. It was re-kindling of the separation anxiety, like what happened when I was little after Father died and Mother left me."

Although he tried to persuade himself that he was facing the possible loss of Alice without depression, and although he denied feeling guilty about her being close to death, he said, "If I hadn't taken the trip — but no, that is absurd — then the dog would have stayed with me and would not have been infected [that is, in the kennel]."

A few days later he arrived at my office attired in mourning — black suit, black tie, black socks, black shoes. "Alice died yesterday," he told me. "I'm very upset. She was right beside me all through yesterday morning. I fed her milk and water every fifteen minutes." (Then the patient had to go to work.) "But she was alone when she died, that's the horrible part of it. When I returned I knew — because Roter (a male toy poodle) didn't run to the door. He [the dog] was very depressed and snuggled in my arms against me. He loved her [Alice] very much. He would sit for hours and lick her face and kiss her. I was afraid to go and see her. She looked very very beautiful. She must have died easily. I touched her: rigor had already set in (here the patient began to weep) and then I went out and cried."

The death of his dog and the patient's feelings about the dog's death brought back a memory following his father's death which until then had remained obscure. I shall not report the incident itself because it could identify the patient. Suffice it to say that it could now be analyzed, and in this way an essential part of the patient's infantile neurosis was lifted into the light of day. Once again a dog had done his master a good turn.

"Let's throw them and have a little fun around here. I'll start acting dependent as hell and you start acting aloof as all get out!"

FOOTNOTES

1. *Psychoanal Quart, 25*:568, 1956.
2. Louis Linn in a discussion of my above-mentioned paper, quoted from Searles, H. F.: *The Nonhuman Environment.* New York, Int Univs, 1960, p. 17.
3. April 11, 1958.
4. Searles, H. F.: *op. cit. supra* note 2.
5. Teplitz, Zelda: On the function of the pet in the development of the sense of identity. Paper presented at the Annual Meeting of the American Psychoanalytic Association, Philadelphia, April 24, 1959.
6. Lorenz, K.: *Man Meets Dog.* Boston, Houghton-Mifflin, 1955.
7. Jan. 10, 1959.
8. June 2, 1955.
9. Cited in my aforementioned paper.
10. Sexual response in women. *J Amer Psychoanal Assn, 11*:375, 1963.
11. Schmidtbonn, Hund und Mädchen: *Garten der Erde.* Leipzig, E. P. Tal & Co., 1922.
12. Similarly, in the case I described in my aforementioned paper, *supra* note 1, the anger of the patient and the distemper of the dog were closely associated.

PART SEVEN
COACHING

INTRODUCTION

THE ROLE OF THE COACH, as Thomas A. Tutko and Bruce C. Ogilvie point out,[1] is a many-faceted one. The coach must not only be thoroughly versed in all aspects of his particular sport, but he must also be able to put his knowledge into operation on the playing field (or with his athletic team). These are his obvious responsibilities, and they are readily apparent to both layman and coach.

There are additional roles required of the coach which will, either directly or indirectly, affect the motivation of his athletes. For example, he must be a salesman who is selling not only his tactics but his philosophy of the game. The job of recruiting makes it essential that he sell his organization as well.

The coach is also a public relations man and must act as a liaison between the team and the public. In college football especially, the coach is in a key position. It is he who directs the general policy on schedules, choice of plays, selection of players, relation to other athletics and educational relationships with his college administration and other college or university officers. He must consider the public relations of both the student body and the alumni, as well as the support of the public. When a team fails to have a good season year after year, the alumni are likely to take action and bring pressure to bear on the university administration for a new coach. It is easy to understand how criticism of a university football team may be directed against the coach. In one law case,[2] where a coach brought suit against a newspaper publisher, the court held that the criticism of the team was fair comment and that it could amount to libel only if the coach could establish actual malice on the part of the publisher.

Frequently, the coach acts as counselor for those of his athletes who are having personal problems. Another responsibility of the coach is that of expert in individual and team motivation. The way that these roles are carried out is in large part dependent on the coach's own individual personality.[3] The coach's personality characteristics determine the nature and extent of his involvement in each of these roles, and they will in turn determine how successful he will be as a coach. One coach, when he was about to be burned in effigy by a disgruntled student body, said, "If I had known this was going to happen, I would have brought the rope." So successful was the coach's tactic that the attitude of the student body mellowed toward him, and they never again complained (although his teams continued to lose games).

Teachers might take a lesson from coaches. Some of the best teaching actually goes on in athletics. The goals may be different (*e.g.*, gate receipts), but many of the techniques used in coaching can be helpful in education. Let us illustrate. The player is regarded as an individual whereas the student is often regarded merely as a number. "I am a Berkeley student. Do not fold, spindle, or mutilate me," one protestor wrote on a sign during a demonstration. On the other hand, consider the personal interest that the coach takes in his players. Even the ordinary coach has a file on the strength and weakness of each and every player. He knows what the player has for dinner, and what he does for entertainment. Only in the one-to-one psychoanalytic situation is so much attention paid to the individual. On the other hand, teachers so often do not even know the names of their students.

The coach's job depends on the development or success of his players, but so often teachers on the other hand hardly care whether their students pass or fail or make any progress. Teachers often say, "This would be a wonderful place — if there were no students!" Student development is hardly a criterion in promotion of faculty.

Other techniques used in coaching might also be employed in education. Television is used in football with great success. Each maneuver is played back over and over. Classrooms likewise ought to be provided with video equipment.

The player rarely misses a practice session, he does not hold the team back, but so many students cut or reluctantly attend classes. The player is out on the field, even if he has a wife who is having a baby; the student though has a "doctor's excuse" or has to do one of a million things. Attending class apparently has lowest priority. A player exercises initiative in improving his performance (*e.g.*, he works at a lumber camp during the summer), but it is only the exceptional student who is regularly prepared and does some extra research.

The problem to some degree may lay in the selection process of player or student. The player who is a detriment is cut from the squad. Yet, whatever the stated ideals, people always do what they want to do. They may be conditioned into wanting to do one thing or another. A task is rarely done for "its own sake." External reinforcement is always helpful. Thinking is hard work and for it there ought to be reward. A reward tends to lead a person to want to do something, while a punishment tends to make him refrain. A player, apart from the coach's close attention, is immediately rewarded for his efforts. He is honored, acclaimed and feted. But a student is rewarded, if at all, only by a grade at the end of the semester or possibly by a dull job upon graduation. A good classroom performance might be rewarded then and there by, say, a bag of luscious grades or a bottle of wine. In grade school, he gets a gold star.

Students, like players, might be kindly greeted, but teachers, especially those who have tenure, feel that they can take out their venom on students. A nice greeting makes a person feel welcome. Each classroom entrance might be provided with cheerleaders who would greet students each morning much in the way that football players are greeted as they come out of the dressing room. If such a practice were followed, students would literally tear their books apart by hard study, and probably cover four years of material in one! Students would prefer cheerleaders to any money loan or scholarship that might be made available.

Thomas P. Johnson demonstrates the complexity of the selection and approach to a life work — in particular, coaching — by analyzing some of the factors operant in one coach, Knute Rockne.[4] Rockne is chosen because he was totally dedicated to coaching and was one of the most successful coaches of all time. Perhaps more material has been published about him than about any other coach. He was beloved Notre Dame football coach, and he has been symbolized as "the true spirit of America." The Rev. Edmund Joyce, vice-chancellor of Notre Dame University, recently said, "Knute Rockne was able to achieve the kind of affection and respect he holds in the minds of many Americans because he represented the best in America. Rockne was a leader of men because he knew human beings. He was a past master in the knowledge of men. He recognized that football was a game of brains and that he could build character and personality through its playing." The memorial to Rockne, erected by the Knute Rockne Club of America on the Kansas turnpike where he died in an airplane crash in 1931, reads: "To Knute Rockne, Notre Dame Football Coach 1918-1931, who inspired athletes and the youth of America by his remarkably successful leadership and stamped himself as the greatest inspirational coach of all times."

In Johnson's essay, the reader is first given a brief introduction to Knute Rockne; then the author, acknowledging the limitations of an investigation that relies mainly on the published observations of others, develops his dynamic understanding of the man. This is not done by any means with the intent of detracting from the legend of Rockne. Rather, the author hopes the reader will feel an increased admiration and respect for a man who overcame difficult circumstances.

The only valid parallel that can be drawn from the study to other coaches — indeed to any person — is that the early struggles, frustrations and needs of a man can make his career-choice and his success or failure in that career understandable.

This is not to imply that only one career will satisfy an individual, nor that all people in a particular field are there for the same reasons. The won-lost record of this football coach was only a part of the evidence for the author's conclusion that for Rockne, the choice of coaching was a good one. In Rockne's case, personality and profession meshed beautifully. If he had not been a coach, the world would have been denied as outrageously as if Karl Menninger had become a podiatrist.

FOOTNOTES

1. P. 355.
2. Hoeppner v. Dunkirk Printing Co., 254 N. Y. 95, 172 N. E. 139 (1930) (high school football coach). See Harper, F.: Privileged defamation. *Virginia Law Review, 22*:642, 1936.
3. Sorry to say, some coaches carry out their sadistic impulses on the team. "The coach instructed players to pick up one boy who had fallen out and drag him along. . . . The boy 'was on his way to death' for one hour and 20 minutes 'in an unconscious condition'." *New Orleans Times-Picayune,* September 30, 1966. The exception, of course, does not prove the rule. Some sick people are unlucky enough to have poor doctors and they die. Some law-breakers are unfortunate enough to have a poor lawyer. And some players are unfortunate enough to have a poor coach.

   The coaching situation and the psychotherapeutic situation have a "surprising number of points of correspondance." *Medical Tribune,* October 10, 1966, p. 28. Cmdr. Ransom J. Arthur, MC, officer in charge of the Navy's Medical Neuropsychiatric Research Unit, San Diego, Calif., observes: "In both situations, there is explicit talk about emotions. For example, in psychotherapy the psychiatrist might say to the patient, 'You seem to be angry today,' and then the psychiatrist might interpret the meaning of the appearance of this emotion at this particular time in terms of the psychiatrist's theoretical framework and his appraisal of the totality of the situation. Similarly, the coach might say to the [athlete], 'You seem to be angry and downcast today.' He then might interpret this emotion in terms of both an event in the immediate past and his appraisal of the [athlete's] character.

   "In both situations psychological maneuvers are used to achieve certain specific goals. For example, in psychotherapy the patient may be asked to recline upon a couch in the hope of increasing the flow of free associations. In coaching such devices as 'pep talks' of varying character may be deliberately used in an attempt to produce a given emotional state in [an athlete]. In another instance, what amounts to siblings rivalry may be exploited between several members to increase their output of effort. . . . Another attribute of successful coaches is a quality that might be termed authenticity. By this is meant a sharply demarcated character structure that is all of a piece, internally consistent, and quite free from cant and hypocrisy . . . The clear definition of character is most important in a coach's success. Indecisive Hamlets make bad coaches." Quoted in Medical Tribune, *supra.*
4. P. 362.

THE ROLE OF THE COACH IN THE MOTIVATION OF ATHLETES

THOMAS A. TUTKO AND BRUCE C. OGILVIE

WITHOUT DOUBT, SPORTS ARE BECOMING increasingly important in the life of the average citizen. From little league baseball to professional athletics, there are ever more urgent demands for expansion. In international sports, as for example the Olympics, athletics have become a major political influence. The increasingly competitive nature of sports and the growing emphasis on winning have placed a heavy burden on the shoulders of the owners and managers of athletic teams; eventually, however, this burden is transferred to the shoulders of one man — the coach.

This chapter is dedicated to that underpaid and overworked man, the coach, who leads a hectic life for at least two months out of each year and possibly for the entire twelve months.

It is our purpose to attempt to clarify the multiple roles the coach must play in motivating his athletes and further to point to some of the reasons why there is a special meaning, a special feeling and a special reverence for the man who has been honored with the title of coach.

Although the coach prefers to see himself as an encyclopedia of knowledge and master of strategy, he is called upon to perform the roles of salesman, public relations man, counselor and psychologist. Of course, the personality of each coach determines how he performs these roles. Let us explore some of the roles a coach is expected to perform.

First of all the coach is, of course, expected to be an expert in his particular sport. He is expected to know the rules, the regulations and be familiar with the latest literature. He must, in fact, be somewhat of a walking encyclopedia. The coach's training has been primarily centered here. In fact, for many coaches this is the only area in which they have been trained. If anything beyond this is asked of coaches, they have usually had to pick it up on their own. If this requirement for such extensive knowledge were carried to its extreme, the coach would spend all of his waking hours exploring the many thousands of pages that are produced annually in his sport alone. In his reading, the careful coach must be able to separate the facts from mere opinion. Furthermore, he must be aware of each individual athlete and of his team as a whole. He must know its potential and be able to apply what he reads to the type of team he coaches. It would be foolhardy for a coach to adopt a new technique simply because it has worked for another team or is the fad. He must be able to weigh the merits of a new or different system with the capabilities of his own club. But by the same token he must be aware of changes and must be able to see the merits of a new system in time to employ it; otherwise he will lag behind. He must change with the times, but only as his talent and his team will allow. However, knowing the sport and its strategy is not enough. A highly related requirement of the coach is that he be a masterful tactician and strategist. The successful coach knows how to apply the knowledge. Furthermore he must be able to time its application.

The coach is like a general who is expected not only to know all the strategies of battle but how to apply them as well. He must be able to cope with any spontaneous occurrence with a minimum of mishaps. It is the coach as the athletic general who determines how the battle will unfold and eventually what course it shall take. It is in the role of masterful strategist that the coach prefers or is willing to risk his career. It is unfortunate, however, that he really fails in others roles, which may appear on the surface to have little if any relation to the sport itself. Moreover, it is unfortunate that the coach has not been trained where perhaps he fails most. What are these areas?

The modern coach finds himself in the necessary position of being a public relations man. Because he is seen as the public spokesman for his team, what he says and how he says it may have a profound effect on the team. The popular image of many a team has resulted not so much from its type of play but from the way the coach has conducted himself in public. Often the coach's attitude has a subtle effect on various members of his team and this, in turn, affects the team as a whole.

The coach may make public statements that certain members of the team consider to be unfair, or they may feel that such comments belong only within the team. The coach may publicly criticize a member of the team. For example, the coach may say, "Joe Smith would be a better athlete if he would concentrate on the sport and spend less time on his outside interests." Such a statement made in public by the coach may alienate not only Joe Smith but the team as a whole. They may feel exposed or betrayed at the very time they are in need of support. We have talked to many athletes who were critical of the coach who publicly exposed their personal weaknesses. This resulted in their never feeling totally confident in him. They found it hard to put out that little extra for the coach or the team in general. In contrast, some coaches by their manner in public relations have been able to instill confidence in the team and develop even greater motivation. To be supportive when the team is having a rough time or publicly to express confidence in an athlete who is having a temporary setback may bring either the team or an athlete through a rough spot. The public relations aspect of coaching is a demanding one since it taxes the ingenuity of the coach. He must be able to motivate two different groups in a single message. On the one hand he must motivate the fans to continue to support the team. On the other hand, he must try to inspire the team to do its very best. The problem is less difficult when the team is winning. If, however, the team is losing, he must reassure the fans as well as the team. Such a task is as simple as walking a tightrope blindfolded while wearing splints.

One distasteful job for a coach is his responsibility as a salesman. This job is a many-faceted one. For example, he must sell his fellow coaches on his ideas — whether they be strategy or a general philosophy of the game. Such a task can be a relatively simple one if the coaches working together have all played on the same team at the same time under the same coach. If they have not worked together previously, there will be differences of opinion and the coaches will challenge one another. How this is handled can have a profound effect upon the team.

The coach's second sales job is selling his tactics or philosophy to his players. He can push for a hard nose, dogmatic, forceful sale or a sale involving persuasion complete with logic as well as evidence. There will arise such fundamental questions as a wide-open attack or a conservative attack, a concentration on offense or defense, etc., etc. As if this were not enough, the coach must sell all interested groups, whether it be faculty, financiers, fans or friends.

For some coaches there is a "third" job of salesmanship — that of recruitment. In this domain, the coach must sell his team, the school or his organization the team philosophy and, above all, himself. He may find that he is competing with a few or many other salesmen who are trying to do the same thing. When he is competing for top athletes, he must sell as he has never sold before. If he succeeds, his job carries a sense of accomplishment. If he fails, he must pick up the pieces and start again, hoping he will have better luck on the next try.

To some coaches this job of selling is a natural, and they seem to thrive on it. Many, however, have little to sell and must put forth an extra effort. But whether or not he is a natural salesman, the coach who has something to sell is in the most favorable position of all. The job is not an easy one, and it is a job most coaches would prefer not having. At times the selling job may even backfire. The athlete may have enrolled because the coach sold the parents on his particular school. The coach may feel he has won a victory only to find later that the athlete himself has not been sold on the school. The selling must then start all over again, but this time with the athlete himself. This selling job will be more difficult since the athlete feels he is an unwilling partner of a bargain he never agreed upon. Such a situation demands that the coach use his most persuasive powers.

One role that each coach must face, by the very nature of his job, is that of the team problem-solver or counselor. Many coaches fail to recognize this role as their responsibility and may therefore delegate it to their assistant coaches. On many teams this responsibility is even ignored or dismissed as unimportant by the coach. It is perhaps the responsibility that most coaches accept reluctantly if at all. For one reason, he may have little if any training in dealing with problems of human relations. A second reason, one that may be more threatening to a team leader, is that team problems may very frequently involve the coach himself. When directly involved, it is difficult for a coach to arbitrate and remain objective.

It must be remembered that, as head of a team, the coach should realize that he represents different things to different athletes. He represents the chief authority figure, and with this distinction go the many attitudes toward authority which include everything from humbleness and respect to hostility and open rebellion. In one sense he becomes the father of the team, and he finds that the feelings each team member has for him will depend primarily upon that particular athlete's attitude toward his own father. In some of his athletes he will find a genuine desire to learn and achieve in the same sense that a son strives to earn the approval of his father. Others may simply want to be liked or accepted. From still other players there may be an open attempt to outwit him or to expose him as being incompetent or inadequate. Thus, it is apparent that the coach may very well find himself dealing with as many attitudes as he has players. The success of a coach may well depend upon his ability to satisfy these complex and varied needs of his men.

The most puzzling and complex responsibility for the coach is that of motivation of his athletes. He is expected to be an expert in motivation. Of the hundreds of coaches we have interviewed, all have agreed that motivation was anywhere from 50 to 90 per cent of his responsibility. The coach who comes up with a new game formation cannot prevent his opponents from adopting it in due time. In this way teams tend to become equalized, and motivation remains the deciding factor.

However, the belief that a pep talk sparks a team to victory or that the coach ignites a team with a few well-chosen words is simply a myth. At times, such gimmicks may help, but these incidents are more the exception than the rule. Moreover, motivation may often be more implicit than explicit. A coach may be able to motivate his team without exerting special effort to do so. In fact, he may be unaware of motivating them. By the same token, he may be unable to motivate, even though he is exerting a great effort to do so. Frequently, coaches are aware of the need for motivation of the team and yet feel totally incapable of providing the spark. Many coaches have approached us for help saying, "I know something is bothering the team. We aren't up for this game and no matter what I do, I don't seem to be able to get them up."

"Bert, darling. I know you've tried everything else. But do you really think *that's* going to exhort your players to a greater team effort?"

To begin, the task is a twofold one. The coach must know how to motivate individuals, and he must know how to motivate a team. In order to do the former, he must be sensitive to individual differences. This requires knowing each of his athletes as well as he knows his closest friend. The coach may employ one of several techniques in order to motivate his athletes. He may be very encouraging and complimentary and make certain that he recognizes each individual athlete as a person. He may take special pains to give him personal praise after each noteworthy performance. On the other hand, he may feel that the best method to motivate is to treat the athlete rough — "chew him out" after he blunders or make an example of him. A coach may apply both methods — praising or punishing — when considered appropriate.

Other coaches try still different methods. Some feel that being a buddy or a benevolent brother is a better way of motivating players. Some believe that they provide a good model by being "godlike," and they remain aloof and impersonal. Whether the coach is authoritarian, democratic or even *laissez-faire* is a function of his personality and how he views his responsibility. While all coaches are aware of the role of motivation, each coach seems to implement it in his own way, chiefly by means of trial and error.

Motivating the team presents an equally challenging problem, and the same approaches may be taken. Just as each player is different, the makeup of each team is different. The interaction of the players as well as their uniqueness as individuals account for differences in groups. Here too the coach must rely on his experience and must use hit or miss techniques until he finds the right one.

Problem athletes or, to state it another way, athletes with problems, require a different motivational technique. Because he is not trained in psychology, the coach finds himself at a decided disadvantage. The many problems and the unique ways in which they must be handled often pose for the coach his major task in building motivation.

Psychological motivation is the most neglected area of the coach's training. When one considers the importance of motivation, it is unfair that the coach should be expected to be an authority here without this special training. Since it is totally lacking, he can rely only upon those experiences which have grown out of trial and error methods.

The one unique quality that the coach contributes to the motivation of his team is his own personality. The coach ought to be aware of his own personality and his own potential. No matter how he may attempt to be objective or to minimize his personal influence, his personality manifests itself. In some instances this influence can be a great motivating factor for the team or, conversely, it may be highly detrimental to team motivation. In essence, the coach, by the effect of his personality, can be a "winner" or "loser." The team eventually becomes an extension of the coach's personality. The way he himself responds in a variety of situations inevitably molds the team's behavior. Members of the team find themselves being rewarded for some behaviors and reprimanded for others. Furthermore, the coach serves as a model for what he wants done both on and off the athletic field.

This personal aspect of coaching may be the toughest of all since a coach is not in a position to change what he has become over the years. His background has been such that he has become a coach, and this in itself has been rewarding; therefore, he is reluctant to change, even if he finds that the team's lack of motivation may be a result of the kind of person he is. Many coaches, even if they were to find themselves responsible for the team's lack of motivation, would rather change their playing personnel than change themselves.

One may wonder why the coach continues in a profession which makes so many demands upon him. Why would someone remain in a profession that is so taxing physically, emotionally and psychologically? The authors have been continually impressed by the number of admirable traits displayed by these men. Their dedication to and genuine love for athletics, their pride and ambition for their teams, their willingness to give unselfishly of themselves in order to bring about success for their teams, their eagerness to meet a challenge and, above all, their ability to derive real pleasure from their work stand out as qualities that can be matched by few other professions. These are, in fact, the intangible qualities they convey in subtle ways to their athletes. What better models can we ask for than these? But to be "a great coach," all you have to do is win.

NOTE

Information contained in this chapter is based on hundreds of hours of interviews with coaches who were employed at the time in either high schools, junior colleges, universities or the professional ranks.

The authors have worked most closely with George Haines and James Counselman, Olympic swimming coaches, Tokyo; Payton Jordan and Bud Winters in track and field; Alex Hanum, San Francisco Warriors, professional basketball; Rene Hererias, University of California, Berkeley, and Stu Inman, San Jose State College, basketball; as well as numerous college football coaches. They have been consultants to one national league baseball team.

FOOTNOTES

1. Obviously all of the possible demands upon a coach cannot be included within this chapter. It is doubtful if even a book could cover such a large area. Some publications, such as Griffith, C. R.: *The Psychology of Coaching*. New York, Scribner, 1929, and Lawther, J. D.: *Psychology of Coaching*. Englewood Cliffs, Prentice-Hall, 1951, have attempted to do so. The nature of coaching itself has been explained by A. A. Strauss in an article entitled "Mirrors and Masks" in the book, *The Search for Identity*, 1959. Perhaps a thorough integration of all of these works could more clearly shed light on this complex profession.
2. In a book by the authors, *The Handling of Emotional Problems in Athletes*, many kinds of problems a coach must face are described along with the specific ways these various problems may be handled.

KNUTE ROCKNE AND COACHING

THOMAS P. JOHNSON

ON THE 31ST DAY OF MARCH, 1931, at approximately 10:45 A.M., a giant trimotored Fokker fell from overcast skies to the Flint Hills of Kansas carrying eight people to their deaths. Response to the crash was worldwide, bringing messages of condolence from kings and presidents because one of the eight was Knute Kenneth Rockne – perhaps the greatest coach the game of football has ever known. The crash, while beginning a legend, ended an amazing career that vaulted a Norwegian immigant boy to national prominence. In his thirteen years as a coach, Rockne compiled a record of 105 wins, 5 ties and 12 losses against the finest opposition.

A paradox in the midst of all this fame was the mystery of Rockne. Francis Wallace, one of his biographers and closest associates during the early years of his coaching career, expressed the view that even those close to him did not really know him.[1] Wallace comments, "he seldom spoke or wrote about Rockne; nor did he want people probing around for the real Rockne, not even with friendly probes." He also writes, "The thing within Rock . . . must have been constantly agitating, gnawing, prowling. This could well explain his intensity. There was so much that wanted to be expressed; and which found release in so many activities. Rockne's autobiography is almost barren of his real thoughts as a student and player. There was the same familiar refusal to uncover himself."

Another paradox in this man who was the acknowledged leader in a highly competitive field was his apparent lack of confidence. His mother once said of him that he was never quite so sure of himself in new things as his aggressive exterior indicated.

Westbrook Pegler in his column "Nobody's Business" in 1930 commented,

> I see Mr. Rockne as a modest man who does not think much of himself, who is constantly amazed to find himself a great national celebrity, and who therefore wants to make all the money he can while he can, lest the public suddenly get next to him. He has a certain kind of confidence but not much assurance, as though always apprehensive that someone will put him to the necessity of proving that he is a great man. Sometimes, when he predicts that his team will lose a football game, he merely wants to tighten up his players, but I imagine that most times, when he says such things, that he is actually low-rating his own as he privately low-rates himself. If he were fully assured of his importance he would not burden himself with some of the obligations he constantly assumes.[2]

This column, according to Wallace, "irritated Rockne more than any other single piece of writing because it touched on certain things Rockne thought nobody's business but his own."[3] Wallace indicates he feels there may be some truth to Pegler's column and adds that Rockne seemed a "shy lion" who "needed to run from fame."

Let us attempt now to fit together and understand these superficially contradictory pictures of Rockne by applying psychoanalytic theory to data collected on his life. The analysis is placed at this point to give meaning to the supporting material that follows.

Rockne attested to a deep love for his mother all of his life. However, his feelings for his father were markedly ambivalent. He admired him and recognized his need to be protected and accepted by him, but his father was a threatening figure with whom to have to compete. Attempts to be like him were ridiculed by his father, resulting in Knute's feeling insecure, frustrated and angry.

Consequently, Rockne never felt the self-confidence to rival openly his awesome father for his mother. In angry rebellion Knute was unable to identify with his father, for he confused identification with subjugation. Instead he tried to win his father's love in a passive "feminine" manner. However, because of his contemporary culture and upbringing, to be passive and "feminine" was taboo; he countered this tendency with a reaction formation of hypermasculine pursuits. He seems to have sublimated his heterosexual curiosity into a quest for knowledge, becoming a voracious reader and memorizer. The feelings of anger and competitiveness for his father were displaced to daredevil, aggressive activities and rebelliousness as exemplified by his stunts, gate crashing and caustic wit.

He found athletics, especially football, an ideal vehicle for symbolically competing with his father. It was an activity which his father opposed; thus playing it offered him a chance to rebel against his father, and yet it did not threaten him with the prospect of directly rivaling his father.

Success was still success, however, and even isolated from his father's field as he was in football, he felt the danger of incurring his wrath as a rival. He handled this by humorously low-rating himself and by being so naive that others frequently imposed and took advantage of him. By these self-depreciating actions, Rockne hoped to project an image of himself as an ineffectual rival and also to "pay a price" to his superego for the success he did achieve.

A residue of this unresolved oedipal conflict was the love for his mother (whom all women symbolized), for whom he could not compete because to do so would require identifying with and rivaling his awesome father.

We then have the struggle of a basic wish to resolve things with father through a passive "feminine" life style in conflict with a culturally dictated masculine role in which he never felt completely secure nor comfortable, but through which he found ample opportunity to vent his anger, competitiveness and rebellion symbolically. While many other determinants undoubtedly also played a part, this conflict seems to have touched many aspects of his life.

LIFE HISTORY OF KNUTE ROCKNE

Knute Rockne was born March 4, 1888, in Voss, a Norwegian village, where he lived until the family moved to America when he was five years old. His father, a stern, persistent man, a firm disciplinarian frequently at odds with young Knute, was a carriage maker, and his craftsmanship won a medal at the 1893 World's Fair in Chicago. In Voss it was the custom for a son to learn his father's trade. Carriage making had been a three-generation tradition in Rockne's family. Knute did not seem to have the aptitude for the trade, however, and was nick-named *klureneve* (all thumbs) by his father. Mrs. Rockne was a very religious woman, and Knute's characteristic attitude toward her was considerate, loving and helpful.

Details on his life before five are scarce, but the flavor is of an extremely energetic, mischievous, daring child. He was rescued from a drifting ice floe, saved from drowning after a fall from the dock at Bergen, and once he scaled the rigging to the ship's crow's nest on the Atlantic crossing.

His father settled the family in a two-story brick house in a modest Chicago suburb, and his early years there were filled with adventure. He was always involved in some sort of stunt or dare, and admits that one of his common pastimes was gate crashing. Teachers recall him as "chock full of mischief,"[4] and there are many stories of his exploits to support this characterization.

Although he enjoyed reading and read a great deal, he spent most of his free time on various sports. Football, his favorite, was played surreptitiously, for it had been forbidden by his father as being too rough. His father permitted baseball, however, and according to Rockne's autobiography,[5] his famous flattened nose was the result of being struck by a baseball bat during a disputed call. Blinded by tears and pain, he recalled running home to point out that father was wrong about baseball and therefore ought to reconsider his ruling on football.

As a teen-ager, Rockne was told that he had a weak heart. His response was to maintain, even increase, his activities and to joke about it when he would find himself on the bottom of a football pile-up.

He often related how he crashed the game between a Chicago and a Brooklyn team for the national high school football championship. There he finally found a male figure with whom he could identify. Starring for the victorious Chicago team at quarterback was Walter Eckersall who was small and quick like Knute. Rockne said of this, "For the first time I went home with a hero. Dreams of how I someday might shine as Eckersall had shone were my lonesome luxury."[6]

In high school he tried out for football but was turned down because of his small size. He turned to track and tennis to build himself up, and it was pointed out that he might have a future in track, but football, the forbidden sport, was his challenge. He had little interest in school and was a below-average student.

His rebelliousness increased during his high school years, and he was frequently truant – usually to practice athletics. At one time when it appeared that the track team would be disbanded because the boys were staying out of school to practice, Rockne threatened to quit school. His father, tired of arguing, finally encouraged it so that Knute could go to work. Then instead of giving up school, Rockne decided to make college his goal.

His senior year was stormy and ended in his dropping out. His high school principal observed that "during his senior year teen-age readjustment became a problem; he desired a new freedom and liberty that conditions could not fully accord to him. He seemed to have no male figure to tie to." This unusually stormy period with authority figures corresponds to the teen-age resurgence of the oedipal conflict.

After he dropped out of school, Rockne drifted to various odd jobs for short periods of time. His goal was to save $1000 and then go to college. He felt he had neither the desire nor the talent to follow his father. He seems to have made an interesting compromise by taking a job with a symbolic father, the government, as a post office employee. There he played out a repetition of the conflicts, attitudes and frustrations he had experienced with his own father. He attacked the job ambitiously, memorizing the complicated schedules for more efficiency, while the older employees ridiculed him for his industry. He said it was "unfair . . . veterans smiled at youth and industry . . . merit meant nothing."[7] He often became discouraged during this period.

Rockne entered Notre Dame University as a twenty-two-year-old freshman in the fall of 1910, but his uncertainty about being able to make good is reflected in the fact that he didn't resign his position with the post office until several months later. He also selected pharmacy as his major as it had the lowest entrance requirements. He was pleased with what he found at Notre Dame. Away from home and his father, he seemed to feel more accepted as a man. Of this he remarked, "A boy entering Notre Dame from prep school finds himself at once part of an organism complete within itself, a wholly masculine democracy . . . animated by a single spirit."[8] He was in college at his own instigation, and under these circumstances he underwent a marked behavioral change, although old problems of being unsure of himself seemed accentuated by his being on his own.

In contrast to his high school record, Rockne presented no discipline problem in college. His roommate, Gus Dorias, recalls him as being sensitive and easily hurt. "He seemed to have more problems than the rest of us. He was always threatening to quit school for one reason or another, but of course never got around to it."[9] His attitude toward women was described as Victorian. He avoided much of the social life and was opposed to time-wasting dances and coeducational schools. He was revolted by a proposed contest to select the best ladies' man on campus. Although he had little time for girls, he collected a fee for use of his ground floor room as an after-hours entrance and exit for those who made time, and probably felt a vicarious pleasure from thus being associated with those actively involved with women. He seldom dated and was tongue-tied around girls. A classmate who double-dated with him recalls that he would scarcely say a word, blushed frequently and rarely dated the same person twice, seeming to be uncomfortable in a close relationship with a girl.

Knute was active in the Notre Dame Players Association, specializing in female roles. His most popular impersonations were those of a squaw and a Negro mammy. This was the only acceptable way in which he could experience a passive feminine role.

He was the campus clown who told jokes on himself and relished lampooning others in this clown role. The clown role served him well, for in it he could safely express his hostility by appearing harmless and incapable of seriously threatening others — his father. By accepting the role of a clown, he acted out a compromise in his oedipal conflict. It represented a passive rather than active role that would not cause his father to see him as a rival and retaliate. The resentment for his father's forcing him to live out the passive clown role is vented comfortably from the clown position.

His football career, after an unpromising start, was highly successful. With Dorais he is credited with perfecting and popularizing the forward pass. The pass is symbolic of achieving a goal by cleverness and by-passing, in a sense not by identifying with and competing directly with father, but competing indirectly by circumventing. Knute competed with his father not by trying to be a better craftsman, but by being a success in a field his father disliked.

The big unveiling of the perfected forward pass came in a game against Army, the government-father team. He faked a limp for several plays prior to catching the touchdown pass to throw the Army team off-guard — in effect saying, "Don't fear me; I'm impotent." Then when the defense had discounted him as a threat, he flashed by to take a surprise pass for a touchdown. "At that moment when I touched that ball, life for me was complete."[10]

Write-ups described him as a "fierce, reckless tackler."[11] He especially liked to be matched against a much bigger man, or the opponent's star. These battles always featured a great deal of verbal sarcasm, and Rockne always had to have the last word. Even as a coach he would go into a blocking duel with a much bigger man taunting him into his best effort. Then Rockne would treat the effort with sarcasm such as, "Is that the best you can do?" These episodes are best shown in his widely publicized encounters with Jim Thorpe, the then acknowledged king of football, who while more than a match for Rockne physically, was no competition for his quick wit. In these symbolic battles with his father, while taking a physical beating, he would manage to get in the last word, making the victory sour for his opponent, yet taking punishment himself.

He related how important it was for his mother to see him do well, so he picked a game against a weak opponent and had her come. He had a great day, but with humorous disgust reported that his mother was most impressed with the cheerleader — a nonparticipant symbolizing his father.

It is believed that his wife, whom he married in 1914, was his first and only girl. Little is known of their life together. Rockne never allowed publicity about his family life. His marriage can perhaps be best typified by the amount of time he was away from home. A usual work day ran until 7:00 P.M., when he would return for supper, unless he had a speaking engagement or meeting. Nights when he was home, he often invited players to drop in, and they were encouraged to use the home much as their own. Rockne frequently traveled all over the country, and even vacations with the family were seldom uninterrupted. It would appear that he found it difficult to make a heterosexual adjustment without the burden of oedipal guilt, and that he used his work and other people to gain distance from his wife.

In 1918 he was appointed head coach at Notre Dame. As a coach, he was a perfectionist. He was a whirlwind of activity, doing everything but blowing up the footballs for the team. "In the heat of battle he could be ruthless and cruel to his players. In calmer periods he could be petty and suspicious of his subordinates."[12] Players recall him as a master psychologist. He often humiliated his men. For example, he once assigned a player who was anxious to do well before his home-town fans the job of marking first downs.

After such episodes he would seek the man out and indicate that some purpose had been served — in a sense, he would make friends. He was also concerned with being on good terms with the opposition before and after the game. Despite his success, it is remarkable that he aroused very little jealousy among the other coaches. This is accounted for by the clown's need not to be taken seriously no matter how strong the attack. The clown must not provoke enemies, for then the clown role has failed.

The feigning of impotence extended into his coaching, and his methods were dramatic. Once in an early season game against a weak team, he intimated to officials that he wanted them to penalize Notre Dame as frequently and heavily as possible because he didn't want the strength of his team known. For similar and other reasons, he usually started his second team so that his true strength would be underestimated by opponents.

As his coaching reputation grew, he was courted by other schools, and there were reportedly a number of contracts signed by Rockne for other schools. He was seductive in these affairs, seeming to need the assurance that came with knowing he was wanted elsewhere. Once this got out of control, and Notre Dame offered to let him go to Columbia. Wallace recalls that when his bluff was called, Rockne was frightened of the possibility of leaving his Notre Dame home. He reports that Rockne seemed "a weak, uncertain little fellow looking for help."[13]

He was known as a gentle, naive, generous man. Many stories that substantiate these traits are offered by his biographers. He once made three speaking engagements for the same night in three different cities because he couldn't say no. He was a soft touch for time or money to anyone who praised him or treated him in a way seen as complimentary. He was known to change his pronunciation of a word in the middle of a speech if another mispronounced it.

He was a poor businessman, of whom it was said money meant little. He relied on friends to protect him. He was frequently taken advantage of in this manner. To Wallace it seemed he was very concerned about the reactions of others, and he would often secretly seek the opinions of others without revealing his interest. He always seemed eager to prove that he belonged and was accepted. The above characteristics were geared to winning this acceptance. He tended to become moody and depressed when a frustration wasn't quickly cleared up. On one occasion he publicly broke down in tears. His first worry after composing himself was what others might think.

Once before a big game, Rockne had a chance to visit with Walter Eckersall. Rockne said the game was no longer important after the chance to be with his boyhood hero. This reaction to meeting Eckersall indicates that what was important after all was not winning games, but being accepted by his father. Through Eckersall, Rockne was thus symbolically accepted in a field shared by both men, and the competitiveness of the game was no longer necessary.

As he grew older he seemed to mellow. He became kinder, less turbulent, less intense. Some rebelliousness remained, however. During several life-threatening bouts with phlebitis, he coached games and made personal appearances against strong medical objections. Even the last plane flight was against medical advice.

Some of Knute's comments on his philosophy of life are interesting, for example: "Build up your weaknesses until they become your strong points."[14] This suggests the hypermasculine reaction formation upon which his life seemed built. When questioned on fear of flying, he replied, "If you are going to meet death, you will have to meet it at the appointed time, whether it comes to you in the air, on land, or in the water."[15] He was fatalistic in his belief that if things were going to happen, they were going to happen and he could do nothing to stop them. When they came, however, he would be prepared to give them battle.

This paradox seems understandable in terms of his constant active-passive conflict. The basic passive leanings said that things are as they are and can't be changed; yet the active, masculine reaction formation is demanded anyway, even though the masquerade is seen as futile.

Rockne wrote a novel, *The Four Winners*. It seems to be a projection of the intrapsychic struggles and changes that took place in Rockne, and a discussion of it is therefore pertient. The hero is Elmer Higgins, a small, bright, hard-working young man whose goal is to be a quarterback. He is opposed by several characters who exemplify various aspects of Rockne's own father. In college Elmer is aided by a kindly, accepting coach who represents the father for whom Knute wished. Mr. Higgins is a brusque man who wants Elmer to forget football and follow in his footsteps to become a lawyer.

In high school he tries out for the team over his father's objections, only to find in Coach Smith a man who does nothing but ridicule and discourage him. Only Elmer's mother has confidence in his yet undiscovered potential. The counterpart of Walter Eckersall is a football star named Hunk Hughes who becomes Elmer's idol and friend. Elmer has a girlfriend, but the relationship is distant. Elmer's philosophy is that only sissies actively pursue women. The real man stays with football, and the girls eventually pick the gridiron heroes over the sheiks.

Elmer goes to Dulac University and says "The only reason I ever want to make the football team at Dulac is to show him" (Coach Smith). "He was determined to avenge himself personally and to humiliate the swaggering Smith. He confided to his mother all his hopes and fears and ambitions and humiliations; she was the only one who seemed to understand him."

That Elmer is Rockne is clear. They shared a similar parent-child relationship, analogous attitude toward football and girls and a physical similarity. Both dreamed of playing quarterback, both attended French-named universities, and both spent vacations working at a summer camp.

Finally Elmer gets recognition from his new, kindly college coach and is named the team's quarterback. ". . . at last he had aroused the coveted attention of his chief and had passed through those stages of ridicule and grief through which every young fellow has to go before he arrives." Although outwardly pleased, inwardly Elmer is obsessed with the fear that he is not equal to the task. He fears the coach has overrated him. This seems to fit with Knute's fear that in spite of the clown's role, his father might see him as a threat.

As a senior Elmer successfully directs his team through an undefeated schedule. "Though Elmer outwardly appeared to be quite settled and adjusted to things, within him were smouldering fire which would not out."

The book's climax is a final game with State University where Smith, their new coach, has one of the country's greatest teams led by Hunk Hughes. Elmer says, "I don't care if we lose every game on the schedule. If we could beat Coach Smith 40-0, it would be the greatest day of my life." This indicates what football is all about to Rockne — a personal, symbolic battle with father. As the game approaches, Elmer's father finally warms up to his son's football success. Elmer, who has been emotionally stoic, gets a note from his parents at the last moment before the final game letting him know that they are at the game and saying, "Good luck, Mother and Dad." Elmer's response is tears.

Elmer's coach directs the team to play the game so hard that the opponents "will begin to think of home, mother and sidelines." This seems to say once again that football for Rockne was a reaction formation against passive wishes to be home with mother.

Thanks to Elmer, the Dulac squad ekes out a last-minute, narrow victory. After the victory, Rockne through Elmer tells of the resolution for which he had been striving.

> After his shower bath, as Elmer was putting on his street clothes, he was surprised to feel no particular spirit of exultation, after all his years of preparation for this greatest event of his life. True, he found a certain sense of satisfaction in the victory; but that was all. He felt sorry for the State team and for Hunk Hughes, his old friend; and he even felt sorry for Coach Smith. He began to see things more at their true value; he began to realize that a football game is just a football game, and not a thing of vital importance after all. He found that what he had imagined was hatred for Coach Smith had been purely boyish emotion, and that it had grown simply because he had made no attempt to check it. He realized now that he no longer hated Coach Smith — the idea was absurd! — and that so far as average human beings go, Coach Smith, after all, was not such a bad fellow. He was a man with certain frailties — but no one is perfect.

Elmer felt "quietly happy in a new and restful way. He felt happy because of his parents, who seemed to take such a keen pride in his achievements."

At the last victory dinner of the season, Elmer announces that he is going into a law firm and part-time coaching. His father says, "Elmer's mother and I are glad . . . but we're not quite sure of the coaching work. But Elmer has already done things so well, we're willing to let him decide." At this point Elmer and his efforts have been accepted by his father, and Elmer in turn has been able to allow himself to become a lawyer like his father.

In the last scene in the book, Elmer for the first time takes the initiative with his girl friend. He leads her aside and states his preference for her over the congratulating crowds. For Elmer, at least, the oedipal conflict is over. He can leave the "congratulating crowds" which include his parents because he has made peace with his father and taken another woman in place of his mother.

During his own life, Rockne seems to have at least partially resolved this central oedipal conflict. That he did can be inferred from his book and mellowing changes observed by others during the last years of his life. Further, he developed interests outside of football, becoming a powerful public speaker and accepting a position as sales consultant for the Studebaker Corporation. In a sense the latter brought him the full circle, for Studebaker was an outgrowth of a family project of wagon and carriage building.[16]

FOOTNOTES

1. Wallace, F.: *Knute Rockne.* Garden City, Doubleday, 1960.
2. Quoted in Wallace, *op. cit. supra* note 1.
3. Wallace, *op. cit. supra* note 1.
4. Lovelace, D. W.: *Rockne of Notre Dame.* New York and London, G. P. Putnam's Sons, 1931.
5. Rockne, K.: From Norway to Notre Dame (1930) ; serialized in *Collier's* 1930, vol. *86,* Oct. 18, pp. 7-9; Oct. 25, pp. 20-21; Nov. 1, pp. 14-15; Nov. 8, pp. 20-21; Nov. 15, pp. 22-23; Nov. 22, pp. 14-15; Nov. 29, pp. 26-27; Dec. 6, pp. 20-21.
6. *Ibid.*
7. Wallace: *op. cit. supra* note 1.
8. Rockne: *op. cit. supra* note 5.
9. Quoted in Wallace: *op. cit. supra* note 1.
10. Wallace: *op. cit. supra* note 1.
11. Quoted in Wallace: *op. cit. supra* note 1.
12. Wallace: *op. cit. supra* note 1.
13. Wallace: *op. cit. supra* note 1.
14. Stuhldreher, H.: *Knute Rockne, Man Builder.* Philadelphia, Macrae Smith and Co., 1931.
15. *Ibid.*
16. See generally Hurt, H. W.: *Goals, The Life of Knute Rockne.* New York, Murray Book Corp., 1931; Huston, M.: *Salesman from the Sidelines.* New York, Long and Smith, Inc., 1932; Rockne, K.: *The Four Winners.* New York, Devin-Adair Co., 1925; Tarachow, W.: Remarks on the comic process and beauty. *Psychoanal Quart, 18:*215, 1949; Trussell, P. L.: *The Life of Knute Rockne.* New York, Wonder Publications, 1931.

PART EIGHT
TEAM SPORTS

INTRODUCTION

To open this section of the volume, Adrian Stokes presents some psychoanalytic reflections on the development of ball games. He speculates about the history and origin of sports. He sees games as a substitute for warfare. In ball games, he says, "the context is always one of potency," and in bat and ball games, "the genital issue is predominant." These games "serve to reflect the emotional alterations which are typical of the adolescent in the process of controlling and directing the rush of genital feelings; the quick change, for instance, from active to passive, from attack to defense, from feelings of omnipotence to those of lurid disaster." Football, soccer and other teams, when they enter the field, "canter out of the natal tunnel beneath a stand," where crowds applaud and "surrender to them the field of play." On the field each team

> . . . defends the goal at their back; in front is the new land, the new woman, whom they strive to possess in the interest of preserving the mother inviolate, in order, as it were, to progress from infancy to adulthood: at the same time, the defensive role is the father's; he opposes the forward youth of the opposition. From the point of view of the attack, it is beyond question that a genital aggressiveness characterizes ball games whose players possess feet, hands, stick, bat with which to manoeuvre the ball, the semen.

Robert Ardrey in his recent book, *The Territorial Imperative,* argues for the existence of an inborn drive to defend an area of space: the territorial drive. Territory, he feels, fills an animal's need for identity, security, and stimulation. His personal association with an area of space fulfills his need for identity; the heartland or nesting center provides security; the fights on the border offer stimulation. In the human world, the intrusion of one juvenile gang on the "turf" of another gang and the resulting mayhem are considered just as much an expression of the territorial drive as is the behavior of the lemur. Protecting a territory also gives the defender a psychological advantage. Animal studies show that the intruder rarely wins, even if he has advantage in size and strength.[1]

Although Ardrey does not discuss games, there are implications of land boundaries in many of them. Most team sports are organized territorially. A team defends a home goal and the opponents intrude on its ground in an attempt to reach the goal line. Baseball players score by getting home after intruding on the opponents' territory. One of the most popular of the non-active games, Monopoly, is based on the acquisition of property, and chess also concerns invasion and defense of area.

Team sports call for cooperative effort. It is difficult to form a good team out of individuals unable to work together. Counselors at industrial schools for delinquents point out that it is well-nigh impossible to develop a good team. On the face of it, teams from industrial schools would appear to be unbeatable — there are so many big and tough fellows in the line-up — but they do not think in terms of the team, they are unable to identify with the team, and as a result they fare poorly in team games.

Games and sports played in teams are characteristic of postoedipal play. The anxieties are related to the struggle for independence and equality. Reassurance is sought in being a member of a group, following a chosen leader, observing the rules of the game, and in the knowledge that the game can be repeated as often as wished. All of which brings us to Abner Doubleday, the reputed father of baseball, whose invention is analyzed by Thomas A. Petty.[2] Doubleday, Petty points out, was "given credit for creating a game that provides for a safe expression of the fantasies and impulses of rebellion against the primal horde father, competition with the oedipal father, and rivalry with the brothers while retaining the prospects of displacing the father as the son and brother. Crucial to this view is Freud's hypothesis concerning events in the primal horde as described in 1913 in *Totem and Taboo* — the banished brothers joined forces in order to drive father out, and so too in team sports, the players have to join together."[3]

Petty in his study of baseball advances the hypothesis that the game's basic motivation lies in the pristine facets of the father and son relationship. Crystallized into the plot of the game and the roles assumed by the players is the son's successful rebellion against the father.

The plot of the game is considered to have three simultaneously expressed, interwoven and mutually dependent fantasies or themes. They are: the rivalry between the teams of brothers, the duel between the pitcher/-father and the batter/son, and the insured triumph of the batters/primal-horde-sons over the pitchers/primal-horde-fathers. The ambivalence between the father and son is expressed in the first two fantasies or themes by directing all of the aggression toward the opposing team and all of the libidinal drives toward members of the same team. And in the third and more deeply unconscious theme the ambivalence is resolved by directing all of the aggression against the pitcher/father by identifying the pitchers of both teams as the father and directing the libidinal drives toward all the batters of both teams as the brother horde.

The pitcher, ostensibly favored by the rules and supported by the fielders, dominates the field and (with rare exceptions) initiates every play. Yet regardless of how effective he is in retiring the batters, he cannot win. No points are scored for put-outs.

The batters, handicapped by the rules and beset by the pitcher and fielders, are destined by the plot of the game to win. Regardless of how many times he is put out, only the batter can score.

Scoring is primarily a team function, and the rally represents the essence of the batter/horde's triumph over the pitcher/father. The home run is the pinnacle of attainment. With one stroke, the batter seizes the potential for scoring and winning the game by himself. Thus simultaneously he vanquishes the father by himself on behalf of the brother horde and wins the oedipal duel.

The only direct violence sanctioned by the plot and the rules of the game has been displaced, condensed and concentrated in the explosive contact between ball and bat. The ball is simultaneously a surrogate of the pitcher/father and a missile or weapon by which the batter can be vanquished. The bat is simultaneously a surrogate of the ambitious batter/son and the weapon of attack.

When Yogi Berra stepped into the batter's box, he probably did not realize that baseball is, in the words of Petty, "a duel between the father and the individual son, that is, in the game between the pitcher and the batter." And Berra probably never stopped to consider what happens when he hit one out of the park. "The home run represented the pinnacle of attainment. The batter achieves the fulfillment of both fantasies concurrently, that is, he vanquishes the father by himself on behalf of the brothers and wins the oedipal duel." And Petty adds: "Soon, instead of returning to the mother, the toddler ventures from a first to a second substitute base of securtiy and eventually to a third and so on. By the time a fourth base is reached, the anxiety over toddling of both mother and child has almost vanished." It is believed that Leo Durocher made this clear to Bobby Thomson before he smacked his miracle shot at the Polo Grounds in 1951.

Sports — individual or team — are generally considered as a "social safety valve" whereby hostility can be blown off. The theme is explored in several papers in this volume.[4] One of the important tasks of society is to provide devices which will allow the channeling of aggressive and sadistic impulses into nonviolent form. Play and work activities are generally regarded as methods of safely getting rid of aggressive feelings — of "blowing off steam." Thus, among other activities, the Romans provided gladiator and chariot spectacles, the Spaniards provided the bullfights, and the British and the Americans have provided football and other games.

Thus, according to this theory, through sports and other activities, the participant directly and the spectator vicariously express aggression and thereby "cleanse" themselves. Professional team owners, advertising the sale of tickets, urge people to buy a season ticket and yell out their aggression instead of taking it out on their families.[5] The word "kill" is used frequently in a ball game — "kill the clock," "kill the referee," "kill him." Cheerleaders shout, "Kill, kill, kill." Samuel B. Haddon's observations in defense of boxing appearing in the *Pennsylvania Medical Journal* are pertinent here:

> Hostility will seek expression in one way or another, and to provide young men in their late teens and early adult life a means of expressing their hostility in controlled combat, such as boxing, serves a very useful purpose not only for those who participate but the spectators as well, because they vicariously discharge their hostility. It is my firm belief that if boxing is not legally permitted, and should the number of participants and spectators be reduced, additional manifestations of hostility on our city streets by rowdyism, vandalism, mugging and other aggressive acts will markedly increase.[6]

Tommy Steele, the bright young star of the musical *Half a Sixpence,* says, "Soccer is wonderful — takes all the gripes out of you, and tones you up," and a newspaper columnist remarks, "Looking at Mr. Steele on stage or off reveals a good argument for soccer. He is a winning young man who doesn't seem to have a gripe in the world. If soccer is responsible for his sunny disposition, a lot of people would be better off for having a fling at it."

One person, perplexed at widespread vandalism, wrote to Ann Landers, newspaper counselor, for an explanation:

> I know you are not a psychiatrist but you seem to have a lot of answers. Can you please tell me what is wrong with people who destroy property?
>
> I am a junior in high school. All around me I see so much destruction in our school that I am dumbfounded. Last year money was raised to buy a new curtain for the stage in the auditorium. It cost almost $1,000. A few weeks ago somebody deliberately cut holes in the new curtain. I was sick when I saw it.
>
> Yesterday the teacher announced that a typewriter had been knocked off a desk and that it could never be fixed. Kids carve their initials on desks, tables, lockers, and write on the walls. They take seats apart in the auditorium and throw away the nuts and bolts. Why are people like this?

Ann Landers, although not a psychiatrist, gave the usual psychiatric explanation in her syndicated column:[7]

> People who get satisfaction out of destroying property are angry — at their parents, their teachers, the world and themselves. They are frustrated and unhappy. They feel they cannot create anything so they have an urge to destroy what others have created.
>
> The only solution is to find constructive outlets for these rebellious and unhappy ones. And retraining destructive people to rechannel their energies is far from easy.

William C. Menninger, the late President of the Menninger Foundation, said in 1948 in a speech on recreation and mental health before the National Recreation Congress:[8]

> The psychiatrist uses recreation extensively in the hospital program of his patients. For at least twenty years in our hospitals in Topeka, we have prescribed the specific types of recreational activities that we believe to be most suitable to alleviate specific symptoms of patients. The aim of the psychiatric prescription is to direct troublesome feelings into a socially approved outlet. In some personality disorders, the symptoms conspicuously express hostile feelings. Intense feelings which the patient harbors, that were probably directed originally toward some member of the family, have become displaced and may be expressed toward any person, or even any object in the environment. We have conducted many experiments in redirection of emotions. For instance, there was a patient who was very hostile to his father even though he maintained that he loved him. We drew a face on a punching bag and suggested that the image was that of his hated parent. Thereupon, he tied into the punching bag to the extent of his feelings. In another instance, practice on a driving range was enhanced by giving each golf ball the name of some disliked person. This particular patient had a long list of people he thoroughly disliked and, as one watched, it was apparent that varying amounts of energy were invested in each drive, depending on the intensity of the feelings towards the person whom the ball represented. In the majority of instances this direct approach is impossible, either because the hostility is too diffuse or because the patient feels too guilty to express his hostility in more subtle, unrecognized forms. He "blows off his steam" in a baseball or a volleyball game or a tournament with an obvious release of tension.

Some individuals, it has been said, have to direct at a single opponent "where the object of rage is obvious," while others prefer the more anonymous sport, such as football, where the target is several people and the aggression is relatively undisguised. Certain people apparently prefer to maintain more "civilization" over their native aggression and thus are inclined toward "the gentleman's game of tennis or golf." Left to their own play habits, boys turn to competitive sports when they are mature enough to give up war games. In adolescence, boys are more prepared for organized team and individual competition and here, sports provide another value, "an escape outlet for frightening and confusing sexual urges." With greater age, a person is able to step back a bit into the world of the observer, retaining competitor rights in more gentle games.

How valid is the theory that sports offer an opportunity to dissipate aggressive and sadistic impulses? Is aggression a matter of quality or quantity? Admittedly, it is better to beat someone at tennis than to use this same psychological and physical energy in a fist fight. But does one *replace* the other? Were the ancient Romans made better men as they viewed the early Christians thrown to the lions, or was their blood lust made all the worse?[10] Do people have a certain amount or quantity of aggression which can be dissipated, or is aggression a quality of the individual which colors all of his behavior? Do those who are not aggressive have any use for sports?[11]

Fritz Redl and David Wineman in their study of aggression, *Children Who Hate,*[12] observe that toys, gadgets and tools or the fascination of ongoing game and activity structures "bind" loose energies of children as efficiently as supervising adults might, and without such structure, especially when impulsivity runs high, even well-adjusted children sometimes have trouble containing themselves. Everyone, to some degree or other, requires "outside controls." Thus, a teacher leaving the room may find confusion and horseplay occurring between the end of a game and transition to the next one. In their work with aggressive children, Redl and Wineman observed:[13]

> Even after we had the children so far advanced that only mild structural supports were needed some of the time to keep them well functioning in a game, the end of that game or any interruption of structure would usually find them incapable of dealing with whatever submerged impulsivity had been kept in check. This means that an unusual amount of planning for adequate program structure was needed, that even when things were going well, the presence and relatedness to adult figures directly on the scene was indispensable. For a long time careful arrangements for other substitute controls had to be mapped out strategically to avoid total ego breakdown in transitional moments of their lives.

For some persons, significant outer structure must always be present in order to control impulses, and they must always have an outlet for their aggression. A person may get worn out chopping wood, but as soon as he is physically refreshed, he is ready to chop again. Individuals need some structure and some outlet all of the time. Aggression is not a matter of quantity that is once and forever discharged.[14] Redl and Wineman illustrate by the following incident in the life of a group of boys:[15]

> On the way home from school, in the station wagon there was some incipient scapegoating of Larry and also a good deal of aggressive throwing. This forced us to stop the wagon several times. After treats, following our arrival home, the counselors suggested a game of dodge ball in the backyard. The group is quite keen about this game, only they call it "murder ball." The game went well. Larry was forgotten and they did not select him unnecessarily as a target. The few rules which this game has — such as waiting until the "target" knows you are going to throw and admitting when you are hit, etc. — were well kept. There was obvious keen enjoyment of all the throwing. Their ability to stick to rules was especially amazing in view of the ugly mood they were in before the game. Just before dinner we stopped, and, as though by magic, the offensive pre-game disposition returned and Larry again became a target for group attack. He was accused of doing things wrong in the game which while it was going on were completely ignored — if they were not even being manufactured now. Even his "baby" behavior at school was hauled out as an issue. . . . Mike climbed up on the garage roof and started heaving debris at him and then fanned out to a more generalized "bombing" and Danny began lumbering to chase Larry around, calling him "Larry, the berry," a phrase which for some reason infuriates him and by this token is relished by the group as an insult.

In this volume, Alan Stone considers the psychological and social significance of football, a sport which permits (almost to the degree of boxing) the overt expression of aggression.[16] The significance of this contact sport for the developing boy is discussed, and the framework is structured around the concept of identity and superego formation and control of aggressive drives. Developmental changes in this respect are outlined.

A psychological study of the fantasies of varsity football players is then presented, comparing fantasies before and after a scrimmage and contrasting fantasy behavior and overt aggressive behavior as the latter is revealed in filmed material. Stone's study suggests that the concept of catharsis is oversimplified as it has been applied to the social situation. Opportunities for overt aggressive behavior do not result in a reduction of fantasy aggression, but rather are associated with several different vicissitudes, only one of which seems to be associated with a reduction of aggression.

Stone describes four patterns of aggressive behavior and fantasy. One type illustrates the outstanding football player who is neither unnecessarily aggressive on the field or in his fantasy. The second type consists of players who are unnecessarily destructive both on the field and in their fantasies, with overt aggression becoming a significant part of their personality structure. The third group consists of players who are less aggressive and less effective on the football field and show heightened fantasy aggression. The fourth group consists of relatively disturbed young men who are often inept in their football but who have intense fantasy aggression and who use football as an opportunity for venting uncontrollable aggressive impulses.

The next sport that we discuss in this section of the volume — basketball — has strictly American roots and differs from most sports in that it was deliberately conceived by James Naismith, an instructor at the YMCA College in Springfield, Massachusetts. He ostensibly sought to create some kind of competitive game that could be played indoors, still be exciting for players, and afford practice in teamwork.[17]

Do the motivations underlying basketball play differ from those of other sports? To Oreste Carvahlo of Brazil, a psychiatrist, just about every sport represents one or more of three drives: incestuous desires, the desire to return to the womb or, what amounts to the same thing, the sexual act itself. In a long paper published in 1960 he gives a sexual interpretation on basketball, swimming, diving, golf, water polo, hunting, catching popcorn in the mouth, cricket, croquet, discus and hammer throw, fishing, flinging stones from slingshots, hockey, skiing, trapshooting, quoits, billiards, volleyball, badminton, marbles, throwing hoops over bottles, fencing, boxing, tennis, table tennis, murder, war, "competition of any kind," roulette, rugby and leaping through fiery hoops (this list is incomplete).[18] "If it symbolizes coitus, any game will become popular," he says, and adds that the more apparent the symbol, the more popular the game. It is for this reason, he says, that "billiards have been dethroned by pool." He points out the extremely "obvious" sexual symbols involved in basketball (consider Naismith and his peach basket!) and other ball games. He tells us that "all aquatic sports symbolize the return to the womb." In fishing, hook and bait are masculine symbols, the fish's mouth, feminine; but when caught by a net (feminine), the fish becomes masculine. In field events, distance becomes the feminine symbol to be ravished by the jumper or thrower. In racing, it is the finish line. The symbolism is obvious in "passing through a hoop . . . particularly a fiery hoop" which alway "diverts the human being."

In the same vein poet and essayist T. H. Ferril in *The Rocky Mountain Herald* commented about football, "Football obviously arises out of the Oedipus complex. Love of mother dominates the entire ritual."[19] He calls attention to the curious opening ceremony which is reminiscent of ancient phallic rituals, and which "begins with colorful processions of musicians and semi-nude virgins." Each virgin "carries a wand of shining metal . . . with which she interweaves her body in most intricate gyrations." The "millions of worshippers" who attend these weekly ceremonies "are seeking an outlet from sex frustrations in anticipation of violent masochism and sadism about to be enacted by a highly trained priesthood of young men." Over the center's "back quarters hovers the 'quarter-back.' The transposition of 'back quarters' to 'quarterback' is easily explained by the Adler school. . . . Actually, of course, the quarterback symbolizes the libido, combining two instincts, namely (1) Eros, which strives for even closer union and (2) the instinct for destruction of anything which lies in the path of Eros." In describing the oedipal conflict in football, he says, "The stadiums without exception are dedicated to Alma Mater, Dear Mother. (Notre Dame and football are synonymous.) "

Willard Manus, who writes in our volume on basketball, focuses on the social aspects of the sport.[20] He looks at the sport from a nonanalytic vantage point and gives us the benefit of the perspective of a social theorist. Of course, what he says about basketball applies to other sports in the same way that many of the psychoanalytic interpretations on one sport in this volume may apply to other sports.

America is a country, Manus says, which takes its basketball seriously, as it does many sports, and kids become serious about it at a young age. They learn early that basketball can be a means to an end. The gifted basketball player can expect to be well rewarded for his talents, for we have developed a caste system that favors him to the exclusion of the average participant. This is an inevitable result of modern-day society, which has brought about a fusion of work and play.

"How can you be proud of a losing team?" Manus says that America's mania for winning has brought about a corruption of sporting principles. Colleges recruit players to build winning teams. With recruiting comes tampering and, as we have seen over the past two decades, the fixing of games. Thirty-two players were arrested in the first major postwar scandal of 1951 alone. The big business ethics of the game prompted them to steal. The game, he says, continues on a dollar-merry whirl.[21]

Those who participate in basketball today do so for various reasons — depending on the nature of the game, the kind of athletes they are and the things they hope to get out of it. But too often and with too many, basketball offers little pleasure. From the top down, basketball is aggressive. And this aggressiveness which basketball has bred, Manus says, has infected the whole American scene. Fairness and playing according to the rules help in superego formation, that is, the development of a conscience, and without fair play, a sport is no longer considered a sport but rather, a racket.

FOOTNOTES

1. Ardrey, R.: *The Territorial Imperative: A Personal Inquiry into the Animal Origins of Property and Nations.* New York, Atheneum, 1966; Goodrich, F. W.: Drive for Possession. *Medical Opinion & Review,* January, 1967, p. 38. Konrad Lorenz, ecologist, says: "If we know the territorial centers of two conflicting animals . . . all other things being equal, we can predict, from the place of encounter, which one will win: the one that is nearer home." Lorenz, K. Z.: *On Aggression.* New York, Harcourt, Brace & World, 1966. See also Tinbergen, N.: Aggression and fear in the normal sexual behaviour of some animals, in Rosen, I. [ed.]: *The Pathology and Treatment of Sexual Deviation.* London and New York, Oxford, 1964, p. 3. Sports dopesters, too, give the home team an edge.
2. P. 400.
3. Freud, S.: *Totem and Taboo (1913),* in Standard Edition, Vol. 4. London, Hogarth Press, 1955,
4. E.g., Reider, N.: *Preanalytic and Psychoanalytic Theories of Play and Games,* p. 13; Beisser, A.: *Tennis,* p. 450; Stone, A.: *Football,* p. 419.
5. In one cartoon, a woman says to her husband swinging a golf club, "The ball, I presume, is me." *New Yorker,* June 20, 1964, p. 29.
6. See also McIntosh, P. C.: *Sport in Society*. London, C. A. Watts & Co., Ltd., 1963, p. 53.
7. Copyright 1965, Publishers Newspaper Syndicate.
8. Recreation and Mental Health, presented at Omaha, Nebraska, September 28, 1948, and published in *Recreation,* November, 1948.
9. In a college newspaper, one student protesting the Vietnam war complained that his fellow students were paying too much time to athletics and little or no attention to national and international political events. Satirically, he hypothesized that those students who prefer football — an aggressive, slam-bang, man-killing type of sport — also would favor a get-tough, "give-'em-hell" position toward the Communists. Since baseball games are rather lengthy affairs which often extend into extra innings and require a great deal of rear-end fortitude from the spectators, he figured that those expressing a preference for this sport which combines a degree of physical activity and discussions among participants and umpires would also enjoy long, protracted brushfire wars, followed by long, protracted negotiations. He believed that those who expressed a preference for basketball would favor a complete American withdrawal from Vietnam. Many aspects of the game, he said, obviously indicate a desire to withdraw or retreat. It is noted that

after each basket all players run at top speed to the opposite end of the court. Also, all physical contact and violence are prohibited and subject to strong disciplinary measures. Finally, it is not without significance that the game is played on a floor called a court — obviously related to respect for the rule of law as opposed to force.

In concluding, the writer said he would be interested in knowing whether football fans can be converted into basketball fans, and if such a conversion is possible, if they would modify their aggressive attitudes in the area of foreign policy. If such a "double" conversion is possible, those who advocate peace at any price might do well to consider a means for increasing interest in basketball throughout the country. Also, he wondered whether foreign policy attitudes may be subject to seasonal changes such as those that accompany the changes in sports.

So much for satire. The crucial question remains: how valid is the theory that sports offer an opportunity to dissipate aggressive and sadistic impulses?

10. Consider: "Furious fans rioted at an international football [soccer] game here [Lima, Peru] and 300 to 500 persons were stamped and trampled to death and suffocated in the panic. At least 500 others were injured in what is believed to be history's worst sports event disaster. The toll of dead may go higher." *AP news-release,* May 25, 1964.
11. It should be noted that a satisfactory phenomenology of aggression has not yet been established, and much of the confusion could be eliminated by more precise use of terms. The terms aggression, hostility and destructiveness are often used interchangeably although they surely designate psychologically different contents. The rebel and the delinquent, for example, are "aggressive" in different ways. See Lederer, W.: *Dragons, Delinquents, and Destiny: An Essay on Positive Superego Functions.* New York, Int Univs, 1964.
12. Redl, F. and Wineman, D.: *Children Who Hate.* Glencoe, Free Press, 1951.
13. *Ibid.*
14. Norman Reider in his paper "Preanalytic and Psychoanalytic Theories of Play and Games" states: "It is generally held that play and games discharge aggression, either as catharsis or sublimation. . . . I doubt that 'repressed' hostility is drained in play. Perhaps 'suppressed' hostility can easily find partial discharge in play and games. Second, it is uncertain whether all cathexes can be displaced by derivatives and thereby find complete discharge in sublimation. . . . Moreover, if hostility is discharged via play, it cannot be any complete discharge, or why the need for repetition? Why must the play be indulged in over and over if hostility is fully discharged in Play?" *Supra* at p. 13.

Helen Ross observes: "Therapy with children called 'play therapy' misled some into thinking that play in itself was therapeutic, overlooking the necessity of the verbalization of insight." Ross, H.: The teacher game. *Psychoanal Stud Child, 20:*288, 1965.

Bruno Bettelheim, writing on modern art, has some pertinent things to say: "To the psychoanalyst it is an appalling story how progressive education, and art teaching in particular, has responded to the insights of psychoanalysis. It is a response that shows an equal confusion both about art teaching and psychoanalysis. It is especially hard to see how art teachers came to harbor the notion that to give the unconscious free rein can be of value, either as education, aesthetics or therapy. To those interested in so-called art therapy, I might add that there is hardly a human interaction that cannot lend itself to therapeutic use: some priests serve as therapists for troubled people, but this hardly makes religion therapeutic. Some art teachers endowed with personal skill have had a great therapeutic impact on this or that student while teaching him art; but so have some football coaches, and we do not class football as a therapeutic activity.

"So much has been made of art education's freeing the emotions that I feel I should say a bit more about this idea of its therapeutic potential. It should be obvious, for example, that if artistic efforts could cure emotional disturbance, then the greater the artistic achievement, the more likely should be the cure. I need only remind you of Van Gogh, whose artistic achievement was certainly great but who, as he reached the height of artistic achievement, first cut off his ear, and then committed suicide. His artistic progress neither led to a schizophrenic break nor did it prevent one. . . . Thus it is not the outpouring of the unconscious, but rather the mastery of unconscious tendencies, the subjecting of creative ability to the greatest aesthetic discipline which alone makes for works of art. . . ." Bettelheim, B.: Art: A personal vision, in *Art,* Symposium published by the Museum of Modern Art, New York, 1964, p. 41.

15. *Supra* note 12.
16. P. 419. "Football is a game of violence, and people like violence," says Coach Vince Lombardi of the Green Bay Packers. *Supra* part 3, at p. ——. See also Smith, M.: Bad boy of the pros. *Life,* October 22, 1965. Numerous writers have been impressed with the many symbolic meanings represented by the game of football. For a humorous but by no means absurd discussion, see Ferril, T. H.: Freud, football and the marching virgins. *Reader's Digest,* November 1961, pp. 152-54, condensed from the *Rocky Mountain Herald,* December 28, 1957.
17. Grombach, J. V.: *The 1964 Olympic Guide.* New York, Avon Books, 1964, p. 131. For a man of his stature, comparatively little has been written about James Naismith, who by title was a Christian minister, a medical doctor, and a teacher. One of the few documents is an unpublished thesis by Jack G. Hamming, *A Historical Sketch of Doctor James Naismith,* University of Kansas, 1962. This study points out that when James Naismith was nine, both his mother and father died, within a period of three days. He went to live with his uncle and maternal grandmother. She too "left" him; she died three years later. He felt guilty about attending school, and felt that he should help with the burden put upon his uncle. He worked in lumber camps, but after two years of this, he had a change of mind and returned to high school. He entered McGill University in Montreal, in 1884, with the thought of becoming a minister. It was here that he first came into contact with organized athletics. He became a member of the football team.

Athletics and gymnastics at that time were considered by many people as inventions of the devil, intended to lead young men astray. Naismith felt that if athletics had power to attract young men, that power should be used to attract them to better ways of living. The idea of athletics and clean living stayed in his mind. How to unite the two was his problem. Then, in 1887, an incident occurred which changed his career from ministry to that of teacher of physical education. One day during football practice at McGill, something went wrong, and the guard next to Naismith let loose a stream of profanity. Suddenly the player stopped and exclaimed, "Excuse me, Jim, I'm sorry." Naismith suddenly felt that clean living could be achieved *through* athletics. The incident set him to thinking, and after talking to the Y.M.C.A. secretary he decided to go to Springfield College, then known as the College for Christian Workers and later the Y.M.C.A. College. He did not, however, leave McGill immediately. He graduated from McGill in 1887 with an A.B. degree, became an ordained minister, and stayed on there for three years, 1887-1890, as an instructor in gymnastics, and as a preacher.

In 1890 Naismith entered the Y.M.C.A. College in Springfield, Massachusetts. After one year at Springfield he was appointed to teach a physical education class of prospective Y.M.C.A. secretaries. No problems arose as long as he could take his class out of doors for exercise, but when winter came, his worries began. There was no question that formal gymnastics did not appeal to the students. Dr. Luther H. Gulick, Head of the Department of Physical Training of the College, was also aware of the problem, and was determined to do something about it. He put the task squarely up to Naismith.

Naismith, then 30, began to recall his boyhood games, and to study the problem in that light. The following is an account of how Naismith arrived at the game of basketball: "I recalled from my boyhood in the lumber regions of Canada that when we played the game called Duck on a Rock, a hurled ball might send the 'duck' farther, but that a tossed ball was far more accurate. The ball, I decided, must be soft enough not to harm the players, yet it must be large enough to be seen, and not to be concealed. Like 'Duck on a Rock,' the goal should be one that could not be rushed, and that the ball could not be slammed through. This called for a goal with a horizontal opening, high enough so that the ball would have to be tossed into it, rather than being thrown." Naismith's favorite game was lacrosse, and this suggested the original position of the players.

In 1895 Naismith left Springfield to accept a position as Physical Education Director in the Denver, Colorado Y.M.C.A. He served there three years until 1898, and during this time he also completed study toward a degree in medicine. In 1898, he was awarded an M.D. degree from the Gross Medical College, Colorado. In 1898, at the age of 37, he accepted a position at the University of Kansas.

Naismith often jokingly stated that he was hired at the University of Kansas because he could pray. Chancellor Snow of the University called his friend Amos Alonzo Stagg at Chicago asking for a recommendation of someone to head up the Department of Physical Education — someone who could lead the prayer during chapel exercises. Naismith was just the man. He came to the University of Kansas in 1898, and remained active there until his retirement in 1937. Under the supervision of Naismith, basketball caught on very quickly at the University of Kansas. The Kansas University Weekly made the following report of its progress: "Everyone who is at all interested in athletics is now talking basketball. Yet it does not stop here. Those who hitherto have manifested no interest, in any sports of skill and strength, seem now to be enthusiastic over the new game. It is talked at the club; it is discussed in the corridors; it is practiced and played in the gymnasium and on the campus. Even the professors have become actively interested in the game and are giving their time of recreation over to this pastime." Kansas University Weekly Newspaper, Feb. 4, 1899, p. 1, c. 4.

Along with his basketball classes, Naismith taught hygiene and kinesiology courses at the University of Kansas, and he also taught fencing and gymnastics with a great deal of enthusiasm. He has made a lasting impression at the University (its basketball teams have annually ranked foremost in the nation), and upon the world (basketball is probably the only truly worldwide sport).

Naismith died in 1939, stricken by a cerebral hemorrhage. His memory is cherished by all who knew him. One of the two large boulevards on the University of Kansas campus is named in his honor. The Basketball Hall of Fame, recently built at Springfield College, has a large bronze statue of Naismith in the center foreground. In 1961 a stamp was published which paid tribute to him. Hamming, J. G.: *A Historical Sketch of Doctor James Naismith.* Unpub. thesis, University of Kansas, 1962.

18. Carvalho, O.: Psicanalise do futebol e de outros jogos (Psychoanalysis of soccer and other games. *Hospital (Rio), 57:*109, 1960, reported in Coogan, J. P.: Take me out to no ball game. *SK&F Psychiatric Reporter,* March-April 1964, no. 13, p. 13.
19. Ferril, T. H.: Frued, football and the marching virgins. Condensed in *Reader's Digest, 79:* 152, Nov. 1961.
20. P. 435.
21. Sportswriter Paul Gallico's "Farewell to Sport" is a bitter indictment of the perversion of sports. See also Cousins, N.: Football and the college. *Saturday Review,* September 28, 1963, p. 36; Glansville, B.: The sportsman as victim. *Punch,* September 11, 1963, p. 366; Mallalieu, J. P. W.: Sport in the Modern World. *New Statesman,* November 8, 1958, p. 638; Manus, W.: Basketball: The fix is still on. *The Nation,* January 9, 1960, p. 32; Youngert, E.: College athletics. *The Atlantic,* October 1958, p. 35.

THE DEVELOPMENT OF BALL GAMES

ADRIAN STOKES

ONE COULD ARGUE THAT games, a substitute for warfare, have become one of modern warfare's opponents: sprung from Homeric conflict, they recall a very old-fashioned fighting, the pitting of one body with another. Greek athletes in classical times battled nude. At the Olympic and other panhellenic games, none the less, there were races for men in armor. It is significant that these were among the few events for which Spartans were encouraged to enter. Whereas more than one competitive game was played by youths at Sparta itself, the Spartan authorities were not otherwise in favor of such triumphant exertion with no killing of the state's enemies in view; nor were the Lancastrian nor the Tudor governments in England where football was repeatedly proscribed. The church has been hostile to popular sports until recently; the best time for games is Sunday.

It is obvious that considerable aggression may be discharged innocuously by games and that a corresponding masochism achieves an outlet also. The loser, we say, is beaten, and very often by himself as well as by his opponent. During any close lawn tennis match one is likely to observe what appears to be a compensatory losing that balances luck, even dishonesty or hard-won gain; for instance, the player who finally breaks through his opponent's service often immediately loses his own; that is to say, his opponent effects at once a similar breakthrough. He, for his part, has been inspired, in that guilt was assuaged by his previous loss. Each point in a hard match epitomizes perhaps a triumph, perhaps disaster, disappointment, frustration and other emotions which, in turn, influence subsequent play. At each turn the player tends to be dominated by a different inner object; for games are a continuous test of qualities in a fluctuating confidence: the opponent senses and seeks to redouble humiliation and doubt. No less than children, adults at play harp on the vagaries of life and death. In ball games, the context is always the one of potency, often the cover for anxiety concerning the good inner object.

In a paper on the psychology of sport — the only piece from the literature I have been able to discover — Helene Deutsch refers to a patient who suffered in infancy from a recurring dream of a castrating, clutching hand.[1] At the age of fifteen a phobia emerged which Deutsch calls a kind of agoraphobia: the patient feared that a ball with which he or someone else was playing might fall on him and either mortally injure him or make him an idiot. A short time after the phobia had disappeared, the patient developed great keenness for ball games; displacing inner danger outwards, he awaited the ball in a state of tension, to master it. "The sport situations," wrote Helene Deutsch, "provide most ideal conditions for release from fear, namely, expectant readiness, contempt of the danger which threatens, a trial of the subject's own powers and rational attack and defence." She does not mention what is perhaps no less important, the repeated endurance of symbolic castration, as when bowled or caught out in cricket, and the power thereupon sometimes developed in the terms, perhaps, of team or collective effort to resurrect the sense of potency after smashing defeat (since considerable luck in games fluctuates at great speed as well as from year to year), for which the English have of late been renowned in wider fields.

The ability to endure defeat and extensive, unexpected tribulation as well as victory with undiminished grace has for some time been considered the essence of sportsmanship. A myth underlying the team games developed by the British proposes in the face of innumerable, heart-rending contests that there is no such thing as irreparable loss if one genuinely plays for, identifies oneself with, the team; nor consequently, is there victory for all time. I think this may help to explain the frequent antipathy between artist and sportsman; it would be in accordance with the standpoint that those who suffer from what is called artistic temperament should not always be good losers. Foreigners were once thought to suffer loss and enjoy success badly; hence, perhaps, the confusion at one time in more insular minds between artists and foreigners, since the artist, of course, must be distinguished in this matter by his steady, undimmed sense of loss and by the omnipotence of his answering re-creation. So far as it is fostered on sport, the English ego-ideal has little use for either. Thus, I am not to be much elated by man-made surroundings, the hidden philosophy seems to urge; I prefer to have some pretty beast to govern, whether in the form of vulgar building or chaotic avenues. Indeed, let there be the recurrent, though not invariable, sense of contingent acerbity or defeat since it helps me to pay off the sense of absolute loss or absolute cruelty without employing a manic defence; my counter can be good-humored.

A liking for understatement is perhaps not unconnected. However that may be, it is remarkable that the individual movements of team games in contrast with athletics are in themselves rarely of more beauty, except in cricket, than those of a man driving a car; grace is at low premium in any of the English styles, whereas athletics once inspired classical Greek sculpture. I myself have the feeling that the psychology of ugliness is even more subtle than the psychology of beauty. In tune with the healthy catharsis of aggression implicit in organized games, some reserved or even pretentious kinds of ugliness, an external moderate manifestation of aggression, of the unconverted sense of destruction, as well as a share in beauty, seem to be not only well tolerated, but actively needed by the ordinary man under modern conditions. Moreover, I think that as well as avoiding art, modern team games can serve as a substitute for it, being in some ways a parallel re-creation, though composed largely of a crude genital sublimation that ignores the sustained feminine receptivity whose collaboration is needed for aesthetic experience. Games must dramatize the unrhythmic chanciness of reality; a large element of luck is essential to their wide appeal; the player makes trial of his good fortune as well as of his skill; he is "chancing his hand," his potency and his power to compel.

Everyone will agree that the issue of potency provides constant and various libidinal themes in ball games: a total inhibition of any desire to exercise dexterity in this or other ways must be canvassed in psychoanalysis not only from the side of inhibited aggression but, as Melanie Klein indicated in a paper of 1923, from the side of inhibited libido. I want, however, to suggest that the libidinal content of some ball games is by no means genital only, that the more various the libidinal outlets they normally offer, the more civilized are the games, the better they contribute to culture.

Very little is known about team games in the past. Polo has undoubtedly the most ancient direct descent. There will have always been street games of ball and games derived from them in wider spaces, played by adolescents: that is, ball pastimes which were not merely the occasion for free fights of one district with another as in the instance of the old football. It is likely that cricket is the only popular survivor in this country of such pastimes with bat and ball that were indulged in by girls as well as by boys. I class cricket with street games, with tennis, with the many derivations from tennis, because I find that all these games have long afforded a notable outlet for pregenital as well as for genital drives. That is not to deny that the genital issue is predominant. Our games serve to reflect the emotional alternations which are typical of the adolescent in the process of controlling and directing the rush of genital feelings; the quick change, for instance, from active to passive, from attack to defence, from feelings of omnipotence to those of lurid disaster. They reflect also the huge patience to be learned in our civilization for the attainment of propitious genital satisfaction. Thus, the rather eccentric game of croquet provides for the strict hierophant a sado-masochistic alteration, now as the father enlarging upon the frustration of the offspring's hope, now as the son prevented by the father from passing even one hoop. A very valuable feature, all will agree, is the catharsis in modern games — it is more a catharsis than a sublimation — of aggression, controlled by the superego and harmonized with the libidinal content. To be any good, one must freely want to smack the ball. As in war, the aggressive component, already contingent perhaps in the very fact of taking violent exercise, is more apparent than the libidinal.

Now for the libidinal. Whereas in hide-and-seek there is only one "home," the adolescent search for objects should be more adventurous. In team games "home" is not to be won but to be defended against all, by the father in fact, while the boy seeks to conquer farther afield. At the same time the boy is allowed to exercise this paternal role. These games reenact the feelings of the male participants particularly in the internalized oedipus situation while blurring the sense of absolute loss — the sense of loss in the depressive position described by Melanie Klein, which I have mentioned already in contradistinction with ballgames, as a positive spur to art — while moderating in the pursuit of a limited outward aggression the superego's cruelty. Generally speaking, the paternal role, at the center of many games, is defensive. The batsman, not the bowler, is the king of cricket. He combines the positions of both father and son whose prototypes are, for the first, a punishing, bearded giant, W. G. Grace, for the second, a compact, swift little man, the young Hobbs, Hendren, Bradman. In his later years the epithet most usually applied to Hobbs was "majestic." Hammond, another master, was a "majestic" bat, notable particularly for his forceful shots off the back, defensive foot. I think it is of considerable importance that such a batsman wins hero-worship from millions in this country, through several generations. The authoritarian or superego aspect of the great batsman is much tempered by his boy's role and by the modest paternal aim of his defensive actions. As autocrats go he is benignant, even-tempered considering his authority, his openness to attack, possessing much elegance and little frenzy. Indeed, it is because the inelegant Bradman was so seemingly mechanical that his ruthlessness appears foreign to cricket.

Doubtless, most cricketing stories are but stories: sometimes, in view of an almost startling feebleness, one is aware of nothing but the deeper inspiration. Thus, it is said with relish of another idol, Compton, that once when well set he blocked six half-volleys delivered by a distinguished elderly bowler, and that he did so in the interests of his (the bowler's) dignity. But usually the bowler, more primitive son than father, backed by his brothers in the field, is a less complicated figure of far less imaginative appeal in spite of the fact that it is the stronger bowling, rather than the stronger batting, side that wins matches as a rule, in spite of the fact that every change of style and of tactics has been dictated throughout the history of cricket by the resource of bowlers, if we except a short period in which W. G. Grace almost drove fast bowling from the field. The batsman, beautifully weaponed, faces attack as might a priestly autocrat who reigns until the moment he shows a physical flaw; he is then cut off in his prime: while he remains he personifies also youth, powers that flow freely, that find the gaps between those who would school him. Of course, every player bats and every batsman in his turn fields, some bowl. Identifications multiply between teammates especially, bringing into the game not only homosexual motifs but also, as I shall try to argue, an all-embracing element linked with life at the breast.

When football teams canter out of the natal tunnel beneath a stand, the crowds applaud, surrendering to them the field of play. Then each team defends the goal at its back; in front is the new land, the new woman, whom they strive to possess in the interest of preserving the mother inviolate, in order, as it were, to progress from infancy to adulthood. At the same time, the defensive role is the father's; he opposes the forward youth of the opposition. From the point of view of the attack, it is beyond question that a genital aggressiveness characterizes ball games whose players possess feet, hands, stick, bat with which to manoeuvre the ball, the semen. More generally, the ball is itself the phallus. When contact is made, the ball, no less than foot, bat, racquet, will be the instrument of intended phallic splendor, in more general terms, of genital deftness, male and female. That is said from a libidinal point of view. On the other hand, it is obvious that considerable aggression is used in hitting, kicking and flinging the ball; indeed, here lies the principal opportunity for the catharsis of aggression since no one will suggest that this hitting of the ball expresses as a rule an attack upon the genital of the hitter, though it frequently represents such an attack upon the ball's sender, a problem arises concerning the fusion of libidinal and aggressive outlets insofar as the opposing instincts are separately expended, as well as fused, in one context. I think that in organized games, unlike blood sports, we rarely encounter *as a dominant theme* so blended a fusion as we call sadism. My impression is that whereas an overt, though of course disciplined, aggression laps all games, some of the more hidden satisfactions are at most only tinged by a particularized negative force; and that this may well be true for the majority of cultural activities at their best.

Now, if playing with ball, if timing, the coordination of muscle with eye, if swift opportunism, the seizure of an opening, are manifest exercises in phallic deftness, control of masturbation, particularly in isolated play, is no less evident. I am reminded that as long ago as the second century, Galen, renowned physician and moralist, wrote a treatise called *Exercise with the Small Ball.* But we should not forget that the traditional inventor of ball games is the Homeric princess, Nausicaa, whose play with her maidens can be interpreted as nuptial practice also. Her game was catch, doubtless the clear clasping with both hands above the head as we still see it performed during the barefoot playing with golden apples of the princess and her attendants in the ballet *Fire Bird.* (Egyptian paintings at

Beni-Hassan, *circa* 2500 B.C., depict games of catch. These performers also are women.) The cricketer dismissed by a catch suffers symbolic castration; nevertheless, it is often less painful to be caught than bowled; there is even a sense of fulfilment if the hit has been hard, away from the slips and wicket-keeper. Nausicaa's embrace is not to be despised, but she holds on too long; does she let go, one is aware that the pleasure has been acute, apart form the relief.

In an account of a cricket match, one may read that so-and-so hooked the ball straight down the throat of square-leg (a fieldsman). Before the change in the soccer offside rule in the nineteen-twenties, one could read very often of halfbacks feeding the ball to the forwards. In cricket, a batsman is said sometimes to farm the bowling, to nurse his partner; he arranges so that his partner feeds on the potentially beneficent enemy semen only. Such an episode emphasizes that in other games as well, players are not only threatened by, but are dependent for their own prosperity upon, the ball activities of the opposing side in addition to their own. The one side serves up bowling, for instance, to the other; the batsman who leaves alone dangerous rising balls outside the off stump and despatches the well pitched-up ball to the boundary, an act that nourishes his score, has made judicious selection between good and bad breast. This is not said to the exclusion of a genital interpretation. The more civilized the game, the more varied the combination of libidinal targets in a single, neat episode, similar to a work of art. In the true cult of games, a significance will be enjoyed beyond the more immediate satisfactions drawn from rivalry and exhibitionism, aggressive and genital, whose content alone would often be dire. What interests me most is that the sum of so many modes of identification between the players contributes to the formation of a breast relationship by which they merge themselves with the game itself, in the manner that is more typical of a corporate ideal. There is a profound unity, in cricket at least, of which players and seasoned spectators are aware. It is not only the unity of action that may exist in any parable of changing fortune, but also a unity of place. A cricket match can be a most exciting contest; yet those writers who with wearisome exaggeration concentrate on this point are the first to insist helplessly that cricket is more than a game, since they would point to some constant element that feeds every dramatic episode.

I trust I need not dwell on the fact that the state of the pitch and the degree of moisture in the air determine conditions for the game from hour to hour. Rain in the night is a cricketing event of the first importance, and so on; the game is enriched by the weather, by some degree of fitfulness from which in adult life we had best learn to contrive nourishment. Not long after it was discovered that Nottingham marl could make a wicket almost indestructable, its extreme use was officially discouraged. A pitch

not only an outlet for aggressive energy in harmony with a genital symbolism, for animal spirits as they are called, for exercise; but also, in the wake of the new order, a libidinal bond with the school whose body they explored thereby. In a still wider sense both teams share an absorption of the mother as do the players in a squash court. Is there a more subtle improvement upon warfare than such games? Surely they exceed in emotional subtlety intellectual games: chess, for instance, a mimic warfare like medieval football or the joust.

The first manifest consideration in the evolution of Association football, or soccer, is likely to have been the value of clothing whose interests could not be reconciled with mimic warfare. Then there was the hardness of the playground. The Charterhouse boys, I have said, had no ground for play but the cloisters. Westminster boys were similarly placed. It is directly from these two schools that the dribbling game — note the adjective — soccer was evolved. It is said that the rules of the principal winter game, whether at Eton, Winchester or Harrow, were determined by the shape of the field in each case. This applies, of course, to the Eton wall game as well. Old public school boys soon founded clubs. After considerable debate and after secessions, both rugger and soccer had been codified much as we know them today by the sixties and seventies of the last century. Popularization was extremely rapid.

Team games have elaborated the genital symbolism of earlier games; in unifying this variety they have enlarged an all-embracing element, a principle of nurture more particularly associated with what I have called the architectural games which alone were organized in every detail.

Amid many alterations in the laws of cricket, the length of the pitch, twenty-two yards, an agricultural unit of measurement, the chain, is constant. This agricultural link may recall the magical foundation on which fortune was once believed to depend. I hope I may have said something that will help to explain the homage of the spectators who approach and stare silently at these twenty-two yards during the lunch interval at Lord's. Even in so ugly an urban ground as the Oval we may become aware of a telluric significance to which potency of all the players, whether on the field or blazered in the pavilion, has contributed. What once was a preliminary religious observance on a separate day at Olympia, or at Siena for the palio, is now immured, part and parcel of the contest.[3]

FOOTNOTES

1. Deutsch, H.: A contribution to the psychology of sports. *Int. J. of Psycho-Anal.* 7:223, 1926, reprinted *supra* at p. 91.
2. Cf. Melanie Klein's *Contribution to Psycho-Analysis 1921-45* (London, 1948), particularly the Oedipus papers of 1928 and 1945.
3. Unlike football, it is probable that from an early time cricket was a game for boys as well

as for adults: it continued to be so — Byron played for Harrow against Eton — and doubtless provided one model for the development of other team games. Cricket had already been accepted in some exalted circles of the seventeenth century, had become a national game, cultivated by the aristocracy in that far from democratic age, a taste acquired, it has been suggested, during the Civil War and Commonwealth at a time when some more expensive sports were in abeyance. Keenness for the game during nearly two hundred years was to be bound up with the huge gambling for which a match was the occasion. The yeoman cricketer could obtain heroic stature in the company of his overlords under summer skies, without much risk to life or limb. This was something to set against, as well as set beside, the heroic eventualities at Agincourt.

It is difficult to realize today that a hundred and fifty years ago London was one of the most beautiful cities in Europe, and that for several hundred years the English people had been accounted by the majority of visitors to be the most brutal, both in their manners and in their occasional sports (see *German Travellers in England,* 1400-1800, W. D. Robson-Scott, 1953) . Maybe cricket had a part in fostering not only the controlled though often rough aggression of other team games -- a habitual catharsis that sweetens the temper — but our national, unaesthetic, homely cult in screening the danger of absolute loss with the easy acceptance of conditional loss.

Some believe the origin of the wicket to be the detachable gate to a fold, used on down turf. It is very uncertain, however, whether the early game had a wicket, even in the seventeenth century. Up to 1750 or so the ball was rolled along the ground, bowled in fact. The bat was curved like a hockey stick. At one time in some districts, though more likely universally, there was a hole in the ground where the stumps now stand. A batsman was dismissed either by a catch or by a run-out if a fielder put the ball in the hole before the batsman could jam in his bat. Hurt to fieldsmen's hands may have brought about the substitution of a stump for the hole: soon there were two stumps with a lintel upon them, the forerunner of bails; but, whereas the batsman could now be bowled by the ball hitting either stump, he was not bowled by a ball passing between them. It is obvious that the new gap between the stumps was not equivalent to the previous hole in the ground; the stumps provide a new phallic image as they guard the hole which for a time survived between them. They are extensions of the batsman's defensive bat, of the father's phallus which is knocked away and broken when his prowess fails. Cricket became a play more various than that race to occupy a hole which is so grimly disguised by the bleak slow-motion of golf. The long to-and-fro of cricket, often protracted over several days, illustrates very well a point I have tried to make concerning modern team games as evolved by the English, namely that, while allowing considerable catharsis for aggression, there is the tendency to mask any extreme outcome of basic themes, though an eventual winner be passionately desired in this test of potency, of good fortune, by fan and player alike: to withhold, then, any extreme outcome from the oedipal situation and from the sense of loss, particularly perhaps the emergence of the superego's overweening cruelty. Today cruelty is no more sporting than is art.

"I, Kil-Roa, ask this: Should this new game, tiki-taki-toa, be tabu or not tabu? That is the question!"

BASEBALL

THOMAS A. PETTY

BASEBALL IS A FATHER AND SON'S GAME. Its basic motivation, I believe, lies in the pristine facets of the father and son relationship. The scope of this chapter is limited primarily to a study of the plot of the game itself and the player's role and with which the fan identifies.[1] It is concerned only secondarily with the consideration of the personality of the player or the fan himself. A strong suspicion is held that for the fan and the player there is a basic fantasy implicit in the structure of the game, and further that this fantasy is realized by each player and fan, that is, winner and loser alike in some measure. Through the specifications of the field of play and the rules and regulations of the game, the realization of the fantasy is simultaneously insured, limited and sanctioned. The discovery of the fantasy is based upon a consideration of the features of the game, its evolution and emergence as an institution of American life, its myth of origin, relevant observations of children's play, and pertinent mythology and archaeology. All are viewed in a way comparable to the day residue of a dream and the associations. The interpretation of the fantasy underlying baseball rests upon the psychoanalytic knowledge of play and Freud's hypothesis concerning the primal horde. Although not explicitly stated, my own experience and associations are implicit in the fabric of the study.

In circumscribing the study, it may be well to specify what it is not. First, baseball, like other forms of play, may be readily utilized by the unconscious of the participant and spectator to express a broad range of unconscious fantasies. This purpose is easily accomplished by the symbolic use of the paraphernalia of the game: bats, balls, gloves and their pockets, home plate and other bases, foul lines, fences, uniforms, etc. Most of the fantasies are not specific to the game and may as readily find expression through other play, games and sports and their accouterments. Although of interest and pertinent to a broad study of the game, these fantasies will be of only incidental concern here. Thus what baseball shares in common with other forms of play will not be a particular consideration of this study.

Second, this is not a clinical paper. Obviously the validation of my hypothesis would be the discovery in individual patients of the externalization of similar psychic conflict in the roles of the baseball player and in the plot of the game. I do not choose to follow this course here for reasons which I hope will be made clear in the following discourse. In addition, I believe that the hypothesis is supported by other impressive evidence which serves my purpose in conducting a reflective study.

The psychological complexities of the personalities of the fan and the player would necessitate too elaborate an exposition if they were to be unequivocally contributory to this study. Baseball is a tension-action game which does not easily yield its essence to verbal translation. To the extent to which the true fan or player is gratified by the action of the game, dreams and other forms of substitute gratification, which are the usual materials of study, are unnecessary. Frustration in the game, which would serve as the stimulus for the dream and substitute gratifications, tends to find expression and surcease through the use of other symbolic representation than baseball. A simple example may best illustrate:

> An adolescent ball player with ambitions to be a home run hitter had not had a base hit in two games. Frustrated and angered, he dreamed: He was driving golf balls straight down the fairway two hundred yards and more. His associations made clear that the immediately pertinent meaning was that the player wished to hit the baseball as frequently and as easily, as far as he hit even short drives on the golf course. A baseball travelling the same distance as a short drive of two hundred yards would be a home run every time in every baseball park in the country. The unconscious meaning of the home run for him was expressed in an earlier association and was not immediately interpretable.[2]

The incompatibility of sanctioned gratification and dreaming was aptly expressed by a young ball player who intuitively grasped the significance of the question as to whether he dreamed about baseball when he answered: "When I play baseball, I enjoy myself." "Why should I dream?" was unstated but clearly implied by the context of his answer.

Indeed, it is the sometime or casual fan or player who dreams about baseball and who tends to utilize baseball symbols in the relatively indifferent material of a manifest dream. It seems that the more meaningful baseball is to the individual at a given moment the less likely it is to appear in the symbols of the manifest content of his dreams and substitute gratifications. Thus with these illustrations and information in mind, the reader will appreciate why this pertinent and complicated material will be dealt with at another time and in another place.

MYTHOLOGY AND ARCHAEOLOGY

Although the determinants of the early evolution of the ball and bat-ball games are lost in antiquity, mythology and archaeology offer clues. Stokes reminds us that Nausicaa, the Homeric princess of the *Odyssey* (B.C. 550-150), was the mythological inventor of ball games.[3] He interpreted her ball playing with her maidens as a nuptial practice. Certainly marriage was a preoccupation when she coquettishly attracted Ulysses' attention by deliberately throwing her ball into the water for him to retrieve.[4]

Henderson traces the origin of all modern games played with bat and ball to the ancient fertility rites observed by priest-kings in the Egypt of the pyramids.[5] He calls attention to Herodotus' report of one of the earliest of these contests. At the temple of Papremis in Egypt the priests and the people enacted a traditional drama: "More than a thousand" men, votaries of the god Osiris, lined up at some distance from the temple. A previously prepared image of Osiris encased in a gilded casket had been prepared and rested on a four-wheeled cart. The object of the group was to rush the image of Osiris through the temple door. Those stationed in the gateway of the temple opposed its entrance, and mock combat ensued. Both sides were armed with clubs, and many heads were broken. Contrary to probability, the Egyptians claimed that no one was ever killed. Herodotus also reported the Egyptians' own account of the festival.[6] They said:

> The mother of the god Ares once dwelt in the temple. Brought up at a distance from his parent, when [Ares] grew to man's estate he conceived a wish for intercourse with her. Accordingly he came, but the attendants, who had never seen him before, refused him entrance, and succeeded in keeping him out. So he went to another city and collected a body of men, with whose aid he handled the attendants very roughly, and forced his way in to his mother. Hence they say arose the custom of a fight with sticks in honour of Ares at this festival.

And, I might add, Freud's hypothesis of the primal horde is foreshadowed.

OBSERVATIONS CONCERNING CHILDREN'S PLAY

My own observation of infants and children as they learn to recognize and to use their hands suggests that the stick, club and bat were initially an extension of the arm and hand and that the ball was a substitute for the hand or more specifically the fist. The small child, constantly prodded by the limitations of his strength and skill, by frustration and proneness to hurt, soon discovers that the arm's reach can be extended with a stick and that things may be struck and propelled with it without hurting his own hand. And further, he discovers that a toy may be a missile when thrown. These articles become a part of the self and share in its narcissistic investment.[7] It does not seem far-fetched to assume that similar developments contributed to primitive man's discovery of the precursors of the bat and ball.

The "Diamond," that is, the field of play in baseball, must have had many antecedents before reference to it in illustrations and rules appeared in 1810.[8] Diagrams of the immediate precursors of the modern diamond appeared in 1842 and 1845.[9] With its three bases and home plate, the diamond is remindful of the four-cornered area in which the infant takes his first tentative steps, that is, the crib, the playpen, the room and the back yard. Commonly the first steps the crawler takes without the support of his mother or other assistance are to a substitute base of security, for example, a chair, table, etc., and the next steps usually are back to the mother.

This first roundtrip of the infant resembles a forerunner of baseball called "One Old Cat." In it there was a pitcher, a catcher and a batter who struck the ball with a bat and ran to a base and returned to the home goal. (When more players participated, one or two more bases were added, and the game was named accordingly "One, Two, Three Old Cat.") Interestingly, children learning to play baseball among themselves often improvise a game that closely resembles the Old Cat games.

Soon, the toddler, instead of returning to the mother or father, ventures from the first to a second substitute base of security and eventually to a third and so on. By the time a fourth base has been reached, the anxiety over toddling of both mother and child has almost vanished. And the corners of the room and the furniture bases have been exhausted.

The relief of anxiety, the joy of accomplishment and the resulting elation are the natural responses to the completion of the circuit. The resemblance to the Two, Three, etc., Old Cat games is evident. The toddler's hesitant completion of his excursion around the room with its consequent emotional response of child and parent has a striking parallel in the home run of the baseball player with the resultant emotional response of teammates and fans.

The oedipal significance of the father and son game is emphasized by the fact that the first formal instructor and the first pitcher in the life of every batter is a father or surrogate. Only he has the incentive, patience and gentle skill to throw a ball so that it will hit the bat regardless of where it is swung by the little batter. This experience not only lays the groundwork for the thrill of the batter but accounts for the fact that the role of pitcher is the most popular one among young ball players. A couple of years later the mama of the Little Leaguer, who reminds him of practice sessions and is in regular attendance at his games, provides incentive and acclaim. The managers and coaches of the teams are father and surrogates.

Baseball, according to Peller's psychoanalytic survey of play activities,[10] would fall into the group of postoedipal play. During this phase, which starts about the age of six, the central theme of the play is sibling relations and fear of superego and superego figures. Up to this time the members of the immediate family have been the center of the child's emotional world. Prompted by biological development and the frustrations of oedipal fantasies and drawn by an improving appreciation of reality and libidinal attachments to playmates and new parental figures (teachers and older friends), the child of the "latency period" seeks modification of the familial attachments.

Games and sports played in teams are characteristic of postoedipal play. The anxieties are related to the struggle for independence and equality.

Reassurance is sought in being a member of a group, in following a chosen leader, in observing the rules of the game, and in the knowledge that the game can be repeated as often as wished. Emphasis is on the formal elements of the play; that is, the plot is codified, the roles are fixed and conventional, and the rules are inflexible. Ceremonies and rituals are essential features. Well-organized cooperation and a common unconscious fantasy are shared by the teammates. The emotional gains consist of the dissolution of oedipal ties and the gratifications associated with learning to cooperate with brothers, followers and leaders. The fact that baseball fits into the category of post-oedipal play does not imply an exclusion of oedipal and preoedipal play elements.

MYTH OF ORIGIN

In the past baseball has been popularly conceived as embodying the ideals of American democracy. Through fair and free competition in an arena of equal opportunity, every man should have the right to prove himself and realize his ambitions. The "self-made man" "picking himself up by his own bootstraps" and becoming a "Horatio Alger hero" pervaded the popular ideals of the times during which baseball evolved. Utterly consistent with these ideals is the myth of origin which attributes the creation of the game to a heroic adolescent.

According to discredited history but popular myth, the game of baseball was created and named by Abner Doubleday in 1839 in Cooperstown, New York. The designated creator was an ingenious school boy of eighteen to twenty years who matriculated at West Point a short time later and became the man who sighted the first shot fired on Fort Sumter that initiated the rebellion of the southern states against the North. Subsequently he rose to the rank of major general in the Union army, an achievement that enhanced his value as the innovator of the national game. He supposedly had been a crusader as well, who had virtuously persuaded the boys of his town to play baseball rather than another game.

Historically the myth rested upon the testimony of Abner Graves, a younger boyhood playmate of Doubleday, who was over eighty years old at the time he was recalling events sixty-eight years past. In 1907, this myth was established as history by a committee of six prominent public-spirited fans,[11] inspired and supported by A. G. Spalding, former star player (pitcher), manager, club owner and sporting goods manufacturer. In spite of a barely audible dissident opinion[12] it remained unchallenged for twenty-five years. Finally it was recognized as a "harmless legend," the result of an "innocuous conspiracy."[13] But with the establishment of the myth as history the actual origins of baseball in the English game "rounders" and its essential relationship to "cricket" were denied. Simultaneously an American father or patron saint of baseball was founded and the foundation for a shrine established. And in 1939 at Cooperstown, the shrine became a reality as the Hall of Fame was dedicated amidst a pageant of historical highlights and an all-star game between teams of all-time great players. The U.S. Post Office also commemorated the event with a stamp portraying a sandlot scene with a house, barn and school in the background; thus associating symbols of wholesome American life with the symbols of baseball. In 1952, the Celler Report of the US Congress considered baseball "a game of American origin."

How ironic it is that the myth of origin which denied the English parentage of baseball attributed its creation to an adolescent who had become a patriotic hero in the war to preserve the union of northern and southern states. Today the myth persists. Sportswriters, sportscasters and fans speak affectionately of Abner Doubleday as the father of baseball in the same way they might speak of Santa Claus and Christmas. The relationship of baseball to the English games is never mentioned, thus attesting to the overriding popularity of the myth and the persisting effectiveness of the original denial.

THE PRIMAL HORDE

Crucial to the view of baseball I am suggesting is the reader's familiarity with Freud's hypothesis concerning events in the primal horde as set down in 1913 in *Totem and Taboo.* A review of the original text or even of just Part IV would enrich the reader's appreciation of baseball immeasurably. The following is offered as the briefest summary of its relevant features:

Freud hypothesized that in the prehistory of man a most significant event occurred — an event which determined the form and organization of the family, the community and the religious life to follow.

Originally, for purposes of survival, man lived in small hordes. Each was under the domination of the strongest male in the group. He was the father or master and wielded his power ruthlessly and brutally. All females were his personal property including wives, daughters and those stolen from other hordes. In order to enjoy the protection and provision of the horde, the sons had to renounce all claim to the women. If they aroused the father's jealousy, he ruthlessly killed, castrated or drove them out. If driven out, the brothers by the exigencies of the times were forced to live in small communities and to secure wives by stealing them. Subsequently one of the sons might succeed in creating his own horde.

It was under these conditions that the significant event took place: the banished brothers joined forces and killed the father and devoured his body. The act of cannibalism was intended to assure each brother magical identification with the father by incorporating a part of him. The sons had not only hated and feared the father but had envied and idealized him as a model to be emulated.

A decisive change in the social organization followed. When brother after brother attempted to supplant the father and met the same fate, the brothers in the interest of self-preservation again joined forces and declared all the women of the horde taboo. Simultaneously, driven by the moralistic reactions to the failure to attain their aim and overcome with guilt for having killed the father, they replaced and deified him with a substitute, i.e., the totem animal. This was a powerful, dreaded animal which retained the ambivalence originally felt toward the father. On the one hand he was the guiding and protecting spirit of the horde and was worshiped. On the other hand he was killed and eaten (totem feast) by the brothers at regularly recurring festivals. The latter was a celebration of the victory of the sons over the father.

The dead father proved to be stronger than the living one. What his existence had prevented, that is, the sons' possession of his power and women, the repressed wishes of the Oedipus complex, were now forbidden under the threat of death by the taboos of totemism. The deed was revoked by forbidding the killing of the totem, the substitute for the father, and their claim upon the women was renounced in "deferred obedience" to the father.

Thus a social organization based upon renunciation of instinctual gratification, binding mutual obligations and sacred institutions emerged. And with the beginnings of morality and law, murder and incest became the first crimes of the primitive society.

Totemism was the first form of religion and was followed by a humanization of the worshiped totem animal. Thus the resulting human god supplanted the totem but retained a transparent relationship. The god may have been represented as an animal, may have resembled one, may have had one as an inseparable companion, or in myth may have vanquished the animal whose place he had taken.

An interim mother god probably appeared before the male gods, who made their first appearance as sons beside the great mothers. Later the son gods assumed the features of the father. These were the male gods of polytheism and of patriarchal times. They shared their authority and were often subject to a higher god.

Parenthetically, the reader may find it an interesting coincidence that while Freud was living and contending with an age of authoritarianism and writing about the consequences of authoritarianism in *Totem and Taboo,* baseball was evolving and emerging as "America's national game."[14]

Although Freud had doubts and hesitation about publishing this hypothesis in 1913,[15] by 1921 he regarded it as his best written work. *Totem and Taboo* remained a favorite throughout his life, and he summarized and discussed the hypothesis with particular care in the sixth chapter of his autobiographical study (1925) and again summarized and quoted it extensively in his last published volume *Moses and Monetheism* (1939).[16]

Although there has been a tendency on the part of anthropologists to relegate Freud's hypothesis to a "symbolic statement," Margaret Mead in 1963 reconsidered it with insightful respect.[17] In addition, anyone aware of the family, social, business, professional and recreational machinations of contemporary life cannot help but be impressed by the intimations of Freud's hypothesis in them.

A HISTORICAL CONSIDERATION

A reflective view of nineteenth century American history leads me to make the following comments. Regardless of the historical rationale for the War of 1812, which does not contradict these thoughts, it was a war that reasserted American rights and independence from its psychological parents Britain and France, and especially the paternal country Britain. The Civil War, which followed approximately fifty years later, was an internecine conflict with psychological implications which have hardly been explored but which are certainly suggested by the consideration of Freud's hypothesis. The game of baseball as we know it today was evolving during this same period, as pointed out previously, and by 1911 had been proclaimed and accepted as "America's national game."[18] Granted, the relationship between the game and history is conjectural; it is also relevant to this study.

THE GAME

Baseball as played by the organized professional player and viewed by the paying fan is the specific subject of study. The players are of the highest proficiency, and the mechanics of the game have been mastered by them so that the particular roles they fill are most likely to be executed in the ideal way.[19] Thus player and fan are insured of a minimum of distraction in the fulfillment of their fantasies, and the reader will be spared the task of considering the many variations of the game. Errors, which are certainly an important part of the game and often determine the outcome, introduce such a range of considerations that they will not be specifically dealt with here.

Baseball is a bat, ball and base contest between two teams of nine players vying for victory by scoring the most runs.[20] Each team has nine alternating turns at bat (innings). Three outs represent one turn. Each team's strategy and tactics are usually directed by an older non-player who frequently assumes a paternal role in relation to the players, not only on but off the field of play. The efforts of the pitchers are unambivalently supported by his teammates. There is no allowance for antagonism toward a teammate on the field of play. Team victory and defeat of the other team are emphasized. *Espirit de corps* is virtuous, as is animosity toward the other team. Friendly association, called "fraternization," between players of the opposing teams is prohibited; and aggressive hostile actions between them are promoted, though rigidly circumscribed and regulated. Teamwork is a prerequisite of effective performance. Although emphasis is on the individual's performance, it is most valued in terms of team victory. Team loss is a loss for each player. Fixed rules and regulations are enforced by a nonparticipating impartial judge (umpire) who insures fair play. Sportsmanship is extolled but is less favored than victory. Cheating is vociferously denounced but tolerated if carried out adroitly. The field of play, that is, the baseball diamond with its three bases and home plate, is laid out upon a well-cultivated plot of level ground. Looked at from behind and above home plate, the diamond looks like a half-opened Chinese fan.

Cliché-ridden, prosaic and repetitious in these terms, the game seems dull to anyone but an ardent fan or player. How then could it capture the imaginations of millions of fans, become "the national pastime" for about a century, become "big business,"[21] and enjoy special exemption in relation to the labor and antitrust laws of the land. The answer is found in a more perceptive view of the game which brings into focus the essential drama underlying its superficial structure.

Baseball is a game whose plot has three simultaneously expressed, interwoven and mutually dependent themes. They are:

1. The first theme corresponds to the superficial view just discussed, that is, of a contest between teams.
2. The theme of the duel between the pitcher and the batter of the opposing teams is the focus of attention for fan and player, who have limited awareness of its implications while thrilling to its outcome.
3. This theme is the insured triumph of the batters over the pitchers. It is obscure and rarely discernible to the fan and the player. It is, like the latent content of the dream, the unconscious fantasy.

With the umpire's command of "play ball," the world of baseball is brought into being for player and fan. In the center of that world stands a pitcher on a mound made of clay rising fifteen inches higher than the rest of the field (it is reminiscent of the childhood game "King of the Mountain"). The mound is in the middle of the diamond (actually it is a 90-foot square) or infield with an outfield and foul territory extending beyond it in all directions.

The pitcher, more than any other player, determines the course of the game. With the pitched ball he not only initiates the action of the game but each play that follows.[22] He is usually one of the biggest, strongest and best athletes on the team.[23] With his size, strength and skill he dominates the field and hopefully the batter. His position on the mound inevitably means that he can pitch the ball faster, trickier, and with better control than any of the other eight players. Thus he dominates his own team, first of all. And he retains his position in the game for as long as he (actually his team, although by custom he receives the credit) is able to retire the other team with a minimum of runs scored. His function is to throw the ball, a rock-hard missile, so that the batter will be unable to hit it and reach base safely. He is the only player on each team who is in almost continuous direct contest with the players of the opposite team. For all the other players direct contest is either remote or infrequent.

The pitcher's position and home plate are separated by a distance of sixty feet six inches,[24] which seems like a safe enough distance to fix between contestants. But from his position on the mound the pitcher may throw the ball so fast (at speeds up to 98.6 mph) that it is almost unhittable,[25] or he may employ a variety of tricky deliveries and cause the ball to hop, sink, curve or flutter as it approaches the batter.

The pitcher also may resort to the use of a variety of illegal devices, such as applying sputum to the ball (spitball) or roughing up or cutting the cover to cause the ball to break sharply as it approaches the batter. If the umpire does not detect the illegal deception, it is accepted by player and fan even though they may protest. Such trickery is usually associated with veteran pitchers who have lost some of their "stuff" and are enviously considered wise or clever.

If the ball passes through a zone over home plate extending between the batter's shoulders and knees and covering a seventeen-inch truncated square rubber home plate, the umpire will call it a strike whether or not the batter swings. Even if the batter succeeds in hitting the ball fairly, the pitcher has eight fielders to assist in putting him out. Any of the fielders can retire the batter by catching the ball on the fly or by fielding it when otherwise hit fairly and throwing it to the appropriate base (usually first) before the batter or base runner can reach it. In addition, the batter may strike out, be called out on strikes, foul out, or be caught off base after reaching it safely. In all, there are nineteen ways a batter may be declared "out."[26] In contrast, there are only seven ways the batter may reach base safely.[27]

The diamond is prohibited to the batter until he has walked or hit the ball fairly and safely, although he is tolerated briefly in the base path between home and first while he is attempting to reach base safely.[28] Otherwise he has no place on the field of play except in the "batter's box" or in the "on-deck circle." Both are in foul territory and, like all other foul areas, may be used by the fielders in putting him out.[29] Even when he has successfully reached base, the area he may tread is limited to a three-foot-wide path between the bases.[30] If he strays he is automatically out. He is never safe unless touching a base. Even then, he may be forced out by a subsequent batter's failure to advance him. Such tentative accessibility to the batter suggests that the diamond possesses a most significant symbolic meaning.

In spite of all that favors their roles, the pitcher and supporting fielders cannot win the game. At best the pitcher and fielders can only keep the other team from winning. Even the "perfectly pitched and played game" could result in no better than a scoreless tie, which does not count in baseball.

Although beset by the skill and dexterity of the pitcher and fielders and the rigidly imposed rules which regulate and circumscribe his actions, the player in his role as batter is destined to win by the rules of scoring. Only in the role of batter is the player in a position to score and win the game. The batter has two harmonious aims which overlap and may be accomplished simultaneously. The more exciting one is to win his duel with the pitcher by hitting safely. The more significant one is to score runs in any way possible. These aims correspond to the second and third themes of the game and are two levels of the oedipal conflict, the latter being the more primitive one.

Scoring is primarily a team function. With one exception it requires the coordinated efforts of two or more batters. Each player, regardless of his size, strength and skill, exercises his democratic right and shares responsibility (and guilt) in the batting by taking his turn in the proper order. No matter how often the individual batter has failed previously there is always another time at bat, another game, and even "next year" when he may prove himself (phallic proficiency) and deny his fears (of castration).

The exception is the home run. By hitting the ball on the fly fairly out of the field of play,[31] the batter transcends the limitations imposed on his teammates by their own abilities, by the rules and by the pitcher. He assumes the scoring function for the whole team, scores by himself, and figuratively seizes the potential for winning the game by himself. The latter is actually realized when he hits a home run to win the game in the last half of the last inning of play. The home run then represents the pinnacle of attainment. The batter achieves the fulfillment of both fantasies concurrently; that is, he vanquishes the father by himself on behalf of the brothers and wins the oedipal duel.

The rally, that is, a series of offensive actions by which a cluster of runs is scored, represents the essence of the batter horde's triumph over the pitcher/father. It often results in the pitcher's removal from the game, that is, his being "knocked out of the box."[32]

The best batters are able to average three to four safe hits out of ten times at bat and may become so effective at batting in runs or scoring them that they preempt certain aspects of the primal father.[33] The pitcher's remedy for this audacity is the intimidating "beanball" or "brush-back pitch," that is, a pitch thrown directly at the batter. Under this threat the batter's effectiveness may be seriously impaired. The pitcher may further frustrate the batter by intentionally walking him when first base is open and a hit might score tying or winning runs.

In baseball the violence of the contest is concentrated in the contact between the ball and the bat in or near the strike zone. The ball is simultaneously a surrogate of the pitcher/father and a missile or weapon by which the batter is to be vanquished. The bat is simultaneously a surrogate of the ambitious batter/son and the weapon of attack. Intimately related to this action is the easily overlooked fact that the pitcher is throwing the ball not to the batter but to the catcher, who receives the ball into his large deep-pocketed mitt. They would like to be able to ignore the batter's presence beside home plate but cannot. He intrudes upon and may interrupt the pitcher's phallic exhibition of "stuff," that is, the game of catch between the symbolic primal parents.

Mounting tension accompanies each pitch as player and fan anticipate and await the action of the game. All eyes are focused upon the pitcher, who compulsively carries out one or more of the following rituals: massages the ball, rearranges the dirt on the mound, juggles the resin bag, gazes into the outfield, tugs at his cap, shirt, or pants and then takes the signal for the pitch from between the squatting catcher's thighs.

The batter has completed a comparable series of rituals. He has carried out one or more or all of the following: put resin on his bat handle; stretched and flexed his shoulder and arm muscles by wiggling, waggling, and swinging the bat; tapped the dirt from the cleats of his shoes with the bat; pulled up his pants; adjusted his belt and protective helmet; looked at the third base coach for a signal; and scratched around in the clay of the batter's box with his cleats. Finally he is settled in a guarding, defiant position beside home plate. Occasionally in a challenging gesture he taps the plate with his bat.

As the pitcher winds up and flings the ball plateward, the tension rises sharply and all eyes turn to the batter. A sharp crack as the bat strikes the ball marks the explosive instant of maximum violence of the game and its essence. But once the ball has been hit, the action continues until the umpire declares the ball "fair" or "foul" and the offensive player "safe" or "out."[34] The batter and base runners advance on the bases as far as the play of the defensive team permits. Then the action is punctuated by a brief lull as the ball is returned to the pitcher. Thus alternating periods of mounting tension and relaxation follow for a minimum of nine turns at bat for each team. The tension reaches its peak during the last three innings of play.

Chance, luck or fate is a major determinant in the outcome of every action. The sun, the wind, the weather, the condition of the turf and the stadium all may prove decisive in a given play. The emotional and psychic state of each player at a given moment of play is the most influential factor; yet the resulting effect of that state upon the play must be accounted to "luck." Fascinating though these considerations are, their influence on the outcome of the game cannot be dealt with here.

The only direct aggression sanctioned by the plot and rules of the game has been displaced, condensed and concentrated in the explosive instant of action of bat striking ball. All other aggression must be disguised as an accident[35] or be inhibited or protected against by gloves, sliding pads, chest protector, helmet, etc.[36] Any other outbreak of aggression, whether physical, verbal or simply a gesture,[37] is punishable by ejection from the game and field.

The possibility that the proscribed aggression will break out and sometimes does adds zest to the game. Fan and player are reminded that flashes and echoes of man's most primitive heritage and his deepest most ungovernable instincts are within an instant of expression.[38] The serious injuries incurred in the game receive brief widespread attention and then are forgotten. Sportswriters and fans tend to shift the emphasis and to promulgate the idea that no one "really gets hurt" in a fight between players.

Although enjoyed by women as player and fan, there is no actual place for them on the professional field of play. Baseball is not a bisexual game. Yet the importance of women to the game is attested by the symbolization of the field of play, the function of the catcher and the fact that the first fan of every ball player was a mother or surrogate.

The catcher's position after those of the pitcher and batter is the most significant one. Since it is the most dangerous position from the standpoint of bodily injury, the catcher is the most armored. He wears a face mask, a chest protector, shin guards and a big padded mitt with a deep pocket. He participates actively in every play. With his fingers between his legs he calls for a curve, fast ball or other pitch from the pitcher. Then he receives the pitch or "stuff" into the deep pocket of his mitt. Simultaneously the catcher is a fielder supporting the pitcher's every effort and like the other fielders a privileged spectator to the duel between the pitcher and the batter. At the same time he is engaged in the oedipal struggle on the side of the pitcher and guards home plate against the scoring base runner.

From the standpoint of emotion and performance, the catcher has the most complex and demanding of positions. His is the one position with obvious bisexual implications. This consideration is obscured by the fact that the catcher is usually one of the toughest and most rugged players,[39] one who is least likely to be associated with anything feminine. Member of the brother-fielder-batter horde, on the one hand, he is in a receptive alliance with the pitcher on the other hand. It is also the least popular position among younger ball players.

Although this is not a clinical paper, illustrative are the observations of Helene Deutsch concerning a patient with a ball phobia, who following analysis developed a keep interest in ball games. The patient had had a recurrent anxiety dream since early childhood. His dream was: "A round object, a ball, a balloon, a circular building, a Roman column, a cloud of a round shape, a strange bird . . . was hovering over his head and threatening to fall down and destroy him . . . [he] sought in vain for help, and awoke with anxiety." At age four, while struggling against masturbation accompanied by sadomasochistic fantasies, his anxiety had been associated with a hand extended menacingly toward him. Analysis revealed the menacing hand to be his father's threatening him with castration. At age eight, he feared that a ball might fall on his head and either mortally injure him or so hurt his head that he would become an idiot. Wherever he went he dreaded the event (agoraphobia). The threatening hand of the father had been replaced by a ball, and the phobia had embodied the dread of castration. The ball corresponded to the anxiety object, the father, who was simultaneously loved and hated. After the phobia had been analyzed, the patient developed an extensive interest in ball games. The phobia had been converted into a play situation and a source of pleasure. "The sport situations," said Deutsch, "provide [the] most ideal conditions for release from fear, namely, expectant readiness, contempt of the danger which threatens, a trial of the subject's own powers and rational attack and defense." Considering the repetitious pattern of the sport, Stokes adds the endurance of repeated symbolic castration as a means of resurrecting the sense of potency after smashing defeat.[41]

IMPLICATIONS

To consider the implications of Freud's hypothesis for baseball: The primal father and primal horde have striking parallels in baseball — in the sponsor or owner and his team, in the manager and his team, in the pitcher and his teammates, and more subtly in the pitcher and the batters. It is in the latter permutation that the overthrow of the father is insured and reenacted.

The killing is displaced to and represented by the explosive contact between the bat and ball in or near the strike zone and the rally. Guilt is distributed over the players who must take their turn at bat and who take part in the rally. The retaliatory threat is epitomized in the "beanball."

The previously forbidden females are represented by the pitcher's mound with its rubber and hole dug by the pitcher's toe on every pitch, by the diamond, and in a larger sense by the field of play.

The "deferred obedience" of the brothers to the will of the primal father in relation to the females and the barrier to incest is symbolized by the plot and rules which establish the odds against the batter's victory and, if won, restrict his presence and action on the diamond to the straight and narrow base paths and only for the time it takes him to complete the circuit of the bases. Also, the winning team is always the last one on the field (in possession of the diamond) but only for defensive purposes.[42]

The loved aspect of the primal father finds expression in the role of the team sponsor and in the benign paternal roles of the team manager and coaches. Both the primal father and the totem animal find representation in the nicknames of the teams, e.g., San Francisco Giants and Detroit Tigers.

The totem feast is acted out continuously during the game by the fans, who eat tremendous quantities of popcorn, peanuts, hot dogs, etc. and drink enormous volumes of pop, beer, etc. Because of the time chosen to play (about 2:00 P.M. and 8:00 P.M.) and its usual duration (2 to 3 hours), the game's termination is brought into juxtaposition with a meal or snack time which as a consequence often assumes the aspects of a totem feast for player and fan alike.[43] Thus the guilt is further shared and dissipated.

The moral and religious heritage of the primal father is symbolized by the umpire. At his station behind home plate, the batter and the catcher, the umpire enforces the rules and makes a decision on every play.

The ambivalence toward the primal father is expressed by channeling love toward the pitcher of the same team, whom the player supports in the field, and the hatred toward the opposing pitcher, whom the player hopes to defeat in the duel and is foreordained to vanquish as a participant of the batter horde. The denial of the whole transaction is seen in the custom of giving the pitcher official credit for winning or losing the game.

The most obvious aspect of the game, that is, the competition of the brother hordes under the guidance of benign paternal managers who were usually recently players themselves and who are voluntarily accepted as leaders, is remindful of the son religion which Freud hypothesized as a late development in the reaction of the primal horde to the killing of the primal father. In the process of atonement the son attained his wish against the father, that is, he became god. The brothers identified themselves with him.[44] The ambivalence previously felt toward the primal father has been split so that there is an effective cooperation among the brothers of one team and an expression of hostility against the brothers of the other.

DISCUSSION

Abner Doubleday as the idealized American school boy (son), defender of the Union (family and brothers) and creator of baseball does not make a very illustrious god as gods go, but it is appropriate that he should be the first deity of the religion of baseball. He was given credit for creating a game that provides for a safe expression of the fantasies and impulses of rebellion against the primal horde father, competition with the oedipal father, and rivalry with the brothers while retaining the prospects of displacing the father as a son and brother[45] — no mean achievement. Margaret Mead comments that:[46]

> In some human societies the culture consists of a large proportion of reliance upon institutionalization of some kinds of the primary process and the unarticulated experiences of early childhood. Although the texture of our modern culture is postulated upon an orderly articulation, either through repression, or protective enactment and satiation of these childhood impulses and primary process types of thought, it is obvious that the full potentiality for embodying them in social forms still remains — as in the mass murders of the Nazis, the Communist assumption that thought is equivalent to deed, and in the variety of cults that are spreading over the world — such as the flying saucer cults or religious cults like Jehovah's Witnesses.

Baseball is one of the institutions to which Mead refers. The game affords a familiar congenial framework for the fan and player to use in the recreative solution of instinctual conflicts. It also offers a direction subsequent generations may follow in solving similar instinctual conflicts. Through the plot and action of the game, fantasy and instinct find fulfillment and expression while potential antisocial strivings and behavior are dissipated and limited. For the individual who is struggling with authority, rebellion, independence, responsbility and self-determination, baseball offers a time-polished, socially approved structure for mastery.

"Since you're losing your stuff, and since that dastardly primal-horde-son-batter, Higby, is coming up, I'm going to play percentages and replace you with a left-handed primal-horde-father pitcher."

CONCLUSION

Based on a reflective study, the suggestion is made that the game of baseball evolved as a means of expressing the unconscious fantasies and strivings related to the primal horde killing of the primal father, the oedipal competition of the father and son, and the rivalry between the brothers. Now it exists as an institution of American society which facilitates the realization of these fantasies safely in play. Regardless of which team wins, the player and fan are assured of enjoying a triumph on at least one level of fantasy, that is, the brother horde's overthrow of the primal father. If his favorite team wins, he may enjoy fantasies on all three levels, and his joy will be bountiful.

NOTE

A preliminary version of this paper was read at the May, 1963, meeting of the American Psychoanalytic Association in St. Louis, Missouri.

FOOTNOTES

1. The colloquial term "fan" was probably derived from fanatic and designated "an enthusiastic devotee or follower of a sport, hobby, etc., esp. baseball." Mathews, [Ed.]: *A Dictionary of Americanisms.* 1951. Fanatic is most pertinently defined in its obsolete form, i.e., a) "a lunatic; b) a religious maniac; c) an English nonconformist." Neilson, Knott and Carhart [Eds.]: *Webster's New International Dictionary of the English Language,* 2d ed. 1949.
2. The association referred to how far a boy could go with a girl in baseball terms: To first base meant necking, which confined the caresses and kissing to the neck and above; second base meant petting, which was caressing from the neck down; third base meant digital manipulation of the genitals; and the home run meant intercourse.
3. Stokes, A.: Psychoanalytic reflections on the development of ball games, particularly cricket. *Int J Psychoanal, 37*:185, 1956, appearing supra at p. 387.
4. Homer: *The Odyssey,* in Hutchins [Ed.]: *Great Books of the Western World,* No. 4, 1952, p. 214.
5. Henderson, R. W.: *Ball, Bat and Bishop: The Origin of Ball Games.* New York, Rockport Press, 1947, p. 4.
6. Herodotus: *The Persian Wars,* Book II, translated by Rawlinson, G. 1942, pp. 147-148.
7. Ted Williams had his bats cleaned daily and discarded one the moment it had a nick. Danzig, A. and Reichler, J.: *The History of Baseball.* Englewood Cliff, Prentice-Hall, 1959, p. 240.
8. Henderson, R. W.: *op. cit. supra* note 5, at p. 140.
9. Menke, F. G.: *The Encyclopedia of Sports,* 2d ed. New York, A. S. Barnes, 1960, p. 82.
10. Peller, L. E.: Libidinal Phases, Ego Development, and Play. *Psychoanal Stud Child, 9*:178, 1954.
11. "A. G. Mills, of New York, an enthusiastic ball player before and during the Civil War, and the third President of the National League. The Hon. Arthur P. Gorman, Senator from Maryland, who died before the Commission rendered its decision. The Hon. Morgan C. Bulkeley, at one time Governor, and at that time United States Senator from Connecticut. He was first President of the National League. N. E. Young, of Washington, D. C., a veteran ball player, the first Secretary and afterwards the fourth President of the National League. Alfred J. Reach, of Philadelphia, head of the sporting goods house, known as the 'Business Genius of Base Ball.' George Wright of Boston, a former

player of note and later a leading business man in sport." Henderson, R. W.: *op. cit. supra* note 5, at p. 174.

12. Irwin, W.: *Collier's,* May 8, 1909.
13. Henderson, R. W.: *op. cit. supra* note 5, at p. 195.
14. Henderson, R. W.: *op. cit. supra* note 5, at p. 180.
15. See Jones, E.: *Life and Work of Sigmund Freud,* Vol. 2. New York, Basic Books, 1955, p. 355.
16. Freud, S.: *Standard Edition,* Vol. 4. London, Hogarth Press, 1955, editor's note, p. XI.
17. Mead, M.: Totem and taboo reconsidered with respect. *Bull Menninger Clin, 27*:185, 1963.
18. Henderson, R. W.: *op. cit. supra* note 5, at p. 180.
19. The ideal performance is epitomized in World Series play. Even non-players and non-fans are intrigued by the spectacle of two championship teams playing for a mythical world championship.
20. Run is scored by the player's completing the circuit of three bases and touching home plate.
21. UPI release in *Detroit Free Press,* Oct. 20, 1965: "Major League baseball owners Tuesday accepted a $30.6 million offer from the National Broadcasting Co. for television rights to the 1967 and 1968 World Series and All-Star games and a game-of-the-week program from 1966 through 1968. . . ."
22. The exception is the base-runner who may initiate a play by attempting to "steal a base." However, he usually does not exercise this option but waits until the pitcher has started his motion before making the attempt.
23. Outstanding exceptions in professional baseball are Whitey Ford of the New York Yankees, Frank Lary of the Chicago White Sox and Orlando Pena of the Detroit Tigers. All are smaller than most of their teammates.
24. In 1893 the unconscious of a surveyor was responsible for increasing the pitching distance from 50 feet to 60 feet 6 inches. The intention was to increase it to 60 feet and the diagram read 60'0". The Surveyor read 60'6". These 6 inches have been retained ever since. Henderson, R. W.: *op. cit. supra* note 5, at p. 94.
25. It would not be remarkable if the pitcher on the mound reminded the reader of the mythological father gods Zeus, Jupiter and Thor with their thunderbolts.
26. Official Baseball Rules. *The Sporting News,* 1963, pp. 35-37.
27. The batter may reach base safely by walking, by being hit by a pitched ball, by having the catcher or fielder interfere with his play, by having a fairly hit ball touch a runner or an umpire before touching a fielder, through an error by a fielder, or by forcing a runner at the next base. But only by hitting safely does he win a clear-cut victory in the duel.
28. In an early version of the game of baseball, the base runner was put out by being struck by the thrown ball rather than by being tagged.
29. Fly balls may be caught in them. Also the player may be tagged out in the batter's box.
30. The base paths from home to first and from third to home plate are six feet wide, three feet on each side of the foul lines.
31. A home run inside the park is infrequent but even more surprising and exciting. However, it is tainted since it depends not only upon the skill of the batter to hit the ball hard and far and the speed to scamper around the bases, but also upon such lowly regarded factors as a favorable bounce or a misjudgment or lapse of a fielder.
32. The customary expression is that the pitcher pitches from the mound, but when he is removed from the game as a result of a rally or wildness, he is said to have been "knocked out of the box." This expression actually is derived from the fact that his name is removed from the box-score when he leaves the game. In contrast, when the batter has been taken out of the game the expression is frequently used that he has been "dropped" or "has dropped out."
33. By fouling off balls pitched on the edge of the strike zone, a clever batter may coax the pitcher into throwing the ball over the plate where it is easier to hit solidly.
34. Indeed every action on the field is subject to the umpire's judgment and decision.
35. This is subject to the interpretation of the umpire.

36. Even the symbolic aggression implicit in treading upon the turf of the field in spiked shoes is liimted for the offensive player to the on-deck circle, the batter's box and the base paths.
37. A player making a verbal hint to the umpire that he favors the other team or by grasping his own neck with his hand suggests that the umpire "choked up" on a decision has offered provocation for being ejected from the game.
38. In 1920, Ray Chapman, brilliant shortstop of the Cleveland team, was killed when hit by a pitch by Carl Mays of the New York Yankees. In 1937, Mickey Cochrane's career as outstanding catcher, hitter and manager was terminated by an errant pitch by Bump Hadley of the New York Yankees. In 1957, Cleveland's great young pitcher Herb Score was hit in the eye by a line drive from the bat of Gil McDougald of the New York Yankees. In 1965, Juan Marichal, leading San Francisco Giant pitcher, attacked with his bat catcher John Roseboro of the Los Angeles Dodgers, inflicting head injuries. In 1965, Tony Gonzales of the Cleveland Indians attacked with his bat Detroit pitcher Larry Sherry after two brush-back pitches.
39. Red Smith, sportswriter for the *N. Y. Herald Tribune,* after reading a summary of the preliminary version of this paper wrote a column, Sept. 27, 1963, entitled: "Somebody's Yogi." The first sentence read: ". . . Yogi Berra is somebody's mother."
40. Deutsch, H.: Contribution to the psychology of sport. *Int J Psychoanal, 7:*223, 1926, appearing *supra* at p. 91.
41. Stokes, A.: Psychoanalytic reflections on the development of ball games, particularly cricket. *Int J. Psychoanal, 37:*185, 1956, appearing *supra* at p. 387.
42. The lone exception is when the home team scores in the last half of the ninth inning to win the game. Then the winning team does not possess the diamond at all.
43. "Post-mortem" is the term humorously used by fan and player for the baseball conversation or the "rehashing" of the game over a meal.
44. Freud, S.: *Totem and Taboo (1913);* in *Standard Edition,* Vol 4. London, Hogarth Press, 1955, p. 13.

FOOTBALL

ALAN A. STONE

AMERICAN FOOTBALL IS ONE OF THE most overtly aggressive team games played in civilized society. Its growth since the end of World War II (eclipsing the less violent game of baseball, once the national pastime) is not without important social and psychological significance. Football, in the course of its growth, has become an event of central importance in the "mass culture" of the United States. Television and professional football have dramatically enhanced this development, creating a level of interest and expertise previously unknown in this increasingly complicated sport.

Critics usually emphasize the violence and physical dangers in this contact sport; they cite death rates, approximately 17.28 per annum (an officially recorded total of 271 deaths "directly" attributable to football during the years 1947-1963), and the incidence of crippling injuries. A recent study of high school football revealed that one out of every four players each season receives an injury reportable to an insurance carrier, and approximately one in a hundred receives a head injury.

It is surprising in view of such evidence that changes in rules and equipment have been slow in coming. For example, the protective face guards and mouthpieces which have saved countless nasal bones and teeth from destruction were not systematically introduced until the middle fifties. Many a football player of those earlier generations now unnecessarily "sports" a dental plate and a flattened nose as the price of his former glory. When one considers the rules of football, it is also striking that relatively small penalties are assessed for intentional fouls as compared to other equally rough sports such as hockey, where a team temporarily loses the service of one of its players because of such an infraction.

The violence of the game and the apparent reluctance of its audience, its rulemakers and its participants to have it less so have been in evidence throughout the history of this sport, producing many public controversies. The most glaring instance was the investigation instigated by then President Theodore Roosevelt, which actually considered abolishing the game because of its dangers. Subsequently, in 1931, the football death of a West Point cadet led to the establishment of a committee by the American Football Coaches Association that ever since has conducted an annual survey of football fatalities.

Advocates of football cite its character-building aspects and emphasize particularly the cathartic value of getting aggression out on the field. They suggest that though rough, football is less dangerous statistically than walking to school, and certainly much less lethal than automobile driving in the same age group. It is also true that some of our most successful Americans of recent vintage were collegiate football players. Many of these men attribute to football important influences in shaping their capacities for success: competition, resourcefulness, leadership and useful aggressiveness. Ambiguous as the causative factors may be, there is little doubt that many men who have won distinction on the gridiron have distinguished themselves in other important areas of endeavor as well.

Whatever the relative risks may be, the data in regard to injury and death prove beyond doubt that football is a rough and potentially dangerous sport. The popularity and high value placed on this sport suggest that its directly aggressive, combative and openly violent aspects appeal to the mass of Americans. Furthermore, the supporters of American football believe that this rough game builds worthwhile and successful character.

These facts can be considered the broader background for this paper, which explores primarily the motivations of football players. Since direct aggression seems such an important aspect, this analysis will emphasize this sector of motivation. It discusses both on a general level and in an in-depth individual psychological level the effects of the sport of football on character formation, particularly as it affects aggressive drives and tendencies.

SOURCE OF DATA

The data to be presented originate in two sources: objective data systematically collected and evaluated, and clinical data.

Detailed Study of College Varsity Football Players

1. Thematic Apperception Tests were administered at three points in time; before practice, after practice and after the football season. The Thematic Apperception Tests were given by the group method, utilizing questionnaires in the technique described by Stein. The results were scored utilizing a method adapted from McClelland and Whiting.

2. Detailed analysis of overt aggressive behavior in football films was made. Approximately ten hours of film for each player were carefully scored to determine measures of effective plays and destructive acts of aggression. A group of observers familiar with football, after brief training for inter-rater reliability, carefully evaluated the behavior of a particular football player on each play. The behavior was categorized as (a) effectively performed his assignment, (b) failed his assignment, (c) clearly utilized "unnecessary" hostile destructive acts, (d) clearly avoided aggressive contacts.

3. This material was complemented by rating scales filled out by coaches

and players. These scales ranked an entire football team on their capacity and tendency for hostile acts along various vectors.

A great deal of data was thus collected; subsequently, to confirm the data, Thematic Apperception Tests were repeated on another varsity football squad. The total sample of subjects for which projective data were available is 60.

Clinical Data

A second source of this paper is clinical data gathered as a psychotherapist of several adolescent football players. This data is supplemented by my own knowledge and experience as a former football player at the sandlot, high school and varsity college levels. The following interpretation relies heavily on the method of functional analysis both on the psychoanalytic and the interactional level.

THE DEVELOPMENT OF A FOOTBALL PLAYER

Children begin to play football when quite young, and today it is not uncommon to see preadolescents involved in well-organized games in leagues supervised by adults. Before such organized football begins, still younger boys, seven to eleven, find in "sandlot" or "pick-up" games an opportunity to try their motor skills and to invest the game with certain emotional charges. It is a chance to act the hero and to belong in a group. It is a chance for close physical contact, and the game often ends in a wildly exciting melee of wrestling bodies, a pile that no one wants to be left out of and that may have obvious erotic overtones. There is laughing, giggling,

tears and anger. There are strategies of revenge and counter revenge which are played out. There are wild, complicated plans for hiding the football under your shirt or winning the game by some similar ultimate act of razzle-dazzle. Football at this level has much less purposeful destructive aggression than it will eventually develop; it lacks venom, though it may have anger and rage. It is spirited and passionate, but it is not yet a way of life; both teams may race off the field, leaving the game, if a child arrives with a new toy or if someone comes up with an interesting idea for some other activity.

STRATEGY

RAZZLE-DAZZLE

NEVER SAY DIE

CRYBABY

Similarly, it is perfectly acceptable to run home to mother if you get hurt; in fact, if you do not, some friend in terror may run home for you. In adolescence, however, a Spartan attitude develops quickly, and tears become a source of humiliation rather than a release.

The psychomotor equipment is not sufficiently lethal at these earlier ages to cause serious injury. To a certain extent this contributes to the playful quality of the game. The child has not yet had the terrifying experience of withdrawing from a blow which has produced injury or serious pain in his victim or himself. In addition to the lack of physical strength, it seems at this age that the superego can, without guilt, still tolerate these clumsy direct aggressive attempts when they are thinly disguised as play. Furthermore, children at this age, perhaps for the last time in their lives, knowingly and intuitively accept mutual cowardice.

However, there are some boys who, because of personal aptitude or special need, begin to devote time to developing their special football skills early in life. They are less willing to end the game, and their fantasies of heroic acts on the football field may become more and more important in their mental economy. Gradually the value system of their peers and families begins to have impact. Their fathers relive their own dreams of glory and may become over-involved and over-identified. I have heard fathers talk seriously of their preadolescent sons' future college football scholarships. Reality issues come into play as well, group status is allotted to those who are better players, and boys who are not natural athletes may be deeply hurt.

A very important social rating scheme develops, based on when you are picked in "choosing up sides." Phallic narcissism, social acceptability, membership in the gang, status and self-esteem at all these levels are directly involved. For some children, basic attributes of their self-esteem, social role and identity will germinate and harden in part out of these pressures. I have seen in consultation a number of preadolescents who were themselves not good football players or athletes. They suffered constant feelings of rejection by the group. Their adjustment to school and life generally was also pathologically passive, while in their fantasies they were active, courageous and heroic athletes. Thus they became inadequate in their important life adjustments, and only in fantasy active and potent. These boys are often referred to child guidance clinics for schoolwork difficulties and particularly learning problems. Such boys are addicted to their football fantasies and may spend long unrewarding hours trying to develop a skill they will never attain and never gain satisfaction from. The advent of televised football games has even made it unnecessary to go through the active process of developing one's own fantasy. The child (and many adults) sits passively for hours watching the intense activity of others. Through television as well as fantasies, such children preserve an image of themselves as active, while in reality they are hardening the passive aspects of character. Obviously such character disturbances are not created by this one competitive game, but it does play an increasingly important part in crystallizing the defect.

Football at the preadolescent level does not have in it an ultimate devotion to winning, and in the middle of a one-sided game it is not unusual for some fair-minded boy (who is losing) to suggest an exchange of players which will even the sides. Though a boy may cry about losing, the devotion to goal-directed winning is not all-consuming. Although he is a member of a team, he strongly thinks of himself as an individual; the team pressures are less. In his games he usually has divided loyalties; his best friend may have ended up on the opposite team when they chose sides. This creates an attitude of *reciprocity,* which also modulates aggression. Reciprocity implies the exchangeability and alternation of roles. The player opposite you today may be beside you tomorrow. Furthermore, usually everybody in such football games gets to try all positions (roles). Structure of the role relations is fluid, and intense aggressive competition is less clearly defined or required. The formation of football leagues for smaller boys quickly, and I believe unfortunately, ends these aspects of reciprocity.

Inherent in the nature of organized football is the institution of specific aggressive goal-directed achievement and team unity. When one is beating a weaker team, one may send in the second stringers, but one doesn't lend them better players. The competition gets rougher, tears are not permitted, players may be congratulated for injuring an opponent or threatened by teammates for doing poorly, players are assigned a specific unvarying role. A missed pass means not only letting oneself down but letting the team down. The individual pressures to perform are multiplied by the group pressures which are so particularly powerful for adolescents. Cowardice becomes the object of scorn and ridicule. The structure of the group intensifies aggression and sanctions its overt expression when directed to the opponents.

In adolescence, the role of the football player changes. The outstanding high school player has a certain status among his peers which gratifies his need for approval. It is assumed that he is strong or agile, which gratifies his phallic narcissism and strengthens his feeling of masculinity during the turbulent uncertain period of adolescence. Most important in our society, it temporarily solves his identity problem. Erik Erikson has delineated the adolescent quest for a personal and social identity and has emphasized both the terrible stress connected with this achievement and the creative possibilities which are contained in this transition. The high school football player knows who he is in a way that his classmates do not. Furthermore, his success as a football player elevates his status in the group. Thus in the transitional phase of adolescence he finds a temporary and highly gratifying solution to the identity crisis.

He wins respect and praise both from the age and social stratifications below him and above him. Siblings, parents and peer group are all apt to be in the stands cheering for him on Saturday afternoon. Furthermore, in his rebellious rivalry with his father and the adult world in general, he is able to define an area in which father and society will express admiration as well as approval for his aggressive performance. It is therefore easy to understand how a sense of triumph and prominence comes to the adolescent football player. In psychoanalytic terms, the boy at one level seems to have gratified his oedipal rivalry. The father now admires the powerful and aggressive son.

This oedipal experience has an important effect on character, sometimes creating a strange admixture of arrogance and insecurity. Social success is attested by his increased status within the dating hierarchy of his school; in fact, for the culturally deprived and the racial minorities, football is one of the rare avenues for significant vertical social mobility. Further proof of his achievement is the large number of colleges who vie with each other for his interest, a situation which his less athletic student friends can only envy.

As the status goes up and the role becomes defined, the demands of the game increase; a commitment has to be made. The other players are increasingly good, and a successful performance requires a devotion to the game and to the physical development of one's body. Further, it becomes apparent, particularly in the type of line play which accompanies the modern wide-open T formation football, that the old-fashioned shoulder block wastes a man who is a potential downfield blocker; therefore, the forearm charge predominates.

The forearm charge is an important aspect of modern line play. Boxers use their fists, and their blows are transmitted through a number of fairly fragile bones, the metacarpals and the intricate complex of the nine wrist bones. Boxing gloves, together with tape, not only lessen the danger to the opponent, they prevent injury to the hands and wrists of the puncher. Nonetheless, serious injuries still occur. The bones of the forearm, the radius and ulna, are in comparison much larger and sturdier; and in a football player they are encased in a firm pad of muscle. The forearm thus is an incredibly powerful weapon without being fragile. It is not hard to conceive, therefore, of what can in fact happen. A lineman can and does break noses, jaws, etc., which are unprotected. Football officials have recognized the particular dangers of the forearm charge, and the rules relating to it recently were made more stringent, but they are seldom rigidly enforced. It was the widespread transition to this type of blocking in the various T formation offenses and the defenses necessary against them that made face guards for all players imperative by any standard.

Recently a number of televised football games have ended prematurely in a melee of uncontrolled fans rushing onto the field. Occasionally a player is engulfed in such a crowd and will be caught on the television camera as he is mauled by fans. Then one can clearly see the football player in his anger turn not to his fists but his forearms, and rapidly clear a swathe through the crowd.

It is the forearm charge, a lethal weapon, that among other things changes the happy pile of half wrestling children into dangerously equipped and potentially brutal men. Modern football tactics sometimes justify and encourage a kind of aggression which borders on sadism; indeed, it may become part of a cult of success. At this point the college football player is no longer just out for fun. This is evidenced in terms of the amount of time he must commit, the risks he must take, the energy he must put into it and the large segment of the community which is economically dependent on his performance.

The football player in college has an enormously exacting role to fill. He must compete not only on game days against the opposition, but all week long as well against highly competent teammates. He must continually and openly compete against his peers while group feeling and solidarity are maintained. When he commits himself to the absolute goal of winning, to the cult of success, a new code of ethics develops. This code has earlier beginnings, but it emerges full blown in highly competitive college football. The code clearly condones violence, and it is not uncommon to see teammates congratulate a player who has injured a crucial opponent. An equally symptomatic phenomenon is illustrated by the famous athlete who recounted proudly that he used to wear a cast on his arm for the sole purpose of using it as a weapon. Such behavior suggests an underlying code that implies, "It is valuable to hurt your opponent so as to win." All coaches do not make this explicit, but it is an implicit part of the élan. Furthermore, this code can be applied whether a team is winning or losing. Thus you hurt the other team to weaken them in order to win, or when you are losing you thereby obtain your revenge.

The whole spirit of football cannot and should not be described in this way. Not all players behave in this manner; however, a player is seldom criticized by his own teammates for aggressive acts which hurt opponents. I suggest that the reason for this is that hurting through destructive aggression has become part of winning, and winning is the absolute credo of modern football.

For purposes of further clarification, it is useful to divide aggression into two general categories: aggression limited to accomplishing a specific instrumental or goal-directed act, and aggression which is destructive in addition to or at times without instrumental or goal-directed value. In the terms to be used in this paper, the former is *instrumental aggression,* and the latter is *destructive aggression.*

Winning is not only linked with hurting and destructive aggression; winning means achievement, standing out, being a star; instrumental acts of aggression are by themselves compatible with this goal. It is the nature of football that backs and ends can be more frequently involved with such issues, and less directly with the violence of so-called "hard nosed" football.

The identity of the football player qua football player is bound to harden and increase in significance as he channels this enormous investment of his energies. Furthermore, as he gains recognition in the university, others identify him as a football player. Although there are those who denigrate this role, the majority respond with some measure of respect. The development and crystallization of such a personal identity brings immense narcissistic satisfaction, and therein lies a potential danger which is the converse of the usual identity crisis. The adolescent who solves his developmental problems through the hardening of an identity and an accompanying set of values as a football player has, by solving one difficulty, created perhaps a more insurmountable identity crisis. How can he now give up this glamorous image of himself won at the expense of such hard work and at the cost of so much of his adolescent energy and drive, and through which he may have felt the triumph of surpassing his father? To give up this identity and seek out a new vocational and social role is often a difficult and sometimes impossible task. It represents a narcissistic loss in terms of sources of status and gratification as well as habitual patterns of instinctual discharge. He must give up his identity and develop a new and often, at least temporarily, much humbler identity, with a concomitant loss of self-esteem. Many football players are unwilling or unable to make this shift. They cling to their connection with organized athletics and may feel inadequate to compete in business, scholastic or professional life. For some the touchdown they scored against Princeton is truly the high point of their lives. (This syndrome has been depicted movingly by John O'Hara in a short story called "The Eighty Yard Run.") The extreme of this picture does not occur with all football players. Some are able through better perspective to relegate football to a limited time and place in their lives, but to a certain extent it is present in all and must be dealt with.

A consideration of the aggressive behavior of football players should not restrict our attention from other potential instinctual gratifications inherent in the game. Not only are there the diffuse libidinal ties generated by membership in the group with common goals, there are also opportunities in the locker and shower rooms for exhibitionism, voyeurism, phallic curiosity and sexualized horseplay and joking. No doubt some of the football players eroticize the physical contact of the game as well.

This leads back to the point already mentioned, namely, the narcissistic blow engendered by giving up the identity as a football player. At the same time the identity is given up there is also (1) the loss of the group with its gratifications, (2) the loss of important channels for aggressive and sexual instinctual discharge, (3) the obsolescence of certain ego apparatus which previously played a significant part in ego organization and self-esteem, and (4) the possible retention of a primitive superego layer condoning direct aggression.

The transition required by these processes is no doubt a critical task for maturation and comes at a time when there is a loss of group identification.

DETAILED ANALYSIS OF AGGRESSIVE BEHAVIOR AND FANTASY

There is little doubt that a wide variation exists for individual players in the amount of hostile behavior. Aggressive behavior is illusive to define, but from an analysis of films taken of college football games one can describe three stages along a continuum.

1. First, there is domination of the other player by skill or force without any specific devices directed toward hurting the opponent. Such "non-hostile instrumental aggression" is most frequently seen among the highly skilled and competent players.

2. Second, there is domination of the other player by skill and force, including destructive techniques which are effective. This hostile destructive aggression is also seen among highly competent players, some of whom, but not all, may tend to be less skillful than those in category 1.

3. Finally, there is destructive activity without domination or instrumental success. This, though rarer, is a distinct phenomenon. It occurs both in players who, though big and strong, lack competence, as well as in others who seem only to function out of viciousness for its own sake.

These distinctions were obtained by rating each player in his filmed behavior as to the percentage of times he was effective in his assignment and relating it to frequency of directly destructive aggressive acts. Such data were supplemented by rating scales in which the college coaches' and players' impressions of instrumental and destructive potential were considered.

This data has been interpreted as follows: In the first group outlined above are certain excellent football players who focus on the development of their skills; their aggressive behavior is part of this skill and is goal-directed. Their hostility is more neutralized and in the service of a specific ego-directed motor act (or game-related objective). The second group of football players, who may or may not be less skillful, use their hostility in a less neutralized way. They not only perform the ego-directed motor act, but the hostility spills out in the form of a destructive attack. Thus the ego activity makes use of less non-hostile aggression and more destructive aggression. It is not in psychoanalytic terms a conquest by the ego over instinctual aggression, but rather a case of the aggression's using an ego route; it becomes an aggressivized ego function. This seems to be a particular example of how football can channelize hostility, pacifying the superego by the social acceptability and commendation. The hostility, as in the first group, is still instrumental and goal-directed, but more diffusely; since the possibility of being penalized occurs, it is probably less functional. But a penalty is often acceptable if the other team loses an important player in the process. Many students of aggression have noted the correlation between "need achievement" and "need aggression." Something of this order seems present in the case of these football players. Destructive aggression becomes linked with achievement, and they mutually reinforce each other. This point will be amplified in the discussion of fantasy aggression. The point to be established here is that hostile aggression becomes egosyntonic, compatible with ego ideal and with reality testing. It results in the development of certain aggressivized ego functions. Simultaneously the superego may develop a layer in which primitive acts of aggression are condoned.

The third group seems to represent an example of destructive aggression without relation to meaningful ego function. It tends to occur in players who are less capable of performing and who either out of frustration or direct sadism use football as an opportunity for hostile instinctual discharge. The group code justifies this to the individual despite the fact that on occasion it may be highly nonfunctional for the team. This type of behavior seems to illustrate a still less "tamed" form of hostility, little related to ego aims or ego functioning; it does not coincide with effective technique and seems an almost direct and impulsive expression of raw aggression.

Before discussing the fantasy aggression of these three groups, let us consider a fourth group, (4), namely, those players who are neither effective nor hostile. They are poor players and can readily be detected in the films as they avoid aggressive interaction by submission or by various other stratagems. They frequently are the objects of aggressive attacks. There is in this group direct evidence for the predominance of overt masochism in the sense that they repeatedly expose themselves to a competition in which they are hopelessly outclassed and in which they make no attempt to succeed. (This is not meant to imply that masochism is confined to this group or sadism to others. Rather, in all cases a predominant tendency is being emphasized.) [1]

The study of the fantasies of football players before and after playing, as well as during the off season, was originally undertaken in an attempt to examine the catharsis theory of aggression. In general, one was asking: does catharsis of aggression occur? Will the football player have less fantasy aggression after the expression of overt aggression in a football game or scrimmage than he did before it? This question implies that there is a connection between overt and fantasy aggression such that they are directly related, so that when overt direct aggression is possible, covert indirect aggression diminishes. This hypothesis is based on a simple closed system hydraulic model. What the evidence showed was that there is no quantitative difference between a football team's fantasy aggression as measured by the Thematic Apperception Test before and after practice nor did it differ from that of a matched control group. These observations were confirmed when experimental data were added from a second football team in a different setting.

If the measures are valid, then the data indicate that playing football and expressing overt aggression do not appreciably diminish fantasy aggression. The hypothesis that football helps boys let off steam would have to be restated. Perhaps it is fairer to say that football seems only to channel aggression, not diminish it.

Let us turn now to the four groups previously described and consider their characteristic fantasy productions. The better football players of group 1 showed both low destructive aggression in the game situation and low fantasy destructive aggresion. For these players the hostile instinctual impulses seem more controlled both at the level of action and fantasy. The directly hostile aspect seems diminished. Both overtly and covertly these players are interested in mastery rather than hostile discharge. Football seems to be of value to them as an outlet for ego mastery, achievement and eminence rather than for hostility and destructiveness.

The second, third, and fourth groups all had relatively high fantasy aggression when compared to the first.

The second group consists of players who are both effective and destructive. They seem to illustrate the situation of hostility being linked with achievement. This group is the embodiment of the vicious code of football previously described. Football, it appears, helps train them to be destructively aggressive. These destructive and successful individuals are an important part of that group who will later have trouble giving up their identity as football players. Football not only provides an area for achievement, but also supplies the important instinctual channel for aggression.

The third group, consisting of those who are destructive without their aggression being instrumental, will not be discussed at length. First, it is small, and secondly, it is apparently composed of disturbed individuals who are atypical and on follow-up turn out to be suffering from gross psychological disturbances.

The fourth group consists of players who on the field neither used their aggression for mastery nor for destructive purposes. These players showed a relatively high quantity of aggressive fantasies.

My interpretation of this data is as follows: Group 1 demonstrates an egosyntonic non-hostile aggression which has strong elements of self-mastery as well as mastery of others. In psychoanalytic terms, this group probably would be described as having a relatively large amount of neutralized aggression. The goal of this aggression seems to be instrumental rather than destructive. As such it seems to represent one example of a useful process of integrating aggression in an acceptable personal and social manner. Such players are often respected by their teammates and show outstanding qualities in other areas as well.

The second group, 2, has found a route for destructive aggression *and* mastery. In psychoanalytic terms, they seem to be expressing both instinctual aggression and neutral aggression. The ego behavior is aggressivized in a socially acceptable framework. However, it retains a direct destructive quality. This represents an example of acculturation contributing to a superego defect. The football player is rewarded for his destructiveness and expected not to generalize it to other situations. This expectation is not easily met. Attempts to meet it will result in the person's having to evolve new ways to cope with aggression at a time when he has less esteem to draw on. Such an interpretation would explain the difficulty such individuals have in giving up football, where they get both instinctual discharge and narcissistic gratification.

The third group, (3), have not been able to use their aggression in the service of mastery of self or other; they have little neutralized or "tamed" aggression. Football is a stimulus situation permitting a sudden and meaningless act of destructive aggression under the guise of the socially acceptable code. These individuals generally have a personality disorder which they bring to football, and their behavior is marginally asocial, even within the social code that prevails. It is my opinion that these outbursts provided by football have little constructive value for the individual.

The fourth group, (4), are comparatively poor football players. They have little purposeful mastery of the game skills; however, they have managed to control direct aggressive discharge. This is the only group which seems to show a reverse relationship between overt and fantasy aggression.

The members of this group are similar to the passive adolescents described earlier who in their fantasies are active, aggressive and at times sadistic. These players seem to get particular satisfaction from the membership on the football team both in terms of being a member of the group and as it reassures them of their manliness. Their uneasy status is underlined by the coaches' shopworn platitude that this scrimmage will "separate the men from the boys."

"Coach, I'm afraid I've run plumb out of overt aggressive behavior – as a matter of fact, I've developed an acute yellow streak about a *thousand* yards wide!"

This separation of the man from the boy is the task of adolescence. Football, although it helps some in this developmental task, is not the sure road some have claimed. One can become a man too soon, and thus a caricature of manliness.

NOTE

Appreciation and credit are given to Random House for permission to reprint cartoons from Steig's *Dreams of Glory,* at pp. 421-423.

FOOTNOTE

1. Each of these four groups must be considered as described only in relation to the specific situation in which they operated. A member of the fourth group, (4), for example, if transferred to intramural football might become a type (1).

BASKETBALL

WILLARD MANUS

When you are a kid you play basketball mainly because everyone else is playing it, and because it is fun to play. This goes for any game. Stickball and punchball and ringelevio were just as much fun for us city kids as the more regimented games like basketball and baseball, with their uniforms and practice sessions and hollering coaches. We were young and strong and stuffed with vitamins; it did not matter what the action was, as long as there was plenty of it.

When we did play basketball we mostly played in a knockabout choose-up style — in the park after school, three men on a side, scrapping like heck, losing team giving way to those "picking next." It was a primitive kind of basketball — lots of elbowing and shoving — but we had a great old time out there, clobbering each other, arguing like mad. In our raucous unselfconscious way we loved the game — loved it with all the purity and ferocity of youth. However, it wasn't long — say age eleven or twelve — before we lost our innocence and began to play the game for a complex set of new reasons.

It starts that early. Because America is a country which takes its sport seriously, kids become serious about it at a young age. They soon see that a game like basketball is, among other things, a means to an end. A kid who shows promise as a ballplayer immediately learns that he can expect to be well rewarded for his talents, for America has developed a caste system that favors the gifted athlete. But the favors will not come unless he works long and hard.

Next time you are near a playground in the early evening, look and see who is out there in the gloom shooting baskets. Chances are you will see a solitary kid, a skinny gawk running up and down the court, tossing up endless shots — hook shots, jump shots, set shots. Up and down, trying his left hand, then his right; thudding the ball up there with weary monotony, driving himself to the point of exhaustion, legs wobbling under him, breath coming hard. There is your gifted neighborhood basketball player, your potential star. Already he knows he can make the high school team, perhaps earn a college scholarship. But he also knows that he has got to be a slave to the game, that he must pay his dues.

So the game is not entirely for fun any more; it is more like work. No more knocking about; intensity and purposefulness are the order of the day. "He's crazy about the game," is what his parents say — and they are right.

Anybody who spends half his life shooting balls into a basket has got to be a little crazy. But don't laugh; out of such "nuts" grow giant All-Americans.

What, you ask, becomes of the average participant, the kid who is not a basketball fanatic? He too learns a lesson at an early age, that he would do better to say farewell to sport and turn to other endeavors. He may remain a fan and watch others play the game, of course. He may read about it, but he won't play it. No amateurs need apply.

What this means is that in order to maintain our caste system of athletics we sacrifice the physical culture level of the nation. This is an inevitable result of the industrialization of modern society, says Henry Morton.[1] In countries like America and Russia, "sport is the medium most fully comprehended and enjoyed by the great multitude," he writes. "Urbanization, increase in population, technological advancement, leisure time; modern transportation, making inter-area and international competition possible; modern communications, television, the sport page; improved equipment and sport structure — all have contributed toward focusing millions of eyes upon sport arenas large and small."[2] Morton asserts:[3]

> Characteristics of modern sport, mass organization; rules which have become highly elaborate and complex; the emphasis on winning and setting of records at an unparalleled rate; the army of specialists, from the athlete who performs a single function (the place kicker in football) to the coach who is hired to supervise only a specific facet of the game (the pitching coach in baseball); corruption of sporting principles by the demands for victories at any cost — all are a reflection of the industrial process which in effect has brought about a gradual fusion of work and play. Sport has become a serious business; even in friendly matches between individuals a premium is placed on winning. And as we work at play, we play at work. Business competition and individual performance have taken on sporting elements stimulated by the dissemination of statistics which publicize production records and sales achievements; the whole economy is in a constant race to overtake last year's figures.

The emphasis on winning, professionalism, a fusion of work and play — this is an accurate picture of basketball today. Most of the five or six million kids who play basketball have had these values instilled in them, but this doesn't necessarily explain why they have chosen this game over another. Obviously there must be something about the nature of it which has a particular appeal.

Sports Illustrated once described the essence of basketball as "a fluid rhythm with the underlying mathematical symmetry of a fugue by Johann Sebastian Bach. What to the spectator may seem merely hectic anarchy is designed to be a smoothly integrated pattern demanding dexterity, endurance, fine timing and continuous split-second appraisal of percentages and alternatives." Pretty fancy stuff, but it means that those who are attracted to the game must be graceful and well-coordinated athletes, boys who like to run fast and jump high and who can think on their feet.

The terminology of basketball also conveys some of its drama and appeal: fast-break, man-to-man, drive-in, jump shot. Basketball offers the swiftness of ice hockey with none of its brutality, the fierce competition of football with none of its mass confusion. It is a slick game to play and a pretty game to watch. (Not all would agree with this. Sports writer John Lardner once described basketball as "a back-and-forth goal game with a built-in stall or sputter . . . [it] has as much fascination as a leaky faucet.")

Basketball requires tall speedy boys, which rules out 90 per cent of the human race right there, most of us being well under six feet and a little on the heavy side. (No matter: there is always golf.) Height is probably a shade more important than speed; in the pro game, anyone under six-foot-five is considered a small man. Here attention must be paid to the psychology of the tall boy who is drawn to basketball. As a giant in a diminutive world, he is the traditional object of much attention and derision. People point him out on the street, girls laugh at his size sixteens and call him the Green Giant. But nobody laughs when he steps on a basketball court; here he is respected and admired, able to overcome his sensitivity and feel normal. ("He had nothing to tie him to school," said one West Coach sports writer of seven-foot-tall Wade Holbrook, former star of Oregon State College. "Ultimately basketball gave him the tie.")

The tall and the small alike get good things out of the game. There is pleasure and pride in having used your body and talent in a clean, hard, honest way. A deep abiding sense of camaraderie comes too. Playing as a team in the heat of day-in, day-out competition does something to a group of boys, imparts something special. They depend greatly on each other, share in the frustration of defeat and the exhilaration of victory. Strong friendships often develop. Pride of teamship surrounds them like unspoken affection at a family reunion.

All right. We know that the game appeals to the gazelles and whippets among us who enjoy chucking a ball at a hoop. We know that the game builds character, teaches how to get along with others. On the other hand, we also know that in the last two decades not everything about the game has been sweetness and light, and that for every boy whose character has been improved by participation in the sport, another has run the risk of having his destroyed.

If this sounds melodramatic, remember the many dozens of boys who were arrested in the 50's for fixing games. Remember too than an ordinary kid – a pubescent goon from the Bronx or Sheboygan or Tuscaloosa – can suddenly, at age eighteen, have his head turned by fame. National magazines will display his picture. Sports writers will ask him what he eats for breakfast. He will play before packed houses in New York, Boston, Philadelphia, Lexington, San Francisco. Ed Sullivan will ask him to stand up and take a bow. Co-eds will go willingly and deliriously into the back seat with him.

The stakes are high for a good college basketball player. They are even higher for a good pro basketball player. A twenty-one-year-old rookie entering the National Basketball Association can count on making no less than $8500 for six months' work. The stars of the game make four and five times that much. Any wonder why that gifted kid in your neighborhood stays out until after dark every day, maybe even in the rain, shooting baskets?

But, again, dues must be paid. The colleges put terrible pressure on their pampered charges to win, again and again. To stay where the money and prestige are, a college must turn out successful teams. Not every three years — the peak of a team's natural performance cycle — but every year, one after the other. This means they must recruit the best players on the market. Round and round it goes: they recruit players to build winning teams, to attract crowds, to get gate receipts in order to recruit more players to win more games to recruit more players.

With recruiting comes tampering — a college offering a star player more fringe benefits in order to entice him to their camp. When there is recruiting and tampering, there will inevitably be fixing of games. They are but different forms of bribery.

"Recruiting. That's the start of it. How they went out and got us to play," said Ralph Beard, ex-Kentucky and professional star, when he was arrested on fix charges in 1951. "It got so big. Too big."

The NCAA and the various other college athletic councils have at one time or another passed sanity codes that call for severe penalties for such things as "subsidization eligibility infractions," but, as the euphemism indicates, the issue is never met head-on, the codes are eventually emasculated and the game continues its dollar-merry whirl.

All this has been said before, even as far back as twenty-five years ago by the Carnegie Foundation study of college sport. But criticism of this kind runs full smack into the roadblock of the American success ethic, behind which most of the men who control college basketball hide. "We do not wish merely to *participate* in sports. We wish to be *successful* in sports!" So proclaimed Adolph Rupp, for thirty years the basketball coach at the University of Kentucky (and the man who recruited Ralph Beard).

To be sure, Rupp's teams have always won for him, and he has had the kind of success which has enabled Kentucky to build recently a four-million-dollar memorial coliseum seating nearly fifteen thousand people. He talks freely about the coliseum but never about Beard or the other five Kentucky players indicted in 1951 for fixing games. Obviously he refuses to admit any connection between the conquistador philosophy of the game and the corruption of its athletes.

This connection has already been analyzed by Judge Saul S. Streit, who tried fourteen of the thirty-two players arrested in the first major postwar basketball scandal of 1951. Seven colleges and a good dozen fixers provided the headlines then; today, as I write this article, the newspapers carry reports of a new scandal at Seattle University. Streit said that by bribing players in the first instance to choose one college over another, the player's "ethical standards are destroyed, and his moral armor pierced at the very act of entering college. The player begins to compare the adequacy of his compensation with the financial returns to the institution. The self-justification which so often is a prelude to crime is thus created."

But as Streit himself admitted, he only scratched the surface of the corruption: "Four-fifths of it is as yet beneath the level of legal proof and indictment." This is corruption which ranges from the coaches and athletic directors collecting payola from promoters to the whole complex and fantastic gambling apparatus surrounding the game. Bookmakers handle an estimated fifteen million dollars a day in basketball wagers. This illegal operation involves the phone companies, the banks, Western Union, politicians, police chiefs and gangsters, as the Kefauver committee investigating the transmission of gambling information proved several years ago. Basketball odds are determined by the various clearing houses around the country, where professional handicappers study inside information on the games supplied by local sports writers, students, tipsters, and, it is rumored, by players, trainers and coaches. The bookmaking syndicates then begin taking bets at these opening odds, which have declared one team a favorite by a specified number of points. It is this difference in points — called the point spread — which makes basketball more vulnerable to the fix than any other team sport.

Given this pool-hall atmosphere of doubt and cynicism in which they must perform, and given the corrupt internal structure of the college game, is it any wonder that the players sometimes go for the dump? Remember, these are but tall children in a commercial world which often forgets the meaning of integrity. Above all else, college has taught them how to steal and get away with it. And so what has made them special may very well destroy them.

Obviously, only a handful of the five or six million kids currently playing basketball in America will be destroyed by the game. Few of them will become totally corrupted by the mercantile values. But there is no question that their motives for playing — and the way they play — have been seriously influenced. Ideally, those who participate in sport should be encouraged to play the game above victory — "it's not who wins the game but how you play it" – but this is not an ideal world. Our mania for winning has produced a new style of basketball that is totally devoid of love and joy. "White-boss style" is how Jeremy Larner described it in his recent Delta prize novel, *Drive, He Said,* whose hero is a college basketball player. Opposed to this is the "loose lost Negro style, with its reckless beauty," he writes.

> It is the more joyful to watch or play . . . but it is the white-boss style that wins. . . . Even the Negroes must play white-boss basketball to win, though fortunately the best ones can't, and end up with both, the Negro coming out despite themselves right on top of the other style. . . .
>
> Hustling . . . is the first essential of white-boss basketball. He who wants to relax and enjoy it is gonna be left behind, or knocked over and his ball ripped away from him. For white bosses play very rough. Unlike Negroes, they will not back off and let a man keep the rebound he has jumped for; they'll tackle him, lean on his back, slap at his hands, tie up his arms, hoping to wrestle away his prize. And even before the rebound, the grim jostling and bumping for position. A good white-boss basketball player is a good football player – deadly, brutal and never satisfied. What keeps him going is the thought that he and no one else must always win, every instant. Let him win twenty games and he will sulk and cry and kick down the referees' locker room door because he did not win the twenty-first.

As Larner indicates, the psychology of the Negro basketball player is a significant factor in today's game. Up until a decade and a half ago, the doors in most white colleges were shut to the Negro. Unlike his white counterpart, he could not count on being allowed to participate in the mainstream of American sport. He could not hope to share in the glory and excitement and material rewards offered by a game like basketball; all he could do was play it for the fun of it. Hence his "loose lost style."

Today, however, the Negro has been well integrated into the game. It is a rare college team (except in the South) which does not have one or more Negro players on its roster. The three highest-paid players in the pro league are Negro – Wilt Chamberlain (estimated salary $70,000), Bill Russell and Elgin Baylor (estimated salary $50,000 apiece). The best pro team, the Boston Celtics, is 75 per cent Negro.

The reason the Negro is so good at basketball and other sports has been well documented[4] by studies which show that the desire to achieve and excel in sport is intensified in the Negro because of economic and social pressures. He tries harder to win out of a need for revenge and compensation and out of a desire to identify with the white race.

This was borne out in a story related to me recently by one of the top Negro players in the game. "When I was eight each class in school was having a basketball team and so I brought in fifty cents for uniform money," he said. "But the teacher said, 'Oh, we're not letting colored play this year.'

I'll tell you, I wailed. There were two high schools in town, one mostly white and one mostly colored. I chose the colored one, and I played every sport I could."

"How did you do against the whites?" I asked.

"I wrecked them," he said.

The Negro athlete is not only satisfying his hunger and anger today but is lifting himself up to the financial and social level of the Negro elite, as George Frazier, author of *Black Bourgeoisie* points out. Even the minimally successful Negro professional athlete is far better off in the material sense than most of his fellow Negroes. The statistics prove it: only one-half of 1 per cent of America's seventeen million Negroes make more than five thousand dollars a year.

Contained in these figures is the reason why the Negro has become supreme in basketball — and why he too has begun to play the game in the white-boss style Larner so vividly described. Thanks to integration, the Negro basketball player is becoming grim and deadly and hungry for victories. In the modern industrial society it is the way of all flesh, whether black or white. Query a hard-bitten Negro pro basketball player as to motivation and his reply will be sharp and succinct: "I like money." But at the same time you will see that before a game he is so keyed-up as to be unable to hold food on his stomach.

There you have it. Negro and white alike have adapted themselves to the system. They go out there and play the game expected of them. They play to win, play with all their hearts and might, for this is not a game, it's life. It's hard to tell where one leaves off and the other begins, as those of us up in the stands know so well. For we too are white-boss basketball players, and play the game expected of us. How could it be any different? If America is to remain powerful and stay on top, it must have citizens who are dedicated to winning, who worship success. So not only are black and white, life and sport one — but player and spectator too.

By definition there can be little enjoyment in the game for adults. Only children get any fun out of basketball — or life.

"Can't you hear those bloodcurdling screams from the stands where thousands are tied in by their legs?" asks Jeremy Larner in *Drive, He Said.* "They scream not for pleasure but revenge. Revenge for a crime that is committed fast as it can be wiped away. Because for every winner there is a loser, and it is the winner who must pay, sooner or later, and on and on and on, right up to heaven versus hell."

FOOTNOTES

1. Morton, H. W.: *Soviet Sport: Mirror of Soviet Society*. New York, Collier, 1963.
2. *Ibid.*

3. *Ibid.*
4. As far back as 1943, by Maynard Holloman in the *Psychoanalytic Review,* and as recently as 1964, by J. M. Tanner in *The Physique of the Olympic Athlete.*

"If we move him a little to the right, we can toss baskets and hit the official at the same time!"

PART NINE
INDIVIDUAL COMPETITIVE SPORTS

INTRODUCTION

THE SPORTS ARENA IS LIKE A STAGE. The athletes are the actors and the script their personal histories condensed into the moment of competitive struggle. The rules, although restrictive, allow for personal style and individuality. Those aggressive acts not explicitly forbidden by the rules allow for behavior which elsewhere in society is considered deviant. Fans often place a premium on these personal dramatizations of psychotherapy and encourage them. What society represses on the streets it may sponsor in sports. Sports provide some outlet for men to act out psychological conflict about aggression and competition in a society which largely constricts these expressions.[1]

Tennis, like other sports, provides a vehicle for men to act out psychological conflict. Arnold R. Beisser, a psychiatrist and former ranking tennis player, presents some observations of that sport.[2] He confines his comments to the behavior of champions. They are "a select group, and their relative mastery of the mechanics of play make unique behavioral characteristics stand out in bold relief." Furthermore, since they are separated from one another by a net, they can be studied in "relative isolation." Beisser says, "Tournament tennis is an especially good sport for observation. The sterility of the atmosphere, separation of players by the net, the dictates of 'good sportsmanship,' and the fact that tournament players have mastered the rudiments of the game make unusual behavior stand out in bold relief."

The symbolic equivalence of the polite ritualized competition to murderous aggression is revealed in locker room talk and the intricate protective maneuvers of the players. Although disguised, the murderous wishes cause fear of retaliation and guilt. To protect themselves, players engage in bizarre attempts to make believe in a magical way that they are not winning. One tennis champion insisted that his opponents were unfair in order to justify his hostile fantasies. The historical significance lies in the competitive relationships between fathers and sons and is symbolized by young champions and "old pros." The origins of the competitive conflict that many tennis champions undergo may be traced to the fact that they were taught to play by their fathers (ruling officials are known as "tennis fathers"). Beisser writes:[3]

> It is interesting to note the difficulty that young champions have had in dethroning old ones even though they were superior players. At the last Wimbledon championships the biggest upset of the tournament was recorded in such a situa-

> tion. America's most outstanding young player was one of the tournament favorites. He was playing superbly, and in his first two matches beat outstanding champions of two countries. In the third round he lost to the oldest tournament player. This was a man in his later forties who is called "Dad" by the other players and whose age has kept him from being a serious contender for years. Although once an outstanding player, he is far beyond his prime. In a stunning upset he defeated his young opponent whose wild play was considered "unexplainable." It is worth noting that the young player's father is a tennis professional who has always acted as his coach, but was absent from the match.

In sum, Beisser says: "Most tournament players demonstrate much inhibition and guilt in competition. They have not resolved their problems about aggression, and a great deal of their overt behavior can be explained as being defensive."

Carl Adatto writes on play and the psychopathology of golf.[4] His paper is based on actual case histories. From the psychoanalysis of patients who play golf, it was discovered that the game of golf has many possible meanings, depending on the kind of emotional conflicts with which the individual is struggling. Through the game he enacts and attempts to work out these conflicts such as children do in their play. Viewed from its unconscious meaning, in addition to being a pleasurable recreational activity, the game is also seriously used to master the anxiety a person has concerning himself and his close relationships. This perhaps explains the mental well-being as well as frustrations experienced in playing the game. Examples are given from psychoanalytic case material to document this view.

Golfers are challenged by the game because of the feeling that they can never consistently master it. One of the reasons for this challenge lies in the fact that they intuitively realize that they are working out their inner conflicts which during the course of life are never mastered completely. At the same time they experience the pleasure and achievement in mastery. By using the unconscious meanings of the game, it can be seen that golf is more than a holiday from work and the vicissitudes of life and that there are no simple psychological explanations for the game or its errors.

The thesis presented by Adatto is that play activity has the same function throughout life: mastery over the environment, mastery of painful experiences and pleasure derived from bodily and psychical functioning. In childhood play, these functions are more openly discernible because of the naiveté of children. In adult play, with its sophistication and rules, the obscured underlying meaning can only be deciphered through psychoanalysis.

John S. Oelkers, veteran and outstanding track coach, discusses in his paper the motivations in track and field.[5] The complex motivations of modern man at work or play find their counterparts in the drives that make him seek perfection in personal achievement in track and field. Running lacks the excitement of other sports – no bones are broken, no one gets kicked on the head; and running is a lonely experience, even when the runner is out for a cup or medal. Oelkers points out that man in his struggle to stay alive developed numerous skills, and some, such as running, jumping and throwing, coupled with his ability to reason, were his earliest bridges to survival in an extremely hostile world. At first man was motivated only by the need for swift and skillful movement as a means of avoiding the constant threat of violent death with which he found himself surrounded and also as a means of providing food for himself and his group. His sole interest in developing proficiency in these movements was to avoid annihilation. He soon found that perfecting his ability to move about in various ways not only kept him alive but also set him apart; it made him a leader and gave him power which increased his chances of survival. He was quick to realize also that with this power came privilege and fringe benefits which made his life much more interesting and pleasurable – so he practiced.

This growing awareness of the need for warlike skills throughout his development and the urge for superiority over his environment and his

Coach John Oelkers and Ralph Slovenko at Tulane, 1947.

fellows have led man to continue throughout his history to seek to perfect the skills which have made him predominant among the creatures of earth. Oelkers says that the mature athlete is found in the sport of track and field.

Bowling, our next topic, is truly a psychosocial phenomenon. What does it mean? What do bowlers get out of it?

Sue Stone discusses bowling,[6] and she does it in terms of its ritualistic and obsessional aspects. The addictive nature of the sport is examined, as well as its exhibitionistic gratifications and dangers. The simplicity of bowling is stressed as an active yet paradoxical psychological facet of the sport. Psychological differences in the amateur and the professional are noted and illustrated. Voyeurism as a concomitant of exhibitionism is outlined. She comments upon some of the symbolic aspects of the game and upon various differences in the psychological attitudes seen in the two sexes. She analyzes the social structure of the game itself and the environment in some detail.

Herbert C. Modlin of The Menninger Foundation, a bowling enthusiast, observes:[7]

> The mushrooming popularity of bowling during the last decade is one of the striking evidences of middle-class leisure and affluence. BOWL beckons in neon from a myriad of emporiums in city, suburb, town, and along highways between. The polished expanses of 32, 48 and even 100 maplewood alleys are adorned with comfortable spectator seats, juke boxes, pinball machines, billiard rooms, restaurants, bars, lounges, and nurseries complete with baby-sitters and bottle warmers.
>
> There are variations, but a characteristic pattern of neighborhood patronage develops in these new community centers. On weekdays housewives deposit their pre-schoolers with the nursery attendant, then roll two or three lines of conversational tenpins. Adults abandon the premises in late afternoon to screaming hordes of adolescents who invade the center to consume tremendous quantities of snacks and cokes, speculatively inspect peers of the opposite sex and, incidentally, throw a few balls.
>
> In the evening it's a man's world as teams of gladiators, striving for nonchalance in their gaudy shirts and shoulder patches, bombard the hall's acoustics with the incessant explosions of colliding balls and pins, clanking beer bottles and cries of joy when a teammate doubles. Saturday is quieter; some schoolchildren in the morning, solitary men grimly practicing to raise their averages in the afternoon. Saturday night is for dating couples and Sunday is family day, including mixed leagues of married couples.

Long played only by men, bowling today is probably the top competitive sport for women. As one bowling alley owner said exultantly, "We've become the people's country clubs, and it's the girls who have made it that way." Bowling was struggling along like an old tugboat until someone decided to take it out of the basements under barrooms or the back rooms behind the bars and glamorize the sport. The fancy treatment caught on and spread rapidly. The bowling establishment of today, at the very least, provides a restaurant, a cocktail lounge with music, and baby sitting service. Today it is a place that caters to mother and the children as well as to father, and the unmarried. It is a place for relaxation, recreation, exercise and romance.[8]

FOOTNOTES

1. It is to be noted that, as elsewhere in the volume, we raise here the long-term therapeutic value of sports as well as its being a temporary outlet for aggression. Doubt has been expressed that "repressed" hostility may not be drained in play. Norman Reider observes: "Menninger holds that play's most important value is to relieve repressed aggressions. Any sort of organized play is full of aggression. All physical games, card games, and board games, especially chess, are a highly sublimated battle. . . . Thus play is a method of carrying out aggressions in a socially accepted form. Since Aristotle wrote of the emotions becoming purified by play, common experience has attested to that belief. . . . Yet the question is not so simple. . . . I doubt that 'repressed' hostility is drained in play. Perhaps 'suppressed' hostility can easily find partial discharge in play and games." Reider, N.: *Preanalytic and Psychoanalytic Theories of Play and Games, supra* at p. 13, and see Stone, A.: *Football, supra* at p. 419, of this volume.

   It is also to be noted that in this section on individual sports, the term "individual" is not intended to mean isolated or asocial activity, but rather that emphasis is placed on individual effort and performance.
2. P. 450.
3. *Ibid.*
4. P. 458. For a history of golf, see Price, C.: *The World of Golf.* New York, Random, 1962; see also Price, B.: Golfers get angry but seldom fight. *AP news-release,* December 1, 1966; Mandell, A. J.: Golf and Psychotherapy. *Arch Gen Psychiat, 16:*437, 1967.
5. P. 471.
6. P. 484.
7. Personal communication.
8. The same is true for the "billiard lounge." See Baker, R.: Observer. *N. Y. Times,* May 30, 1963; Goodrich, D. L.: Girls Take the Cue. *Sat. Eve. Post,* April 18, 1964, p. 25.

TENNIS

ARNOLD R. BEISSER

IN COMPETITIVE SPORTS MEN COMPETE physically with each other. In its primitive form, competition was a fight for survival, with death the fate of the loser. Such fighting was pervasive, and for primitive man this law of the jungle was dominant. The process of civilization has greatly limited the opportunities for such overt competition. As society has become more highly organized and complex, the physical fight has had more restrictions placed on it. The restrictions are personal and intrapsychic as well as social. Competition has become more subtle and symbolic. The present-day psychiatric patient reveals conflict over competition and aggression in his mental life. In psychoanalysis the nature of the conflict is explored through the verbal retrospective accounts in a setting which purposely limits physical action as much as possible. This is the source of most psychodynamic observations. In competitive athletics, the rules allow physical competition to occur within limits. The sports arena affords a rich opportunity to observe psychodynamic interaction, for the player can actually be seen in competitive struggle. He can be watched as on a stage as he enacts his personal drama. In this setting the athlete can act out some conflicts with a personal and social acceptance which in other situations would be unacceptable. What might be considered "sick" in ordinary behavior is often seen as "color" in sports. Fans, in fact, often place a premium on the deviant behavior of a competitor.

Sports have received only limited attention from psychologists, psychiatrists and psychoanalysts. Helene Deutsch has described the psychoanalysis of a patient in whom an infantile ball phobia had led to a special interest and ability in sports.[1] The method of study is office psychoanalysis. Adrian Stokes has described some psychoanalytic reflections on the development of ball games.[2] This is accomplished through speculations about the history and origins of sports. Francis Ryan has used questionnaires to examine the psychology of track and field athletes who performed well or poorly under pressure.[3]

The relationship between sports and psychology may be seen as one of opposition and thus account for the limited psychological literature on sports. "Only when action fails to satisfy human needs is there ground for thought."[4] Sports provide an avenue of easy access to physical activity for

Americans. The availability of sports for the satisfaction of the need for action in a sense removes the necessity of thought about them. As will be seen from the material which follows, even very serious conflicts in an athlete can be turned into acceptable action.

The sport to be considered here is tournament tennis. The author has been closely associated with this sport for twenty years and has had ample opportunity to make observations from the viewpoints of a psychiatrist, a sports writer and a ranking player. The observations which follow refer to the best players of the world during a period of two decades. They are well known to the author as acquaintances and were former opponents on numerous occasions.

When two opponents enter the court for a tournament match, they enter a very restrictive setting with a myriad of inhibiting psychological factors, both conscious and unconscious. Although their avowed purpose is to win and defeat the opponent, this must be done in a sportsmanlike manner. Sportsmanship dictates that outward signs of aggression towards one's opponent be suppressed. The gentlemen's game requires spotless white attire and polite praise of a rival's good shots, and the loser is expected to congratulate the winner with a handshake and a smile. Audience participation is limited by custom to muted applause for "placements" but never for errors. This sedate atmosphere is generally adhered to and rarely violated.

By contrast, in the locker room after a match there are fewer social restrictions and the facade of politeness is removed. Here the intense competitive spirit of each player is revealed. It is especially interesting to note the terms used to describe defeat: "It was murder." "He slaughtered him." "He killed him."

One is struck by the contrast between these expressions of primitive carnage and the polite cultural setting in which the action occurred. Murder, killing and slaughter are apparently quite foreign to the cultural setting of a tennis match, but the selection of these terms to describe the game betrays the unconscious accompaniments of the apparently controlled aggression of the match. As we shall see later, the actions of tennis champions sometimes make the destructive elements and their defenses quite transparent.

There are several advantages to making observations here. Champions are a select group, and their relative mastery of the mechanics of play make unique behavioral characteristics stand out in bold relief. The rules provide for the separation of opponents by a net. This allows for observations to be made of the individual player in relative isolation.

Unconscious murderous impulses do not escape the restrictions of the adequately developed superego. They are forbidden and must be transformed to gain acceptance, or conflict results. The player who in defeating an opponent is unconsciously killing him is also faced with the fear of retaliation of the talion principle.[5] A variety of defense mechanisms can be observed in the behavior of players.

A national champion of the last decade was the most popular player with the other players. He was always friendly with his opponents, even in the heat of battle. He was known never to have said a harsh word about an opponent, either on or off the court. Yet, in contrast, he was probably the most unpopular champion with fans, for during a match he constantly berated the ball boys. Each of his important matches was held up by his criticism of them. On more than one occasion he was known to strike a ball boy with a ball or with his racket. He could, however, tolerate the displeasure of the fans and the antagonism of the ball boys. This displacement of destructive fantasies to a less threatening object allowed him to compete successfully against his opponents.

All of the major tournaments in the world have the same participants, so that the players know each other intimately. Although coming from different countries and having strong rivalries, there is a firm *esprit de corps* among tournament players. Many follow the sun and play the year round. They are with potential opponents almost constantly and even room together. This poses a serious problem for the player who has difficulty in distinguishing between his destructive fantasies and the competition in a tennis match. A player who was ranked as the world's best amateur a few years ago handled this problem in an interesting way. As the tournament progressed and he could see who his next opponent would probably be, he would undergo a personality change toward him. He would avoid the potential opponent and not speak to him. If, as was inevitable, they met socially, he would glare angrily, utter hostile and sarcastic remarks, and in a most unrealistic fashion accuse his "victim" of unfounded and petty things. This could be particularly uncomfortable if, as often happened, he were staying in the same hotel room as his opponent. His anger disappeared immediately after the match, whether he won or lost. He was once again affable. This pathology was sharply circumscribed to the opponent and the match. When asked about his bizarre behavior, he would pass it off lightly and deny that it had happened. Projection, in this paranoid manner, was his way of dealing with the aggressive conflict aroused. It also served the purpose of a mandate to "fight."

In a recent finals match of the United States National Championships, two players from the same foreign country met. One of them had won the year before and was favored. His opponent was the same player he had beaten the year before. The match was very close, but soon he gained the upper hand and forged into the lead. He needed only a few points to complete his second consecutive championship. Then, during a particularly hard-fought point, his challenger fell and apparently sprained his ankle. The match was delayed as the officials rushed to see how seriously he was injured.

The pained expression on the injured player's face was far surpassed by the anguish on the champion's face. He hung his head and paced back and forth, the picture of dejection. As it happened, the injury was minor. The match was quickly resumed, but now the defending champion missed easy balls. He did not regain his high standard of play and lost the match.

Although there were probably several determinants in the sudden change in this match, one was most apparent. When his opponent injured himself, the champion's appearance was one of dejection and anguish. He hung his head. His expression was one of great guilt, as though he had committed a serious crime. It was apparently this guilt that caused him to lose the match. An athletic injury is the calculated risk of anyone who competes. Separated by a net, if one player turns his ankle, it is hardly the responsibility of the other. In this case the injury was so minor that play was quickly resumed. The defending champion behaved as if it had been his intent to injure his opponent. In the fantasy of the player, the match was the "killing" expressed in locker room talk. When his fantasies were realized, he was overwhelmed with guilt.

There are several world caliber players who exhibit a consistently predictable kind of behavior when they are winning. They begin to castigate themselves. They speak to themselves critically, as to another person, with expressions such as, "You're terrible," "You're lousy," "You can't play." This is indeed surprising to hear after a player makes a brilliant shot. It is incongruous to see a player on one of his best days behaving this way, especially when on a bad day he has no need to do so. It is a magical gesture in which the player denies his strength and potency. He says, in effect, "Look, I am not really strong as it appears, I am weak; I am not winning as it appears, I am losing." By this gesture he hopes to avoid the retaliation which unconsciously is certain to come to him if he wins.

A variation of this same activity was seen regularly in another famous Wimbledon and Forest Hills champion. He could never win an easy match. His first round score against a weak opponent was just as close as in the finals against the best player. He appeared just as disheveled after an "easy" match as after the finals. There was an expression among the other players that if his clothes weren't dirty from his falling on the court he hadn't played. When chided about this, as he often was, he would rationalize, "This is how I keep in shape." He attempted to deny his potency by always having the same narrow margin of victory. If he barely won, he demonstrated that there was little difference between him and his opponent. This served as an unconscious protection. The punishment he had to face would then be small or overlooked.

One of the players who has been mentioned sought psychoanalytic treatment with a colleague. Although therapy was brief, it helped him to shed

"How could a miserable weakling like me be one point away from winning the tournament?"

some light on the origins of the conflicts described. He was taught to play by his father. The competition between father and son was intense. At about the age of ten he asked his father if, should he beat him in a love set, the father would give him something he wanted. He then did beat his father 6-0, to the father's great surprise, for he did not know the boy could do it. They did not play after that or, if they did, it was but rarely. Later the competition between father and son was resumed in business.

That the origins of the competitive conflict lie in the oedipal competition between father and son is further substantiated by the fact that nearly all of the champions mentioned here were taught to play tennis by their fathers. The ruling officials of tennis are known popularly as "tennis fathers." It is interesting to note the difficulty that young champions have had in dethroning old ones even though they were superior players. At a recent Wimbledon championship the biggest upset of the tournament was recorded in such a situation. America's most outstanding young player was one of the tournament favorites. He was playing superbly, and in his first two matches beat outstanding champions of two countries. In the third round he lost to the oldest tournament player. This was a man in his later forties who is called "Dad" by the other players and whose age has kept him from being a serious contender for years. Although once an outstanding player he is far beyond his prime. In a stunning upset he defeated his young opponent whose wild play was considered "unexplainable." It is worth noting that the young player's father is a tennis professional who has always acted as his coach but was absent from the match.

In a recent Davis Cup match, the United States captain chose a little-known player to represent the country. It was a surprising choice which was sharply criticized. The player had never won a major championship and, although there was no doubt about his ability and talent, he could not win important matches because he lacked the "killer instinct." He astonished his critics by winning all of his matches and the Cup. He beat players who had always been his masters. His explanation for his brilliant play was that he had done it for the team captain who had done so much for him in the past. He took no credit himself but attributed it all to the captain. By so doing he had transferred the superego responsibility to another and said, in effect, "I am not responsible for winning, he is; any retaliation should not be directed to me." His father, too, is a professional and had been his teacher.

The "killer instinct" has been considered essential to the personality of a champion. It is supposed to allow the champion to defeat an opponent relentlessly. When the opposition's weakness is exposed, the attack is even more vicious. When the champion's behavior is closely scrutinized, however, victory is fraught with conflict. Most tournament players demonstrate much inhibition and guilt in competition. They have not resolved their problems about aggression, and a great deal of their overt behavior can be explained as being defensive. Some of the mannerisms seen when a player is losing or playing poorly are even more impressive than the behavior of the players described above who were victorious or on the threshold of winning.

There is a belief among players and fans that the player who becomes angry will play poorly and lose. There are many sports axioms about keeping a "cool head" and admonitions against angry displays. Although this is true in many cases, the contrary appears to be so in others. Several top ranking players, when losing, show a fascinating kind of predictable behavior. As the match progresses, the player misses easy shots and falls behind. He begins to talk to himself, at first softly under his breath, then louder until it is clearly audible to the fans. The content is critical of himself, "You're no good, you're terrible, you can't play." The self-castigation gradually increases in intensity. Generally at some point this self-maligning seems to have a positive effect; and he begins, surprisingly, to play better. The player speaks to himself like a critical demanding father who insists that his son must win.

The player's appearance between points is one of despair as he hangs his head. The appearance, the despair and self-castigation are strongly suggestive of a depressive reaction. If the player's game does not improve, he may do something even more dramatic. In the framework of the tennis match, he will make a "suicidal gesture." He will appear to give up totally. He may not even attempt to return balls but simply watch them go by. He may hit balls wildly on purpose or even over the fence. He exclaims, "I give up, what's the use, there is no point in going on." Such dramatic gestures are almost always followed by improvement. This is similar to the clinical improvement shown in the depressed patient after a suicide attempt. The player castigates the bad image within himself and finally even tries to kill it. The bad image is that part of him which was disapproved by his teacher-father when learning. Once destroyed, play is resumed and he plays better. The self-criticism, maligning and "suicidal gesture" appear to have a restitutional function. They are almost always followed by improvement.

Secondary gain may play a role in the tennis "suicidal gesture" as it does in the psychiatric patient. Several years ago in the world championship at Wimbledon a player seemed clearly headed for the championship. He had beaten the favorite and was now considered the choice by most to win. In the semifinals he played an opponent he had met many times before and always defeated. In the match he played so well that his opponent won only one game in the first two sets. He had never beaten him so decisively before. The opponent in his despair castigated himself severely and finally seemed to give up. He hit several balls indifferently and finally let one go by without trying. He was clearly heard to say, "I quit, I'll never play again." The near champion then suddenly altered his game. He seemed very concerned about his discouraged opponent. He missed several easy shots and lost his high standard of play. He eventually lost the match and the championship.

In contrast to the highly civilized setting in which a championship tennis match occurs, players have unconscious destructive fantasies toward opponents. These fantasies interfere with the player's realization of the goal of winning. Behavior can be observed during matches through which a player distorts or justifies his fantasies. Some players attempt to demonstrate weakness while winning, in a magical way, in order to deny their destructive intent and the potency to carry it out. The origins of these competitive conflicts lie in the relationship of players to their fathers who taught them to play and set standards. Some players, when failing to realize these standards, act toward themselves as castigating fathers. Tennis is an especially useful sport on which to make psychological observations. The individuality of the players, separated by a net in a social setting which deliberately seeks to channel and restrict aggression, presents a unique psychological "laboratory" situation. Tennis, like other sports, provides a successful vehicle for men to act out psychological conflict.

NOTE

Sections of this paper are reprinted from *Psychoanalysis and the Psychoanalytic Review, 48*:69, 1961, through the courtesy of the Editors and the publisher, National Psychological Association for Psychoanalysis, Inc.

FOOTNOTES

1. Deutsch, H.: A contribution to the psychology of sport. *Int J Psychoanal, 7*:223, 1926, reprinted *supra* at p. 91.
2. Stokes, A.: Psychoanalytic reflections on the development of ball games, particularly cricket. *Int J Psychoanal, 37*:185, 1956, reprinted *supra* at p. 387.
3. Ryan, F. J.: An investigation of personality differences associated with competitive ability; in *Psychosocial Problems of College Men,* Wedge, B. M. [Ed.]: New Haven, Yale, 1958, pp. 113-122; Ryan, F. J.: Further observation on competitive ability in athletics; in *Psychosocial Problems of College Men, supra* at pp. 123-139.
4. Whyte, L. L.: *The Next Development in Man.* New York, American Library, 1950.
5. Fenichel, O.: *The Psychoanalytic Theory of Neurosis.* New York, Norton, 1945. Webb B. Garrison in his book, *Why You Say It,* discusses the use of the word "love": "One of the puzzles of modern sports is that 'no score' in tennis is called 'love.' Scholars poring over the problem of how this got started have suggested several alternatives. Perhaps the most common explanation is that a person who fails to score is playing for love of the game.

   "Far more plausible is the theory that 'love' came into being when English imported the game of tennis from France. In that language 'no score' was frequently termed *l'oeuf* (egg), because a zero resembles an egg. Stumbling over the French term, English sportsmen quickly transformed *l'oeuf* into *love.*" Garrison, W. B.: *Why You Say It.* Nashville, Abingdon, 1955, p. 160. Perhaps the transformation of the term into "love" stems out of a reaction formation.

GOLF

CARL ADATTO

During the analysis of a patient whose primary recreational activity was golf, a surprise occurred due to a change in the course of the analysis, centered around the unconscious meaning of golf. This and another case will be discussed, together with data from other golfers who have been psychoanalyzed, to support a thesis that play activity in the human being serves the same function at all ages.

There is no intent either to review completely the psychoanalytic literature on play or to do more than superficially comment on the psychology of golf. The primary purpose of this chapter is to apply some of the psychoanalytic theories of the meaning and function of play to the following clinical findings, so as to include more fully adult play. Freud's position regarding play stressed the concept of the enactment of wishes in preparation to growing up, and also the mastery of traumatic experiences.[1] Melanie Klein interpreted play as the discharge of masturbatory fantasies and its wish-fulfillment expression, but also noted the analogy existing between means of representation used in dreams and play.[2] Waelder later summarized the psychoanalytic theories of play in terms of the instinct of mastery, wish fulfillment, assimilation of overpowering experiences according to the mechanism of the repetition compulsion, transformation from passivity to activity, leave of absence from reality and from superego and fantasies about real objects.[3] He includes the attainment of functional pleasure in play activity. Erikson sees childhood play as the infantile ego's effort at synthesis; the purpose of play is to hallucinate ego mastery.[4] However, he infers that the comparison of adult and child's play is somewhat useless because adult play is recreation while that of the child is preparatory. Greenacre states that one of the main functions of play in connection with creative imagination is that it aids in "delivering unconscious fantasy and harmonizing it with the external world."[5] She comments that not enough attention has been paid to the differences between content and underlying drive in play. Kris views adult play in part as "a holiday from the superego," while play in childhood supplies a bridge enabling instinctual satisfaction to take a form of adapted reality.[6] He considers children's play to perform two tasks: "acqurinig mastery over the environment and warding off unpleasure (mastering 'painful' experience)," in addition to having a motive of promotion of pleasure in function.

Free play in a two-year-old or a golf game in an adult differ *manifestly* as a result of differences in maturation and development, but unconscious drama is present in both. Like dreams, play must be understood in terms of its latent rather than its manifest content and allow for differences in symbolization and ego development. With analysis one can see the widest possible range of unconscious activity enacted in the game of golf, depending on the conflicts with which the individual is coping at the time. There has been a tendency to attach specific symbolic meaning to games and treat them as a special kind of play instead of considering games to be a more sophisticated type of play retaining all of the richness of play as understood in children.

Because adults are reluctant to admit having overt pleasure in play, and because they need to demonstrate diligence in work and intellectual pursuits, psychoanalysts may not hear much regarding such activity. In addition, if it is a game of action, it lends itself poorly to verbal description. However, analysts know the need to cull every bit of material available for the purpose of understanding the intrapsychic processes. We scrutinize dreams, character traits, bodily gestures, personal interactions, and in fact all aspects of the person's life.

Studies of childhood play have been fruitful in revealing considerable data regarding psychic development. Therapeutic techniques using play were adopted early by child analysts in the treatment of children because this was the natural medium with which to communicate with children. In commenting on play techniques, Anna Freud states: "In this way we have the opportunity of getting to know the child's various reactions, the strength of its aggressive impulses or of its sympathies."[7] By the time adulthood is reached, play recedes into the background of the individual's activity and manifestly becomes more ritualistic and mechanical. Peller describes how it changes from unrestricted play to organized games with libidinal and ego development.[8] Among other reasons, free play becomes taboo because it represents too great a threat to instinctual break-through. In most adults, play usually takes the form of games which are not only acceptable but desirable. In recent years golf has achieved such status for the average person.

Through understanding the psychoanalytic productions of golfers, it is hoped that a further contribution to the vicissitudes of play can be made. The golfer's game becomes a crucial arena for adaptation and working out conflict, widening ego activity, working through the infantile neurosis; in addition, it may become neurotic behavior in itself. Golf, despite certain obvious features, has no single meaning within the framework of the game; individual meanings are worked out. Data from this group of patients failed to yield any specificity. On the contrary, even for the same patient, the game would have different meanings. This is not to say that specific anxieties, such as castration anxiety, are not common in golf. However, to limit the meaning of the game to specific areas fails to recognize the wide range of psychic activity. Golfers are frequently heard to say that the challenge of the game lies in the fact that it can never be mastered. No doubt this is their intuitive way of recognizing that they enact their interminable unconscious conflicts and continuing development in playing the game.

Certain aspects of the game are noteworthy. Golf is a game in which the individual primarily struggles with himself and secondarily plays with others as participants, competitors, partners or witnesses. One must master new motor skills to learn the game, with the result that muscular mastery and its psychic counterpart of active mastery become a central part of the psychology of the game. The intermixing of shots of power with those of "touch" or finesse opens up the possibility for performing various kinds of motor skill. Golfers are apt to play well one day and poorly another, or do so during the same round; nevertheless, it is characteristic that their performance shows an overall constancy. Equipment (bag, clubs, ball, etc.) and components of the golf course (fairways, greens, rough, hazard, etc.), as well as such phenomena as the trajectory of the ball, permit a ready-made focus for unconscious symbolism. In order to swing the golf club correctly, it must anatomically become an extension of the left arm, even though the right arm along with the rest of the body furnishes the power required to execute shots of distance. The fact that the left arm becomes trained in a new way presents great difficulty to the beginner, who has customarily used the dominant right arm to engage in similar activities. For instance, swinging a baseball bat is more "natural" in this respect. Children, however, learn to do this as easily as they learn other motor skills. This is a common envy of the adult beginner. Remarks such as "If only I had learned this as a child" or "I'll teach my children to play the game early so they won't have my trouble with it" are often heard on the golf course. This sort of wish to achieve the ease of childhood motor mastery cloaks also the regressive aspects of the game. The novice requires considerable practice and instruction before the game can become enjoyable. Only those who are bent on such bodily and psychic mastery withstand this period of indoctrination. The manner in which this is approached and accomplished tells much about the individual. For instance, one golfer intensively worked at the game in all of his spare time for about a year before he felt sufficiently free to play on a golf course. This was similar to the way he studied in school and earlier in his life mastered poor motor coordination, which had been the bane of his existence.

The golf professional who teaches is aware of resistances to learning, and discusses the need to "practice psychology" with his pupils. His use of the relationship with the student in the teaching situation becomes highly important. As with other teachers, it is necessary for him to be aware of the student's inner struggle in order to teach successfully.

CASE ILLUSTRATIONS

The following clinical illustrations are selected from the analyses of six golfer patients. License is taken in describing the cases for the purpose of concealing the identity of the patients.

Case 1. An unmarried woman, thirty-two years of age, came to analysis because of recurrent periods of apathy and disinterest in her work and her friends. She had become progressively uncomfortable during the previous few years because of embarrassing outbursts of anger in social gatherings. When she sensed that these outbursts were exaggerated, she developed increased feelings of uneasiness and guilt. Her history revealed that she had always been a self-sufficient person with the feeling that she could ultimately overcome these difficulties on her own. The loss of control over her feelings was the factor which precipitated sufficient anxiety to motivate her to seek treatment.

She was the oldest of four children, having two brothers and then a younger sister, all of whom were married and leading what she termed normal lives. Her father died when she was six years old, and her mother remarried when she was twelve. She was always close to her mother, and evidently had taken on an assistant's role in helping with the siblings. This role persisted until she came for analysis, and according to her description she had become more a grandmother than an aunt to her nieces and nephews. On the surface, her adolescence presented nothing unusual. She apparently separated herself from her mother in many ways and had the usual conflicts centering around independence, boy friends and sexuality. When she was seventeen, a boy friend taught her the game of golf, which she immediately liked and mastered fairly well. From then on she continued to play fairly regularly and later won many trophies in competition. In her analysis it developed that learning the game was based on an identification with her boy friend. Her attempt to recapture her father, who died during her oedipal period of development, revealed itself in the analysis of this relationship.

When she was in her third year of college she became engaged to be married. During this period her mother developed a malignancy and died. Even though she had continued her education during her mother's illness, she had spent much time nursing her. Her mourning reaction was intense and was later followed by her breaking her engagement. Ultimately she obtained employment as an executive assistant to a businessman, a job which she held at the time she sought treatment. Other attempts at serious relationships with men never materialized due to disinterest on her part.

During the immediate mourning period for her mother she abandoned golf, but resumed it with vigor afterwards. Early in the course of the analysis it became evident that she was playing a bisexual role when she played golf, and that she was attempting to master her passive-dependent longings through mastery of her golf game, work and efficient dealings with people. An unusual bit of data came out in one session when she reported a dream: "I bought a new golf bag, but found out I couldn't put the clubs in easily." When her associations brought out her preference for oval-shaped bags, she laughed and said, "I've been looking at myself as an old bag recently." Difficulty in placing the clubs in the bag eventually delineated more clearly than before her conflict regarding her sexual identity and inhibitions.

Later on in the analysis, at a time when oral material was the central theme, she complained about her golf game with much disgust. First she reported that she was frequently losing her ball in the rough, and then that she developed intense anxiety about going out onto the golf course. To make matters worse, she developed a "slice" which frequently carried her ball into the rough. In an attempt to correct this error, she took additional lessons which helped somewhat; however, when her anxiety persisted, she gave up the game for a few weeks. With considerable determination, she reported: "I'm not going to let this damned game get the best of me." The obsession with her golf game permitted no other material to come into her analysis, and previously understood meanings of the game were of no help in resolving this dilemma.

A point was reached when it seemed that her use of golf had become a massive resistance to the analysis. This impression was conveyed to her, and she was inclined to agree with it. A few sessions later she reported a dream which brought out a surprise meaning in all of her activity, and what she was enacting on the golf course: "I dreamed that I was walking through a cemetery, then through some fields looking for a golf ball I had lost. I was alone and felt intense panic." Her associations promptly led her to her mother's burial and her grief reaction at the time. She also recalled that at the time of her father's death, her mother was alone in her room for long periods of time, and according to her fresh recollection of the period it was then that she began to nurse her mother and look after her siblings. The golf ball itself, rather than being an obvious genital symbol, became identified with her mother's body. She was searching for it and afraid of finding it at the same time.

It was easy to see all of it once her associations became clear, in view of the nature of her neurosis; nevertheless, it was a genuinely rewarding surprise. As more analytic productions evolved, looking for her mother's body was more specifically a wish for the breast and her fear of having destroyed the breast. This was in sharp contrast to her apparent central use of the game of golf, which focused on the problems of bisexuality and body mastery. Previously she had used her golfing companions to help her act out her unconscious oedipal and maternal strivings. In this part of her game, the companions were for all purposes nonexistent to her, and she was alone. Once this analytic material was worked out, it became obvious that she was using the game for enacting and working through her entire constellation of problems. It reminded me of a child patient who would bury small objects in clay repeatedly and then hide the clay until the following session. This ultimately was discovered to be the child's reenactment of the loss and burial of a sibling.

This patient's attempt to get the golf professional to correct her "slice" was an attempt to split the transference. This and her agoraphobic symptoms on the golf course were patent enough for her to see as a defense, so that it was not difficult for her to return to the analysis of the transference to work through her destructive aims and oral dependency.

Following this episode, although her "slice" disappeared, her golf game became less exact for a while. At the same time she noted a new quality of enjoyment in the game, indicating a predominance of pleasure in the activity of the game.

Case 2. A twenty-eight-year-old married man presented himself for analysis because of increasing difficulty in concentrating on his work and the fear that he might jeopardize his future because of this. In addition, he had developed insomnia, cardiac palpitation and other somatic symptoms. After a medical workup proved to be negative, he himself recognized his bodily disturbances to be signs of anxiety. He was married, had three children, and in general had no serious complaints in this sphere of his life. He was the middle of three children, having an older brother and a sister four years younger than himself. The brother evidently had a birth trauma with slight spasticity which was fairly well overcome by persistent exercise and training. As a result of this difficulty the father, who himself had always been athletically inclined, stressed exercise for all of his children. The patient learned to play golf in early adolescence and was encouraged by his father, who was a proficient golfer and a student of the game. His mother also played golf well, but his brother concentrated on swimming, and his sister on tennis. The whole family were avid football and basketball enthusiasts, and both boys played these sports in high school. As the patient reached his college years, he worked on his golf game and was constantly the object of praise by his father who pointed out to his cronies how his son could outdrive him and frequently beat him in a golf match. The history and description of these matches revealed a poorly veiled oedipal problem which was intense but well managed.

After finishing his professional education, he married a girl who was of his own culture and economic background. He reported that during her first pregnancy he initially became aware of his cardiac palpitation. In the analysis of this episode he brought forth memories of the birth of his sister. Upon discussing this event with his parents, he was told that he became sullen and morose at the time. His own principal recollection of the event was being told not to touch his sister. There was further anxiety during his wife's subsequent pregnancies, and he reported that he managed his feelings during these episodes by working harder and assuming a position of more responsibility. Upon realizing in the analysis that his work record was quite satisfactory, he moved into more personal areas of his life.

During his marriage he continued to play golf regularly and reported that in the two years prior to his analysis he had "attacked the game with ferocity." He took intense pleasure especially in coming from behind to win his match with "cool control" and executing exceptionally difficult shots. If he played poorly toward the end of a round of golf, he became irritated regardless of whether he won or lost his match. It developed that his rivalry with her brother and guilt over winning favor with his father by playing his father's game well screened his competitive rivalry with his sister. The eighteen holes in a round of golf became a reliving of his maturational years, with greater skill and control expected of him in the later years, or the latter part of his game.

Only when this material was analyzed did he report a long-standing symptom of periodic sexual impotence. This was equated with losing a hole due to his poor performance. If his opponent won the hole with superb play, he would merely pass it off as the fortunes of the game. The negative oedipal problem and the identification with the aggressor came out in analyzing his golf, work and relationship to his father. It seemed that the essential rationale for his golf game in terms of his neurosis was playing and replaying the game in an attempt to master his oedipal conflict. The use of a round of golf to reenact his total development gave the clue that the game had more meanings.

As his analysis progressed, he developed a period of intense anxiety which almost paralyzed him in his work. His symptoms became aggravated, and he complained bitterly that his analysis, rather than helping him, had made him worse. During this period he continued to play golf fairly well, but he terminated playing abruptly when in a fit of temper after missing a short putt he threw his club away in a rage. Many times he had the impulse to do this, but he had always deferred and controlled the impulse because of his contempt for those who did throw their clubs. On the spot, the incident evoked severe censure from his fellow players, which added to his embarrassment. He stopped playing on the golf course and spent his evenings compulsively hitting golf balls at a driving range, to the point of developing blisters on his hands. He was difficult to approach analytically due to the intense resistance during this period until he reported an outburst at his oldest child, a girl, whom he adored. She accidentally soiled herself, for which he impulsively whipped her and then experienced remorse. This incident led to memories of his own bowel accidents, some of which had occurred after the birth of his sister, when "I was too old for that sort of thing." The anxiety-ladened family ideal of muscular control and its relationship to his own sphincter mastery were a part of his golf game. While the game had been a source of sublimating and working through this conflict, it had not fully succeeded. When this was partially analyzed, the game itself became a threat. The failure to make a short putt (a bowel accident) evoked his rage and sadistic impulses. It was probable that his daughter emphatically responded to his own conflicts when she soiled herself. Through her he was able to gain insight into his own conflict. The compulsive nature of his work and sexual activity was opened up further by play on the golf course.

In this case, as well as in the previous one, it was apparent that the deeper meanings of the game were covered over by the more obvious later maturational conflicts. To have considered the game only as a phallic, competitive sport would have bypassed the wealth of intrapsychic meaning it carried. Other aspects of his neurosis were enacted on the golf course, although with less drama than the incident reported.

These two examples of analyzed golfer patients are not unusual. In all such patients I have analyzed, I found that golf has a wide variety of meanings for each patient. In one instance the problem of exhibitionism was reached only through the analysis of the golf game itself. This was brought out when the patient began joking about the way he hit some of his best shots when many other golfers were watching. The analysis of this observation led to information regarding his fantasies about phallic exhibition. Another patient, who was threatened by ego disintegration and a fear of a psychotic episode, tenaciously hung on to her golf game as proof of her psychic mastery during a period of intense external stress. Merely playing the game and controlling her swing were proof to her that she was intact. On several occasions this patient demonstrated how the golf club itself became a part of her body image, and that it was not only a weapon of attack but also proof of adequate bodily functioning. One golfer learned that when he developed a certain error in his swing, namely, a bending of his left elbow, it was a sign that he might be experiencing castration anxiety. In an interesting way his golf game became a signal device to which he paid serious attention. Still another player abruptly stopped using a caddy when he was working out the resolution of his infantile dependency on his wife, who had always nursed him rather carefully.

To document this thesis further, a case which Oberndorf reported is quoted:

> When the patient's compulsion to work gradually weakened and he began to play golf he once remarked that golf is really a solitary game, for there is no comeback from the ball such as one would receive if one approached any living thing with equal aggression. Golf reminded him of earlier days when he spent much time playing solitaire at cards and would alternate the game with frequent masturbation. In golf his primitive impulses to violence reappeared, and he said that he actually felt temporarily "crazier" on the golf course than he had been during some phases of his serious mental illness. To him the only pleasure derived from golf consisted in the moment when he struck the ball and all his viciousness, bitter aggression and latent sadism found release. To him, walking around the golf course represented only arduous work which he hated, but any form of play had to have an element of work for him if he were to indulge it at all."[9]

In this brief description Oberndorf notes a central theme, that of handling aggression in the golf game, but infers other uses as well.

COMMENTS

The above clinical material demonstrates that golf has a useful role in the lives of the individuals who play it. As a game it carries the complexity of the intrapsychic conflict, and the working through and physical enactment of this conflict with the self and the environment. In the two cases presented, it can be seen that the analysis of the patient was expedited by information regarding the golf game. The overdetermined role it played in the life of each patient was a factor which led to the analyst's knowledge that the attitudes to golf constituted significant data. In contrast to play techniques with children, the golf game is played with others and then brought into the analysis. The analyst's understanding of the game permitted easier communication on the part of the patients, who as golfers were more than happy to report the details of their play. It also enhanced empathic understanding of the unconscious material through a common medium, and at the same time alerted the analyst to the problems of identification and countertransference. It became a source of valuable information and a delicate indicator of anxiety and conflicts such as Bond described in aviators.[10] This made a strong impact on the patient and added to his conviction of the workings of his unconscious by understanding the psychic determinants of playing the game. The surprise factor in the two cases reported was noteworthy. At a point where it was considered that their golf game had been fairly well understood, the abrupt change in how the game was played revealed meanings which had previously not been recognized. These episodes could be considered creative analytic work.

The first patient assumed she had worked through her mourning for her mother, until the game and the dream revealed facts to the contrary. Then it became clear that with the death of the mother, she had suppressed the earlier oral problems, which in turn had made it impossible for her to continue with her developmental task. Only after she was able to complete her mourning and continue the analysis of her conflicts did her life change appreciably. She was then able to reestablish relationships on a plane consonant with achieving pleasure in her own right, rather than through being a parental substitute.

The second patient's rage reaction and the dissolution of the compulsive aspect of his game were the signal for the breakthrough of important anal-sadistic data. His fear of being castrated, as he considered his brother to be, led to an elaborate constellation of defenses involving identification with and excelling his father in an approving way. When he sufficiently overcame his fear of castration, he was able to permit himself to be impulsive, uncontrolled and a "poor sport." Then he could see that he was defending in the game itself a fear of having no muscular independence, which to him meant being feminine. By acting out the soiling in the game, he was more easily able to cope with it and thereby analyze it. The analysis of this material permitted him to begin to restore his body to himself.

It is convincing that this game, which occupied a strong interest in the individual's life, must be laden with meaning, and that in essence it fulfilled the same psychological role as play of childhood. Analysts are in danger of accepting the concept that play is permissible only for children. It would seem that this notion has at its roots, in part at least, the need to keep play free from the encumbrances of revelation and thereby preserve it as a reservoir for the fantasies of childhood. The very fact that adult games become so well structured and bound by rules shows how the free activity becomes modified by the ego in a way which is acceptable by the superego and environment. In addition, the respectability cloaking the game of golf and its wide acceptance make the underlying meaning less suspect. However, despite this obvious organization, the player can openly dramatize his conflicts and share them with others with the comment, "It's only a game." The private games adults play with themselves, and which they usually reveal only in the privacy of the analysis, indicate a need for stricter defenses.

It has been observed that to some patients the game becomes compulsive activity, losing the element of enjoyment and serving essentially a defensive role. This was exemplified by a patient who routinely plodded through many rounds of golf with an attitude: "Thank God it's raining today so I don't have to play." In other words, it can become principally neurotic behavior and have the characteristics of such action. Some individuals give up the game at this point, only to return to it again for a fresh start. Invariably, when some of the defensive meanings of the game were in the process of being analyzed, patients would either temporarily abandon the game or their skill would deteriorate for a period of time.

Players apparently use the game constructively in a sense of working out their problems, although they are not fully aware of it. This is similar to the way children play in the course of their daily lives, an activity which has been described by Freud as "normal."[11] These adaptive ego functions are observed in the use of the game and have profound significance. However, the scope of this paper precludes anything but mentioning this point. Reports in the literature vary as to what motivates individuals to play games, and usually stress specific conflicts or developmental tasks.[12] Chess, however, has received more psychoanalytic interest than any other adult game. Jones in his study of Paul Morphy proposed that the theme of father murder is prominent in the game of chess.[13] Reider in an extensive study of the game states: "Chess is the royal game for many reasons. It crystallizes within its elaborate structure the family romance, is replete with symbolism, and has rich potentialities for granting satisfactions and for sublimation of drives."[14] Going beyond Jones, who admits that impulses behind the play are of a mixed nature, Reider opens the game to all of its rich psychological potential. No generalization could be drawn as to why golfers take up the game; nevertheless, identifications in the two cases mentioned did play a crucial part in learning the game. The two patients described began their interest in golf in adolescence, but each had a different reason. Many individuals take up the game in middle age when they cannot stand the vigorous activity of other sports, or when they feel the need for reassuring themselves of their physical potency and functioning. One patient who started playing golf in his forties remarked that he felt he was "finally entitled to have some fun," as though it was his due for years of hard work. He discovered it was work of another kind, but he could approach the resolution of certain infantile conflicts only through muscular action.

Even though the thesis of this paper is based on data from a small number of patients, the information is convincing enough to the author to postulate generalizations regarding all play activity. Analysands who have played different kinds of games such as tennis, bowling and bridge yield the same sort of findings. Instead of continuing to confine play to "children's play," as is frequently found in the literature, or to limit adult play for the most part to a recreative activity in which leave is taken from reality and the superego, it is felt that *play should be considered a lifetime activity of the human being, and its latent unconscious meanings rather than its manifest structure should be used as a basis for understanding and comparison.* The analysis of these patients' golf games demonstrates the existence of the meanings of play described by Kris: mastery of environment, mastery of painful experience, and pleasure in function.[15] In the analysis of patients one focuses on the first two functions, especially the second, since these are interwoven with neurotic behavior. The pleasure in the action of the game was frequently reported by the patients and is easy to verify by listening to golfers as they relax in the clubhouse. The feeling in executing a good shot, described as an effortless impact of the club on the ball, is a sensation which the golfer tries to achieve. Not only does he enjoy the pleasure of executing a good shot, he also experiences a general vigor following the psychic and physical activity in a round of golf which is relatively free of neurotic activity or results in some diminution of neurotic conflict. While this paper has focused on the psychopathological processes in patients, I do not wish to imply that the pleasurable aspect of the game is unimportant. On the contrary, I believe that this very pleasurable function permits the player to withstand the hard work of mastery of inner and outer conflicts. One can observe the same sort of thing in children in whom the pleasurable sensations of play act as a stimulus for their continuing the serious task of mastery in which they are involved.

Since play does have such an important role in the adult's life, continued and expanded studies of the meaning of this activity deserve attention. Our culture permits more time for recreation and leisure than before, as is evident in the great spurt in building new golf courses, bowling alleys and other similar recreational facilities. The analyst has a valuable method by which these activities can be understood. From a clinical viewpoint a broader understanding of play should permit a more complete analysis of patients.

SUMMARY

This paper attempts to document through analytic material from patients that the game of golf has a wide range of intrapsychic meanings to the patient. Because of maturation, the adult's play differs manifestly from that of the child, but like the dream the latent unconscious meaning is similarly active and should be used as a basis for comparison. Analysis demonstrated that while a game may have certain common symbolic meanings, golf has no single meaning, even for the same individual. It is proposed that the theories of the function of play, especially those emphasizing mastery of the environment, mastery of painful experience and pleasure in function, should be uniformly extended to include play activity throughout the life of the individual, and not be limited to childhood or special categories of adults.

NOTE

This paper was presented at the New Orleans Psychoanalytic Society, Jan. 11, 1963, and at the Annual Meeting of the American Psychoanalytic Association, May 4, 1963, and was published in the *Journal of the American Psychoanalytic Association, 12:*826, 1964. Included in the paper are ideas suggested by many discussants, especially those of Drs. Fred P. Robbins and W. C. Thompson.

"If I could putt like you, Simpson, I'd probably regard golf as a *fun* game and yell *'Olé!'* too."

FOOTNOTES

1. Freud, S.: *Writers and Day-Dreaming (1908). Standard Edition,* Vol. 9. London, Hogarth Press, 1959, pp. 142-153; *Beyond the Pleasure Principle (1920), Standard Edition,* Vol. 18. London, Hogarth Press, 1955, pp. 7-64.

2. Klein, M.: The psychological principles of infant analysis (1926), in *Contributions to Psycho-Analysis (1921-1945)*. London, Hogarth Press, 1948, pp. 140-151.
3. Waelder, R.: The psychoanalytic theory of play. *Psychoanal Quart, 2*:208, 1933.
4. Erikson, E. H.: *Childhood and Society*. New York, Norton, 1950, pp. 182-218.
5. Greenacre, P.: Play in relation to creative imagination. *Psychoanal Stud Child, 14*:61-80, 1959.
6. Kris, E.: *Psychoanalytic Explorations in Art*. New York, Int Univs, 1952, pp. 182-183.
7. Freud, A.: *The Psychoanalytic Treatment of Children (1946)*. New York, Int Univs, 1959, p. 28.
8. Peller, L. E.: Libidinal phases, ego development, and play. *Psychoanal Stud Child, 9*:178-198, 1954.
9. Oberndorf, C. P.: Psychopathology of work. *Bull Menninger Clin, 15*:77, 1951.
10. Bond, D. D.: *The Love and Fear of Flying*. New York, Int Univs, 1952.
11. Freud, S.: Writers and day-dreaming. *op. cit. supra* note 1.
12. Beisser, A.: Psychodynamic observations of a sport. *Psychoanal Rev, 48*:69, 1961, appearing herein; Deutsch, H.: A contribution to the psychology of sport. *Int J Psychoanal, 7*: 223, 1926, appearing herein; Peller: *op. cit. supra* note 8; Phillips, R. H.: The nature and function of children's formal games. *Psychoanal Quart, 29*:200, 1960; Stokes, A.: Psychoanalytic reflections on the development of ball games, particularly cricket. *Int J Psychoanal, 37*:185, 1956, appearing herein.
13. Jones E.: The problem of Paul Morphy: A contribution to the psychology of chess (1931); in *Essays in Applied Psychoanalysis*. London, Hogarth Press, 1951, pp. 165-196.
14. Reider, N.: Chess, Oedipus, and the Mater Dolorosa. *Int J Psychoanal, 40*:320, 1959.
15. Kris, E.: *Psychoanalytic Explorations in Art*. New York, Int Univs, 1952, pp. 182-183.

TRACK AND FIELD

JOHN S. OELKERS

FOR SEVERAL HUNDRED THOUSAND YEARS, throughout his evolution from a tree dweller to his present level of civilized living, man has been faced with the necessity of being able to run, to jump and to throw — first as a means of survival and, as he progressed, for a variety of other reasons only partly concerned with staying alive. To borrow from the motto of the modern Olympics, he was always having to improve his skills to the point of "faster, higher, further" or perish, or at the very least suffer loss of face in his social order.

When Australopithecus, man's remote ancestor, decided to spend most of his life on the earth's floor rather than in the treetops, he immediately added many new problems of survival to an already most hazardous existence. His tools and weapons were few and very crude, his skills in using them limited, and improvement possible only through trial and error experimentation which often ended abruptly for all time where he was concerned. Even when he was successful in postponing for a time the fatal outcome of his curiosity, the knowledge gained at great risk to life and limb was often useless and always dangerous to a hominid who was just not equipped physically and mentally to cope with the overpoweringly lethal environment in which he now chose to live.

Although it was imperative that he become an upright creature in order to broaden his ability to see about him and free his forequarters for the use of tools and weapons, he was not yet anatomically capable of moving with the speed his new surroundings often required of him. Certainly he could not meet on an equal footing creatures who had roamed this terrain for hundreds of thousands of years before his first timid steps took him farther and farther away from the great trees which had been his home and his protection. Often as not, he was at a great disadvantage in size and strength and found himself as tempting a morsel of food to as many of these creatures as he himself regarded other and smaller game. He was, on most occasions, the hunted rather than the hunter and soon found himself concerned almost entirely with survival. He began to develop skills which have come down through the ages in almost pure form, such as running, jumping and throwing, which are today the fundamental skills of our modern track and field program, although motivated by completely different reasons.

At the Australopithecus stage of the evolution of the creature who would hundreds of thousands of years later become Homo erectus and eventually

Homo sapiens, he and his contemporary paranthropus and later advanced Australopithecus were not anatomically designed to run with the speed or elusiveness that later became one of man's basic survival tactics. His ability to jump and throw, while somewhat more advanced skillwise because he undoubtedly had some use of these skills even while living in the treetops, were still rudimentary by any standards. In fact it is a wonder that he survived at all in an environment that had seen the failure of creatures similar to himself that had preceded him and the eventual extinction of his contemporary paranthropus.

When the evolution of man had reached the advanced Australopithecus stage, it found him with two growing powers that were to be the cornerstones of his survival and development — reason and communication. The greatly increased ability to reason possessed by the advanced Australopithecus as compared to his predecessors and his improved ability to communicate with his fellows gave him an ever growing advantage over his contemporaries, both hominid and animal, which largely compensated for his lack of comparative size and strength and his still rather clumsy efforts in the basic survival skills of a land creature. In fact, it is thought by some scientists that this lack of superior reasoning ability was a strong contributing factor which may have hastened the extinction of paranthropus who competed with advanced Australopithecus for dominance.

Whatever the reasons, and there have been a number of theories, the decisions of the tree dwellers to become land creatures and the subsequent need for the increased use of tools and weapons of a diverse nature made it imperative that they learn and practice new skills which their changing mode of living made a part of a daily survival pattern. He ran to capture or escape, he jumped to reach or avoid, he threw to kill or to defend; and over the hundreds of thousands and millions of years of his development he ran ever faster, he jumped in new and complex ways, and he threw, not only more accurately and farther, but with a larger variety of implements. His growing powers of reasoning told him he could do all of these things better with more skillful control of his body and that this control came with constant repetition of the required movements. Therefore, as he evolved, he devoted more and more time to perfecting skills in handling tools and weapons while not actually engaged in survival activity — in short, he practiced.

Some naturally became more skillful than others and liked to demonstrate this superiority not only in cases of necessity but also in practice before the group or tribe. They soon noticed that their superior strength, speed, agility or skill impressed everyone, particularly the desirable females, and so the faint stirrings of many of the motives behind man's actions, as we know them today, began to play a part in how well the primitive creatures performed these physical acts.

War and its constant threat to survival were also motivating forces that further enhanced man's physical powers throughout his evolution, stemming from the need of military training and preparation for war. In fact, many of his peacetime physical competitions have their roots firmly fixed in the warlike skills developed in the various civilizations that have existed throughout the world. These civilizations have merely refined what was passed on to them by the primitives, adding here and subtracting there, as the needs of their environments dictated the things to be learned and the physical and mental improvements necessary to perfect them.

Some of these skills, while not in themselves concerned with running or the other activities of the modern track and field program, nonetheless require the high level physical condition, coordination and dexterity that are the by-products of such a program and often are the bases upon which the successful individuals in our modern society build the disciplines and drives which carry them to the top in their fields.

As man becomes increasingly concerned with the meaning behind his actions in a civilization whose complexities have made it imperative that he know the workings of his mind and its direction of his activities, it is most important that we find out as much as possible about ourselves and the various motivations which lead us to do the things we do. Many of these motivations we are conscious of; for some we need professional help and analysis of our unconscious minds to discover the real, and sometimes unhealthy, reasons for our behavior. But all of them, conscious or unconscious, play a part in our everyday lives and make us the individuals we are.

The tremendous growth of track and field since 1950 and its emergence as not only a top international sport but also as one of the most important means of communication between the world's peoples have increased the interest of a vastly greater number of participants than ever before; and in addition, and perhaps in some quarters more important, it has come to be considered as a prime propaganda medium for the ideological thinking of certain nations. Because of this, it is possible that the motivations of many of the participants are the result of some new pressures of comparatively modern origin or merely seem so. It was with this in mind that an opportunity to talk with many of the great stars of modern track and field was most welcomed in an effort to determine what they felt they were expressing or achieving through participation in this most demanding and lonely of sports.

Over the past two years the writer has had the opportunity to observe, live with and talk at length on a variety of subjects with many of the young men and women who have been in the international headlines for their outstanding performances in world competition in track and field; and while not a trained psychologist, he is a trained professional in the track and field area with almost forty years of experience in sectional, national and international track and field competition. With this background, the writer feels that he has been able to recognize and sort out not only the conscious motivation, but also some of the deeper determinants of behavior of many of those athletes. At the same time, the lesser athlete whose lack of natural ability has confined his competition to local contests has been a no less rewarding source of interesting and often amusing material. In fact, in the opinion of this writer, it is often the casual participant, more concerned with fun and an occasional small triumph, who provides both himself and the investigator of his id with the healthiest motivational patterns.

Since the nature of track and field competition in the various social structures of the world makes it predominantly a sport of the young, and since it is in turn readily available to school and college age groups, it would seem to be and in fact is the sport most apt to attract the student, the scholar and the intellectual. The origins of many of its traditions, closely bound up with the Olympic games of ancient Greece and the intellectual life of that great civilization, made it natural that a continuous knowledge of and interest in track and field sports be a part of the life of the student. He found much to help him relieve the tensions, mental and physical, that build up in long hours spent in study in close quarters and trying class sessions. But the intellectual was not alone in his need of the therapeutic effects of track and field training and competition. Many men holding jobs requiring a varied amount of physical labor find the outdoor exercise and, in some cases, the very hard physical activity a welcome change of pace from the everyday working grind. Even people keeping very long working hours in the various professions have sometimes taken to running as a means of recreation and relaxation. In addition, the track and field type of conditioning is often the basic preparation for participation in many other sports, many of which were the original goals of the participants.

The wide variety of physical types demanded by the full program of track and field events opens the door to all kinds of physical development in the individual competitor. One world-famous athlete recently mentioned his own completely unimpressive size and build. He pointed out that, although too big to be a jockey, he had probably been too small or too slow to be successful in the sports he had tried to participate in until he had decided to give distance running a try. He is now one of the great distance runners of the world and is able to win his share of races in international competition. He is also one of the most relaxed, happy and perfectly adjusted persons encountered in this survey. He finds the variety of competition and the comradeship he has encountered in the many countries in which he has competed to be extremely stimulating both mentally and physically. He feels that in no other sport in the world is there such a constant flow of ideas, methods of training and living, personal problems to be solved, sacrifices to be made, and self-discipline to be enforced, and at the same time the possibilities of reward to the participant in health and peace of mind coupled with a sense of real accomplishment.

Another international star, speaking of his own development, pointed out his lifelong pleasure in running. Blessed with great speed, he ran successfully almost daily in grade school, high school and in his first year of college; he then found to his dismay that his increasing size was slowing him to the point of being an "also ran" in the sprint races. Happily for his peace of mind, his coach was a great believer in relay teams and converting big sprinters into shot and discus throwers, and he soon became one of the great weightmen of the area and eventually of the country, all the while running on various sprint relay teams on occasion. Although he was considered to be All-American material in football as a high school player, it did not give him the same feeling of satisfaction that a win, no matter how unimportant, gave him in track, and he eventually gave it up. Even running on winning relay teams did not seem to be the answer; he was far more interested in perfecting his technique in the weights. It seems obvious then that the real attraction of track for him was that it was single-handed combat, not team play, he was interested in and in which he had a very great drive to succeed. Even running, for which he professed a great love, and which in his training for the weights he still did a great deal of, was not the major motive, but rather the desire for single-handed victory.

The reasons men and women submit themselves to the rigorous, often painful, regimen of modern-day training for running are probably as varied as the basic motivational drives of the human race. It is only rarely that the combinations of motives for such personal dedication to what often seems to the outsider as paying an exorbitant price for a relatively unimportant reward are the same, but there are some basic determinants of the behavioral patterns of the runner. You quite commonly hear trackmen say that they enjoy the good fellowship and friendliness that seem always present when a group gets together to train for a meet, even a meet in which they will be striving against each other for a major championship. Others point to the improved social and economic environment to which the successful trackman finds entry with the corresponding opportunities for personal improvement. A number of top-flight American athletes freely admit that there was little hope of a college education for them until their track ability opened the academic doors. As one put it, he had always wanted to attend a good engineering school but had little hope of realizing his ambition because of the size of his family and the fact that he was a younger son. An early recognition of his potential as a runner by an understanding coach and the knowledge of what he could expect in the way of college scholarships if that potential were developed to the fullest extent led to two years of completely dedicated academic and athletic efforts which brought many offers of college scholarships and a chance to attend the school which had been his original inspiration. Today, after a very successful college career as a student and athlete and a few years of postgraduate competition, he has made a tremendous success in his chosen profession and is well on the way to becoming a very wealthy man. He is firmly convinced that the very real contribution made by his years of competitive running to his character and education was made possible by the strong motivation to enter the academic world through what was at the time the only open door.

In talking to the athletes during the course of this study, it becomes readily apparent that the motivation described above was a factor to some degree in the competitive careers of many of our better trackmen. Discussion brought out the fact that there were many reasons for the desire to attend college, but a common denominator was the ability to solve financial problems with an athletic scholarship, which in turn was a strong incentive for athletic success. In fact, it seems likely in some cases that the rigid self-discipline necessary to carry a trackman through a tough training and competitive season was bearable only for this reason. Others might have felt that this was so in the earlier stages of their exposure to the track program, but, as many say, they rapidly became aware of the many intangible contributions made by track participation to their way of life which made it much more satisfactory.

Many trackmen will talk at great length of the pleasure they derive from the many lasting friendships which spring up between the various competitors at all levels of track competition. One great runner who has made numerous trips to all parts of the world to compete talked of the beauty of the places he had visited and the friendliness of the people. He has made close friends of many of the foreign athletes whose countries he has visited, many of them his toughest competition for world rank; and he spends a great deal of time corresponding with them, exchanging new ideas on training and personal and other news of interest mutually. Over the years he feels that this in itself has contributed greatly to his education and his knowledge and understanding of the world's peoples. Because his activities are mostly out-of-doors, he has become familiar with and greatly impressed by the natural beauties of the countries he has visited; his growing knowledge of the topography, the social and economic structure and the political climate of these nations has made him an informed observer of their problems and their ambitions. The excitement of being on the spot while the history of these countries is being made, the lasting friendships and the stunning beauty of some of the areas he has visited are strong motivations, he feels, in his decision to continue on for a few more seasons with the running competition which provides him with his magic carpet.

In recent years the great performances of many world class trackmen around the globe and the visits of foreign athletes to many lands have touched off a great acceleration in the exchange of ideas on training and techniques in the track and field program. These training methods and technical information on the various form events of track and field competition have, in most instances, found their way into print, and in turn have strongly motivated the interest and participation of thousands of young boys and girls in many lands — so much so that today we are on the threshold of the greatest upgrading of individual performance in the long history of man's attempts to run, jump and throw better than his fellows. More and more, too, coaches with great athletes under their direction have been willing to discuss the day-to-day activities of these athletic heroes, who rival all the popular idols of history in the minds of the growing numbers of young people who have found and profited by the school of hard, vigorous exercise as a means of satisfying the various drives that fill them with such great nervous energy. Perhaps not yet as well known in some areas as the Beatles, these track and field heroes and their records are nonetheless familiar to the young athletes to whom the name Ringo is vaguely associated with the old-time American West.

The great upsurge of new knowledge has been most beneficial to the many young athletes who have had the patience to try all of the new developments, but it has also been a motivator that has produced, paradoxically enough, a great deal of nonconformism and original thinking among the athletes of all ages, which has in turn produced some very sound and exciting new methods of training and techniques in all of the various events of the track and field program. One by one, many of the old taboos have been broken and forgotten. Some techniques have changed so much as to be almost exact opposites of the form used in the earlier stages of the development of modern track and field. Training routines have expanded in all directions, producing fitness for competition fantastically ahead of that reached by the greatest athletes of only a generation ago. The modern track athlete consumes all of the latest information about his event as he would consume a tasty beefsteak, and true to the nature of the current crop of athletes, remains hungry for more. Quite often he decides he could do a better job as cook. He respects the true "cordon bleu," but he must be shown and his respect must be won. He will accept tried and true methods as long as they are getting him where he wants to go, but if his goal is the top he also must have a bit of a go at his own ideas. He often horrifies his elders with his radical thoughts but is quick to admit their superior knowledge when they are right and to share his successes when they come.

It seems inevitable, therefore, that this independence of thought should have provided strong motivations to many young athletes with inquisitive minds who are willing to subject themselves to many long hard hours of training to test new methods which they hoped would lead them to world class ranking.

One of the great stars of distance running has told of his lack of success in his early running career and the strong feeling that he could be much better if only he could find the way. This strongly motivated his search for methods of training by which he could realize his maximum potential. He feels that his eventual success in reaching that goal was this drive which gave him the determination to carry on until he found the right training program, supervised by the right coach, that brought out the best efforts of which he was capable and made him one of the great runners of our time. It is quite possible that this athlete would never have reached his eminence if he had conformed to the average pattern and lacked the independence of thought that is so often the hallmark of great champions. He freely admits that he was strongly motivated by the many articles he found had been recently written on various methods of conditioning for running, which kept up his interest and his hope until he eventually sought out and trained with a coach who could open the right doors of knowledge to him.

This inspiration derived from the stories of the successful runners, field men and coaches of the present is becoming an increasingly common story behind the successes of many of the great young athletes of today and is a major contributor to the great upsurge of quality performances throughout the track and field programs of the world. Olympic champions are once more among the popular idols of the young people of many lands and many races, and the urge to emulate them is bringing thousands of new participants into the sport strongly motivated by a desire to one day achieve an equality with their heroes in the running, jumping or throwing events. It is an exciting time for these young people and is producing fantastic results.

The worldwide social acceptance of the world class track and field athlete, so greatly increased in recent years, has had a strong effect on the athletes of many races in motivating their search for the greatness they feel will be a short cut out of the pit into which racial prejudice has cast their lot. There is very little racial consciousness among track and field competitors, and a good performance is cheered regardless of the color of the performer's skin or his national origin. He becomes one of the group and finds friends and wellwishers from all backgrounds who will share their ideas, their table and their quarters with him and enjoy his company. To many athletes whose backgrounds have made them familiar with the hurt and the anger made possible by bigotry, this has been a very strong incentive to persevere in their efforts to become great in track and field. Many great colored athletes have played a most inspiring role in the lives of some of the fine crop of young track stars of all races now making new track history all over the world. Young Negro athletes have made heroes of Jesse Owens, Ralph Metcalf, Bob Hayes, Henry Carr and the great Ralph Boston, among others, and sought to copy their training methods and techniques with considerable success.

The achievements of these great champions has also been a continuing inspiration to colored athletes in other countries and in other sports. These young people, many coming from homes of great poverty, have been quick to realize that their God-given talent is the magic wand that can open many doors to social and economic opportunity which have always been closed to them in the past, and that these doors will remain open so long as they make themselves worthy of all that these opportunities imply. The vast majority of them have accepted the challenge in a way that speaks well for the relationships that will make for greater understanding and acceptance by all who come in contact with them. Their ready acceptance of the responsibilities, self-discipline, and the hard work that goes hand-in-hand with greatness in track and field is indicative of a very strong determination to win the dignity and respect to which they know they are entitled, particularly since the ability that they are blessed with has made it possible for them to further their education in directions which would have been economically impossible in most cases. They are acutely aware that the soundest way to make and keep the great gains that they and other members of their race are striving for is by the example of productive and responsible citizenship that will earn for them the respect of their fellows.

Many of these young athletes, traveling as they do in foreign countries, are becoming some of our finest good-will ambassadors. They enjoy the scenic beauty and cultural heritage of the countries they visit and the people they meet, and usually they have succeeded in making the people like them because they show their own enthusiasm and enjoyment in what they are experiencing. It would not be true to say that this is always the case, but the times when the contrary is true are, to their everlasting credit, rather few.

They all speak of this facet of their track and field life as a most rewarding phase of their young lives and well worth all the toil and effort that provided them with their transportation to these wonderful new experiences in such a way that one cannot escape the strong feeling that the desire to return and continue these foreign tours will be a strong incentive in their decision to continue to pay the price in the self-discipline and hard work that will take them back. But most of all, one is conscious of the deepening feeling of appreciation for their own country for itself and what it has to offer, without in any way disparaging the beauties and worth of the countries they have visited or the good intentions of their people. For it is the people and the countries that leave the good impressions, and they have little time to think of heads of state and governments. There is a remarkable absence of political talk or discussion of ideologies among the athletes when they gather for these international meetings that test only one thing, the worth of the champion and his challengers. There is a shared feeling which generates its own good will among all races and creeds.

Throughout the development of man from the primitive to the present, the great hunter, the heroic warrior and now the famous athlete have each been an object of admiration by all his fellows, especially by the female of the species. He has always responded with greater efforts and has not been slow to take advantage of the edge his fame gave him in satisfying his sexual urges.

The fact that the trackmen of today tends to live a rather Spartan life for most of the year and is even monkish in his habits in the last stages of his preparation for championship and international competition does not in any way imply he is undersexed. Quite the contrary, he has a lively interest in, and perfectly normal approach to, the satisfaction of his sexual urges. He is not unaware that the effect of his superabundance of good health and vitality upon the females he comes in contact with improves his chances with them.

It is quite true that a few of those so aware have been somewhat inclined to excess and have let sexual adventures seriously affect their competitive ability in some crucial situations. In general, however, the track athlete reacts in a perfectly normal way to the give and take of the relationship between the sexes which is today's standard, and such sexual episodes as result from these relationships are usually seen in their proper perspective and treated as one of the pleasant sides of a full and interesting life pattern.

The happy and healthy adjustment to society that most athletes make indicates that the place of the sexual drive in the behavioral pattern of the present-day track and field star is in the normal pattern. If at times it seems out of proportion, it is usually because of the greater physical awareness the highly conditioned fitness of the athlete's body brings to his mind and senses.

Track athletes, male and female, usually have one thing in common, however, in their sexual attitudes. They are not attracted to, and are sometimes positively repelled by, the small groups of individuals who sometimes are a noisy part of our college campuses. The men like their girls to look and dress like girls and to be on speaking terms with soap, water, hairbrushes and combs. And they don't think dark cellars, bad coffee, flat beer, sick poetry, guitar players who can't play and singers who can't sing are recreation and prove anything but a waste of time. The women athletes feel much the same about the bearded, unwashed men and almost unanimously avoid them in their sexual and social contacts. These young athletes are practicing liberals in the truest sense of the word, having shared quarters, showers, dinner tables, recreation facilities, knowledge, and good fellowship with all nationalities and races, all creeds and political ideologies, wthout wasting thought on equality. They feel they do not have to prove anything by outlandish behavior or dress and do not have to seek the company of those who do in order to satisfy any personal need.

The many motivations of the track and field competitor are the need to satisfy ego by being the best in the world; the need to triumph over hardship and pain; the need for social acceptance and economic security; the many drives to identify with, and be a part of, a group; the sexual drive; and the need to achieve individual excellence. In short, these, and all of man's normal motivations that made him the complex individual he is are present to a greater or lesser degree in the track and field performers of today.

Thinking as they do, they sometimes find themselves regarded as "kooks" or arch-conservatives by the various angry young men of today's college campuses. These observers think anyone who gets up two hours before breakfast to run several miles before returning to shower and eat with an appetite they, themselves, can never summon up at that time of day must surely be abnormal, and a waster of time better spent in improving one's mind or fellows. Not really understanding him, they taunt him with epithets, often more nearly self-descriptive, such as "animal," "slob," etc., and regard him as some kind of nut because he finds it important to maintain a balance of high level mental and physical fitness and to achieve competitive excellence on the athletic field as well as the classroom. They find it even more to be decried against that he is ready to spend most of his spare time doing it, and are much taken aback that he is so strongly motivated he usually achieves his goals both academically and physically with something to spare.

It is very true then that he does not conform to the pattern regarded by some as the norm for the young intellectual, but as one great track star currently working on his Ph.D. puts it, "it is our privilege in this country not to conform, particularly not to conform to the mediocrity or sloth of the immature and uninformed groups of lazy thinkers who are sometimes mistakenly thought to be representative examples of the present-day student and the hope (sic) of the country." His years of college life, his intellectual accomplishments and his wide travel in the rest of the world make his comment seem most pertinent.

In general then, the modern track athlete is motivated by most of the reasons his fellows in all sports have for their acceptance of all the extra hard work, self-discipline and dedication needed to reach the top, but the writer thinks one of the strongest reasons the greats in sports will accept all of these things was expressed to him by one of America's youngest and greatest track stars. When asked to pinpoint the strongest single motive behind his fantastic success at such an early age, which had obviously required long and dedicated training and self-denial, he gave it such a long considered period of thought that it seemed he was not going to answer the question; then he replied, "I guess I just love to run." And so must all who follow this hard road to the ultimate achievement — love to run, or jump or throw.

"He says it's great sport — calls it pole-leaping, or something like that — and *I* think it's a new wrinkle worth learning!"

REFERENCES

Bannister, R.: *The Four Minute Mile*. New York, Dodd, Mead & Co., 1955.
Cofer, C. N., and Appley, M. H.: *Motivation: Theory and Research*. New York, Wiley, 1964.
Doherty, J. K.: *Modern Training for Running*. Englewood Cliffs, Prentice-Hall, 1964.
Doherty, J. G.: *Modern Track and Field*. 2d ed. Englewood Cliffs, Prentice-Hall, 1963.
Elliott, H.: *The Golden Mile*. New York, Nelson, 1961.
Hewson, B.: *Flying Feet*. New York, Arco, 1962.

Pirie, G.: *Running Wild*. 1961.
Van Dalen, D. B., *et al.*: *A World History of Physical Education*. Englewood Cliffs, Prentice-Hall, 1953.
Watman: *The Ibbotson Story*, 1958.
Time-Life Series: *The Origin of Man*, 1964.
Periodicals on track and field include *National Collegiate Track Coaches Association Clinic Notes* and *Track and Field News*.

BOWLING

SUE S. STONE

THE KEYNOTE TO BOWLING'S popularity as a modern sport is in its simplicity. The technique of the game is basically one exercise repeated over and over again with an attempt at machine-like precision ("the approach," as it is called) . Grace and timing are as relevant in this sport as actual strength. The fact that strength and energy are not necessarily related to high scoring can be adduced by anyone willing to sit for an hour and watch a group of high-spirited school boys bowl: Tom, with broad shoulders, hurls the ball with great force, but the jerkiness of his approach and the speed of his ball repeatedly leave him a series of "splits" (random pins with open spaces between them) instead of a clean sweep of pins in a series of "strikes," the object of the game. Nine out of ten of the boys, all vigorous and healthy, will not have the powers of concentration to reduplicate their pattern of approach more than once, and yet all will have the intelligence to assimilate some approximation of the technique of the game and its object. The sport's lure is its ease, and paradoxically this simplicity is its greatest challenge.

Bowling is then first and foremost an *exercise,* and psychological submission to that fact is a requirement for excellence in it, as it is, for instance, in the practice of classical ballet. Self-expression and individualism are only variables in success at a very high level of play. The person who loves to bowl enjoys the mechanization for its own sake, as the classical dancer is willing to restrict himself to five basic positions. The bowler may not realize as clearly as the dancer does that he is participating in a little ritual, but the fine bowler must be as ritualistic as the fine dancer.

It is a much advertised fact that bowling in the United States has in certain socioeconomic classes helped eliminate the vise the local tavern has on the male members of the community. Once the ritualistic nature of bowling is clearly understood, we can have a more profound psychological understanding of why this has been possible. The obsession of bowling replaces the addiction of alcohol. And bowling itself becomes for the more obsessional player an addiction. There is no bowling alley without its large core of regulars. Although this phenomenon can be studied in the framework of social science as a lower-middle class, middle-class club, from the psychological point of view each of these individuals is grappling with his obsession and being lulled by his addiction. Many bowlers bowl beyond their financial resources, as gamblers do who cannot resist one more card, and, as in gambling, the desire to win does not seem the primary element. For there is, within this sport, the same simple playing with acceptance and rejection that we see in our psychological formulations of gambling.[1]

If you wish to note the obsessional aspects of bowling, there is no better way than to watch a televised match between two professional bowlers. There, in your armchair, away from the noise and peripheral confusions of the bowling alley, you can visualize more clearly how controlled the actual environment of the sport is, how limited the variables. Bowler A will start each time from exactly the same spot; he will roll the ball over exactly the same board; his stance and the position from which he pushes off with the ball and begins to move are all minutely stylized. Bowler B may well demonstrate for you the fascinating mechanism of the minor obsessions blossoming within the framework of the major obsession, the sport itself.[2] We observe his repetitive forearm contractions at the start of the approach, his special towel, half for wiping the perspiration from his forehead and half for the heel of his left shoe so that he will grip properly at the release of the ball.

Another important psychological factor in this game is the way the personality must adjust to its own wish to be exhibitionistic and the concomitant fear of this desire. For this sport is exhibitionistic in its gratifications. Bowling takes place in a crowd; week after week, bowlers participate in league play with the same team members; match play takes place before an audience. Even in so-called "open bowling" no bowler "strikes" without at least a small turning of the head, a shy blink, a whoop, a leap, meaning clearly and childishly, "Look at me." The professionals can usually permit themselves this exhibitionism and its attendant gratifications. Some have developed highly stylized body mannerisms which display satisfaction or disgust without words. Interestingly, one of the most common movements after a strike is a punching movement.

In amateurs, the importance of the audience is clear. Many can bowl beautifully in the morning when the bowling lanes are empty but become tense and awkward during league play. There are all kinds of subtle variations in how much exhibitionism, and how large an audience, the various personalities can tolerate: Jim can bowl well with his wife, but not with his team members; John is excellent in match play as long as it does not take place before the television eye.

The exhibitionistic joys and vicissitudes of bowling are accompanied by a voyeuristic pleasure special to this sport, that of releasing the ball and watching it roll toward the pins. This moment of hopeful suspense is lacking in the "contact sports" where you cannot pause to see the punch you land or the beauty of your tackle. Even in baseball, the batter must follow up his hit with the greatest possible speed. There is evidence from the dreams of bowlers that the ball itself is a phallic symbol, and this would be an interesting study to pursue. Certainly in our culture the ball is a masculine symbol, presented to the little boy at the earliest possible age; the common differentiation is to give the little girl a doll.

There are therefore, as I see it, certain psychological differences in the meaning of bowling for men and women. For men, bowling is a socially acceptable masculine sport which allows them to express and develop their impulses toward rhythmic movement and grace. For women, this sport offers satisfaction of their masculine cravings in a carefully limited setting where they can realistically compete with men.

It might be added here that for women educated with men and habituated to the competitive modern society, sports such as bowling which are neither very expensive nor very time-consuming provide, after marriage and childbearing, an outlet for their competitive needs which is not simply a service to the woman herself, but to her husband and children, who may well be bearing the burden of her projected masculine wishes.

For the "solitary," both male and female, bowling offers a therapeutic recreation. The social opportunity is available, but the social demands are minimal. A host or hostess employed by the bowling alleys will place you in a league; instruction is free for those who wish it; no special skills or personal qualifications are required. You do not need an introduction or a passport of social charms or wealth to enter a bowling emporium. People come from all walks of life and do not probe or press into each other's backgrounds. You may volunteer personal information if you so desire, but the milieu invites friendship without the more threatening aspects of intimacy.

Bowling, as one of the "handicap sports," allows the average bowler to participate in competition without allowing the competition to overwhelm him. In handicap leagues improvement counts more than natural excellence. The expectations are always realistic, for the goal is simply to do a little better this time than you did in your last performance. For those who excel in bowling, there are "scratch leagues" and multiple opportunities to compete in situations where nothing counts but superiority of performance, whereas "handicap play" encourages the average bowler to improve his skill slowly.

The method of scoring in bowling allows the man discouraged with his current performance to hope that luck will come to his aid where skill has failed. A game in bowling consists of ten frames with two balls thrown in each frame except for the tenth, where the player is permitted a bonus ball if he "spares" or "strikes." If the player knocks down all ten pins with his first ball, he "strikes" in that frame. If he succeeds in knocking down all the pins with his two allotted balls, he has "spared." There is the possibility of adding ten additional pins to your score every time you spare, and double this many if you put two strikes together. There is, therefore, always the possibility of transforming a bad game with a series of strikes.

Although many bowlers have faith in the concepts of "luck," "fate," "chance," bowling is not a game of roulette. Good fortune can influence the play of a single night but is usually balanced out by an evening of ill fortune later in the season. In this respect it is not unlike poker, a game which is superficially easy to grasp but in reality difficult to play well, a game in which luck seems to play a much more predominant role to the beginner than it does to the veteran player. But, whereas the experienced poker player hides his knowledge, the experienced bowler announces his by mentioning "his average." A good bowler's average of play over the previous season is his merit badge, his passport, his letter of introduction to his comrades. The averages of current play are posted weekly upon bulletin boards in bowling alleys. The values inherent in this emphasis on a man's average are numerous: esteem is given on the basis of total performance, reliability and stability of temperament, conscientiousness and even punctuality. The objective light of a larger reality illuminates the occasional current disaster, for "all is never lost in a single throw of the dice."

"I notice that usually his predelivery ritual is sort of a Highland fling — but when he's got several strikes going for him, he flops on the floor and does this sort of thing."

To sum up, bowling is a comforting sport. Easily accessible, these bright, safe nurseries for grownups where children are also welcome provide, along with the snacks, soft drinks and music, a simple, yet fascinatingly difficult game. The chances of bowling a perfect game of three hundred are minimal, but the childish pleasures of handling a big ball, the jubilance experienced when the pins collapse, and the calm infant-like acceptance of their peaceful resurrection, are available to us all.

FOOTNOTES

1. Fenichel, O.: *The Psychoanalytic Theory of Neurosis.* New York, Norton, 1945, p. 272.
2. Freud, S.: Obsessive acts and religious practices; in *Collected Papers,* Vol. 2. London, Hogarth Press, 1924, p. 25.

PART TEN
FIGHTING SPORTS

INTRODUCTION

ORDINARY FIGHTING IS A BASIC human physical activity requiring little or no preparation. Boxing, on the other hand, is regarded as a form of sport (as are bullfighting and hunting).[1] Boxing enthusiasts say that boxing, unlike fighting, is an art or skill and requires a long period of training. Karl Menninger says that boxing would fit into the definition of play "only to the extent that it is not actually destructive."[2]

Boxing is apparently "actually destructive" when its prime and direct object is the physical injury of the contestants. This and other charges against boxing are well known: that it is crooked, that gamblers and gangsters move in the shadows of the game, that men die in the ring, damage their brains, stumble through the rest of their lives. Anthony Quinn in the film *Requiem for a Heavyweight* brilliantly portrays a battered boxer, a pugilist who practiced the trade too long. And boxing crowds are known to roar with joy when blood is spilled and the boxer is knocked into a coma, near death. On the other hand, on the positive side, it is said that boxing is a useful substitute for brawling in life, that a polite society needs its public punchers to sublimate and expiate its violence.

Hunger and poverty are commonly considered as the reasons for some boys going into boxing as a career, but the real reasons, former boxer Max Novich says, come closer to such things as feelings of inadequacy, fear of lack of masculinity, lack of pride, dependency needs and failure of acknowledgment by parents. Problems arising from sibling rivalry and jealousy as well as oedipal situations account for persistence of hostile feelings with a predominantly sadistic and masochistic coloring. Exhibitionism, the need to be looked at and admired, is an additional factor. Other boys go into boxing to escape any identification with effeminacy. There are innumerable factors that compel men to become boxers. "Hungry" fighters seem to be better fighters, but this hunger is not for bread alone.[3] Vernon Scannell, who writes on boxing in this volume,[4] is not concerned with the medical and moral cases against boxing, as powerful as these may be. He is concerned with trying to explain the potency of the appeal of boxing both to the spectator and to the participant.[5]

Gregory P. Stone and Ramon A. Oldenburg write on wrestling,[6] which is an activity engaged in by man since his appearance on earth. Throughout its history, wrestling has undergone a series of profound transformations.

It probably began at once as work and play, but early technological developments in hunting and warfare removed the work component from wrestling, and it persisted for centuries primarily as a play form. By the end of the nineteenth century, at least in the United States, wrestling was transformed once more into work with the rise of professional sports. After World War I, the professional sport underwent its final transformation — it emerged as drama. Indeed, it is now best conceived as a passion play. But professional wrestling is also a business, and a lucrative one. Moreover, it is undoubtedly the most financially rewarding career that any professional athlete can undertake in the United States (wrestlers recently unsuccessfully sought admission as entertainers in the American Guild of Variety Artists).

As a sport, wrestling has largely commanded the interest of lower status followers in Western civilization for eight hundred years, and this continues to be true of the dramatic entertainment we call wrestling today. The largest proportion of followers and fans is found in the lower socioeconomic stratum, and, within that stratum, among older women. Social psychological characteristics of lower income groups combine to make them particularly credulous. They tend, more than others, to be gullible about appearances, and they express what has come to be called "working class authoritarianism" so that they are prone to assess the world about them in clear-cut black-and-white terms. Thus, they believe in the good and evil represented by the actors in the wrestling arena, though they are uninterested in the plot of the drama that is performed. Yet, why professional wrestling in the United States should fascinate older women remains a mystery. We can only speculate, and any informed guess is probably as good as ours.

William R. Sorum's essay on the Oriental fighting arts is a narrative account of the author's interest and participation in judo and karate with brief mention of some of the other martial art forms.[7] He attempts throughout to correct some of the misconceptions concerning these activities. In the section devoted largely to judo he describes the methods by which its techniques can be mastered. He discusses the motives of the devotee which range from a need for knowledge of self-defense, a need for a means of physical conditioning, and a desire for competitive achievement to a desire for self-mastery in acquisition of proficiency in technique. He goes on to discuss the psychological and philosophical aspects of the sport. In the section on karate he discusses some of the similarities to judo which he feels are largely superficial. He describes the forms by which one learns the techniques. He points out the importance of psychological and philosophical basis of this discipline. He concludes that these activities are beneficial in proportion to the effort expended, and that for the average participant it is an excellent means of physical conditioning in a disciplined activity.

"Who desires peace, let him prepare for war!" is an old philosophy, and appears to be the philosophy of some warrior schools, as the following newspaper advertisement by one school illustrates:[8]

> Is your son a sissy, or less of a real boy than you would like him to be? Does he run home crying when he should stand and defend or assert himself? Does he shy away from contact sports or other activities that require a little daring? Judo can develop confidence and poise in the shy or timid child. Judo is a spirited sport with a gentlemanly touch. It teaches children to fall and tumble scientifically and safely, and actually toughens them up physically as well as emotionally. Self-defense is the basis of Sport Judo. After the basic movements are developed, any of the Judo throws, locks, holds or submission techniques that are practiced in the sport style have numerous practical applications for self-defense. When a child isn't afraid of being hurt, or has nothing to fear from the bully or antagonistic type, he will accept more challenges and enter into the more rugged and virile sports and games and become a *real boy* and a *real man.*

The term "martial art forms" and such advertisements may be misleading. Judo, karate, and the other martial art forms are indeed exceptionally clean sports; they emphasize respect for the opponent, and they teach control of aggression.[9] Gichin Funakoshi, the founder of present-day karate, says that "the ultimate aim of the art of karate lies not in victory or defeat, but in the perfection of the character of its participants." He maintains that even though effective self-defense is one of the chief purposes of karate (and the other martial art forms), it is of secondary importance. After only a few months instruction in karate, a student can learn to defend himself to a considerable extent, but if a student takes pride in karate and perseveres with the repetitious instruction, that perseverance can in turn instill character and pride in the student. Karate, he says, can also build confidence: "We teach that in karate you should not flinch from an attack, but face up to it. This can give the student confidence in himself where he will not shy from the responsibilities of life but stand up to them. I have seen students who in the early stages of their instruction were shy and lacked confidence. After several months of training they are different persons."[10]

The word "karate" comes from the Japanese and literally means empty hands. Thus, karate is a weaponless martial art based upon techniques of striking, kicking and punching. There are two types of karate: the kata (form) contest and the kumite (sparring) contest. In the kumite contest, two opponents face each other and are free to use any offensive or defensive techniques. A winner is determined when one of the contestants executes a "focused attack," that is, a powerful, precise punch, strike or kick. In the kumite, actual hitting of the opponent is prohibited. Therefore, a contestant executes a focused attack when he stops his technique immediately before actual contact with the target area; the ability to stop the technique calls for a high degree of simultaneous mind and body discipline. In the kata there are no opposing contestants. The kata performer defends himself against a simulated attack. The kata contestant is judged on the same basis as diving. Points are given for speed, power, form, spirit, attitude and the contestant's understanding of the kata.

With Barry J. Pariser,[11] we turn to fencing — *"En garde!"* Fencing in this country has become popular in high schools, colleges, private clubs and organizations such as the YMCA. Whereas in its youth fencing was practiced by the military for combat purposes and also was a gentleman's sport, today it is easily available to everyone. There are local tournaments held all over the country in addition to the national championships.

Women only fence foil, but men can compete in all three weapons — foil, sabre and epee. Different classes of fencers in each weapon are based on achievement. The lowest to the highest class, in order, is unclassified, C, B, and A. Attributes that benefit a fencer are intelligence, ability to be taught, athletic ability, stamina, strength, speed, timing distance, ability to concentrate and discipline.

There are many reasons motivating people to start fencing. High on the list is the swashbuckling motif; people are influenced by the movies and books on the subject. Another motive is that a person knows someone who had fenced or is fencing. It is also an excellent means of staying in shape, building coordination and increasing athletic achievement. It provides another way to meet interesting people, both ben and women. It is also a good means of acting out hidden hostilities and relieving daily tensions in sport.

A fencers' club for young psychiatric patients was initiated in 1963 in the recreational therapy program at the University of Michigan Medical Center. Prior thereto the sport apparently had never been employed with psychiatric patients, so there was an added spirit of adventure and special caution in inaugurating the program. Staff members had many questions that apparently could be answered only by experience: How would disturbed boys, with complex problems of fear and hostility, react to the threat of three feet of steel coming at them? How would these patients cope with the need for controlled aggression? Would the frightened, insecure youth bolt and run before he could accept the sport as a game of skill? The therapists established some general ground rules, along with a plan for overcoming the patient's initial concerns and fears, and after the first several months of the program, the staff began to see tangible evidence of results. The children acquired skills and interests they could take with them when they left the hospital; they had an added measure of self-assurance; they learned that aggression can be channeled in a nondestructive fashion. Staff members also observed that each fencing session afforded a mirror of the patient's experiences earlier in the day – whether on the wards, in school, or in sessions with the doctor.[12]

FOOTNOTES

1. It may be noted that cockfighting, which is not covered in this volume, has recently gained a covert but rapidly growing popularity in several midwestern states. Cockfighting captivated the Romans as early as 200 B.C. and was known in Asia more than 3,000 years ago. In cockfighting, rarely does a cock raise his hackle — this is the sign that the chicken has "chickened out." From this act, which reveals a row of white feathers beneath the hackle, came the old saying, "showing the white feather," an accusation of cowardice. *Kansas City Star,* January 15, 1964, p. 1.
2. Menninger, K.: *Love Against Hate.* New York, Harcourt, Brace & World, 1942, p. 173. Menninger says that play has an unrealistic nature which affords the opportunity for the relief of repressed aggressions. "It enables us to express aggression without reality consequences: we can hurt people without really hurting them; we can even kill them without really killing them. 'It is all in play.' We say that we do not really mean it, although this is not quite true. We do mean it, but we know and our victim knows that it has no dangerous consequences and he can therefore tolerate it and (usually) forgive us." Menninger, K.: *op. cit. supra,* at p. 172.
3. See Liebling, A. J.: *The Sweet Science: A Ringside View of Boxing.* New York, Grove, 1963; Novich, M.: A physician looks at athletics. *JAMA, 161:*573, 1956; Mayhem in the ring puts doctors on the spot. *Medical World News,* December 2, 1966, p. 84.
4. P. 496 .
5. See also Scannell, V.: Why I enjoy boxing. *The Listener,* June 20, 1963, p. 1040.
6. P. 503.
7. P. 553.
8. Advertisement of Bushidokan, Kansas City, Mo., in *Kansas City Times.*
9. Judo-Mayhem with a gentle touch. *Reader's Digest,* September 1965.
10. Interview with Gichin Funakoshi. *New Orleans Time-Picayune,* October 11, 1964, sec. 1, p. 24.
11. P. 541.
12. Child psychiatric hospital finds fencing therapeutic. *Medical Tribune,* January 27, 1965, p. 20.

BOXING

VERNON SCANNELL

BOXING AS A SPECTACLE AND A PASTIME has attracted equally passionate defenders and opponents since William Cobbett wrote *In Defense Of Boxing* in 1805, but in the past both factions were drawn from an articulate and leisured minority. As the game became more democratic, international and sophisticated and promoted with all the techniques of modern showmanship, so its hold over the imagination of a large public and the indignation of a much smaller one increased until the invention of television brought the roped arena right into our living rooms and a whole new army of enthusiasts was created. Men and women who had never before seen a fight came to accept the battling homuncules behind the glass screen as a natural part of their cultural landscape, and for every person who was indifferent or hostile to the spectacle there were hundreds who developed toward it a real and sometimes ardent attachment and who found that watching the sport provided them with an excitement and release that they would find difficult prescisely to explain.

I am not here concerned with the medical and moral case against boxing however; powerful as these may be, I believe that persuasive counterclaims can be advanced in favor of the game. I am concerned only with trying to explain the potency of its appeal both to the spectator and to the participant, an appeal which is more widely exerted today in most parts of the world than ever before.

First, then, the appeal to the spectator who has not himself boxed and who in all likelihood would be appalled at the idea of active participation, yet who is an enthusiastic supporter of boxing; why is it that this game rather than another captures his imagination in the way that it evidently does? I suggest that it satisfies the common need for a hero figure at a point in history when the traditionally heroic activities of explorer, soldier, sailor, have lost their mythopoeic power, since, in the twentieth century, we have most of us been soldiers or sailors, we have flown with our briefcases like plump middle-aged Icaruses through the skies, and we have few illusions about the romance of war. The battlefield as a testing ground of those primeval human values of strength, courage, honor and stoicism has become too vast, too complex, impersonal and mechanized to operate effectively; boxing, like most violent competitive games, is a minuscule war, a war between two men, but it is a war cleansed of the filth, grief, indiscriminate carnage and technological heartlessness of war as we have known it in this century. It is a quintessential conflict, and its violence is partly real and partly theatrical, and this peculiar synthesis of sophisticated theatricality and atavistic conflict is responsible for much of its appeal to minds and sensibilities of such varied levels of depth and refinement as are to be found among boxing enthusiasts. And the curious, quasi-heroic mythology of the prize ring cannot, I think, be paralleled by any other sport. This mythology was already firmly rooted in the English consciousness in the days of Cobbett and Hazlitt, and George Borrow's great paean to the Heroes of the Ring in *Romany Rye* was written over a hundred years ago; in this century it has been further enriched internationally by figures like Battling Siki, who prowled the streets of Harlem with a pet leopard on a leash and died with a knife in his back; Georges Carpentier, the handsome Frenchman who fought with the grace and ferocity of a panther; Dempsey and Tunney the savage fighter and the icy perfectionist; Jimmy Wilde, "the ghost with a hammer in his hand"; Tony Galento, the "Boston Beer Barrel," a Falstaff of a fighter who trained on a diet of beer and cigars and hired superannuated pugs to do his road-runs for him while he regally followed in the back of a limousine urging them on to more strenuous efforts, yet who put the great Joe Louis on the canvas and fought with fantastic courage despite his natural and self-imposed handicaps. Mythopoeic figures such as these abound in the history of boxing, and they exert a powerful influence over the imagination of the true aficionado of the boxing-ring.

Not all followers of boxing are equally susceptible to the rough poetry of its mythology, but all respond to the theatrical elements that exist in the actual fight: the formalized ritual of the introductions, the colorful dressing-gowns, trunks and gloves, the calling together of the contestants for the liturgical homily of the referee, the acolytes in white sweaters, the mounting tension before the clang of the bell for the first round. All experience, too, something very close to the Aristotelian catharsis after they have witnessed a really good bout. For, however civilized we may appear to be, the aggressive impulse exists in all of us, and it finds exultant release through identifying with our heroes in the ring. The fact that we are rationally aware that, outside the ring, the boxer may be anything but an admirable human being increases rather than minimizes our sense of glory and release at his splendid performance, for we are seeing a man transcending the limitations of his own nature, becoming nobler, braver, more generous in victory or defeat than ordinary men could be, and indeed, than he himself could be except in the practice of his art.

Identification with the heroic fighter is probably the most ubiquitous and most radical single motivation for the male who regularly watches boxing. W. H. Auden writes in his poem *Prothalamion*: "Tonight the asthmatic clerk shall dream he's a boxer"; not a bullfighter, big-game hunter, racing-driver, jockey or ball-player, because the expert performer in any of these activities, however admirable, is not participating in something as primeval, as conclusive, as symbolically rich as proving his superior strength, cunning and bravery over a single human challenger. Auden's asthmatic clerk regards the role of boxing champion as the summit of human endeavor though no doubt in his waking hours he would deny that such was his view. The boxer symbolizes male power and bravery; he is elevated and admired. But more than this: he is generally of fine physique, so that the clerk in his fantasy inhabits that splendidly muscled torso and dotes upon himself with narcissistic admiration.

The overtly homosexual interest in watching boxing is rare. Anything approaching a full appreciation of the sport involves a good deal of technical knowledge and an enjoyment of the often unspectacular finer points of the game, of ringcraft, footwork, in-fighting and so on. The violence, when it is properly unleashed, is genuine, controlled, ruthless and of a kind from which most homosexuals would recoil in horror. Many of them would be far more likely, like women, to take pleasure in the sham violence and melodramatic contrivance of commercial wrestling. It is relevant here to note that most of the women I have seen attending fights are genuinely interested in and well informed about the techniques involved; and unless they are emotionally related in some way to one of the participants, their attitudes are no more subjective than the male spectators. So, while obviously one cannot discount sexual interest as a probable element in the motivation of both the man and woman who watch boxing, it is likely in practice to be less potent than many neat hypotheses too readily assume, and while it is a fact that some of the jargon of the fight enthusiast might carry what seem to be homosexual or heterosexual overtones (one hears, for example, of a fighter being "a sweet mover," "a lovely boxer," "pretty to watch,"), we must remember that all games have their metaphorical language and almost invariably these metaphors have oblique or direct sexual connotations.

The mention of metaphor brings us to another human need which is, in some cases, satisfied by the spectacle of boxing; and this need, while connected with our often unconscious hunger for ritual and drama, goes beyond these things into the realm of the metaphysical: it is the need to see the drama and complexity, the horror and grandeur of the human condition reduced to a quintessence and to a scale upon which the contemplative regard can focus. Many people are able to fulfill this need through religion or one or other of the arts, but the power of religion to present man with a coherent and plausible image of himself and the universe he inhabits has declined generally all over the world; and, for that huge majority who are not able to find a meaningful and harmonious microcosm in science, the arts or religion, sport in general and, I believe, boxing in particular can in some measure function as a substitute and thereby perform a valuable service to the individual and to society. To say that any sport can present a total *weltanschauung* is manifestly absurd, but to claim that it might act as a crude but effective substitute for religious, philosophical or aesthetic experience is at least arguable. Camus has said that he learned more about ethics on the football field than from all the moral philosophers, and he is here regarding the game as a metaphor, a formal activity that mirrors action beyond itself, no less than the conflicts, failures and achievements of daily life. But boxing, it seems to me, can be seen as a metaphorical activity reflecting not the broader conflicts and resolutions of life but the more circumscribed ones of art. On reflection one sees that both the artist and the fighter must be dedicated to their tasks; they must both submit to the harsh, unremitting preparation for the encounter; they must both exercise the same watchfulness in action, both must refuse to play to the gallery. The good fighter, like the good artist, must have mastered all the basic orthodox techniques, but he must also be inventive and resourceful enough to adapt and modify these as new and unexpected problems are set before him; the boxing contest, like the poet's, painter's, or composer's struggle with his medium, must be conducted within the limits of strict rules, and both artist and fighter are heroic figures: each is the lonely man, fighting it out high above the heads of ordinary men.

Much of what has so far been said may seem fanciful, but if it is now less certain that all fight spectators are simply part of a barbaric mob howling for blood, then at least reference may be made to the cathartic effect and the aesthetics of boxing without provoking instant derision. For the spectator who probably quite unconsciously attends fights as substitutes for the experience of art and ritual enjoys considerable aesthetic satisfaction which is not to be explained away in terms of aggression, sado-masochism, *schadenfreude* or compensation fantasy. A fighter of the calibre of Sugar Ray Robinson at his best combined the qualities of the expert fencer and the great dancer, but no movement was executed for its own sake or simply to impress the spectator. The beauty was a consequence of functional economy.

The principal motivations then for the spectator are the needs for a hero figure with whom he can easily identify; for an activity which can offer myth, drama, ritual and excitement; for a cathartic spectacle and for an experience which can take the place of aesthetic experience which would be beyond his intellectual and imaginative capacity to enjoy. But the motivating forces which send the actual participant into the ring, though occasionally closely related to those of the spectator, naturally require separate examination.

The boy who takes up boxing will first have been attracted to the heroic and dramatic aspects of the game, but unlike Auden's clerk he is not content to dream that he is a boxer; he will set out to become one. Once he is boxing, even as an amateur novice, he feels at once removed from and superior to those who merely watch. Exhibitionism and the need to assert his masculinity and to be admired contribute to the total motivation, but these drives in themselves are not enough to keep a boy at the bitter disciplines of training and the fierce and often painful ordeals of competitive bouts. Many other less arduous games could fulfill these needs. He continues to box because he finds in the experience an excitement that no other game can supply.

My own feelings toward the game, when I boxed as an amateur and later as a professional, remained to the end highly ambivalent. Immediately before a contest I would be stretched on a rack of nervous anticipation and apprehension; the fear had little to do with the possibility of pain or injury. It was much more like the sensations experienced by actors before an important debut; it was the fear of being publicly humiliated. Yet this feeling, or complex of feelings, was also pleasurable in a febrile way, and one could become addicted to it as if it were a drug. This accounts for those fighters who continue to perform long after they have passed their best and when there is no economic necessity for going on fighting.

The financial rewards of first-class professional boxing are, of course, substantial, but it would be a mistake to think the desire for such rewards is a primary motivation for the boxer. Few boxers enter the professional ranks without first serving an apprenticeship as amateurs, and only a tiny percentage of the amateurs ever do in fact become professionals, by which time they have already proved themselves as accomplished performers. As with artists, few if any boxers have begun their careers simply for the financial gains involved; some have found that economic necessity has forced them to go on fighting after the real enthusiasm for the game has died. These men present as sad a spectacle as the spent writer who goes on churning out pot-boilers long after the joy of creation has crumbled to dust.

It is tempting to theorize about the complexity of the motives which send a boy into the boxing-ring, but in practice I believe that the drives are relatively simple. Sheer physical pleasure in executing the various maneuvers required cannot be ignored, and if impulses of sadism are present then they are usually effectively sublimated, for it is a fact that the boxer rarely feels personal animosity toward his opponent but, on the contrary, tends to regard him almost as an abstraction — a problem to be solved. After a contest both boxers almost invariably feel a bond of affection, a sense of having shared an ordeal, and they are further united in mutual regard for each other's skill, toughness, courage and the sense of their apartness from the noncombatant spectator. They feel that they are members of a gladiatorial elite. The danger of injury, even fatal injury, must be present. It is interesting that protests against the brutality of the game and the exploitation of the boxers and the cries for greater safeguards to protect the fighter from damage to the brain, to the eyes, etc. never come from boxers themselves, for they know, at some level of consciousness, that if the very real dangers of the sport were removed, then it would all become meaningless. The opportunity to demonstrate heroic courage, generosity, strength would be gone. To ask that the boxer should engage in contests where he could not be seriously hurt seems to him as absurd as asking the big-game hunter to go on safari with blank ammunition in pursuit of stuffed lions.

The attraction of the danger element is, I think, stronger than is generally allowed. Nearly all other sports which are obviously dangerous and from which the participants derive the intense excitement of confronting the last enemy, Death, are not accessible to the boy of humble background. I am thinking of mountain climbing, skiing, motor-racing, flying and big-game hunting, all occupations reserved for the more or less wealthy. This may well be the reason boxing has always been a sport for the underprivileged; even in these democratic days, one does not often find boys from prosperous backgrounds taking up boxing seriously. The children of wealthier parents can experience their exciting confrontations with death less primitively, more comfortably, and without the rigorous preparation for the encounter that the boxer has to undergo. Boxing is one of the few violent and risky activities that a poor boy can legitimately pursue. However, although the majority of boxers come from the less privileged social groups, it would be a mistake to believe that the desire for escape from his milieu or to gain the applause of those who belong to higher social categories is a primary motivating force in his becoming a fighter. As with the prospect of monetary reward, it may later become a decisive influence in the choice to continue boxing or to turn professional, but the primary motivations are deeper and, in a sense, purer.

To recapitulate: the young male is first attracted to boxing by its dramatic and mythopoeic power; he sees the boxer as a heroic figure to be emulated. He finds that his natural aggressive instincts are not only sanctioned but actually admired and encouraged; he finds the ordeal of nervous tension before going into the ring exquisitely exciting and, probably unconsciously, knows that his life would be impoverished without this intensity of experience. As he learns the skills of his chosen sport, he comes to enjoy their practice; he believes that his masculinity has been established beyond question, and he is happier than his non-boxing friends who are nagged by the need to prove their manhood and their toughness. The disciplines of training, though they may be exacting and often painfully so, nevertheless supply an order and discipline for which he probably craves. He is splendidly conscious of belonging to an elite. He is braver, stronger and nobler than the majority of men, and he will wear the scars of his trade like medals. The asthmatic clerk could dream of worse things to be.

"The Champ, my grandfather, attributed his stance, great reach, strong arms and ability to bob and weave to having owned and operated a pub."

WRESTLING

GREGORY P. STONE AND RAMON A. OLDENBURG

SEVERAL YEARS AGO ONE OF us took a friend to the railroad station. We arrived early and went to a nearby tavern to kill time. Those were the days when wrestling was getting its big play on television, and the set at the bar was presenting the then current struggle — the Russians (Kalmikoff brothers, one since deceased) versus the local heroes (good, clean-cut Americans). We chose to ignore the spectacle in favor of conversation, but were suddenly interrupted as a lone beer-drinker slammed his fist on the bar and shouted: "I don't give a damn if it is a fake! Kill the son-of-a-bitch!" We have pondered those lines ever since: how can the wrestling fan who seemingly has penetrated the facade of the match still be caught up in the "heat" of the performance? This is the primary question that orients this chapter. The question seems simple, and perhaps it is. But the answer is highly involved and complex. It requires a consideration of the historical transformations of wrestling, the social organization of the enterprise, wrestling careers and, of course, the social and social-psychological character of the audience and the wrestling fan.

HISTORICAL TRANSFORMATIONS OF WRESTLING

Wrestling as Work and Play

There is archeological evidence that wrestling existed in human society five thousand years ago, but by that ancient time it was carried on almost exclusively as sport or play.[1] Wrestling is certainly as old as the appearance of man or quasi-man on earth and probably older. If we indulge in a bit of anthropomorphism, it becomes easy to imagine that beasts "wrestle" their prey to the ground or that kittens and cubs "play" at "wrestling." We can speculate, then, that wrestling in human society began at once as work and play. Wrestling is the most primitive mode of combat and, at its inception, was probably a type of work carried on in the struggle man waged with beasts and other men. Wrestling play could undoubtedly be found at the same time in what we think of today as childish pranks. Body control is an essential dimension of poise (one way we signal to others our readiness for interaction) and is unknowingly cultivated in young people as they push, trip, tickle, tackle and otherwise grapple with one another. With the development of a more efficient combat technology, the *work* of wrestling ceased, and wrestling persisted in society as a play form, except, of course, in emergencies and other uncontrolled situations. An important function of play is the *re*-creation and maintenance of obsolete work forms, making history a viable reality for mankind. Thus canoeing, archery and horseback riding persist in society today as play. Wrestling is no exception.

Before the twelfth century, wrestling was a universal play form in Europe, engaged in by all strata of the male population without reference to social rank. After the twelfth century, with the crystallization of an aristocracy, the character of play underwent a change.

> This marked the beginning of the idea that noblemen should avoid mixing with villeins and taking their sport among them: an idea which did not succeed in imposing itself everywhere, at least until the eighteenth century, when the nobility disappeared as a class with a social function and was replaced by the bourgeoisie.[2]

Wrestling was one of the earliest sports set apart and marked off by the aristocratic stratification of European society. It became a common sport and not a knightly game in the twelfth century. Of course, there are many exceptions – Henry VIII was a skilled wrestler – but, by and large, wrestling has been a lower status sport in Western civilization for eight hundred years.

There was probably an element of snobbery in all this. Ariès cites a sixteenth century account which reports some protest at the continuing mixing of nobles and peasants in festival games: "If there is anything which is too ugly and shameful for words, it is the sight of a nobleman being defeated by a peasant, especially in wrestling."[3] Yet, an additional reason for the relegation of wrestling to the lower strata is to be found in precisely its "primitive" character. It is the least elaborated of all sports with the possible exception of walking and running. Even in these instances, a comparison of, let us say, the equipment of the Japanese sumo wrestler with that of the track athlete suggests that the technology of wrestling is impressively less complex. In general, the more elaborate the technological paraphernalia of a sport, the higher its social status. There have been some attempts to extend the equipment of wrestling, as with the *schwingenhosen* of the Swiss and Tyrolese or the canvas jackets used in Cornwall wrestling, but these have not caught on widely at all. In contrast to sumo wrestling, judo wrestlers do have a uniform, and, perhaps more than anything else, this betrays the fact that ju juitsu developed among the samurai in Japan, while sumo was the national or common sport.

In its early history, then, wrestling was quickly abandoned as a form of work in society, but was retained as a play form. In Europe it was established as lower status play long ago, and, as we shall see, with the exception of wrestling play, it persists as a lower status spectator sport today.

Wrestling as Sport and Drama in the United States

Sport is a transformation of work and play forms. Amateur sport is usually a transformation of work into play; professional sport, a transformation of play into work. Precisely when wrestling became a professional sport in America is not known. Quite likely it emerged along with other professional sports in the last half of the nineteenth century. If we do not know

THE VIKING
—Photo by Bill Mobley.

when professional wrestling originated in America, we do know that the last sporting wrestler was Frank Gotch.[4] Gotch wrestled for thirteen years, winning 156 out of 160 matches (about one match per month – compare the schedules of present day wrestlers, often four or five matches a week). He retired in 1912.

After Gotch, the character of the sport changed dramatically, for it became a drama. It is very difficult to arrive at any definitive explanation of the transformation of wrestling into commercial drama,[5] but at least four factors contributed to the change: (1) the nature of the sport itself; (2) the urbanization of the United States; (3) a general revulsion against violence in sport which arose shortly before Gotch's retirement; and (4) the development of wrestling "trusts."

Wrestling is a dangerous sport. The risk of severe injury to the participants is high. As a consequence, with the evolution of wrestling as play, rules were devised to mitigate the physical risk. The result was to define victory in amateur wrestling contests as a disturbance of the opponent's poise – tripping him, upsetting him or forcing him out of a sharply demarcated play area. This persists today, not only in amateur wrestling, but in wrestling play – "Indian wrestling" and "arm wrestling." However, this kind of match does not command great audience enthusiasm, though it might well enthuse the participants. The alternative mode of victory is submission of the opponent, and this is the mode professional wrestling has adopted. Although it *may* command great and extensive enthusiasm among spectators for reasons we shall discuss later, earnest attempts at submission can be very boring indeed for the onlooker. It can hardly command the enthusiasm of the participants over the long run. Gotch left an incredible string of broken legs in the wake of his 156 victories, and a broken leg forced his own retirement. This is just the point: wrestlers can not anticipate *any* extensive career, if submission of the opponent is the test of victory, and the match proceeds on the basis of catch-as-catch-can.

Submission holds are easily established and *impossible* to break. This fact has a dual consequence. First, spectators must resign themselves to long periods of inactivity, and this must inevitably depress their interest. Specifically, when Gotch finally met Hackenschmidt for the world title in 1904:

> Gotch followed his strategy rigidly with the result the match developed into a dull pull-and-haul affair with the champion and the challenger on their feet for two hours. The crowd of 18,000 who paid approximately $70,000 to see the match . . . booed the contestants for lack of action.
>
> After two hours and three minutes of tussling, Gotch finally maneuvered to get behind Hackenschmidt to whip a waistlock on him. The Iowan then lifted the Russian off his feet and banged him down on the mat. "Hack" immediately informed the referee . . . he would forfeit the fall to Gotch.[6]

The tedious achievement of submission bores the audience. Second, the consequence of early severe bodily injury to the wrestlers is highly probable. We have already mentioned the frequency of fractures that attended early professional wrestling in the United States; but, in this respect, the superiority of wrestling over boxing as a combative technique has been unambiguously established. William Muldoon, the "greatest Roman of them all," defeated the great John L. Sullivan in 1887, and it took Ray Steele, a heavyweight wrestler of no great merit, thirty-five seconds to subdue King Levinsky in 1935. By 1937, "Strangler" Lewis, Jack Dempsey, Benny Leonard and Dean Detton all agreed that wrestlers could defeat boxers, each fighting his own style.[7]

Our point is that, when professional wrestling opted for the alternative of submission to adjudicate victory, it sharply curtailed the "life expectancy" of the business. No economic enterprise in America is established with the prospect of going out of business, and the continuity of business presupposes the continuity of the clientele and the *gradual* replacement of key personnel. Consequently, wrestling as a professional sport, that is, play transformed into work, was primed for some kind of transformation when it seized upon the option of submission as the mark of victory.

Since professional sports must build up followings, fans must identify with the symbols or representations of the sports. The representations of combative sports are the individual combatants, and identifications with combatants (unless the fan is caught up in the snares of nostalgia, or, as we shall see below, the relationship between fan and combatant is relatively intimate or bolstered by other bonds) can only persist as long as the combatant is active. In team sports, on the other hand, the name of the team with which the fan identifies typically persists beyond the career of any given individual player. The players represent the collectivity. In the case of wrestling, then, a way had to be found to extend the careers of the wrestlers or to cloak the sport in representations that transcended individual wrestling careers.

This exigency was made all the more urgent by the rapid urbanization of the United States in the early twentieth century. When wrestling was a young sport, wrestlers followed a circuit of small towns where almost every resident knew almost every other. Local heroes were pitted against alien villains, and identifications with local representatives were strong and long established. Interest ran high in such matches, as manifested in extensive gambling, so that fairly large turnouts could be anticipated, despite the fact that the outcome of matches was usually decided by upsetting rather than overwhelming the opponent. Beginning in 1828, Abraham Lincoln wrestled throughout the Mississippi and Ohio river country, and it has been estimated that he engaged in some three hundred matches before his political career precluded further participation. The mark of his extensive wrestling remained as a lifelong imprint — the huge cauliflowered left ear. He was a kind of representative of the wrestling of his time, and it is significant that his outstanding championship match took place at Coles County, Illinois, two counties south of what is now Champaign-Urbana, hardly an urban center.[8] With the rise of cities and the relocation of the wrestling "market," wrestlers could no longer appear as representatives of local small towns, but were forced to establish themselves as representations of larger, nationwide, or worldwide social units which could cut across and mobilize the identifications of anonymous spectators.

Shortly before Gotch's retirement, a wave of revulsion against violence in athletics swept over the nation. In 1905, Teddy Roosevelt was so enraged by the bloody brutality of a Swarthmore-Pennsylvania football game that he threatened to abolish that sport by executive edict, unless extreme measures were taken to reduce the violence.[9] Boxing had not been legalized at that time in most of the states, in part because of the attendant vehemence. This public temper may well have accelerated the trend to reduce the probability of grave bodily injury in professional wrestling by making wrestlers even more keenly aware of the vary real physical risks that their profession entailed.

Finally, to explain the transformation, we must consider the whole network of events touched off by the problem of effecting a transfer of power after Gotch's retirement, for the way in which this was done culminated in the formation of the great wrestling "trusts." When Gotch retired, he designated two wrestlers to engage in an elimination bout for his title. The winner was defeated in 1914 by Charles Cutler, who proceeded to subdue all significant opposition.[10] In a desperate search for a worthwhile opponent, Cutler located a young Nebraskan, Joe Stecher, who was a good wrestler but, because of his inexperience, hardly of championship caliber. In 1915, Stecher defeated Cutler in straight falls, and wrestling fans lost thousands of dollars in wagers. This initiated a steep decline of public confidence in the sport. The fate of wrestling as a sport was undoubtedly sealed in 1917, when, for as yet unstated reasons, Stecher refused to appear for a third and deciding fall and lost his title to Earl Caddock. Again the betting public took a severe beating. Clearly, the "fix" was on. Wrestling could no longer be conceptualized in the public mind as a sport with genuinely uncertain outcomes, and today the absence of any large-scale betting on matches is one clear sign that wrestling has been transformed from a sport into a drama. To revive and sustain a wrestling following — to make money — wrestlers joined with promoters and managers to form "trusts."[11] These trusts sought to bring as many wrestlers as possible under their control and arranged dramatic, colorful encounters, called "working matches" in the trade, on extensive circuits across the nation. An outstanding trust was known as the "Gold Dust Trio," comprised of Ed "Strangler" Lewis, Joe "Toots" Mondt, both topflight wrestlers, and Billy Sandow, one of the shrewdest promotors and managers in the history of American professional wrestling. At one time, this trust had five hundred wrestlers under contract.[12]

It is not as though there were no real or "shooting" matches. Where there are trusts, there are "trust-busters," and wrestlers would often sign to "work" a card but would "shoot" instead. To lessen the likelihood of this kind of double cross, "policemen" were used to test the ability of wrestlers whose motives were suspect, prior to matching them with a champion. It is said that Mondt was Lewis' policeman.[13] Moreover, wrestlers would at times become discontent with their status in the trust, and shooting matches would be arranged. Even today, there is probably a chance of an occasional double cross or an indefensible complaint so that shooting matches may still occur. Our guess is that this is rare.[14]

No better documentation of the fact that wrestling had become drama is to be found than a reference to the career of Jim Londos, who belonged to one of the most lucrative trusts in wrestling. Londos, born Christopher Teophelus, was a mediocre wrestler whose career began before World War I and lasted until the mid-thirties. He had been defeated countless times by countless wrestlers until 1930, when he became *a* world champion in a Philadelphia match. Griffin says: "Perhaps no greater betrayer of a people ever appeared bofere the public,"[15] and he proves it! *Ring* magazine marked October, 1934, as the end of wrestling as a professional sport in the United States.[16] That was the year Londos shared the "title" with Ed Don George. But Londos was most significant for the transformation of wrestling into drama. First, he was "box-office."

> Londos met his hand-picked opponents in bouts night after night, sometimes locking grips with the same wrestler four times in one week, in different cities, of course.
>
> The number of times he "wrestled" Ray Steele, Rudy Dusek, Gino Geribaldi, Sammy Stein, Karl Pjello, Jim McMillan in "matches" advertised for the title runs into the hundreds.
>
> The gates for these bouts totaled thousands of dollars. In fact, after meeting Steele in some sixty-eight "contests" Londos "wrestled" the latter in an open air "match" at the Yankee Stadium, New York. The bout drew close to seventy thousand dollars, a new high for wrestling gates in New York, a record never since equalled in the New York metropolitan area in money or gullibility on the part of meat-tossing enthusiasts.[17]

Second, Londos introduced the "freak" into the drama — the contest between "beauty and the beast" remains in the wrestling repertoire at the present day. Third, he lured women into wrestling fandom.

Londos was *a* champion and a significant catalyst in the transformation of wrestling, but the trusts promoted different personalities in different parts of the country, and there were regional as well as national trusts. In 1933, there were six "world champions"; in 1934, two; but, by 1943, the list had swelled to fifteen; and today there are at least five world champions and probably as many regional champions as there are television viewing areas. Verne Gagne is affectionately dubbed by at least one sport columnist in the Twin City area "world champion of the five county mosquito control district." This multiplication of champions was enabled precisely by the removal of wrestling from the world of professional sports. It meant that sports writers lost interest, with the result that the national wire services ceased to report wrestling results.[18] Wrestling is played down in the local press as well. Glancing at the Minneapolis *Tribune* sports section for Sunday, February 7, 1965, we found the first page primarily given over to accounts (continued on the inside) of University of Minnesota hockey and basketball games. Attendance at those matches was 5,093 and 6,273, respectively. The "world championship" wrestling match between Verne Gagne and "Mad Dog" Vachon received two and one half column inches on page four. Attendance was 6,389! Almost two and a half months later, the situation had changed very little. On April 18, 1965, the front page was mostly concerned with the Minnesota Twins 3-0 victory over the Cleveland Indians. That game attracted 4,492 spectators. The rematch between Gagne and Vachon was reported on the third page this time and given three and three-fourths column inches. The rematch attracted 8,900 spectators, about twice the attendance of the major league ball game! This, of course, rankles the wrestling audience, and sportswriters are also disturbed. Sportswriters feel a strong obligation to all sports fans, but they also have a great pride in their craft. They are critics. Long ago they concluded that there was nothing left to criticize in professional wrestling, so perhaps two or three inches on page three or four of the sports pages is the best compromise they can make. They're damned if they do report wrestling and damned if they don't. At any rate, the lack of any national or interstate press coverage facilitates the drama. Drama permits a single actor to play many roles, and wrestlers use different names in different places. Thus, the dedicated fan can not discover, except fortuitously or by an unlikely search, that the world champion of his own local area is not, in fact, *the* world champion.

This overview of the transformation of wrestling from work to play to professional sport to drama has touched upon some of the facets of the social organization of professional wrestling in the United States, but important details have been omitted. It is to these that we now turn our attention.

SOCIAL ORGANIZATION OF WRESTLING

When the sociologist first attempts to probe the present-day social organization of wrestling, his reaction is one of wonder at the fantastic extent of a marvelously controlled "conspiracy of silence." As he continues his study, the wonder gives way to consternation at the impenetrability of the conspiracy. Finally, his attitude becomes one of dull resignation and reluctant acceptance of the fact that many of his conclusions will be more inferential than demonstrative. The imperviousness of the conspiracy is attested to by the reaction of a local sports editor to an interview with the writers. The editor had been in the "trade" for thirty-five years, and his career included a stint in New York as well as the West Coast and other midwestern cities. In a Sunday column, he admitted publicly that he had no answers for most of our queries. Apparently the deepest "penetration" he had made of the conspiracy was securing an admission from a local promoter that he had "never told a wrestler to lose a match" — scarcely more than a knock on the door of the inner sanctum. Moreover, sportswriters often make friends of professional athletes and, in the give and take of friendship, become party to trade secrets. This may not be the case with wrestling. One of the reporters on the editor's staff established a close relationship with a wrestling tag team, accompanying them on fishing trips and participating with them in other leisure activities, but he never became privy to the secrets of the sport. Our analysis of the inside organization of wrestling, then, is necessarily deductive. For the outside organization, it is, of course, a simpler, more direct matter.

Size of the Industry

In 1952, there were approximately fifteen million paying spectators of professional wrestling. By 1959, the number had risen to 24,000,000 and had exceeded 25,000,000 by the early sixties. Not only does this latter figure exceed the paid attendance for such other professional sports as major league baseball, professional football, professional basketball and horse-racing, but the number of wrestling spectators (excluding the TV viewers) has risen at a rate greater than our overall population increase. The number of active professional wrestlers has been variously established at between two and four thousand. There are more than five hundred regularly used wrestling arenas in the nation. Gross gate receipts in the early fifties exceeded twenty million dollars, and today they probably come close to doubling that figure. Moreover, wrestling in the American fashion has spread to other countries, notably Australia, Great Britain and Japan, and there are currently signs of the development of an international circuit which attracts the top wrestlers. In short, professional wrestling is big business.

Regional Organization in the United States

Although the *Encyclopedia of Associations* does not list a single professional wrestling organization, there are certainly four and probably five which organize wrestling on a regional basis in the United States: the World Wide Wrestling Federation, centered in New York; the National Wrestling Alliance, located in St. Louis; the American Wrestling Alliance, headquartered in Amarillo, Texas; and the World Wrestling Alliance, located in Los Angeles. A fifth organization quite probably organizes the southeast, perhaps centered in Miami, Florida. The Minneapolis Club, from which most of our observations have been drawn, is in the AWA.

How these organizations function is not completely clear. They *may* exert sanctions on participating wrestlers. As an example, Larry Hennig and Harley Race were recently declared southwest tag-team champions by Sidney Blackburn, president of the American Wrestling Alliance. Following a conversation with Blackburn, Hennig asserted that he had been assured that top tag-team combinations would be dropped from title contention if they declined to meet the southwest champions.[19] How much of such talk is ballyhoo and how much is factual reporting is impossible to determine. Our guess favors the ballyhoo. Yet, reports do appear, from time to time, of fines and suspensions exacted by wrestling alliances or commissioners against recalcitrant and "berserk" wrestlers.

Certainly, the alliances do see to it that matches promoted by affiliated clubs remain within the letter of state legislation. For example, a Texas statute declares that it is a criminal offense

> knowingly [to] conduct or give or participate in any sham or fake fistic combat match, boxing, sparring, or wrestling contest or exhibition except it be as burlesque.

Legally, therefore, wrestling is defined as burlesque in Texas, although, of course, the definition is not publicized. There is no statutory regulation of professional wrestling in Minnesota.

In a general way, the territory staked out by each regional association sets boundaries marking off contiguous television viewing areas within which canned performances of regional heroes and villains are circulated. Today, the area in which any given wrestling league is popular is determined almost wholly by the exposure of the area to televised wrestling. Promoters have found that interest in the sport cannot be maintained without televising wrestling matches regularly.[20] One of the major decisions to be made in any region is the allocation of time to the televising of wrestling matches. In one region it was decided that a minimum of two hours per week is essential, but that it would not be judicious to exceed two and one-half or three hours.

All major professional wrestlers follow their canned performances around the country. From the Twin City area, for example, canned shows are sent regularly to Illinois, Nebraska and Colorado. When fan appetite has been sufficiently whetted, the wrestlers who have been viewed on television in those areas make live appearancs. Fan interest can also be diverted by the sponsorship of canned matches originating in rival regions, though this rarely occurs. When it did happen in one area, the local promoter remarked, "Well, of course, he (the rival promoter) doesn't give a damn what happens to us here." Probably alliances establish treaties about the distribution of canned performances, and this may be a major function. If wrestling were more popular as a national television attraction, and advertisers sought to sponsor it, a "battle of the leagues" could develop. Instead of engaging their respective "world champions" in frequent decisive combat, the war would be waged by sending canned matches into rival territories. Again, we can see how the "conspiracy of silence" operates to maintain the status quo. The lack of national press coverage makes the "battle of the leagues" an extremely unlikely eventuality.

Whether or not the above functions characterize the operation of the alliances, one function is certain. The existence of diverse alliances reduces the probability of embarrassment for the champions. When we asked Verne Gagne to explain the multiplicity of wrestling champions on the national scene, he scarcely raised an eyebrow. "Is that so unusual?" he asked. "The AFL and the NFL each has its own champion. Why shouldn't that be the case for each wrestling league?"

Local Organization

Regional wrestling alliances seem to be loose, wispy federations of local clubs. Perhaps, at best, they demarcate audiences for whom passionate dramas between good and evil are enacted. However, when one takes a hard look at local organization, the structure seems to come alive. The metropolitan club is the core organization of professional wrestling. Viewed from the outside, the club tightly organizes the relationships among the promoter, the matchmaker, the wrestlers, an announcer, referees and lesser figures, such as seconds, (off-duty) policemen and badge-wearing arena ushers. In local television presentations, most of the personnel play a part in the ongoing drama. Will the promoter bring in some new and rugged hero to threaten the reign of a devilish villain? Will the matchmaker arrange a meet between the two "bad guys"? Will the commissioner act on the referee's request to suspend the villain who has hospitalized two fine young wrestlers? Such questions are planted in the fan mind by the announcer and those he interviews between bouts. The announcer stresses two themes: (1) he is instructed by the local promoter to "boost" each wrestler who appears in the ring; and (2) he continually echoes and inspires the sentiments appropriate for developing identifications among the fans. "My goodness, ladies and gentlemen," he will say, "this is the most barbaric thing I have ever seen in the ring! I don't know why they allow him to get away with that." Of course it is the referee that permits the barbarism. Referees are as important a part of the drama as the wrestlers themselves, and they assume as many different identities. These range from local sports heroes, through national sports heroes who are "over the hill," to figures like "Blind Anthony," who is led into the Chicago ring by a seeing-eye dog. Obviously referees are not those who oversee what goes on; they overlook it.

Promotion

At the heart of the local organization of professional wrestling is the promoter of the metropolitan club. Most of the money is made in the metropolitan arenas, and all of the topflight wrestlers regularly appear in those rings and on the metropolitan television station. Wrestling no longer depends to any great degree upon the small town carnival or the fair to attract its paying audiences. Indeed, as we have shown, it cannot. Nevertheless, an important function of the metropolitan promoter is to maintain a liaison with small town promoters and fans. Small towns often act as feeders for metropolitan clubs, and, consequently, wrestling is cultivated there. They also form the "fringe sectors" of television viewing areas. Fan loyalty in the fringes is typically high and must be sustained, for fans in remote places add to television ratings.

Therefore, some wrestlers still make appearances on the carnival scene. Usually they appear in what has come to be called the "ad show" (from "athletic show," somehow). Besides touring "pros," two kinds of wrestlers are likely to be found in the ad shows. There are the younger and non-college-educated wrestlers who use this opportunity to establish professional wrestling careers. By appearing in these shows, they come under the watchful eyes of club promoters who keep a constant vigil for new box office attractions. Then there are those who have retired from the more strenuous activities of the metropolitan arenas. Wrestling matches at carnivals are usually short in duration, often carried on under a five-minute time limit.

Carnival wrestlers frequently issue challenges to club wrestlers who may be in the area, and if scheduling permits, they usually accept such challenges. Of course, it's an "extra buck," but also, as one club promoter told us, "They never know what they're going to meet in that kind of ring." Thus, for the club wrestler, the occasional carnival or ad show match can serve as one guarantee against "going stale."[21] Moreover, as we shall see, the appearance of the club wrestler in the small town is a vital part of the promotion process.

A far more lucrative carry over from the old days of carnival wrestling is the fair date. Fair dates are regarded as "sure things," since such celebrations are always insured against nonattendance. Usually, the participating club is given the lion's share (60% is common) of a guaranteed $1,500 gate.

Other than club promoters, the promoter of a wrestling event may be a person, a corporation, an established religious group, a city council or a local chamber of commerce. Any duly recognized person or group may be the occasional promoter of a wrestling match. In almost all cases, the occasional promoter will work with the metropolitan club in the promotion of wrestling and vice versa. The established club will usually have at least two small trucks or "panel jobs" which carry collapsible rings and whatever other paraphernalia is necessary. This "set-up" is always ready to go. Should inclement weather make traveling difficult or mechanical trouble cause a late arrival, there is seldom any real problem. Though the panel truck may be an hour late in arriving before a frustrated audience, once there, it is possible to set up for the event in fifteen minutes' time.

While the local club rarely refuses to cooperate in the promotion of a small town event, there are often problems. At times, the total gate may be as little as $600 or less, and this hardly compares to the $900 guaranteed to the club at a fair date. Moreover, compared to the routine $10,000 arena gates, the small town "take" is ridiculously small. Small town engagements, then, are construed as profitable in a long-run promotional sense, and the main problem is that of providing a suitable card of wrestlers for the small audiences. It is seldom that a "world champion" will undertake an engagement for less than a guaranteed $100, and the current world champion of the AWA, "Mad Dog" Vachon, demands $750 for each appearance. Understandably, every occasional promoter would like to have the "champ" on his card, and regional associations often make this possible. The "champion" is the one wrestler over whom the alliance does exert control in the scheduling of appearances. Champions have always been reasonably willing to comply with the schedules set for them by the association which has awarded them the crown.

Be these things as they may, the journey of the club wrestler to the small town is a powerful technique for solidifying the market. Whether the "champion" appears or not, it is certain that some notorious hero or villain will put in a personal appearance in the small town. The sport figure who appears on television can, at any moment, become a living reality for the small town viewer. In only one other professional sport is this the case, and the consequent loyalty of the fans is brute testimony to the efficacy of the device as a rhetoric of identification. Probably no other sport organization commands the pervasive support of the fans than that of the Green Bay Packers!

Offhand, it would seem that the club promoters and matchmakers sit at the seat of power in professional wrestling. At times this may well be the case. Matches in adjoining metropolitan centers, e.g., Minneapolis and St. Paul, run the risk of box office competition, but a "gentleman's agreement" usually obviates this possibility. As Riesman has observed of the nation, so it is with professional wrestling: "free trade" has given way to "fair trade."[22] When a neighboring promoter offers a competing card at the same time another promoter has scheduled a "big match," fireworks may ensue. Ordinarily, there are threats to build up the competing match with "championship blood" from rival television viewing areas. In the "give and take" of threat and counterthreat, compromises are formed, and the market remains undisturbed by the existence of spectator choice about which of the competing matches to attend.

WRESTLERS' CAREERS

Like all occupations, wrestling is characterized by careers demarcated by the stages of recruitment, maintenance of position and termination. Moreover, wrestling, like other occupations, has its sidelines and is, on occasion, a sideline itself.

Recruitment

The recruitment of new blood into the profession is accomplished, in the main, by the watchful eye which established promoters keep over college and university athletic departments. The majority of professional wrestlers have had careers as college wrestlers, college football players, or, quite often, both. Any lineman or back on a college football team, if he is both big and agile, comes under close scrutiny as a potential professional wrestler. The proposition put to him is usually directly to the point: "Do you realize," the promoter may ask, "just how much money you can make in this game?" And, indeed, the inducement is formidable.

While many promoters insist that wrestling gates are lessened during the height of football enthusiasm, football and professional wrestling are complimentary in many respects. Via football, many local wrestling heroes win that fame with which so many wrestling fans will come to identify and pay to watch. Further, we have already cited the problem which the active wrestler faces — that of "going stale." Many professional athletes work six months at professional football and the remaining six at professional wrestling. One activity keeps the body in shape for the other.

The great majority of professional wrestlers are fine athletes, and, as we are suggesting, most recruiting is done in communities of trained, well educated, amateur athletes. There are two notable exceptions to this convention: the "freak" and the "physique." In recent years, however, professional wrestling has moved anxiously away from the freakish, the "physical" and the feminine in terms of the identities it presents to its fans. One still sees a liberal enough sprinkling of atavistic monstrosities, awesome behemoths, golden tresses and smooth bodies among the matmen, but the recent emphasis is on the masculine, clean-cut, Frank Merriwell type.

A few men find their places among the ranks of professional wrestlers because of their physiques alone. Thus, an occasional weightlifter may appear in a series of (to us) unconvincing bouts which consist mainly of muscle-flexing and the use of "naked power" in breaking holds. In contrast to some of the great men of the game who become "Masters of a Thousand Holds," these fellows may manage but three or four. Also enjoying some popularity is the three-hundred-pound-plus pachyderm whose simple gimmick may be that of falling upon his hapless victims, repeatedly "crushing" them amid all the blubber. Yet these "wrestlers" are the exception rather than the rule, and the fan seems to bestow most favor upon the accomplished wrestler and imaginative performer. Organized wrestling recruits mostly ability and intelligence and recruits the body only for occasional color.

Identity-work

Once recruited into the profession, the major task of the wrestler is identity-work — building and husbanding an identity that can mobilize the appreciations of the audience and maintain them over time. Identity-work is perhaps the most crucial activity of the professional wrestler. The very mention of the task to Verne Gagne in an interview enthused that occasional world champion. He stated that decisions about identity — whether to be a hero or a villain, a "wrestling dentist" or a "mad dog" — are all up to the wrestler himself, as is his choice of other marks of identity — distinctive holds and techniques of "hooking" (maneuvering an opponent into an inescapable position). Wrestlers often lose sleep perfecting their remarks and styles of delivery for television interviews. Gagne waxed poetic about the high points of creativity required for working up an identity that permits the wrestler's "real self" to emerge in the contest or the appearance.

While the idea of matching a worked-up identity with the "real self" — the "virtual" with the "actual" identity, as Goffman would have it[23] — poses an unenlightening chicken-and-egg paradox,[24] there is no doubt that *becoming* the worked-up identity may carry serious risks for the wrestler. The "cover story" can become an efficient trap, once it is accepted by those to whom it is presented, for there is a reverberating influence upon the one who presents the cover. Fans *place* the wrestler in his *announced* identity, and there is no more powerful identity cement than consensual validation.[25] Harley Race, after he was designated southwest tag team champion, believed he was a champion and championed the cause of an underdog at a Minneapolis bar early in 1965. Race was shot and seriously wounded for his heroic effort. Becoming the worked-up identity may even mean death. Rikidozan, the highly popular Japanese champion, was convinced of his professed invincibility and walked six blocks to a hospital after an assassin had completely transfixed his torso with a sword in December, 1963. He left his hospital bed against medical advice, aggravating his wound, and that was the end of the invincible champion.

One reason that the intelligent and educated wrestler is organizationally superior to the "meathead" is that he will be able to exercise imagination in working up an identity which fans will find attractive, or at least attracting. Moreover, the intellectual superiority of the professional wrestler permits him to maintain a lack of emotional involvement while effecting a good dramatic performance, a capacity that can be extremely valuable whenever a good deal of fan "heat" is being generated. Wrestlers appear to go berserk in almost every event; understandably, it is essential that they do not go berserk. Many fine wrestlers make relatively few appearances and have otherwise illustrious careers precluded, simply because they do not "draw," but intelligent and educated imagination can handle such problems.

A case in point is that of Bill Miller,[26] a licensed veterinarian and ex-Ohio State Rose Bowl football player. Miller, an excellent wrestler, consistently failed to draw. Conceiving that the failure indicated an identity problem, he proceeded to make his identity problematic and became the masked "Mr. M." The result was a rapturous fascination on the part of fans and a novel business success for Bill Miller. Indeed, a fan became so mesmerized by the villainous identity of Mr. M that, when the spell was broken by the inevitable unmasking, he smashed Miller on the head using a two by six inch plank with a one inch cleat fastened on the end. Miller was knocked unconscious, rushed to the hospital, found suffering from a brain concussion and transferred to the Mayo Clinic. Luckily, Miller was able to return to the ring after an extended convalescence. Besides eliciting mayhem, the unmasking of Mr. M mobilized revised appreciations of Bill Miller. Identities, then, can be established by revelation, and this may also serve to resurrect identities that have died. As Ernest puts it:

> Don't be surprised if Big Bill does go back to a mask someday if his pursuit of the title flags down a bit. Only this time he'd probably assume a dual personality — and wrestle as a masked man in the same territory as the real Bill Miller.[27]

Identities may have been worked up so well and appropriated so completely that they persist beyond the active career of the wrestler. Lou Thesz was a hero during his career,[28] and this identity persisted beyond his retirement. When a villain, Buddy Rogers, became "world champion," Thesz felt it was necessary to come out of retirement: "Buddy Rogers' wearing the World's Heavyweight Championship belt was just too much!"[29] In 1962, Thesz did come out of retirement, "defeated" Rogers for the NWA crown, and had this to say:

> With Rogers out of the way, I feel that wrestling has taken a big step toward eliminating a character with which wrestling has, to a degree, become identified in recent years. I am as proud of having helped to bring this about as I am of having won the title for an unprecedented sixth time.[30]

Terminations

There are two terminal points in the wrestling career: one, temporary and local; the other, permanent and total. Temporary local terminations have to do with movements away from metropolitan clubs, generally to other television viewing areas. Taken together, such terminations, demarcating appearances of varying lengths, constitute the wrestler's itinerary. Wrestlers may stay with any given club for as short a time as two or three months. Thus, Sailor Art Thomas, "a nice enough guy, but not very bright," in the words of an anonymous authority, will probably never learn to wrestle. Unskilled in identity-work, the "meathead" can never command audience appreciations for any extensive length of time. Nice guys never win ball games – without talent! Art Thomas remained on Minneapolis cards somewhat more than two months. In contrast, the "Crusher" remained on the Twin City scene for two years, "cooled it" for a short time in Milwaukee and recently returned to the Twin Cities, where his identity has been reworked from simple villain to the "good-bad guy."[31]

Probably the success or failure of identity-work is the crucial variable determining temporary local terminations, but there are others. There is the matter of the overall strength of the card. Too many mediocrities – *not* failures – mean that the card must literally be "beefed up" and that some mediocrities must go. Wrestlers may, for various reasons, lose rapport with the local organization. Won-lost records may become monotonic with a consequent loss of audience heat. Better offers from other clubs may lure the wrestler away. Finally career contingencies[32] – the opening of the football season – may bring the wrestler's local appearances to a temporary halt.

Except for the wrestler who simply fails to become a draw, permanent and total terminations seem to be exclusively physical. By the mid 50's, the bones become brittle, the spring is gone from the muscles, and it is better that the wrestler take his business elsewhere. This is precisely what he does. Wrestlers whose careers have persisted until this age are generally quite well off and have accumulated considerable business experience which they generally invest into proprietorships. However, there are more abrupt permanent and total terminations—compound bone fractures and fatal heart attacks. We have no data on the frequency or fate of wrestlers whose careers are ended by extensive physical damage, but Verne Gagne estimated for us that two or three of his associates, usually in their forties, die of heart attacks each year (the fate of "Gorgeous" George Wagner, who died in December, 1963, at the age of forty-eight).

Sidelines

Wrestling, as we have said, is a sideline for some football players; however, when the shorter football career ends, wrestling may well become the central vocation. Yet, wrestling has its own sidelines. The successful wrestler often markets health products such as vitamin preparations on the side, and can use his television appearances to promote those products. Indeed, in at least one case, the sideline became the sponsoring agency for the televising of local live wrestling bouts. Health clubs and hair salons are other examples of sidelines carried on profitably by successful wrestlers. All wrestlers, however, receive some additional income from the sale of photographs. Consider this excerpt from a field report:

> I had waited for about twenty minutes in the front office of the Minneapolis Club when a smallish man in a neat summer suit came in and energetically began examining all the pictures of wrestlers covering three of the four walls of the outer office. Of approximately one hundred photos, he seemed to recognize all but three. When he didn't recognize a wrestler, he would call the secretary over to get the name. In all, he made her leave her work five times in the ten minutes he was there. He purchased two 8" x 10" glossy prints which the club stocks for the more avid fans. "What I do is put them in real nice albums," he explained. He asked the secretary for directions to a local pornography shop and left. When he was out of earshot, the secretary took off her glasses, put her head down on the desk, and laughed almost hysterically. We had both placed him as a homosexual, and she said that this sort of photo-collector is not rare, but that women purchase most of the photos, with high school-age boys who have taken up wrestling running a close second.

All in all, for the players, wrestling is probably the most lucrative of American professional sports, and certainly it is the one sport in which the athlete exercises greatest control over his own destiny. As Verne Gagne put it:

> It's the only free enterprise left in America. You wrestle when you want to, whom you want to, and you take a vacation whenever you want to. You come to the match, and you bring your own soap and towel.

THE FASCINATION OF THE FANS

In the trade it is generally recognized that wrestling is entertainment. It is defended on that ground and rightly so. Catch-as-catch-can wrestling, as it was fought prior to World War I, could not hold the attention of large numbers of spectators, nor did that style of wrestling-in-dead-earnest permit the economic growth of the professional sport. Defenders of professional wrestling, however, draw a sharp line between entertainment and fakery. That wrestling is artfully contrived has, as we have shown, been established for a long time. And, if doubting Thomases persist, let them note that there are no acknowledged critics of the sport, there is little speculation about outcomes, there is no betting, and there is no supersitition among wrestlers.[33] Yet there is a certain honesty about the deception, for the fan may rest assured, at least, that the wrestlers will remain in character during their performances.

Consequently, we can dispense with the distinction between fakery and entertainment. *Wrestling is drama,* and no member of the dramatic audience accuses the actors of misrepresentation. James Arness is not accused of fakery when he appears week after week as Marshall Dillon, nor is Laurence Olivier disesteemed because he presents himself as a long departed Shakespearean hero. On the other hand, the response of the wrestling fan to the drama is rather more like that of the child at the Saturday matinee – audibly warning the cowboy hero that the villain lurks ahead in ambush – than the response of the critical viewer of the legitimate theater. The fan is fascinated.

Many forces combine to establish this fascination. Matches are brilliantly staged;[34] but, as we shall see, the effectiveness of the staging is underwritten by the attitude of the audience. The audience comes to the arena primed for blood, or, more mildly, to see justice done. The entire drama emerges as a magnificent fugue. The theme is set by the match; the audience provides the contrapuntal impetus – a rule is violated; the referee doesn't notice; the crowd roars; the referee looks; the villain "covers up." Another contrapuntal passage may be established in the mockery of the fans by the wrestler, and this is a powerful weld, for wrestling is one of the very few sports where the mutual recognition of the fan and the athlete seemingly catches each up in an ascending spiral of affect. At any rate, the fugue generally culminates in an awesome chorale – the main event – after which there is little left to be said. And, indeed, there is little recounting of matches by spectators after the matches, contrary to other sports, for the fugue has run its course in a climactic, exhaustive and probably exhausting denouement.

It is not as though there is no expertise on the part of wrestling fans. Fans claim they can distinguish the "real" from the "fixed."[35] However, the very distinction coerces the fan into a defense of his fandom and tightens his attachment to the sport. As in any sport, the fan can distinguish play from display, or over-stepping the "practical norms" from over-stepping the "formal rules," and this makes him something of a critic.[36] The audience can discern the "bad actor," but this is different from the villain. In wrestling, the villain must be a very good actor. As an example, in a "championship" bout we witnessed, the challenger — a villain — consistently failed to press obvious advantages and was greeted by cries of "chicken" from the audience. In the vernacular of hot-rodding teen-agers, the challenger had veered off the course of confrontation — had "hit the curb" — too long before the collision was imminent. Villains, in the view of the audience, are not very convincing if they abandon their role too soon — before the climactic phase of the drama. In all this, the fan is not concerned, as Denney has so cogently observed,[37] with the story structure. He is rapt in identities. This is a point to which we shall return.

Much drama re-presents the activity of the larger society, and this is the case with wrestling. At the wrestling match, one can view and become caught up in re-presentations of the class or status struggle, the eternal conflict between beauty and ugliness, the battle between the sexes (including the third and fourth sexes), the "cold war" or the bitter antagonism between local provincialism and cosmopolitan sophistication. Such struggles cut across the hostilities and loyalties of the nation and operate as powerful attractions for an anonymous mass audience, for all these struggles feature one common denominator — the universal agony of morality, the passionate tension between good and evil. For this reason, the drama of wrestling is best conceived as a passion play. Here again, wrestling is set apart from other professional sports. With few exceptions, e.g., the long passé quest for the "white hope" in boxing, other sports do not represent the larger struggles of the society *in their performance.*

Nevertheless, the drama of wrestling does not catch up all the members of society. The spectators of wrestling are drawn from clearly definable segments of the population. There are, first of all, the deviants, but our estimate is that these represent a relatively small proportion of the wrestling audience. They include homosexuals, voyeurs, women with a perduring hostility towards men, and the "touchers." The latter came to our attention in an observant conversation with a knowledgeable fan:

> I talk "homesy-folksy" about imaginary problems, and we become good friends, because I listen well. She tells many incidents about her hated high school bookkeeping teacher whom she disliked intensely "because he was too free with his hands." This business of touching bodies was brought out again when she talked about other female wrestling fans who like to touch the wrestlers as they walk by. They seem, she insisted, to like to touch sweaty bodies after the matches, more so than dry bodies before the matches.

A larger block of fans is made up of teen-agers, and, while we have no first hand data on them, we have estimated that as much as one-eighth of those attending wrestling matches are teen-agers. For the bulk of the audience we have more precise data.

Characteristics of the Audience

Several years ago, in 1958, we completed a survey of 566 adult married residents of the Twin City metropolitan area.[38] The sample was not a random sample of the population, but an analytic sample which endeavored to select approximately equal numbers of respondents in each of twenty-four cells generated by the cross-tabulation of four variables: sex, age (over and under 40), residence (urban-suburban), and socioeconomic status (upper, middle and lower). Among the questions asked was "When you hear the word 'sport,' what activities do you think of?" Fifty respondents — almost one tenth of the sample — mentioned wrestling.

Unlike mentions of most sports, sex proportions were about the same — 9.5 per cent of the men mentioned wrestling, as did 8.2 per cent of the women. Residence showed a somewhat greater discrepancy with 10.6 per cent of the suburban residents mentioning wrestling, compared to 6.9 per cent of the urban residents, but that difference is not statistically significant. It is a different matter for age and socioeconomic status. The proportion of older respondents mentioning wrestling (11.7%) was almost twice the proportion of younger people (6.1%), and the largest proportion of mentions was found in the lower socioeconomic stratum, as the following table shows.

TABLE I
PROPORTION OF RESPONDENTS IN THREE SOCIOECONOMIC STRATA MAKING SPONTANEOUS MENTION OF WRESTLING AS A SPORT

Stratum	*Per Cent*	*Total in Stratum*
Upper	6.8	192
Middle	6.0	183
Lower	13.6	191
Totals	9.0	566

These data indicate that wrestling is a salient sport for older, lower-status people and that women, although not significantly differentiated from men in this respect, are probably overrepresented in comparison to the attraction that other spectator sports ordinarily hold for them. That this latter contention is likely is confirmed by Vance Packard, who has reported that "a Nielsen check of TV fans watching wrestling matches revealed that ladies outnumbered men two to one."[39] Moreover, the sports editor of the St. Paul *Dispatch,* commenting on the avidity of wrestling fans, surmised that fewer complaints would follow the failure of the sport page to report major league baseball results than the failure to report wrestling results. When his paper did occasionally fail to report wrestling matches, about seven of every ten complainants, in his estimate, were women.

In combination, age, sex and status generate the largest proportion of respondents mentioning wrestling as a sport. Almost a fifth (19.9%) of forty-six older lower-status women mentioned wrestling as a sport. This proportion was followed by older, lower-status men (16.0%), then by younger, lower-status men (12.8%). One other category of respondents contributed more than 10 per cent of its numbers to those who mentioned wrestling as a sport: 10.6 per cent of the older, upper-status women. However, there is a possibility that the women in that category included amateur wrestling in their ken, and this is most unlikely for the lower-status respondents. Whether or not this is the case, lower-status is the definitive characteristic of those for whom wrestling has saliency as a sport. This has also been confirmed by an interview we conducted with the matchmaker of a local club. He expressed some guilt about the considerable sacrifice made by most people who attend wrestling matches, and we have observed that spectators in the most expensive seats appear to be those who can least afford it. Status is followed by age and sex, respectively, as differentiating variables, but the three variables operating conjointly generate the greatest relative frequency of those who include wrestling in their conception of sport.

Fans

In addition to the fifty respondents who mentioned wrestling as a sport in our Twin City survey, thirteen were classified as fans, i.e., spectators who mentioned wrestling as their favorite sport. The social characteristics of these fans did not differ markedly from those of the larger audience. Eight were older, eight were women, and eleven were lower-status. Again, the convergence of sex, age and status placed the largest number (5) in the category of older, lower-status women. In only two other categories — older, lower-status men (2) and younger, lower-status women (3) — were there more than one fan. The remaining three fans were scattered. One was a younger, lower-status man; another, an older, middle-status man; and the last a younger, middle-status man. There were no upper-status fans.

Intensive analysis was made of the interviews taken with these fans. This established the relatively low education of the fans compared to the larger audience. Specifically, no middle-status member of the larger audience had acquired less than a high school education, while the average year of school completed by the three middle-status fans was 11.6 years. In the lower stratum, the difference was not as striking but was, nevertheless, in the same direction. The average year of school completed for the lower status audience was 9.1 years; for the fans, 8.5.

Fans relied mostly on television for their information about wrestling.

For seven of them, television was their most important source of information; for four, attendance at the matches; and for the remaining two, the newspaper. This finding, of course, is hardly startling and is quite logically congruent with the other characteristics of the fans, the sparse reportage given professional wrestling by the press and, of course, the way in which the drama is promoted.

An additional finding disclosed by the interview analysis is of particular significance. Fans are people who rely more than others on appearances in their assessment of people. They seldom seek to penetrate the facades and masks that the members of our society conventionally offer to others in their day-to-day encounters.

Besides raising questions about sport, the interviews taken with the residents of the Twin City area focused on the variety and use of status symbolism in the anonymous situations of urban life. Respondents were asked:

> If you met a stranger downtown and took a strong personal liking to him (her), what kinds of things would you want to know about him (her) before you would invite him (her) to your home?

Afterward, they were asked how they would go about finding such things out. It is this latter question that is pertinent here. People can either be subtle about such matters, for example, engaging the stranger in seemingly unrelated conversation; they can be blunt, i.e., employing direct questions; or they can rely on appearances. Of course, any or all of these approaches may be used in combination. None of the wrestling fans relied exclusively on the blunt approach; four were primarily subtle and indirect, but nine depended primarily on appearances to provide the information they desired about the stranger. In short, there was a pronounced tendency for the fans to accept appearances at face value. Moreover, this seems to be generally characteristic of lower-status people. The same questions were asked of 125 adult respondents in Lansing, Michigan. In that study, more than a third of the lower-status respondents (38.1%) used observation to validate their inferences about the hypothetical stranger, compared to 11.8% of the middle-status and 21.9% of the upper-status respondents. Lower-status respondents resorted least often to subtle probing — 23.8 per cent, compared to 60.8 per cent of the middle-status and 62.4 per cent of the upper-status respondents.[40]

The "Mentality" of the Wrestling Audience

Pulling together all the information we have assembled on the wrestling audience and fans permits considerable insight into the attitude of the wrestling spectator, into just what it is that is expected at the match or on the television set.

As we have shown, those who make up the wrestling audience are predominantly lower-status, and, as such, their stance is probably pervaded by what Lipset has termed "working-class authoritarianism." He points out that

> The social situation of the lower strata, particularly in poorer countries with low levels of education, predisposes them to view politics in simplistic and chiliastic terms of black and white, good and evil.[41]

Later, he remarks:

> All of these characteristics combine to produce a tendency to view politics, *as well as personal relationships,* in black-and-white terms, a desire for immediate action without critical reflection, [and] impatience with talk and discussion.[42]

To the extent that this is the "set" of the wrestling spectator, then, he comes to the match primed for the active immediate struggle between good and evil. Nor is he concerned with the development of the plot:

> This concern with the immediate perceivable, with the personal and concrete, is part and parcel of the short time perspective and inability to perceive the complex possibilities and consequences of actions which is referred to . . . as a lack of social sophistication.[43]

The wrestling spectator is rapt in the identity of the wrestler *at that moment* and *in that place*. Moreover, in the counterpoint of the match and audience response, the relationship is personalized and further concretized, thereby heightening the rapture. That the lower-status person sees the world in black-and-white terms also helps explain why the greatest audience "heat" is generated "not so much [in] the indeterminate moments of the contest . . . as the moments in which one contestant is very much ahead,"[44] and why the long hours of indecision in many of the bouts carried on before World War I failed to hold the audience.

Recently, Lipset's observations on working-class authoritarianism have been criticized on the grounds that the authoritarian perspective is more a function of inadequate education than working-class membership, although the two variables are highly correlated.[45] How this constitututes a critique somewhat escapes us, since Lipset explicitly stated the priority of education over occupation as a determinant of authoritarian attitudes.[46] Nevertheless, low education does seem to play a more influential role in establishing the authoritarian perspective than does occupational status, and this permits the inference that our remarks about the wrestling spectator are all the more true of the fan. His lower education increases the probability of his authoritarian stance.

Lower-status persons seldom question the concrete world about them. Consequently, they are more susceptible to staging than persons on higher status levels. Indeed, among the middle classes, individuals often see staging where there is none. "Why do they have these things at this time of day?" queried the middle-class lady, inconvenienced by the time of a solar eclipse.

We suspect, too, that Candid Camera is most successful with working-class people and children. Lower-class people have less control over staging and are less familiar with it.[47] There is evidence for this. As a part of a study of dress, 172 married men and women were shown a picture of a woman with an emphatic bustline clad in masculine-appearing dress and presenting a masculinized hairdo. Twelve per cent of the respondents misplaced the woman as a man, but this proportion included 16.8 per cent of the lower-class, 9.8 per cent of the middle, and no upper-class persons.[48] In other words, more than people in other strata, lower-status persons seem inclined to believe that people are what they appear to be. This being the case, we can deduce that wrestling spectators, and especially wrestling fans, believe that the wrestling hero is *really* good and that the villian is *really* bad.

This reliance on appearances also increases with age. With reference to the picture discussed above, 6.6 per cent of the younger respondents misplaced the woman as a man, 11.5 per cent of those between thirty-five and forty-seven years of age, and 20.0 per cent of those forty-eight years of age and older.[49] Although a second portrayal depicting a man clad in the jacket and skirt that is common male attire in southeast Asia, but feminine appearing to unsophisticated Western eyes, elicited no marked status differences in sex misplacement, age differences persisted. Almost a third (31.8%) of the respondents misplaced the man as a woman, and this proportion included exactly half of those forty-eight years of age and older, but only 26.2 per cent of those in the middle age range and 23.0 per cent of the young respondents.[50]

There were no significant sex differences in these misplacements of sex (as we would expect, men were more often "taken in" by clothes than women, themselves skilled in the arts of deceptive dress), but there is some reason to suspect that women are more easily deceived in other areas of life than men. Specifically, Bloch, in his discussion of the "con-game," mentions that about 10 per cent of the victims of the "long con" (where the "mark" must leave the scene, collect his money and bring it back to the scene) are "repeats," and most of these are elderly women.[51] Geis has also noted that middle-aged women are frequent marks.[52] Despite the fact, then, that women see through clothes more easily than men, they are not unsusceptible to apparent misrepresentations. On the other hand, we suspect that much more research must be done to develop a convincing explanation of the appeal that wrestling has for the female spectator.

Lower-status and older age, therefore, generate a whole complex of social and social-psychological conditions which both ready most spectators for the harsh violence of the match and lend a credibility to the performance which is difficult to comprehend in other social circles. Most spectators are prepared for a bloody clear-cut struggle between good and evil (in whatever form) in which an overwhelming victory will be won from whatever quarter; for the victory of either good or evil serves, in the final analysis, to reinforce the sentiments that are expressed by the audience. Unaccustomed to questioning appearances and extremely susceptible to staging techniques, the great majority of the audience is caught up by the rhetoric of the match and establishes strong identifications with the performers. This is all the more the case with the fans whose social characteristics render them even more prone to the fascinations of the drama. The rapturous devotion of women to the sport is more difficult to explain. Though they can be conned, there are other features of staging with respect to which they display more sophistication than do men.

On the other hand, in our society, women are the traditional custodians of morality, and this may account, at least in part, for their captivation by the blatant struggles between good and evil in the wrestling ring. There is some probative support for this contention in our interview materials. When we asked our Twin City respondents how important "morality" was in their assessment of other people's social standing, we found that women attached significantly greater importance to morality than did men. The findings are presented in the following table.

TABLE II
SEX DIFFERENCES IN THE DEGREE OF IMPORTANCE ATTACHED TO "MORALITY" IN THE APPRAISAL OF SOCIAL STANDING

Importance	*Males*		*Females*		*Totals**	
	Number	*Per Cent*	*Number*	*Per Cent*	*Number*	*Per Cent*
Very important	131	48.1	175	60.3	306	54.4
Important	113	41.5	96	33.1	209	37.2
Unimportant	28	10.3	19	6.6	47	8.4
Totals*	272	99.9	290	100.0	562	100.0

$X^2 = 8.89$ $.02 > p > .01$

*Two men and two women did not respond to the question. They are not included in these computations.

However, even these data may be misleading. When we examined social class differences in the importance attached to morality, differences approached but did not meet our criterion of statistical significance. In this case, the greatest differences were provided by lower status respondents who played down the importance of morality in greater proportions than could be expected by chance. Moreover, sex differences in these respects were not characteristic of lower status respondents. Finally, we found that, of our thirteen wrestling fans, only three felt that morality was "very important" in appraising the status of others. When we compare that proportion (23.1%) with that for the sample as a whole (54.4%), we see immediately that we are treading on dangerous ground if we employ these data to explain the fascination that the sport holds for its followers. The mystery of lower status feminine rapture continues to elude us.

CONCLUSION

Yet, wrestling can not be construed as a con-game. At least there is no larceny in the heart of the fan, though there may well be mayhem. Wrestling is a drama, and, concerned as it is with morality – the breaching and upholding of moral codes – it is perhaps best conceived as a passion play. It is a passion play, however, in which the plot is irrelevant, and only the character of the cast of characters matters, together with the "passion" that the characters must undergo. For the audience has little concern with the sequence of events, but is very much concerned with the concrete persons who enact them and the agony that they suffer for the punishment of their sins or the vindication of the good life. Moreover, the audience *believes* in the

"My God, Sybil, are you sure you just got the right channel? I swear I've never seen wrestling like *that!*"

performers, and the belief is passionate, mobilized by simple and powerful sentiments. In short, they *don't* give a damn if it (the match) is a fake. Kill the (*really* evil) son-of-a-bitch!

FOOTNOTES

1. Except as otherwise noted, we have relied on various encyclopedia accounts for our discussion of ancient, preindustrial, European and Asiatic wrestling. The sources are standard.
2. Ariès, P.: *Centuries of Childhood.* New York, Knopf, 1962, p. 93.
3. Ariès: *op. cit. supra* note 2, at p. 93.
4. With the exception of a few encyclopedia references, we are almost totally dependent upon the work of Griffin, M.: *Fall Guys.* Chicago, Reilly & Lee, 1937, for the early history of wrestling in the United States. Of course, responsibility for the interpretation of Griffin's materials is our own.
5. Probably some drama, like work and play, is found in all sport, as in the dramatization of fouls in basketball. It is a question of which predominates and, of course, why.
6. Barton, G. A.: *My Lifetime in Sports.* Minneapolis, Olympic Press, 1957, p. 304.
7. Griffin, M.: *op. cit. supra* note 4, at pp. 27-28.
8. Griffin: *op. cit. supra* at pp. 24-25.
9. Denney, R.: *The Astonished Muse.* Chicago, U. of Chicago, 1957, p. 112.
10. Possibly World War I contributed in a minor way to the shortage of suitable contenders.
11. In our view, the joint participation of wrestlers, themselves, with promoters and managers in promotional and matchmaking operations both enhanced that transformation and marked off the history of professional wrestling from that of professional boxing in the United States. In the first instance, we merely note that the career of the dramatic actor is notoriously longer than that of the professional athlete and that it is in the *interests* of the professional wrestler to prolong his career. In the second instance, it is important to keep in mind that, with few exceptions and until recently, boxers have *typically* had no control over their own professional destinies. Indeed, boxing managers are said, in the trade, to run "stables." This lack of participation by most boxers in management, promotion and matchmaking accounts in no small measure for the much greater occupational and economic success of professional wrestlers as contrasted with that of professional boxers. We must add, as a final consideration, that, as some boxing champions do undertake management functions or at least participate in them, we can expect more fiascoes of the Clay-Liston caliber, *unless* the sport is transformed into drama (and we see tendencies in this direction in the shenanigans of Cassius Clay — pardon us — Mohammed Ali) *or* the sport is regulated at the national level.
12. Griffin: *op. cit. supra* note 4, at p. 50.
13. Griffin: *op. cit. supra* note 4, at p. 56.
14. This is a commentary on the business enterprise, not on the ability of wrestlers. There are many cases of skeptical observers whose challenges were quite effectively met by professional wrestlers. A local sports editor has told us about one of his staff, a two hundred pound ex-marine who challenged a local wrestling mediocrity. The challenge was met, and the ex-marine was pinned in a matter of seconds.
15. Griffin: *op. cit. supra* note 4, at p. 104.
16. Griffin: *op. cit. supra* note 4, at p. 170.
17. Griffin: *op cit. supra* note 4, at p. 107. Griffin was writing in the depression years, so the $70,000 gate is doubly impressive, and he was writing about New York, where wrestling has never enjoyed the success it has enjoyed in other parts of the United States. As early as 1911, some 25,000 fans paid $87,000 to watch Gotch defeat Hackenschmidt in Comiskey Park. See Barton: *My Lifetime in Sports.* Minneapolis, The Olympic Press, 1957, p. 305. Probably the largest gate that professional wrestling has enjoyed occurred in 1961, also at Comiskey Park, where 34,995 fans paid $127,000 to view the Buddy Rogers-Pat O'Connor match.

18. Griffin: *op. cit. supra* at 89.
19. *Wrestling Facts*, Vol. 1, p. 4 (Oct. 10, 1964).
20. It will become evident later on that interest in the televised matches, particularly in fringe areas, cannot be maintained without the promotion of live matches. Actually, the live match and the canned performance mutually enhance one another in the eyes of spectators.
21. The danger of "going stale" is one of the distinct career hazards of the popular wrestler, that is, one who may wrestle on an average of three to five times a week for as many as forty-eight weeks of the year.
22. Riesman, D., *et al.*: *The Lonely Crowd*. New Haven, Yale, 1953, pp. 157-161.
23. Goffman, E.: *Stigma: Notes on the Management of Spoiled Identity*. Englewood Cliffs, Prentice-Hall, 1963, p. 2.
24. By this time, the drama of Pirandello and the novels of Malcolm Purdy, not to speak of Nigel Denis, ought really to have silenced all queries asking us to distinguish between "real" and "false" identities.
25. Stone, G. P.: Appearance and the self; in Rose, A. [Ed.]: *Human Behavior and Social Processes*. Boston, Houghton-Mifflin, 1962, pp. 86-118.
26. Ernest, M.: Why Big Bill Miller wore a mask. *Wrestling Confidential, 1:*15-17 and 62-64, July 1964.
27. Ernest: *op. cit. supra* at 64.
28. Indeed, a local sportswriter fantasized nostalgically that Thesz was the last of the "real" wrestlers.
29. Hogan, J. R.: The real reason why Lou Thesz returned to wrestling. *Wrestling Confidential, 1:*48-55.
30. Hogan: *op. cit. supra* at p. 55. Ed "Strangler" Lewis held the previous record of five championships. We have placed "defeated" in quotes to indicate some skepticism about all this. Since his retirement, Thesz has never wrestled in California, which forbids wrestling competition after the age of fifty. Moreover, Thesz's purge of the wrestling ring has not been extensive. At this writing, "Mad Dog" Vachon still rules as "world champion of the five county mosquito control district" — pardon us! — the AWA.
31. Wolfenstein, M., and Leites, N.: The good-bad girl; in Rosenberg, B. and White, D. M. [Eds.]: *Mass Culture: The Popular Arts in America*. Glencoe, Free Press, 1960, pp. 294-307.
32. Becker, H. S.: Some contingencies of the professional dance musician's career. *Human Organization, 12:*22, 1953.
33. Weinberg, G. K., and Arond, H.: The occupational culture of the boxer. *Amer J Sociol, 57:* 460, 1952.
34. Goffman, E.: *The Presentation of Self in Everyday Life*. Garden City, Doubleday, 1959; Gross, E., and Stone, G. P.: Embarrassment and the analysis of role requirements. *Amer J Sociol, 70:*1, 1964.
35. Denney, R.: *op. cit. supra* note 9, at p. 133.
36. Denney, R.: *op. cit. supra* note 9, at p. 134.
37. *Ibid.*
38. The study is as yet unpublished, but a preliminary report of early results may be found in Stone, G. P.: *Some meanings of American sport*. Sixtieth Annual Proceedings, National College Physical Education Association, Columbus, Ohio, 1957, 6-29. For making possible some of the results that follow, we are indebted to a grant provided by the Graduate School of the University of Minnesota.
39. Packard, V.: *The Hidden Persuaders*. New York, David McKay, 1957.
40. Form, W. H., and Stone, G. P.: Urbanism, anonymity, and status symbolism. *Amer J Sociol, 62:*504, 1957.
41. Lipset, S. M.: Democracy and working-class authoritarianism. *Amer Sociol Rev, 24:*482-483, 1959.
42. *Supra* at 495. Our emphasis.
43. *Supra* at 494.

44. Denney, R.: *op. cit. supra* note 9, at p. 133.
45. Lipsitz, L.: Working-class authoritarianism: A reevaluation. *Amer Sociol Rev, 30:*103, 1965.
46. Lipset, S. M.: Democracy and working-class authoritarianism. *Amer Sociol Rev, 24:*482, 1959.
47. One reason, of course, is simply that the symbols used in staging cost money. Clothing and furniture serve as examples, and these are ordinarily purchased. If we think of such items as constituting a kind of vocabulary of apparent symbolism that is implemented in the staging process, we can see that the vocabulary of the lower-status levels is limited, indeed. That they often must wear hand-me-downs underscores the paucity of their staging vocabulary.
48. Stone, G. P.: Clothing and Social Relations, Unpublished Ph.D. dissertation, Dept. of Sociology, Univ. of Chicago, 1959, p. 36.
49. *Supra* at 35.
50. *Supra* at 34.
51. Bloch, H. A., and Geis, G.: *Man, Crime, and Society*. New York, Random, 1962, p. 578.
52. Maurer, D. W.: *The Big Con*. New York, New American Library, 1962, p. 116.

ORIENTAL FIGHTING ARTS

WILLIAM R. SORUM

It is hard to recount just what combination of childish fantasy and physical need led me to study that which the initiate loves to call the oriental fighting arts. This discussion of the subject is written at an embryonic stage of my development as a participant, and at a relatively advanced age in life. The title may be somewhat fraudulent as my experience has been with judo and karate, while the term oriental fighting arts covers such wide-ranging disciplines as *aikido,* the art of psychic self-defense; *kendo,* the art of sword play; *sumo,* the sport of the tremendously obese wrestlers; and *kyudo,* an archery form. The real devotee can also drop such exotic terms as *kungfu* and *tai-chi-chuan,* disciplines of Chinese derivation.

Recently there has been a large number of books on the American market which discuss these activities from all points of view, from the physical to the philosophical and even the mystical. These tomes range in approach from how-to-do-it to the somewhat more elevated mind-over-matter; from "how to master the village bully" to "how to become an expert on life itself through concentration and control of the mind." My effort here will not be a contribution to either end of this spectrum, nor yet a record of my accomplishments in the field of judo and karate. Rather, it will be a partial chronicle of my addiction to these endeavors because — let us face it — I am hooked!

As a child I had the same exposure as did many others during the prewar years to countless advertisements in many magazines concerning jujitsu. These often featured tiny orientals or small, clean-cut, young men throwing huge, coarse-featured, hulking brutes on their backs, disarming them or otherwise reducing them to impotence, often in the presence of women. Of course this last factor was determined by the nature of the magazine in which the advertisement appeared, whether pulp or *The Open Road for Boys.* There were also plays and movies in which the Japanese valet with apparent ease would quickly throw the murder suspect. The myth — as I have, with experience, found it to be — which these all conveyed was that with the application of an esoteric knowledge and skill, the small man could always win.

As a serviceman in World War II, I took an interest in a different approach to the subject. Available books on dirty fighting based on jujitsu stressed the more lethal techniques of gouging, kicking and choking. This more pedestrian approach, lacking the glamor of punish-the-bully, was instead just plain kill-the-bastard-now-you-have-him-down.

With the passing years, the need for techniques of such simple utility lost any urgency it might once have had for me, and again my interest shifted to a new aspect of the subject. This time a curiosity about zen, shared by all sorts of acquaintances, from the socially-defiant unwashed to the serious student, led to a perusal of philosophical works in which the words judo, karate and aikido appeared. My earlier fantasies were rekindled, tempered this time by maturity.

All of these contacts with the oriental fighting arts played some part in pointing me toward active participation, but it was actually the chance remark of a fellow sufferer in a steam bath which led me bodily to a judo instructor. Like many middle-aged men with rolls of fat and growing bulk, I had been driven to a local health club where the usual huff-and-puff routine of calisthenics had left me hoping that there might be some other means for body conditioning.

So I found myself entering the *dojo* (a derivation of the Buddhist term meaning a place of study), as the gymnasium for the practice of judo is called. It was soon evident to me that the place not only had a special name but a special impact on the anatomy as well, for the novice begins with the practice of falling.

JUDO

Judo exercise and competition take place on a large matted area with the participants dressed in pajama-like outfits belted with sashes of different colors denoting the individual's rank in proficiency. An air of politeness pervades, as each individual bows to the mat and to his opponent at the beginning and end of each exercise and upon taking leave of the mat. I took some comfort in this, feeling that if I were to be thrown about, it would at least be among gentlemen.

It soon became apparent to me that the impression of effortlessness conveyed by the skilled *judoka,* or practitioner of Judo, was the result of hours of endless repetition of movements and intensive physical training, rather than some esoteric secret of invulnerability. The techniques used in judo demand considerable attention and involvement in learning and good physical condition in execution. The exercises for this conditioning involve flexibility, coordination and strength.

Another misconception I had shared with most laymen was that size and strength are of no consequence in judo. The truth of the matter, that a skilled large man has tremendous advantage over the skilled small man, is evidenced in official competition by the grouping of the competitors according to their weight. My large size, modified by clumsiness and lack of skill, gave me advantage over no one.

The chief judoist of the Louisiana Judo Club, to which I now belonged, is Jacques Legrand, a fourth degree Black Belt. His power and strength are apparent at a glance, and little more observation is needed to become aware of the tremendous skill and quickness which have brought him to his present high rank. His seeming callousness discourages any self-pity on the student's part, though he couches most of his brusqueness in mumbled French expletives in order to conform to the tradition of politeness with regard to the student's feelings.

Progress in judo seemed quite slow. Weeks of instruction went by before I was considered ready to be taught even the most elementary of throwing techniques. Despite this slowness, I was alrady aware of pleasing side effects; an increased firmness at the waistline, a loss of weight and a greater flexibility. In addition to these benefits, the perfection of form in judo requires such intense concentration that any immediate personal and professional problems have to take a back seat, at least for the moment.

As is often the case in taking up a new subject or activity, textbooks on the principles and practice of judo began to have meaning only after I had had some instruction. Now I was able to read with some comprehension both the philosophical discussions and the explanations of routines.

According to publications of the Kodokan Institute in Japan the skills of Judo can be mastered by two methods: the practice of *kata,* a formal system of prearranged exercises in throwing and grappling; and participation in *randori,* free-style exercises in which the opponents test each other's skill in throwing and in taking falls. A training session might be comprised of a warm-up period followed by time spent in both of these activities. Periodically, members of a club take part in a *shiai,* or contest, with progress in rank determined by grading on form as well as the outcome of the matches. Matches are won by successful throws; hold-downs, or controlling the opponent's body on the mat for at least thirty seconds; as well as strangle-holds, or armlocks which cause the opponent to resign.

The throws which may be used can be divided roughly into hip throws, shoulder throws, neck throws, foot sweeps and sacrifice throws in which the momentum of the opponent is utilized to the maximum. These spectacular affairs may be observed in some action movies where the victim, apparently helpless, falls to his back, then, planting a foot in his assailant's abdomen, sends him flying through the air.

Though all the techniques are not equally usable in all competition, a thorough working knowledge of them is required. Every good judo competitor develops three or four key holds which he seeks an opportunity to use on his opponent. In addition, he strives constantly to develop quickness, balance and control, and to learn the situations which might vary the application of technique. Judo is obviously an open-ended sport, one in which the individual can spend a lifetime in mastery and perfection of skill.

The desire for this very proficiency seems to be one of the prime motivating factors for continued study. Self-defense might seem at first thought to be the primary reason for taking up judo, but this motive is soon replaced by others if the beginner is to survive the hours of seemingly endless repetition required to develop skill. Some participants value judo as a form of relaxation. Others come to look upon it as an ideal system for achieving and maintaining good physical condition — I for one feel it is unsurpassed for the purpose. Still others, with attainment of the upper levels of rank, become trophy-oriented, directing their efforts toward top judo competition.

The philosophical gains should not be overlooked in discussing the psychological aspects of judo and other martial arts. A contributor to *Black Belt* — the "bible" of judo and karate men — in an article entitled "Serenity Through Violence,"[1] states that the object of this training is not primarily self-defense, but serenity arising from self-confidence. This serenity makes the practice of violence for its own sake unnecessary, essentially beneath one's dignity. Another author in the same publication stresses the fact that one's only adversary is oneself and the purpose of the martial arts is the achievement of the wisdom of self-mastery.[2] He defines this as "no mind," a state in which no conscious thought need be given to one's movements. This attainment seems to be reserved for adepts with years of training. The closest that I seem to have come to feeling it was after a particularly hard fall.

Kyuzo Mifune in *Canon of Judo*[3] (a comprehensive but poorly translated textbook) devotes considerable space to the meaning of judo for the practitioner. He contends that in principle judo is in accord with "consistent natural law." So in action it must be consistent and reasonable, avoiding the destructive element of the irrational act. For him this principle implies the idea of mutual benefit. He regards each match as something to be approached seriously, but maintains that victory is secondary to development as a person.

There is a modern trend, particularly in the United States, towards an emphasis on judo as a competitive sport, moving away from the idea of an art form for art's sake. Some authorities consider judo to be the leading Amateur Athletic Union sport in the US in terms of number of competitors. Experts who are not in favor of this trend would prefer to see judo practiced with greater emphasis on the recreational and philosophical aspects.

The late Jigaro Kano, originator of the sport and founder in 1882 of the Kodokan (mother institute of judo in Tokyo), conceived of it as "a system of training mind and body for the most efficient use of mental and physical energies."[4] Ishikawa and Draeger see this best implemented, rather than contradicted, by the development of the physical strength that has been characteristic of such competitive champions as Geesink, DeHardt, Matsumato and Kimura.[5] These authors give lip service to the idea that competitive judo is simply a means to the end, higher self-development.

In some judo clubs considerable emphasis is placed on contest judo, and great pride is taken in the resultant array of club championships. Ideally, however, the recreational aspect of the sport should be maintained, with each student regarded as individual in his potentialities, thus meeting the needs of the average participant for companionship, exercise and recreation.

KARATE

Another member of the family of the oriental fighting arts which has interested me to the point of active participation is karate. The Louisiana Karate Association, an affiliate of the Karate Association of Japan, is headed by Takayuki Mikami, fifth degree Black Belt, former All-Japan Champion, whose wife holds the rank of second degree Black Belt. To one whose expectations are based on television and movie portrayals of karate, Mikami's appearance might be disappointing. His manner is not at all sinister; it is pleasant and somewhat businesslike.

At first glance there seem to be many similarities between karate and judo. The uniform one wears is almost the same. Some of the Japanese terminology is the same. They share in misconceptions on the part of the layman. Karate is often thought of as a sport of thugs who spend their time smashing bricks and boards with deformed, calloused hands when not otherwise occupied in delivering lethal neck chops. A recent example of this mistaken idea is the fictional character "Odd-Job," the karate expert in the James Bond book and movie *Goldfinger*.

In karate as in judo, an introduction to the sport dispels any ideas of sudden mastery of an esoteric knowledge imparting overwhelming powers. This too is a system of strenuous training, demanding hours of repetitious practice.

Further involvement with karate reveals that the similarities to judo are superficial. The term martial art seems more descriptive of karate, for the confrontation in competition is much less direct. Though it does have some aspect of sport, experts in the field feel it is a way of life, considering the aim of the physical and mental training to be unification of body and spirit.

For the novice the emphasis of the first few months is on correct positioning and basic methods of defending, thrusting and kicking. He learns several standing positions, basic blocks, punches and kicks. These moves are then woven into combinations and practiced as *katas*, formal exercises conceived as defenses against an opponent. These *katas* are similar to dances. Indeed, Masutatsu Oyama, a master of the sport, has said that karate cannot be learned without the innate sense of rhythm and basic flexibility required for dancing.[6]

A typical class begins with warm-up exercises followed by practice of the basic techniques of kicking, punching and striking in various stances. In more advanced classes a sparring session called *kumite* might follow. In these sessions the emphasis is on speed, accuracy and power. Some schools, the Louisiana Karate Association among them, permit no bodily contact. The attack is stopped just short of the target. Other schools permit some contact, using protective padding to prevent injury.

It has been said that there are as many schools of thought on karate as there are instructors. This may be a slight exaggeration, but since the introduction of the sport to Japan from Okinawa forty-five years ago by Funakoshi, there has been a proliferation of schools. Each of them professes to have the same aims, but considers its techniques the only true way of achievement. To the reader familiar with the various schools of psychoanalysis and their regard for one another, this attitude may sound a familiar note.

Competition in karate takes two forms. The individual is judged according to his form in performance of the *kata*. He is judged for preciseness of attack in *kumite*. Even in contest, the attack is stopped short of contact.

Karate requires different abilities than does judo. There is greater need for flexibility, agility and grace. The single most important element is control. Perhaps the difference in requisite abilities accounts for the number of women one finds participating in karate classes. It is possible for them to learn techniques of self-defense without the physical strength and ability to fall necessary for judo.

The basic principle of karate is focus, or the ability to concentrate the energy of the body in an instant on a specific target. According to Nishyama and Brown in *Karate: The Art of Empty-Handed Fighting*,[7] the psychological basis of karate is *mizu no kokoro* (a mind like water), referring to the necessity for an undisturbed state of mind which like undisturbed water reflects without distortion what comes within its range; and *tsuki no kokoro* (a mind like the moon), referring to the necessity for an awareness of the totality of that by which one is confronted, as the moonlight falls equally on everything within its range.

In literature on the subject, considerable stress is laid on the philosophical aspect of karate. Oyama emphasizes the relationship between this discipline and that of Zen Buddhism, stating that, "Zen is Karate, and Karate is Zen."[8] That is, the aim of one as well as the other is to lose and extinguish oneself in concentration on a discipline as a means of self-mastery.

At this point in my involvement with karate and judo, I lay no claim to self-mastery or any of the other spiritual rewards they offer. I do observe a slimmer mirror image, and I am aware of a greater sense of physical and mental well-being than I possessed before beginning this participation. Perhaps anyone might claim these benefits for the sport they enjoy. It is

"No, he's not hooked on karate – he's a perfectionist and has tantrums when things go a little bit haywire!"

as a football coach once told me, "You get out of anything what you put into it."

So there is no great secret I can pass along whose practice will insure omnipotence. I keep looking nonetheless. As a matter of fact, I have begun reading about aikido. Now, there is an art which purports to be a combination of physical relaxation and mental control enabling the performer to project a so-called *ki*-force or spiritual strength, supposedly unstoppable. Perhaps this is the secret knowledge. It is more likely, however, that again the strength will be the result of endless hours of training.

Try judo or karate if you are looking for recreation in disciplined physical activity and not invincibility. As so skilled a judoist as Legrand put it, when asked how he would deal with a gun-bearing assailant, "Consider, if there is time, the techniques one has learned and the possibilities therein, then surrender or run!"

FOOTNOTES

1. Lee: Serenity through violence. *Black Belt, 2*:42, 1964.
2. Zalle: The zen 'unconscious' — highest attainment of the martial arts. *Black Belt, 3*:39, 1965.
3. Mifune, K.: *Canon of Judo — Principle and Technique*. Tokyo, Seibundo-Shinkosha, 1960, pp. 27-29.
4. Draeger, C. F., and Ishikawa, T.: *Judo Training Methods*. Rutland, Tuttle, 1962, p. 19.
5. *Id.* at pp. 20-25.
6. Cited in Gluck, J.: *Zen Combat*. New York, Ballantine Books, 1962, p. 31.
7. Nishiyama, H. and Brown, R. C.: *Karate: The Art of Empty Hand Fighting*. Rutland, Tuttle, 1959, p. 20.
8. Oyama, M.: *This Is Karate*. Tokyo, Japan Publications Trading Co., 1965, p. 320.

FENCING

BARRY P. PARISER

FENCING PROBABLY BEGAN WHEN the first cave man grabbed a club and swung at another. When the second man grabbed a similar weapon and tried to defend himself in one manner or another the sport, or the type of combat, was born. Times progressed, sharp stones were added as tips to these primitive weapons, and the combat evolved to a poking or thrusting. When it was discovered that various metals could be used, the art of combat again changed. The metals were stronger, more durable, kept their sharpness, and in addition, allowed for the edge of the weapon to be sharp, something which a club or spear did not provide. Various types of weapons evolved: the dagger, short sword, broad sword, rapier, foil, sabre, epee and even the bayonet. Various swords lost their popularity for different reasons; the dagger and short sword because they were too short, the broad sword because of its clumsiness and heaviness, the rapier also, because it was too long and an infighter would quickly dispatch the rapier-wielder. Of course, the use of gunpowder and firearms soon became more advantageous in warfare, and swords became articles of dress. The sabre, with its sharp point and cutting edge, was used in cavalry because on a horse it was easier to inflict a wound with the whole side of a blade rather than with the point alone. The foil was used for teaching the other weapons, hence the name "the practice weapon." The epee is also called "the dueling sword." I will leave the reason to the reader's imagination.

Eventually fencing changed from a means of combat to a sport, when it was realized that practicing for combat could be fun in itself and no one would get hurt. It provided an opportunity for a safe means of expressing aggression in the form of physical exercise and sport. The military and nobility were the groups which participated most during the earlier stages of the sport. Since it is an exacting sport and one which requires a long time to perfect, it became necessary for long periods of tutoring. As a result, usually only the wealthy could partake of this sport, and it became a "gentleman's avocation." Since the European countries started the sport, it is logical that they became leaders in fencing, both from a standpoint of style and success. However, it has been enjoying more popularity in the Western hemisphere in recent years.

The styles of the sport are almost as numerous as the various individual fencers. Also, different countries are known for the styles they teach. Thus, there is the athletic and acrobatic style popular with the Polish and Russian fencers, the smooth cat-like style of the Hungarian sabremen, the lightning fast style of the Italians and the technically classic style of the French. The Americans, being the greatest imitators, have been using a mixture of all of these styles.

The weapons, too, have a great deal of variety. In foil, there are French handles, Italian crossbar handles, Belgian, American and Spanish types of pistol grips. The guards are also of various sizes, but always the weight of the weapon, the maximum length and bend of the blade are within regulation limits.

The sabre has undergone a tremendous change since the turn of the century. The blade has changed from a wide and heavy type to a thin and very light one so that faster actions, cuts and counter-cuts, are more easily executed. The weight has become less, the guards vary according to style and individual preference, the blade bends, but again, all within very precise regulations and limitations. The same holds true for the epee. By far the greatest advance for the epee has been the introduction of electrical weapons. This advancement has made the utilization of ink on the tip of the weapon to ascertain the touch obsolete. The foil is also fenced electrically. The sabre has not yet been electrified, so that a full complement of judges is still required. The use of electricity in the foil especially has changed the technique of the game. It is just a matter of time before engineers arrive at a solution to make the sabre electric.

Today, in the United States, fencing has evolved so that it is no longer a sport of the elite. Many high schools, private schools and colleges have fencing teams. Teen-agers have been exposed to this sport more than ever before, and they have the opportunity to compete against other teams. In addition, there are many private fencing clubs throughout the country. YMCA's, YWCA's and camps teach fencing; thus there is the opportunity for those interested to be exposed to it. Intercollegiate fencing is a major sport in many colleges, not just a group that gathers occasionally and dabbles in it, but a varsity sport to be practiced seriously. There are intercollegiate fencing meets, Regional Championship Tournaments and the National Athletic Association Fencing Championship.

The Amateur Fencers League of America (AFLA) is the organization that manages most of fencing in much the same manner as the AAU governs other sports. It is a subsidiary of the AAU. The AFLA, through its divisions throughout the country, runs competitions in the various weapons and in the different classes within the weapons. There are no weight classes in fencing as there are in boxing or wrestling, but rather categories of A, B, C and unclassified fencers, starting from the highest to lowest class. A higher ranked fencer cannot enter a lesser ranked tournament, whereas a lower classified fencer can compete in higher competitions usually and gain experience. The AFLA also has an important task in selecting the Olympic team. In short, its job is to improve fencing and govern non-school fencing throughout the country. The National Championships are the ultimate competitions in the country and provide National Ranking for all its finalists. In addition, the New York Athletic Club holds an annual International Tournament where great fencers from all over the world and Olympic and world champions can compete.

Although men can fence with any or all of the three weapons, women are restricted to foil. Their bouts are for four touches, while the men compete for five touches, the winner having touched or scored upon his opponent the requisite number of touches before he has been scored upon the same number. Thus, a bout can be decided by 5-0 or by any amount of touches to 5-4 for men, and up to four for women.

In foil and epee, the object is to hit or touch with the point of the weapon. In epee, the whole body from head to toe is the target, while with the foil only the trunk is fair target, the arms, legs, and head being off target and not considered a valid touch. In sabre, every part of the body above the hip line is fair target. The bout is fenced on rubber strips or mats of regulation size. In foil a fencer must remain on the strip, for if he goes off the end of the strip, a touch is scored against him. In epee and sabre a fencer is allowed off the end of the strip once. He is then brought back to the center of the strip, and if he goes off again a touch is scored against him. In foil and sabre there is the concept of a right of way. In other words, if a fencer starts an attack, his opponent must defend or block his opponent's blade before he can score on a counterattack. This defense is called a parry, and there are many types of parries just as there are many kinds of attacks. Once the parry is made the fencer can then launch a counterattack, or riposte, which then has to be parried, and so on. A rapid and prolonged series of attacks, parries, ripostes, and counter-ripostes is called a phrase. Usually, however, touches are scored either on a direct attack or the riposte. In contrast to the foil and sabre, where the right of way is used, the epee game is completely different. There is no right of way in the epee, the touch going to the guy who"gets there fustest with the mostest." In other words, a fencer can start a straight attack, and his opponent can thrust into the attack without parrying if he feels he can hit first, the touch being awarded to the fencer who "draws first blood" to to speak. This goes along with the concept of the duel and the dueling sword. If both fencers hit simultaneously, then a double-touch is awarded against both fencers.

Being a sabreman, I am naturally most familiar with this weapon. When I enter a bout against someone I have never met on a fencing strip before, I have to figure out some form of strategy to beat him. Usually I do know most of the people I compete against or I know about him by reputation or by having watched him fence, thereby scouting him. However, for those competitors I have never before met, my thought processes might go something like this.

"Let's see if he can parry well." I'll then make an attack or a feint to either his head, flank or chest. If he ignores the right of way, doesn't parry the attack, and cuts into my attack, then the touch will be scored against him. If, on the other hand, he parries the attack, he may be off balance and not able to make a riposte; but if he does, I will try to parry it. However, in this last instance I have learned some valuable information from him. "I see he can parry, now let's see if he can parry a feint to one line, and then the cut into another line." I have set up my opponent to parry, so now I will make a false attack to the line I want him to be in when I deliver the real attack to another line. Now let us suppose that my opponent is not just acting as my defenseless target (as they rarely do), but starts attacking me. I have to be ready at all times to interrupt my thoughts to be able to outmaneuver him. Most of these actions are pure reflex, caused by years of training, taking lessons and practicing what I have learned in the fencing room against practice opponents. In a bout, a lot of actions are second nature because of these ingrained reflexes. In actuality a bout is much more complex, the actions are much more varied than I have mentioned, and the possibilities are countless.

Since the best fencers are Olympic team aspirants, there are no professionally paid fencers except for the coaches and fencing masters, or maestros, as they are often called. Many of these fencing masters have come from Europe and settled in this country to teach the sport. Probably the most famous is Georgio Santelli, who coached many of our Olympic teams. Most of the American coaches have in some way or another, either directly or indirectly, benefited from Georgio Santelli's teachings. His father, Italo Santelli, coached many Hungarian world and Olympic champions and prior to his death was considered one of the best fencing masters who ever lived, if not the best. Of course there are numerous successful native-born coaches.

As one may well imagine, fencing is not a prominent spectator sport. One reason is that it is so complicated that a certain amount of knowledge of the sport is necessary in order to enjoy it. The actions are so quick that an inexperienced observer may miss the touches and after a while lose interest. As a result, most spectators are fellow fencers, or friends and relatives who want to observe someone they know in action. This is in great contrast to some of the European tournaments, where I have been told that thousands of spectators turn out to watch their fencing heroes, in much the same manner as an American would go to a sporting event to watch a Mantle, Chamberlain, Palmer, Gonzales or Hornung.

What makes a fencer good? The answer is the same for fencing as it is for all sports. He must be able to be taught, to take direction. He should have athletic ability, stamina, strength, speed and muscular coordination. He has to have a feel for the sport, to understand the right of way concept, and should be intelligent (this does not hurt in any game, or game of life). He has to learn timing, and when to go. He should have a good sense of distance. I have seen fencers who consistently step back and avoid being hit by as little as an inch or less. He should have the ability to concentrate intensely on his opponent, and in that way be able to take advantage of the moment the opponent makes a wrong move. He should have the discipline necessary to correct his own mistakes and to force himself to want to improve. He should be able to train and take lessons frequently and be able to enter competition often, in order to gain experience against all types of opponents and their styles. Having all these attributes will enable an athlete to become a champion. Few people possess all these traits, and although they would be desirable, they are not completely necessary as long as an individual has most of them. The variation in these traits is one of the things that makes for different styles.

What motivates the fencer? In citing a few examples of ideas which motivated some of my friends to start fencing, it is not my purpose to explain fencing motivation one hundred or even fifty years ago, or fifty years from now. Times change and so do ideas of motivation. What I will attempt to do is to relate, through the eyes of some of today's competitors, the motivation of fencers today.

I started fencing at Columbia College quite by accident. I thought I would go out for the swimming team, but during freshman orientation the fencing coach gave an exhibition with the team captain. The coach had a terrific sense of humor, and his demonstration was so interesting that a friend and I thought we would give fencing a try. The coach had demonstrated in his previous years his ability to make champions out of inexperienced men. All we had to do was work and train hard. This idea of being a champion appealed to me. I was determined right then and there to become an NCAA champion. Incidentally my friend never got as far as the door of the fencing room.

There is nothing typical motivating different individuals, although in speaking with many fencing friends I have found that a majority of them became interested in the sport through reading swashbuckling literature and seeing theatrical swordplay in the movies. One friend told me he was actually "shanghaied" from a gym class by the fencing coach in college. The coach learned he had boxed in high school. The similarity in tactics and footwork between boxing and fencing is apparent. They are both combative sports and the individual is important.

One foilsman started in high school because his friend was on the school team. After he started fencing he became "bit by the bug." Several other fencers had older brothers or fathers who fenced; they were drawn to the sport primarily because of this relationship. There have also been brother-sister, father-daughter, and husband-wife combinations in the sport. In fact, whole families have participated as an enjoyable pastime.

Since many of the clubs or *salles d'armes* are "co-ed" the opposite sex angle interested some people. I know of quite a few fencers who met their spouses at the fencing salles.

One foil champion claims that he was a skinny, anemic, sixteen-year-old kid with a congenital heart murmur. He liked sports and wanted to compete in one, but because of his weak stature he wanted one where his strength did not count. With a fencing weapon one does not have to be strong or tall to be successful (although it helps). It is timing, distance technique, experience and tactics that are important. Today, in his forties, this fine foilsman has made the Olympic foil team for the fourth time, and to look at him you could never imagine him as a scrawny teen-ager. He is as solid as a house, and his overpowering game, strong defense and infighting have earned him the nickname of "ironfist."

An older *sabreur* that I know saw actual duels as a youth in Hungary and become interested in fencing as a sport because of its excitement, rhythm, beauty and timing. When he came to this country he had the opportunity to start fencing. He started fencing at the age of twenty-nine, and by persevering, by the time he was thirty-six he had earned positions on two Olympic teams and was a national sabre champion. Today, in his seventies, he still works out two or three times a week and is a definite challenge to younger and stronger competitors, especially when the evening is young and he is still fresh. After awhile he tires more rapidly. This was not the case a few years ago when he could be seen in tournaments, often in the final round of local competitions at the age of sixty-nine. An epeeist I knew was a strong competitor in his mid-seventies and even earned a national epee team medal at this age. Although his legs and stamina were not strong, his point was so deadly that he could hit an opponent's hand if he opened up a target of one quarter of an inch. He was an excellent competitor for a key three or four bouts. These examples are few and far between, but they illustrate that fencing is a sport that can be practiced into late age.

Another fencer began fencing in his late twenties because he wanted a relief of daily tensions. He works in advertising and finds that working out after a day at the office gives him an opportunity to unwind. This I have found to be true also. In college, I often found it easier to study after a workout, and as a physician I find I can forget some of the day's problems and tensions during a good two- to three-hour fencing session. Even though I may be tired, I find that by pushing myself to the club, working hard and then taking a cool shower, I leave the gym refreshed.

I know one woman who wanted to understand the sport so that she would not be bored while watching her husband fence at competitions. She began taking lessons and "loved it"; she also liked the idea of getting exercise and being able to stay in shape. Unfortunately, motherhood cut short what might have been an ardent enthusiasm. This is one instance where I can definitely say, "She ain't no lady, she's my wife."

A baker friend did not start fencing until he was thirty when he saw a newspaper article about fencing classes in his community. He also was motivated to fence because of swashbuckling movies and books. He became an Olympian at the age of thirty-seven. To tell of his motivation to succeed, all I have to do is to state that he would travel two or more times a week from New Haven, Connecticut, with some of his friends, to New York City, work out for two or more hours and then return to New Haven where he would go back to his bakery and work until five or six o'clock in the morning. This unusual and dedicated athlete had the stamina and physique of a man in his early twenties. He also taught his daughter to fence, and she too would travel with him to New York City to take lessons at a rival club.

Psychologically, I suppose a lot of people are able to act out their aggressions and hostilities on a fencing strip, a chance to "kill" someone without actually doing so, a chance to have an old-fashioned duel without anyone getting hurt. I know that when I started fencing, my coaches tried to instill the idea of "kill or be killed." This made me all the more wary and dangerous in a bout. After years of fencing, however, this element disappeared, and the challenge became more of a purely competitive one. Fencing is a game of outwitting your opponent; it is almost a physical game of chess. This mental game is always apparent even though fencing is becoming more physical; reflex actions of technique, stamina and the ability to cover ground quickly, both in advancing and retreating, are assuming more importance. It is not as graceful a sport as many people think. The sport of fencing has about as much similarity to theatrical swordplay as competitive wrestling does to television wrestling. The only aspect that remains the same is the idea of hitting your opponent before you are struck. However, in one the objective is to win; in the other, it is entertainment.

These are some examples of the early motivations in learning the sport. Once experience is gained, there are other motivations, the main one being the love of the sport. Other motivations are the enjoyment of working out regularly, keeping in shape, seeing old friends with whom you have a common interest, and if you are good, the enjoyment of doing well and perhaps the enjoyment of being idolized by your *confreres.* Fencing also provides the opportunity to meet many interesting people, frequently college graduates and professional men. With the close ties that one makes in the sport, I have found that many of my closest friends are from rival clubs, as well as my own club.

"Your fencing is progressing nicely, Madame. Remember to keep your left arm well back and present the smallest possible target when you pass the mustard!"

The art of fencing is by and large an individual sport in that you have to do your own thinking and fighting. Your friends or coach may be able to give you some tips before or even during the bout, but it still comes down to one man clearly against another. Despite the individuality of fencing, team competitions have always been more interesting and exciting to me. It gives the opportunity of fighting not only for yourself but for your friends and teammates, enabling you to pull together and cheer a teammate on and to get the same cheering stimulus when you are on the strip. I have always felt that the excitement of winning a team event with the celebration of the victory with my teammates and our friends afterward is far more full than the relative emptiness when only one individual wins. This is my personal feeling, and it by no means reflects the feelings of other fencers. There have been many excellent individual competitors who perform relatively poorly in team competition; the reverse is also true. Some individuals just can't get "up" for team sports, whereas others are extended to their maximum with the incentive to produce for their team, club, school or even country.

Likewise, there are excellent competitors who are good individual and team performers. Either they are just too good, or their disposition is even for both events.

NOTE

I wish sincerely to thank Major "Joe" Velarde for his patience and invaluable help in the development and writing of this chapter.

PART ELEVEN

NATURE-ORIENTED ACTIVITIES

INTRODUCTION

THIS SECTION OF THE VOLUME includes papers on a variety of nature-oriented activities – camping, cowboying, hunting, fishing, mountaineering, skiing and sailing.

Expressions of solitude and sociability in everyday life are found in camping. William R. Burch, Jr., discusses the sport form of camping.[1] A particular ethic motivates a person to opt for one style of action rather than its alternative. It is thus important to define the social and work ethics and to indicate the historical and social sources of these motivators. This task accomplished, Burch then tests whether these ethics do in fact structure a person's leisure behavior.

It is argued that there is an intimate connection between the meanings assigned to nature and those values which prevail in everyday life. Two styles of forest camping – easy access and remote – are described and used to illustrate different approaches to nature. Then the social sources of motives such as Protestant and social ethics are examined. Burch suggests that such ethics are not so much attributes of particular historical epochs as fairly constant attributes of particular work, leisure, status, occupational and locational groupings. It is suggested that this modification in the theories of David Riesman, William S. Whyte and C. Wright Mills permits explanation as to what motivates persons to select different styles of camping. The "other-directed" and sociable attitudes characteristic of blue collar and lower white collar workers are continued in their easy access camping. Professional and managerial workers continue their "inner-directed" quests for solitude in remote camping. And many persons who have been "uprooted" from the rural, small town ways are able to reconstruct an identity in their remote camping.

Of most interest for an understanding of motives in camping is Max Weber's study of the relation between the Protestant ethic and the spirit of capitalism.[2] Certainly, Weber's ideas might be fruitfully applied to motivation in other sports, and some of the ideas expressed in Burch's essay apply not only to other sports but to the wider social dimensions of work and family life. That is, motives in sport cannot be adequately understood if sport is separated from the wider historical and social setting.

Most sports other than camping do not permit the option of solitude and therefore do not provide as useful a test as to whether work and social ethics motivate one to seek a particular style of action. Certainly the rhetoric used by football coaches to justify the "character building" qualities of the sport may take on aspects of the Protestant ethic. However, it is highly questionable whether so highly organized a team sport permits scope for expressing individual variation which is at the core of the Protestant or work ethic.

The western story is next considered. Stories based on the history and legends of the Old West not only retain immense popularity in the United States but through the media of film and printed page have become the most pervasive and uniquely American cultural export. They have given rise to sports and games which appeal to children and adults alike all over the world.

With occasional minor variations, the stereotyped western story goes as follows: The cowboy hero and his "sidekick" happen upon strangers in peril; after fast and furious confrontations with the villain and his henchmen — chases, gun battles, saloon brawls — the cowboy eventually and inevitably triumphs in personal combat over the villain. Declining the grateful offers of those he has saved (a position of respect and authority in the community and/or marriage to the rancher's daughter), he and his companion ride off into the sunset.

Warren J. Barker's examination of this stereotyped western story, with the aid of psychoanalytic insights,[3] reveals that the ostensible struggle to bring law and order to the frontier serves as a colorful but relative unimportant facade behind which a far more ancient, universal and personal battle rages, the battle that every child must wage within himself to master the dark forces that run counter to the most fundamental moral prohibitions.

Besides being symbolic representations of "good" and "evil," the characters of the western romance are psychological extensions of the reader's or participant's unconscious childhood conception of the members of his family and their interactions. Generally speaking, the hero represents the son; the rancher or sheriff, the father; the rancher's daughter or school ma'am, the mother. Moreover, by an unconscious psychological process called decomposition the attributes of each of the members of the family are dissolved and reassigned among the characters of the story so that, for example, the good rancher is invested with the desirable qualities of father, while the villain is invested with those aspects of the father which are most condemned. While the spectator of the western film or the participant in the "Cowboy and Indian" game identifies mainly with the hero, he also surreptitiously identifies with the others in the cast and thus can give vent, vicariously, to impulses which are alien to his idealized self-concept. Thus, the western story is a ready-made fantasy which the viewer can borrow temporarily, and by identifying with the various characters in the story can express both his constructive and destructive impulses and in the end see the triumph of the former. The fascination of the western story among people of all ages is that it gives momentary hope, even vicarious realization, that one can prevail not only over external enemies but over internal ones, and points up the fact that the deepest and most universal yearnings of childhood are never completely repudiated.

Stonewall B. Stickney's account of hunting began as a psychoanalytic essay. It was completed, delivered as an address, and promptly lost (by the author). In the process of several rewritings two years later it began writing itself into its present form, adding to itself recent dreams, old experiences and childhood rumors.[4] It began using the psychoanalytic tripartite splitting of the ego into the experiencing, the reporting and interpreting functions. In the hunter's soliloquy there appears the dreamy, rambling, allusive quality of free-association, with its repetitions of significant themes. Much of this material is readily subsumed under the well-known oral, anal, and especially phallic stages of psychosexual development. An aggravated and tragic form of the oedipal conflict appears in the story of the two "accidents"; the more common resolutions by self-castration, failure, and masochistic character formation are alluded to, as well as the institutionalized one of cutting off the hunter's shirt-tail when he misses his buck. Stickney further hints at a resolution of the conflict by the symbolic destruction of the bad paternal introject and the dream punishment of the killer. The dreamer survives to tell the tale. The reader may enjoy examining the drowning dream and using all the rest of the account for associations to explain the dream. Totemic, regressive and atavistic allusions will help.

Beyond the psychoanalytic frame of reference, there appears the search for the ineffable "it" – the wild, divine, mysterious, beautiful force of life itself – and with it, the terror of becoming the hunted and facing the mystery of one's own death. The joy of killing, like that of orgasm, is admitted, described, but remains as mysterious as life and death. Hunting as the primary "scanning model" of elemental thought is fancifully described by Stickney.

Once the hunter sought to kill game for food, but this need no longer exists. Hunting is now deemed a sport, when certain rules are followed. A machine gun is not allowed – the odds would be unreasonable, and in such a case, it would be slaughter, not sport. Theodore Roosevelt observed that "the mere size of the bag indicates little as to a man's prowess as a hunter and almost nothing as to the interest or value of his achievement." A challenge (some call it fairness) is an element of sports (thus, one admires the coach who sends in the subs when his team is enough ahead). But however hunting is accomplished, some protests are made against it. Anti-hunters say that the enjoyment of hunting lies in the expression by brutal men of their most hideous traits of character. For example, Karl Menninger says: "Hunting is the sheer lust of destroying something by magic (a deadly piece of magic – a gun) and skillful aim – something wild and unsuspecting, something innocent usually, and often beneficial. But the great thrill of seeing it fall after I touch the trigger is a piece of dangerous childishness which many men never outgrow."[5] Joseph Wood Krutch says, "To me it is inconceivable that anyone should think an animal more interesting dead than alive."[6] (Underlying violence may have a relationship to police work, and a study of the interests of one police force may provide some clue to the motivation for police work. The study showed that a majority were fond of hunting and fishing; about a third made collections of guns or other articles; only about a fifth of them were interested in various forms of athletics.)

It may be noted that a feeling of power can be obtained through a control of animals, as well as through destroying them.[7] Earl Nightingale put it this way: "My daughter used to ride in horse shows, until she discovered boys are more interesting than horses. And while this is, in many cases, debatable, it often brought to mind an interesting parallel. Between events, I used to hold and walk her horse for her. He was a magnificent thoroughbred hunter, alive with nervous energy and tremendous power. With one hand I kept his nearly one thousand pounds under control – just as my little girl did when she took him over the jumps. He was controlled by our minds, certainly not by our strength."[8]

It is necessary, however, to make some distinctions among hunters. There are, after all, millions of hunters; not all of them are motivated by killing. Hunters are various sorts of men, and from the activity they take various sorts of pleasures, as Vance Bourjaily points out in his recent book, *The Unnatural Enemy*.[9] Some hunters like the exercise, the open air, relaxation of tensions, identification with tradition, the challenge.[10] Often a man may begin hunting everything at random but gradually comes to specialize on a particular sort of game and hunting situation which best suits his personality. Traits of character are often reflected in the choice, and this may offer some revelation of the hunter.[11]

Some persons prefer hunting to fishing because the catch can be seen. And the hunter can be more active in its pursuit.

Sport fishing, our next topic, is immensely popular; yet its appeal is not explained by the value of the catch, the exercise it affords, nor by any other superficial attribute. Viggo W. Jensen and Douglas A. Sargent in their paper say that the excitement of angling depends upon the opportunities it provides for the gratification of unconscious psychological needs.[12] These needs represent substitutes for impulses which were repressed in childhood and which persist into later life as unconscious mental tendencies. With examples from clinical psychoanalysis, literature, films, cartoons and myths, they illustrate how repressed childhood tendencies reappear later, in disguised form, in the sport of fishing.

The main forces which contribute to the pleasure of fishing come from the period of life when the developing infant struggled with his attachment to his mother. Dependency upon his mother conflicts with his need for independence; the wish to bite and devour conflicts with his need to be loved; his aggressive drives lead to the fear of punishment. Traces of these conflicts can be seen in the fisherman's tendency to identify with the fish and to go fishing as a means of avoiding threatening relationships with women. These conflicts also appear in the disguise of jokes in which the fish chases or bites the fisherman. Other repressed childhood needs which find symbolic expression through the sport of fishing have to do with sex and reproduction. Sea serpent and mermaid myths are vehicles for the expression of unconscious infantile theories about sex anatomy. Pulling fish from the water symbolizes childbirth. Competitive fishing expresses the oedipal conflict between a young boy and his father.

We next take up mountain climbing. What are the motives of mountain climbers (and also of ocean sailors, explorers, aviators, sky divers and "other suchlike cranks")? Why do the great risk takers do it? It was a mountain climber who coined the phrase "because it is there" to explain why he wanted to climb a particular peak (and some say we are eager to get someone to the moon simply "because it is there"). Man is the restless animal, apparently never satisfied. Why? Calvin S. Hall, Director of the Institute of Dream Research at the University of Miami, says:[13]

> Why do such things as faucets exist which can be used to symbolize the penis? No, we are not being prankish. Obviously, the faucet did not invent itself. It was invented by someone or by a number of people independently. Why was it invented? Common sense answers, "Because it serves a useful purpose." In our opinion, all purposive explanations are rationalizations. The motive power for behavior is a wish, not a purpose.
>
> The faucet was invented for the same reason that the young man dreamed his penis was a faucet. The inventor of the faucet was acting out *his* fantasy of a penis which could be turned on and off at will. That his fantasy proved to have utility is a consequence, and not an antecedent or cause. . . . The faucet was invented by a man who wanted a better penis. Money was invented by someone who wanted to accumulate a bigger pile of feces. Rockets to the moon were invented by a group of dissatisfied oedipal animals. Houses were invented by wombseekers, and whiskey by breastlings.
>
> What we are proposing is a *tabula rasa* — not of the mind which asserts that

objects evoke fantasies — but a *tabula rasa* of the environment which asserts that fantasies create objects.

At birth, a baby whose mind is filled with fantasies enters an *empty* world. Out of his fantasies, he fills the world with faucets, fountains, hoses and sprinklers. He invents the world. He is still inventing the world. . . .

Thanks to the acted-out fantasies of previous generations, the world is well-stocked with things. . . . Man is led to things that already exist by his fantasies; he is led to invent new things by his fantasies.

One would think that enough things had been invented to satisfy all of the fantasies that man has or possibly could have. If one thinks this, then he doesn't understand the dynamic of progress. The dynamic is dissatisfaction with what exists. He finds a horse but that doesn't satisfy his fantasy of having a more powerful penis, more powerful even than father's. He invents the automobile but that doesn't satisfy him for long. He invents the airplane (winged phallus), which is better than an automobile, but not as good as a jet, which in turn is not as good as a rocket, and so on *ad infinitum*. Progress is spurred by unsatisfied infantile wishes.

Man is the dissatisfied animal. Why is he dissatisfied? Because money is not feces, a rocket is not a penis, the moon is not one's mother, whiskey is not mother's milk and a house is not a womb. Perhaps I can satisfy my infantile wishes by some new invention, so thinks man, the eternal optimist. . . .

Man is what evolution has made him — the metaphor-making animal. The metaphors that he makes and acts out are all of them motivated by infantile wishes. Progress is a euphemism for regression.[14]

There are, naturally, other explanations. The challenge of the impossible, Charles S. Houston says, is the strongest urge to climb.[15] Man, he says, is always reaching beyond his grasp to test his limits, and "mastering one's faculties" is a private way of "mastering the world." Yet mountains are not enemies to be beaten; rather, he says, they are friends to be visited. Men do not conquer mountains any more than mountains conquer men; either is but a momentary victory snatched from prevailing circumstance. Adding to the thrill of large challenge is the heady sense of danger, a strong fascination. The adventurer is pleased by the sense of keeping danger under control through the application of skill. The blinding beauty of the world below, seen through the high thin air, the feeling of wonderful fitness, the appreciation of crisp snow, firm rock, hot sun all add to the pleasures of mountaineering. It is a way of reaching Nirvana.

Some men like to put themselves in tight spots because of the teamwork it imposes on them and their fellows. Shared dangers and shared satisfactions build strong friendships. The profit motive is present to some degree, because personal and national prestige is enhanced by ever larger, ever more risky climbs. Those who equate drama, fame or size with the richest rewards of climbing are themselves the losers; the sport is unchanged. Houston says, "Climbing is the expression of man's aspiration to be better than he is."[16]

James A. Knight's study on skiing, which next appears, is based on interviews with many skiers, supplemented by personal participation.[17] A multitude of motivations can be identified as contributing factors in the widespread interest in skiing. The social environment of the ski community also has a very special attraction for many.

Accomplishments on the slopes range from mastery and control of the body to the curing of a peptic ulcer, from a sensitivity to the beauty of nature to a feeling of closeness with ultimate reality, from a feeling of independence to a feeling of "godlike" power, from joy in participating in a thrilling sport to a greater joy as skill and involvement increase.

The ski community has been credited also with many accomplishments. Among these are helping one overcome his feelings of separateness and isolation, furnishing a type of group psychotherapy, discovering a new sense of values and enabling one to free himself from hectic tensions and the bondage of former unrewarding relationships.

Skiing has become the winter fashion. Mechanical devices such as ski lifts and snow-making machines have aided in the development of many ski resorts. The female on the ski scene has accelerated the development of *aprés-ski,* the other-than-outdoor aspects of the sport. Skiing furnishes a blend of exposure to danger, muscular exertion, creative skill and individual expression which in combination may neutralize certain disintegrating aspects of modern civilized living.[18]

Next we go out to sea. Ships are but boards and sailors but men; yet boatmen say, "Happiness is a boat." "There is nothing," British author Kenneth Grahame wrote in 1908, "absolutely nothing half so much worth doing as simply messing about in boats, or with boats. In or out of 'em, it doesn't matter."[19] Many boatmen refer to the time when they put to water as "the time we start living." Russell R. Monroe writes about sailing in this volume.[20] The reasons that people sail, he says, must be as numerous as sailors themselves because sailing provides an endless variety of experience, ranging from the intense competitiveness of a triangular race to the lonely vigil of a single-handed transatlantic crossing. Like many sports, sailing is man's response to the challenge of nature; but more than this, the sailor has the added satisfaction of converting natural forces into useful motive power. This pleasure is further enhanced because the participant possesses and controls a microcosm (the boat and its equipment) which has been carefully planned to anticipate every possible contingency. The captain of a boat is both coach and player in that while being a participant, he must develop a devotion among crew members so that every command is obeyed automatically and precisely. The vagrancies of the elements and the complexities of the maneuvers mean that despite years of experience, each day brings something new and exciting. When the harbor is finally reached, the boat safely anchored in quiet waters, the excitement of the challenge to nature ceases and the pleasure of peaceful contentment takes over. Sailing becomes an all-consuming passion just because it appeals to all that is self-reliant, independent and daring in human nature; yet at the same time it nurtures all that is regressive and dependent, the boat in a snug harbor providing symbolically a retreat to the warmth and tenderness of mother's arms.

FOOTNOTES

1. P. 562.
2. Weber, M.: *Protestant Ethic and the Spirit of Capitalism.* New York, Charles Scribner's Sons, 1948.
3. P. 573.
4. P. 582.
5. Menninger, K.: Totemic aspects of contemporary aspects of contemporary attitudes toward animals; in Wilbur, G. B. and Muensterberger, W. [eds.]: *Psychoanalysis and Culture, Essays in Honor of Roheim.* New York, Int Univs, 1951, p. 45. See also Menninger, K.: *The Vital Balance.* New York, The Viking Press, 1963, p. 214.
6. Krutch, J. W.: Confessions of a square. *Saturday Review,* May 9, 1964, p. 23.
7. Several papers containing psychoanalytic interpretations of bullfighting have appeared in *American Imago.* Desmond, W. H.: The bullfight as a religious ritual. *American Imago, 9:*173, 1952; Hunt, W.: On bullfighting. *American Imago, 12:*343, 1955; Ingham, J.: The bullfighter — a study in sexual dialectic. *American Imago, 21:*95, 1964. See also Verissimo, E.: *Mexico.* New York, Dolphin, 1962, p. 341; Kothari, U. C.: On the bullfight. *Psychoanalysis, 49:*123, 1962.
8. The Earl Nightingale Program, copyright Earl Nightingale, Chicago, Ill. On boys and the meaning of the automobile, see Joseph Noshpitz's essay in Slovenko, R. [Ed.]: *Sexual Behavior and the Law.* Springfield, Thomas, 1965, p. 204. See also Nearles, J., and Kinokur, G.: The hot-rod driver. *Bull Menninger Clin, 21:*28, 1957.
9. Bourjaily, V.: *Unnatural Enemy.* New York, Dial Press, 1963. See also Bourjaily, V.: Hunting is humane. *Sat. Eve. Post,* Feb. 15, 1964, p. 6.
10. *But cf.:* "All these rationalizations cannot disguise the fact that hunting exploits the pleasure of causing fear, suffering and death in other living creatures, who have as much right to live as we unless their death furthers human welfare in some respect other than amusement. However, to call such individuals sadistic, uncivilized and psychopathic is just as untenable as to call their opponents idealistic, fanatic and sentimental." Menninger, K.: *The Vital Balance. op. cit. supra* note 5, at p. 214.
11. Bourjaily, V.: You can tell a hunter by what he hunts. *New York Times Magazine,* November 29, 1964, p. 38. But consider F. Gerstacker's comment, quoted *supra* at p. 241, n. 10.
12. P. 597.
13. Hall, C.: Out of a dream came the faucet. *Psychoanal Rev, 49:*113, 1962.
14. See also Slovenko, R.: Television cameras in the courtroom; in Slovenko, R. [Ed.]: *Crime, Law and Corrections.* Springfield, Thomas, 1966, p. 661.
15. P. 626.
16. *Ibid.*
17. P. 637.
18. David Cort points out that skiing is the reverse of mountaineering. He writes: "Skiers do not climb at all; they are lifted to the heights by a mechanical contrivance. They then descend as quickly as possible: Whee! It is like sliding down the banister without ever

having to climb the stairs. With the ski tows, all the seriousness has gone out of skiing. Practically nobody now uses skis that are fit for cross-country; that is, nobody skis. 'Seriousness,' on the other hand, seems to be the password of mountaineering." Cort, D.: Mountaineers: Dilettantes of suicide. *The Nation,* May 18, 1963, p. 423.

19. Grahame, K.: *Wind in the Willows.* New York, Charles Scribner's Sons, rev. ed. 1933. See also: Happiness is a boat. *New York Times,* May 2, 1965, sec. 73, p. 1. Water has long been regarded as a healer of psychological and physiological difficulties. Hydrotherapy and other practices of immersion have a long history. We all know that a nice bath relaxes the body and mind. We may recall the theme of ablution as it relates to the rites of purity and rebirth. Water, the simple and primitive liquid, is considered to belong to all that is purest in nature. The return to water's limpidity assumes the meaning of a ritual of purification. Tissot, a disciple of Rousseau, said: "Nature has prescribed water as the unique beverage of all nations; she gave it the power to dissolve all sorts of nourishment; it is agreeable to the palate; choose therefore a good cold water, fresh and light; it fortifies and cleans the bowels; the Greeks and Romans regarded it as a universal remedy." Tissot, S. A.: *Avis aux gens de lettres sur leur santé.* Lausanne, 1767, p. 90. In the Middle Ages, the traditional treatment of a maniac was to plunge him several times into water "until he had lost his strength and forgotten his fury." Foucault, M.: *Madness and Civilization.* New York, Pantheon, 1965, p. 167. During the Renaissance, it is reported that the mentally ill were put on a ship and entrusted to mariners because folly, water, and sea, as everyone then "knew," had an affinity for each other. Thus, "Ships of Fools" crisscrossed the seas and canals of Europe with their comic and pathetic passengers. Some of them found pleasure and even a cure in the changing surroundings, in the isolation of being cast off, while others withdrew further, became worse, or died alone and away from their families. Barchilon, J.: *Introduction* to Foucault, M.: *Madness and Civilization. Supra* at pp. vi-vii.
20. P. 649.

CAMPING

WILLIAM R. BURCH, JR.

On a cool summer day in 1883, President Chester A. Arthur mounted his horse and with other members of his party set off on a leisurely 350-mile camping trip into Yellowstone National Park. Seventy-nine years later, in 1962, members of the Kennedy family hurried on their helicopter-supplied "camping trip" into Olympic National Park. As "wilderness" trips these two journeys reflect more than technological change. Arthur and his immediate successors were concerned with turning the great empty expanse of the West into settled land. Members of the Kennedy administration hoped to preserve some remaining empty spaces from the progress of settlements. Yet in both eras men have paused to wonder at the tumbling land and the stretching sky.

Each generation of Americans has expressed the mood of its times through its attitudes toward nature. Nature has not only served as a stage for the great dramas of conquest, settlement and defeat, but has provided a setting for intensifying the expressions of companionship and solitude. This essay, by exploring the motives and meanings associated wth styles of camping, may suggest something of the continuing significance of nature.

Camping uniquely expresses the apparently paradoxical behavior of those who seek to live *in* and *with* nature, when the whole tenor of their social order seems to pronounce nature as a controlled if not irrelevant factor in human existence. Interestingly, those persons whose affluence and, therefore, comfort is greater than the average are the ones most likely to be campers who most passionately value the discomforts of temporary privation.[1] Such behavior suggests paradox and ambiguity in motives, with perhaps a heavy touch of reverse snobbery.

However, the construction of "free time" rewards from actions which run counter to the publicized "goals" of society may reflect neither paradox nor ambiguity, but an intimate connection between the motives and meanings assigned to nature and those values which prevail in everyday life. In the following sections I will attempt to clarify the argument. We will first examine two styles of camping which represent opposite approaches to nature, then we will examine some of the sources of social values such as solitude and sociability, while the concluding sections will attempt to relate social values to actions and suggest that there is but a thin and arbitrary line between the world of play and the everyday world.

THE PLAYWORLD OF CAMPING – APPROACHES TO NATURE

Camping, as suggested above, is a unique play form which may take on the aspects of work and whose pleasure is often measured by the amount of privation endured. Camping broadly refers to those human actions which take place in a relatively natural environment free from the artifacts of established year-round human settlement. In this essay our main interest is in those family groups who, primarily for recreational purposes, live temporarily in a tent, trailer, or outdoors without shelter. Further, these family groups go camping for the varied recreational experiences offered rather than using camping as simply an inexpensive means of getting from one place to another. Camping differs from other play in that the campers, though isolated from the commitments of everyday life, pursue many of the routines of everyday life – such as cooking, sleeping and so forth. The family unit for the duration of its engagement is a relatively self-sufficient unit containing the resources of existence without immediate dependency upon others. Within the broad confines of the camping activity system there are many different styles or approaches to nature. To aid understanding I will compare two quite different camping styles – easy access and remote.

An important characteristic which distinguishes these two styles of camping is the mode of transportation. Easy access campers enter the forests with automobiles and rarely stray far from their machines. Remote campers backpack or canoe or ride horseback into roadless areas of the forest. Therefore, these camping styles, roughly divide on the dimensions of relative personal comfort and discomfort. Further, the camping styles present distinctive social milieus with the easy access style offering extensive sociality with outside groups, while the remote style is characterized by intensive sociality within one's own group. It would appear that the selection of one or the other of these alternatives expresses different commitments to nature and society and is directed by a different "vocabulary of motives."[2]

In an easy access area one can come equipped with many of the conveniences of home or, in fact, haul in his "mobile home." One's group is situated within a setting that opens privacy to the observation of numerous strangers, and the congregation and closeness of most campsites encourages interaction and adjustive behavior for these strangers. It is often far less quiet, private or comfortable than the time one spends at home. Easy access campers could be characterized as people who carry out routines under slightly different conditions: there is some privation; many private functions are subject to public review; and it is easy to enter the forests, and therefore, easy to leave if weather or social relations are unfavorable. Further, the easy access camper is often more closely linked to specific activities associated with forests – water skiing, hunting – rather than the total experience of nature which is a characteristic motivation offered by many remote campers.

Remote campers have the opportunity for the relative isolation of their group from all other groups. There is the demand for a fairly systematic division of labor if there is to be any success to the trip. The opportunity for disengaging oneself from the area due to poor weather or poor social relations is at a minimum. One is most dependent upon the moods and values of the other members of the party. There is a continual demand to exert unfamiliar labor which under everyday circumstances would be defined as unpleasant work. Consequently the contrast between the comforts of everyday life and the privation of leisure is at a maximum. Remote campers, then, are characterized by limited equipment, considerable deprivation, effort of a more demanding nature, isolation of one's group with attendant intensive sociality, and more direct subjugation to the whims of nature.

Moreover, remote campers consistently express an involvement, often of poetic depth, with the many facets of their camping experience. Such depth of expression is occasional rather than characteristic of easy access campers. A recurring theme among remote campers emphasizes that the rewards of play are to be found in one's personal struggle to overcome difficult obstacles. As a forty-five-year-old remote camper put it:

> I would like to see the few remote wilderness areas [preserved] . . . so that the youngster of today may have the opportunity to shoulder a pack and feel the sweat run down his back and trail dust caked on his face and stand on the rim of a high mountain lake after five or six hours of hard work and know the feeling of accomplishment and self-assurance, knowing that he got there by his own efforts and that he is strictly on his own. No policeman, no fireman, no doctors, just hard work and his good sense . . .[3]

In general the remote camper believes that pleasure is best found by paying costs in terms of feeling and effort while the easy access camper generally prefers paying his costs in the impersonal terms of cash. Such divergent approaches to nature suggest equally divergent sources of motive. The next section will indicate some of these sources.

ATTITUDES TOWARD LEISURE: "PROTESTANT" AND "SOCIAL" ETHICS

One prevailing theory of recreation behavior suggests that people desire a "change of pace" or "new experience" in their off-work time.[4] This seems to be an unsatisfactory explanation as to what directs a person to select one style of camping over another. It is unsatisfactory as all styles of camping provide "new experiences" for the well-paid and well-housed urban worker. Further, how long must one engage in a new experience before it becomes an old and familiar experience? Sex play for a newly joined man and woman may quickly lose its novelty, though one could hardly say there is a corresponding loss of interest. A large number of campers have been camping for a considerable number of years; yet attachment to the play form seems to increase rather than decrease. The new experience theory assumes a terribly flat, unidimensional notion of man which sees him randomly flitting from this to that, ever pushed on by impulse and whim, forever unable to derive durability and satisfaction. It would seem more useful to consider that man lives in a symbolic environment whose nature permits, in fact encourages, depth of expression in all human endeavor — whether it be tinkering on a new symphony or tinkering on an old machine.

Certainly it is doubtful that the "motives" for expressions such as the creation of a symphony or the creation of a camping style are to be found either in impulses for new experience or quivering somewhere within the viscera. It is more likely that the motivation is to be found in those symbolic constructs we call social values. The argument is important enough that we will need to outline some of the discussion most closely related to our concern with "motive" in sport.

The German social scientist Max Weber has provided an inspiring source for most present-day explorations of the relation between social values and social action. Weber, in challenging the strict economic determinism of Karl Marx, produced a series of painstaking historical studies which demonstrated that social values such as religion could as likely be seen as the factors which determined the economic system. Weber, though careful to indicate that he had no desire to substitute a one-sided spiritualistic interpretation for a one-sided materialistic interpretation, was able to demonstrate the intimate connection between social values and attitudes toward work and play. Of most interest for our understanding of "motives" in camping is Weber's study of the relation between the Protestant ethic and the spirit of capitalism.[5]

Weber, building his ideal type of the capitalist spirit on the maxims of Benjamin Franklin, argued that material acquisitiveness was not unique to western capitalism. He believed that the uniqueness of western capitalism was that its moral attitudes were colored with utilitarianism and an imperative that one avoid spontaneous enjoyment of life as one's duty was in one's vocational calling. Weber saw this moral imperative toward work as being in direct contrast to traditional attitudes which viewed labor as an onerous duty to be avoided whenever possible. In the traditional period labor was seen as man's punishment for his fall from grace; labor was something which one endured, not something to which he piously devoted himself so as to demonstrate his right to salvation.

In discussing the struggle between the King and the Puritans over the *Book of Sports,* Weber links the ethic to the new classes. "The feudal and monarchical forces protected the pleasure seekers against the rising middle-class morality and the anti-authoritarian ascetic conventicles, just as today capitalistic society tends to protect those willing to work against the class morality of the proletariat and the anti-authoritarian trade union."[6] Weber says that for the Puritans:

> Sport was accepted if it served a rational purpose, that of recreation necessary for physical efficiency. But as a means for spontaneous expression of undisciplined impulses, it was under suspicion; and insofar as it became purely a means of enjoyment, or awakened pride, raw instincts or the irrational gambling instinct, it was, of course, strictly condemned. Impulsive enjoyment of life, which leads away both from work in a calling and from religion, was as such the enemy of rational asceticism, whether in the form of seigneurial sports, or the enjoyment of the dance-hall or the public-house of the common man.[7]

Weber, though believing that Puritan values may have been instrumental in forming the spirit of capitalism, suggests that such ethical rewards are no longer available to modern industrial man. The industrial order with its rationalization of time, money, men and machines has secularized such values so that they are part of existence for all persons, regardless of their religious affiliation.

In summary, Weber argued that the morality, or Protestant ethic, of the rising middle classes gave dignity to work and not to leisure. Such an ethic places greatest stress upon the process of struggle for gain rather than upon the actual amount accumulated. With the passage of time the emphasis upon effort, hard work and devotion to one's calling became no longer associated with a specific religious group but was diffused throughout the capitalist industrial order. Our question remains: What of today when the issue is not one of scarcity[8] but of a surplus of goods, and the encouragement of production is less important than encouraging higher levels of consumption? Within this changed context are those who still hold the older morality able to carry out their devotions to struggle? Perhaps motivation for demanding sport, such as remote camping, is derived from the older work morality while motivation for easy access camping is derived from the equally old sociable morality of the "common man"? Recent social research suggests something of this pattern.

Two students of religion in American life, Gerhard Lenski[9] and Will Herberg,[10] have attempted to extend, test and refine Weber's ideas. For example, Lenski's studies in the Detroit area offer empirical evidence that positive attitudes toward work are more likely to be associated with white Protestants and Jews, while negative attitudes toward work are more likely to be associated with Catholics and Negro Protestants.[11] That is, those groups who are traditionally overrepresented in the lower social positions of American society evidence attitudes toward work and play which are similar to the attitudes which Weber attributed to the "common man" at an early stage of the industrial order. It would seem that the morality of hard work and personal struggle still confronts the morality of social ease and relaxation. However, the nature of the confrontation may be changing.

Of particular interest is Herberg's argument that Catholics and Jews have been concentrated in urban areas while Protestantism has been primarily a rural expression. Herberg believes that Protestantism was well adapted to meet the challenge on the rural frontier of the West; however, Protestantism was never able to conquer the city frontier. He develops an impressive argument that Protestantism was the religion of the frontier proletariat which became transformed into a more or less conventional denominationalism. As the frontiersman moved up the social hierarchy, so too did his religion. Protestantism, however, remained primarily a rural, small town religion. As he says, using data of the Federal Council of Churches:

> No Protestant group, not even the Episcopalians, were as urban as the Catholics, or the Jews, and of course neither Catholics nor Jews were anywhere as rural or 'small town' as the Baptists, Methodists or Lutherans. Protestantism as a whole showed a higher proportion of residents on the farm and in smaller towns, and a lower proportion in big cities, than the national sample.[12]

The writings of Weber and Herberg suggest two patterns: (1) the "Protestant" ethic is associated with "rising middle classes" in the early stages of industrialization, and (2) Protestantism in America is most vigorous in rural and small town areas. However, America has moved from a scarcity economy to one of abundance and from a rural frontier nation to an urban-industrial nation. It would seem that these changes should have an impact upon social values. There are numerous analyses of these changes, but three studies seem most relevant for an understanding of changing attitudes toward leisure. These critical analyses are to be found in the writings of David Riesman,[13] William S. Whyte[14] and C. Wright Mills.[15] All three authors develop their examination of contemporary society through expanding Max Weber's discussion of the Protestant ethic.

The studies of Riesman, Whyte and Mills, all evidently pursued independently, seem to come up with a similar set of interpretations and a similar set of dichotomies for their analyses of the changing American society. Whyte is concerned with shifts from a "work ethic" to a "social ethic"; Mills is concerned with shifts from the dominance of the "old middle classes" to the "new middle classes"; and Riesman is concerned with the shifts from a society composed of "inner-directeds" to a society more and more composed of "other-directeds." Each of these sets of analytical categories would appear to be a different piece of the same animal. Whyte places emphasis upon the shifts in value orientations, Mills upon shifts in the social structure, Riesman upon shifts in patterns of socialization and social control.

In short, these authors are essentially talking about directions away from the "Protestant ethic" toward something akin to a highly complex system of catholic feudalism. The parallel is not unfair, for each is somewhat shocked by the white collar serfs in bondage to corporations, the increasing corporate and national parochialism with its fear of individualistic and innovating initiative, the increasing rigidity of inherited social positions and the strain toward human standardization. Each believes that the new generation of technocrats and bureaucrats is foregoing the competitive struggle of ascetic capitalism to embrace the cooperative morale of organizational dedication and personal anonymity. The move is one from privacy and solitude to other-direction and sociability.

CAMPING STYLES AND SOCIAL VALUES

It would seem that the aforementioned authors provide the necessary explanation of "motives" in camping. If new and old middle classes, work ethics and social ethics, inner-direction and other-direction exhibit the configurations attributed to them, then styles of camping from easy access to remote should follow the predicted patterns. One would expect the new middle-class, other-directed persons holding a social ethic to predominate in easy access areas and the old middle-class, inner-directed persons subscribing to a work ethic to predominate in the more primitive activities.

I explored some of these ideas in a study of 740 family camping groups. I assumed that if a Protestant or work ethic were still associated with a particular religion, then one might expect a demanding camping style, like remote camping, to be more attractive to Protestants. However, I found that remote camping actually attracted more persons who had no religion (48.6%) than persons who were Protestants (45.0%), while almost 55 per cent of the easy access campers had Protestant affiliation. Further, members of the major faiths were represented in camping at about the same proportion as they were to be found in the general population, though members of the Jewish faith were somewhat underrepresented in camping.[16] These findings are in harmony with Herberg's contention that the three major American religious groupings are fairly similar in their world views. However, this argument does not deny the possibility that value systems such as Protestant or work ethics and social ethics may be relevant in shaping an individual's line of action.

In this same study I asked campers for their opinions on a series of statements, some of which emphasized the values of solitude and challenge found in forests, some which emphasized the opportunities for sociability, and some which emphasized the instrumental qualities of forests, such as the opportunity for good fishing. A five-point intensity scale from "strongly agree" to "strongly disagree" provided a means for scoring the responses.[17] An analysis of the scores found that almost 76 per cent of the remote campers emphasized a work ethic, while only 56.8 per cent of the easy access campers saw solitude and meeting challenge as prime rewards of camping. The contrast is even sharper when we consider attitudes toward sociability; only 15 per cent of the easy access campers received low sociability scores, while 46.8 per cent of the remote campers obtained low scores. These respective scores, as responses to several other questionnaire items, furnish evidence that remote campers are guided in their play by a work ethic, while easy access campers are guided in their play by a social ethic.

However, a closer examination of the scores revealed that *both* camping style and social status are associated with particular value systems. As I have reported elsewhere:

> In general, the lower the social status and the less primitive the camping style, the more likely one holds a social ethic and the less likely he holds a work ethic; while the higher the status and the more primitive the camping style, the more likely one holds a work ethic and the less likely he holds a social ethic. However, regardless of camping style, high status persons along with primitive campers are most likely to hold a work ethic; low status persons, regardless of camping style, are more likely to hold a social ethic; lower and middle status easy access campers are less likely to hold a work ethic and most likely to hold a social ethic.[18]

In other words, we find that those persons in the lower social strata — clerical and blue collar workers — have attitudes toward leisure similar to those of Weber's "common man" at the beginning of the industrial era. They stress "groupness" and emphasize the pleasures of sociability rather than the pains of solitude — which are all the symptoms of the social ethic which Whyte found in his organization man. Yet, as Richard Hoggart's study of English working class culture demonstrates, a social ethic is a fairly pervasive working class value.[19] And this value is in marked contrast to the work ethic held by those persons in the upper social strata — professionals and managers — whose attitudes toward leisure are very much like those of Weber's Puritans. Obviously, such ethics are not so easily attributed to particular historical epochs as Mills, Whyte, Riesman and others would suggest.

Perhaps these authors have drawn too much from comparing the life styles of their friends and themselves with those now sharing rising levels of living, and then assumed that such escalation of material standards for whole classes of persons marks technology's complete triumph over the dignity of effort. What they may actually be recording is the great mobility in terms of material opportunities for those in the "working classes" (classes whose values are now more visible) rather than the decline of a hallowed ethic. Further, it appears that what they are recoiling from is the reestablishment or expansion of the superficially sociable values of small town business boosterism so ably reported by Sinclair Lewis and the Lynds' 1920 study of Middletown. The appeal of such belongingness would seem natural to those caught in the unstable stability of increasing material advance, as it is and was to the small Junior Chamber members.

Such a "sociable" ethic is less appealing to certain professional classes whose occupational associations and training stress difficult struggle, facing odds and getting ahead via the educational ladder, and who tend to emphasize the privacy and solitude of the individual. One would anticipate such values to prevail in the liberal arts faculties whose antipathy toward boosterism is as clear as their reflection of the inner-directed, self-sacrificing values of the hard-working humanist who is transcendentally ambitious. It is an ambition which may be best called "aristocratic" as it advances special status claims which by nature are restrictive rather than equalitarian in their proposals for a meritocracy of endeavor.

Given this understanding, we should not look solely to value shifts between historical epochs to explain "motives" in sport but expect that leisure behavior such as camping style, though framed within historical time, will reflect the everyday values found in certain occupational and social strata groupings.

However, cutting across the tidy assignment of values to social strata is the fact that camping style is also associated with either a social or work ethic. Therefore, we may have a lower stratum camper who should exude sociability but we find that he only talks of challenge and struggle and solitude because he is a remote camper. Perhaps this deviation from our expectations may be understood by returning to our discussion of religion.

Both Lenski and Herberg, as other students, have argued that the third generation members of American immigrant groups, particularly those of the "new immigration" (from Southern and Eastern Europe), have been unable to retain their ethnic identity. These writers believe that what has been retained is the parental religious affiliation: Pole may now marry Irish, but both are Catholic. Herberg sees the recent resurgence of religious affiliation as being bound to a general quest for identity in contemporary America. He says of the immigrant person that it was ". . . through his religion that he, or rather his children and grandchildren, found an identifiable place in American life."[20] He believes that religion has served to link the generations while language and cultural traditions have tended to be lost by the third generation.

Though his study, as many others, offers sympathetic concern for the "new immigrant's" quest for identity, seldom is there a suggestion that perhaps children of the "old immigrants" have similar, if not as crucial, problems. It would appear that the spiritual home of these old immigrants — the small town, rural area — is being overwhelmed by urbanization, mechanization and the growth of large centralized corporate enterprises. The old immigrants find they are compelled to seek occupational opportunity outside the rural ways; thus they drift to the city. "Uprooted," spiritually and physically, they may find the rural values of effort and self-denial guiltily contrasted to the ease and comfort they have bought with their jobs in the urban bureaucracy. It would seem that for this group the problems of discovering continuity with past generations could be an even more difficult quest than that faced by the "new immigrants," as the Protestant religion of the fathers, if there was any, is not adaptive to urban patterns. Perhaps this group turns to leisure forms such as remote camping in order to construct a continuity with the past values.

If this is the case, then it is an indication that an important function of play is the opportunity to carry out roles and values which no longer are available. Here then is an important argument that it is socially valuable to protect "playgrounds" such as wilderness areas which allow the performance of archaic roles and values, to take up the slack for those whose life cycle is caught in a social cycle.[21] Certainly it is an issue worthy of future research.

"No, I'm *not* 'enjoying camping' — I'm a bum and I live this way all the time!"

CONCLUSION

I began this essay by suggesting that nature has had a continuing importance in American social life. What I am suggesting is that the members of each generation have explored the meaning of their times through posing attitudes toward nature. By their posing — in fear, in arrogance, in destruction, in humility and in wonder — they speak of those motives deemed significant in their times. It is not in paradox but in doubt that men wander from the clamor of their day, bringing with them the tag ends of their daily existences. Nature furnishes a broad spectrum of physical and social stage settings amidst which men can perform purified dramas of those values which give meaning to everyday routines. In camping those riding the escalator of higher levels of living can explore the sociable frontiers of equality, while those trained to value the solitude of personal challenge can extend their expression to the tangible face of mountain and alpine meadow; and those uprooted from the soil of the hinterland values may reconstruct personal continuity. Motives in camping as the hills upon which they are played, furnish a future by reflecting a past.

FOOTNOTES

1. For empirical support of this assertion see Burch, W. R.: Nature as Symbol and Expression: A Sociological Exploration of the Meaning of Nature in American Social Life, *Univ. of Minnesota,* unpub. Ph.D. dissertation, 1964, ch. 7.
2. Mills, C. W.: Power, Politics and People, Horowitz, I. L. [Ed.]: New York, Ballantine Books, 1962, p. 452. Burke, K.: *Permanence and Change, An Anatomy of Purpose.* Los Altos, Hermes Publications, 1954, pp. 20-25.
3. For a detailed examination of these themes see Burch: *op. cit. supra* note 1, ch. 9.
4. de Grazia, S.: *Of Time, Work and Leisure,* New York, Twentieth Century Fund, 1962.
5. Weber, M.: *The Protestant Ethic and the Spirit of Capitalism,* translated by Parsons, T. New York, Charles Scribner's Sons, 1958.
6. Weber: *op. cit. supra* note 5, at 167.
7. *Supra* at 167-169.
8. Galbraith, J. K.: *The Affluent Society.* New York, New American Library, 1958.
9. Lenski, G.: *The Religious Factor.* Garden City, Doubleday, 1961.
10. Herberg, W.: *Protestant, Catholic, Jew.* Garden City, Doubleday, 1960.
11. Lenski: *op. cit. supra* note 9, at 96.
12. Herberg: *op. cit. supra* note 10, at 213.
13. Riesman, D.; with Glazer, N., and Denney, R.: *The Lonely Crowd.* Garden City, Doubleday, 1956.
14. Whyte, W. H.: *The Organization Man.* Garden City, Doubleday, 1956.
15. Mills, C. W.: *White Collar.* New York, Oxford, 1956.
16. Burch: *op. cit. supra* note 1, at 345-352.
17. Readers interested in more details concerning research techniques, analysis of data, and additional findings should see Burch: *op. cit. supra* note 1.
18. Burch: *op. cit. supra* note 1, at 365-366.
19. Hoggart, R.: *The Uses of Literacy.* Harmondsworth, Penguin Books, 1958, p. 33.
20. Herberg: *op. cit. supra* note 10, at 28.
21. Sullivan, H. S.: *Conceptions of Modern Psychiatry.* New York, Norton, 1953, pp. 223-224.

THE WESTERN STORY, SPORTS AND GAMES

WARREN J. BARKER

THE STIRRING HISTORY OF THE American West, especially that of the nineteenth century, has served as the basis for thousands of short stories, novels, radio programs, cartoon "comic strips," motion pictures and television programs. Over the years the production and dissemination of these derivatives of the western saga have steadily increased throughout the world. Expressed in this colorful variety of ways, the legend of the American West reaches and affects, for better or worse, more people than jazz, the other authentic and uniquely American cultural export. To millions of people throughout the world, America is almost synonymous with the Wild West. At any moment of the day or night, someone, somewhere, in equatorial Africa, in Greenland or in Micronesia is looking at an old western film or video tape. Out of the legend of the West, there have evolved numerous so-called western sports in which one can either passively or actively participate. The *culte de l'Ouest* attracts many devotees in Europe where western clubs are popular. Their members affect western dress and trappings and congregate regularly to play "cowboy and Indian" or practice the "quick-draw." It has been said, almost solemnly, that the first words ever put together by children learning to speak, the first phrase in any language, can be translated as "hands up." It's possible.

It is common knowledge that the passage of time has seen the history of the American West contaminated by some rather fanciful legends. While this history was happening, such figures as Ned Buntline were disseminating their unique version of life in the West through the medium of "dime-novels." Some of the authors of western tales during that period never set foot west of the Mississippi. As a matter of fact, one who created a tenacious and lurid image of the West for millions of Germans never saw any part of America. Karl May[1] wrote such western classics as *Helden des Westens* and *Old Surehand.* His plots and characterizations are similar to those used by many American authors, present as well as past.

It is well at this time to examine the stereotyped version of the western legend because it is from this that a better understanding of its perennial fascination can be achieved — and of course such an examination is important to a better understanding of some of the unconscious motivating factors in some of those who indulge in so-called western sports. A run-of-the-mill film version of the western story which was extremely popular on television in this country during the 1940's and 50's, and which presumably about now is reaching some of the far corners of the earth, can be described as follows:

> A young wandering cowboy astride his handsome gelding rides into view on a lonely western landscape. He is accompanied by one or two male companions. The sound of gunfire in the distance introduces the fact that the stagecoach is being held up, or that a local rancher — a complete stranger to the hero — has been murdered or his life menaced, and his property unlawfully wrested from him or from his rightful heirs. Without a moment's hesitation the cowboy springs into unrelenting retributive action. After a number of desperate pursuits on horseback through desolate and forbidding terrain, after gun battle and saloon brawls, with almost superhuman effectiveness he overcomes the villain in personal combat, avenges the crimes and restores the undamaged gold-dust, ranch or herd to the rightful owner. Having performed these services he rejects the offer that he assume office as sheriff, or become the foreman of the restored property with the rancher's daughter or the school ma'am as his bride. With complete self-effacement, the laconic cowboy tips his hat politely and gallops away, accompanied still by his faithful companion.

Another adventure inevitably follows in which the whole drama is repeated with minor variations. Like the mechanical figure that strikes the hours on a medieval turret clock, the western hero seems obliged to gallop jerkily and repeatedly around an unchanging orbit. Robert Warshow has made this cogent observation:[2]

> Once it has been discovered that the true theme of the western movie is not the freedom and expansiveness of frontier life, but its limitations, its material bareness, the pressures of obligation, then even the landscape itself ceases to be quite the arena of free movement it once was but becomes instead a great empty waste, cutting down more often than it exaggerates the stature of the horseman who rides across it; we are more likely now to see the westerner struggling against the obstacles of the physical world than carelessly surmounting them.

The central figure in the frontier myth is certainly not the stump-pulling, land-tilling, patriarchal settler who was probably the really significant person in the westward expansion of the United States, nor is it the artisan, businessman and industrial organizer who followed in his path. It is, rather, a man who caricatures the pioneer virtues of self-reliance, courage, initiative and fraternal interdependence in the face of common danger. In the western myth one easily recognizes this central figure as one who in other times, other costumes, other dramas has struggled in the valleys of the Euphrates and the Nile, Greece, Spain, Scandinavia and Camelot; he is the Hero. In the western legend he has exchanged his shining helmet for a ten-gallon hat, his breastplate for an embroidered shirt, and his lance for a pair of six-shooters. The scene has shifted to the American Southwest; ranch houses and sheriff's offices have replaced castles, and saloons and hideouts have been substituted for lairs of dragons; but the hero's interminable adventures follow the ancient pattern. It is apparent that the cowboy hero is the eternal son, repetitively and compulsively acting out an archetypal fantasy. It is interesting to note that Karl May used the same plot for novels about the Orient as he did for his "Westerns." The stereotyped Western is a morality play. The issue is "good" versus "evil." If the ethics of the hero are more ambiguous, and if his "native hue of resolution is sicklied o'er with the pale cast of thought," then we are dealing with what has come to be called an "adult" Western. Fortunately for art's sake these are becoming more common.

The cowboy hero in the old-time Western is at once proud and modest, bold and shy. His courage, agility and reckless self-confidence in righting wrongs and defending his "honor" are in marked contrast to his respectful backwardness in the presence of women. He is decoratively and conspicuously dressed, wearing a large white hat, embroidered shirt, skintight trousers and high-heeled boots. From his hips hang two large pistols. He is never profane, rarely smokes and rarely drinks intoxicating liquors. He adheres rigidly to the code of the prairie, never taking unfair advantage, even of the villain, his worst enemy. When the latter is ultimately disarmed, the cowboy tosses aside his own pistols and subdues him with his bare fists, sometimes undergoing what appears to be unnecessary punishment in the process.

The western hero is usually accompanied by one or more male companions who are faithful to him from one adventure to the next. Ordinarily, the companion is of approximately the same age as the hero but frequently is considerably younger, or sometimes much older. This person is dependent on the hero for leadership and is inclined to be indecisive, inept and impulsive. He is patronized and dominated by the cowboy even when old enough to be his father. At times his ineptitude jeopardizes the cowboy's safety or his own. Reciprocal rescues are frequent. This "sidekick" is often permitted to make innocent, abortive, romantic advances toward women but always retreats and remains faithful to the hero; his comic misadventures at the end of the story are greeted with derisive laughter from all the good people, and the glee of his idol is more conspicuous than that of any other. This companion is the "comedy relief" in these mirthless films.

The villain is an absolute contrast to the hero. He is often portrayed as a saloon keeper. No action is too dastardly for him to contemplate or attempt. His activity is perpetually counter to conventional morality. When thwarted and brought to justice, he remains defiant and sullenly unrepentant. He drinks, gambles and stares lasciviously at his dancing girls. His loutish hirelings are encouraged to imitate his behavior. Wearing a black hat and suit, lurking behind a black cigar, he broods, scowls and schemes to get the worthy rancher's property and his virginal daughter. When the villain is a banker or a sheriff who pretends to be an upright and law-abiding citizen, his mendacity is all the more odious. It is noteworthy that in this instance only the hero seems to have a clear conviction from the outset of the villain's duplicity and evil intentions. This worthy has duped the locals for years, but at their first encounter our clear-eyed cowboy looks deeply and intuitively into his black and dissembling heart. More on this curious talent later. In more elaborate western productions the villain is in alliance with hostile Indians, surreptitiously selling them firearms and "firewater" and inciting them to attack the wagon train or the homestead.

In a common variation of the western film, the sheriff is one of the law-abiding inhabitants but is weak, vacillating and ineffectual in the performance of his function of maintaining law and order. When this is so, the cowboy reluctantly usurps his duties temporarily for the purpose of rescuing the imperiled and bringing the arch-criminal and his gang to justice. All offers to retain this position of authority permanently are declined, just as the cowboy also refuses to marry the rancher's daughter.

The rancher who must be protected or avenged by the hero is cut from the same cloth as the ineffectual benign sheriff, and he plays a minor role. If he survives the opening moments of the story, he is occasionally permitted to organize a posse and assist in the capture of the villain's henchmen. If the rancher has a son, he is depicted as spoiled or perhaps even treacherous, and secretly in league with the villain. The daughter is traditionally proud, courageous and fanatically vengeful. Her independent efforts to redress the wrongs of the villain are premature and planless; consequently, she usually falls into his clutches, is roughly handled and carried off, struggling, to the villain's lair. When ultimately she is rescued by the superhuman efforts of the cowboy, she is chastened and worshipfully grateful. In her new-found shyness she tends to simper excessively.

The question arises as to the source and nature of such universal fascination with the western legend. It is a truism borne out by clinical psychoanalytic experience that every item of behavior is multiply determined. That is to say that its motivational roots grow from various levels of the personality. It is intended to serve several goals simultaneously. The resultant "item of behavior," whether it is an overt act, a dream, a symptom or a myth, is a compromise of id, ego and superego needs. Some of these are conscious and others are unconscious. For example, an individual who consumes alcoholic beverages to excess may do so for a number of reasons. In any given instance these might include some or all of the following: the wish to relieve tension and avoid feelings of insecurity, the wish to conform to the behavior and mores of his social group (or the opposite), the wish to impress his friends with his imbibing prowess, the wish to harass his wife, and at a deeper unconscious level, a wish to satisfy some insatiable, infantile, oral wish, or even to serve as a means of subtle self-destruction.

For another individual who exhibits this type of behavior these motivating forces may vary both as to number, intensity and relative importance. An example closer to the theme of this investigation is the individual who has a compelling need to ride a horse. Here again there are numerous possible motivating factors of which some are more cogent in one instance than in another. First of all, a horse may be the only means of transportation between point A and point B. Or the rider may be riding because it is healthful exercise, and not only for the horse. Or riding may be fashionable in his social circle. Maybe the rider is basically afraid of horses and must ride to overcome his feelings of fear and shame. Perhaps he rides because it gives him an exhilarating feeling of power. It is a common observation that pubescent girls often have an intense obsessive interest in horses and horseback riding. This usually conceals a desperate unconscious wish to deny their feminity. The horse replaces a missing phallus. Obviously the context in which each individual rider rides must be studied in order to determine which factors, for him, are most pertinent. But the fact does remain that most behavior serves several purposes simultaneously and that there are motivating contributions from both the conscious and the unconscious levels of the personality. We must accept the fact of multiple-determination. It must be left to others to elaborate upon the social, cultural and other implications of the western legend. It is the purpose here to explore certain of the popular western phenomena mainly in terms of their *unconscious* meaning and function.

However, it is with trepidation that we apply some of the insights of psychoanalysis to such a universally popular and widely revered institution as the "Western." One can expect a few howls of outrage from the more dedicated devotees. Even though our investigation is undertaken good-naturedly and without any solemn pretense of infallibility, some readers may react as they once did when first brushed by the unsettling rumor that Santa Claus was, in reality, just old prosaic Dad. So we shall pursue our examination of the Western in spite of the anticipation that some might hurl the accusation that "head-shrinker says Cowboy Hero is just a rotten kid!"

Turning again to the western film, one is forced to doubt that the manifest narrative content, despite its furious action and striking setting, can entirely account for the widespread and tenacious interest in it. One can justifiably suspect that the ostensible historic struggle to bring law and order to the geographical frontier serves as a relatively unimportant facade behind which a far more ancient, universal and personal battle rages, the battle that every child must wage to master the dark forces in himself that run counter to the most fundamental moral prohibitions.

For the spectator or the reader of the western romance, and to some extent for the active or passive participant in so-called western sports, the myth of the American West can be looked upon as a ready-made fantasy. If we approach this "fantasy" much as we would the manifest content of a daydream reported by a patient in the consulting room, one picks up a number of clues which have a ring of familiarity to the psychoanalyst and from which he can draw a number of conclusions about the latent or unconscious forces behind the manifest fantasy.

The cast of characters in the stereotyped western romance are psychological extensions of the spectator's or reader's unconscious conception of, and can be analogized with, typical members of the family. Generally speaking, the hero of the western is the son; the rancher or sheriff, the father; the rancher's wife or the school ma'am, the mother. But these are not simple one-to-one equivalents. By an unconscious psychological process which has been called "decomposition," the entire family group consisting of the son (hero), parents and siblings with their various attributes are dissolved and several other individuals invented. Onto these newly invented characters who are the ostensible characters in the story have been projected – at first glance, seemingly willy-nilly – a number of the original attributes of the various (now dis-membered) members of the family. In this sense each of the newly invented characters may possess composite attributes derived from those which originally belonged to one or another of the members of the family. The mental mechanism of identification is extremely important in trying to understand the source of the individual's absorption in the story or the games derived from it. While he identifies himself mainly with the hero, it is also true that at the same time and to a greater or lesser extent he is identifying with the other characters.

If one can assume further that every person in the story represents to a lesser extent some aspect of the hero in relation to those characters who also more obviously represent the father, mother and siblings, the elements of the western romance seem to fall into a more or less consistent pattern. As one might expect, the cowboy hero is overtly invested with the egosyntonic characteristics of the child in the family who aspires to quick but pseudo-adulthood, and his ego-alien tendencies are displaced onto others. Other personal attributes of the original family members are symbolized by animals and inanimate objects. The cowboy's faithful horse – the object of such solicitude, pride and respect – probably represents the hero's narcissistically overvalued phallus, and at the same time may represent the father as totem animal. The six-guns are obvious phallic symbols.

The dreamer of a dream, as its creator, has to be considered responsible for all that happens in his dream. Similarly, we must hold the hero of the western story "responsible" for every action and counter-action that takes place in the romance. The hero's compulsion to redress wrongs committed against the rancher — a father surrogate — suggests that there is a certain amount of guilt that he feels, although manifestly the crimes are attributed to the villain. Like these hostile tendencies toward the father, incestuous, oral and hostile tendencies toward the mother are also displaced mainly to the villain. The villain of the piece represents the bad father; bad, because it is father who deprives the narcissistic "king of the nursery" of his heart's desire, the good mother. In overwhelming the villain, our hero is simultaneously doing two things — he is reenacting the oedipal crime against the father and avenging both his father and himself. By rescuing the maiden — the mother, by the way, is forever young in the unconscious — the hero puts a stop to any lecherous hanky-panky which he suspects might be agitating the villain's mind. Since the hero has unconscious and forbidden designs on this maiden-mother himself, he must make doubly sure that these intentions are not carried out.

The hero's loyal companion represents another aspect of the hero as well as a brother-figure; sometimes he is like the hero's father. The hero both loves and depreciates him; always, however, the companion's wayward tendencies are kept under control, and the hero is reassured that he has nothing to fear from him, and that in fact he is always superior to him.

The good father is represented first and most often by the rancher, next by the benign but ineffective sheriff, and of course by the hero's own restitutive and protective virtues. The good mother is not clearly personified although sometimes the rancher has a wife who fulfills this role to a minor degree. In a sense the ranch itself represents the providing mother. The idealized mother is personified principally by the rancher's daughter or by the school ma'am; the seductive bad mother is the fickle mistress of the saloon keeper. All these women also represent to some extent the hero's own unacceptable feminine tendencies. Like the arch-villain himself, the disloyal son of the rancher personifies those ego-alien tendencies in the hero that are subject to the strongest repression.

The cowboy hero's arrival from nowhere at the beginning of each adventure suggests the child's feeling of mystery and confusion about his own origin.[3] In the typical ancient myth, and in the so-called family romance, the hero is a foundling, the long lost son of noble parents who have abandoned him to the care of beasts or a humble family. In the western legend it is significant that the code demands that no one express any curiosity about the identity, origin or parentage of the hero. His lonely existence at the beginning and at the end of each adventure is a commentary on the child's recurrent but vain wish to return to a blissful symbiosis with mother, to a childhood Garden of Eden from which he was exiled as a consequence of the awakened knowledge of sexual and hostile impulses.

What Ernest Jones[4] said of Hamlet also applies to the western legend; it is "a highly elaborated and disguised account of a boy's love for his mother, and consequent jealousy of and hatred for his father"; and, "the picture here presented of the son as avenger instead of the slayer of the father illustrates the highest degree of psychological repression, in which the true meaning of the story is concealed by the identical mechanisms that in real life conceal both repressed hostility and jealousy in so many families, namely, the exact opposite attitude of exaggerated solicitude, care and respect." The lowly Western also reflects a number of other universal personal

"Like you, I was a knight in shining armor, western style. The bad guys gunned me down when my back was turned. They say the good guy is not supposed to get killed, but everything seems to be mixed up. How did you get *your* unjust desserts, Podner?"

conflicts, some that precede, some that are concomitant with, and others that derive from the more obvious oedipal struggle. Among these is the apparent endeavor to get rid of both parents — the same wish that arises in the fantasy of the child when he is trying to establish his independence. Other interwoven conflicts grow out of the relationships of brother with brother, brother with sister, and sister with father. This multiple determination and these subsidiary conflicts permit the ego of the reader or viewer or participant in western sports some choice, as it were, in concentrating unconsciously, first upon one and then another of these universal conflicts.

One is justified in believing that these stereotyped western myths can serve an integrative educational function, especially for the young child, and that they are by no means entirely a passive, regressive or purposeless pastime. Like the military commander who engages his troups in tactical maneuvers with an imaginary or simulated enemy, the boy or child utilizes the framework of the Western to anticipate difficulties, to experiment and to seek socially acceptable and tolerable answers to his most urgent and pressing unconscious emotional conflicts. Toy pistols and a cowboy costume help him, momentarily at least, to believe it is possible to prevail not only over external enemies but over internal ones. The fact that grown men and to a lesser extent grown women also have been known to play these "cowboy and Indian" games and to practice the "quick-draw" points up the fact that the deepest and most universal yearnings of childhood are never completely repudiated.

NOTE

Acknowledgment is made to the *Psychoanalytic Quarterly* for permission to reprint parts of the author's article, The Stereotyped Western Story; Its Latent Meaning and Psychoeconomic Function, *24*:270, 1955.

FOOTNOTES

1. A brief account of Karl May and his works is to be found in the *Columbia Dictionary of Modern European Literature*. New York, Columbia, 1947, pp. 528-529.
2. Warshow, R.: The gentlemen with a gun; in *Encounters* (an anthology from the first ten years of the magazine, Spender, S., *et al.* [Eds.], sel. by Lasky, M.). New York, Basic Books, 1963, pp. 229-239.
3. Compare the nursery rhyme:
   "Where did you come from baby dear?
   "Out of the everywhere into here."
4. Jones, E.: *Hamlet and Oedipus*, New York, Norton, 1949.

HUNTING

STONEWALL B. STICKNEY

A CURIOUS MANUSCRIPT WAS DELIVERED to me not long ago, one I'd half expected would appear some day. The name and some fragments of the history of its unfortunate author, but little more, were known to me for many years. Now his memoirs, in a sense his testament, were to provide me the opportunity to analyze his hidden motives. I had often wondered what he was hunting for, and what he ultimately found.

Two tragic accidents brought the bulky manuscript to my hands. (Now, when I consider all that he wrote down, I have some feeling that he sent it to me expressly.) It is not an exaggeration to say "tragic" here, even if the actors in this drama were obscure people. When the mallard is shot down in all his swiftness, cleanly killed or slowly drowned, it is the end of the world. It is tragedy, even as when the cunning hunter dies or is himself shot down.

No mallard, no hunter, will ever see that particular world again.

Some years ago in the high water swamp of the Tombigbee, an aging and experienced turkey hunter was returning to camp about dusk with a big gobbler slung over his shoulder. He usually got his bird, and this one had been felled with a .222 slug at slightly over a hundred yards: his usual clear shot over an oat patch on the high ground. He had latterly grown so deaf that he now relied upon his tracking skill, his eyes and his rifle with its telescopic sight. There was no point in wasting time trying to hear a turkey gobble or fly off the roost.

The old man's grown son, hunting with a 12-gauge Greener double, must not have been so successful. No gunshot had been heard from the low swamp where he had been waiting hours to hear a turkey fly up to roost. He had in fact heard one, seen him fly up, and waited very still in a storm of mosquitoes till he could see the gobbler move behind a clump of Spanish moss. Then, after paddling across the deep slough on a log to get in range, he had fired, but no bird had fallen. Pondering, he recalled that maybe a quarter hour previously he had heard one soft clap, as of a felt hat against a man's thigh. Now it seemed only too clear that once again a sly old gobbler had outfoxed him, had seen him move. With one flap he had probably sailed a hundred yards, slanting soundlessly down like a buzzard from his perch.

With a wry expression and some obscene remarks about turkey hunting, the unsuccessful young turkey hunter had paddled back across the darkening water and started slogging back to camp. He was prepared for considerable rough humor at his expense when the time came to dry out his clothes and he had nothing to show.

Somehow the paths of the two hunters converged, one on the dry ridge, the other on the edge of the swamp walking soundlessly on the deep carpet of leaf mold. There was a rustle, the bronze glimpse of a turkey on the ridge, and a shot. When the son ran up the side of the ridge to get his bird, which had dropped instantly, he found his father dead.

The old hunter had died very suddenly and cleanly, struck behind the ear with a close patterned charge of #2 chilled shot. A fine bearded gobbler, already cold and showing no mark from the sudden blast, lay beside the dead man, who had pitched forward on his face. He was probably dead when he hit the ground. The leaves and twigs were undisturbed where he lay. His rifle with its scope was slung over his left shoulder, and one gaunt grey leg of the gobbler was still clutched in his right hand.

It was not an unheard-of hunting accident, and the officials concerned carried out a perfunctory and largely commiserative inquest. The death was accidental; there was no motive for murder that they could conceive of. Of course, the son was cleared. He didn't even lose his hunting license, since he was known to be a careful hunter. However, he did not seem to recover well and was evidently not comforted by the condolences he received, among them my own. Morose, and more solitary than ever, he kept to his room when he was not busy with his medical practice. For some time he didn't hunt at all, and when he resumed he would only hunt alone. This was the more striking since he now confined himself to duck hunting, which is enough work for at least two men anytime. There's the skiff, and the several dozen decoys to place in the icy water, and the unruly wind, and rowing, and the cutting of bamboo for a blind; and then there's the trouble of hauling it all back to shore when sundown comes. And however lovely the sky of dawn, however breathtaking the swing of teal and pintail, duck hunting is often chill, dull, lonely as all hell without a partner.

One freezing wet, grey day the ducks were moving nicely up and across the blustery north wind — miserable to be out in, and ideal because it kept them from rafting in the middle of the bay. That day the lonely hunter went forth long before dawn to his old blind in the marshes. He did not return. His skiff was found the next day, a mile or so down the bayou from his stool of decoys and his unfinished duck blind. The oars were neatly shipped — empty otherwise, and drifting.

There was some halfhearted dragging for the lost hunter's body, but the hunt was unsuccessful. Usually the bodies floated up later anyway, down the bay or against the causeway, driven by tides and north wind. This one was found much later by a fisherman's anchor, in deep water near the bend of the bayou where the man had been hunting. Now it was late spring, and whole families of shrimp, blue crab and catfish had by this time paid their last respects to the lonely hunter. The strength of their feeling for him had left little to show who this gleaming frame of bone had been in life.

There was little doubt now though, and the finding of the gun would confirm the identity that was almost certain. Where was it, and had it been fired? The remains had shown no sign of gunshot or powder burn, but so little was left. . . .

The gun was soon found in the mud near the marker where the fisherman had anchored. It was the same Greener double, slim, graceful, its engravings now embossed with barnacles and the stony tracks of sea worms. It had not been fired.

In a deep channel under a bank of bamboo, the body and the gun had lain in twelve feet of water. It now appeared that the hunter had rowed from his shallow blind toward the bank to cut more bamboo for his blind before daybreak. With gun in hand he had stepped toward the bank, into the black water. Somehow he had never come up again. As is customary in such accidents, the survivors of the deceased all recalled that he had been an excellent swimmer.

Strapped to the bony shoulders of this enigma was a stout canvas rucksack, of the sort commonly seen on the backs of hikers in Europe. Not standard equipment among duck hunters. The pack must have weighed sixty pounds or so, and it contained nothing useful to life. Three packets of, say, twenty pounds each were inside, two of them filled with #2 chilled shot.

The third was wrapped securely in several layers of oilskin and contained the bulky manuscript in question. It was written in a familiar scrawl on heavy waterproof chart paper in waterproof ink. The sacks of shot had no good reason to be on a hunter's back. Perhaps they had reminded him to stay down in the blind when the wise mallard, the shot-shy teal turned on the wind's edge. Or perhaps they had only made certain he would stay down at last.

The third sack — what was its purpose? The author had surely been concerned lest water wash away his history after claiming his life. He provided against that disaster as he had not against the others.

Perhaps he provided us with some clues about hunters, especially those Ahabs whose hunt is unfortunate, somehow doomed. About himself he left more puzzles than answers, so we shall try to content ourselves with analyzing that part of his strange life that flowed into hunting, into killing, and into the final dark waters.

For some reason the family of the deceased chose not to read the manuscript, or at any rate had it sent to me first. If he had ever confided in any person, it was in me, on rare occasions. At times, I had been his friend. Besides, the family guessed he must have lost his mind to have died in the clumsy and unnecessary fashion he seemed to have chosen. They never thought much of psychiatry, but they believed I might be interested in the document for obscure psychiatric reasons. The old turkey hunter had often quoted to me in his scoffing laugh, "That's the kind of doctor that don't help nobody!" This was alleged to be a comment an illiterate had made upon learning that the old man's brother, a professor of English literature, was not a medical doctor. So much for higher learning among turkey hunters.

According to my custom, I left the manuscript unread for some time, until it had aged sufficiently or I was ready to read it. Perhaps I wasn't sure, myself, that I wanted to know what my late friend had suffered. I already knew he was a man who had no faith, never told whom he loved, and had no devices to avoid thinking once he started. He used to say, "Once you start thinking, you're up the creek." Hunting alone in an indifferent universe. . . .

The manuscript, like the writer, turned out to be impersonal — available when sought out, at times very generous and helpful, but not to be known intimately. Like him, the testament was undisciplined, chaotic, sometimes poetic, often prolix — hence its bulk. It contained notes, plans, dreams, hopes, fears, guesses, theories, memories, anecdotes, with occasional snatches of old ballads he had loved. My friend had read widely, even deeply, in his planless illogical fashion, and at times some of his observations had an almost psychoanalytic flavor — psychoanalytic more in the manner of Groddeck than of Freud, be it said.

Since he was essentially a lonely hunter, I have chosen to relate to you those parts of his story that tell of seeking, finding, killing and missing. In some perverse way he had made it appear that true seeking and killing were both inseparable and insolubly antithetical. We must grant that he had explored both modes, sometimes simultaneously with the one of healing. He seemed, also, to harbor the same confusion about finding and missing. These confusions were accepted with a mocking stoicism or with the dire levity he had often aimed at himself and life in general. At times he called himself "the fitfully dangerous agent of the Audubon Society, a largely harmless bird watcher." Sometimes in the notes he referred to himself in the third person as "Salvo." Scattered associations seemed to tie in the name with saving and salvation. Then in other contexts he merged with the salvos of cannon. The most scornful reference made his name mean the salver, the soother or soothsayer, the quack, the faith healer who has little faith himself.

There were trial titles scribbled about the first page, titles such as "Hit or Miss?" "Memoirs of an Unsuccessful Hunter" and "Ecce Salvo."

Now I shall let him speak to you in his own words:

"For thirty years I have done my puzzled research on hunting, hunters and myself as a hunter. At first the field work was involuntary. If a boy didn't hunt in my hometown he might soon be suspected of secretly playing tennis, listening to classical music, or having an unhealthy interest in girls. Those were the depression days, too, and even a few grey squirrels or a rabbit were appreciated, as were the occasional doves, shot out of a pine tree with my .410 dogleg.

"My father, of course, was the successful hunter, and spent most of his spare time at it, providing us with bearded turkey gobbler, venison, doves, quail and his favorite game — wild duck.

"One of his recurrent jibes had it that when I was born, my mother turned her face away, murmuring, 'My God, another duck hunter.'

"But she sure knew how to cook game. I can recall Sunday breakfasts of doves smothered in brown gravy, with hot biscuits aplenty, as well as grits to put the gravy on. Sometimes, eating squirrels prepared the same way, we ate the jaw muscles then cracked the skull with a knife and ate the brains. Now, incredible.

"We weren't raised to be squeamish. A fair amount of what today I'd call 'sadism' was then allowed or encouraged. Every summer from age seven to eight on I spent the long hot days killing mockingbirds. With a slim hickory slingshot my father made for me I shot all manner of lovely songbirds as well as woodpeckers, jaybirds, pigeons and swallows when I could. They fell from our fig trees, from the scuppernong arbor, the mulberry tree, the pecan and the wild cherry trees in our huge backyard. The pigeons were tough, but I occasionally knocked one from the roof of our tall two story house. Some of the birds I ate, but not many. Mostly I killed for the joy of killing — like a weasel in a hen house. Once I killed a fine brown thrush at a hundred feet as he sat singing in my neighbor's backyard. This was poaching, and sometimes got me into trouble, the same as breaking windows or roof slates. One time I astonished myself by knocking a flying catbird out of the air some fifty feet off the ground. In those days things were simple and I was a successful hunter.

"Where did I get *permission* to kill? Obviously, from my father. I suspect most hunters today were taught by their fathers. I mean, mostly, permitted. The rest of the people, those who shudder at the killers, have hired killers at the stockyard or poultry farm. Now I remember our cook wringing the chicken's neck till it came off, or rather the chicken did, and ran and flopped and spouted blood for a good while before it kicked and lay still. Those days it was clearer that the women killed too, and did it to feed me, so it couldn't be too bad. I doubt if I ever thought that then. I just looked forward to doing the next neck-wringing myself, then scalding, plucking and drawing the hen as I'd been taught.

"Once I read a memoir by an old poacher. From time to time it said in heavy print, *'I shall poach until I die.'* That's how I feel about hunting. I know too that every hunter worth a damn is a good conservationist and is also ready to poach or overshoot his limit, or take game out of season any time he thinks he can get away with it. We're all of us outlaws, we know we're doing something savage already, and our law-abiding tendencies are not especially powerful when temptation comes. It's a wonder we don't kill one another more often, considering this lawless strain. It does happen often enough. (The government says it's fine, as long as your target is a foreigner, or someone described as a condemned murderer.) Speaking of that, one of my clearest memories of hunting shows me about eleven or twelve years old out in the woods walking behind my father. I'm trying to keep up, to step quietly and to look and listen around me, all very intensely, and my pulse is fast. At the same time, somewhere in my mind the thought is forming, all of itself and without dramatics or horror: 'I could blow the back of his head off from right here. Nobody would know. "Some fool shirt-tail boy going along with his safety off and his trigger finger inside the guard; must have tripped and fired." Never get caught.' Only years later, when I read all about Oedpus and Hamlet, did I wonder how I could have had that thought so easily, with so little fanfare or battle within. Perhaps by the same device we use when we kill lovely birds and harmless deer — we keep our feelings separate from our intent, we act swiftly and coldly. Later the skinning and dressing or drawing and quartering of the prey are carried out with almost surgical detachment and without revulsion. My young friends and I served our apprenticeship of several years picking ducks and doves, skinning squirrels and gutting the carcasses for our fathers when they returned from the hunt. Our fathers gave one another long, drawling understated accounts of their experiences, their hits and misses. We understood they were letting one another brag, and we learned how this was to be done too, so we wouldn't sound like fools when we started bragging on our own guns, our marksmanship or our luck.

"My best friend's father sent to England for his son's first shotgun, a Greener, and it arrived with the boy's name engraved on the rib. Old Mister Nick said, with a knowing twinkle, 'Now, son, here's a gun you can bring out in any company and never be ashamed!' I had wanted a Greener ever since, but it took about twenty-five years for me to find one. It appeared after months of scanning the want ads, and came at a very good price. When my old man saw it, he examined it narrowly, threw it up and swung it, and said 'Some people have all the luck.'

"He started a pretty nice Greener collection himself not long after that. One day he sent me a postcard saying, 'Don't think I've gone crazy when you receive the Greener I'm sending. It's the mate to the one you have, and I missed a turkey with it last week.' I was properly appreciative and later learned that he had talked a fellow collector out of an even prettier model to replace the one he sent. From my now advanced state of analytic knowledge it is hard to tell whether he was competing with me or I with him. Both, no doubt, but I see now that both of us could have showed more restraint and things might have ended differently.

" 'Model' recurs to my mind, and models, and the calling of guns, like boats, by female names. 'She' or 'Old Betsy' turn up quite often in the hunter's language. This is odd, considering the plausible notion that guns in dreams are phallic symbols. I never needed an analyst to tell me that; the times I have dreamed dismally of shooting at some big animal, only to have the slug fall harmlessly out of the barrel, taught me all I wanted to know about that equation. Or just watching the gun fancier oiling and stroking his piece before or after a hunt. Once I heard the old man say about an especially beautiful double with gold chasings on the breach, 'I don't shoot it much. I just like to take it out and pet it once in awhile.' This would be a middle-aged or elderly hunter, not quite so keen on killing as formerly, but full of memories of old hunts and hunting companions, famous shots at long distances and hoary jokes at the expense of those who missed their buck and had their shirt-tails cut off when they got back to camp. Youngsters and fools.

"And why is it always a buck or a gobbler down here, not a doe or a turkey hen? Local hunters just shake their heads wisely when the yankee conservationists prove that every year thousands of female animals starve to death through over-population. Their people shoot at does and turkey hens and get away with it, but it doesn't set well with the hunters down here. Sometimes it makes me feel we're dreaming, and not sure what we're shooting. Or whom? It begins to remind me of things I've read about totem animals, totem feasts, the Eucharist and taboos. I remember too, that Eskimo women weren't allowed to go on a whale hunt — the whales would be mortally insulted and never return to the coast to be hunted. Down here I never saw a woman on a hunt, but once up north on a goose-shoot on James Bay I saw one. All the men in the party shut up immediately when she arrived with her sheepish husband. There were no more jokes, no customary affectionate obscenities, no belching and farting aloud, no big drinking and eating, and no fun. The taboo had been broken and the male ritual was not to be.

"And if the woman had remained, but invisibly, she would have heard all those happy noises of boyish relaxation and camaraderie, but little or no talk of women, or of adult sex. Much talking and joking and pleasurable, emphatic enactment of all the other body functions, preferably publicly, would have been heard instead. Playful invitations and nicknames referring to homosexual acts would have been offered from time to time (especially on drunken deer hunts), and nobody's masculinity would seem to have been impugned by all this loose talk. To my knowledge the suggestions were never acted upon, at least during the hunt, but the openness and innocence of them were astonishing.

"Perhaps they only seem so now, after a few recent years of reading and observing, just as it now seems hilarious that many people down here will call a man a sissy or an 'Aunt Puss,' and never imagine that he may be a practicing homosexual! Still less can they imagine that such virile characters as hunters and athletes could harbor such tendencies. Their manly recreations proclaim their virility and aggressiveness.

"Maybe I started being curious about this on one of my first deep-sea fishing trips. The fishermen were camped in tents on the beach, full of beer and merriment, and I saw a curious scene in one tent. A man pretended to have sexual relations with a fat man who lay on his back pretending to be a woman while the onlookers cheered them on, 'Give him leg-room Bubber!' My old man was embarrassed and pulled me out of the tent without comment. I knew he couldn't speak of such matters.

"There is some pristine quality about all those memories that reminds me of the happy days in the big back field, with all boys, when girls were despised and avoided. Our sexual talk and games and exposures were all with each other — no Eve intruded on this Eden of naked Tarzans. And in later years my father and other men on weekend deer drives would jokingly refer to having escaped from wife and home as if his companions were all accomplices in truancy.

"No question, this return to boyhood, and to the customs of the primitive hunting pack or horde, was a great part of our pleasure, but there were many others. Sheer beauty, of the woods, its sounds and smells, the sky, the animals — this was always a deep part of it about which we were mostly too shy or inarticulate to tell each other. The stillness, wildness, strange timeless primeval quality of a Tombigbee swamp, where you could walk soundlessly among gumtrees and cypress and see a quarter mile. Or sit all day on a stump in a slough and watch a family of raccoons washing and dipping their food in the water's edge not over thirty feet away.

"Some of the loveliest times I recall were fleeting chances to kill when I failed to shoot — I stood transfixed, gazing at the animal or I fired and missed an obvious kill.

"Once on a deer drive I deceived myself by becoming over-impressed with a club rule that anyone firing at anything other than a deer would be fined five dollars for disturbing the drive. (The Cheyenne had a similar custom on buffalo hunts, but with much stiffer penalties). As the baying of hounds, the shouts and tin pan clatter of the Negro drivers drew near, a large fat woodcock walked up in range, stared and walked on. A few moments and many pulse-beats later a magnificent pearl-grey wildcat padded up within eight feet of me; he gave what seemed an ironic look at my motionless face and form, then silently disappeared. As usual, no buck came by me, only a succession of fleet does and a spotted fawn. Judging from my heartrate, fine tremor and my pleasure, nobody would have known that this was another unsuccessful hunt of mine.

"A few days later I was on a deer stand in a swamp just forty yards over the ridge from an oat patch. I could just hear the dogs coming when they were drowned out by a rush of heavy wings and a soft thud. There on a log at close range was a huge old gobbler with a red blue neck and a long beard on his breast. I froze. He looked at me cynically, with one eye, then with the other. I moved one finger to click off my safety and he was gone in a thunder of feathers and speed. This fiasco I reported to no one, for it was too personal. It was the only real shot I'd ever had at a gobbler. He was too beautiful.

"The beauty of that moment was marred a few instants later. Moving over toward an irregular, noisy thrashing, up the hill from me, I saw a wounded spike buck crawling through a barbed wire fence. One snap shot at his neck and he went down, seemingly, but disappeared over the edge of the rise. When I arrived at the fence I saw a strange and ugly sight. The stricken animal, breathing and moaning desperately, was pushing itself across the muddy oat patch. Both its forelegs were broken. My friend Gideon, who had broken the first foreleg with a bad shot, came panting up just then and we each urged the other to go put the animal out of his misery. I recall firing two barrels at close range at the buck's neck, and missing him clean. My friend, torn between laughter and revulsion, had to finish him off with birdshot at a range of inches because he and I had run out of buckshot. The aftermath for me was something close to nausea, but not in the stomach. All over.

"Later when another hunter arrived with a station wagon to haul the carcass to camp, he got stuck in the soft patch and it took hours of work to get the vehicle out. Meanwhile, we recalled that the weekend's whiskey supply was in this wagon, and by the time we had torn down a board fence and an old shed to build a causeway out of the mud, all of us were obliviously drunk and hilarious. Somehow, since that time I've had little zest for deer hunting, and haven't killed another one. They do look at you.

"Now I recall my most obvious miss on a close range shot at a buck; it was the day I saw the wildcat. I'd just heard a shot from the nearby stand of Harvey, but no halloo came and I figured he had missed. A half minute later I saw a magnificent buck with a rack like a rocking chair picking his way toward me, slowed to a walk. Just asking to be shot. About thirty yards away he paused for five or ten seconds, in profile, a clear shot through an opening the size of a window. I took careful aim at his neck and fired. He ducked his head and disappeared. When I walked over to his tracks I was dumbfounded to find not one drop of blood. I had carefully fired right over him. Harvey came over shortly after I returned to my stand and we commiserated, with some half truths about how we'd missed the buck. I was not at ease with this man, since he had been my successful rival in a very painful love affair some years before. In fact, I preserved the amenities only because he was a friend of my father. Come to think of it, my father had been unusually patronizing and obnoxious earlier on this hunt. Only now does it occur to me why I had to miss that particular buck. It would have felt too much like murder. I didn't deserve the pleasure.

"A psychiatrist friend of mine I used to shoot trap with had missing all figured out. When you were 'on' you were aggressive, out to kill without reservation, feeling cocky, cheerful and murderous. Even though the targets were clay pigeons, I think he was right. When you were 'off,' missing frequently, you were dubious, tense, depressed, and, as he said, 'ambivalent' about killing. Perhaps this also meant what I've puzzled about: confusion as to what we were shooting at, or whom. This isn't the sort of idea I could discuss with the old man or with other hunters. Some of my friends who don't hunt might be interested. I always had the two sets of friends. Perhaps the successful hunters have no such division in their friendships, or in their feelings about killing.

"Anyway, I'd much rather shoot doves, geese, ducks; something that flies by swiftly, beautifully and impersonally. It doesn't look at you, and you never hear it breathe or moan, or see it bleed. When it falls, it is usually dead. The fall itself is a beautiful thing, a sudden and artless surrender to death and gravity, as if without regrets. From my earliest days with the slingshot I recall the sheer joy of killing in this fashion, and the thrill of pleasure when I picked up the fallen bird. Only very gradually and secretly did I realize that a great part of my pleasure was in capturing beauty, wildness, mystery. I could not be it, seize it alive and question it, or get close to it. Yet in killing it I had the brief illusion of capturing beauty. Perhaps later, when I sometimes ate the bird, I imbibed beauty. Thus the 'savage' eats the heart of the lion in order to be imbued with his courage. I have begun to understand even such strange people as the birdwatchers and the former hunters who now mount telephoto cameras on gunstocks and go 'turkey hunting' with them. Even the Catholics, who absorb godliness from the communion Host, are kin to me in this magic.

"Once on a goose-shoot for Canadas on the coast of North Carolina, I saw a snow goose flying some distance away, and called him in to sit unharmed among our decoys. Our guide was astonished because I was a 'sport,' not a guide, and I logically could not have done what he'd just seen and heard me do with my voice. For some time I held off telling him I had learned it from the Cree Indians of James Bay, where even the small children could do it. I was savoring the feeling of magic, of talking with the wild goose, of *being* one. This must be very close to what an expert turkey caller feels as he talks a gobbler in toward his blind to be shot. Or the skillful duck callers of Stuttgart, Arkansas, who can make mallards peel out of a fast flying 'V' like dive bombers, and pitch in through the pin oaks to be shot – all by a few eloquent quacks on wooden callers.

"And the big game hunters, the safari fanciers, what are they after, going clear to Africa to shoot animals they can't eat? Then they bring the remains back at enormous expense, courtesy of some London taxidermist who must be a millionaire, and hang the heads on the wall. With a little encouragement they will show films proving they were there and had indeed shot the lion and the buffalo, the leopard, the elephant, the guileless kudu. They developed an interest in prize heads, horns, tusks, and recalled the measurements more fondly than golfers do their score on a tough course.

"When I questioned my psychiatrist friend who went on safari, he soon understood I was envious. Then he added, 'Shooting kudu is *good!* Have you never heard of sublimation, displacement, projection – things like that?' I assured him I indulged freely in all of them when I could do so unobserved, but still had no urge to go kill a lion, *et al,* under the illusion that I'd be challenging the beast on even terms. (This seems to be one of the myths of big game hunters.)

"If you'll read magazines catering to 'outdoorsmen,' you'll find some hunters fancying themselves endangered by moose, elk, old fat bears and crazed grouse attacking from behind. Now, some of this is true, no question. White hunters in Africa fairly commonly do get killed or maimed by lions, buffalo and rhinos. Some men, like Hemingway, seek out such dangers as a form of transcendence. They live, if successful, in the fullness of a timeless moment wherein there is no doubt or weakness, but the clean joy of doing well the only thing there is to do. It is a substitute for war or the bullfight or the prize ring – ordinary life is too tame beside it. The joy is the danger. The close brush with death – then, giving instead of receiving death. Even the boy with the slingshot knows this joy of killing. It asserts his life, his strength, his invulnerability.

"The old, the tired, the jaded know – a different pleasure. When they kill, it does not assert their springing life, it denies their coming death. Or, it denies they are mostly dead already. Quite a bit of this sham comes through in Robert Ruark's writing about big game hunting, as compared with that of Hemingway or Corbett or Hunter.

"And what of the stories and movies like 'Francis McComber' — all those heroic triangles where the poor weak husband is outshot by the white hunter and is lucky to escape with his life, much less his wife? These seem to get funnier every year. They seem more and more like reruns of the childhood love triangles, and the noble ambition to kill the old man and have his wife. Of course, the author somehow gets us on his side, i.e., the hunter's side.

"This reminds me of old Bob Larkin, who was a taboo-breaker among hunters. I was turkey hunting at his lodge once when he casually mentioned that he and his mistress often had come there together for the weekend. 'I never heard of taking a woman on a turkey hunt,' I remarked. Bob smiled gently and explained, 'When I go hunting I like to take along everything I need.'

"For some reason this recalls the 'Hunting of the Snark' to my mind, and the mysterious refrain: 'They sought it with thimbles, they sought it with care, they pursued it with forks and with hope. They threatened its life with a railway share; they charmed it with smiles and with soap.' What was 'It' that we all hunted from boyhood to old age? I remember in the poem one of the hunters suddenly disappeared — he had become the hunted. 'It' was a Boojum, a beast dreaded by all, and like Moby Dick, indestructible.

"Sometimes I've heard it in the clamor of geese flying south, rousing me out of sleep at midnight as they flew low under scudding black clouds. Once or twice I've felt it on the end of my line when a big fish sounded deeply, nearly pulled me overboard, and snapped the line. The language of it is unequivocal and fierce, like the something in myself that dreams strangely and loves to kill, sing, dance, fight, or make love to a strange woman.

"I see myself and fellow hunters at all our ages from boyhood to the time of the old palsied man, Mister Frank, carried out to the deer stand by colored servants. He got his buck every year till he died. Some of us sought it in hunting, some in war, some in whiskey, some in women. Or we got greedy and tried all of them, like a gamehog.

"The mortal stricken fall of the mockingbird from the original fig tree recurs to me insistently. Whom did he mock, and why me, armed as I was with my sling? That small David knew no mercy. He would sit for hours wide-eyed and still under the fig tree, under the scuppernong arbor. He was as mindlessly receptive and scanning as a photographic plate or a radar receiver. The entire pattern of leaves, twigs, green light and blue shadow was imprinted on his retinae, on the still surface of his soul. The slightest tremor of a twig, even the quiver of a dragonfly on a leaf's edge, would infallibly focus the scanner like a deadly gunsight on the moving form. The lethal thud of the pebble against the grey feathered breast or neck was so swift and automatic as to be an afterthought. Then 'It' burst forth from inside and ran to seize the warm body, sometimes wet with hot blood, or still pulsating. The fierce joy then was and remains indescribable. It may be a thing in itself, like orgasm — but so different. Once, in such a mood, I bit the head off a bird I'm not sure was alive or dead.

"There was something there below and beyond the joy of killing for its own sake, way past that positively sensual part. It was something primeval, something that was Mind, searching. Maybe my first animal ancestor, detecting through his very skin the pattern of light and shade — then the slightest intrusion on the pattern and the sudden, reflex, probably sluggish pursuit of the prey. This was thought's beginning: first, the near-blind search and struggle to catch food. Then, the birth of something like meaning from the learning of patterns. Finally, thought itself — the search for cause and continuity, motion, discontinuity, pattern and change, cause of motion; the search for meaning regardless of consequence of gain or loss of sustenance! This is beyond me, but it won't let me alone . . . Mind.

"Now it reminds me of the nameless fear I have known in the woods at dusk or after dark. Or even in the daylight, still-hunting the harmless squirrel at Faun Luce and yet feeling my heart pounding in my throat fit to choke me. The mosquitos sang insanely. They never seemed to bother my old man, or else the fumes of his pipe kept them about a foot from his face. They assaulted my eardrums and rushed to be inhaled, swallowed or smashed against my neck. 'That pounding in my throat sounds like a buck crashing through the woods. I don't seem to belong here in this quiet oak grove. While I watch and wait to kill something, my hands tremble, my mouth is dry. What *am* I going to kill, feeling so excited and glad?'

"It was important in those days not to waste shells; to be a good shot, to come back to camp with something to show for every shot. Pride was at stake, and the wish to be praised by my father and his friends. God knows that praise was scarce enough, and ridicule was there in plenty anytime.

"But those small matters were not the thing that eluded me, at times shook me all over, alone at dusk. As first-dark deepened, the harsh scolding notes of ground birds, the distant cry of an owl, the merest twig snap and rustle of dry leaves were magnified with menace. The dark and the depth of woods grew vast and trackless as I grew smaller and humbler and more vulnerable.

"Strangeness, wildness, darkness, space, nothingness. These trees and thickets, low swamps and piny woods ridges knew me not. The world entire, the whole dark universe was indifferent to me, to my very life; pure luck if I survived this time. Great gratitude to be back near the fire, and food. Never mind the jokes. . . .

"At dark, the hunter, who deals death, becomes the hunted. No, he *knows,* for the few agonizing instants he can bear to contemplate the truth, that he too is doomed, marked to be slain, he knows not when. Then his godgame of holding life and death in his own hands is over.

"In the dark are strange lives with feral eyes and claws and teeth, to whom his life is nothing. Just a little smaller and he'd be bitten through the neck and delicately devoured by a weasel, without remorse. This fear of death becomes the fear of what is stranger still — life.

"Hunting means a long time alone, time to think, daydream, remember — or to merge with the woods and your own sensations. Even on the communal dove shoot or the feudal deer drive, the hunter is alone for hours. This is a great solace, especially in a time and country where solitude is not highly regarded or easily found.

"But it can be terribly lonely in a solitary duck blind, with the north wind to talk to, and your thoughts. I notice I no longer say we. I'll try to recall it, the feeling of being with — someone. We stand, sit, crouch, kneel motionless for hours. Waiting for that change, sound, motion. If we relax our alertness or get up to stretch or urinate, that moment is the time when the clever animal appears and is gone again before we can reach the gun.

"The wind blows, hands and feet go numb with cold and stillness, joints cramp, stomach growls for food, for love. Surely these torments and trials, these proofs by ordeal that we are fit to join the company of men, surely they must toughen the candidate for initiation, for the universal hazing, for life's indifference? Or, as my psychiatric friend might say, these rigors must 'augment our ego strength, or develop autonomous ego functions and strong character traits' to a high degree? Patience, independence, courage? I am not so sure.

"It has seemed to me that when disaster strikes the hunter down, he is not prepared against it, any more than the next man.

"What am I hunting for?

"What am I waiting here for?"

This was the inconclusive and wondering, not to say pessimistic way the manuscript ended. There were no dates, so it was impossible to say how closely connected in time were the last thoughts inscribed and the final act in Salvo's career. He was timeless, as always.

EPILOGUE

The time has come to confess to the reader that I have no intention of analyzing this hunter. At least, not in public. That would be an impertinence to his memory and might turn out to be entirely too personal, besides. He has analyzed himself and his melancholy history right before our eyes. Let him who has eyes to see do his own hunting, and he will find what he will find.

If he is a successful hunter, he'll find what he was seeking. If, like our unfortunate and lonely hunter, he is not successful — then perhaps he will learn something from his history. He may learn to consider deeply a crucial question: What are you hunting for?

". . . and if I can't get rid of my frustrations by bagging a big, old cotton-picking elk, maybe I ought to shoot my wastrel son, Ralphie, when I get home!"

FISHING

VIGGO W. JENSEN AND DOUGLAS A. SARGENT

On any summer day an observer hovering in a helicopter high above almost any body of water on earth could see small craft, some anchored, some slowly crisscrossing the water's surface. They contain motionless figures in characteristic hunched positions. The adjacent shoreline, jetties, docks and wharves are dotted with other figures frozen in similar attitudes. Dropping lower, the observer could see that most of them are male. Their faces are fixed in uniform, rapt expressions. They are not paralyzed, for they stir occasionally. They can be seen to breathe. In their hands are poles, long and short, with thin lines attached which dangle in the water, at whose heaving surface the men stare, entranced. What can be wrong with them? Well, nothing, really. These men (and an estimated 30,000,000 others like them in North America alone) are engaged in one of the most popular forms of recreation: sport fishing.

Abandoning his helicopter for a jeep or a pack-horse, the observer could explore the globe's wilderness areas where he would find fishermen of a different sort than those whose frozen forms he had seen from the air. These men are pursuing the fish into remote hiding places. From a submarine he could see yet more venturesome men with spears in their hands chasing the elusive prey into the very depths, at great risk to themselves.

Sport fishing is almost exclusively a male activity. Those addicted to the sport (for intense, even intoxicated devotion is characteristic of fishermen) can be divided into two broad groups: the "still fishermen," who sit and let the fish come to them, and the "moving fishermen," who pursue the quarry.

If these broad groups are further subdivided according to *modus operandi* (jig fishermen, trollers, fly casters, spear fishermen etc.) they can be arranged along a gradient from passive to active. The gradient also corresponds, roughly, to the inner mental state of the fishermen while they are fishing. The more sedentary the fisherman, the more he tends to be engrossed in fantasy; the more active the fisherman, the more he tends to act out the content of his inner world.

WHY SPORT?

Radcliffe cites archeological evidence which shows that the origin of fishing is "Neolithic, certainly post-Paleolithic" and, further, that "the spear, line, rod flourish synchronously . . . about 3500 B.C."[1]

No one can tell precisely when this life-sustaining activity first was transformed into a sport. Many other human activities which originally served to sustain life tend to persist in altered, symbolic or degraded form (often as recreations) long after they have ceased to play any obvious role in man's vital economy. It is likely that hunting and fishing could become forms of recreation only when food production advanced to a stage where freedom from constant foodgathering allowed time for play. Thus, Stone Age warfare became shot-putting, hammer-throwing, boxing and wrestling; fighting with sword and bow became fencing and archery; jousting became polo, etc. Swords were not simply beaten into plowshares; rather, swordsmanship became a game. This peaceful transformation is always tentative and in danger of being reversed; Wellington said that the Battle of Waterloo was won on the playing fields of Eton. How easily sport threatents to revert to war is shown in this example:

> Bluefish are warriors of the first order, and when they are in action, it would be impossible to restrain my boys and myself from fitting our boat with the proper weapons and provisions and cruising out to sea for a couple of broadsides.[2]

But why should a once-vital activity linger on like some vestigial organ whose function is no longer appropriate? Dangerous, exhausting feats of

WARNING

FISHING POX

VERY CONTAGIOUS TO ADULT MALES

SYMPTOMS: Continual complaints as to the need of fresh air, sunshine and relaxation. Patient has blank expression, sometimes deaf to wife and kids. Frequent checking of tackle catalogs. Hangs out in the Sporting Goods Stores longer than usual. Secret night phone calls to fishing pals. Mumbles to self. Lies to everyone. NO KNOWN CURE.

TREATMENT: Medication is useless. Disease is not fatal. Victim should go fishing as often as possible.

Courtesy of Komic Kards, Pan American Pub. Corp., P.O. Box 717, North Miami, Florida.

skill and endurance are easy enough to understand when they put food in the belly or clothes on the back, but once the threats of starvation and similar dangers recede, why doesn't this anachronistic activity simply disappear? Why does it survive in altered form as a sport? Why does an otherwise sensible man spend hundreds of hours and a lot of money in order to pursue a sport described with only moderate exaggeration in the following document?

We will attempt an answer to these questions by exploring the psychological meaning of fishing to the fisherman, uncovering some concealed (unconscious) motivations and describing some of the hidden purposes which sport fishing serves in man's *psychological* economy. We will submit evidence drawn from literature, films, myths, jokes, cartoons, as well as material from clinical psychoanalysis.[3]

WHAT IS SPORT FISHING?

Despite variations which often have ritualistic significance for the fisherman, most forms of sport fishing have these features in common:[4]

1. A fish is tricked (or persuaded) into biting a baited hook, is caught by the mouth and pulled from the water.

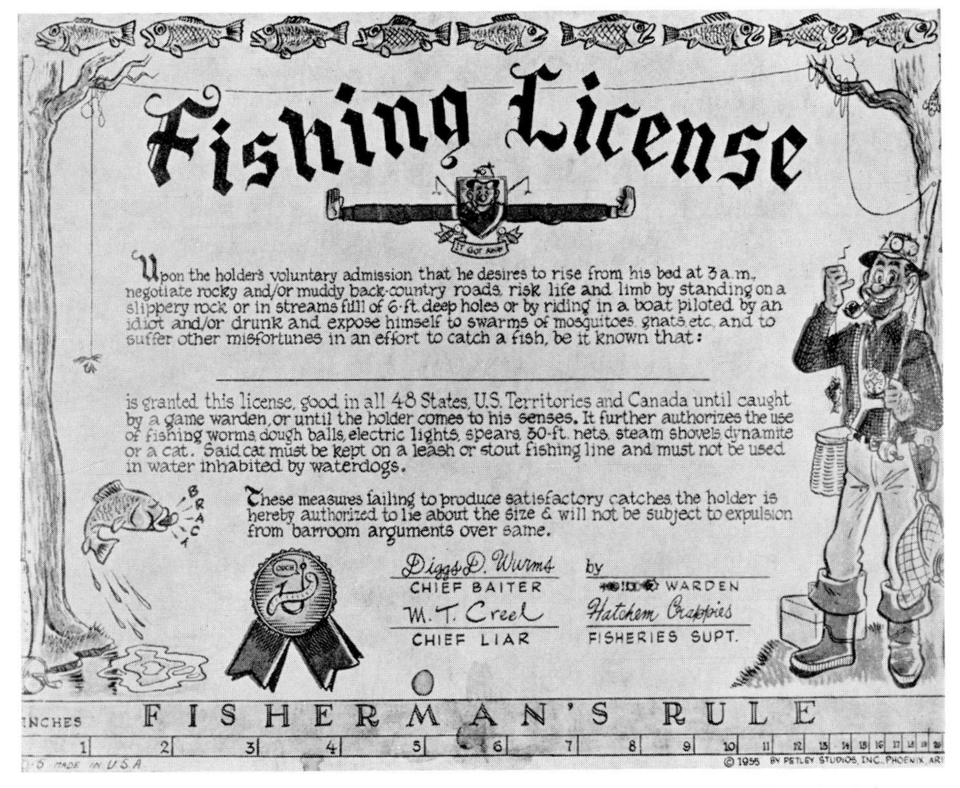

Fishing License

Upon the holder's voluntary admission that he desires to rise from his bed at 3 a.m., negotiate rocky and/or muddy back-country roads, risk life and limb by standing on a slippery rock or in streams full of 6-ft. deep holes or by riding in a boat piloted by an idiot and/or drunk and expose himself to swarms of mosquitoes, gnats, etc. and to suffer other misfortunes in an effort to catch a fish, be it known that:

____

is granted this license, good in all 48 States, U.S. Territories and Canada until caught by a game warden, or until the holder comes to his senses. It further authorizes the use of fishing worms, dough balls, electric lights, spears, 30-ft. nets, steam shovels, dynamite or a cat. Said cat must be kept on a leash or stout fishing line and must not be used in water inhabited by waterdogs.

These measures failing to produce satisfactory catches, the holder is hereby authorized to lie about the size & will not be subject to expulsion from barroom arguments over same.

Diggs D. Wurms
CHIEF BAITER

M. T. Creel
CHIEF LIAR

by ________________
WARDEN

Hatchem Crappies
FISHERIES SUPT.

INCHES F I S H E R M A N ' S R U L E

1 2 3 4 5 6 7 8 9 10 11 12 13 14 15 16 17 18 19 20

MADE IN U.S.A. © 1955 BY PETLEY STUDIOS, INC., PHOENIX, ARI

Courtesy of "Fishing License," copyright 1955 by Petley Studios, Inc., Phoenix, Arizona.

2. In order to equalize the struggle between himself and the fish, restrictions (such as limiting the number and kind of hooks, strength of line, etc.) are placed upon the fisherman which reduce his effectiveness.
3. In order to guarantee that his efforts cannot be regarded as having any purpose except that of sport, limitations are placed on the number of fish he may catch. (The elite among sportsmen release their catch unharmed.)

WHY IS FISHING FUN?

The excitement, the relaxation, the pleasure of fishing cannot be explained by any of the superficial characteristics of the sport (fresh air, enjoyment of nature, thrill of the chase, etc.), nor by the value of the catch (fly-caught salmon often cost their captors hundreds of dollars a pound). To understand the nature of the joys of angling we must look below the surface where we can discover the hidden forces which give this activity its unique intensity and zest. When we do this, we can see that fishing is a *game* providing multiple opportunities for gratification of a variety of unconscious psychological needs. These needs find indirect gratification through an activity which lends itself uniquely to their symbolic expression. Fishing facilitates the acting out, or the discharge through fantasy, of derivatives of unsatisfied infantile desires which have persisted into adult life as unconscious, repressed tendencies.[5]

The relatonship between fishing and fantasy is well known:

> Padding swiftly along the old trail — over windfalls, under others, I sometimes recapture the fantasies of my boyhood; once again, perhaps, I am a lithe young Indian brave — the seventh son of Chief Booze-In-The-Face, a modest lad who can wheel and shoot the eye out of a woodcock at seventy paces — now bound riverward to capture a great copper-hued trout for a demure, copper-hued maiden, or more sensibly, I am returning from the river simply to catch the copper-hued maiden herself.[6]

What is not so well understood — and what we hope to show — is that these fantasies receive their energy from the fisherman's need to express, in disguised form, the adult residuals of several great issues which once confronted him and all other children. These issues are (1) the infant's primal attachment to his mother and the subsequent need to separate from her and establish his own separate identity; (2) the biological mysteries of sex and reproduction; (3) the child's wish for exclusive possession of his mother against the rivalry of his father and siblings (the "Oedipus complex"). The sophisticated observer can see, disguised in the sport of fishing, derivatives of the infant's struggles to master these issues.

THE FISHERMAN AND HIS APPETITES

Often the lunch the fisherman packs in the morning outweighs the catch he brings home at night. That fishing affords vicarious satisfaction of the fisherman's hunger through identification with the hungry fish is implied in the joking comment often heard in tackle stores: "That lure looks so good I could eat it myself." Fishermen have a legendary mania for collecting lures, and their choice of lures is more often determined by personal taste than by any known principles of fish biology. Manufacturers of fishing tackle utilize this phenomenon in their advertising.

Courtesy of "Tenite" advertisement.

Hemingway's classic story, *The Old Man and the Sea,* is rich in allusions to the gratification of the fisherman's appetite through identification with the feeding fish. In fact, at times, the images of the two fuse and the fisherman too eats raw fish. With a gourmet's attention to detail, he describes the lure that is to deceive the great marlin and is to be his undoing:

> Each bait hung head down with the shank of the hook inside the bait fish, tied and sewed solid and all the projecting part of the hook, the curve and the point,

Courtesy of Larier, L., You've Got Me on the Hook, Dodd, Mead & Co., N.Y., 1954, p. 47 (Millar cartoon).

> was covered with fresh sardines. Each sardine was hooked through both eyes so that they made a half-garland on the projecting steel. There was no part of the hook that a great fish could feel which was not sweet smelling and good-tasting.[7]

Then the Old Man exhorts, pleads, teases and cajoles the great fish to take the bait, like a mother trying to get a reluctant baby to take his food:

> ". . . Eat them, fish. Eat them. Please eat them. How fresh they are and you down there six hundred feet in that cold water in the dark. Make another turn in the dark and come back and eat them."
>
> He felt the light delicate pulling and then a harder pull then a sardine's head must have been more difficult to break from the hook. Then there was nothing.

"Come on," the old man said aloud. "Make another turn, just smell them. Aren't they lovely? Eat them good now and then there is the tuna. Hard and cold and lovely. Don't be shy fish. Eat them."

He waited with the line between his thumb and his finger, watching it and the other lines at the same time for the fish might have swum up or down. Then came the same delicate pulling touch again.

"He'll take it," the old man said aloud. "God help him to take it . . ."[8]

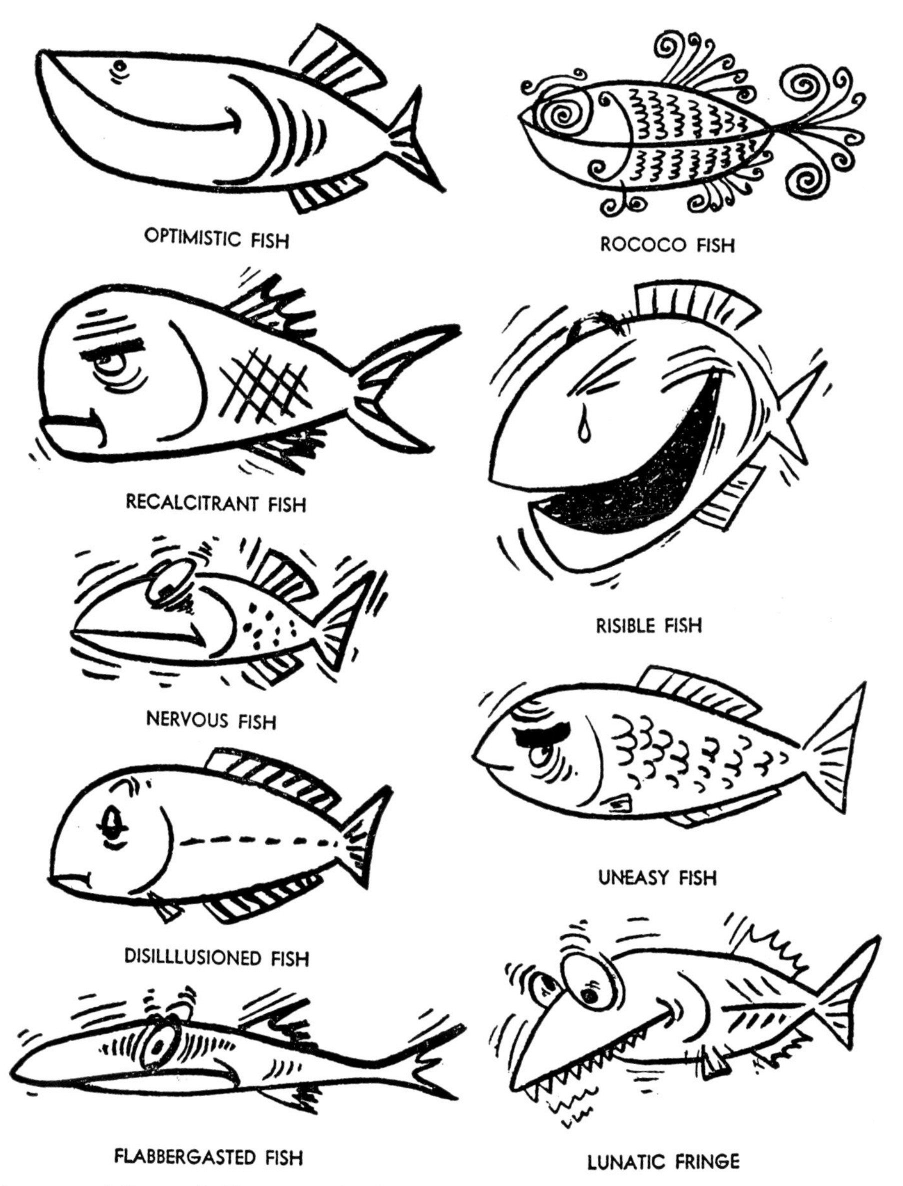

Courtesy of Zern, ed., How to Tell Fish from Fishermen, D. Appleton-Century Co., Inc., N. Y., 1947, p. 5.

Another of Hemingway's stories, "The Big Two Hearted River," is commonly considered to be a fishing tale. It really is a pastoral idyll about a young man's return to a loved area (mother earth) of his childhood. It contains vivid descriptions of the succulent meals he prepares for himself alone in the wilderness. The topic of fishing itself receives relatively little attention. The same thread of orality runs through the author's last pub-

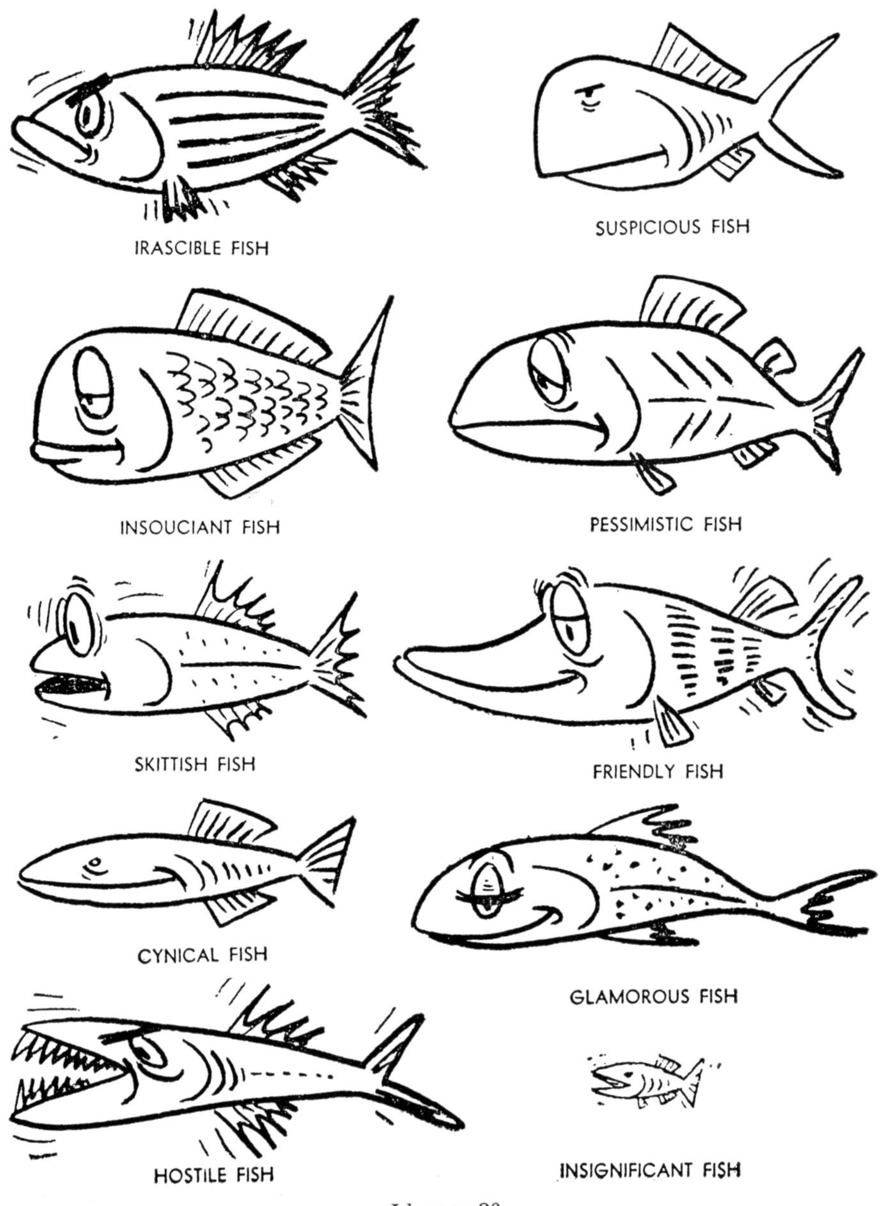

Id. at p. 23.

lished work, *A Moveable Feast,* and emerged with appalling force in his final tragic act of shooting himself in the mouth.

Another aspect of *The Old Man and the Sea* claims our attention: at times the distinction between man and fish blurs so that the Old Man's *identification* with the fish is unmistakable:

> You are killing me, fish, the old man thought. But you have a right to. Never have I seen a greater, or more beautiful, or a calmer or more noble thing than you brother. Come and kill me. I do not care who kills who.
>
> Now you are getting confused in the head, he thought. You must keep your head clear. Keep your head clear and know how to suffer like a man. Or a fish, he thought.[9]

And, later:

> . . . his head started to become a little unclear and he thought, is he bringing me in or am I bringing him in? . . .[10]

These excerpts are the literary counterpart of the old fishing myth: in order to catch a fish, one must *think* like a fish. (In a lighter vein see Millar's cartoon and the book by Ed Zern entitled, *How to Tell Fish From Fishermen,* which includes many pictures and text which illustrate identification with the fish.)

THE SEARCH FOR THE MERMAID

The mythological figure of the mermaid, the alluring and elusive half-woman half-fish, provides a remarkably suitable figure upon which to project unresolved remnants of the child's first attachment to his mother and to her breast. This aspect of the mermaid seems to represent the longed-for, unobtainable, full-breasted, nurturing, loving, "good" mother of childhood.[11] Every mammalian infant first reaches out, catches hold of and relates to his mother with his mouth. Her breast (or its substitute) provides him with both a source of nourishment and an object upon which he focuses his feeling about her. The human infant, in whom the phase of oral attachment to the mother lasts longer than in most other species, experiences attraction, satisfaction and love, as well as frustration, repulsion and hate, literally at his mother's breast. The breast comes to stand for the mother and for the infant's longing for food, love and comfort.

Often in fishing cartoons the figure of the mermaid represents, in a condensed fashion, several aspects of the infant-mother relationship. The mermaid is obviously more mammal than fish, and her mammalian attributes are the most important aspect of her appeal.[12]

In this mermaid cartoon the artist has captured the essence of the infant's wish to convert his passive position into one of active mastery. The fisherman (infant) catches the mermaid (mother) and pulls her in to him.

Like a fish out of water, the mermaid is now helpless and subject to his will. In this manner the fisherman reverses his infantile experience wherein he was hopelessly caught by his (own need for his) mother and subject to *her* will, regardless of whether she was loving or rejecting toward him. In the cartoon he measures her breasts, and finding her deficient, he discards her by throwing her back into the water. He thus (unconsciously) revenges himself on his mother for a thousand childhood humiliations. This represents the infant's ultimate victory (control) over the mother and is achieved

Courtesy of *True* magazine, March, 1962, p. 82.

through identification with her. The *fisherman* now has the lure (allure), and *he* can decide how the mermaid (fish-mother) shall be treated.

The late psychoanalyst Sidney Tarachow has demonstrated that, in the Jewish myth of Leviathan, the giant fish is a symbol for mother and her breast. He equates belief in this legend with an unconscious wish to remain "at the breast forever."[13]

Our everyday language contains many references to the parrallel between a psychological state of longing and the plight of a fish at the end of the fisherman's line; in the case of the dope addict, he is "hooked"; the gullible person who is attracted to goods of dubious value is a "sucker" who falls for such false attractions "hook, line and sinker."

In the fishing scene of *Anthony and Cleopatra,* Shakespeare uses the analogy of the fisherman and the fish to convey this irresistible attraction of one human being for another.

Cleo:

. . . Give me mine angle; we'll to the river: There —
My music playing far off — I will betray
Tawny finn'd fishes; my bended hook shall
Pierce
Their slimy jaws; and, as I draw them up,
I'll think them every one an Anthony,
And say, "Ah, ha!" you're caught.[14]

An example from clinical practice:

> A patient dreamed the following dream during the first year of psychoanalysis: "I am angry at my mother and I tell her that I am going to get my milk creamed by Mrs. M. from now on. Then M. (a figure representing the analyst) is rowing me across the lake in a boat; at the same time he is fishing and catching a lot of fish. One little fish asks, in a high-pitched voice, to be thrown back, but M. puts it on the stringer." This dream linked up the patient's feelings of having been deprived of love (milk) in childhood with the present-day feeling, revived in relationship to the analyst, that he is not giving enough (love, milk) to the patient, and is charging too much. The patient literally feels like a poor fish who is being victimized and strung along.

Although such childhood "dependency" feelings are commonly revived in psychoanalytic treatment, they are rarely expressed as clearly as in the following poem, a fishing allegory, in which the writer also portrays the psychoanalyst as the angler, and herself as the "poor fish":

Pechez La Femme

Now this time, dear old Angler, I have swallowed your hook,
Often enough before, you have lured me forward
Under the rocks of sleep and I have been hooked
Lightly in the mouth and bled no more than from a good kiss
By tearing away.

This time your catch is certain. The struggle is all play
And no suspense. You will surface me through
Dark and glimmering heights of pressure and pain from where
I guarantee — and I can remember — I was once oddly alive.
Reeling one in to you, is almost just mechanical — the
turn of the screw.
To me something happens bodily, resembling an embrace.
I am pulled wholly upward; I leap into it
If only to avoid being turned inside out.
And yet my eagerness is as sincere
As though your face, seen through a disturbance of water,
As though your face were very dear —
You, who fish up the wily landlocked truth of me.
Becoming to me and your lovely lures:
The Supervisor or the Warden's Worry,
The Green Ghost, the Gray Ghost, even the Silver Doctor.[15]

"Gee! Lilacs in bloom, katydids chirping, full moon — makes a guy want to get out and cast for bass!"

Courtesy of Lariar, L., *op. cit.* at p. 79, Wetterberg cartoon (originally in *Sat. Eve. Post*).

Of course, it is widely recognized that simply *going* fishing is an effective and commonly employed means of avoiding women. This persistent theme (simultaneous attraction to the woman and defensiveness against women by going fishing) is condensed in the cartoons by Wetterberg, Syverson[16] and Lariar.

In this context, we can see that the fisherman who selects the tempting lure, who casts it into the water, who lures, catches and keeps — or releases — the fish, is unconsciously exercising magical, omnipotent, active control over

Angleworm: A smart-aleck nimrod who knows all the angles.

Courtesy of Lariar, L., Fish and Be Damned, Prentice-Hall, Inc., Englewood Cliffs, N. J., 1953, p. 36.

Courtesy of Lariar, *op. cit.* at p. 38.

a childhood relationship which he once experienced passively as the "sucker." Thus the fisherman repetitively reassures himself that he is no longer the "sucker." Instead, *he* is now the one who teases and tricks. He is no longer helpless in the face of the painful pricking of his hunger, for he is the one who wields the hook and line, and who reels in the fish at will. He is no longer the "fish out of water," who can do nothing against his longing, his need for, his absolute dependence upon his uncontrollable mother; instead he now has the gasping victim on *his* string.

At a somewhat different level the fisherman also asserts that he is "in control of himself," of his own instinctual drives. This, too, is a most satisfying activity.

DafFISHnitions

SURF CASTING: Trying to land one in the breakers.
Courtesy of Lariar, *op. cit.* at p. 83.

Courtesy of Lariar, You've Got Me on the Hook, *op. cit.* at p. 25, Pearson cartoon (originally in *Colliers*).

BITING AND BEING BITTEN

And the Shark has teeth
And he wears them in his face
And Macheath, he has a knife,
But the knife one does not see.[17]

Cartoons as well as jokes, legends and just plain tall stories abound which clearly deal with the theme of the fisherman's fear of being bitten or even eaten by the fish. Question any fisherman closely and he is likely to recollect squeamish reluctance to wade in certain streams, or occasional phobic trepidation at the thought of putting his hand into some dark underwater hole. He knows that these fears are "silly"; he would not mention them if he were not questioned about them, but would relegate them to some seldom-visited corner of his mind.

Courtesy of Lariar, *op. cit.* at p. 79, Brogden cartoon (originally in *Colliers*).

Many people have a similarly unreasonable fear[18] of fish (or something) nibbling at their toes while swimming. In reality, the sport fisherman rarely encounters a fish large enough to harm him. The fear has no rational basis. Yet it cannot be dismissed; it is too universal not to warrant an explanation. The fear of becoming the fish's victim is often associated, in cartoons, with the fear that the fish will attack the fisherman with his own weapons – hooks, gaffs, etc. – and is related to another strange idea, namely, that the fisherman may attack the fish with his teeth.

This odd combination of ideas is found also in a particular stage of the child's development, the "oral" stage, during which his attachment to his mother is the predominant feature. This stage is divided into two parts: the first, "sucking" stage with its emphasis on passive, dependent pleasure, and the second, "biting" stage which features active, aggressive pleasure-seeking. The event which divides these two is the eruption of teeth. The conflicting emotions and impulses of this stage are handled in a variety of ways which are never wholly successful so that traces can be found especially easily in the sport of fishing. The activity is "tailor-made" for the purpose. At this oral stage of personality development, and for some time afterward,

"To be perfectly honest, *it* caught *me*!"
Courtesy of Lariar, *op. cit.* at p. 85, Hagglund cartoon.

the infant's mode of dealing with conflicting emotions is governed by a principle of mental functioning which has been called the Law of Talion ("an eye for an eye, a tooth for a tooth"). Accordingly, if the infant has a voracious impulse to bite someone, he automatically expects that he will, in turn, himself be bitten. Because at times his hunger seems unassuageable and his urge to bite, to tear with his teeth and to devour seems impossible to contain, the infant is driven to great lengths to check it or to drain it of its dangerous intensity.

Erikson has described the dilemma which this stage of development presents to the child:

> . . . At this stage, however, not even the kindest environment can save the baby from a traumatic change — . . . For it is here that "good" and "evil" enter the baby's world. . . . It is, of course, impossible to know what the infant feels, as his teeth "bore from within" — in the very oral cavity which until then was the main seat of pleasure. . . . Our clinical work indicates that this point in the individual's history is the origin of an evil dividedness, where anger against the gnawing teeth, and anger against the withdrawing mother, and anger with one's impotent anger all lead to a forceful experience of sadistic and masochistic confusion leaving the general impression that once upon a time one destroyed one's unity with a maternal matrix. This earliest catastrophe in the individual's relation to himself and to the world is probably the ontogenetic contribution to the biblical saga of paradise, where . . . they bit into the apple and made God angry.[19]

A recent short comic film about fishing illustrates this childish fear of retaliation with clarity and force.

> A fisherman is surf-casting for striped bass. Between casts he takes sandwiches from a magically inexhaustible lunchbox and devours them voraciously. Finally the supply of food runs out. He stops fishing and searches about desperately for something more to eat. His gaze alights on a package lying in the sand. He fumbles in his eagerness to unwrap it. It is a sandwich. After an experimental nibble, he stuffs the entire sandwich into his mouth, only to be jerked off his feet and be dragged swiftly seaward across the beach at the end of a line; a barbed hook is seen protruding through a wound in his cheek. The fish has caught the fisherman!

The fisherman in this example was betrayed by his own savage appetite. While in the midst of his attempt to take advantage of the hungry fish, the tables are turned and he is caught (and presumably eaten) by the fish. The fisherman's unconscious fear of retaliation could hardly be expressed more forcefully.

The following example drawn from clinical practice sheds additional light on the origin of the fear of being bitten and its relationship to fishing.

> A young married man entered psychoanalysis because of extreme, almost overwhelming anxiety. From the beginning of his treatment he had nightmares of lions or tigers threatening to eat him or to gnaw off parts of his body. As he slowly came to understand his unconscious conflicts about his childhood relationships to parents and sisters, the frightening dream animals diminished in size until they were smaller than himself. Still later the biting dreams became pleasant, as the animals were now menacing someone else. These "others" usually turned out to be disguished representations of his parents and sisters whom he could now more openly resent. Finally the dream animals became alligators, then muskelunge and finally harmless panfish, which he caught and killed. At this point, in reality, the patient began to go fishing for the first time since childhood. Only when an argument with someone close to him aroused his anger did he again suffer "punishment dreams." (In these the fish bit his fingers or jumped out of the water after

him.) Although fishing became possible for him only after he had conquered his infantile rage and especially his fear of this rage, the fishing, in turn, provided him with an exciting activity which was an acceptable, harmless means of gratifying sadistic impulses and of warding off fear of retaliation for those impulses.

This subtle, simultaneous experiencing of sadistic impulses and the fear of retaliation (which never comes) probably contributes to the great excitement that fishing provides to many people . . . a state combining both anxiety and euphoria. This resembles the young child's excitement when someone plays the "cannibal game" with him. (Adult threatens to bite child; child is first apprehensive and then, excited, laughs.) This game is a harmless acting out of the wish to bite and to be bitten.

In fact, one of the authors was expounding on this theory to a colleague one day while they were fishing together. The friend apparently had a "strike." Hearing a commotion behind him, the author turned just in time to see his friend lose his balance in his excitement and stumble into the water.

In this connection a writer of popular fishing stories has said, ". . . a feeding fish excites me. And in my excitement to toss out a bit of weighted feathers I . . . yep, I tossed the whole damned rig, — rod, reel and all, right into the [water] . . ."[20]

This same excitement is described in a more subdued style in this extract from a classical fly-fishing article:

> . . . There are those occasions, which are very frequent on the Letort, when I can observe every movement of a feeding trout — see him aquiver the instant my artificial lands a foot in front of him, watch him detach himself from his observation post, undulating backward and lifting slowly to take the fly at the precise instant they both meet at the surface, as though the trout had calculated the interception by triangulation! These are the worst times for me. Being somewhat nervous by temperament, I cannot subdue the building up of nervous pressure engendered by the visible and deliberate rise. . . .[21]

Finally, an example in which the original theme of the fear of retaliation returns virtually undisguised:

> Any fisherman can spend a few days, a week, a month or longer in this area if he has his trip timed with the seasonal runs of his favorite fish. He should have a barrel of fishing fun besides enjoying the unspoiled rugged terrain. *If he's lucky, he may even be caught and played by a sturgeon.*[22]

ON THE STRING

At this point it is appropriate to comment on another aspect of fishing which is related to the end of the oral stage of child development. Under the pressure of weaning and the stimulus of growth and maturation, the infant is forced into an awareness that he and his mother are separate beings, and not a unity. This process of individuation is aided by several "games," familiar to all parents, which most children "invent" out of a need to practice new-found skills. The first of these is "peek-a-boo," in which the child enjoys exercising control over the disappearance and reappearance of his parents.

"Oh, that's just Irwin with his realistic practice."

Courtesy of Lariar, *op. cit.* at p. 33, Filchock cartoon (originally in *Today's Health*).

This game is soon followed by a more active one which affords both him and his parents more exercise. The child throws all of his toys out of the crib in the expectation that his parents will retrieve them, which they usually do to his obvious delight. Still later this control finds wider scope in a variety of toys which are pulled around at the end of strings (yo-yos, tops, etc.) and which can be made to perform by remote control. As the child's own motility and range of action increases, he graduates into kites, airplanes and sailboats which "come back" from progressively greater distances and which permit the child's control to operate over an increasing area. Many of these games persist into adulthood as sports. Casting a fishing lure is one form of this mastery-over-distance. Repetitively casting-out and retrieving a fishing lure has a pleasure all its own which is readily distinguishable from the other aspects of fishing. In fact, competitive casting for distance and accuracy on dry land with a hookless weight has become a sport in its own right, and has lost any appreciable connection with fishing.

In this section, then, we have demonstrated a variety of ways in which the sport of fishing becomes the vehicle for the mastery of the troublesome, unconscious residuals of infantile conflicts revolving around the "oral" relationship to the mother; namely, the attraction for the primal love object, the wish to bite and the fear of being bitten and, finally, the establishment of a sense of individual identity.

THE MYSTERIES

The pleasure of fishing also owes a great debt to a later phase in the development of the child, for some of the excitement of angling derives from unconscious remnants of this period. This phase confronts every child with a great developmental task, which he must master, namely: unraveling what are, for him, the great mysteries of life. These are:

1. What is the nature and significance of the anatomical differences between the sexes and how did they come about?
2. Where do babies come from? How are they conceived and how born? This leads directly to the third mystery.
3. Why does the child's beloved mother prefer the father to the child? What is the nature of the parental relationship?

In his struggles to solve these mysteries, every child develops theories and working hypotheses which are based on his limited experience and incomplete mental development. These theories are never wholly replaced by the more accurate knowledge he acquires later, but are only repressed. Traces of these infantile theories as well as other attempts to master "the mysteries" can be detected in the activity of fishing.

What Little Girls Are Made Of (Now You See It, Now You Don't)

Legends of sea monsters generally take two forms. The "Loch Ness" or *mysterious* variety holds that some local body of water conceals a sea serpent whose existence defies logic and description. From time to time people catch glimpses of the monster and are amazed and awestricken at the sight. Almost every local fishing hole has a similar but less spectacular myth about a huge fish which no one can catch, although from time to time a few privileged fishermen are amazed to encounter it. This elusive, giant fish is a stock figure in every fisherman's fantasy life, and every fishing expedition is enlivened by the possibility that someone (maybe I!) may catch – or at least catch sight of – this elusive prize. It is evident that at one level this fish-serpent represents a penis, "hidden" in the feminine body of water, and that the myth is an attempt to cope with the residue of infantile shock, amazement and disbelief over the absence of a penis in females. The refusal of both sexes to believe that women lack penises is expressed by the insistence that something (a penis) does exist where logic says that it cannot. A clinical illustration:

> While undergoing psychoanalysis, a woman (whose problems included a jealousy of men and an ungratified wish to emulate them) had surgery on her reproductive organs. Following surgery she had a dream in which she found herself pulling endless numbers of small fish from the water. Analysis of this dream led to memories of a tonsillectomy in early childhood and the recovery of the "forgotten" childhood conviction that when the doctor took out her tonsils, he also removed her penis. Catching the fish was symbolic expression of the wish to regain the lost penis.

"Beginner's luck!"
Courtesy of Lariar, *op. cit.* at p. 38, Norment cartoon (originally in *Saturday Review*).

Gallagher Saturday Evening Post

"Looks as though Ed's hooked into something."

Courtesy of Lariar, *op. cit.* at p. 12, Gallagher cartoon, (originally in *Sat. Eve. Post*).

The Kraken Will Get You If You Don't Watch Out

The other variety of the sea monster myth, the *threatening* type, is that of the giant squid, octopus of kraken.[23] This version emphasizes a dangerous monster lurking in the deep, a frightening, spidery something that may grasp with uncanny power, pull down and engulf the unwary sojourner on the sea's surface. This myth is found, in adumbrated form, in relationship to many freshwater lakes and ponds which are said to contain weird, nameless creatures at the bottom of some "bottomless" section of the lake. (Every district contains some lake reputed to be "bottomless.") This version of myth represents a derivative of the infantile fear of the female genital,[24] which he regards as a mysterious, spidery, unfathomable trap which may close on objects (especially penises!) and injure them. This is the fear of the notorious "castrating female."

The fishing expedition becomes a thrilling joust with these monstrously frightening "things," whose threatening presence beneath the surface of the water turns each encounter with the water into a brush with death and consequently a magical victory over the unconscious fear of death or mutilation.

Where Do Babies Come From?

Ingmar Bergman's film masterpiece *Wild Strawberries* contains a poignant scene which depends, in a large part, for its compellingly evocative effect upon the symbolic equation: fishing = childbirth. An old doctor's journey to the city to receive an honorary degree is the skeleton upon which is hung a series of reminiscences of his childhood. These alternate with incidents foreshadowing his approaching death. The dominant theme of the film is that as he nears the end of his life the old man's wish to live on grows in intensity. He is disappointed in his son's troubled marriage which has robbed him of the vicarious immortality of grandparenthood. A side trip to the summer house where he had played in his youth induces a vivid reverie; on the beach he sees his mother, obviously pregnant, sitting in a chair sewing. His father is standing near her, fishing pole in hand, and pulls a large fish from the water, so that it lands behind him at his wife's feet. The message is clear, and the psychological economy of the symbolism adds immeasurably to the impact of the message: at the end of his life the old man would like to be reborn, to do it all over again. He is the fish his father catches out of the sea.

A nineteenth century scientific theory held that in the depths of the sea there existed a primordial generative substance (*Urschleim*) which continually produced new forms of elemental life which matured and evolved as they slowly ascended to the surface of the water. This theory was promulgated by many of the most respected scientists of the day. Their mistaken notion even extended to the belief that a gelatinous substance which they dredged up from the ocean depths was this same *Urschleim* and that they could actually see it move under the microscope. (It later proved to be an artifact, an inert, inorganic precipitate formed by the addition of alcohol to sea water.) Nevertheless, the concept that there is a mysterious, hidden source of perpetual new life was, and is, so seductive, and the need to believe in it so great, that it was able to delude these eminent scientists.

It is obvious that water is a symbol for the mother, from whose mysterious interior new life emerges from time to time. The fisherman who, with his rod and line, implants a little fish (bait, lure) in the sea and pulls out a bigger fish is at one level practicing symbolic fertilization of the female and delivery of a child.[25] In this way he attempts to exert magical control over birth, a process which in childhood presented him with only a frustrating, insoluble riddle. (He also mimics his father's biological role in this process.)

Sports fishing is often openly competitive. At all times there is an element of rivalry in the quest for the biggest fish, the possession of secret knowledge of the best fishing hole, the most seductive bait, etc. This competition has elements derived from the child's unresolved rivalry with his father. To illustrate:

> An eight-year-old boy whose mother had died of asthma when he was four years old ran away from his father's care. He was picked up by the police and placed in a detention home, where he had the following dream: "I am a skin diver and am fishing with a spear. I see a man in a regular diving suit with a

huge fish. I fight with him, cut his air hose, take the fish away from him and take it home to the man's wife. . . ." The boy's association to the dream revealed that he wished (unconsciously) that his father had died (suffocated) rather than his mother, so that his mother could still take care of him. At a deeper level, the big fish he wrests from his father represented the father's large genital which he wanted to have so that (according to an infantile concept of sexual attraction) he could win his mother away from his father and present her with a child.[26]

"You should have seen the one that got away!"
Courtesy of Lariar, Fish and Be Damned, *op. cit.*, frontispiece.

"Charlie! Tom! Bill!"
Courtesy of Lariar, You've Got Me on the Hook, *op cit.* at p. 32, Shirvanian cartoon (originally in *Sat. Eve. Post*).

When to these other unconscious motives we add that of trial by combat between son and father, the thrill of fishing becomes even easier to comprehend. Few forms of recreation seem to offer less prospect of pleasure at the outset and end by providing more than does fishing.

Through fishing about in the murky waters of the unconscious, we have attempted to show that this apparently most simpleminded of pastimes actually serves a variety of complex psychological functions, and that this unexpected fact is largely accountable for its special capacity to provide pleasure and relaxation.

With these remarks about the element of rivalry, we conclude this contribution to the depth-psychology of sport fishing. This article was written as an outlet for the frustrations which the authors had accumulated since the end of the fishing season just past. We are happy to report that it has been a successful catharsis and that we are at peace . . . but one of our young sons has just rushed in with the news that the ice on Lake St. Clair is thickening. As he is too young to appreciate the concepts of vicarious gratification, etc., there seems to be nothing else to do but to go and help him push the fishing shanty out onto the ice.

NOTE

FOOTNOTES

1. Radcliffe, W.: *Fishing From the Earliest Times.* New York, Dutton, 1921.
2. Blair, F.: Letter in column Where They Fish. *The Fisherman,* May, 1958, pp. 7-8.
3. Sigmund Freud first called attention to the fact that artists (authors, playwrights, painters, cartoonists) can provide us with valuable insights because they often look *directly* into the unconscious, seeing with ease that which others cannot, or *must not* see. It is part of the artist's gift; and it is of value to his audience, who can enjoy the insight vicariously, thus without discomfort.
4. Here we use the term "sport fishing" as roughly synonymous with the term "angling." "The angler rates classification as an artist for his handling of the frail rod, the casting of his line and the special technique in the operation of his reel, whereas the ordinary fisherman is concerned only in acquiring something, and a lot of it, for the frying pan." Menke, F. G. [Ed.]: *Encyclopedia of Sports.* New York, Barnes, A. S. 1963, p. 13.
5. The human mind automatically regulates its impulses so that a tolerable balance of pleasure and pain is maintained at all times. In the process of maturing and becoming progressively civilized, the human infant finds it necessary to relinquish many of his primitive, instinctual impulses (such as the impulse to eat, sleep and eliminate on demand, to possess exclusively whatever he loves and to destroy whatever he hates), to transform them into socially acceptable forms or to regulate them according to the demands of his parents. In this process the child progressively develops the mental capacity (ego) to control these impulses which originally were uncontrollable, and at the same time takes over and establishes in his own mental structure (superego) the social code of permissible behavior which originally was imposed on him by his parents. In this process he comes to pattern himself after the parent of the same sex. As his mind develops the capacity to comprehend and take account of the demands of reality, he progressively abandons the original infantile tendency to wish-away (or to ignore) pain and to replace frustration with pleasant, gratifying fantasies. The reality-testing function is never completely reliable, nor does it work fulltime. Under the pressure of fatigue and stress (or at night when we sleep) we abandon, temporarily, the "reality principle" and allow our mental processes again to be governed by the "pleasure principle," in which wishful fantasies predominate. At such times it becomes possible to infer, from the content of these fantasies, something about the nature of the inner conflicts and mental tensions with which the mind grapples and which the fantasies are designed to minimize. When unconscious mental conflicts threaten to break into consciousness they cause anxiety, which the mind dissipates in a variety of ways, which in turn provides conscious relief and relaxation.
6. Traver, R.: *Trout Madness.* New York, St. Martin's Press, 1960, p. 18.
7. Hemingway, E.: *The Old Man and the Sea.* New York, Chas. Scribner's Sons, 1954, p. 34.
8. *Id.* at p. 46.
9. *Id.* at p. 102.
10. *Id.* at p. 109.
11. The "femme fatale" aspect of the mermaid myth is dealt with later.
12. The other aspect of the mermaid's fascination is that she has a tail instead of female genitalia (to some, the female genital organ is frightening). The fish tail symbolizes the penis which females lack.
13. Tarachow, S.: Judas, the beloved executioner. *Psychoanal Quart, 29:*528, 1960.
14. Shakespeare, W.: *Anthony and Cleopatra,* Act II, Scene V.
15. Pedrick, J.: Pechez la femme. *The New Yorker,* vol. 36, p. 52, March 12, 1960.
16. Syverson, cartoon in Lariar, L.; *You've Got Me on the Hook.* New York, Dodd, Mead & Co., 1954, p. 47.
17. Weil, K., and Brecht, B.: "The Ballad of Mack the Knife." The Threepenny Opera, copyright Brackhouse Music Co., Inc., 1957.
18. We exempt the fear of sharks from the category of unreasonable fears . . . at least in salt water.

19. Erickson, E. H.: *Childhood and Society*. New York, Norton, 1950, p. 74.
20. Seville, J.: Flamingo. *Sports Afield,* October, 1958, p. 152.
21. Marinaro, V.: Fishing the dry fly on quiet waters; in Camp, R. [Ed.]: *Fireside Book of Fishing*. New York, Simon & Schuster, 1957, p. 288.
22. Close, E. P.: The fish that plays you. *Outdoor Life,* October, 1958, p. 117. Italics ours.
23. The story of Moby Dick also seems to contain elements of this myth.
24. The spider is a symbolic representation both of the feared female genital and of oral sadistic impulses. Sterba, R.: On spiders, hanging and oral aggression. *American Imago,* 7:21, 1950.
25. In *Measure for Measure,* Act I, Scene 2, Shakespeare uses the symbolic equation fishing = childbirth:

    Pompey: *Yonder man is carried to prison.*
    Mrs. Overdone: *Well; what has he done?*
    Pom: *A woman.*
    Mrs. Overdone: *But what's his offense?*
    Pom: *Groping for trouts in a peculiar river.*
    Mrs. Overdone: *What, is there a maid with child by him?*
26. At a still deeper level, both the fish and the sea itself represent the mother, and diving underwater represents a wish to rejoin her.

MOUNTAINEERING

CHARLES S. HOUSTON

FOR MUCH OF HIS RECORDED history man has feared, admired and worshiped the mountains. They were to him the home of demons, of gods or of game which he could hunt. Apparently he was not as aware of their beauty as of their danger, for mountain storms and avalanches of rock or snow could kill him brutally. Mountains were a barrier to travel rather than a roadway as was the sea. Through the many centuries when life was a harsh struggle for survival, it was natural for him to avoid the mountains except to cross them for conquest or trade or in search of food or graze.

Eventually he did discover precious stones and metals in the mountains. He learned that the great ranges could be a wall against invaders, but only if the invaders were ignorant of secret passes. Thus exploration became important, to find riches as well as to find routes for attack or to defend. Much later he found in the mountains something which has become a sport, for mountaineering is an old sport compared to others, though not as old as hunting, fighting or pursuit of the opposite sex — and sublimations of these survival activities.

HISTORY

In analyzing the motivations of modern climbing, it may be helpful to review its history, which goes back for several centuries. As in so much of history, the Greeks are our first source; I am not aware of earlier. The Greeks looked on the mountains with awe and reverence. Zeus, they believed, was born in a cave high on snowy Ida. Later his numerous family were housed on Mount Olympus where they watched over all of Attica and dallied with mortals. Down from Olympus came thunderbolts and visiting divinities whose interference was often harmful. The sea was the familiar of the Greeks, object of their love and praise. It was their larder and highway. Mountains were hostile barriers, the home of beasts, storms and gods who demanded appeasement more than love.

There is no indication that the Greeks climbed mountains for sport — surprising in a people so athletic, competitive and fearless. In fact, to the best of our knowledge, Mount Olympus was not climbed until 1913, though only 9,500 feet high and not particularly difficult. The Greeks played games for competition and pleasure, but avoided the mountains except for travel.

The Romans left nothing to show any interest in mountains other than as obstacles. Hannibal in 218 B.C. described his crossing of a 12,000-foot pass with understandable pride in the military and logistic accomplishment. Caesar does not mention mountains; they were in the way, he crossed them, and that was that. The Crusaders do not mention the mountain crossings, which must have been devastating. Not until the Renaissance do we find even a hint of admiration for the mountains.

Then in 1555 Conrad Gessner, physician, scientist and author, wrote a sensitive book *On the Admiration of Mountains,* in which he describes his climbs in the lesser Alps and lauds the delights of climbing. As a physician it is understandable that he should have praised its contribution to good health. As a scientist he was particularly interested in the effects of altitude and in the flora and fauna. Clearly he enjoyed climbing for the sport alone, and for a few dozen years others followed him. This was, however, a false dawn for mountaineering; not for two hundred years did Haller and J. J. Rousseau renew public interest in the mountains.

In Asia the most celebrated mountain is 12,000-foot Fujiyama. Unlike Olympus, Fujiyama has been climbed by countless thousands since the dawn of Japanese history. It is a holy mountain, the objective of pilgrims. It is a beautiful mountain which the Japanese have admired in word and picture for centuries. As a climb, it is a long tedious grade whose only hazard is sudden, often lethal storm. It is interesting that the Japanese who have climbed Fuji for all of their national lifetime have only in recent years begun to climb the beautiful Japanese Alps, and only in the last twenty years turned to the ranges of other countries. Climbing for the Japanese has become a sport only in this century.

Both Hindus and Buddhists regard many Himalayan peaks as holy. Kailas is the home of Shiva and Parvati. The native name for Everest is Chomolungma — "Goddess Mother of the Earth." Nanda Devi is known as "The Blessed Goddess," and near it is one of the great pilgrimage spots of Asia — Gaumukh (Cows Mouth) where the holy Ganges originates. Nanga Parbat may be translated as "The Naked Goddess."

The Himalayas are dangerous because of weather, and their great altitude makes residence insupportable for long. It is not surprising therefore that those who live near these mountains should avoid them except for essential activity. Less than one hundred years ago the British began to explore the mighty valleys, at first for military or political reasons, later for the hunting and fishing. More recently, as the European Alps became "overrun," British climbers explored and climbed. Still the village people near these mountains showed no interest. Only in the last fifteen years have the Indians begun to climb their own hills.

The great mountains of Africa are so veiled in cloud, so surrounded by tropical rain forests or dreary wastes that they are extremely difficult of access. Though high, the climbing is not hard, but the weather is. The primitive peoples who live near the base have accepted the mountains with neither fear nor reverence nor any urge to climb. Again it has been the restless European who has travelled here.

The North American Indian and the Eskimo worshiped the primitive gods of Sun, Moon and Rain. Even those who live in the mountains seem to accept them as part of life, a barrier, home of storms, protection against the enemy and source of hunting. We know that they travelled extensively but apparently never climbed for sport. We late arrivals in North America have been too occupied with opening up our land to do more than search for gold and silver, lumber and pasturage in the mountains. We have mapped and explored the Rockies so that we could penetrate them with transportation to extract their wealth or to reach the Pacific. Only in this century have we begun to climb for sport.

The civilizations of South and Central America were as brilliant as any in man's history. They have left a testament of art and architecture which still delights our admiration. They travelled widely. They knew and used gold and silver and precious stones better than we. Their history is lost in time. They too worshiped natural gods of Sun, Rain and Moon, but so far as we know the mountains were only a refuge, and not sacred. There is no evidence that they climbed except for utilitarian reasons. Their conquerors, the Spaniards, climbed 20,000-foot volcanoes to obtain saltpeter and sulfur, and penetrated the lower peaks in pursuit of the natives, their gold and their women. But they did not climb for sport.

In Europe during the Middle Ages, mountain valleys were inhabited by a sturdy peasantry whose superstitions kept them out of the mountains. Pontius Pilate was believed to have lived in torment on Mount Pilatus until Gessner disproved this myth with his scientific expedition of 1548. The valley people believed that most Alpine peaks harbored demons, some with scales, some with tails, some merely breathing fire, but all dangerous. Eye witnesses wrote lurid reports. Intrepid hunters of chamois, or rock crystal, often received more attention by their narrow escapes from dragons than from their finds. As recently as 1730 we find serious accounts of these strange creatures, fully illustrated by eye witnesses. These are somewhat comparable perhaps to reports in our own times of the man-ape called the Abominable Snowman in the Himalayas.

Alpine climbing began seriously in 1754 with the ascent of the highest peak in Europe — 15,800-foot Mount Blanc — by a party from the village of Chamonix at its foot. Although attempts on the mountain dated back for a dozen years, apparently motivated by adventure and curiosity, the successful ascent seems to have been motivated primarily by competition for notoriety and for money; at least this was the main result of the ascent.

More parties climbed this lovely snow peak, frequently and frankly for material gain. Mademoiselle D'Angeville in 1838 was frank in saying that she was bored by the life of a middle-aged spinster and hoped that her climb of a famous mountain would bring money, fame, and — one assumes — suitors; it did not. In 1854 Alfred Smith climbed Mount Blanc and made many sketches so that he could lecture. He became world famous and moderately wealthy for a time, and in the process interested thousands in climbing as a sport. Most Alpine climbs were done by the British, at least in the early days. As we have seen in other countries, those who live at the foot of the mountain seldom climb for pleasure.

But the British, at first by the dozen and soon in swarms, flocked to the Alps for vacation. In the Golden Age of Alpine climbing, nearly every summit was reached and the obvious routes were made between 1855 and 1870. It was a glorious period. The valleys were quaint and picturesque, the people hospitable and the opportunities unlimited. What a marvelous playground it must have been!

Thus was born the sport of mountaineering — in the Alps in the middle nineteenth century, nurtured in its infancy by all the weight of British tradition. The British refined the equipment: ice axes, crampons or climbing irons, ropes, nailed boots, knickerbockers and capes. They established the customs: "A cold bottle on the summit," says Mummery. They interested locals in the new sport — but not for sport alone. The mountain villagers were needy and became professional guides who took the foreigners up the mountain for money. These Swiss, French, German and Italian professionals became the finest climbers in the world, and intimates of the privileged amateurs. Later, as their clients became self-sufficient, the professional guides would themselves become pioneers in ranges of other lands.

Victorian Europeans climbed for sport and for adventure, but had occasional qualms of conscience. There was a strong feeling that a man had no right to enjoy things unless he suffered for them first. One should not do a thing only for pleasure. For several decades few respectable climbers dared to climb a mountain without at least boiling a thermometer on the top! Their voluminous accounts always tried to give some semblance of scientific purpose to what was often a pure and simple lark. Science advanced prodigiously as a result. Between 1880-1900 Paul Bert, Mosso and others built the foundation of modern high altitude science in the Alps.

Thus climbing became a sport during the Victorian age. Its traditions and customs remain today. Every Alpine summit was climbed, and as the obvious routes were made it was natural that the more enterprising climbers should turn to more difficult routes. The standard of climbing rose. More and more mountains passed through the stages described by Mummery:[1]

An inaccessible peak,
The most difficult climb in the Alps,
An easy day for a lady.

Books and guides multiplied, variants were built on variants. Winter climbing became fashionable. Ski mountaineering was introduced. Soon guideless climbing enabled the skilled amateur to travel on his own, sometimes ending in a disaster from which the understandably irritated professionals rescued him or retrieved his body. Danger became a constant companion as more difficult routes were attempted. To control danger, artificial aids were introduced: the nail or piton, used in rock cracks or in ice; the karabiner or snaplink; and direct aid devices such as ladders, prussik knots and pulleys. Clothing and food became better and lighter, enabling longer more exacting climbs.

Soon it was not sufficient merely to write an account of a great climb. Its exact difficulty had to be defined in terms commonly accepted. Suddenly classification was upon the climber. Mountains were graded by their overall difficulty. Routes were subgraded by total difficulty and by difficulty of individual pitches. Conditions during the ascent were also graded. And finally the climber himself could obtain a classification. Based on his accomplishment and his ability, he was given an official number recognized in most climbing circles. The ultimate is now upon us: class 7A2 climbs may be attempted only by climbers whose class is 5A or better!

Today all over the world, people of many nations are climbing mountains for sport. Hundreds every year climb the well-worn Matterhorn, probably the best-known mountain in the world. Thousands tramp over less distinguished hills. And scores of experts attempt impossible climbs on what few virgin faces remain. The most fortunate, with money and with time, explore the less known areas where politics are permissive, maps incomplete, and many summits untried.

MOTIVATIONS

Why do men climb mountains? I have tried in the preceding whirlwind tour through the past to describe *what* has happened in climbing, in the hope that the elusive *why* may appear. But motivations have been mixed and are changing: only the parameters can be defined. Perhaps the following may help.

I will lift up mine eyes to the hills
from whence cometh my strength.

PSALMS[2]

But to me, high mountains are a feeling
Felt in the heart and felt along the blood.

LORD BYRON[3]

Why climb Everest? Because it's there.
George Mallory[4]

At the risk of obvious over-simplification, we may say that men climb for four major reasons: for pleasure, for knowledge, for an answer to a challenge and for gain. Not a surprising or original description surely, but inclusive perhaps.

There is little question of the beauty of the mountains. They are sublime, their heads near heaven, their feet in the sweet greens of daily life. Grynaeus five hundred years ago wrote:

> I say therefore that he is an enemy of nature who so ever has not deemed lofty mountains most worthy of contemplation.

More than a hundred years ago Ruskin said:[5]

> To myself mountains are the beginning and end of all natural scenery.

— but he preferred to look up at the peaks rather than to climb them. Hundreds of lesser writers have praised the clear air, the sparkling snow, the brilliant sunrise and sunset. The diamond brightness of the stars at night, the deep blue-black of the daytime sky, or the rose stain on the snow at sunset — all of these are familiar to the climber. They are not the least of his pleasures, and to feel them is one of the strong urges for his climbing.

There is also the satisfaction of honest rock beneath the hand, the good bite of crisp hard snow under the nailed boot. Trees, grass, flowers are especially sweet when returning from a period surrounded by bare rock and snow. After weeks of Spartan expedition life, daily pleasures are fresher and the senses renewed. On high mountains everything seems more clear, more sharp, more vital.

Strenuous exercise, healthy fatigue, deep sleep, sharp appetites — these are pleasures too, but they may be gained more cheaply and without risk in other sports — running a track to name the most pedestrian. The pleasure of physical fitness, though it results from climbing, is not a prime motive.

There is no denying that the view from the top is often sublime. Looking down to the valleys, across at distant ranges, or up to cumulus towers is a rich reward. No plane or glider can give the same vantage as can a mountain summit. To sit pleasantly tired from the work, back against sun-warmed rock, to look down on insignificant dots below, munching hard bread and sharp cheese, to do this in good company after a long struggle gives a pleasure which soothes in a way offered by few other sports.

But is not climbing often unpleasant too? Indeed it is. Mallory described vividly his own discomfort when climbing above 20,000 feet; he felt "like a sick man walking in a dream," and any who have been there would agree.[6] In that thin, high air every exertion demands breathless panting; thawing boots, melting snow for water, tying a shoe and turning over in bed are major efforts. Bitter storms, bone-deep cold, battering winds, hunger, thirst — all plague the high climber. Surely these are not pleasurable. But the optimist does not anticipate them as he starts his climb. None but a masochist would deliberately seek them. They are the dash of salt which makes the sweet sweeter, and if not avoidable must be endured. Discomfort is not sought, and if all climbing were unpleasant, only the psychopath would climb. The pursuit of pleasure in its richest sense offers stimulation of the senses as can few other sports, and is I believe one of the major reasons why men climb. Godley put it simply:[7]

> I appear then as a member of that class of not altogether respectable persons who ascend hills merely for pleasure. We have no particular principles except the general maxim that it is better to be at the top than at the bottom.

The search for knowledge led many to the mountains during the eighteenth and nineteenth centuries when little was known about barometric pressure and the effects of altitude. From the studies of these pioneers came basic knowledge now enormously enhanced by laboratory work. Still, it is hard to believe that science was the main spur for the pioneers. It seems to have been more of a respectable reason to do what they wished to do anyway but regarded as frivolous. Haldane and Barcroft, for instance, contributed more to high altitude physiology from their unromantic laboratories than from the mountain summits. Physics, geology, cartography, and more recently the study of cosmic rays and magnetism demand field work, often the ascent of peaks. Many such workers have climbed mountains everywhere in the world for science and for knowledge, and perhaps for no other purpose. And yet one feels that the search for knowledge is not a strong motive in mountaineering.

But wait, great ventures may bring self-knowledge. Many climbers freely recognize how much better they have come to know their inner characters through climbing, most frequently after a disaster has tested them. Men who are seldom called to exert the last traces of strength and courage in daily life may do so in the mountains. From knowledge of these inner reserves may come better understanding. I doubt if one may properly include search for self-knowledge as a motive in climbing, but it is surely a reward, and one of the most important. Mallory expressed this beautifully in one of his letters. Writing of a successful climb he said:

> Have we vanquished an enemy? None but ourselves. Have we won a kingdom? No, and yes. We have achieved an ultimate satisfaction, fulfilled a destiny. To struggle and to understand, never this last without the other.

There are those who see the mountain as a personal antagonist to be beaten. They speak of "conquering" a summit and feel each ascent to be a victory. For them mountaineering is a contest between the climber and nature. To the few for whom this is a prime motive, wise Julius Kugy has written a gentle reprimand:[8]

> The mountains should not be our enemy. How distasteful it is to read of a man throwing down the gauntlet to them, setting out to conquer, speaking of them as enemies against whom he pits his own strength. Mountaineering is not a battle. . . . there is a note of arrogance and presumption like the chatter of dwarfs. I cannot imagine any place less suitable to choose than the high mountains wherein to display the mastery of mankind. . . . When we enter their palaces let us do so as modest guests in the house of the great. In my whole life I have leaned on them as upon some stronger friend. They were so kind to me as to bring me comfort and restoration after grave earthly sorrow. Such is the mountaineer's life as I see it; such was the love and trust with which I turned to them, and thus in the destined hour will I bid my farewell to the everlasting hills.

Knowledge of one's physical capacity is a different matter, a strong motive in climbing. Climbers deliberately seek to test their ability, trying harder and harder climbs to find the limits of their tolerance. Though this is a search for knowledge, it is more precisely a response to challenge. And this response is perhaps the overriding motive in mountaineering.

"To solve a problem which has long resisted the skill and perseverance of others is an irresistible magnet in every sphere of human activity. There is no height, no depth, that the spirit of man, guided by the higher spirit cannot attain." – thus said Sir John Hunt, after Everest.[9] Nansen wrote of "Man craving to get beyond the limits of the known." In this, mankind seems different than animals. Established, he may deliberately leave the comforts of home and the daily round to make a storm-tossed voyage, reach a pole, climb an unknown mountain, even knowing that hardship is certain and that he may not return from the risk. And he does it again and again.

Bonati, having shared the ascent of K2, went on to ever more difficult Alpine ascents until his incredible climbs verged on the impossible. Buhl, who qualified himself by night ascents, alone in winter, of the most difficult faces in the Alps, climbed the last 3,500 feet to the summit of Nanga Parbat alone, and later went on to increasingly daring climbs until at last, in storm, he fell. There are many of these challengers:[10]

> *We are the pilgrims, master, we must go,*
> *Ever a little farther, it may be*
> *Beyond that last blue mountain rimmed*
> *with snow.*

"Man must reach beyond his grasp" may not be a safe maxim for him who is struggling on a steep cliff, but it is the way to advance in all frontiers.

The bright face of danger has appeal also. Few sensible people do a thing *only* because it is dangerous, but few avoid an activity because danger is involved. Some few of those who climb alone have acknowledged that the thrill of great fear is the thrill they seek. Many climbers testify that in fear they have reached high performance and equally high appreciation. When one comes back from near death, life takes on new meaning. The smell of danger is intoxicating stuff, and there are climbers whose main urge to climb is the risk of death. But they are few, and even they are not completely foolhardy. Otherwise we would find them climbing blindfold, with one hand tied, through winter storms, or only at night. We do find such climbers, but they are the aberrant.

Climbers are not masochists, and they are as eager as the next man for the hot bird, the cold bottle and the warm bed. On major climbs one accepts thirst, hunger, cold, sunburn or frostbite, poor sleep and great fatigue as part of the game — not as the goal.[11]

Challenge is the great magnet for climbers. Something difficult to do — go and do it. Something lost beyond the ranges — go and find it. Try to do what others have not, perhaps cannot. Challenge is the clean word; competition is less so. But to do the undoable is a worthy undertaking for anyone. This is probably the strongest urge to climb.

Personal gain there may be also. As I have mentioned, the search for gold and precious stones led many early climbers. Fame and notoriety called others in the early days. Between our two great wars the dispairing youth of Europe sought personal and national identity by trying spectacular ascents, and medals were given by the state to the most daring. Higher mountains and more dangerous routes were climbed, and the "victors" became national heroes, much as astronauts of today. World tours were arranged, royalties poured in, and the sweet fruits of fame were bought by great daring in the mountains.

A major expedition became a costly undertaking. Some countries demanded an admission fee and issued a "hunting license" whose cost increased with the height or fame of the mountain. Though transportation became faster, it was also more expensive. Equipment was better and more costly; special precooked and prepackaged food could be bought. Air supply became fashionable. It saved time, they said, and time is certainly money. An air-drop did eliminate the tedious caravan to base camp with attendant worries and expense. Only those who knew the good old days appreciated that the march in was also a great pleasure.

As costs of climbing rose, new sources of income were found. Movies, television, advertising testimonials and lecture tours yielded substantial sums. A famed climber could often get a prestige position in some large firm or gain a large trade in sporting goods. There is even a tale of the village entrepreneur who made an "arrangement" with a climbing team about to tackle a prodigious and dangerous face, best visible from the inn he owned. I can picture the time not far off when fees may be charged of those who watch human flies nailing a way up sheer cliffs, as was done for the daredevils who walked a tightrope over Niagara Falls. Though mountaineering is not yet a commercial sport, soon, like baseball, golf or horseracing, its heroes may be salaried and spectators may watch "live" ascents of a perpendicular from the comfort of the television room.

Is this bad? Only, I believe, for those who, seeking material rewards, lose what the mountains uniquely offer. The sport is not prostituted; its protagonists may be. Only those who crave the payoff lose the real rewards in climbing. The pleasures of riding, sailing or tennis are not diminished for their amateurs because professionals have gained. I am not among the Cassandras crying "Shame" as climbing turns commercial. The eternal hills are untarnished and unchanged, though some climbers are.

"To answer your question, did I achieve the summit 'because it was there'? The answer is frankly no. Ten Ting and I were utterly lost. We didn't know we were anywhere *near* it, let alone *on* it, until we discovered that we could ascend no farther!"

While the great mountains attract the adventuresome and daring, there are multitudes who walk more modest hills with equal joy. They may never venture above timberline or leave a travelled path, but these hill walkers are enriched by peace and beauty, by physical fitness and the milder challenge. No fame is theirs, little risk and no tangible gain. But they are true lovers of the mountains, and theirs is perhaps the purest motivation to climb.

ENVOI

We are drawn to climb by many motives. Beauty and splendor may be found in the hills more than anywhere in nature. As we conceive heaven to be above, so mountains approach the divine, and so men have seen them. Self-knowledge, self-conquest, good health and wisdom may be gained in climbing. Fame and material rewards may come too, but sharply pursued, cause loss of the richer intangible gains.

Above all is the challenge to be met, the risk to be taken and won. A burning desire to do the impossible has led man alone of all the animals to the blessings – and the burdens – of civilization. To reach beyond his grasp has always been and will long remain man's unique spur. Men never conquer mountains any more than mountains conquer men. In the pursuit of what the mountains offer, men find more than victory.

FOOTNOTES

1. Mummery, A. F.: *My Climbs in the Alps and Caucasus.* Hollywood-by-the-Sea, Transatlantic Arts, 1951.
2. Psalms CXXI.
3. Byron, A. L.: *Childe Harold's Pilgrimage.*
4. Mallory, G. L.: *The Assault on Mount Everest.* 1922.
5. Ruskin, J.: *Modern Painters,* 1850.
6. Mallory: *op. cit. supra* note 4; Mallory, G. L.: *Alpine Journal,* vol. 32, 1917.
7. Godley, A. D.: *The Alpine Journal,* vol. 23, 1879.
8. Kugy, J.: *Alpine Pilgrimage,* 1925.
9. Hunt, J., Jr.: *The Ascent of Everest.* New York, Dutton, 1954.
10. Flecker, J. E.: *The Pilgrims.*
11. Noyce, W.: *The Springs of Adventure.* Cleveland, World Pub. Co., 1958.

SKIING

JAMES A. KNIGHT

SINCE WORLD WAR II the sport of skiing has become extremely popular. It is the fastest growing sport in the United States. Gregory Stone, in his searching inquiry into sports and status, investigated adult attitudes toward a number of sports in widely divergent socioeconomic areas in Minneapolis.[1] His findings revealed that the most generalized or mass sport was skiing. There were no age, sex or class differences among those who expressed an interest in it.

Skiing has become the winter fashion. Each masculine newcomer is usually matched by a feminine beginner in molded stretch pants. The female on the ski scene has accelerated the development of *après-ski*. This delightful French phrase summarizes the other-than-outdoor aspects of skiing.

Two mechanical devices have also aided in the development of ski resorts — the ski lift and the snow-making machine. Twenty-five years ago, the skier got to the top of the hill by slogging up the slope under his own power or by holding on to the endless rope of a motor-powered ski tow. Such a tow was tough on the arms and a strain on the muscles. We are now in the painless era of the ski lift. Also the helicopter, extensively used in the Alps for transportation to the remotest mountain peaks, is now being used to a more limited extent in the United States.

Snow droughts or destructive thaws have always threatened the skiing season of many resorts. In these areas, the snow-making machine is standing by as emergency or supplementary equipment. Through a maze of aluminum piping, propelled by compressed air, water is sprayed through nozzles. Whenever the temperature is 32° Fahrenheit or lower, this sprayed water turns to snow. Thus skiing can be virtually guaranteed all winter long.

Another mechanical device, although simple, should be mentioned as contributing greatly to the success and popularity of skiing; that is the safety release on skis which saves many skiers from serious accidents when they fall.

I have interviewed a number of skiers, both amateur and professional, regarding their views of skiing and the ski community. Although informal interviews and conversation often elicit only conscious motivation, one can see in the material a number of unconscious or deeper determinants of behavior.

A physician speaking in a general way stated that

> the almost total distraction which skiing requires has been given credit for the healing of peptic ulcer by some of my friends. I believe the medical profession is represented in the skiing field to a greater degree than any other group, and it is a common story that they find this sport a most effective means of getting unwound from the professional pressures. There are so many factors which are peculiar to this sport. There is an exhilaration in the environment, a sense of satisfaction in having control of motion, and certainly gratification in an accomplishment which I have observed.

Another physician, a prominent skiing enthusiast, feels that essentially the same motivation exists in skiing as in a number of other sports such as mountain climbing, water skiing, sailing, ice skating and gliding. He states that the basic factors of out-of-doors activity — speed, danger, body appreciaton and comradeship — are fundamental to all of them. He feels that there is only a slim chance of finding any one common tendency of mind in skiers, for to him "skiing is not a sport, but a philosophy of living *with* and not *against* the elements."

Those interviewed listed a multitude of motivations to explain their interest in skiing. A very stable, attractive ski instructor stated that prior to learning to ski she had been an introvert; skiing had opened a new world for her and had given her the ability to relate to people, to be sociable, and to change her personality from introversion to extroversion.

A former chief secretary to one of the world's greatest surgeons emphasized the thrill of body coordination in skiing. She mentioned that there was a special type of body sensation that was associated with the coordination of skiing movements similar to that of dancing and ballet. She went on to say that possibly this represented the mastering and control of the body which was so important to the skier. She listed other factors such as sensitivity to the beauty of nature and the feeling of worship and closeness to ultimate things. She felt that the great heights involved in skiing and the overcoming of such height and fright were both meaningful features of skiing. Also this was a socially acceptable way for those sensitive to social pressures to participate in the sensation and thrill of speed. While one could not legally speed in a car, one could subject himself to great speed and the thrill of it in skiing, without the legal or social stigma associated with auto speeding. This talented and beautiful secretary had worked for years — seven days a week — for this surgeon. She finally sacrificed this important position, took a vacation at a ski resort and, significantly enough, remained there to work and ski.

Although dedicated to fine skiing, a good percentage of those addicted to skiing find the sport irresistible probably because it offers escape. This is especially true for those who work all the time at ski resorts. They are running from the nine-to-five job and from responsibility. Sometimes this need to escape may be an effort to free oneself from the bondage of unrewarding relationships and situations. At other times it may stem from feelings of inadequacy and lack of confidence. In skiing ability, there may be no lack of confidence. Thus if the person succeeds in becoming a part- or full-time ski instructor, he has truly succeeded, for in the ski resort the ski instructor is a god.

Environment and atmosphere were mentioned by many people as the two chief motivations behind the sport of skiing. A girl's extended visit to a ski resort brought forth this testimony:

> Aspen was fabulous, marvelous, delightful, grand, and all other superlatives which could possibly apply. . . . It's the inexplicable, strange, exhilarating thrill of swooping down a mountain in the sunshine as well as the happy, *friendly* people connected with both ski and after-ski that lead to such quick addiction. . . . Unless one has ever been to a ski resort, the atmosphere is difficult to describe: open, honest, extroverted friendliness is as close as I can come. It's tremendously easy to meet dozens of people.

Many mentioned the beauty of nature and the beauty of God's world, as well as the closeness one feels both to nature and to people in such an environment. Some spoke of the skiing world as having created in them a sense of worship and closeness to God which they had never been able to experience in a man-made cathedral; they found worship easy in the "cathedral of God's world."

In such a cathedral in nature the biblical declaration comes to life: "All thy works shall praise thee, O Lord."[2] One person stated that since skiing takes place only in a majestic setting, one seems to hear at times the whole world of nature cry out, "For thine is the power and the glory." A girl mentioned the joy of skiing alone, away from the crowds, and being wrapped in the silence of the hills. She feels that she now knows what the Psalmist experienced when he sang, "I will lift up mine eyes unto the hills from whence cometh my help."[3]

Those skiers who find a closeness to God when they are on the mountainous slopes may have something in common with a mountain climber and poet such as Wilfred Noyce who once wrote: "There is a streak of madness in these men and women whose eyes are fixed on the stars, but it is a divine madness."[4]

In discussing Noyce's statement with a skier, he mentioned that in skiing he often felt a strong sense of creative power and grandeur as if he had control over, or even created, everything that was below him. He experienced this when skiing high in the mountains, alone and early in the morning. Although he did frequently feel a closeness to God, at other times the emotion was one of such power he could describe it only as "godlike" or that of himself as a creator.

Many spoke of the dynamic factor of proving oneself. The process of skiing is somewhat dangerous and difficult. Therefore, if one is successful, it is a way of proving oneself in this type of dramatic performance.

Somewhat related to this was another point stressed by many — the element of death. Since skiing is a very dangerous sport, the skier almost defies death in the chances he takes and the treacherous situations which he gets into on the slopes. Thus, possibly it is a means of defying death and overcoming it, and in this way getting rid of one's fear of death. "Survival euphoria," therefore, may be a factor — a desire to win out over the near-death that a dangerous situation may involve. The Chinese have a saying that narrow escapes are like cutting off the Devil's tail.

An amazing thing about skiers is their resistance to giving up the sport even in the face of illness or crippling injury. Many know the story of the courageous Austrian skier, Bruno Wintersteller, who was slated for Olympic honors when a skiing accident cost him his right leg.[5] The first winter after he lost his leg he hobbled out to the Austrian hills and began trying to ski. Today, on one leg, he is again a champion. He has been the winner several times of Austrian ski meets for crippled skiers. He gained a perfect balance and flawless control over the limb. He was described in *Skiing* magazine in these triumphant words: "He had conquered himself. He was no longer handicapped."[6]

There are many handicapped skiers on the slopes. In contests, they are grouped in many classes: skiers on crutches, skiers on wooden legs, skiers with no arms, skiers with paralyzed knees or hips, skiers with no arms or legs but with artificial limbs instead. Once the mayor of Innsbruck, when giving out race trophies, stated that all handicapped skiers are winners, for they have won over life itself. The mayor's words possibly tell us something of the motivation in *all* skiers.

A recent issue of a medical journal carried the story of a forty-nine-year-old surgeon, a veteran skier and outdoor sportsman who was stricken with an acute massive coronary infarct.[7] Within six months after his heart attack he was skiing again in the high thin air of the Taos Ski Valley, 11,200 feet above sea level. He does his skiing with a special oxygen rig strapped on his back. Since then, wearing his translucent face mask and portable oxygen rig, he has become a familiar sight on the slopes of the Taos Valley. Again, life is being conquered.

Exhibitionism was another point mentioned. Many skiers have a wide variety of attractive ski clothes, especially the girls. They dress in very seductive fashions, in the new type of stretch ski pants, and exhibit their sex in stimulating ways. This, plus the whole process of graceful body movements, rhythm, the mastery of control and many other factors make exhibitionism very important in skiing.

An interesting point was mentioned by an unmarried girl who stated that skiing was one great opportunity for independent performance. "When I ski, I am on my own. You either succeed or fail, and nobody can help you or ski for you." This independent performance is very important for many people. The girl who made this statement comes from a wealthy family and is an only child. Possibly there have been very few situations in life where she has been allowed to express her individuality and independence. One can speculate that probably her parents have frequently sought to overprotect her. On the ski slopes, she could express herself unhampered by parental control, be independent, and fail or succeed on her own merits. Thus, for her, skiing had become a very meaningful part of her emotional economy.

Many people have asked about the sexual implications of skiing and have attributed sexual meaning to various aspects of skiing activity. Of course, competition, the need to excel, aggressive performance and the comradeship on the slopes are sexually flavored in the broad Freudian sense. Two west Texans, an independent oil operator and a lean, successful internist, were fascinated by schussing the slopes. They described the skier, schussing the slopes, as a giant human rocket shooting the mountainside at the delirious speed of sixty to ninety miles an hour. At this point their sexual symbolism became so bold that it would have gladdened the heart of Sigmund Freud had he been around to hear it.

Psychologist Ernest Dichter, a motivational research specialist, has said: "There is a sort of defloration involved . . . of the virginal snow. Conquest. You make your own tracks. Stretch pants can be compared to a sweater of the lower extremities. . . . Skiing also has a similarity to getting drunk. You're discovering, as you do when you're intoxicated, another part of yourself. Is this really me? You ask yourself: Am I capable of this kind of enjoyment? Perhaps there is a relationship here to sexual release."[8] Dichter goes on to stress that skiing also involves the moment of truth — complete absorption away from the complicated trials of modern life. Alone in the winter landscape, one becomes very important to himself.

One physician skier mentioned that it is easy to equate the skiing resort with the full measure of ski activities. He went on to say that this is an erroneous conclusion in spite of the fact that the skiing resort invites the eye toward the body forms of men and women more than it does any other sense. Yet a great amount of skiing is done in separation from ski resorts — maybe more in Europe than in the United States. At this point I could not help recalling my conversation with some of the Swiss whom I visited and interviewed in the communities around the Jungfrau and the Matterhorn.

Many mentioned how they grew up on skis, which they often used first as a means of transportation. They mentioned the joy of skiing alone and how deeply they were fulfilled by such an experience.

The physician skier mentioned above feels that motivation for many skiers may relate more to "body appreciation" than "sex appreciation." Thus one may be an enthusiastic member of the ski community without any need to rebel against the sexual or other mores of society, for his motivation evolves out of a different life orientation. This physician stated:

> Very socially respectable people, with or without sex drive, are participating in skiing merely for reasons of finding a new approach to nature, which separates them for the first time from the machinery of daily life, and finally gives them a chance to touch "untouched" nature, meaning newly fallen snow. Here is a factor which is similar to that found in climbing on difficult rocks and in skiing. This possibility of touching nature as the first person since the evidence brought down by newly fallen snow precludes any contamination of this evidence of nature by anything else — so the climber feels able to touch the rock wall as the very first person, and has in this way a very close contact with nature itself. Whenever such a basic feeling is introduced, the understanding of skiing reaches into a depth which has passed the obvious feeling of sex appreciation.

Someone witnessed to the fact that the sport of skiing and the ski community enable one to overcome his feelings of separateness and isolation. This type of statement is not far removed from the basic concept of the psychoanalyst Erich Fromm, who has stressed in many of his writings that man, in developing his individuality, broke his primary bonds to nature. After these ties were broken, he then felt alone and isolated and spent his life trying to overcome his aloneness.[9] One can speculate that skiing and the closeness to nature which is required in this activity help one reestablish his primary bonds to nature. In addition, the interpersonal relationships in the resort community help further to overcome one's isolation by nurturing a type of human solidarity.

THE SKI COMMUNITY

The ski community furnishes a special environment for analysis and study. In fact, it seems that living there is almost a form of group psychotherapy within itself. People with various types of needs, goals and problems gather there for work and recreation. Possibly those who come to stay fall into a different motivational group than those who come once or twice a year for a week or two of skiing. A mixture of rich and poor people is found in these communities, but money is usually no badge of status, for people are evaluated on other terms. Perhaps the people who ski well are the ones who have the highest status. At any rate, one cannot help noticing the democratic spirit which generally prevails in the ski community. Regardless of creed or economic background, when one is on the skiing slopes, he stands shoulder to shoulder and on the same level with everybody else.

"Thrilled to know, Mr. Carstairs, that something's bugging you, too!"

In speaking of the democratic spirit and sense of community which exist in many ski resorts, I do not mean to imply that there are not in certain places distinct social groups and a variety of social climbing on the slopes. Gay Talese describes the social climbing at the chic snow spa of Sugarbush, Vermont:[10]

> The slopes of Sugarbush are superbly conditioned for social climbing. At the very top, though the group numbers fewer than one hundred of the 2,400 who ski Sugarbush on a busy day, is café society's heralded jet set, which does not come by bus. The jet set, which travels to Europe a great deal and insists on having to its parties at least one Greek shipowner, a Ferrari auto racer and a cocktail of countesses, was not lured to Sugarbush through any enticement by the center's thirty-six-year-old president Damon Gadd, a congenial but not effusive Yale man. It came, rather, because it was seeking a new cold-weather playpen and because one of its very favorite people was Sugarbush's chief ski instructor, Peter Estin, a slim, rich, thirty-five-year-old former Dartmouth ski hero, tennis player and wine-taster, a linguist, a cartoonist and a climate-hopping *bon vivant* whose current girl friend is a French baroness. Estin has had as many as three Greek shipowners to a single party.
>
> With such credentials, Peter Estin had no difficulty getting the jet set to Sugarbush, and soon they decided that they liked the place so much they built their own small chalets on the mountain near Estin's. Sugarbush quickly achieved its posh, cosmopolitan image. Each weekend this winter the mountainside has been climbed by rising new cliques, but the jet set remains the envy of many of those below.

Just below the jet set at Sugarbush is another group of skiers who are a little younger, a little less continental. They have not yet made it in the professions but are on the way up. They are described by Talese as belonging to the turbo-prop class or the tourist-class jet set.

Most of the skiers at Sugarbush, however, are not trying the hills solely for social status. The higher status that most are seeking is the status one enjoys when he is an excellent skier in fast company.

Another group at Sugarbush is a small society of skiers who remain apart from all other groups. They rebel against everything the jet set stands for. They are mostly college boys who bunk in run-down ski lodges. They often wear blue jeans instead of ski pants or ski while wearing long red underwear over their blue jeans. These college boys, however, are fighting impossible odds, for the world of high fashion has conquered the slopes of Sugarbush.

An excellent ski instructor in her early twenties described how she came to a ski community. Her story illustrates some of the personal fulfillment certain individuals find in this type of life. She was reared in a straight-laced conventional family in Los Angeles and went to a religious school. She managed to extricate herself from this school when she was nineteen and discovered at that time "smoking, dancing and sex." Ever since, she has found these to be very interesting and exciting forms of activity. She emphasized that everybody in her ski town who was working there seemed to be running away from something and that "the running away" was the one common denominator which all of the permanent or semipermanent residents shared. She mentioned that a great spirit of nonconformity existed among these people, and life in such a town permitted them to express their individuality. She also emphasized that there was a great deal of free love going on in this type of community, and the majority of people participated in this without any compunction of conscience but as a very natural expression of human fulfillment. She then went on to say that the four chief pastimes of her ski community were (1) skiing, (2) drinking, (3) people, and (4) sex. She testified that she participated in all of these with great enthusiasm and interest.

She was a very personable individual, and her emphasis on people as a significant psychic ingredient in her life seemed genuine and important. This girl was obviously a true rebel and was rebelling against the value systems of her family, of society, and all the conventional forms of morality which at times seemed artificial and unnecessary to her. Yet there was a sense of integrity, fidelity and understanding in her life, as well as a need to help people and show compassion for those in trouble. These virtues were very evident and genuine in her own life. In many ways she portrayed the existential point of view in her need to live today, since this was the only time that had been allotted her. Whether or not tomorrow would come was not for her to predict, for the filling of today with meaningful living consumed all of her time. Thus, she was content to spend the day in skiing and the night in dining, dancing and good fellowship. Her motto is "life is for living."

The problem of rebellion versus conformity is seen in a girl somewhat similar to the one just described. This girl epitomizes the conscientious, well-disciplined type of person. She is an only child and the sole object of parental scrutiny. Her parents have always insisted on the very best from her, and she has never failed to give it to them. She is of superior intelligence and, to all outward appearances, socially quite well-adjusted. She has always been a conservative and a conformist, even while excelling in the liberal environment into which her art training and background have led her. This, coupled with the fact that she achieves absolute perfection in everything she does, makes her a target for criticism for a plethora of reasons, such as jealousy and misunderstanding. Yet she has maintained every one of her high standards.

Recently she had been working as an apprentice in an art studio and everyone anticipated that her performance would be consistent with her previous pattern — she would persevere until eventually she would be promoted to a top position. In the midst of all this, however, she took off for a ski community with a vagabond type of boy whom she had been dating. They planned to stay until their money ran out. This adventure seems utterly incongruous with her previous behavior pattern. She seems to have experienced a metamorphosis, shedding the straight-laced conservatism and emerging as a daring liberal. Her restraint and high standards had formerly provoked a "spiritual isolation," as it were, from her contemporaries, and possibly she always secretly admired people who were capable of rebellion. At any rate, it would seem that this sojourn in a ski community is an obvious act of conformity to the rebellion ethic in an attempt to show everyone that she had been miscast as the conservative. Anyway, such a person gives one an opportunity to review some of the aspects of rebellion and conformity as they are seen in certain members of the skiing community.

Although we may look upon some of this nonconformity with mixed feelings, the sobering lesson of history is that almost every great soul has been a nonconformist.

In his article "Ski-Bum Artist," Stan Fischler tells the story of Leon Vart, a seventy-five-year-old fugitive to New York from Moscow. Vart's philosophy is quite simple: "If you want to live like a dog and die like a man, get married. If you want to live like a man and die like a dog, then be a ski bum like me."[11] He has been ski bumming since 1917. He thanks the Russian government under Kerensky for launching him on his colorful career. Then an art student, he was sent to the Orient in 1917 to buy 300,000 shoes for his comrades in Moscow. Once he saw the snow on Fujiyama his wanderlust took possession of him and he was no longer interested in purchasing shoes. Kerensky never heard from him again. He has spent his bachelor life skiing at most of the ski resorts of the world. He offers his paintings in exchange for life's necessities. If his paintings do not suffice, he resorts to a variety of odd jobs from writing to interior decorating. He claims to have found in his way of living the truly abundant life.

The character of the ski community is further enhanced by the number of successful people who give up their primary vocations, go to a ski resort and become ski instructors. As a ski instructor, such a person makes a very modest living and has to live simply. One example of this is an excellent engineer whose father is famous in the same vocation. Yet he gave up his vocation and his place in the family engineering company to devote his life to skiing. He is happy in his new pursuit and free from the hectic tensions and artificialities of his previous way of life.

CONCLUSION

If one studies the relationship of evolution to present-day physical and emotional health, he is painfully impressed by the diseases of civilization.

"They don't come any poshier than Sir Alexander, the big wheel distiller. Hosting three Greek shipowners and five Baronesses at the moment!"

Primitive man participated in strenuous muscular activity as a means of survival. Frequently he was stimulated suddenly by the threat of danger. He was forced to flee or fight. His body prepared itself for strenuous muscular activity, and no matter what course of action he chose, it expressed itself in muscular exertion. But in our civilized society today we are faced frequently with dangers, threats, insults and verbal attacks of one kind or another. Yet seldom can we deal with any of these dangers by muscular exertion. While our endocrine system has prepared us for fight or flight, all that polite society permits us to do is sit quietly with a thousand storms churning within us. This state of preparedness, which seldom finds expression in physical activity, is almost certain to manifest itself in some way in the human organism. Probably this is not a definitive explanation of some of our psychosomatic illnesses, but it may well be a part of the picture. In what way does this relate to skiing?

A physician has said that skiing is not a sport but a way of life and mentioned that a fellow physician had recovered from his peptic ulcer on the slopes. Possibly skiing furnishes the right combination of exposure to danger, muscular exertion, creative skill and individual expression to give man an opportunity to use his physical and mental endowments in the way in which nature intended him to for survival. Also the skiing community furnishes man the freedom to express himself as an individual yet gives him a sense of relatedness to and solidarity with his fellowman. Thus, skiing may be one of the best forms of activity (or "ways of life") for neutralizing certain of the disintegrating aspects of modern civilized living.

Regardless of the motivation, skiing is here to stay. Its ever-increasing popularity can be witnessed by the number of ski resorts that have sprung up in all parts of the United States and Canada, by the publications devoted to the subject, by the unending conversations of ski enthusiasts, and by the fact that if nature does not provide snow on the slopes man will manufacture it. Possibly a study of motivation will enhance further the enjoyment of this activity.

NOTE

Sections of this paper, with revisions, are reprinted from a guest editorial in the *Western Journal of Surgery, Obstetrics and Gynecology, 69*:395-398, 1961.

FOOTNOTES

1. Stone, G. P.: Some Meanings of American Sport. Sixtieth Annual Proceedings, National College Physical Education Association, Columbus, Ohio, 1957, pp. 19-20.
2. Psalms 145: 10.
3. Psalms 121:1.
4. Quoted in *Newsweek,* Aug. 13, 1962, in reporting the death of Noyce who fell while descending from the peak of Mount Garmo, high in the rugged Pamir Range on the Russian-Afghanistan border.

5. *Skiing,* Feb. 1961, pp. 24-26.
6. *Ibid.*
7. M. D. cardiac on skis. *Roche Medical Image,* Dec. 1964, vol. 6, no. 6.
8. Quoted in *Playboy,* Nov. 1963, p. 93.
9. Fromm, E.: *Escape from Freedom.* New York, Rinehart, 1941; Fromm, E.: *Man for Himself* New York, Rinehart, 1947.
10. Talese, G.: Social climbing on the slopes. *Sat. Eve. Post,* Feb. 9, 1963, p. 30.
11. Fischler, S.: Ski-bum artist. *Pictorial Living, Journal American,* Feb. 2, 1964, p. 11.

SAILING

RUSSELL R. MONROE

SHIVERING WITH COLD IN THE COCKPIT of my sailboat, while the rain trickles down the back of my neck, hands blistered from hauling lines and back aching from cranking sheet winches, eyes burning from the salt spray, I often wonder what I would be doing with my weekends if my grandfather had not taught me the joys of sailing at a tender and impressionable age. I can imagine myself comfortably ensconced in an easy chair, a beer in one hand and a cigar in the other watching the Sunday afternoon baseball game. Yet on the next day of rest I, like millions of others, will be gleefully back on the water having easily forgotten the miseries of the preceding weekend.

Why do people sail? Like no other sport it means many things to many people. To one it is the endless hours of practice summer, fall, winter and spring, sailing single-handed in a fourteen-foot boat in the rough waters of the North Sea, feet hooked under hiking straps, body suspended far over the windward rail, driving in the blustering winds in pursuit of an Olympic gold medal. To others, sailing means a boat with a deckhouse large enough to accommodate stereophonic equipment and a card table. It can be the excitement of twenty to thirty boats simultaneously approaching the windward end of the starting line of a triangular race, or the peaceful, silent gunkholing in the winding rivers of the Chesapeake Bay's Eastern Shore. It is the challenge of a single-handed thirty-day sail across the Atlantic, solitary confinement on an inadequate diet, soaked or at least damp all the time, sleeping fitfully as life is always in peril. It is the blissful peace of stretching out in the cockpit while quietly anchored after a long day's run, sipping a cool drink or eating a warm meal while the seagulls cry overhead and the sun sets on the distant horizon. What is there — or, in fact, is there anything — common to such varied experiences? Like many sports, sailing is man's response to the challenge of nature, as climbing Mt. McKinley, shooting the rapids of the Albany River or conquering the head wall of Tuckerman's Ravine on skis. In fact, the land-locked sailor often takes to the skis, mountains or rivers. Man's need to respond to this challenge, to see the unseen and to do the undone, is as old as his own history and is part of what is uniquely human.

There is something different in this challenge as expressed by the sailor in his boat. To sail is not only to challenge nature but to harness the elements, wind and water, tide and current. The sailor is the sportsman most effective in converting the natural forces from wild threats to human existence to useful motive power. Although I would not know from personal experience, I suspect the pilot in his glider is the sportsman most nearly akin to the sailor in his boat. When the uninitiated is told that the maximum hull speed of most displacement boats is seven or eight knots (no more than 10 mph) he wonders how this can be an exciting sport, particularly in an age where speed is measured in Mach units. Experience alone can convey the exhilaration of feeling one's boat leap ahead, heeled at a 20-degree angle with the lee rail buried in the boiling foam, while one's face feels the sting of the wind and spray. Nothing is heard but nature's sounds — wind singing in the rigging, sails fluttering, the splash and gurgling of water and the pounding of waves. This is the exhilaration of utilizing natural forces without destroying or being destroyed by such forces. This is an experience we have too seldom in our modern world. Only a few can manipulate an atomic pile and get the same exhilaration from harnessing nature. Perhaps it is for this reason that sailing as a sport is relatively young — only a little over one hundred years old. It is during the same epoch that our increasingly complicated technology has robbed man of the direct satisfaction of harnessing nature.

Of course, there are other aspects of sailing which contribute to the gratification one obtains from this sport. Whether he is in the middle of the Atlantic or in Long Island Sound barely twenty miles from Manhattan, the sailor has the feeling of being in a world of his own, in fact, not only of his own but of his own choosing — a small world where all the elements needed to control these natural forces are at his finger tips and completely under his control. He has selected the boat, spent many hours equipping it, anticipating every contingency. Supplies and gear are stowed in a precise place where they are convenient for immediate use should an emergency arise. There is an extra anchor, extra tiller, a paddle, a sail repair kit, tool box, foul weather gear, a compass, a radio, charts, tide-tables, almanac — everything the sailor needs for a late afternoon sail to Lloyd's Neck five miles away or a winter rendezvous in the Bahamas. Complex as the modern cruising auxiliary is, it is a microcosm compared to our weekday world — a microcosm that can be thoughtfully kept in immaculate order, and without omnipotence — a world that is completely under the sailor's control. Here is a world where every man is a king.

This world provides the sailor with the opportunity for an expression of a myriad of other hobbies and interests. The mathematician becomes the navigator; the electronic buff designs and builds his own transmitters, direction finders, depth recorders, etc.; the carpenter equips his cabin; the painter varnishes his bright work; the mechanic tinkers with the engine. In fact, the attraction of the boat as an end in itself is so great that some boat owners hardly use their sails but spend their leisure time at the mooring, always getting ready to sail but finding the preparation itself so enjoyable that they seldom weigh anchor.

Most sailors do not go to sea alone. There is a crew as well as a captain. The relationship between the captain and the crew, as everyone with a movie acquaintance with Captain Bligh knows, can spell the difference between a successful voyage and catastrophe. The close confines of the ship strips every man of his facade. No experienced captain will go on a long voyage without knowing his companions well, for nothing can be more miserable and, at times, even dangerous than three or four incompatible people unable to escape each other's company for days on end. On the other hand, nothing can be more satisfying than the intimacy of such a voyage with close friends. Sailing today is becoming a family enterprise which can either lead to family cohesiveness or rip it asunder. Some families, all sailors, cope with this by each having his own boat crewed by friends of his own choice. Other families have been spending their summers boating since the time the children were toddlers in playpens on the foredeck or restrained by harness and line made fast to the mizzenmast. Such togetherness is not the calamity that one might presume because the immediacy of crew and boat coping with the elements dramatizes the need for family cooperation and unity which is not so obviously required in today's suburban living. One of my fondest memories of family life will always be long winter months when my wife, my two daughters and myself looked at pictures and discussed specifications of the boat we were going to charter for the following summer. Having made this decision, we then secured charts, determined tides and currents and plotted alternative courses for our forthcoming cruise. Before long we were thoughtfully packing our limited personal belongings, ingeniously devising convenient but tasteful menus and then scouring the community for the appropriate supplies.

Finally, the time came when we boarded the boat, but we still had to restrain our impulse to get on with the voyage until we had spent a day stowing the supplies, learning how to use the equipment, assigning duties, checking the compass and running a measured course so that after all these months of joint effort we could cruise with confidence that in sunlight, darkness or fog we would arrive safely at our point of destination. Mutual respect develops as each individual sees the other carry out his particular function in a thoughtful and thorough manner. There is new admiration for father who plans the cruise with precision and flawlessly handles the boat regardless of how difficult the situation. Mother can cook delicious meals at home equipped with an automatic electric range and supplied by a neighborhood supermarket via the refrigerator and freezer, but there is a special appreciation when she cooks a meal on a gimbled stove in a galley 15 degrees from the horizontal. Even the eight-year-old finds particular status mixed with anxiety when she discovers that she is the only one suited to go up the mast in a bosun chair to retrieve a lost jib halyard. There is something poignant about the experience of being caught in a bad storm and finally entering a harbor of refuge to have your nine-year-old child turn to you and say: "Don't worry any more, Daddy, we can swim for it now."

In this day of permissive child-rearing and pride in individual independence, sailing provides an experience which is both unique and valuable — that is, submitting to the authority of the captain-crew relationship. It does not take many voyages before family crews are convinced of the need for immediate obedience to the captain's orders. They soon discover that these orders are not just unreasonable demands of an inconsiderate adult but necessary for the safety, pleasure and sometimes survival of all those aboard. Woe be unto the skipper, however, who does not show the proper appreciation for the part his crew plays in a successful sail. One such skipper received his just reward when, having victoriously crossed the finish line of a race in a brisk breeze dead before the wind, spinnaker billowing before him, he was horrified to see his indignant and much maligned crew jump overboard, leaving him alone with a scant two hundred yards between himself and an onrushing seawall. Because he was an expert seaman he managed to douse his spinnaker, trim the mainsail and reach the tiller again just in time to avoid running hard on the rocks. He learned the lesson well because he is now one of the most appreciative and considerate skippers afloat.

Too little has been said of the competitive aspect of sailing — that is, the weekend series of races against competitors with identical or nearly identical boats. Like all competition, sailing requires coordination, physical endurance, practice and, for the winner, that indefinable something that distinguishes him from the second best. To be a champion requires a highly developed sense of space and direction — a three dimensional mind's eye view of wind direction, course, position of numerous competitors and one's own relative position in respect to all these. He must combine this with a precise knowledge of the intricate right-of-way rules and aerodynamic principles in order to plot his winning maneuvers. He must possess the verve of the automobile racer to keep on his collision course until the very last second, tacking with precision and fullest cooperation from his crew to backwind this competitor or to establish an overlap at the windward mark. In light airs the champion literally feels what to others are imperceptible wind shifts. He concentrates on the sails and the motions of the waves, gently manipulating the tiller to squeeze the utmost out of the wind, waves and current, slowly inching ahead of his less talented competitors. His crew must keep alert to all that takes place from horizon to horizon while the skipper concentrates on his boat. It is the crew's responsibility to see what is happening to other boats close by and in the distance, noticing whether some are being picked up by the wind shifts so that they can lay the mark while others are thrown off the course so that they must tack again before reaching this same mark. The skipper, like the coach, must have the capacity in his interpersonal relationships to develop a devotion among crew members so that they will practice until every command is obeyed automatically and with a precision that would do justice to synchronized swimmers.

Races are often won or lost long before the boat reaches the starting line. In today's one-design competition, the boats are allegedly the same; yet in certain national championships where all competitors rotate boats it soon becomes apparent that certain one-design boats are duds and others exceptionally fast. To obtain the latter status every effort is made to keep the boat just as light as the rules will allow. The hardware must not only be strong but in smooth working order. The lines and sails must be in perfect condition because breakdowns are no excuse, and except in long series, are usually disastrous. Hulls must be polished until they look like the living room piano, and the proper sails must be selected on the basis of anticipated wind strength. In fact, the precision and devotion that goes into the pre-race tuneup reaches fantastic proportions. As an example, consider the competition among the twelve-meter boats for the American Cup. These are seventy-foot boats weighing sixty thousand pounds; yet, before a crucial race, the boat may be hauled out of the water and electric heaters placed below deck to dry out the few pounds of water that have been absorbed by the hull during the preceding days. Just such precision can make the difference between the winner and the "also ran."

Part of the excitement of sailing is that no matter how skillful the skipper and crew or how perfectly tuned the boat, there is always the element of unpredictability of the wind which, in a split second, can change one's position from first to last. Of course, such a disastrous outcome from a windshift happens least often to the experienced skipper, but it is the very unpredictability that increases the excitement of the race. No matter how far ahead one is, he cannot be sure the race is won until the finish line is crossed and the race committee gives the gun. This is the excitement that keeps the "duffer" racing, although day after day he comes in last or near last. There is the anticipation that sooner or later his skills will develop so that he will be among the top of the fleet; but more immediately, there is a hope that, this very day, some fate will favor the ill-starred skipper so he will end up at the top of the fleet. It happens just often enough so that this hope is not completely irrational. What other sport is like this? Can one imagine the weekend golfer beating Arnold Palmer?

The unlimited complexities of sailing sustain the interest of sailors year after year. I have been sailing for thirty-five years; yet there is hardly a weekend, whether it is in racing competition or an afternoon sail with congenial friends, that I do not discover something new about the sport of sailing. It was just several weekends ago that I happened upon a maneuver that had never occurred to me before. Since then I learned, with smug satisfaction, that a somewhat similar maneuver was used by H. S. Vanderbilt in the final selection trials of the American Cup series between Rainbow and Yankee in 1934. The maneuver simply described is this. It is not unusual, particularly if one has become negligent or unobservant, to find that suddenly your jib is being backwinded and the boat is being thrown on the opposite tack, even though you do not desire this to happen. The skipper then shoves the tiller hard to windward and hopes that his forward momentum will suffice to carry him back on course without the unwanted tack. Often it is too late. The boat does not have the required headway so that it rapidly falls off on the other tack and one finds himself proceeding on a course 100 degrees from the one planned. This means freeing the jib sheet, trimming it on the opposite side of the boat, waiting patiently while the boat regains headway, and then coming about again which means retrimming the jib sheet. Minutes later, and after much commotion, you are back on your old course, cursing yourself for such carelessness. This maneuver requires considerable effort and time particularly in these days of large Genoa jibs that demand strong backs and mechanical winches to trim the sail properly. If one's crew is composed, as mine has been in recent years, of wife and children, such a maneuver can become a real chore. The last time this happened to me, perhaps because of laziness, I left the sails trimmed as they were while the wind, backwinding my jib, spun me around like a top. I not only went 100 degrees off my course, but I turned a complete 360 degree circle — that is, first I came about and then I jibed but without any more effort than pushing the tiller hard to windward and keeping it there until the maneuver was completed. In no time at all I was back on my course — no lines were freed, no backs were aching and no curses uttered. A simple maneuver, yet one I had never thought of before; and I expect many others have not thought of it, probably because it appears at first glance to be an unseamanlike procedure. As it turns out it is a simple and efficient trick — one that Commodore Vanderbilt found useful as a planned maneuver to gain valuable time against his opponent when rounding a mark. It is such discoveries that sustain the excitement of sailing year after year.

We have talked about the wind and the water, the captain and crew, but have saved the most important aspect of the sailor's world until the last. That is, the "ship." It is seldom that a member of the crew is content to remain "crew" at all times and in all situations. He gets the itch to buy a boat of his own. This may be no more than an eight-foot sailing pram, but the pride of ownership overwhelms him so that soon he is the possessor of his own "ship." What is this need to have one's own boat?

"To you, your sloop may be a girl, but, to me, mine's just a big, irresponsible, naughty boy!"

No matter how strong a man is, how exhilarated he becomes in challenging and harnessing nature, how independent he feels in ruling his own world, in the quiet moments after the storm he longs for the arms of his sweetheart or wife, and having surmounted one crisis gains strength for the next by symbolically returning to the lap of his mother. In his isolation, of course, it is not really his sweetheart or his mother he turns to but his boat. It is no accident that throughout the ages ships have been designated as female. The love and devotion given to them is paralleled only by a similar love and devotion to sweetheart and mother. There are other parallels, too. The skipper selects a boat after many years of anticipation. But just as the man who proposes to his bride-to-be often does so impetuously, so the sailor purchases his boat and soon afterward begins to worry whether he can afford such an expensive mistress. It is usually a case of love at first sight, and no matter how ugly she appears to others, she seems beautiful in the eyes of the possessor. Like all love, it is irrational. The ship is coveted and adored long after it should be discarded, but then one does not lightly dispose of wife or mother. No expense is spared to keep her beautiful. When, through the skipper's own miscalculations or poor seamanship, she behaves badly, she is cursed and blamed for all the trouble. But at the end of a harrowing day, when the sailor is curled up in his bunk dreaming in the soft light of the kerosene lamp as he listens to the lap of the waves against the hull, there is the same warmth and closeness one felt as a child in mother's arms. It is no wonder, then, that the desire to sail becomes all-consuming. It appeals to such basic human needs. It appeals to all that is self-reliant, independent and daring in human nature. Yet, it succors all that is regressive and dependent, providing a retreat to the warmth and tenderness of mother's arms. It is not surprising, too, that sailing usually has much less appeal for women. For the most part they seem to tolerate sailing because of their devotion to spouse and children and, at worse, may not only refuse to participate but even become intensely jealous of their man's love for his boat and the sea.

PART TWELVE
SKY SPORTS

INTRODUCTION

This section contains two papers on parachuting. But parachuting is only one of a number of sky sports, and so perhaps the reader deserves an explanation of our limited treatment of an important subject.

First of all, we need a definition. Logically and psychologically speaking, we should not be concerned with such altitudinally low-level activities as trapeze acrobatics, tightrope walking, high diving and ski jumping. Without condescension, we may say that in these sports one goes through various physical contortions, however skillfully, at only small distance from the ground. Then, and also easy to eliminate from our consideration, there is an assortment of old-fashioned curiosities: wing-walking, the aerial ballet, the barn-stormer's air show. These are, of course, mere stunts, performed usually by professionals, most often as exhibitions and crowd-drawers at the local county fair.

By contrast, the true sky sport catches something of the spirit of our times, from the Montgolfiers to Ben Franklin and Wilbur and Orville Wright. Flying, soaring, parachuting, ballooning — these are the sky sports, born of man's inventiveness and imagination.

But, sadly, the balloon has had its heyday, and one must turn the pages of Jules Verne (who went up in one) to get an idea of the delights and exciting perils of ballooning. As for that rare and esoteric sport of soaring, it remains as remote and inaccessible as the eagle's aerie. Perhaps the silent flight of the sailplane induces in its pilot a mood of quiet and serene contemplation; at any rate, judging by the meager literature on soaring, too few are prompted to describe its fascination.

Flying, when not primarily to get from one place to another or to carry the mail, passengers, or bombs, can undoubtedly qualify as a sport. Even more, some would say: a love, a passion, a way of life. Such writers as Anne Morrow Lindbergh and Antoine de Saint-Exupéry have given us vivid and moving accounts of their experiences of flying. And, we should say, the classic study on the psychology of flying has already been written by Douglas Bond, *The Love and Fear of Flying.*[1]

Parachuting is in some ways very much like flying, but psychologically, the obvious differences are most important. The aviator has his airplane, the jumper his parachute, and each man's preferred equipment becomes a very real psychological extension of himself. The pilot puts his faith in a complicated mechanical contrivance, controlled by skilled, fine manipulations and guided by a vast amount of technical knowledge. The jumper trusts only a very simple apparatus, his parachute. Characteristically, the one man regards the other's activity with a jaundiced eye, and there are few who can lay claim to equal expertness in both flying and jumping.

Today, parachuting enjoys a great vogue, with an ever growing number of enthusiasts all over the world. But parachuting is more than a popular sport. Mechanically simple, psychologically profound, it can well stand as the model *par excellence* of sky sports. The authors of the two papers to follow have found it so. A psychiatrist[2] and a sociologist,[3] they have arrived at their formulations and conclusions independently and from different professional orientations. This combination, then, provides a contrast between the psychiatric case study and the sociological survey, the former attempting to describe and understand the individual experience, which the latter attempts to define more in terms of standards and larger populations of subjects. Yet, interestingly, the psychiatrist talks of parachuting as social behavior, while the sociologist stresses the solitary character of the act. Also, in an area where folklore is more prevalent than scientific data, the authors are at variance in their assessment of the danger in parachuting, although sharing the conviction that jumpers regularly deny and minimize this danger.

Apart from these few points of difference, however, the authors of the following articles are in agreement on main issues. The reader will find that the different terminologies used are close enough for considerable correspondence, at the same time preserving some important distinctions. Thus, the psychiatrist, who writes about the "anxiety" and "counterphobic pleasure" in parachuting, refers to something very much like "fear" and "enthusiasm" in the act, described by the sociologist. For both authors, the transformation of fear (or anxiety) into pleasure is a process that constitutes the very essence of the experience of jumping. To understand how and why this can occur, the authors assert, is to understand why men jump.

NOTE

This introduction was prepared by Dennis Farrell.

FOOTNOTES

1. Bond, D. D.: *The Love and Fear of Flying*. New York, Int Univs, 1952.
2. Dennis Farrell, p. 661.
3. Samuel Z. Klausner, p. 670.

THE PSYCHOLOGY OF PARACHUTING

DENNIS FARRELL

In 1500, Leonardo da Vinci conceived of a safe means of descent from a great height and drew the first-known design of a parachute. Over four hundred years later, Freud proposed that Leonardo's interest in flying stemmed from a persistent infantile sexual curiosity.[1] Since Freud's work, with few notable exceptions, there has been little interest in the psychology of flying and of allied activities. Yet the air-age is hardly new; the space-age is now upon us. Today, the rocket is no less commonplace than was the airplane when Freud wrote on Leonardo. Even parachuting has come into its own. Over the troubled years of the past quarter-century, a dozen armies have used parachuting with telling effect in the waging of war. As a sport, parachuting claims more and more adherents. Sky-diving clubs now dot the face of America; in France, a trip to the local drop zone bids fair to replace the Sunday afternoon promenade as the weekly family outing.

Despite this widespread and growing interest in parachuting, one encounters two quite different attitudes in regard to it. Parachuting appeals to some as a thrilling adventure; to others, the prospect is the stuff of which nightmares are made. Between these extremes there is a remarkable scarcity of neutral feeling. Whatever the reaction, to most of us the idea of falling or jumping from a considerable height seems psychologically compelling. It has the character of something primitive and obscure to reason, something none of us has quite got over, man's amazing technological conquest of the air notwithstanding.

Perhaps, in the stories of men who love the sport — and of those who fear it — there is some hint of motive and impulse that lie ordinarily beyond our awareness.

THE PARACHUTIST

More often than one might think, the parachutist asks himself why he jumps.[2] His question is prompted by an uncomfortable lack of solid "reasons" for the pursuit of an activity that others see as reckless, crazy, heroic, frightening. For him, it is is none of these, quite. He agrees that what he does is unusual, and that there is an indefinable, irrational "something" which adds to the attraction of jumping. When pressed, the parachutist may finally say that, in jumping, it helps to be crazy.

In contrast to this aura of mystery about parachuting, the histories of many men show a strikingly direct connection between the wish to jump and a much earlier wish, the desire to emulate an admired figure out of the past. This figure — father, uncle, brother — once served as an important model in the formation of the individual's sense of identity and thereby preserved a place for itself in the "ego ideal"; to measure up to these internalized standards became something of value to one's self-esteem. In general, the prototype for these men is the aggressive, masterful man of action. These early identifications have influence on more than a man's general outlook and self-concept; they often dictate specific behavior within his life style.

> One man, volunteering for parachute duty in military service, explained that he "simply had to learn to jump." In connection with this feeling of compulsion, he recalled a number of memories of his father. In his early days, the father had been a cowboy — a role which by itself defines a typically American ideal prototype of strength, independence and individual action. Later, the father became a proud and skillful tradesman in a booming western industrial area, but he did not forget, nor did he fail to pass on to his son, his own love for a life of adventure, of rugged individualism, of physical mastery. Specifically, the father approved of parachuting: he had often said that there was one thing he wished he might have done, that jumping from an airplane must be the ultimate in thrills. His son realized this dream.

The importance of such identifications in motivating behavior deserves emphasis here because of the frequency with which it occurs as a specific determinant in the choice of career and avocation. Examples are easy to find: Almost all the adult males of a certain Indian tribe become structural steel workers on the most hazardous construction jobs; circus daredevils commonly pass on their trade from one generation to the next. There is no reason to limit this mechanism to more pedestrian cases of following in father's footsteps.

Succinctly but in more technical language, Erikson quotes Freud in defining one important source of self-esteem as "such infantile omnipotence as experience corroborates," or the fulfillment of the grandiose dreams and fantasies of childhood.[3] If this self-esteem is achieved through identification with a group, all the better. The present climate of social acceptance of parachuting as a sport creates a strong contagion effect, and this, too, should not be overlooked in considering both conscious and unconscious determinants of many men's motivation to take up jumping. For one thing, it helps that one no longer needs to be a daredevil or an eccentric to jump from an airplane.[4] Nowadays, in certain circles, parachuting is fast becoming one of the "in" things to do with one's leisure time. As social behavior, it offers the comradeship of men exposed to risk and adventure, the attractions of apprenticeship to the more skilled leader, and pride in the exclusiveness of membership in an elite group.

THE EXPERIENCE OF JUMPING

The jump itself takes only a few seconds; the experience, psychologically, begins with the minutes and hours of anxious expectation before that final step. Few parachutists deny this pre-jump anxiety. In fact, within the group, complete denial of fear is taken as evidence of an unbecoming false bravado, or if it seems to ring true, as psychological aberration – such men are "jump-happy." The actual danger is minimal statistically, but it is further minimized in the minds of most jumpers. Injuries and fatalities may occur, of course, through a variety of circumstances; yet the group as a whole clings to the belief that whatever misfortune occurs is the victim's own fault. The parachute is of such simple design that this is most often true, though not invariably so. To translate roughly into more familiar terms, it might be said that the risk in parachuting ranges between the dangers in skiing, at one extreme, and in mountain climbing, at the other.

The usual anxiety is limited within easily tolerable bounds of duration and intensity. It begins, ordinarily, shortly before the jump and mounts in intensity to the point of exit from the door of the airplane.

Parachutists commonly make use of several devices to dissipate this anxiety before a jump. "Talking it out" in countless "jump stories" often told with grisly humor is characteristic. Shouting and stamping within the aircraft just before the jump is another. Talismans are common: a cigar clenched between the teeth, a doll, a scarf, a special pair of boots.[5] Some men are silent on the ride to the "drop zone," some fall asleep. Finally, the roar of the engines, vibration, cold blasts of air from the open door, and above all, the thrill – the mounting anticipation of danger – these are all abruptly escaped by the jump.

The physical sensations of the jump occur as sudden contrasts. From noise, vibration, immobility and confinement, the jump brings rapid motion, and suddenly, as the canopy opens, suspension in what seems for the moment an absolute quiet in endless time and space. The subjective feeling is that of sudden release of tension with a surge of exhilaration.

Parachutists become sentimental when they talk about jumping. Some are reduced to such inarticulate statements as, "I don't know – you just can't describe it." Others rise to the occasion with expressions of some poetic quality. One such man expressed at least something of what most jumpers feel, though with unusual intensity:

> The jump isn't like a roller coaster ride, like they say. You are *free* when you jump. And when that old canopy opens, it's like the hand of God has caught you up. You look down on the world, and you think how nice it would be to stay up there. Just the same, I like to make a good landing. I always feel good after a jump, kind of relaxed and happy. Sometimes when I pick myself up, I feel like I'm ten feet tall. I don't know – you just can't describe it.

Why do men jump? A complex of converging forces determines the single act. A man jumps for many reasons, past and present, within and without his inner world. Ultimately the measure and quality of each must be weighed with the rest; yet each makes its unique contribution to the wish.

And jumping is not "just like everything else." It is not "take it or leave it" behavior. Instead, it is an unusually intense experience and one with special richness in symbolic meanings. The act itself is simple, quick, discrete, and demands full commitment. There must be an urge to jump. "That first step is a long one," the men say, but without this one step there cannot be a jump or a jumper.

Anxiety and Fear

A few years after Freud's classic analysis of anxiety, Alice Balint[6] wrote on a special form of infantile fear which she believed to be of more primitive nature than the earliest danger situations described by Freud.[7] The significance of this fear, that of being dropped and losing support, is reflected in the language by the numerous expressions which identify security with physical stability. Balint's examples of the German idiom are directly translatable: To lose one's grasp or hold on something (mastery, command); to be supported (cared for); to lose one's mental balance. With Ferenczi, Balint saw in the common experience of dreams of flying a wish-fulfilling denial of primitive fear; he who flies need not fall. Mankind's longing to fly, the child's joy in swinging, sliding — often so close to fear — the thrills of skiing and skating, all attest to man's need to encounter this danger, to master it, to reenact his mastery time and again.

Jumpers often describe a "fear of heights," which seems to them something unrelated to the act of parachuting. Paradoxically, these men do not experience a fearful sense of height at altitudes usual for jumping; instead, at lesser heights the fear in many cases actually increases with greater proximity to the earth. For example, one successful jumper recalled his embarrassment on finding himself unable to ride the parachute tower at Coney Island, despite prompting from his girl friend. In contrast, men who fear *jumping* may report greater fear of height with increasing distance from the ground. For such men, the earth exerts a mighty pull on the imagination; quick descent by the safest means, reassuring contact with the ground, injury on landing, fatal impact, not letting go, just getting down — these are the thoughts they describe. The jumper is more concerned with the jump itself, his own performance, staying aloft, himself in the air. He tends to feel more "free," more detached, with increasing distance from the earth. During the jump, his self-interest outweighs all else (e.g., his interest in ground, home, girl friend waiting below). One parachutist described in some detail just such complex feelings of attraction and aversion in regard to space:

> This man expressed a love for freedom in space and motion. He enjoyed parachuting, mountain climbing, skiing, diving; he had always longed to take up the sport of soaring. He described frequent, very pleasant dreams of flying and gliding, activities accomplished in the dream by merely wishing it so; he had never had a dream of falling. Flying in an airplane was not to be compared to these other pursuits — fantasied and real — since "the engine and the noise would spoil it." But for all this attraction to space and to the idea of unrestricted, effortless movement, there was one further requirement: There had to be an object to keep in view and eventually to return to. In looking up at a clear sky at night, he experienced some anxiety, described as a kind of cosmic loneliness at the thought of "all that space with nothing in it." He liked the open country, but a landscape barren of any objects (trees, hills, house) evoked similar uncomfortable feelings. Moving about in space scarcely populated by other objects was an exhilarating experience for this man, but the mere thought of empty space aroused anxiety.

Probably there is no "instinctive fear of falling," but there is certainly an abundance of painful events in earliest childhood to account for the development of such fear; perhaps this is why a later fear of heights seems so "natural," yet often so out of keeping with the degree of real, objective danger. The small child who has taken a fall on a step learns to sit next time before gingerly placing both feet in position. Gradually he becomes brave enough to forego the sitting down. At last, able to anticipate and control the abrupt physical change and sudden flood of stimuli, he jumps joyfully from the same step where before he had met the shock and pain of falling.

The Pleasure

Most parachutists jump because they like to jump. This seems quite obvious, and yet it is a point that has been ignored or misunderstood by some nonparticipant observers. Kepecs, for example, studied neurotic reactions of several paratroopers and states among his conclusions: "All, or nearly all, parachutists fear jumping . . . the essential conflict is between the desire to escape and the demands of duty and personal pride."[8] Such ideas of conflict and struggle do apply to men who fail as parachutists and to those whose performance is adequate only at the cost of distressing symptoms. But the total number of such men is a small fraction of a group distinguished, to the contrary, by an ability to parachute with considerable ease and satisfaction. Ordinarily, the gratification in jumping — far from intensifying any inner struggle — is precisely what makes parachuting desirable. Bond, in his study of airmen in World War II,[9] found that men who took pleasure in their activity (combat and flying in this case) were successful; the ability to find gratification in such action was of much greater significance in determining success than any other definable factors, such as character structure or neurotic disposition. The same is true of parachutists.

But what makes parachuting pleasurable? Paradoxically, it may seem, the presence of anxiety, within limits, is an essential condition of a large element of pleasure in jumping. This "counterphobic pleasure"[10] results from active repetition and resolution of the anxiety situation in the exercise of a function without anxiety, or with less anxiety than before. As a major defense against anxiety, a fundamental attribute of the counterphobic attitude is its tendency to transform a state of passive helplessness into one of active mastery; by this means, it may acquire high value in reality adaptation and in the generation of creative activity. In this sense, all play, sport, art and science derive in part from the counterphobic attitude.

The act of jumping might serve as a model of object loss, of the anxiety-inducing situation. It is no surprise, then, to learn that most parachutists exhibit traits of the counterphobic personality.[11] The jumper's pride in his performance, his seeking of the thrill, his interest in the act as opposed to its result — all bear witness to the presence of this defense against anxiety. Parachutists as a group show an impressive predilection for counterphobic behavior in general — besides parachuting, such activities as auto-racing, rodeo-riding, hunting panthers with bow and arrow, and snake-handling.

The point is that the counterphobic attitude finds special prominence among the psychological attributes of most parachutists. But, if present in excess, it forces men to rigid, extreme and compulsively repetitive behavior. These men, the "jump-happy," obsessively seek fearful situations. They jump as often as possible, with preference for the most varied conditions. For them, jumping is only one of an assortment of thrills; when it begins to pall, a new and more dangerous activity must be found. For these men, anxiety is too great to be mastered, and any possible gratification in jumping is spoiled by the driven character of their constant need to prove that they are not afraid.

For almost all parachutists, however, the jump is an effective way of getting rid of tension. Through the act, one can discharge anxieties collected at random. The elation that follows this mastery of "anxiety" is short-lived, ineffective against major conflict, and, after all, not very rational. Nonetheless, it makes an important contribution to the attractions of parachuting.

A man's anxiety about jumping ordinarily diminishes with experience and, with it, so does the thrill. The jump eventually becomes fairly routine. Then, another element of pleasure is experienced in sharper contrast to the whole. This element of "erogenous" or sexual pleasure derives in a direct, physical sense from a pleasurable use of muscles and the apparatus of equilibrium, and from pleasure in being looked at and admired — the exhibitionistic aspect of the act. Such sensuality is, of course, not lacking in other sports and playful activity in general, but parachuting is hardly matched for prominence of these attributes.

Thus, a host of attitudes and feelings about the pleasure of jumping reflect its partly sensual and impulsive character. Subjectively, parachuting may be experienced as a kind of childish play — as one man said, "just like the fun at the amusement park." Some men describe the sensations of the jump as something closer to the sexual act, to which symbolically it bears a striking resemblance. But by this time, when the jump has been practiced almost to the point of habit, its relation to the deeper strata of psychic life — so obvious in the stories of men who attempt jumping and fail — is usually revealed only in an oblique light, perhaps in a joke, a chance remark or an occasional anxiety dream.

SYMBOL AND REALITY

Salvador Dali speaks of parachutists as newborn children descending from the heavens, "all the while remaining attached to the umbilical cord which holds them suspended to the silk placenta of their maternal parachute."[12] Perhaps such flamboyant language suits the striking symbolic connection between jumping and the act of birth. Hardly less obvious is the symbolism at other levels: The jumper leaves Mother Earth, sure of a safe return; he goes into the sky, the dwelling place of a benign fate, of the Heavenly Father; as he descends, he feels a mounting tension; he stands above all, exposed to admiration from below, approval from above, in prideful omnipotence; he lets himself go in an experience of sudden release and satisfaction; he descends triumphantly to earth. But to the earthbound, the ground may be the only "real support." To rise to a great height may be to defy fate, to challenge jealous gods. The temptation is dangerous; the earth exerts a fatal attraction. One may lose one's balance and fall from grace. The daredevil may meet his downfall.

Probably there are few persons immune to the thrill of vicarious participation in such spectacular performance. The crowd below stifles a guilty wish for the daring to fail and urges the jumper on. Sanctioned by his fellows and leaders, approved by the crowd, he risks everything in one step. The canopy billows out, and he has won his gamble with the gods; Fate has smiled upon him. There is no need to be afraid; he is safe, and there will be no punishment. By some kind of magic, a childhood dream becomes reality.

Like the actor, the parachutist plays out an inner drama on the set of the object-world. His role must adhere to the first principles of reality — that space, time, self and world exist. In jumping, in a fleeting moment of exhilaration, he enjoys the illusion of omnipotence. The trauma of birth, the threat of castration, man's helplessness — these dangers are belied by his magical act. But what is the gain, if only illusion and fantasy? Where is the reality?

In jumping, a man does attain a degree of real physical mastery. He learns skills in the manipulation of objects. Perhaps, in one sense, he learns to differentiate more sharply the outer world from what is within. The jumper turns away from his world in a highly dramatic gesture. Perhaps on second approach, reality is less cruel; one had made it more tolerable by effecting some change within as in the outer world.[13]

But there are psychological perils. One's view of reality is always colored by inner experience. Alice Balint spoke of the unconscious equation — loss of love equals danger to life — as the root of irrationality in the face of external threat.[14] In jumping, there is an illusion of mortal danger. The crux of the matter is whether one feels safe or in danger, loved or unloved. With all its connotations of aggressiveness and sexuality, the idea of the jump grips the imagination. The parachutist thus risks a certain closeness to primitive layers of psychic experience. What helps him skirt this inner danger without losing sight of the real outer world?

Of first importance is the social reality of the group. Though a man is rarely more alone than at the moment of the jump, parachuting is nonetheless a distinctly social phenomenon. The symbol of the jump reaches deep within each man to tap different roots; yet a community of feeling arises to constitute the binding force of the group. The act of jumping then becomes the common bond, the ritual, each man's share in the leader's omnipotence. Then, parachutists say, "We can do anything."

Joining such a group demands of each man a certain degree of psychological regression. From the point of view of the ego, there is a partial sus-

"I'm going to leave Herbert, Julia. The omnipotent feelings he experiences in parachuting are turning him into a big, bossy, insufferable stinker around home!"

pension of critical judgment. Objective danger is partly denied, remaining supports are idealized, and in general, a man comes to share in the pride, prejudice and superstitions of the group. At the same time, a regression occurs on the side of the emotions, with a loosening of usual ties and an increasing identification with the group.

For his part, the parachutist must form a close identification with his group. He must feel both willing and able to accept it and to be accepted by it; only by becoming a part of the whole can he draw upon its strength. The nature of a man's early identification is crucial in this process — the acceptance of the father-like image of the leader who condones a thrilling and dangerous act. Members of the group identify themselves with one another in relation to this collective, externalized ideal image — the jump school instructor, the jumpmaster, "the angel on the wing tip," God, but ultimately, father.

Then, the jumper has his brief moment of exhilaration, his fleeting illusion of omnipotence. But there is more. A man can find a sound and abiding satisfaction in jumping — perhaps a new and better sense of what he is.

FOOTNOTES

1. Freud, S.: *Leonardo da Vinci: A Psychosexual Study of an Infantile Reminiscence (1916);* in *Standard Edition,* Vol. 11. London, Hogarth Press, 1955.
2. Here, "jumper" and "jumping" mean parachutist and parachuting. They are the more explicit terms of the parachutist's vocabulary.
3. Erikson, E. H.: Ego development and historical change. *Psychoanal Stud Child, 2:*359, 1946.
4. In fact, one may even be a tired housewife, a tense executive, or a victim of peptic ulcer or chronic low back strain, according to recent publicity promoting parachuting as a way to health.
5. "Jump boots" have a special place among the badges and talismans of parachutists. There even exist a few pairs that have been preserved in bronze.
6. Balint, A.: Ueber eine besondere form der infantilen angst (concerning a special form of infantile anxiety). *Zietschrift fuer psychanalytische Paedagogik, 7:*414, 1933.
7. Freud, S.: *The Problem of Anxiety (1926);* in *Standard Edition,* Vol. 20. London, Hogarth Press, 1959.
8. Kepecs, J. G.: Neurotic reactions in parachutists. *Psychoanal Quart, 13:*273, 1944.
9. Bond, D. D.: *The Love and Fear of Flying.* New York, Int Univs, 1952.
10. Fenichel, O.: The counterphobic attitude. *Int J Psychoanal, 20:*263, 1939.
11. For an engaging description of such a personality, see Robert L. Taylor's New Yorker profile, "No Feeling of Falling," on the sports parachutist, Jacques Istel. *The New Yorker,* vol. 34, Jan. 24, 1959, p. 42.
12. Dali, S.: *The Secret Life of Salvador Dali.* New York, Dial Press, 1942.
13. Such ideas as these have been developed at length by Michael Balint in his book *Thrills and Regressions.* London, Hogarth Press, 1959. Balint does not discuss parachuting, but this activity might well serve as a model for many of his concepts. See *supra* at p. 243.
14. Balint, A.: *op. cit. supra* note 6.

SPORT PARACHUTING

SAMUEL Z. KLAUSNER

WE THINK OF PARACHUTING EITHER AS an emergency procedure or as a means for sending troops into battle. Yet, some thirty thousands persons in the United States parachute for sport. Frenchmen and Russians were parachuting for sport during the 1930's. American interest blossomed after the Second World War. The Parachute Club of America, the largest organization of these sportsmen, publishes a monthly journal, the *Parachutist;* this club fosters regional and international competitions, and concerns itself with problems of safety, training and federal legislation affecting the sport.

Individual parachutists combine resources to obtain instruction in and facilities for sport parachuting. Perhaps four out of five sport parachutists in the United States are members of local clubs. For others, commercial parachute centers provide a jump area, planes and pilots, equipment and training without the more continuous personal associations of club membership.

Though parachutists combine resources, parachuting is a team sport only in the loosest sense. A parachute jump is primarily the act of an individual alone in the air, subject to the influences of the natural forces of gravity and wind. The pilot is engaged for a fee. He may or may not be a jumper and is generally a member of the club, sometimes honorary. There is a trend toward pilots becoming jumpers. The jump master, usually a senior member of the club, supervises and signals the novice jumper. He is a trainer, evaluator and coach.

The novice concentrates on exiting procedures, body positions during the initial part of the fall, maneuvering during descent, and body control at landing. His static line, attached to the aircraft, draws taut and opens his parachute after he has fallen for about three seconds. The more experienced jumper takes advantage of "free fall" time before pulling his own ripcord. The free-falling body, depending on its attitude, reaches a terminal velocity of 120-170 miles per hour. A dynamic equilibrium is established between friction, gravity and lift force at this velocity. The jumper can then move himself horizontally, essentially fly, by positioning his arms and legs. The skilled jumper engages in complex maneuvers such as approaching another jumper and passing a baton or directing himself toward a predetermined ground target for a precision landing. Not more than twenty per cent of free fall jumps include over thirty seconds of free fall and not more than five per cent include as much as a minute.

Jumping is emotionally exciting. For all jumpers this experience involves some fear and some enthusiasm before, during and after a jump. The anticipation of these emotions is part of their motivation for jumping. This is an exploratory study on the relation between the experience of fear and the experience of enthusiasm. Fear will be assessed in two ways. The first will be a self-report of fear phenomenologically grasped. The second will be an inference from a projective test about predispositions to fear.

SOME FACTS ABOUT SPORT PARACHUTISTS

Method

Replies to a mail questionnaire by 825 sport parachutists affiliated with 103 parachute clubs are the data of this study. Questionnaires were administered by officials of the individual clubs and asked about the experience of fear and enthusiasm, personal and social characteristics of the parachutists, and attitudes relevant to sport parachuting; they included the Ma and Hy scales from the MMPI, a Draw-A-Person Test, and four story-stimulus pictures of parachuting situations. Only the jump experience, an analysis of the stories told about one picture, and a few social characteristics will be reported in this paper.

Where are these jumpers located? What age groups do they represent? What is their marital status? The sponsor of this study, the United States government, requested that items on race be deleted from the questionnaire. Our general impression is, however, that nonwhites account for no more than two per cent of the sport parachutists. Therefore the demographic characteristics of sport parachutists must be assessed with respect to the distribution of these characteristics in the American white population.

Sport Parachuting Is Western

Sport parachuting is not equally popular in all parts of the country. The geographic distribution of sport parachutists and that of the American white population is given in Table I.

TABLE I

DISTRIBUTION OF AMERICAN SPORT PARACHUTISTS AND OF THE AMERICAN WHITE POPULATION BY REGION IN THE UNITED STATES AND RESIDENT IN FOREIGN COUNTRIES

	(in per cents)						
	North-east	*North Central*	*South Atlantic*	*South Central*	*West*	*Foreign & Other*	*N*
Sport parachutists	7	30	16	18	27	2	(805)*
US population	25	30	13	15	16	1	(160,200,000)

*It was not possible to identify residence of 20 respondents.

Sport parachutists are over-represented in the West and in the South and under-represented in the Northeast. Windy or too cloudy weather interferes with parachuting. The higher proportion of clear and calm jumping days in the South and West may influence this distribution. We do not know how the regional distribution of sport parachutists compares with that of other sportsmen such as skiers, scuba divers, and mountain climbers, who tend to be the same types of individuals and are variously affected by climatic and geographic conditions. Figures are available, however, for hunters and fishermen who also tend to be lone outdoor sportsmen. In New England among persons of age twelve and over, 16 per cent either fish or hunt in a given year (1960) while in the South Atlantic states 25 per cent do, and in the Pacific and Mountain states 21 per cent do.[1] This distribution departs from that of the American population in the same direction as does the distribution of sport parachutists, suggesting western and southern regional preferences for those outdoor sports.

Sport parachuting may also be influenced by regional attitudes toward flying. California has 13 per cent of the active civil aircraft in the United States while New York, with a nearly equal population, has but 5 per cent; and Illinois, with about two-thirds of California's population, also has 5 per cent of the civil aircraft.[2] People like to jump from airplanes where people like to fly them.

The three factors of climate, general sport interest, and interest in flying may conspire. The greater interest in outdoor sports such as hunting and fishing in the West than in the East may be channeled into sport parachuting through the greater orientation to the air. Climate may be a facilitating factor. In addition, interest in risk-taking, a psychological factor, may differ in the various regions. The pioneering psychology of the West as opposed to the more stable, conservative outlook in the East may also contribute to establishing skydiving as primarily a western and secondarily a southern sport.

Parachutists Are Young and Think Male

The population of skydivers is quite young. Fifty-four per cent are twenty-five or younger. The greatest turnover, however, is among younger jumpers. They are less likely to remain as serious jumpers. Table II compares new and experienced jumpers according to age.

Older jumpers are indeed more likely to be veteran jumpers. This is not due to the fact that one grows old while becoming a veteran jumper. Three successive years account for nearly all the jumping.

The physical requirements of skydiving do not preclude female participation. Yet, 92 per cent of those in their first year of skydiving and 98 per cent of those who have been jumping for three or more years are males.

Possibly more females have been joining the ranks of skydivers lately; but, more likely, the few females involved are less likely than the males to continue over several years. Skydiving may not be a masculine sport in the physical sense, but it is in the social-psychological sense. Most skydivers are reluctant to admit women to their clubs. This may reflect male jealousy in preserving an area of male courage. Perhaps, in this area of sensed risk, women may be associated with "bad luck," as they were at sea in the days of the sailing ship.

TABLE II
MEAN ORDINAL NUMBER OF YEARS IN JUMPING
ACCORDING TO AGE

	16-20	*21-25*	*26-30*	*31-35*	*36 or over*
N	80	308	213	84	65
Mean	1.39	2.10[a]	3.09[a]	3.52[b]	3.42[c]
SD	.39	2.11	4.82	6.81	6.68

[a]Different from previous age group, $p > .90$
[b]Different from previous age group, $p > .99$
[c]Not significantly different from mean of previous age group

Parachutists Are Single-minded

Skydiving tends to be a consuming interest of its devotees. As such it competes for time with their participation in other social roles such as family roles. Table III sheds light on the relation between marital status and skydiving by comparing the proportion of jumpers who are married with the proportion of their age cohort in the general population who are married.

TABLE III
PROPORTION OF JUMPERS WHO ARE MARRIED COMPARED WITH
PROPORTION IN THE AMERICAN POPULATION WHO ARE MARRIED
BY AGE COHORT

	Age			
	16-25	*26-35*		*36 and over*
Skydivers	27%	54%		72%
	(437)	(306)		(67)
	20-24	*25-29*	*30-34*	*35-44*
American population	45%	76%	88%	89%

Sport parachutists are less likely to be married than are members of their age cohort in the general population. We do not know whether they are less likely to be married than are other intensely involved sportsmen. There is evidence, however, that they are less likely than others of their age to be stable husbands. The proportion of those who have not remarried after being widowed or divorced is high. Of all skydivers in the sample, 12 per cent have been or are divorced or separated and .4 per cent have been widowed. Six per cent of those 16-25, 22 per cent of those 26-35, and 19 per cent of those 35 or over have been widowed or divorced and have not remarried. The proportion of divorced and widowed and not remarried in the general population does not exceed 3 per cent for any of these age groups. This is consistent with the overall tendency of jumpers to be single.

A good proportion of married jumpers may proceed with the sport, despite their wives' sentiments to the contrary. We may examine the relation between the length of time they have been jumping and their spouses' feelings about their activity. Each person was asked whether his spouse approved of, was indifferent to, or disapproved of his being a skydiver. Disapproval takes two principal forms. Some spouses resent the diversion of energies from family to the sport. Others are concerned about the danger to the jumper. Table IV shows the responses for individuals who have been jumping for one, two, or three or more years.

TABLE IV
NUMBER OF YEARS JUMPING ACCORDING TO SPOUSES' ATTITUDE TOWARD SKYDIVING
(in per cents)

Attitude of Spouse	*Number of Years Jumping*		
	First Year	*Second Year*	*At least Third Year*
Disapprove	36	37	31
Indifferent	26	19	20
Approve	38	44	49
	(111)	(93)	(168)

$\chi^2 = 3.95$ df = 4 $P > .30$ when null hypothesis is true

Spouse approval is but slightly correlated with continuing in the sport. The distributions of spouse attitudes do not differ significantly between novice and experienced jumpers. Of those who have been jumping three or more years, almost a third do so over the objections of their spouses. This suggests an independence of or disregard for the opinions of their spouses.

Sport Parachuting Is Dangerous

Sport parachutists tend to deny that their sport is more dangerous than any other sport. Insurance companies, however, have shown reluctance to insure them. Some information on objective danger is available from responses to a question about injuries sustained from jumping. Table V shows the proportions slightly injured (suffered sprains or knocked out) or severely injured (fractured limb) among individuals who had been jumping for one, two, or three years.

TABLE V
INJURIES AMONG SKYDIVERS WHO HAVE JUMPED FOR ONE, TWO OR AT LEAST THREE YEARS
(in per cents)

	Years Jumped		
	First Year	*Second Year*	*At least Third Year*
Never injured	63	35	29
Slightly injured	32	51	44
Severely injured	5	14	27
	(307)	(178)	(266)

Of all respondents in their first season of jumping, 37 per cent had been injured. When they had jumped three or more years, 71 per cent had suffered injury. Among all Americans in this age group about 27 per cent are injured (requiring at least one day's restricted activity) in a given year from all types of accidents including home and motor vehicle.[3] With such an injury rate, the inherent danger can hardly be unknown to the participants.

A picture of sport parachutists begins to emerge. Lone individuals are casting themselves into the greatest of natural paradoxes: the freedom of the firmament in which death inheres deterministically unless the individual performs a single human act – pulling the ripcord. This is a dangerous sport, a male sport. The spirit is the spirit of the West. Parachutists tend to remain free of marital ties or may disregard the obligations of those ties. Younger men test their youth and older men persist in a serious challenge to nature.

THE EXCITEMENT OF SPORT PARACHUTING

The emotional excitement accompanying skydiving is a complex of, among others, two contradictory components, fear and enthusiasm. The contradiction is not that skydivers are repelled by the former and attracted by the latter, that of an approach-avoidance conflict. Rather, the excitement is constituted by a tension between these two components and by a transformation of fear into enthusiasm.

Throughout this report, enthusiasm will be assessed phenomenologically, that is, as it appears to the jumper. In this section we will examine the relation between enthusiasm and fear, also as assessed phenomenologically. The measures of fear and enthusiasm are self-reports of these experiences during the jump. Respondents were introduced to working definitions of fear and enthusiasm constructed by the reasearcher after he himself had parachuted and conducted preliminary interviews with skydivers. Individuals may experience their feelings in many ways. Without some standard only case studies would be possible. Respondents were asked to accept the researcher's frame of reference as a standard. To establish and to test the assumption of a standardized frame of reference, respondents were asked to read the following:

YOUR FEELINGS DURING YOUR EARLY PARACHUTE JUMPS

The following questions are about your feelings of FEAR and your feelings of ENTHUSIASM while parachute jumping. Sometimes these feelings overlap so much that you cannot tell them apart. For example, you might feel so tense at night that you cannot fall asleep. It is difficult to know whether your tenseness comes from FEAR about what will happen the next day or from your ENTHUSIASM in looking forward to the next day. Sometimes, you may be AFRAID and ENTHUSIASTIC at the same time. For example, the first time that you went off a high diving board you may have been AFRAID but at the same time you may have been ENTHUSIASTIC about proving to yourself and to others that you could do it.

For the following questions it will be necessary to distinguish whether your excitement is due to FEAR or to ENTHUSIASM. Here are some signs that will help you recognize which type of excitement you are feeling. When you are SCARED you may feel helpless and you may feel that the world about you is dangerous and is closing in on you. You may wish that you could just shrink away or disappear. You may be worried about the way things will turn out. You may be asking yourself if you are doing the right thing. You, personally, may not feel all of these things, but would feel something like them when you are SCARED or FRIGHTENED.

How can you tell when you are feeling ENTHUSIASTIC about something? When you are ENTHUSIASTIC you may feel very powerful. You may feel that you can control yourself and even control part of the world about you. The world seems to open up before you and you know that you are doing the right thing and feel that things will turn out well.

Respondents were asked to reply Yes or No to six reading comprehension questions about the above paragraph. Only those who scored 5 or 6 on this test, 661 of the 825 respondents or 80 per cent of the group, are used in the succeeding analyses of fear and enthusiasm.

The fear scale was presented as follows:

FEAR

Keeping the above definitions of being frightened or scared in mind, let us construct a scale to help you indicate just how much fear you feel in certain situations. Think of the *left* end of the scale as indicating the *least* fright you have ever felt in connection with sky diving. Think of the *right* end as indicating the *most* fright you have ever felt in connection with sky diving. The *Fear scale* may be represented as follows:

Least									Most
0	1	2	3	4	5	6	7	8	9

FEAR

Following is a list of situations. In the blanks to the right of the statements put the *number from the scale* which tells how frightened you felt in each case.

Avoid using the "0" unless you were *absolutely calm* at that point. Do not use the "9" unless you want to say that you were nearly *petrified* with fear at that point. Go through all of the situations for First Jump and *then return and go through the situations for First Free Fall.*

THINK OF THE FOLLOWING SITUATIONS IN CONNECTION WITH THE *FEAR* YOU FELT DURING YOUR FIRST JUMP AND FIRST FREE FALL

Situations	*FEAR* *First Jump*	*FEAR* *First Free Fall*
1. While trying to fall asleep the night before	______	______
2. On the way to the DZ	______	______
3. Arriving at the DZ in preparation for my jump	______	______
4. Waiting to board the plane	______	______
5. While climbing to jump altitude	______	______
6. When pilot starts jump run	______	______
7. While stepping out of the plane	______	______
8. At the "push off" signal	______	______
The following items should be answered only for *first free fall*:		
8a. While in free fall		______
8b. A second before pulling the ripcord		______
8c. While pulling the ripcord		______
8d. While waiting for the parachute to open		______
9. At the moment my parachute opened	______	______
10. A minute or so after my parachute opened	______	______
11. Seconds before touching the ground	______	______
12. Upon touching the ground	______	______
13. After removing my parachute	______	______
14. Before retiring at night after the jump	______	______

The enthusiasm scale was presented as follows:

ENTHUSIASM

Now, keeping the definitions of enthusiasm in mind as they were described at the beginning (look back if you do not remember what they were), let us construct a scale to help you tell how *enthusiastic* you felt in each situation. Think of the *left* end of the scale below as indicating the *least* enthusiasm you have ever felt in connection with sky diving and the *right* end as indicating the *most* enthusiasm you have ever felt in connection with sky diving. The *Enthusiasm scale* may be represented as follows:

Least									Most
0	1	2	3	4	5	6	7	8	9

ENTHUSIASM

This time, in the following list of situations, enter the number from the scale which tells how *enthusiastic* you believe you felt in each of the situations in each column. Again, answer first for all First Jump situations and then return and answer for all First Free Fall situations. Avoid using "0" unless you were *completely unenthusiastic* at that point. Do not use the "9" unless you were *almost completely overwhelmed by enthusiasm* at that point.

The same situations were listed as for the Fear scale. In the tables and graphs which follow, these situations will be designated by the numbers 1-14 as in the column at their left.

Conscious Fear and Enthusiasm

Graphs I and II trace the means of fear and enthusiasm scores at each point of the jump situation for the first jump and for the first free fall. So that the two curves may be compared, both sets of means have been converted to T scores. The graph of one half of the sum of the fear and enthusiasm means (T scores) at each point is also shown. This represents the joint contribution of these two components to the general level of tension

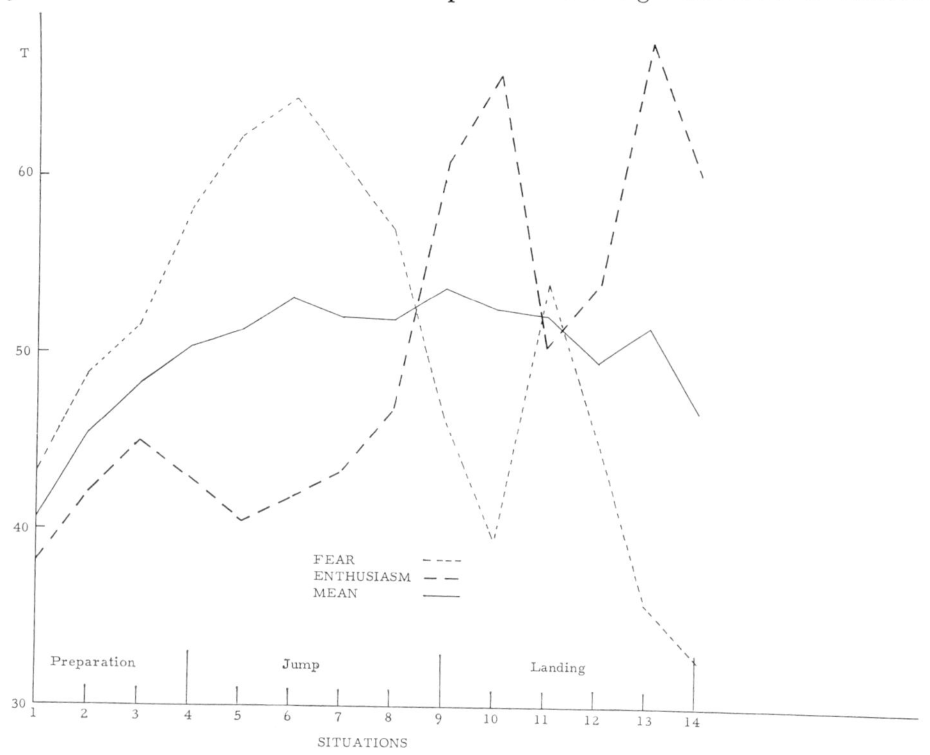

GRAPH I. Profiles of fear and enthusiasm (T scores) and their mean $(\frac{F + E}{2})$ for first jump situations ($N_{av.} = 590$).

or excitement. The general level of excitement gradually rises as the jumper approaches his act, attaining a peak the moment the parachute opens and then gradually trailing off.

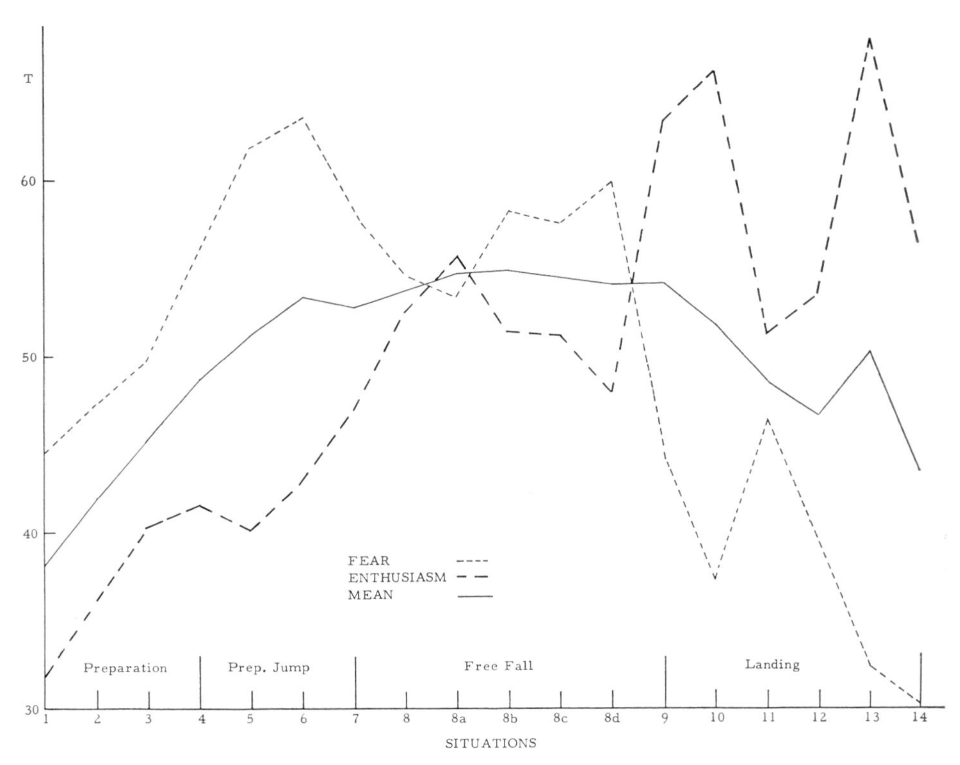

GRAPH II. Profiles of fear and enthusiasm (T scores) and their mean $(\frac{F+E}{2})$ for first free fall situations ($N_{av.} = 490$).

Through most of the jump, mean fear and enthusiasm scores are negatively correlated. They are positively correlated, however, in three situations: prior to boarding the airplane, prior to exiting, and after the parachute is removed. The first two of these are stages preparatory to an act, and the last follows the act. Thus, fear and enthusiasm are negatively correlated when the jumper is engaged in executing, rather than preparing for, the act of jumping or of landing.

The experience may be traced through successive situations. From the night prior to a jump until arriving at the drop zone, both fear and enthusiasm increase. This constitutes a relatively great increase in the level of excitement. When boarding the plane and climbing to altitude, fear increases while enthusiasm decreases. As the pilot starts the jump run, preparation for a new stage of the act, both curves resume their positive slope. As soon as the jumper steps out of the plane, as soon as he commits himself to the culminating act, and through the initial part of the fall, his fear decreases and his enthusiasm increases. Enthusiasm reaches a peak and fear a nadir a minute or so after the parachute has opened. As the landing approaches, fear increases and enthusiasm decreases. This time is preparatory for a new phase of the act, but it differs from preparation for boarding the airplane and preparation for the jump in that the jumper enters upon it inevitably. When the ground is touched, fear drops while enthusiasm increases to its highest point after the parachute is removed. After the jump is over, both fear and enthusiasm and the general level of excitement drop.

The general level of excitement is higher at the end than it is at the beginning of the jump. The relative contributions of each component to this excitement are reversed. At the outset, fear exceeds enthusiasm. At the end, enthusiasm accounts for most of the excitement. The increased level of excitement and its shift of character from primarily fear to primarily enthusiasm are two emotional "payoffs" of the experience.

At about the fifth jump a skydiver attempts his first "free fall." Without a static line to open his parachute automatically, he falls about five seconds and then pulls the ripcord manually. The mean fear, enthusiasm, and excitement curves for the first free fall (Graph II) have essentially the same relative shapes as those for the first jump. During the first jump, however, the period from exit to the opening of the parachute was characterized by increasing enthusiasm and decreasing fear. The free fall time, with the parachute not yet opened, is marked by slightly increasing fear and decreasing enthusiasm. This trend does not reverse until the parachute has blossomed.

Learning To Enjoy Parachuting

Each of the components changes between the two jumps studied. The fear associated with the first jump may be compared with that of the first free fall and the enthusiasm of the first jump compared with that of the first free fall. The actual means for each situation are shown in Table VI.

We might expect that, with respect to the first jump, the first free fall would increase fear and reduce enthusiasm. Countrariwise, we might expect that, since it is at least the fifth jump, the fear might be reduced and enthusiasm increased through greater familiarity. In most of the fourteen situations the mean fear scores were lower during first free fall than during the first jump. Fear does tend to rise, however, during the actual free fall situations (8a-8d). Enthusiasm tends to be higher during the free fall jump than it was during the first jump and continues to rise during the actual free fall situations. This fits the contention of veteran skydivers that later jumps are less fearful and more enjoyable.

TABLE VI

MEANS FOR FEAR AND ENTHUSIASM SCORES FOR FIRST JUMP AND FIRST FREE FALL FOR EACH SITUATION

	Fear		*Enthusiasm*	
Situation	*First Jump* (N = 590) av.	*Free Fall* (N = 490) av.	*First Jump* (N = 590) av.	*Free Fall* (N = 490) av.
1	1.96	2.02	4.29	4.43
2	2.49	2.25	4.63	4.72
3	2.76	2.48	4.85	4.98
4	3.38	2 97	4.69	5.05
5	3.78	3.50	4.49	4.97
6	3.98	3.64	4.61	5.14
7	3.65	3.20	4.72	5.41
8	3.30	2.90	5.01	5.77
8a		2.77		5.96
8b		3.19		5.69
8c		3.15		5.68
8d		3.34		5.47
9	2.30	2.04	6.14	6.45
10	1.63	1.43	6.54	6.63
11	3.01	2.18	5.30	5.69
12	2.16	1.59	5.58	5.83
13	1.25	1.00	6.69	6.75
14	0.98	0.83	6.10	6.01

All differences except situations 1 and 14 significant at .05.

All differences except situations 1, 2, 3, 10, 12, 13, and 14 significant at .05.

The above measures are changes in the magnitude of emotion. Another aspect of the experience is constituted by the emotional ups and downs. The repetitive rising and falling of fear may be emotionally exhausting. The rising and falling of enthusiasm may be exhilarating. This may be assessed by comparing the variances of the first jump and first free fall curves. These variances and F (ratio of Mean Squares) are shown in Table VII.

TABLE VII

VARIANCES OF FIRST JUMP AND FIRST FREE FALL CURVES

	First Jump	*df*	*First Free Fall*	*df*	*F*
Enthusiasm	$\sigma^2 = .651$	13	$\sigma^2 = .411$	17	2.08[a]
Fear	$\sigma^2 = .906$	13	$\sigma^2 = .725$	17	1.67[b]

[a]$P > .90$ [b]$p > .75$

The variances of both fear and enthusiasm scores tend to be less in the later than in the earlier jump. The curve has become smoother. To the extent that excitement is produced by the rise and fall of tensions, it is reduced in later jumps. To maintain the experience of rising and falling excitement may be why jumpers increase their free fall time in successive jumps. They must keep raising the "ante" to get a constant "bang."

Hypothesis

These findings may be viewed in the light of an hypothesis about the source, level and composition of emotional energy. While approaching the act of skydiving, the level of emotional energy is increased through an environmental input to the personality system and also educed within the system. In the execution of the act and consequent to it, the composition of that energy within the system changes as a result of a transformation of one component, fear, into the other, enthusiasm. Another concomitant of the execution of the act is the reduction of the level of emotional energy by its expenditure by the act.

Presuming that the emotional pattern of the first jump and the first free fall typifies that over a series of jumps, it seems that the parachutist initially experiences a low excitement level and a sense of emotional deprivation. The quality of this low level excitement is such that the negative component, fear, outweighs the positive component, enthusiasm. The jump experience both raises the general excitement level and transforms its internal structure so that its positive component is predominant. Following the jump, the parachutists' level of excitement again drops, and he is again troubled by fear. He jumps again and rights the balance. This pattern may be repeated from jump to jump.

To create a feeling of enthusiasm, the person first needs the energy with which to be enthusiastic and some positive self-evaluation or accomplishment to be enthusiastic about. It was noted above that fear and enthusiasm both increase during preparatory situations. The predominant feature at these points is the input of energy to the personality from its environing social structure. Until he exits, the jumper is involved with others who provide support by direct encouragement and implied threat of shame. Entering a fearful situation also generates energy but this is taken from within himself; this energy is educed. As he stands on the threshold of the act of jumping or of landing, the fear component increases markedly. This increases the store of emotional energy available to be converted into enthusiasm. The negative correlation between the fear and enthusiasm scales is associated with the execution of the act. Energy which was bound up in fear is transformed into emotion experienced as enthusiasm. The actual transformation takes place when the jumper has passed the point of no voluntary return. The parachutist first voluntarily endangers or risks the self and then abandons the self to fate. This abandon may be a condition for the internal transformation. The voluntaristic aspect of overcoming the fear produced a positive self-evaluation making it possible for the transformation to go in the positive direction of enthusiasm. Simple abandon of the self to fate without this positive valence might induce that transformation of energy experienced as the obliteration of self as in a mystic type of experience.

An implication of this model is that the greater the degree of fear which the individual succeeds in generating within himself, the greater the enthusiasm he may experience. (This is not to say that fear is the only basis of the energy of enthusiasm.) This may be a basis of the motivation for seeking danger. The conquest of fear through a combination of voluntary act and abandon contributes to a feeling of psychic expansiveness or power.

SUBCONSCIOUS FEAR AND ENTHUSIASM

The remainder of this paper will be concerned with the eduction of energy as an intrapsychic process. The effect of predisposition to fear upon enthusiasm will be the principal focus. Enthusiasm must be about something just as fear must be about something. In this way they are distinguished from the diffuse emotions of euphoria and anxiety. This "something" or cathected object is embodied in the meaning the jump has for the individual. The above hypothesis alluded in a general way to the positive valence given the energy transformation by voluntarily overcoming fear in executing the act. Any jump may have a variety of meanings, and these meanings may have different weights for different individuals. Two meanings will be considered here. The first has to do with the jumper's assessment of the danger to which he is exposing himself during the jump. This is a measure of proneness to fear as a personality factor. The second meaning has to do with the sense of control the jumper believes he has over the outcome of his jump. This is a measure of intrapsychic mechanisms for the control of fear.

Method

The questionnaire included a picture of a parachutist lying prone and apparently hurt. The respondents were asked to write a story about the picture. These stories were scored according to the extent of harm that had befallen the individual and according to the attribution of responsibility for the harm. The supposition is that respondents project into this story the expectation of harm and responsibility involved in their own personal images of jumping.

Of 688 respondents whose stories could be scored with respect to the harm suffered by the pictured parachutist, 43 per cent noted that an accident had occurred but did not specify any harm to the individual; 28 per cent said that the harm was slight or that perhaps he had just fainted; and 29 per cent mentioned that he was seriously hurt, had a broken leg or a broken back, or that he was dead. The experienced parachute jumper could recognize from the outspread parachute that a total malfunction, which would have meant death, probably had not occurred.

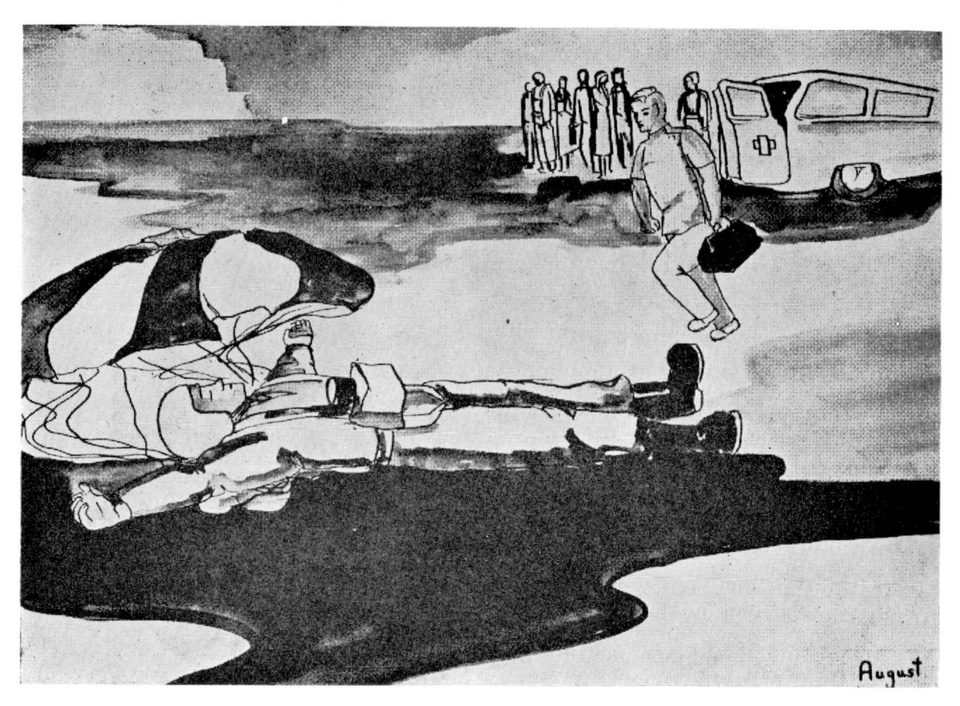

An example of a story scored as an "accident" without specifying the harm is the following:

> Having completely disregarded warnings of more experienced people and all of the safety rules and regulations, he tries a low pull. His parachute deploys, but it is too late to do him much good.

An example of a story scored as "slight harm" is the following:

> This jumper is a competition type and landed downwind in order to gain a few feet on target. As a result, he banged his head on the ground and knocked himself out (most helmets aren't too efficient). There isn't much the medic can do for him. He'll wake up pretty soon and be OK but he'll have some headache. The crowd thinks he is hurt worse than he is and are hesitant to walk over and see what happened.

An example of a story scored "serious" is the following:

> This man appears to have made an improper landing and injured himself. He is probably not thinking anything. The result could be a broken leg or head damage.

Graph III compares the mean enthusiasm scores for each of the fourteen situations of the first jump according to the type of harm perceived. On the whole, jumpers who find the pictured individual seriously hurt report greater enthusiasm during their own first jump than those who do not specify the extent of harm. The differences, however, are not always statistically significant.

The jump will be considered in three stages: *preparatory,* the period until ready to board the plane; the *jump,* beginning with the climb to altitude and ending with the opening of the parachute; and *landing,* from the time the parachute is open through the landing and postlude. For the free fall situation the jump stage is divided into *preparatory for jump* and *free fall.*

The series of situations will be treated like a series of tests and the curve examined as a test profile. An analysis of variance for profile data was accomplished for each of the three stages or groups of situations. The situations are the column variables. The individual scores across situations are the row variables. These scores are arranged in two groups: those who perceived an accident and those who perceived severe harm. There are five sources of variance. Variance from situations is contributed by the increase or decrease of enthusiasm from situation to situation. Variance from groups is that due to a difference between those who perceived an accident and those who perceived the jumper as seriously hurt or dead. Variance contributed by the interaction of groups by situations tells whether the shapes of the group profile curves differ from one another within the range of situations under consideration.

The variance from subjects in groups and the residual interaction term of subjects by groups by situations both tell about variability among individuals within the groups or situations. These will not concern us here. (F for groups is determined from the quotient of Mean-Square groups divided by Mean-Square Subjects in groups rather than from the former divided by the residual Mean-Square.)

The Expectation of Harm

In the preparatory stage, those concerned with serious harm are slightly more enthusiastic than those who only image a diffuse accident. Their enthusiasm drops as they engage in actual preparations at the drop zone. (Differences between the groups are in opposite directions at the beginning and end of the range. The difference between the group means, being averaged out, is not significant, but that between the shapes of the profiles is: ($F[3;1101] = 2.42$, $P > .95$). With the jump underway, those who perceive possible serious injury seem slightly more enthusiastic (for difference between groups $F[1;342] = 5.60$, $P > .95$). It is possible to speculate that the greater the perceived danger to overcome or the greater the perceived risk, the greater the degree of enthusiasm once this danger has been conquered. What has been measured here has not been an environmental stimulus but

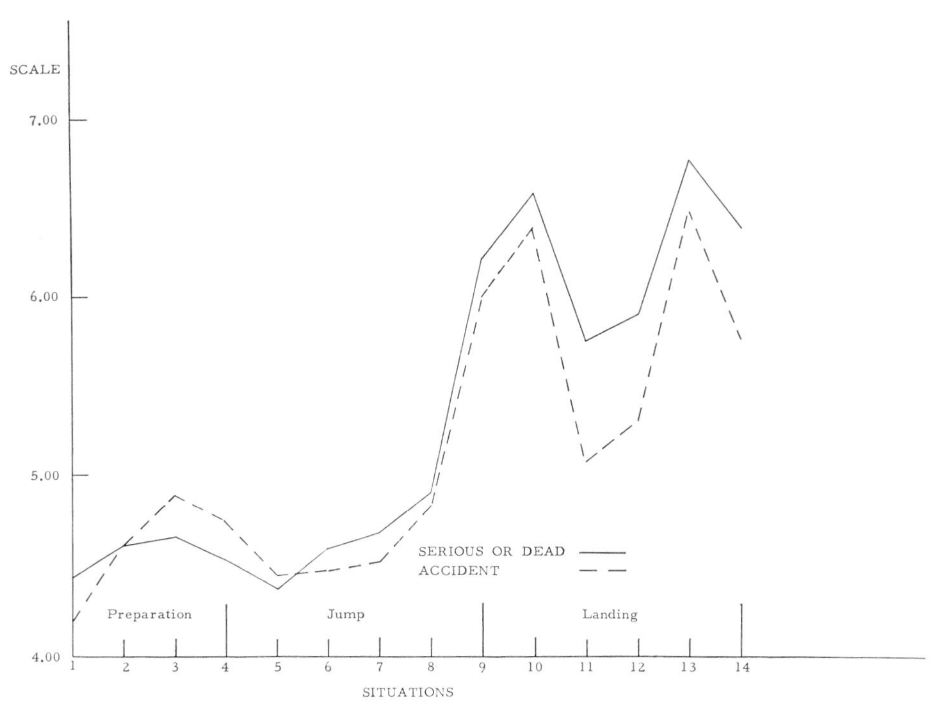

GRAPH III. Comparison between group not specifying harm and group perceiving parachutist as seriously hurt or dead (first jump).

an internal predisposition to perceive a situation as dangerous. Facing this internally perceived challenge educes energy within the system and makes it available for transformation into enthusiasm.

Jumpers attempt their first free fall after four or five static line jumps. Graph IV compares the mean enthusiasm scores for the first free fall among those who perceived diffuse harm and those who perceived a serious injury to the pictured parachutist. Among these more experienced jumpers, there is little difference between those who project the possibility of serious harm and those who do not until the parachute opens. As the landing approaches, however, those who feared serious harm become much more enthusiastic. (There is a statistically significant difference between the means of the groups. $F[1;288] = 5.30$, $P > .95$. The shapes of the profiles also differ. $F[4:1152] = 4.61$, $P > .99$.)

It was shown above that fear decreases in the later jump despite the added element of free fall. The perception of challenge or danger, as represented by the picture story responses, influences the novice during the preparatory stage and during landing. The experienced jumper is influenced by these perceptions about harm only during landing. Personality predispositions are less effective in educing energy when the jumper has had more experience.

COMPARISON BETWEEN GROUP NOT SPECIFYING HARM AND GROUP PERCEIVING PARACHUTIST AS SERIOUSLY HURT OR DEAD

(First Jump)

	Preparatory				*Jump*				*Landing*			
	SS	*df*	*MS*	*F*	*SS*	*df*	*MS*	*F*	*SS*	*df*	*MS*	*F*
Situations	47.88	3	15.96	7.64	679.38	4	169.85	49.35	423.83	4	105.96	61.60
Groups	1.12	1	1.12	NS	3.06	1	3.06	NS	92.41	1	92.41	5.60
Subjects in groups	3289.75	367	8.96		4088	340	12.02		5639.20	342	16.49	
Groups by situations	15.20	3	5.07	2.42	4.09	4	1.02	NS	16.79	4	4.20	2.44
Subjects by situations by groups	2304.05	1101	2.09		3685.43	1360	2.71		2355.67	1368	1.72	
Totals	5658.00	1475			8459.96	1709			8527.90	1719		

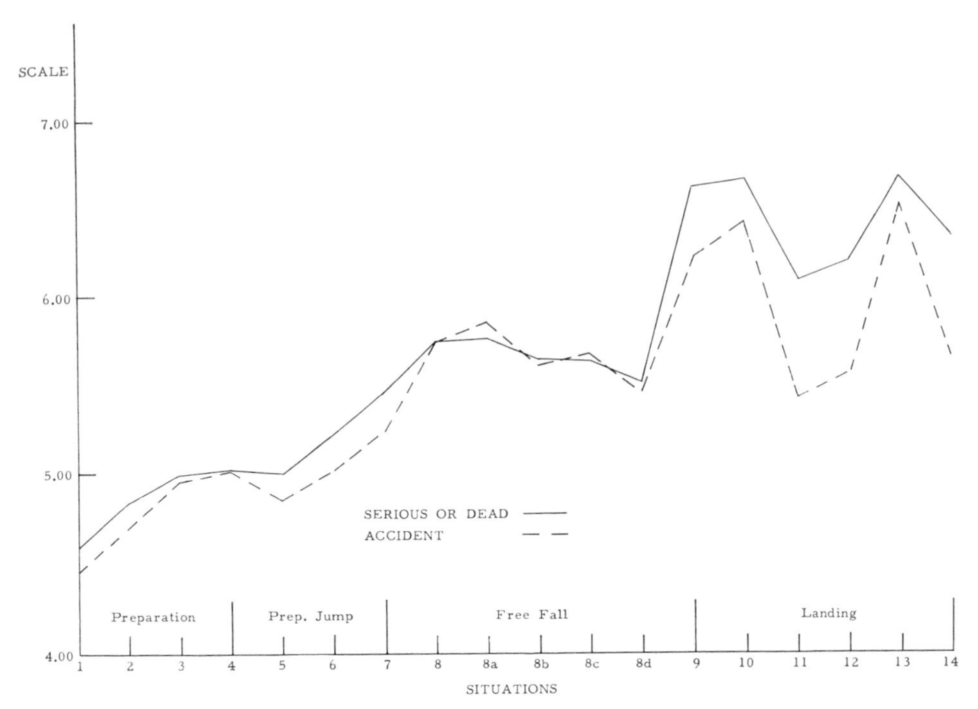

GRAPH IV. Comparison between group not specifying harm and group perceiving parachutist as seriously hurt or dead (first free fall).

Actual experience permits environmental input to structure the jumper's expectation so that he is less subject to his internal predispositions. It may also be said that enthusiasm among experienced jumpers is less related to personality predispositions than to factors realistically associated with the jump experience itself. A selective factor which may be at work here accounts for some of the differences between the first jump and the first free fall. Approximately sixty of the jumpers who contributed responses about their first jump had not yet experienced a free fall. Those who drop out before free fall may differ on this personality dimension from those who persist through the free fall.

The Fatalistic Attitude and Enthusiasm

The stories written in response to the picture of the prone parachutist were also scored according to the way the respondent accounted for the harm that had befallen him. These responses were classified according to whether, on the one hand, the harm was said to have been caused by a mechanical failure, unusual wind, or by the jumper's not having been properly instructed, or, on the other hand, according to whether the blame may be attached to the jumper himself. Perhaps he made an error in judgment or intention-

COMPARISON BETWEEN GROUP NOT SPECIFYING HARM AND GROUP PERCEIVING PARACHUTIST AS SERIOUSLY HURT OR DEAD

(First Free Fall)

	Preparatory				*Jump Preparation*				*Free Fall*				*Landing*			
	SS	*df*	*MS*	*F*	*SS*	*df*	*MS*	*F*	*SS*	*df*	*MS*	*F*	*SS*	*df*	*MS*	*F*
Situations	47.10	3	15.70	16.19	26.07	2	13.04	10.03	142.42	5	28.48	23.15	203.93	4	50.98	34.68
Groups	1.45	1	1.45	NS	7.37	1	7.37	NS	1.41	1	1.41	NS	83.95	1	83.95	5.30
Subjects in groups	3785.25	288	17.01		2904.67	289	10.05		5694.50	286	19.91		4560.20	288	15.83	
Groups by situations	1.70	3	.57	NS	.13	2	.07	NS	10.45	5	2.09	NS	27.08	4	6.77	4.61
Subjects by situations by groups	842.38	864	.97		757.11	578	1.30		1765.96	1430	1.23		1695.07	1152	1.47	
Totals	4677.88	1159			3695.35	872			7614.74	1727			6570.23	1449		

ally violated rules. The first will be termed "fate" since the fault lies with some person or force outside the individual parachutist, and the second will be termed "responsible" since the harm was considered to be a result of factors under the jumper's control. The following is an example of a story scored as harm caused by "fate":

> Damn, this thing is stuck — better go for my reserve — oops — handle. Well, my 'chute finally opened and I have a May West. 'Chute tears in half. My God, here I come! He lands — is dead — the ambulance arrives and takes him to the morgue.

Following is an example of a story scored "responsible":

> This individual is alive but injured and unconscious. (Why else would the doctor run?) The crowd, including jumpers, near the van are muttering angrily among themselves. The jumper has always been erratic and a show-off and at last he's put himself out of the picture; the others swear never to let him jump again. They don't even want to talk to him so they remain at a distance. Our friend collapsed his canopy by slipping in mid-air and held it that way down to the ground — to wow the kiddies. It reopened too slow and both of his legs are fractured.

Of 688 stories which could be scored on this dimension, 33 per cent reported the harm caused by fate, and 67 per cent blamed it on the jumper's irresponsible behavior.

Findings

How do the alternative images that one's destiny is controlled by fate or is in one's own control influence the enthusiasm scores? Graph V compares the mean enthusiasm scores on the first jump for the "fate" and "responsible" groups. Through the preparation, those who feel they are in the hands of fate seem to experience slightly more enthusiasm (the differences between groups are not statistically significant). During the jump, however, the fatalists are significantly more enthusiastic (for difference between the groups $F[1;473] = 5.54$, $P > .95$). During the landing stage there seems to be but slight difference (not statistically significant). After the parachute has been removed and after leaving the drop zone, those feeling responsible experience more enthusiasm (the differences are not significant over the range of landing situations but are at the point of landing $t > .97$).

In the case of the first free fall, the fatalist does not show significantly more enthusiasm during preparation. When actually on the jump run, on the edge of his free fall, the fatalist is considerably more enthusiastic than the one who is concerned about his own control of his destiny (difference between groups statistically significant $F[1;409] = 4.86$, $P > .95$). During the actual free fall experience, while he waits for the parachute to open and until he touches the ground, this attitudinal difference is not reflected in any difference of enthusiasm. Again, however, the self-directed person experiences more satisfaction at the point of landing and after the event (at point of landing, t > .98). Fate seems to be a more comforting attitude when one faces a challenge. During the act of jumping, it makes no real difference whether one feels responsible or is a fatalist. After it is over, the independent, responsible individual experiences greater satisfaction. The sense of expansiveness of the self is available to those acting as responsible selves. In energy terms, the fatalistic attitude may be thought of as a kind of unbinding of energy. Under this attitude, the internal excitement is transformed from fear into enthusiasm during the early stages of the jump. The attitude of responsibility is one of energy control. During the early part of the jump, the energy is bound, builds up and is experienced as fear. Release comes after the act and as a result of the act.

Carrying out an action in which there is a perceived danger contributes to the self-enhancement of the individual. A fatalistic attitude permits greater enjoyment, greater ease in entering the act, and presumably less anxiety, as one moves through the danger. Once the act is accomplished, however, the person who feels in control of himself reaps the greater reward. This is the voluntaristic aspect hypothesized as giving the positive direction to the transformation of energy. The thrill of facing danger and presumably the fear of it lessen as one becomes more familiar with the challenge. The conception of whether one is or is not in control of his own fate is more constant than is the perception of possible harm in its influence on the fear of danger and the thrill in overcoming it.

NOTE

This work was supported under contract AF 49 (638) 992 between the Air Force Office of Scientific Research and the Bureau of Social Science Research, Inc. Appreciation is expressed to Peter Vea for statistical assistance.

FOOTNOTES

1. Table 273, Statistical Abstract of the United States (1962).
2. Table 806, Statistical Abstract of the United States (1962).
3. Table 74, Statistical Abstract of the United States (1962).

REFERENCES

Epstein, S.: The measurement of drive and conflict in humans: theory and experiment; in Jones, R. [Ed.]: *Nebraska Symposium on Motivation — 1962.* Lincoln, U of Nebr, 1962, pp. 127-206.

Fenz, W. D.: *Conflict and Stress as Related to Physiological Activation and Sensory, Perceptual and Cognitive Functioning.* Psychological Monographs, No. 585, Washington, American Psychological Association, 1964.

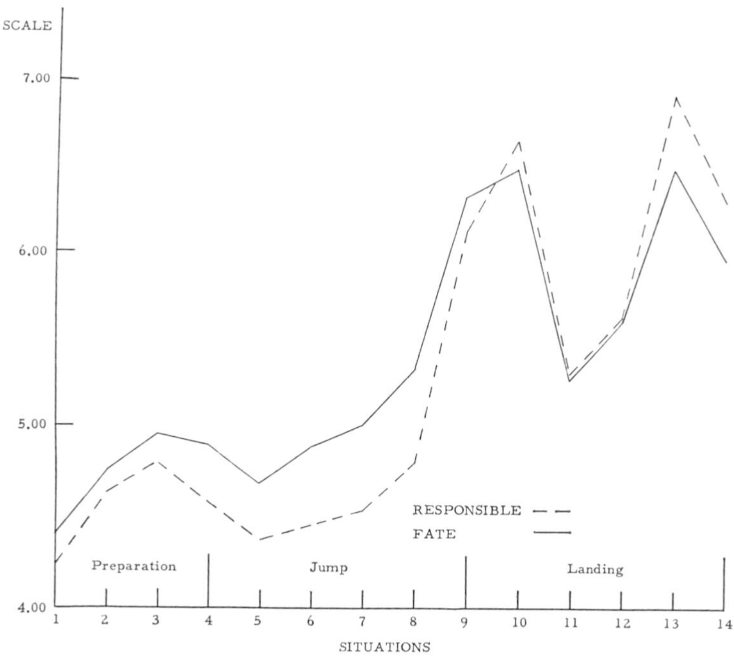

GRAPH V. Comparison between group attributing situation to fate and group perceiving the parachutist as responsible (first jump).

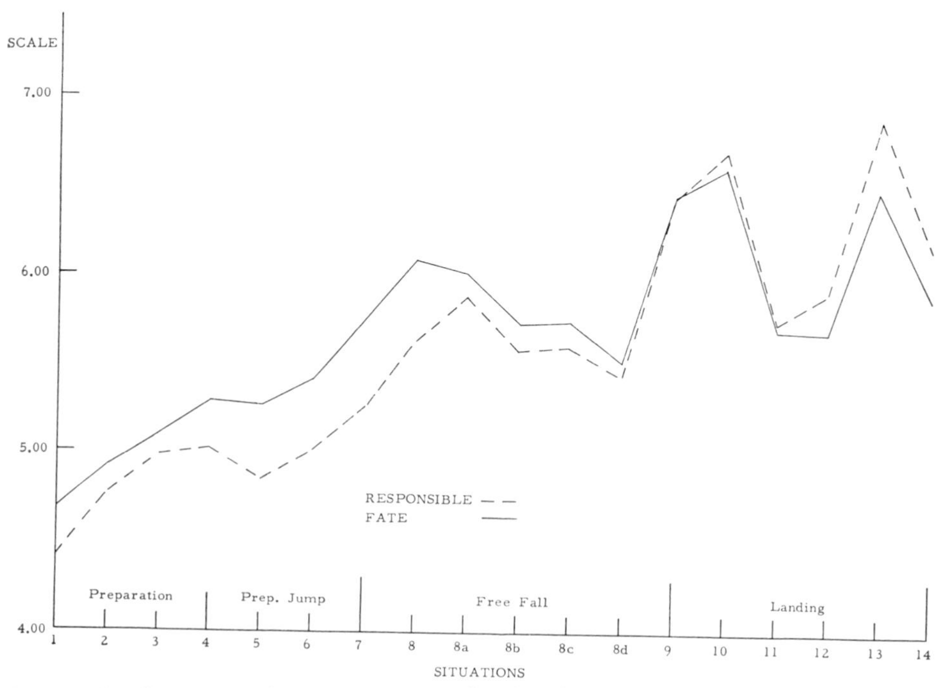

GRAPH VI. Comparison between group attributing situation to fate and group perceiving the parachutist as responsible (first free fall).

COMPARISON BETWEEN GROUP ATTRIBUTING SITUATION TO FATE AND GROUP PERCEIVING THE PARACHUTIST AS RESPONSIBLE

First Jump

	Preparatory				*Jump*				*Landing*			
	SS	*df*	*MS*	*F*	*SS*	*df*	*MS*	*F*	*SS*	*df*	*MS*	*F*
Situations	88.47	3	29.49	23.97	925.27	4	231.32	119.23	744.44	4	186.11	83.08
Groups	16.47	1	16.47	NS	82.98	1	82.98	5.54	21.76	1	21.76	NS
Subjects in groups	6034.60	512	11.78		7087.20	473	14.98		6582.00	476	13.83	
Groups by situations	2.72	3	.91	NS	7.94	4	1.99	NS	1.16	4	.29	NS
Subjects by situations by groups	1894.56	1536	1.23		3667.18	1892	1.94		4269.43	1904	2.24	
Totals	8036.82	2055			11770.57	2374			11618.79	2389		

COMPARISON BETWEEN GROUP ATTRIBUTING SITUATION TO FATE AND GROUP PERCEIVING THE PARACHUTIST AS RESPONSIBLE

First Free Fall

	Preparatory				*Jump Preparation*				*Free Fall*				*Landing*			
	SS	*df*	*MS*	*F*	*SS*	*df*	*MS*	*F*	*SS*	*df*	*MS*	*F*	*SS*	*df*	*MS*	*F*
Situations	89.48	3	29.83	29.91	39.16	2	19.58	28.38	247.02	5	49.40	30.49	374.47	4	93.62	52.60
Groups	14.00	1	14.00	NS	49.43	1	49.43	4.86	13.13	1	13.13	NS	21.62	1	21.62	NS
Subjects in groups	5103.01	407	12.54		4159.34	409	10.17		7621.93	404	18.87		5584.80	407	13.72	
Groups by situations	1.88	3	.63	NS	.32	2	.16	NS	11.05	5	2.21	NS	7.36	4	1.84	NS
Subjects by situations by groups	1217.39	1221	.997		562.76	818	.69		3261.76	2020	1.62		2903.07	1628	1.78	
Totals	6425.76	1635			4811.01	1232			11154.89	2435			8891.32	2044		

Klausner, S. Z. [Ed.]: *The Quest for Self-Control.* New York, Free Press, 1965.

Klausner, S. Z.: The transformation of fear: A study of parachuting; in *Symposium 13: Motives and Consciousness in Man.* 18th International Congress of Psychology — 1966, Moscow, International Union of Scientific Psychology, 1966, pp. 52-55.

News release: "Luis Rios, a Spanish bullfighter, announced plans to parachute into a bullring, shed his gear and fight the bull. When the time came he missed the ring and landed in the city dump."

PART THIRTEEN
SPORT AS SPECTACLE

INTRODUCTION

PROFESSIONAL, COLLEGE AND HIGH SCHOOL teams play before audiences. Organized sports could hardly thrive the way that they do without being spectacles. In this section of the volume, we discuss the sportswriter and the cheerleader — individuals who help make a spectacle out of sports.

Roy G. Francis writes about the sportswriter.[1] The press (and radio and television) promote sports (and reciprocally they devote more attention to sports than the combined coverage given the movies, theater, art and books because of the interest of their audience). Sportswriters (and sports announcers) turn out floods of copy. What motivates them?

The sportswriter is seen by Roy Francis as a special case of man working out a consistent self-identity in the face of uncertain and to some extent inconsistent demands. Motivations of the sportswriter differ along a set of dimensions. One of these is the character of the sport — as hunting and fishing differ from other "individual" sports. Whether the sport is one in which events take place (as in boxing), or regularly recurring games (as baseball), the sportswriter variously involves himself with those making up "sporting news."

In the process, the sportswriter can pursue, accurately as well as in error, a number of more or less explicit images of self. He may aspire to be nothing more than a craftsman, or he may aspire to be a columnist; in either case, he may end up being a "huckster" who is a lackey for those who sponsor the contest.

The sportswriter is caught up in a network of social relations which impinge upon both the identity he pursues and the reputation he achieves. He has a job, and this demands that he get his copy in on time. Hence, he cannot take time to reflect and give a polished literary effort. He needs to prove superior knowledge against even the most erudite fan. So he finds it valuable to have "inside" information — and enters a precarious relationship with the star or the management. Thus, to prove to have superior knowledge, he must get the favor of those "inside" the sport — and that comes at a price. He may have to support an event he would rather not. Thus, as the sportswriter wrestles with the tension between what he does and what he feels he ought to do, he acts out the problem of every man in search of an identity.

Lawrence R. Herkimer in this volume gives us an inside picture of cheering and cheerleaders.[2] In the past fifteen years, cheerleading has become more of an art and a much more organized activity. Activities of cheerleaders have expanded as well as the sports in which they participate. Cheerleading "schools," workshops, camps and training clinics have been initiated in almost every state of the union, and organizations like the National Cheerleaders Association, the American Cheerleaders Association and the United States Cheerleaders Association have been formed. What has brought this about? Why is it such an honor to be a cheerleader, and important to so many junior high, senior high and college students for them to "try out" for cheerleading in their schools? What psychological drives prompt a girl or a boy to want to be a cheerleader? What drives them to expend vast amounts of energy and work performing their cheering duties and preparing for their cheering sessions at the athletic contests and pep rallies? What sometimes drives many cheerleaders to states of approaching hysteria during exciting games? What prompts them to spend many hours preparing for the game, as well as money for uniforms, decorations, equipment, etc.? Why do some schools want only girl cheerleaders, and some only boys, and others a combination of the two? Herkimer discusses these and many other questions.

What are the current trends in cheerleading, how do different sections of the country vary in style of yells, uniforms, activities, etc.? What sports do cheerleaders cheer for? What effect on the crowd do cheerleaders have? What do they do along the lines of "boosting school spirit"? How do they improve sportsmanship; how do they motivate crowds and students in sportsmanlike gestures; and how do they many times spur the team on to greater heights? These are some of the questions that Herkimer studied and inquired about from many of the 100,000 cheerleaders he trained at the National Cheerleader Association summer camps, schools and one-day clinics held during the spring and fall months this past year. Some of the answers were as one would have expected, but others were very interesting and unusual.

And what effect does sport as spectacle have upon the athlete? A sports audience is usually reduced to the lowest common denominator. The sports audience is total and absolute; it possesses no shades of adequacy; its reaction is total acceptance or total rejection. Every activity has its stresses and tensions, but an athlete, performing before such an evaluation board, is bound to suffer increased anxiety.[3] No one at any time likes to lose, but the athlete performing before an audience is forced to "win" instead of playing for "play's sake." Winning becomes the primary motivation.

FOOTNOTES

1. P. 700.
2. P. 727. Miss Sandra Dotson, secretary at The Menninger Foundation in the building where Ralph Slovenko has his office, was a cheerleader in high school, and had a course under Herkimer. She says "he's really great" and richly deserves the title "Mr. Cheerleader."

3. For example, Gale Sayers, Chicago Bears and former University of Kansas football star, says: "Before practically every game, I throw up my breakfast. Usually, I don't eat much either. I order three eggs and ground beef. I eat a fourth of the beef and just touch the eggs. . . . The pregame jitters sort of drains your nervous energy. . . . It doesn't make any difference playing for money." Interview in *Topeka Daily Capital,* October 5, 1966, p. 15.

THE SPORTSWRITER

ROY G. FRANCIS

THE PROBLEM OF THIS CHAPTER is to account for the various motivations of the sportswriter. It is not primarily or even secondarily an effort to explain why writers employ words the way they do. It is not primarily an effort to account for the generally poor writing found on our sports pages. Poor writing scarcely distinguishes the sportswriter from, say, a sociologist; he does have a wider audience, however, so the impact of his poor writing may be the greater. Were we certain that his readers are, or would have been, able to detect instances of poor writing, we would be more certain in our judgment of him. Alas, however, few readers seem capable of noticing or complaining about the poor craftsmanship found in the sports section of our daily press.

The point of view of this chapter is sociological, and this will require that we put the sportswriter in a social context. We will examine him in terms of the kinds of activities about which he writes. We will comment on the major identities which he sometimes pursues. We will discuss the various relationships he enters with his employers, his peers, his fans and those on whom he depends for material.

It turns out, of course, that even the poorest sports writer is a highly complex creature. He becomes trapped in a series of situations, few of which are of his own making. In the midst of conflicting pressures and competing interests, he struggles with the task of discovering a consistent self-image in his career. Like the rest of us, he seldom fails completely or succeeds entirely. The motivations of the sportswriter are, in general terms, surprisingly like those of other people. In terms of content, naturally, he has relatively unique problems. But his struggle is ours, and in knowing the sportswriter, we get a glimpse of ourselves.

GENERAL CONSIDERATIONS

Man, as the consequence of social interaction, may well indeed be the product of a social process. But he does not experience process; that is to say, he is not aware of participating in a process. He experiences *events,* occurrences which rightly or wrongly he perceives as being distinct from other happenings in his life. He recalls events, but not the process. The student cannot remember being educated. He may recall a particular teacher or a small number of outstanding incidents which took place in that teacher's class; but the continuing, on-going pattern he cannot intuitively recall.

In part, I suppose, this is related to the rarity of quality. While some rare things are not, on that account, cherished, the commonplace is most easily put aside. Even when one witnesses an outstanding performer, we must admit that his average may be higher than the average performance of others; but sometimes Ted Williams struck out more than once in a game, and sometimes even he went hitless. This is true in all areas of life. "Great" comics like Bob Newhart and Jonathan Winters may be generally better than others with whom they are compared. Yet even they have a few truly outstanding "routines" which insure their place in our memories.

Now in "real life," including the sports world, there are some events which can be anticipated. A championship boxing match is an event of such a kind. Sometimes the event is unscheduled, as in a "nohitter" or "perfect game." These are recognized immediately as different, and each obtain a special place in our memories. But a season consisting in baseball of some 162 games conveys a different image. Because of the large number of happenings, it takes on the character of a process. Thus the World Series or playoffs, like a Rosebowl Game, take on the added sociological dimension of an "event." The writer covering the routine game is stuck in the midst of a process, and he becomes bored with his task. He forgets that the fan might be seeing only one game a season and hence for him it is an event. Thus in his bored hackneyed account he impliedly tells the fan that the fan is "bushleague." He destroys what to some is a possible great event simply because he does not understand that the routinization of play has dulled his perceptions of the game.

Sociologists often refer to three basic types of relationships which man enters. One we call "personal" because the actors interact as people known to each other. This generally calls for an exchange of names, though the name may be restricted to the particular relationship (i.e., "Poopsie" and "Tweetie Pie") . A second relationship is the structural one, involving an exchange of titles since the actors are involved in an organizational exchange. A third relationship is the categorical one, in which case only the name or label of the category is involved. Thus, most "fans" relate only in the simplest of terms and can share experiences with this minimal identification. It soon turns out, of course, that even in this instance gradations of identity are required to distinguish the novice from the knowledgeable fan.

Insofar as the sportswriter obtains a by-line or even has a picture appearing by his article, he tends to enter a number of asymmetrical relationships. The "fan," for example, obtains his name but does not exchange his own; the fan maintains, most frequently, a categorical identity. Sometimes, of course, the fan may be motivated to claim a personal relation, real or imagined, with a sportswriter; with greater infrequency is the relationship of the sportswriter, for he must "imagine" his audience and rely on accidental outbursts for any "feedback" in his assessing himself.

Related to this asymmetrical aspect of the relationship the sportswriter characteristically enters is the process by which one does become involved in the writer-fan relation. For the writer, this is ordinarily a career decision. He has some real or imaginary image of the sportswriter; he may have had other writing aspirations and drifted to sports by a series of accidents. But once in the network of relations, he is less free than the fan who need merely buy another paper to change his relationships.

Now, it is clear that the writer must, in a sense, *grow* into his part of the relationship. He cannot don the identity simply by accepting a job on the newspaper staff. Rather, if he does, his initial efforts at knowing himself must be faulting and vague. He still must discover his style and which of the various kinds of relationships he is to develop during his career. While the fan may have to "learn" the writer with whom he interacts, he can "join" it in a moment or leave it as easily. The defense which the writer tries to enjoy is in numbers. The larger the number of fans he can respond to, the less he is concerned about any one of them.

It is one thing to appeal to motives to explain behavior. It is quite another thing to explain the motives themselves. A circular argument would explain motives in terms of the behavior to which the motive is appealed to as an explanation. Generally speaking, appealing to a motive makes sense only when alternative actions are possible and the action is seen instrumentally, that is, when a predictable consequence is attached to a particular action. Moreover, motives are customarily appealed to when the action taken is "mysterious," "surprising" or somehow out of the ordinary. That is to say, when the actor engages in activities other than those the observer would probably have engaged in, a motive is sought to explain the surprising activity.

Appealing to motives is a cheap intellectual exercise. Almost any act can be accounted for from a set of "sufficient" motives. Ascribing particular motives is therefore a most difficult task. In the case of relatively unique behavior of a specified individual, one may have considerable evidence favoring a particular subset of motives or favoring the rejection of a particular subset. When one is attempting to explain the behavior of a class of individuals, the subsets are rapidly increased until, in many cases, the number of putative explanations is so large that the entire argument is weakened.

Thus, one is tempted to reject the ascription of motives in explaining behavior. Herein lies a dangerous possibility. One may be tempted to infer that the refusal to specify motives implies a rejection of motive as a theoretical dimension. Though some may wish to take that position, I do not. I find the concept of motive quite useful, and tend to associate it with deliberate action. That is to say, insofar as man can be involved in self-conscious goal-directed behavior, I am willing to admit "motive." In general, then, I connect motives to "ends" to be achieved. In turn, I am required to believe that the actor is thus goal-directed; his attention turns towards various means for the achievement of that end.

In principle, he views a number of alternative means. In some way, the actor must "choose" which of the means will achieve his end, with what other consequences. In facing these alternatives, his action is based on *values*. One may, as a matter of fact, generally define values as the premises upon which action choices are made. What I am doing here, however, is to indicate a difference between *instrumental* values, as those values on which choices of means are made, and *transcendental* or *relatively* transcendential values, as those on which "ends" or "goals" are chosen. The relatively transcendental value is related to an end which, in a broader situational context, may be seen as a means to some more general goal. Thus, one may attend a class as a means to achieve professional training as a means for a higher-income career as a means for a preferred style of life. In my terminology, one is motivated when his commitment to a transcendental (or relatively transcendental) value is so strong as to impel a choice based upon an instrumental value.

The distinction between the "transcendental value" and the motive lies in the commitment to action. One can philosophize about "means-end" relations and can "see" how a given means will result in a given end without any commitment to action. To move from mere "intellectual" concern to behavior more generally regarded as action, we must have some notion that results in manifest behavior. The premise which makes this connection is "motive."

My problem is not a complete accounting for motives of sportswriters, nor even specifying them. I am writing from the point of view of sociology, and hence look to the social world for the "action-inputs" that impel behavior. Now many actions may be the consequence of error on the part of the actor; he need not be deliberate about the intention of the consequence. In such cases, we must look elsewhere for motives and consider what he might have been trying to do when the error took place. Thus, a sportswriter may be "motivated" to write a profound commentary on human behavior and end up with a hackneyed bit of superficial phrasing.

The writer is explicitly involved in communication. He is "taught" some of the elements of "writing." He receives formal training, however badly learned, however ill utilized, in "grammar." He learns, if he goes to a journalism school, a number of conventions of "how to write." He often "unlearns them" on the job and picks up new conventions on lead sentences, organization and the like. While he generally is a poor craftsman, his marketable skill is, ostensibly, writing.

Though he may not recognize it, writing involves three levels of communication. These "levels" occur simultaneously, though one tends to be emphasized. These levels are as follows:

SUBSTANTIVE COMMUNICATION. What the article or story is *prima facie* all about constitutes the substance of the communication. It may be about a football game, a baseball player or a controversy about the duck hunting season. All formal grammar is oriented to this level of communication. As a result, we often are lead to think that this is all there is to communication; the "semanticists" certainly premise their claims to public attention on such a position.

EXPRESSIVE COMMUNICATION. Explicitly or not, the writer conveys a normative position in writing. He gives assent, insinuates disapproval, or otherwise communicates some value judgment in his writing. This he may do by choice of words, by ordering his ideas, by neglecting to report certain occurrences. He may think that he is being objective, not realizing, for example, that "being objective" is itself a normative stance. Thus, regarding a controversial call by umpire, he may try "not to choose sides," being unaware that in so doing he is supporting a particular position or the status of the official. Even choosing to write about a topic lends a value stance to the topic, if not to the content of the article. Since we require deliberateness for the concept of motive, the writer may be unable to recognize his expressive behavior and might deny any scientific explanation of it.

EXHIBITIVE COMMUNICATION. Communication at this level involves the presentation of the self by the writer. While he may not always be conscious of the self he is presenting, and while he may make errors in the sense of attempting to present one image of self and actually present another, the writer is often quite conscious of who he intends to be in his writing career. Thus, he may have strong motivations in this instance and regard substantive communication instrumentally. In part, of course, we are here concerned with the differences between "front stage" and "back stage" behavior, to use a dramaturgical vocabulary.

As we have observed, our grammar refers to substantive communication. Societies tend to develop more or less understood rules for the other types of communication — but we do not have "schooling" in them. Indeed, we may be unaware that we are even engaged in them. Many workers would most vehemently deny "exhibitive" behavior, though every reader would be able to get the message he has essayed.

We ought not leave the impression that, somehow, expressive and exhibitive communication are undignified or unworthy types of behavior.

On the contrary – existentially, they are as significant as is "substantive" communication. It is the manipulation of these forms of communication that often spells the difference between success and failure. This is no less true of the sportswriter.

On the other hand, since the writer is clearly in the "substantive communication business" it would be easy for him to conclude that he is motivated solely in that regard. It is easy to deny accusations of expressive or exhibitive behavior. Since we are not always clear as to how to proceed in these directions, a great deal of confusion regarding meanings and intentions result from the built-in ambiguity of this type of communication.

THE SOCIAL SETTING OF SPORTS

The term "sports" covers such a wide variety of social forms that a strategy for writing about one may fail when applied to another. Some sports are ordinarily thought of as involving individuals, as in the case of hunting or fishing. One can imagine a competitive situation in which teams are organized to see who can obtain the greatest kill or catch. But normally this is not done. Ordinarily, the hunt is an end in itself, and an audience is involved only after the episode is completed. One does not come to watch a person hunt, though hunters of course have been observed. One may watch a fly-casting contest, but ordinarily, one does not become a spectator at the catch.

Hunters and fishers are differently organized than are, say, baseball fans. The ball fan generally has a point about which his attention is focused. While special interest groups may be organized, as Ducks Unlimited, the hunter or fisher generally seeks out and enters individual relationships that are or may be highly personal in their commitment to the sport, as hunting and fishing buddies.

The sportswriter who writes about hunting and fishing is likely to merely supply information (season dates, catch limits, reports of good fishing) or some "event" as when a fisher catches a record-breaking fish or some such thing. There are, of course, advertisers with vested interests in the area; the state may be concerned about a tourist business, so that there is sufficient motivation for some writer to develop a special interest in "sports" of this kind. Since their audience is generally a participating one, few sportswriters attempt to pass themselves off as experts. If an expert does the writing, the process is usually that the paper or magazine sought out the services of a man known to be expert.

One interesting point about the kinds of sports reported on the sports pages of our newspapers is that some are regarded as sports *only* if engaged in by amateurs. When, for example, fishing is engaged in for money, it is regarded as a "job." One reason for this is that in hunting and fishing the object of the search has an economic value as a food. Hence, when engaged in for money the concept of "lowest unit cost" per unit secured is legitimate. From the class-bound notion of the amateur fisherman, there is nothing sporting (i.e., there is no contest by which man is tested) about using a net; nor does "shining a deer" constitute a sport, since this is regarded as "taking unfair advantage" of the animal. From time to time, sportswriters who cover these activities crusade against various "unsportsmanlike conduct" of the hunter or fisher. Some nimrods are criticized for being "butchers," for seeking the kill rather than enjoying the hunt. The ability to buy the services of an expert guide (who may or may not make the actual kill) is hardly a test of a person's skill in the woods. Yet the sportswriter who may condemn such behavior may not acknowledge that in his other reporting he contributes largely to precisely such a mood. An outstanding kill or catch is an event in the sense that it is unusual. Hence, it is a matter worthy of reporting. Moreover, with the emphasis placed on "getting the limit," many hunters and fishers are subtly goaded into getting as many as possible, not in obtaining the least consonant with a self-image of the successful sportsman. News accounts have done much to convey the impression that the good hunter or fisherman always gets his limit – which, in part, is related to the possibility of an overkill of game animals or fish.

Some "sports" are largely individual in the sense of participation rather than spectator but either have a few spectator events or changes are wrought in which the spectator becomes an important element. Thus tennis, golf and more recently bowling involve large numbers of participating individuals and commercial interests to be served. They also have a few events staged as tournaments, which require both expertise in writing them up and which require the writer to have some contact with the participants. Since the potential audience of activities of this kind is rather enormous, no daily sports editor can afford to ignore them. Indeed, local commercial interests may create annual tournaments which require considerable newspaper support for success. In the case of bowling, cities are put into competitive positions to bid for certain of the bigger tournaments. For success, the venture requires good press coverage, the pressure on the sportswriter mounts.

However, sportswriters seldom have any problem with their consciences in supporting efforts of this sort. Their only real problem is to be certain that the tourney is honestly run and not some sort of con game. To find this out, they ordinarily rely on personal knowledge of the sponsors. Since the sportswriter is likely to play a bit of golf or bowl from time to time, his sympathies are easily aroused and he can enter the huckster role with few regrets.

The fact that events of this kind are relatively infrequent enables the writer to share the spectator's image of it as an event. It is out of the ordinary. If the prizes are adequate to attract big names — and the writers frequently use pressure themselves to push local sponsors to increase the purse — the task of writing is made easier. This is especially true when the writer is preparing a feature interview. It gives him a personal contact and enables him honestly to drop a few names, enhancing his own position in the eyes of his fans. Though the knowledge of the performer and any subsequent friendship that might grow up are clearly the consequence of the job and not due to any unique qualities of the writer, the fact remains that the writer is able to enter a personal relation with a person of importance.

One reason boxing is in such ill repute today is found in the kind of person on whom the writer would depend for special information. In the past, a number of boxing writers were extremely good as writers. The eventful character of the boxing championship enabled the writer to become involved in anticipated consequences. While some of the lesser fights involved damaged stumble-bums, the championship fight usually put the writer in contact with "class." Ring Lardner once wrote an engaging story about a champ who was a real bum. In the story, writers hated to relate to him as "champion" and managed to do him in. The point is well taken: the sportswriter wants to be able to admire the champ. If he cannot, he withholds the honor generally associated with the title.

Partly because the writers do not want to be associated in the public's eye with today's handlers of boxers, and because the activity is not attracting the kind of person whom they could admire, they withhold their support, refuse to give the traditional coverage and belittle those who are involved. When a local figure attempts to "revive the sport," he is caught between conflicting emotions. While many writers will defend their practices in the current boxing situation, they generally deny any ability to use similar influence elsewhere. That is to say, they will deny deprecating a baseball player or owner out of personal feelings.

In the case of "spectator sports," such as baseball and football, the fact of organized sponsorship induces the sportswriter to take stands he otherwise would not. At once we must distinguish between the "major" and "minor" leagues; the writers tend to obtain the status accorded their teams. Those who cover bush league baseball are regarded as bush league writers. Bush league writers, on the other hand, may entertain vague hopes of getting to the big time, or are such generalists that they are more likely to think of themselves as sportswriters rather than as, say, "baseball writers."

We are a competing people. Each segment of our society develops its own ways of competition and its own measures of success. In the case of sports, we often pay for the privilege of watching other people compete. In this engagement, we suffer vicarious defeat or enjoy vicarious victory. Yet the pattern of competition varies among the several sports.

In a way, hunting and fishing have the vaguest standards of success or failure. True, the bag limit is some sort of mark of success, but many hunters or fishers compete with the game they seek rather than with other people.

In golf, the individual may indeed try to do better than specific others. But he may also compete simply against a "standard" with no sense of besting another individual. The standard may be of the order of "par" which only a few amateurs can consistently hope to better. It may be a "bogey par" (usually allowing one stroke per hole more than the "real" par). Incidentally, it is interesting to note that as long as golf was the game of the striving middle class, the image of a standard for achievement dominated scoring; when golf became something admitting the working class, the concept of "par" became closer to an empirical average, something more reasonably attained. Returning to our previous point, the standard may be a highly personal one. As a matter of fact, the individual may have a personal standard he wishes to better; he may be tuned enough to his culture to aspire to break par; he may be a realist in the sense of knowing his score is likely to be greater than either.

In tennis, we find a real sense of contest in which one not merely tries to outdo the other but to oppose his chances of success. In track, both runners try to outdo the other, but one does nothing to prevent the success of the other. Moreover, the idea of "team" varies from sport to sport. In track and swimming, for example, the team is a collection of individuals who in aggregate (except, however, for the "relay") constitute a team. In football and baseball, the team members act in concert. Thus we must distinguish those sports which imply opposition as well as competition and those in which the teamwork is a concerted effort rather than sequential.

The consequences for reporting are quite significant. One can more easily describe the action of men racing against each other (or putting the shot; or, though in concert, doing the same thing, as a crew), than to describe accurately concerted action requiring various actions. In this regard, baseball is easier to describe than football since the role behaviors occur in sequence: first the pitcher throws, then the batter hits it, then the shortstop fields it, etc., and is complicated only to the extent of more than one baserunner.

Since football is a difficult sport to describe, writers tend to select out a few "key" players. Normally, these are those contributing directly to the scoring potential — the quarterback, halfbacks, ends and the fullback. Sometimes a lineman is noted for a particular block; but that is identified as an "eventful" thing rather than the normal play. The *accumulated* effort of a defensive player may be noted, but the complicated play of the defense unit is hardly ever noticed in detail by one observer, let alone easily written.

But further distinctions must be made. There is the difference between pro, semi-pro and "amateur" sports. The latter can conveniently be divided between those associated with educational institutions (college and high schools) and those sponsored otherwise. Now sports identified with colleges give higher status to those covering them than those with high schools. Colleges themselves are ranked on some prestige pattern. There is more prestige for a writer covering the Big Ten than, say, a Minnesota Intercollegiate Athletic Conference game.

It is interesting to note that in very few cities is there both an outstanding college football team and a profesisonal football team. With the advent of the television contract underwriting the American Football League and the recent expansions of the National Football League, there will be possibly greater tensions between collegiate and professional football. It will be interesting to see just where the loyalties of the sportswriters will lie; in the case of a conflict, will they identify with the college or with the professional? My hunch is that they will tend to support the obvious play for money teams. The reason is quite simple — more prestige, more power, more money. The competitive bidding of the two leagues for college seniors in the "draft" turned up a surprising number of people from relatively unknown colleges. The writers identified with the college team will find that the competing pro outfit can get talent from lesser college units; hence a loyalty to the college will be negatively viewed by management of the money team.

It is already clear that writers in general relate to such obvious organizations as a corporation formed around a team of some sort. They understand more clearly the roles played by the management, press personnel, scouts and the like than a college or university. They can participate in a minor way by suggesting tips on potential players as sort of amateur scouts. In the case of collegiate ball, however, they encounter a group whom the writers can never understand — the faculty.

Faculty members are likely to suffer from curious stereotypes about the student-athlete. They are likely to be guided by emotions rather than formal information. They are likely to recall the memory-commanding incident rather than the range of student abilities — the hefty behemoth who was dumb survives in faculty imagery many generations after the coaches found him detrimental. Yet the error lies not in the image the faculty has of the athlete.

Of more importance is the commitment the faculty has to the academic tradition, the scholarly attitude. These are the true intellectuals, not the pretenders sometimes found elsewhere. The sportswriter knows intuitively that none of his pretenses are likely to be effective against this group; he can claim no superiority over these individuals except his personal contacts with the sports world. But more important, they do not share his identification with sports. Academic people may well regard sports as "mere games," as something hardly worth the adulation sportswriters pour out.

In this context, the athlete who is a hero to the sportswriter merits no special reaction from his professor. The maintenance of a winning team falls quite low on the professor's scheme of things. If he does not share the point of view which categorizes all athletes as dumb physical specimens, the professor may regret to see this good mind corrupted and taken from its "rightful heritage." Thus the sportswriter tends to condemn faculty senates for insisting on controlling collegiate athletics and often openly condemns the professor in whose course a student achieved a failing mark. Academic ineligibility is something the sportswriter cannot understand; and because the writer has no contact and hence no control over the faculty, he feels free to castigate those who dare to lessen the quality of that from which he achieves his identity.

Thus, also, the sportswriter is baffled by the conflict between the AAU and NCAA regarding the control over amateur athletics. Being unable to place his world in a broad social context, the writer is generally unable to see how changes in society wreak changes on the sports world — or vice versa. He cannot understand how the concept of "amateur" is bound to class position. He writes in essentially an ahistorical point of view and is unaware that at one time such workers as blacksmiths could not compete as amateurs because they had earned money from a physical activity. The sportswriter tends to reify a particular concept of the athlete and is completely unequipped to handle a situation in which this conception simply does not obtain.

Since the sportswriters have no *general* social theory from which to articulate a discussion of such events as "The Olympics," they fall back on the limited strategies of writing that work in the world they do know. The result is an expressive communication of sentiments or moods rather than a substantive argument. They can insinuate a dissatisfaction with the present state of amateur athletics; but none of their pronouncements makes sense to anyone who is aware of the problems of social organization.

Hence, their writing on the *performance* of the amateur athlete is superior to their *analysis* of the games. Since they share neither the intellectual heritage on which the Olympics rest nor the values underlying individual athletic efforts outside of the team-competition framework, writers have invented various scoring systems and have *imposed* the team-competition definition on the games. To claim simple-minded chauvinism as the explanation is, I think, unfair. There is a social process which lends itself to this result.

Writers from each nationality group have, to a greater or lesser degree, the ethnocentrism generated by their various cultures. They have statistical and sometimes personal knowledge of the men and women competing under their national colors. They speak the same language as these athletes, have the same food preferences, same style of clothes, and, in general, identify with them. Thus, in the actual moment of performance, the sportswriter is gently forced to take the role of the athlete from his country. He will tend to identify not with the single performer who naturally wants to win his event, but with each performer from his country that he sees. Hence, the writer tends to have a generalized identification with the team and seeks to have some measure of how well his collective self is doing. The result is a corruption of the purpose of the Olympic games.

Thus, one of the factors necessary to account for the behavior of the sportswriter is the social structure of the moment of performance. The way in which the writer relates to the amateur performance is vastly different from the way he relates to the professional. There are some overlapping similarities, as the analogy between a collegiate conference from which a champion emerges and a "league" of professionals. Whether the individual occurrence is highly repetitive, like one baseball game in a season of 162, or an event such as "The St. Paul Open," or a relatively eventful occasion such as a football game in a season of fourteen, the writer's involvement varies considerably. To prevent boredom, the writer often "creates" events, as the naming of the "mythical" All-Star team.

Most writers are caught up in the day-by-day efforts required to produce a paper. They have neither the opportunity nor the desire to make an objective appraisal of their situation. Hence they have no controls over it; only to the extent that man has articulated the situation he is in can he expect to have control over it. And then, it must be borne in mind, the character of the variables used in the assessment of the situation implies who can do the controlling. If the variables relate to groups, few individuals have such access to power as to make the manipulation — such variables call for group control. If the variables relate to individuals, there is some measure of likelihood that an individual can effect some control. If the variables are discernable only by sophisticated research, control and manipulation become the province of a special group of experts. Clearly, these various alternatives involve us in value decisions of enormous and profound dimensions.

THE SPORTSWRITER AND HIS IDENTITIES

The sportswriter, because of the public character of his work, acquires a reputation. This does not exhaust his possible identities, for he is a member of a work force and may become known as a politician, a man gunning for editor, or whatever. These are backstage identities; his contacts as sportswriter outside of the paper are frontstage. The frontstage identity can be virtually equated with a reputation. Thus, great allowances have to be made for the identity sought — the one for which he is motivated — and the one obtained. They need not be the same. Briefly, the achieved identities are these:

THE SPORTSWRITER OR REPORTER. The image presented here is one who has a job to do — to report something that has happened or will happen in the world of sports. The best adjective one could apply to this identity is that of the "objective" writer. Among the worst would be the "hack." The nonobjective writer may well be a laudatory self-image, if his bias is a moral one.

The claim to this identity insinuates an ability to write. Even as a simple craft, few writers today can claim superiority in writing to their readers. The claim rests ultimately on their having a job. Continuance in the job constitutes sufficient validation.

THE HUCKSTER. The writer is in contact with a number of persons who differentially serve the sports world. One of the categories of such people is that of those sponsoring the sporting event. Such an individual may be a fight promoter, the owner of a professional team, or a member of a Chamber of Commerce committee. They find the writer useful: stories about a pending event have advertising value, for the event itself or for "civic pride."

Now, ordinarily, few writers are willing simply to be advertisers. Too frequently, the event turns out to be a bust, and if they peddled it too obviously, their reputation would suffer. Moreover, they may always desire to have the power to criticize, and this would be greatly endangered if they simply lent their efforts to conning the public into attending forthcoming events.

It should be clear that the identity of huckster involves a network of social relations. In particular, the huckster finds a commitment to the sponsor greater than a commitment to a reading fan. Yet this relationship is fraught with career dangers. Why, then, do sportswriters enter this relation, even if only temporarily?

There are a number of reasons for this. We should not imagine that the sportswriter is ordinarily motivated to be a huckster. Mostly, he may be unaware of the forces that turn out to manipulate him. But he has a recurring problem: his claim to being a sportswriter is *de facto* validated by having a job. This validation is adequate for the hack writer; but for all who are better or who think they are better, a superior basis for validation is needed. The sportswriter must be able to present himself as one who is superior to the fan.

He can do this if he has superior knowledge or if he has access to information not available to the fan. If, that is, he can get the fan to rely on him for certain bits of information, his claims on the identity "sportswriter" would need no further validation. An obvious strategy is to be in a position in which one can report the backstage performance of others involved in the performance. To do this requires that one be privy to "behind the scenes" material. There is only one way to get such material: one must enter the backstage world of those putting on the event.

This requires that the writer enter at least a quasi-personal relationship with the performers and the sponsors of sporting events. The structured relation involves only frontstage activities – the advance man has a role to play, and he isn't about to release true backstage information to just anybody. In general, then, the sportswriter must be willing to do someone's bidding at certain times if he is to obtain prized information. As a temporary pattern of writing, most career men are willing to pay the price. Woe, however, befalls the man who gets so enmeshed that his public reputation is that of huckster.

The Informant. The converse of the huckster is the man who is presenting the "real dope" about forthcoming events. He has the scoop on the trades to be made, the change recently installed on an offensive strategy, on sailing equipment, and the like. His readers are superior in discussing sports than readers of lesser men. He has a following. This is the dream of many writers. It is this identity which motivates the writer who, as we have seen, becomes a huckster if only for a moment to willingly pay a "price" to achieve this self-image.

The Analyst. When sporting events go according to anticipated patterns, the writer can claim superior knowledge. He is capable of analyzing the situation so well that the outcome is predictable. He gets caught when the event turns out to the contrary; but the superior analyst simply faces a new challenge. He "digs out" unknown "facts" which enable him (to save face) to explain the untoward consequence.

Most such writers rely on the general inadequacy of their fans. Thinking is a difficult task, and many fans find it useful to have ready-made answers for them. Yet there are a number of fans who have knowledge superior to the writer. They may be somehow presently involved in the sporting event, or thay may have been active participants in the past. They are freed from the various entangling (e.g., huckster) relations the writer faces. They are freed from making public statements, and, above all, free from making deadlines. They are free from having to continue the task of writing about forthcoming events. They have a certain leisure which the writer either does not have or refuses to acquire – the leisure of connecting past writing with subsequent events.

Few football predictors bother with analyzing subsequent events. Few are called to task. Few bother to connect the analysis of one game with their analysis of another game. I can recall one writer accounting for two football upsets which occurred in the same season. In one game, the underdog scored first and went on to clobber the other team quite badly. In the second game, the "overdog" scored early, but the underdog held on and in the fading minutes of the game lost when they gambled for a two-point try after the touchdown instead of going for a game-tying kick. In accounting for the first incident, the writer argued that "when a team scores early, there is a tendency for the other to relax and show uncertainty and dismay. This lets the scoring team go on to pile up an unsurmountable advantage." For the other occasion, he wrote that "when a team scores early, the other team realizes it has a fight on its hands and stiffens its defense early in the game."

This type of analysis is *ad hoc*. Even when written before the game, it is never presented as a hypothesis which could be proven wrong. Unlike the scientist whose analyses are presented to seek general explanations, the sportswriter concerns himself with the unique here-and-now. Moreover, the scientist deliberately seeks an accumulation of knowledge; there is no similar sense of responsibility to a body of knowledge by the sportswriter. The sports page is read for immediate response. In a certain sense, it is not to be taken seriously.

THE DRAMATIST. Many sporting contests, such as a football game, can be regarded as dramas. The involvement of a team of individuals who are in opposition to another team, acting according to a set of rules (limitations of their degrees of freedom, as it were) and under a finite amount of time, generates a sense of an event. The game begins and it ends. Personal involvement with the performance may indeed be process; but the game, like a drama, has a final act.

In the hands of a Greek writer, many facets of a philosophical nature could be discussed under the substantive commitment to the game. If, for example, football does create "lessons for life," these could be elucidated by the sportswriter. They almost never are. One major reason is that few writers are intellectually equipped to enter such discussions; a second is that their writing skills are so utterly limited that they couldn't carry it off if they tried. A third is that the tradition of the sports page is against it. It takes a rare person and a rarer talent to essay a comment on "the four horsemen of Notre Dame." Yet even that effort, as inadequate as it may appear to a philosopher, stands out like a ninety-eight-yard kick to the coffin corner by a left-footed substitute punter playing for the first time in the third quarter of the seventy-seventh meeting between two cross-town rivals.

Perhaps one final reason for this identity so seldom being achieved, let alone sought, is the chore-aspect of writing. Copy has to be ground out in time for a deadline. Not only does the writer face similar contests week after week, or day after day in the case of baseball, so that the eventful character of the game is missed, he sees it as sportswriter. He is removed from the fans — he is not one of them. He does not permit himself to get involved; he cannot enjoy the game. He can take neither the role of the players, the coaches, or the fans. He must be aloof. He does not, then, see the game that is being played. He sees something else. He has a job and is under pressure to hack out a story. Moreover, there is nothing staler than old football scores, unless it is last season's swimming times. The fan can't wait for the superior dramatic presentation. He wants his "news" *now*.

If the writer is motivated to do anything, he is motivated to find some knowledge no one else had — that the second string quarterback hurt his knuckles so the coach couldn't substitute in the third quarter, etc. He becomes a technician. He is more worried that some other story will crowd his off the page than he is with being dramatic in his presentation.

THE INSTRUCTOR. In the case of the "major sports," as football and baseball, a good ploy is to write "for the women" — Not so much that women necessarily read the stuff, but it provides the male fan with something he can give to the women he wants to impress. The task of writing for women about sports which our culture denies to women is enormously difficult. If the reader can reasonably "take the role" of the sports-figure being discussed, the task is easier. But for a woman to imagine what a tackle does or what a linebacker does is made all the more difficult when she can't put herself in their positions. However, few writers are bothered by such considerations since they can't articulate role theory, anyway. Since they are not particularly well trained to think in terms of generalizations, they find it easier to write about examples — to describe unique actions in certain plays.

More often, however, they find their role as "instructor" better in certain relatively esoteric situations. This may involve rule or regulation changes. It may involve, however, a discussion of an activity which is not well known. Thus, a feature article may be on "curling" or some other "minor" sport.

Since the "instructor-student" relation is ego-satisfying to the instructor, it is a relation which is often sought by those in some "need" of status. In addition, it is a self-fulfilling satisfaction. A capable instructor is able to accept (that is, have a rhetoric to account for) both the success of his student and his failure. Since the instructor is "superior" to the student, his own judgment of the consequence is the more acceptable. Accordingly, the sportswriter, who seeks always to demonstrate a superiority over his fan, may unwittingly fall into the "instructor" style of writing. When the reader rejects the implied position of "student," the writer is judged with negative terms such as "bad" or "failing."

THE MAN OF INFLUENCE. In a success-oriented culture like ours, a common desire is to have influence beyond one's immediate career lines. One tends to seek the widest audience for the validation of his claims on success. The ability to influence decisions not immediately involved in one's own tasks is in many ways the highest accolade one can achieve. This is especially true if one's abilities are sought rather than thrust into the situation.

In the world of sports, the writer loves to believe he influences not mere knowledge of the game and related events but its intrepretation. He likes to think that decisions affecting the team or the selection of key personnel — as in a new coach for the local college team — involve him. He likes to think that rule changes are the consequence of his shrewd insights and analysis. He likes to think that changes in length of, say, a hunting season or a bag limit are the consequence of the leg work he did and of the way he mobilized sentiment.

But he wants influence, not power. With power comes responsibility; with responsibility comes accounting for error. The writer finds it comforting to cleave to the intellectual tradition of essential irresponsibility, of being freed from the actual fact of decision-making. Thus he is free to make use of hindsight, new data, and the like, should later events prove an earlier analysis to be wrong.

THE MAN FROM OLYMPUS. The goal of most writers is to have a column. If it can become syndicated, all the better. Something happens to men of limited ability when they achieve the status of the columnist. I doubt if it is the result of the tradition of having the picture printed at the head of the column, yet that aspect of identity-presentation cannot be too lightly dismissed.

Frequently, the columnist becomes a pontificator. He has achieved a long-sought goal. He grew up on a job which taught him the superiority of the man with the column. Upon obtaining that position, he comes to believe that the words he speaks are really true. As any writer can attest, whatever doubts one had when looking at an edited bit of copy tend to disappear when the clean and orderly publication appears. Yet that is an inadequate explanation.

The clue for the general push towards pontification must lie in the inability of a reader to challenge the authority of the writer. The validation of the claim for being an authority is immediate: the column is printed. It is not like the efforts of a cub writer to get notice. His stuff can be butchered. But the columnist is in a different position. Only the editor (if the columnist is not the editor) can challenge him. This is unlikely, since the editor is most likely to have been responsible for his position. As long as their pontifications are mutually reinforcing, there is no challenge.

The asymmetrical character of the writer-fan relationship is never more clearly seen than in the instance of the pontificating columnist. The individual fan is quite helpless and has little if any effect on determining the behavior of the writer.

Most sportswriters will be motivated to achieve excellence in one of these identities. He may, by the character of his situation and of his personality, present in varying degrees each of these identities. There is seldom any mechanical alternation from one to another of these identities, and he may be converted from one as his dominant pattern to some other. His behavior will be directly affected by the identity involved at the moment he does his writing.

It is noteworthy that at the moment of action, the major "others" of the various relationships he enters are not physically present. The cues relating to his position on the news staff, of course, are there. Insofar as these impinge upon his action, their significance will be felt. But any involvement with his "fans" or "sports stars," or officials of some club must depend on symbolic representations. Indeed, he may self-consciously reject the roles most strongly implied by the cues which are physically present and engage in those whose physical cues are minimal.

THE SPORTSWRITER AND HIS SALIENT SOCIAL RELATIONS

The sportswriter is caught in a network of relations. He must relate to a number of different people who, having different interests in the sport, make different claims upon his talents. Somehow, out of the various pressures exerted on him, he strives to develop a more or less systematic and consistent image of himself. Men develop various strategies to cope with these pressures. Some, to use Riesman's words, seek cues in others in order to locate themselves socially and program their own behavior: these are "other directed." Some seek an image of themselves and marshal their behavior accordingly. These 'inner directed' need not be particularly moral people; they can be highly self-centered and regard others as mere things to be manipulated, a profoundly dehumanizing concept of others. Some seek to learn the traditional role and act in terms of an imaginary setting rather than the uniquely immediate one. Whatever the individual writer's strategy may be, he more or less consciously encounters a number of distinct 'others' with whom he must interact, with whom, that is, he must enter a social relation.

THE NEWSPAPER. He first makes a job commitment. He joins a staff. At this point, his career aspirations become apparent. He begins in a lowly junior capacity and, if he develops proper friendships, gets tips and "trade secrets." Since many writers are paid by the "column inch," he desires to get as much material written as possible. Like most Americans, he is caught up in a success-oriented culture. On the newspaper, he learns a "subculture's standard of judgment."

This success-motive is sufficient to induce a desire to have a column, for the Sunday paper, at least, and preferably daily. Once the writer has a column, his problem is to fill it. A rather common device is to enable the public to make contributions. This is possible in a variety of ways – one is to be so controversial that people write in anger; another is to become a "soap-box" so that many points of view can be expressed. This, in turn, helps create "identities" of the sportswriter some of which are achieved in error.

One paradox of writing is that the more successful one is (until he achieves a syndicated status), the more space he must fill daily. The more he has to write on a daily pattern, the more routine his work becomes, the more "process-like" and less eventful is each bit of writing, the more mundane he will seem to the public. To overcome this the writer must seek wider experiences. Some essay magazine articles; some seek expression on radio or television; some essay internal politics and aspire for editorship.

As a staff member, he must accommodate himself to the intents of the paper's policy. If the paper has a policy (say) to support attempts to land a major league club, he must either support that in his writings, gravitate to some sports area where that is not germane, get out of that organization, or suffer in some way. This is true for a variety of things. The unequal access to power puts a certain pressure on the underlings, especially the newcomers. If the editor of the sports-page has a "thing" about the local college coach, he can express his virulence easily; he may also recruit supporters from other writers on his staff. Like the politician who comes to believe that he can have power only if he is elected and hence will do strange things to secure election, the writer may come to believe that he can do that which he desires only if he is a writer and hence will do strange things to secure that position.

THE SOURCES OF NEWS. These consist of the sponsors, officials and the athletes concerned. Not all possible relations are compatible with each other. The sponsor (club president, say) and an athlete may be at odds with each other; the writer dare not easily take sides. To be "in the know," and hence be valuable to his fans, the writer must cultivate these sources of information. They have in their hands, then, the potentiality of great power. They can, if they choose, virtually destroy a "personality." Most fans know only what they or some friend of theirs have read in the paper.

Hence, the sportswriter by controlling what the fan learns of the personalities involved wields great influence.

Consensus among writers flows from a variety of sources. If the object is clearly an excellent athlete, say, then consensus flows easily. Of course, the athlete himself can get "tagged" or "obtain a definition" with the result that the sportswriter simply follows the mob and accepts what he learns from others. This is probably the greatest source of uniformity of judgment. Another source requires some sort of organized effort. It is difficult, for example, to imagine an entire association of sportswriters deciding to write up a nice guy as a bad guy. It is easy, however, to imagine an editor convincing his entire staff to take their picks on some local athlete or sponsor.

A concerted effort on the part of a sports editor, especially in a single-press town, could wreak havoc on local management. Games can be badly reported and badly written. Highly colored words can be employed to give direction to the possible inferences the reader can draw. Information can be hidden, and contrary points of view either not reported or distorted. One can imagine some writers trying to force a local owner into submitting to the editor's personal desires only to find that the owner has obtained permission to move elsewhere.

The other extreme finds the sportswriter simply a lackey for those involved in the game. Athletes are written up gloriously. Bad plays, dumb plays, boners all can be ignored or explained away. As we saw before, the writer can become simply a huckster with little or no identification with the fan.

The writer may become so blasé, so cynical, that he is devoid of any sense of obligation or responsibility. He may regard the entire range of sports, especially "professional sports," as simply an organized con game the least offensive of which is wrestling. Then the writer would be in it for what he can get out of it. He would accept favors, and be sufficient unto the day. In many papers he would be hard to detect.

The writer for a paper whose supporting town fields a major league baseball team has a particular difficulty. The number of games during the season places a great demand upon his ingenuity as a craftsman. Because of this, he seeks to contrive "eventful things" around which he can have a more interesting task than would otherwise be the case. Often he is neither a clever nor a resourceful man. He too often relies upon the press agent to get unusual stories. He accepts the trade definition that certain people like Casey Stengel or Ted Williams are "colorful." This really means that a sufficient body of knowledge is available for them to write feature articles easily. There seems to be no a priori reason why we must think that a good writer could not develop interesting stories about other players. The major drawback seems to be the difficulty in obtaining the information. The "colorful" player is easy to write about.

Because the football season is arranged for one game a week, football writers can spend more time preparing "feature" stories. Indeed, this is a requirement if the sports pages are to be full of readable materials between games. Hence the writer is compelled to write about individual players other than the obvious stars.

But the demand for copy has another effect during the football season. The opposing team is written about in considerable detail. Specific players are discussed and, in general, the coming game gets a great deal of "house." This is quite unlike the treatment given visiting teams during the baseball season. Unless the team is of the stature of the New York Yankees, the visiting teams often get very little house prior to their coming.

A curious situation obtains in the huckster aspect of the writer's career. He tends to become pro-management in surprising ways. It is true that he always reserves the right to criticize and may even attempt to impose his will upon management. But with the pressure from the Chamber of Commerce who sees Big League Sports as a device to lure spenders into town, the writer tends to identify with the local team. This identification is one reason why failure of the team to succeed creates a flood of negative and critical articles in the local press. The writer loses his objectivity and when the team loses on the field, he suffers from personal defeat. When the team is losing more than its "proper" share of games, the writer has an opportunity to demonstrate his superior knowledge and present analyses of the play, the personnel, and the management. To the unwary reader, he can show himself to be more knowledgeable than the manager. This type of exhibitive and expressive communication is an adverse house, of course, and contributes to a shrinking attendance.

But shrinking attendance is what neither the owner nor the chamber of commerce wants. Ultimately, neither does the sportswriter — for if the town becomes dead, as far as that sport is concerned, the sportswriter loses his identity as a major league sporstwriter and drifts into the nether-nether land of minor league sportswriting. Thus, few sportswriters are ever motivated to contribute to a shrinking attendance. When this occurs, it is simply as an accidental consequent of another set of motives.

What neither baseball management, local officials in civic groups nor baseball writers give any evidence of being aware of is the tremendous mobility of our population. They seem unaware of the adolescence of the adult baseball fan. The fan is hardly likely to have grown up with an emotional attachment to the local team. Indeed, he may not have had an attachment to the league which the local outfit represents. Yet writers go along with management to demand team support. They write up the local team. They deprecate fans who "boo" or razz local efforts.

It seems clear that the price of admission of someone supporting an opposing team brings in as much money as that of a local supporter. As far as management is concerned, he should be indifferent to the team the ticket buyer supports as long as he comes. Yet by not covering visiting teams in any depth, by not giving feature reports about opposing players in the same depth the football writers do, the editors of sports pages make it extremely difficult for local people who grew up identified with other teams to go to a local baseball game. They create a situation in which fans supporting the locals are virtually the only fans in attendance. When this occurs drastic drop-offs in attendance follow a decline in the standing of the local team.

If the baseball writer would give equal space to the visiting team — the same "statistics," the same number of column inches on feature stories, the same effort to get supporters of the visiting team to come out to support them, if they would sell the league if not baseball — the attending fans would be less a function of how well the local team is doing than is usually the case.

Such a change in strategy would require not just a reorientation of the sportswriter. It would require an understanding of the local management and civic groups. For as it stands now, they tend to see articles about the visitors as detracting from the local team. Above all, the local chamber of commerce orients itself to "its city." It cannot think otherwise. The milleni-um seems a far way off.

FELLOW SPORTSWRITERS. Writers belong to a variety of professional organizations. Let it be observed that a major function of professional organizations is the creation and maintenance of identities. Attendance at conferences of the professional assures the person of the opportunity of associating strictly with others of a similar identity. Self-conceptions are clearer and tensions resulting from competing ego demands are less. Of course, one added source of tension is the struggle for position on an internally defined hierarchy. However, a low position on a prized totem pole is preferred to a high position on an undesired pole, so that the internal struggle need not be destructive.

Status within the domain of "sportswriter" depends, of course, upon the personal reputation of the individual. The writer who has achieved syndication has high status. The writer for a nationally regarded magazine or news service has status. Though there will be contention for status between football writers and baseball writers, these two tend to have more status than those who write for minor sports. And, of course, a writer covering a major league team has more prestige than one from a minor league town.

Within the domain of sportswriters, there tends to be a common set of measures of success. The cub reporter spends some time discovering the rules of achievement. If he is lucky, he will acquire the tutelage of some friendly older person. Indeed lucky is the young fellow who is the protege of some well-established person. There is, then, a certain play for some "law of imitation," or the incipient use of flattery. Styles of writing are emulated by the aspiring. One consequence is that a few writers not only dominate in styles of writing but in establishing points of view.

As a result of this, sportswriters write about sportswriters. Thus, if a Kansas City writer blisters local management in a column, this becomes "news" to other writers. Opinions of writers are not merely sought through informal means, but formally as well. Certain contrived events, manufactured from whole cloth by writers, become the subject of news stories and local analysis.

The so-called "All American" football team is such an invention. Of course, with growing disagreement as to whom one should place on such a team generates a series of such teams. Eventually, though there was sufficient over-lap to generate a "consensus team," enough variation in names occurs so that all regional favorites get some distinction and honor.

Another paradox of the sportswriter is the reversal of the attempt to create events where process is experienced. The seasonal event of choosing an "All American Team" resulted in "weekly polls" to determine the "lineman of the week" and "back of the week." This resulted, probably, from the attempt to create an acceptable system of identifying national collegiate football champions. Since there is no playoff in any tournament sense, the championship is entirely in the hands of sportswriters. Obviously, the sportswriter has to rely on secondary sources for his judgment of various teams which he does not see in play. In part his judgment is aided by an intuitive rating of the various conferences; yet, to a large extent, those voting for the top ten teams can base their decisions on impressions gained from the sports pages. Thus, though one analytically knows that one must take into account the caliber of opposition, and the margin of victory, the simple fact of won-loss results often determine ratings. Thus, if in basketball the No. 1 team narrowly defeats the No. 2 team, as it should in most encounters, the No. 2 team often drops drastically in the rating, especially if No. 3 and No. 4 did not lose that week.

Recurring to the reliance on consensus, certain common expectations of performance come into being. This may relate to individuals or to teams. Now, in a success-oriented society one finds rules to account for failure. If a society fails to establish ego-satisfying rhetorics to account for failure, the cost in mental health would be enormous. Just as those who try to predict academic success statistically cover their predictive errors by the rubrics of "over-achievers" and "under-achievers," the sportswriter coined the "upset." If sportswriters could manage to make individual judgments, there would probably be much less consensus. But such is the force of prestige. A judgment made by a highly regarded writer tends to be copied by lesser figures. Indeed, anyone who persistently disagreed with "consensus" would find his motives questioned. And this is the greatest threat to modern man; hence, like the suburbanite, the aspiring young sportswriter finds certain substantial rewards in conformity. A few are strong enough in psychic reserve to achieve the identity of "an odd-ball, but otherwise OK." By definition, they are rare.

THE FAN. Most of this chapter deals directly or indirectly with the way in which the sportswriter relates to the fan. We place it here, again, mainly to complete the picture of the relationships impinging upon the writer. What needs to be emphasized is the asymmetrical character of the relation. The writer has access to a source of power; the "mere" fan does not. The "fan" is such a huge category that further breakdown seems necessary. The most advantageous dimensions would be in terms of amount of participation and of knowledge of the game.

The fan who fishes, for example, wants to see more of that sport in the paper. Similarly for all the so-called "minor" activities as drag racing, boating, curling, or whatever. Those supporting "minor" have relatively little influence, by definition. A "minor sport" is one which commands the attention and allegiance of a relatively small and hence unimportant body of fans. Thus, as the number of teams playing, individuals playing, and fans attending basketball games increased, its status was per force changed from "minor" to "major" sports.

From time to time, fans do get organized in an effort to mobilize greater sentiment for their preference. If they can get some commercial interest also involved, they have a greater chance for success. Then they exert a pressure on the sportswriters to increase coverage. At times, the writers are willing collaborators. Yet unless a favorable sentiment of the public exists, the sportswriter cannot, simply by writing about the sport, automatically increase the number of those willing to support it.

Whether the individual sportswriter is able to engage in a crusade urged by a body of fans, however, depends upon other aspects of his network or relations. Consider fans who may desire to obtain stories of horse racing, presuming that such stories are not now being presented. One is likely to encounter such sources of resistance as the editor who may have a moral thing about horse racing as being connected with gambling and other forms of naughty behavior; or the owner of a local baseball franchise who would feel economically threatened by a competitive sport; or a larger body of highly influential fans who oppose horse racing and stories about horse racing; or some combination of them.

The sportswriter has a continuous hazard that far offsets the advantage he has over other newsmen. For the most part, he reports highly similar events. He can specialize. Baseball games are remarkably similar. Football games show considerably less variation than, say, a political rally. The latter may have a highly simplified format: but the spoken word is the object of the report to a large extent and, hence, considerable variation can be expected unless it is a part of a long, drawn-out campaign. In the campaign situation, the listener is not likely to have heard the speech; the similarity is apparent only to the writer.

In sports, however, there are some fans who are as knowledgeable as the typical writer. Many fans have played the game, have a son playing it at the moment, read about it, think about it, discuss it — and hence are as expert as the ordinary sportswriter. This creates a devastating problem for the writer. He is virtually committed to being a "hack," at least in the eyes of knowledgeable people. He has a way out which, of course, he has developed. He becomes a record keeper. In baseball, a writer becomes the official scorekeeper. He makes decisions as to whether a play was a hit or an error; and, if an error, on whom. Thus, in a tight battle for a batting championship, a vindicative writer can rob a contender of a precious hit. Or he can protect a failing athlete.

But more than that. The writers keep records that no fan would dream of keeping. Now, a fan may have a theory regarding the effect, say, of wind velocity and direction on a pitcher: does a wind from the back "straighten out" the curve of some pitchers? Records of this kind are not kept. But amazing bits of information regarding the number of chances a left-handed firstbaseman has had in a single game are assiduously maintained and sometimes reported. In this way, the writer maintains a semblance of superiority over the typical fan. Unfortunately, some fans *are* impressed by the erudition of writers who rely upon such information for their position.

Thus the writer must not only take into account who the fans are, but the various tensions which exist among the fans themselves. In addition, he must locate himself in his own career-line and his sources of information. Unless he is sensitive to a wide range of social pressures, he is likely to be just a hack writer who can be trusted only to follow orders.

SUMMING UP

The significance of "sports" in American life can be measured fairly well by the amount of space devoted to it in our daily press. Every major paper has a section called the "sports section" and, with varying amounts of space given to advertising, it constitutes a major part of the material available in the paper. On Saturdays, papers may have a page or two devoted to religious news — or less than a couple of columns. The papers may have a page or so devoted to business. From time to time a feature article may appear on "Science," and other topics get varying amounts of coverage. To be sure, traffic accidents get considerable space and politics, in season, does too. But for regular, predictable coverage, sports always gets its own section. The point, I propose, is well taken and clearly established.

The "sportswriter" is not a single social being. He is a bundle of relationships which he must enter and develop from time to time. He is a member of a work force; he has a job to do. He meets people; he writes about some. He addresses his comments to some people. He likes some of those with whom he interacts; he dislikes some. He is a social creature, many faceted, with a highly complex system of motivations as a result.

It may be that out of these various relationships and subsequently contradictory pressures that he develops a preferred image of himself. He may, for example, come to feel that he is essentially a man of noble integrity that he must "call them as he sees them." He may decide that his greatest obligation is to a vaguely defined but keenly felt image of the "sportsman." He may, then, find himself under great pressure to submit to the desires of the sponsor of a sporting event which he considers not exactly kosher. His boss may insinuate economic retaliation if he fails to comply; but his conscience bids him be honest with the public.

It may be, then, that he reluctantly writes an article which hides the doubts he prefers to expose, that he finds plausible reasons why it will be exciting entertainment. He may, against his preferences, be for the moment a blatant huckster. He probably would have a number of "explanations" — I was under pressure; I was not myself; I was shameful, etc. Now, we may be tempted to indicate that he was a "coward"; but we should recall that in addition to his identity as a sportswriter he has other concerns and identities — as, say, "father" or "breadwinner." The point is not to excuse cowardice nor, even, to explain it. The point lies elsewhere.

We often talk about one's real self. In the episode just described, the writer would feel that his "real" self is a brave world-conquering writer of integrity. *Empirically,* however, he was a coward. *Normatively,* he is brave. The point, clearly is this: *one's real self consists of an integrated set of values, of normative preferences.* A recognized difference between one's "real" self and one's empirical self may result in a sense of shame or of guilt. This in turn may result in a motivation to alter some aspect of one's situation.

The normative aspect of one's "real self" runs counter to the demands which the organization may make. The newspaper as an economic enterprise asks that its personnel be true to its purposes; that, at least, the writer be loyal to his formal commitments. These organizational demands for loyalty may run counter to private morality with consequences predictable only with greater knowledge of the individuals involved. Of course, what I have written about the sportswriter is simply a special case of a wider generality. This, in some sense, is the characteristic problem of man.

"Consarn it, Phillips! How come you assigned our Roving Horticulture Expert, Old Granny Peebles, to cover the Big Game while I was off fishing? What kind of sports reporting is this? Quote: 'Unlike honeysuckle, the leering victors jubilantly jumped up and down, sweating like mad and they smelled something *awful!*' "

CHEERLEADING

LAWRENCE R. HERKIMER

Did you ever wonder what motivates a person to become a cheerleader? What makes some individuals want to get out in front of a crowd and strain their vocal cords, their leg muscles, arm muscles, and endanger dislocating their backs, etc.? Is it the thrill of leading the crowd, of hearing the responses one has caused, of being the center of attraction, or the recognition one receives for the title of "Cheerleader"? Possibly it is the notoriety of wearing the uniform, or it could be other reasons. The author endeavored to find this out by interviewing several hundred cheerleaders in all sections of the country who were attending National Cheerleader Association annual training clinics for cheerleaders. Some of the answers were quite unexpected.

The first thing the author noticed was the difference between cheerleaders from various sections of the country and from different size towns and schools. Secondly, the author noticed many similarities regardless of where the cheerleaders came from or what size school they represented. One thing they all had in common, in almost every instance, was that they were definitely extroverts. Some were extroverts to a greater degree than others, but very few were to be considered "shy." The majority were very healthy physically, and probably more attractive than average. The majority were also above average scholastically, and were also leaders in other fields in their school activities. In short, most of the cheerleaders possessed the physical ability, the aggressiveness, the poise, the appearance, and the knowledge to be leaders. All walks of life were found among these individuals. We had the opportunity of observing cheerleaders from schools for the blind, schools for the deaf, private schools, Indian reservation schools, parochial schools, public schools, and even cheerleaders for professional teams who represented no school at all. To the question, "Why did you want to be a cheerleader?" we got many replies. Answers such as, "Because it's so much fun," or "I guess I like the excitement," or "Well, the cheerleaders are really *it* in our school" suggest some reasons. Others were a little more serious in their replies and said such things as, "It gives me a chance to be of service to my school," or "I wanted to do something to help improve the school spirit of our student body and the team." The majority of the answers reflected the desire of the individual to be in the limelight, be popular, be able to display their talents physically such as gymnastics, jumping ability, physical appearance, etc., or their ability to handle a crowd, or to get its attention. Others simply got a thrill that sent chills through them when the crowd roared their response. Also the excitement of being in on the action, so to speak, and close to the playing field and playing court, every game, was a big thrill to many of the cheerleaders interviewed.

Planning of pep rallies and campaigns to boost spirit and advertise the athletic contests were cited as reasons for wanting to be a cheerleader. The author has noticed a change in the general type of student who is now engaged in cheerleading activities from those of fifteen years ago. Now there is much more emphasis in leadership and planned activities for the cheerleaders to do, and their responsibilities are more outlined and set up with standards, etc., than they were fifteen years ago. In earlier years, cheerleaders had to use their own ingenuity in working up routines, planning activities, etc. Because of this, many times cheerleading was not what it should have been, nor was the importance given to it that is today. Therefore, with lower standards and fewer regulations, it did not carry the honor it does today. This, however, was certainly not the case in all schools. Many schools had very fine cheerleaders, just as good and better than the cheerleaders of today, depending upon the faculty help given to the cheerleaders. Generally, however, there is marked improvement in the organization of cheerleader activities today over the period of fifteen years ago.

The big change in cheerleading today was largely brought about by the training clinics and books provided by the National Cheerleaders Association. This organization was formed in 1951 and training clinics were established over the nation for High School and College cheerleaders. At present, the N.C.A. clinics are held in forty-three states as well as in Canada and Central and South America. Over 100,000 students receive training in cheerleading and cheering techniques each year. Standards have been established for the cheerleaders conduct on the field, requirements for being selected as a cheerleader, duties, responsibilities, etc. Also, there has been a philosophy of cheerleading developed, and a close observation of the purposes of cheerleaders at a game, as well as at rallies and other school activities.

The general philosophy of cheerleading is that the main function of the cheerleader is to get response from the crowd, not to merely perform for the crowd. The cheerleaders are actually glorified "choir directors" and the motions they employ and the rhythm they adopt for their cheers have a lot to do with the response they receive from the crowd, just as would be the case with the choir director. The N.C.A. Training clinics stress these points and teach many of the actual techniques of getting the crowd to respond. Another important point in cheerleading is the proper choice of cheer. There are offensive cheers and defensive cheers, and certain cheers should be given at one point in the game, and others at another point. The timing of the yells is also important. There are certain psychological moments for a cheer during a game when the crowd wants to yell and the cheerleader needs to sense these moments and give the proper yell at the proper time. Many ball games have been won or lost due to the fine, or the poor, efforts of the cheerleaders. The players report that they many times give a better effort when the crowd is cheering for them. There is definitely a psychological advantage for the players to have the crowd cheering them on. A good set of cheerleaders can then do much toward success of their athletic teams. Cheering is now being used at more sports than in the past. Now there are cheerleaders for football, basketball, hockey, wrestling, track and baseball. There is also some organized cheering at swimming meets. Hockey and wrestling have particularly grown during the past ten years with the utilization of cheerleaders.

Cheerleaders many times effect the behavior of the crowd and a well-trained squad of cheerleaders can do much to foster better sportsmanship at athletic contests. Little things such as starting the game off with a welcome yell for the other team helps, as does applauding for an injured player on the other team as he leaves the game, or quieting the crowd during free throws at a basketball game all help along these lines. The choice of cheers also makes a difference. The cheerleaders who cheer positively rather than negatively have better behaved fans. In other words, a cheerleader always using yells that praise the home team without degrading the opponents' team has a better effect on good sportsmanship than if derogatory remarks are used concerning the other team. Wording too strong such as "Stomp 'em, Knock 'em cold, Kill 'em," etc., are in very bad taste. At N.C.A. clinics cheerleaders are taught that it is good to yell "Our team is red hot," but not to add, "And their team is all shot." Mob psychology principles lend themselves to cheering situations as the cheerleaders in effect have a mob of cheering students, and the tempo of this cheering needs to be regulated and controlled, which a cheerleader with training can do.

So you see, there are many phases of cheerleading, so one would expect various reasons stimulate a student to want to become a cheerleader. Whatever their reasons for wanting to become a cheerleader, they look as if they do have a great time out there on the playing area doing their jobs, and I for one am glad that so many young people are interested in being cheerleaders and that there are thousands of them across the country, for I see high school and college athletic events very dull without their enthusiasm and colorful demonstrations. Cheerleading builds leadership qualities within the individual. The ability to sway a crowd or talk to a group with authority is a fine trait to have in a young person and it should be very valuable to him or her in life after school is over. As the N.C.A. clinic training usually brings out, this ability often makes the difference in the possibility of the girl someday being president of her local P.T.A., instead of just being another member. For the boys, it sometimes makes the difference of their advancing to head of their companies in the business field. Enthusiasm, devotion to an ideal, good health coupled with a good personality, and quick thinking can many times take students straight to the top in later years. Certainly the experience of being a cheerleader for a fine student body and a fine school gives a wonderful opportunity for one to develop these qualities. So, keep your cheerleaders cheering and possibly they will cheer up more of us.

EPILOGUE

. . . on the other hand, a sports car *could* be merely a sports car.

INDEX

I

J

K

T

U

V